Pine to Prairie
Cookbook
Volume IV

Telephone Pioneers of America
C.P. Wainman - Chapter #18

Purpose

The purpose of the Telephone Pioneers of America shall be to provide a means of friendly association for the longer-service employees and those retired; to foster among them a continuing fellowship and a spirit of mutual helpfulness; to exemplify and perpetuate those principles which have come to be regarded as the ideals and traditions of our industry; and to participate in activities that are of service to the community, contribute to the progress of the association and promote the happiness, well-being and usefulness of the membership.

The proceeds from the sale of this Cookbook are used primarily for community service projects.

Published and Printed By
Cookbook Publishers, Inc.
2101 Kansas City Road
P.O. Box 1260
Olathe, Kansas 66061-1260

OFFICERS

Eileen Rekowski . . . . Chapter President
Robert J. Lewis . . . . Pioneer Administrator
A. T. "Ike" Isakson . . . . Chapter Life Member Rep.
Blanche Masica . . . . Chapter Life Member Rep.
Jerry Abel . . . . Bismarck Council President
Jerry Moyer . . . . Lakes Council President
Ella Fennessy . . . . Duluth Council President
Barbara Fivecoate . . . . Range Club President
Robert Hangsleben . . . . Lake Agassiz Council President
Mary Borrowman . . . . Minneapolis Council President
Barbara Boline . . . . Anoka Club President
James Helgeson . . . . Red River Valley Council President
Alice Dulitz . . . . Rochester Council President
William Nelson . . . . Central Council President
Charles Hardy . . . . Western Plains Club President
Jo Anne Rahn . . . . St. Paul Council President
Clifford Olson . . . . Arrowhead Life Member Club President
Elton Wolf . . . . Bismarck Life Member Club President
William Woods . . . . Harley Forsyth Life Member Club President
Arlene Byrne . . . . Hiawathaland Life Member Club President
Elaine Rolerat . . . . Lake Agassiz Life Member Club President
Telsche Paulson . . . . Minneapolis Life Member Club President
Barbara Kaste . . . . Red River Valley Life Member Club President
Bunny Weidell . . . . St. Paul Life Member Club President

PAST CHAPTER PRESIDENTS

1980-81 . . . . Phyllis Brooks
1981-82 . . . . A. T. "Ike" Isakson
1982-83 . . . . John G. Norton
1983-84 . . . . Gerald R. Hamann
1984-85 . . . . Ronald A. Schwartz
1985-86 . . . . Ron Christy
1986-87 . . . . Mary Hennessy

PRESIDENT'S MESSAGE

I want to thank all of the Telephone Pioneers and Partners who took the time to submit recipes to make this a successful project. Also, thanks to the Celiac Sprue Association and the Midwest Gluten Intolerance Group for special recipes for the Gluten Free Section and The American Heart Association for the Heart Health section.

Thanks to the Arrowhead Council and the Range Club members and partners for accepting the challenge of collecting, sorting and typing the recipes that were submitted, also for their time and effort so Volume IV could be printed.

A big **HUG** is in order for all Council and Club members and partners for their support of the Hug-A-Bear project, the Calendar Raffle and all the other projects that are being done for the handicapped and less fortunate.

Thanks are also due the Chapter administrator and officers of the chapter, councils and clubs of the C. P. Wainman Chapter for their continued support of the many projects that are being done by our members and partners.

Eileen Rekowski
Chapter President
C. P. Wainman Chapter
Telephone Pioneers of America

Expression
of
Appreciation

Since this is our fourth "step" into the kitchens of all our faithful and gracious cooks, we want to thank all of those that contributed recipes for this book and we hope to fill in some of the areas that may have been overloaded or overlooked in previous "steps" in the kitchen.

For everyone involved may you have many hours of good reading, several cups of love, tablespoons of friendship, few teaspoons of calories, ounces of smiles, litres of helping others, bunches of hugs in return and a "pinch" of knowing ourselves.

Take this heartwarming recipe, mix it all well and see the speciality it will bake . . . . Pioneering!!!!!!

Without You . . . . It could not happen!

Cookbook Committee

Clare Baker	Sigrud Johnson
Dessa Clafton	Mary Patalas
Mandy Feiro	Lorraine Sojka
Barb Fivecoate	June Szymczak

The proceeds from the sale of this cookbook are used primarily for community service projects.

All I Ever Really Needed to Know
I Learned in Kindergarten

Most of what I really need to know about how to live, and what to do and how to be, I learned in kindergarten.

Wisdom was not at the top of the graduate school mountain but there in the sandbox at nursery school.

These are the things I learned: Share everything. Play fair. Don't hit people. Put things back where you found them. Clean up your own mess. Don't take things that aren't yours. Say you're sorry when you hurt somebody. Wash your hands before you eat. Flush. Warm cookies and cold milk are good for you. Live a balanced life. Learn some and think some and draw and paint and sing and dance and play and work every day some. Take a nap every afternoon.

When you go out into the world, watch for traffic, hold hands and stick together. Be aware of wonder. Remember the little seed in the plastic cup. The roots go down and the plant goes up and nobody really knows how or why, but we are all like that.

Goldfish and hamsters and white mice and even the little seed in the plastic cup - they all die. So do we.

And then remember the book about Dick and Jane and the first word you learned, the biggest word of all: LOOK.

Everything you need to know is in there somewhere. The golden rule and love and basic sanitation. Ecology and politics and sane living.

Think of what a better world it would be if we all - the whole world - had cookies and milk about 3 o'clock every afternoon and then lay down with our blankets for a nap.

Or if we had a basic policy in our nation and in other nations to always put things back where we found them and cleaned up our own messes.

And it is still true, no matter how old you are, when you go out into the world, it is best to hold hands and stick together.

TABLE OF CONTENTS

Barbecue 1

Crock Pot Cooking 7

Cooking for a Crowd 19

Ethnic Foods 35

Dressings and Salads 127

Microwave 139

Potpourri 189

Helpful Hints 287

**American Heart
Association**

WE'RE FIGHTING FOR YOUR LIFE

Heart Health 367

Diabetic Delights 455

Gluten Free 487

FAVORITE RECIPES
FROM MY COOKBOOK

Recipe Name	Page Number

Barbecue

MEAT ROASTING GUIDE

Cut	Weight Pounds	Approx. Time (Hours) (325° oven)	Internal Temperature
BEEF			
Standing Rib Roast [1] (10 inch) ribs) [1] If using shorter cut (8-inch) ribs, allow 30 min. longer	4	1¾ 2 2½	140° (rare) 160° (medium) 170° (well done)
	8	2½ 3 4½	140° (rare) 160° (medium) 170° (well done)
Rolled Ribs	4	2 2½ 3	140° (rare) 160° (medium) 170° (well done)
	6	3 3¼ 4	140° (rare) 160° (medium) 170° (well done)
Rolled rump [2]	5	2¼ 3 3¼	140° (rare) 160° (medium) 170° (well done)
Sirloin tip [2] [2] Roast only if high quality. Otherwise, braise.	3	1½ 2 2¼	140° (rare) 160° (medium) 170° (well done)
LAMB Leg	6	3 3½	175° (medium) 180° (well done)
	8	4 4½	175° (medium) 180° (well done)
VEAL Leg (piece) Shoulder Rolled Shoulder	5 6 3 to 5	2½ to 3 3½ 3 to 3½	170° (well done) 170° (well done) 170° (well done)

POULTRY ROASTING GUIDE

Type of Poultry	Ready-To-Cook Weight	Oven Temperature	Approx. Total Roasting Time
TURKEY	6 to 8 lbs. 8 to 12 lbs. 12 to 16 lbs. 16 to 20 lbs. 20 to 24 lbs.	325° 325° 325° 325° 300°	2½ to 3 hrs. 3 to 3½ hrs. 3½ to 4 hrs. 4 to 4½ hrs. 5 to 6 hrs.
CHICKEN (Unstuffed)	2 to 2½ lbs. 2½ to 4 lbs. 4 to 8 lbs.	400° 400° 325°	1 to 1½ hrs. 1½ to 2½ hrs. 3 to 5 hrs.
DUCK (Unstuffed)	3 to 5 lbs.	325°	2½ to 3 hrs.

NOTE: Small chickens are roasted at 400° so that they brown well in the short cooking time. They may also be done at 325° but will take longer and will not be as brown. Increase cooking time 15 to 20 minutes for stuffed chicken and duck.

BARBECUE

INDIA JELLIED SNAKE

Any one of our snakes can be used. Rattler is real tasty.

1 medium snake	1 handful mint
2 c. vinegar	2 tsp. salt

Skin snake; remove intestines. Cut into 1 inch pieces; wash in cold water. Put vinegar, mint, and salt in container. Place the pieces of snake on top and cover with water (cold) and let stand overnight. Place the container in the coals in the morning and simmer slowly for 35 minutes; remove from heat and cool. The dish is ready to eat when the jelly has set.

Barb Fivecoate, Virginia, MN

BARBEQUED BEANS

1 lb. pinto beans	¼ lb. bacon
1 Tbsp. garlic salt	¾ c. sliced onion
½ c. green pepper	½ c. catsup
1 tsp. cayenne	1 tsp. chili powder
1 Tbsp. sugar	1 tsp. salt

Cook beans until tender. Saute bacon and onion until tender, not brown. Add to beans, plus other ingredients. Cover and let simmer until tender.

Bernice T. Eugenis, Saginaw, MN

FRESH BARBECUED SALMON
(Alder smoked)

Fresh salmon fillets	1 to 2 onions, thinly sliced
Lemon juice	Butter or margarine
Garlic powder	Snipped parsley
Johnny's Dock seasoned salt	Green alder twigs (size of pencil)
Salt and fresh ground pepper	Heavy-duty aluminum foil (for
1 to 2 lemons, thinly sliced	boats and tent)

Fillet salmon, leaving skin on one side. Make foil boat for each fillet; double thickness, ½ inch longer and wider than fillet. The ends and sides should be 1 inch high and secure enough to hold liquid.

Place salmon in foil boat, skin side down. Pour about ½ cup lemon juice over each fish fillet. Season well with garlic powder, seasoned salt, salt, and pepper. Add slices of lemon and onion to cover. Top with generous dabs of butter or margarine. Sprinkle with parsley.

Scatter twigs on prepared bed of hot coals. Place foil boats on grill about 3 ½ inches above coals. Close lid to barbecue and cover vents with foil, or if no lid, make a tent and cover well to contain smoke. Watch for possible flaming.

Cook about 20 to 30 minutes, depending on thickness, or until thickest portion is fork tender.

Sit back and receive compliments for the best flavored, most moist barbecued salmon ever enjoyed! Done on television when I was working there. Two thousand requests the first day.

Jane Klein, Bellevue, WA

BARBECUED CORNED BEEF

Cover 2 or 3 pounds corned beef brisket and cook until tender (about 1 hour per pound); drain. Place beef on spit and position on preheated grill. Brush with Barbecue Sauce and cook for 20 or 30 minutes until nicely browned.

Barbecue Sauce:

3 Tbsp. mustard
½ c. brown sugar
⅛ tsp. Tabasco sauce

2 Tbsp. vinegar
1 clove garlic, minced

Combine all ingredients and heat.

Elynor Pederson, Montevideo, MN

KABOB (MARINADE) SAUCE

1½ c. salad oil
½ c. Worcestershire sauce
½ c. wine vinegar
½ c. soy sauce
½ c. lemon juice

2½ tsp. salt
2 Tbsp. dry mustard
2 cloves garlic, minced
1½ tsp. parsley flakes
1 Tbsp. pepper

Marinate for 4 hours or overnight: Chicken, turkey, steak, or pork. Put on kabob, with or without, vegetables and grill.

Allan T. Isakson, Fargo, ND

MARINADE SAUCE

This is good for pork or beef.

1 c. oil
¾ c. soy sauce
½ c. lemon juice
¼ c. mustard

¼ c. Worcestershire sauce
1½ tsp. salt
1 tsp. pepper
1 tsp. garlic powder

Mix well with wire whip. Marinate meat for 12 to 24 hours, the longer the better.

Note: Keeps in glass jar for at least 30 days. Be sure to rinse raw meat before adding to sauce.

Renee Ulberg, Bismarck, ND

WORLD'S BEST STEAK BASTE
(From Family Circle Magazine)

1 c. soy sauce
¼ c. browning and seasoning
   sauce
2 tsp. Beau Monde or Italian
   herb seasoning mix

2 large onions, coarsely
   chopped
2 Tbsp. bottled chopped garlic
   in oil

Combine ingredients in blender; cover and whirl for 1 minute until well blended. Store in tightly covered jar in refrigerator (thickens upon standing). To use, baste both sides of steak, burgers, or chops just before grilling. Continue to brush with baste during cooking. Can be used on broiled meats also to create a barbecued flavor.

I use A.1. Steak Sauce, Beau Monde seasoning, and dehydrated minced garlic. This gives all meats a really super flavor. Makes 2½ cups of sauce, 12 calories per tablespoon.

Peggy Mielke, Chisholm, MN

BARBECUE SAUCE
(For chicken or ribs)

Bake ribs in 400° oven for 1 hour and pour off grease.

Sauce:

1 c. catsup
2 Tbsp. Worcestershire
2 tsp. dry mustard
1 Tbsp. liquid smoke
1 tsp. salt

6 Tbsp. sugar
½ c. vinegar
2 tsp. paprika
1 c. water

Put this in pan and bring to boil; pour over ribs and bake at 350° for 1½ to 2 hours.

Joyce McCann, St. Cloud, MN

EASY BARBECUE SAUCE

8 oz. can tomato sauce
¼ c. honey

¼ c. prepared mustard
1 Tbsp. minced onion

Mix together. Very good over spareribs and meat loaf.

Mavis E. Dilts

BARBECUE SAUCE

1 c. finely chopped onion
4 Tbsp. green pepper
4 Tbsp. salad oil
1½ c. ketchup

4 Tbsp. brown sugar
4 Tbsp. prepared mustard
2 Tbsp. Worcestershire sauce
1 tsp. salt

Cook onion and green pepper in oil until tender (not brown). Add remaining ingredients and simmer.

Good on hot dogs, fish, chicken, etc. Will keep in refrigerator.

Mayabelle Morganson, Bemidji, MN

BARBECUE SAUCE

1 Tbsp. brown sugar
1 Tbsp. soy sauce
1 Tbsp. vinegar
½ c. catsup

1 c. hot water
½ tsp. Worcestershire sauce
½ tsp. chili powder

Mix and pour over desired meat.

Anne La Fleur, Duluth, MN

BASTING SAUCE FOR GRILLED CHICKEN

½ c. oil
1 c. vinegar
1 Tbsp. salt

1½ tsp. poultry seasoning
½ tsp. white pepper
1 egg, beaten

Mix with whisk or fork. Brush on chicken while grilling over charcoal. Makes enough for 2 chickens.

John and Barb Jordan, Sartell, MN

BARBECUE CHICKEN

1 c. ketchup
1½ c. water
1 Tbsp. chili powder
¼ c. Worcestershire
Lemon slices

3 dashes Tabasco
¼ c. brown sugar
Onion slices
Chicken

Cut up chicken; lay in pan. Put sliced onion and lemon over it. Mix rest of ingredients and pour over chicken. Bake at 350° for 1½ hours.

Excellent for barbecue chicken wings for appetizer.

Janet Lozon, Owatonna, MN

BEST-EVER BQ SAUCE FOR TURKEY INJECTION

½ lb. butter
1 c. barbecue sauce
1 c. water
1 c. brown sugar

1 tsp. dry mustard
1 tsp. lemon juice
1 tsp. Worcestershire sauce
⅛ c. salt

Combine all ingredients and heat until all dissolved. Inject in turkey and cover outside; cook. (Go to veterinarian and get largest injection needle.)

Lois Thelen, Detroit Lakes, MN

BAR-B-Q'S

4 lb. ground beef
1 c. onion, chopped
½ c. celery, chopped
1 Tbsp. salt
¼ c. lemon juice
2 Tbsp. brown sugar

1 Tbsp. Worcestershire sauce
½ tsp. dry mustard
1 c. water
2 tsp. vinegar
1 (14 oz.) catsup

In large kettle, cook and stir meat and onion until brown. Drain off fat. Stir in rest of ingredients; heat to boiling, stirring frequently. Cover and simmer for 30 minutes. Cool. Makes 5 pints.

Carol Gilbertson, Hawley, MN

CHINESE BARBEQUED PORK

Pork tenderloin or boneless
   pork roast
½ tsp. salt
¼ tsp. pepper
¼ tsp. Chinese 5 Spice

1 Tbsp. sherry
2 Tbsp. soy sauce
3 Tbsp. hoisin sauce
2 to 3 drops red food coloring

If a roast, cut into 2 to 3 inch chunks. Leave the pork tenderloin whole. This is not easy to find, so grab it when you see it. Marinate for 2 to 3 hours or overnight. Bake at 350° on open rack, 25 minutes on each side. Slice in ¼ inch slices; serve with Chinese hot mustard and toasted sesame seeds.

This is the same appetizer you pay dearly for in a Chinese restaurant, but this is so much better! Very tender. This is fabulous and so easy!

Jane Klein, Bellevue, WA

BARBEQUE RIBS

3 to 4 lb. country style ribs   Salt and pepper

Salt and pepper the ribs on both sides and place in uncovered roaster for 1 hour at 350°. Turn so both sides are brown. While ribs are browning, make following sauce.

Sauce:

1 medium onion
¾ c. brown sugar
3 Tbsp. Worcestershire sauce

1½ c. catsup
¾ c. water

Dice onion and saute in oil; cook until transparent. Add brown sugar, Worcestershire sauce, catsup, and water; simmer for 20 minutes. When ribs are brown, drain off drippings, then cover ribs with sauce; return to oven in covered roaster for 1½ hours. Test for tenderness.

Sauce may be used over again and will keep a long time in the refrigerator.

Dorothy Hills, Rochester, MN

BARBECUED RIBS

I use country style ribs. Trim fat and cut into 2 or 3 rib portions. Put ribs in large kettle. Add onion slices and cover with water; bring to boil, then simmer until almost done (fork tender). You can either freeze the ribs or they are ready to barbecue. You can use your favorite sauce.

One of my favorite sauces is:

1½ c. catsup
2 Tbsp. dark corn syrup
3 Tbsp. cider vinegar

2 tsp. salt
1 tsp. paprika
1 tsp. chillie powder

Mix together and brush on ribs. Cook either in broiler or over charcoal grill until brown. Sauce is enough for 4 pounds of ribs.

James Renner, Fergus Falls, MN

Notes

Notes

Crock Pot Cooking

FIRST AID IN HOUSEHOLD EMERGENCIES

POISONING: When a poison has been taken internally, start first aid at once. Call doctor immediately.
- Dilute poison with large amounts of liquids — milk or water
- Wash out by inducing vomiting, when not a strong acid, strong alkali or petroleum
- For acid poisons do not induce vomiting, but neutralize with milk of magnesia. Then give milk, olive oil or egg white. Keep victim warm and lying down.
- For alkali poisons such as lye or ammonia, do not induce vomiting.
- Give lemon juice or vinegar. Then give milk and keep victim warm and lying down.
- If poison is a sleeping drug, induce vomiting and then give strong black coffee frequently. Victim must be kept awake.
- If breathing stops, give artificial respiration.

SHOCK: Shock is brought on by a sudden or severe physical injury or emotional disturbance. In shock, the balance between the nervous system and the blood vessels is upset. The result is faintness, nausea, and a pale and clammy skin. Call ambulance immediately. If not treated the victim may become unconscious and eventually lapse into a coma.
- Keep victim lying down, preferably with head lower than body.
- Don't give fluids unless delayed in getting to doctor, then give only water. (Hot tea, coffee, milk or broth may be tried if water is not tolerated.)
- Never give liquid to an unconscious person. Patient must be alert.
- Cover victim both under and around his body.
- Do not permit victim to become abnormally hot.
- Reassure victim and avoid letting him see other victims or his own injury.
- Fainting is most common and last form of shock. Patient will respond in 30-60 seconds by merely allowing patient to lie head down if possible on floor.

FRACTURES: Pain, deformity or swelling of injured part usually means a fracture. If fracture is suspected, don't move person unless absolutely necessary, and then only if the suspected area is splinted. Give small amounts of lukewarm fluids and treat for shock.

BURNS: Apply or submerge the burned area in cold water. Apply a protective dry sterile cloth or gauze dry dressing if necessary. Do not apply grease or an antiseptic ointment or spray. Call doctor and keep patient warm (not hot) with severe burns.
- If burn case must be transported any distance, cover burns with clean cloth.
- Don't dress extensive facial burns. (It may hinder early plastic surgery.)

WOUNDS: Minor Cuts — Apply pressure with sterile gauze until bleeding stops. Use antiseptic recommended by your doctor. Bandage with sterile gauze. See your doctor. **Puncture Wounds** — Cover with sterile gauze and consult a doctor immediately. Serious infection can arise unless properly treated.

ANIMAL BITES: Wash wounds freely with soap and water. Hold under running tap for several minutes if possible. Apply an antiseptic approved by your doctor and cover with sterile gauze compress. Always see your doctor immediately. So that animal may be held in quarantine, obtain name and address of owner.

HEAT EXHAUSTION: Caused by exposure to heat or sun. Symptoms: Pale face, moist and clammy skin, weak pulse, subnormal temperature, victim usually conscious.
Treatment: Keep victim lying down, legs elevated, victim wrapped in blanket. Give salt water to drink (1 tsp. salt to 1 glass water) ½ glass every 15 minutes. Call doctor.

GENERAL DIRECTIONS FOR FIRST AID

1. Effect a prompt rescue
2. Maintain an open airway
3. Control severe bleeding by direct pressure over bleeding site. No tourniquet.
4. Give First Aid for poisoning.
5. Do not move victim unless it is necessary for safety reasons.
6. Protect the victim from unnecessary manipulation and
7. Avoid or overcome chilling by using blankets or covers, if available.
8. Determine the injuries or cause for sudden illness.
9. Examine the victim methodically but be guided by the kind of accident or sudden illness and the need of the situation.
10. Carry out the indicated First

CROCK POT COOKING

PARTY MEATBALLS

2 lb. ground beef	1 slightly beaten egg
1 large onion, chopped	Salt and pepper

Mix ingredients and form into balls.

1 large jar chili sauce	Juice of 1 lemon (scant)
1 small jar grape jelly	Sugar to taste

When this mixture comes to a boil and jelly is dissolved, add meatballs; simmer for 1 to 1½ hours. Can be done in a crock pot.

Lenora Buck, Fargo, ND

BREAD PUDDING

In crock pot in layers:

¾ c. pressed brown sugar	2 c. raisins
8 slices stale bread cubes or	
lightly toasted bread	

Mix and pour on it:

3 c. milk	4 beaten eggs
1½ tsp. vanilla	

Sprinkle cinnamon on top. Do not stir or lift lid.

Carol Gilbertson, Hawley, MN

BAKED APPLE

5 to 6 medium apples, cored and	1 tsp. cinnamon
peeled about 1 inch down	2 Tbsp. butter
½ c. sugar	½ c. water
½ c. raisins	

Mix sugar, raisins, and cinnamon. Stuff apples with sugar mixture and dot with butter. Pour water into cooker and add apples. Cook on LOW for 7 to 8 hours.

Lenora Buck, Fargo, ND

CROCK POT DRESSING

½ c. onion	½ c. butter
½ c. celery	

Chop and saute onion and celery in butter.

8 c. bread cubes or stuffing	1½ tsp. poultry seasoning
2 c. chicken broth (bouillon)	½ tsp. pepper
1 tsp. salt	

Pour sauteed mixture over bread cubes. Pour chicken broth over that. Cover and set on HIGH for 1 hour. Turn to LOW and cook for 30 to 40 minutes.

Marlys Wendorf

KATY'S HOMEMADE POTATO SOUP

9 c. bite-size chopped potatoes (unpeeled)	½ c. butter
	5 c. water
2 onions, chopped	13 oz. can evaporated milk
1 carrot, sliced	1 Tbsp. parsley flakes
1 stalk celery, chopped	Salt and pepper
5 chicken bouillon cubes	

Put all ingredients, except milk, in crock pot. Cover and cook on LOW for 10 to 12 hours (HIGH for 3 to 4 hours, AUTOSHIFT for 6 hours). Add evaporated milk a few minutes before serving. Shredded cheese can be added just before serving for richer flavor.

Harlan Brekke, Fargo, ND

HEARTY POTATO-SAUERKRAUT SOUP

4 c. chicken broth	1 medium onion, chopped
1 (10¾ oz.) can cream of mushroom soup	2 stalks celery, chopped
	¾ lb. smoked Polish sausage, cubed
1 (16 oz.) can sauerkraut, rinsed and drained	½ c. chopped cooked chicken
8 oz. fresh mushrooms, sliced	2 Tbsp. vinegar
1 medium potato, cubed in small cubes	2 tsp. dried dill weed
	½ tsp. pepper
2 medium carrots, chopped	

In a 3½ to 4 quart electric slow crockery cooker, stir together all ingredients. Cover and cook on LOW heat setting for 10 to 12 hours or until vegetables are tender.

Sue Schindler, Barnesville, MN

VEGETABLE BEEF SOUP

1 lb. soup meat or ground beef, browned	1 (16 oz.) can tomatoes (undrained)
3 c. water	2 potatoes, diced
2 carrots, sliced	1 onion, diced
3 stalks celery, sliced	1 bay leaf
1 small rutabaga, diced	Salt and pepper to taste

Put all ingredients in crock pot; stir well. Cover and cook on LOW for 12 to 24 hours (HIGH for 4 to 6 hours).

The longer it cooks the better it is!

Laila Schroeder

SPLIT PEA SOUP

1 lb. pkg. split peas	1 stalk celery, diced
1 ham bone	2 qt. water
1 carrot, diced	1 tsp. salt
1 onion, diced	1/4 tsp. pepper

Combine ingredients in slow cooker. Cover and cook on LOW for 8 to 10 hours. Remove ham bone; cut off meat, then dice and return to soup. Serves 8.

Marlys Swehla, Albert Lea, MN

CROCK POT BAR-B-Q RIBS

3 lb. country style ribs	2 Tbsp. brown sugar
1/4 c. chopped onion	3 Tbsp. Worcestershire
1/2 c. diced celery	2 Tbsp. vinegar
1/2 tsp. salt	1/2 c. chili sauce
1/4 tsp. pepper	1/4 c. lemon juice
1 Tbsp. prepared mustard	1/2 c. water

Cut ribs in serving pieces; brown. Place meat in bottom of crock pot. Mix remaining ingredients in bowl and pour over meat. Cover and cook on LOW for 7 to 8 hours - on HIGH for 3 to 3 1/2 hours. Serves 6.

Mrs. David Kosmatka, Forman, ND

BEEF STEW

2 lb. stew meat	2 tsp. Kitchen Bouquet
4 carrots (chunks)	Salt and pepper to taste
3 potatoes (chunks)	Garlic to taste
1 onion, diced	1/2 c. tapioca (thickening)
2 celery stalks, sliced	3 c. water

Put all ingredients in crock pot; stir to mix well. Cover and cook on HIGH till it bubbles, then turn on LOW and cook overnight (HIGH for 4 to 5 hours, LOW for 10 to 12 hours).

I've started this at supper time and served the next noon.

Laila Schroeder, Shakopee, MN

HEARTY BEEF STEW

2 lb. stew beef, cut in 1 inch
    cubes
5 carrots, cut in 1 inch pieces
1 large onion, cut in chunks
3 stalks celery, sliced

1 (1 lb. 12 oz.) can tomatoes
½ c. quick cooking tapioca
2 bay leaves
Salt and pepper to taste

Trim all fat from meat. Put all ingredients in crock pot; mix thoroughly. Cover and cook on LOW for 12 hours (HIGH for 5 to 6 hours).

Marlys Swehla, Albert Lea, MN

FORGOTTEN STEW

Cut up:

2 lb. stew meat
3 stalks celery
6 carrots

4 potatoes
1 large onion

Mix:

2 tsp. sugar
2 tsp. salt

2 Tbsp. quick cooking tapioca
1 c. tomato juice

Let tomato juice mixture stand for 10 minutes, then add to other ingredients. Cook in crock pot for 10 to 12 hours.

Sue Schindler, Barnesville, MN

NO PEEK STEW

1 lb. beef stew meat
1 c. potatoes, cut up
1 c. carrots
1 c. celery
1 onion

12 oz. V-8 juice
2 Tbsp. tapioca
Salt and pepper to taste
1 can green beans (add last ½
    hour)

Stir all ingredients. Put in crock pot or bake in 250° oven for about 5 hours (covered). Recipe can be doubled - freeze ½ of it for another time.

Mrs. Cora Mueller, St. Paul, MN

PAT'S STEW
(Crock pot)

2 c. water
4 potatoes, quartered
4 carrots, quartered
1 lb. stew meat (1 to 2 inch cubes)
2 bay leaves

2 Tbsp. soy sauce
1 Tbsp. A.1. Steak sauce
1 shake red pepper
5 shakes paprika (no more)
1 shake garlic salt
Salt and pepper to taste

Combine in order in crock pot. Turn to HIGH for 7 to 10 hours.

Bernice T. Eugenis, Saginaw, MN

BEEF-AND-KIDNEY STEW
(Serves 6)

¼ lb. mushrooms, halved
4 Tbsp. butter
1 c. chopped onions
2 lb. boneless lean beef, cut into 1 inch cubes and dusted with ¼ c. flour
2 pairs lamb kidneys, thinly sliced
2 c. beef stock

2 Tbsp. chopped parsley
1 tsp. dried thyme
½ bay leaf
¼ tsp. freshly ground pepper
Pinch of cayenne pepper
1 tsp. Worcestershire sauce
4 potatoes, peeled and quartered
Chopped parsley (garnish)

Saute mushrooms in 2 tablespoons of the butter in a skillet or a slow cooker with a browning unit for 5 minutes; remove and set aside. Add remaining butter and brown onions, beef, and kidneys. Put potatoes in the bottom of a slow cooker and add meat mixture with remaining ingredients, reducing stock to 1½ cups. Cover and cook on LOW for 6 to 8 hours. Add reserved mushrooms; cover and cook on HIGH for 15 minutes. Garnish with parsley.

Kathy Olsen, Duluth, MN

IRISH LAMB STEW
(Serves 6 to 8)

2½ lb. boneless lamb, cut into 1½ inch cubes
2 Tbsp. corn oil
1½ tsp. salt
½ tsp. freshly ground pepper
4 turnips, cut into ½ inch thick slices

4 carrots, cut diagonally into ½ inch thick slices
2 onions, sliced
4 potatoes, peeled and quartered
2 Tbsp. flour
2 Tbsp. chopped parsley

Brown the meat in oil in a skillet or a slow cooker with a browning unit. Put all ingredients, except flour and parsley, in a slow cooker with the meat. Add 2 cups water and cook on LOW, covered, for 8 to 10 hours. Uncover and turn on HIGH.

Blend flour with ¼ cup water until it forms a paste; slowly add to the stew, stirring constantly, until slightly thickened. Stir in parsley and serve.

Kathy Olsen, Duluth, MN

BRAISED OXTAILS, SPANISH STYLE
(Serves 6)

3 to 4 lb. oxtails, disjointed
3 Tbsp. olive oil
2 onions, chopped
2 cloves garlic, finely chopped
1 Tbsp. flour
2 c. beef stock
1 c. dry red wine
½ c. tomato sauce
6 peppercorns
½ tsp. dried oregano

1 dried red chili pepper, seeded
   and chopped
2 whole cloves
2 carrots, chopped
1 sweet red pepper, chopped
1 Tbsp. chopped parsley
2 potatoes, peeled and cut into
   chunks
Salt and freshly ground pepper
   to taste

Brown oxtails on all sides in oil in a skillet or a slow cooker with a browning unit. Add onions and garlic; cook for 5 minutes. Sprinkle flour over the meat; blend well and cook for 2 minutes. Reduce stock to 1½ cups and wine to ¾ cup and add with all the remaining ingredients and the meat to a slow cooker, placing potatoes in the bottom. Cover and cook on LOW for 8 to 10 hours.

Kathy Olsen, Duluth, MN

MEAT LOAF WITH TOMATO SAUCE

3 medium sized tomatoes (1 lb.),
   quartered, *or* 1 (1 lb.) can
   whole stewed tomatoes
   (undrained)
1 garlic clove

2 Tbsp. chopped parsley
1 egg
1 tsp. salt
1 lb. ground beef
1 c. soda cracker crumbs

1. Set covered pot on base. Preheat at Setting No. 5 while mixing ingredients.

2. In mixing bowl, place tomatoes, garlic, parsley, egg, and salt; beat with electric mixer until smooth.

3. Combine ground beef with cracker crumbs and 1¼ cups of tomato mixture. Shape into a loaf and place in 9x5 inch loaf pan. Pour remaining tomato mixture over meat loaf. Place pan in pot.

4. Cover and bake at Setting No. 5 for 2 hours. Place inverted platter

over loaf pan and turn platter right side up to remove loaf from pan. Makes 4 to 5 servings.

Hint: Meat Loaf With Tomato Sauce may be placed in pot without loaf pan. Preheat and bake at Setting No. 3½ for 2 hours.

Betty Risse, Bismarck, ND

MEATBALLS WITH RICE

1 lb. lean ground beef or chuck	3 Tbsp. flour
½ c. cracker crumbs	1 tsp. paprika
½ c. milk	1 (28 oz.) can whole tomatoes
1 egg	(undrained)
3 Tbsp. minced onion	½ c. sliced onion
1½ tsp. salt	1 tsp. salt
¼ tsp. basil	1 c. raw rice
¼ tsp. savory (optional)	

1. In mixing bowl, combine ground beef, cracker crumbs, milk, egg, minced onion, salt, basil, and savory. Shape into 12 meatballs. Combine flour and paprika; roll meatballs in mixture.

2. Place pot on base. Place tomatoes in pot and break up with spoon to cover bottom of pot. Add onion and salt. Place meatballs on top of onion. Cover and simmer at Setting No. 3½ (midway between Settings No. 3 and No. 4) for 5 to 8 hours. One hour before serving, add rice; stir to bottom of pot and increase heat to Setting No. 4. Keep warm for serving at Setting No 2. Makes 6 servings.

Betty Risse, Bismarck, ND

STEAMED FRANKS

1. Use 1 pound of frankfurters. Place 6 frankfurters crosswise in bottom of pot. Lay remaining frankfurters on top, lengthwise or in opposite direction. Do not add water.

2. Cover and place pot on base. Steam at Setting No. 3½ for 30 minutes. Frankfurters will be hot and brown where they touch the pot. Keep warm for serving at Setting No. 2. Makes 10 servings.

Betty Risse, Bismarck, ND

SWISS STEAK

2 lb. round steak, cut into serving pieces	1 large onion, sliced *or* 1 pkg. onion soup mix
1 tsp. salt	1 (16 oz.) can tomatoes
⅛ tsp. pepper	

Combine all ingredients in cooker. Cook on LOW for 6 to 10 hours or on HIGH for 3 to 4 hours.

Lenora Buck, Fargo, ND

CROCK POT RIBS AND SAUCE MIX
(6 large servings)

1 c. hickory smoked barbeque
  sauce
½ c. red cooking wine (white is
  okay)
½ c. chopped onion
1 can Spanish vegetable soup
  (Campbell's)
2 to 3 Tbsp. soy sauce
½ pkg. onion soup mix
1 tsp. Worcestershire sauce

1 tsp. Mrs. Dash
1 tsp. lemon pepper
2 to 3 rounded Tbsp. brown
  sugar
⅛ to ¼ c. dark Karo syrup (lite is
  okay)
¼ c. chopped green pepper
2 buds (large) garlic, crushed
½ c. water
10 lb. country ribs

Brown ribs in hot skillet with butter. Arrange in 5 quart crock pot. Take skillet and ½ cup of water and dissolve bouillon cubes. Mix this broth with rest of sauce ingredients in a large bowl; pour over ribs in crock pot. If ribs are for next day, place in refrigerator and let marinate overnight.

To cook, place on HIGH for 6 hours (LOW takes about 8 or 9 hours). Ribs are done when the meat starts to separate from the bones.

H. Marxen, Williston, ND

CHILE CON CARNE
(Serves 6 to 8)

2 lb. stewing beef, cut into ½
  inch cubes, or 1 lb. each
  stewing beef and pork butt,
  cut into ½ inch cubes
1 onion, chopped
3 cloves garlic, minced
2 Tbsp. lard
3 c. peeled and chopped ripe
  tomatoes
¼ c. chili powder, mixed with 1
  Tbsp. flour

1 Tbsp. minced oregano or 1
  tsp. dried oregano
½ tsp. ground cumin
2 bay leaves
1 tsp. salt
1 c. pitted ripe olives
Chopped onions (garnish)
Minced fresh green chilies
  (garnish)
Chopped coriander (garnish)
Warm tortillas (accompaniment)

Brown the meat, onion, and garlic in lard in a skillet or a slow cooker with a browning unit. Combine meat mixture and remaining ingredients, except olives, in a slow cooker. Cover and cook on LOW for 6 to 8 hours. Add olives; cover and cook on HIGH for 10 minutes. Garnish and serve with tortillas.

Kathy Olsen, Duluth, MN

EASY CHILI

1 lb. ground beef
1 medium onion, chopped
½ c. chopped green pepper
2 c. (1 lb. can) undrained
   tomatoes
2 c. (1 lb. can) undrained kidney
   beans

1 c. (8 oz. can) tomato sauce
1 tsp. salt
2 to 2½ tsp. chili powder
1½ tsp. prepared or dry mustard
1 clove garlic or ⅛ tsp. garlic
   powder

In a large frypan or saucepan, brown ground beef; drain off excess fat. Add remaining ingredients. Put in crock pot on LOW heat for 10 to 12 hours.

Sue Schindler, Barnesville, MN

CROCK POT BEANS

½ to 1 lb. ground beef
¾ lb. bacon, cut in small pieces
1 c. chopped onion
2 (1 lb. 15 oz.) cans pork and
   beans
1 (1 lb.) can kidney beans,
   drained

1 (1 lb.) can butter limas, drained
1 c. ketchup
¼ c. brown sugar
1 Tbsp. liquid smoke
3 Tbsp. white vinegar
1 tsp. salt
Dash of pepper

Brown ground beef in skillet; drain off fat and put beef in crock pot. Brown bacon and onion; drain off fat. Add bacon, onion, and remaining ingredients to crock pot. Stir together; cover and cook on LOW for 4 to 6 hours.

Marlys Swehla, Albert Lea, MN

GREEN BEAN CASSEROLE

1 (1 lb.) can cut green beans,
   drained
1 (3½ oz.) can French fried
   onion rings, crumbled
1 c. grated Cheddar cheese
1 (8 oz.) can water chestnuts

1 can condensed cream of
   chicken soup
¼ c. white wine
1½ tsp. salt
½ tsp. curry powder
¼ tsp. pepper

In cooker, alternate layers as follows: Beans, onion rings, cheese, and water chestnuts. Combine all other ingredients and add to cooker. Cook on LOW for 6 to 7 hours or on HIGH for 3 to 4 hours. Makes 4 to 5 servings.

Lenora Buck, Fargo, ND

HOT VEGETABLES DISH
(Serves 10)

1 (10 oz.) pkg. frozen broccoli
1 (10 oz.) pkg. frozen Brussels
   sprouts
1 (10 oz.) pkg. frozen cauliflower
1 (10 oz.) pkg. frozen carrots

1 (8 oz.) pkg. frozen onions
1 can mushroom soup
1 (8 oz.) jar Cheez Whiz
¼ c. milk

Mix 1 can mushroom soup and 1 (8 ounce) jar of Cheez Whiz together with ¼ cup of milk. Mix all of the vegetables together and pour mushroom soup and cheese mixture over them. Put in crock pot and cook for about 3 hours on HIGH.

Mary Borrowman, Minneapolis, MN

CHEESE AND POTATO CASSEROLE

2 lb. pkg. frozen hash brown
   potatoes, partly thawed
2 (10 oz.) cans Cheddar cheese
   soup

1 (13 oz.) can evaporated milk
1 can French fried onion rings
Salt and pepper

Combine potatoes, soup, milk, and ½ the onion rings. Pour into greased crock pot. Add salt and pepper to taste. Cover and cook on LOW for 8 to 9 hours or on HIGH for 3 hours. Sprinkle remaining onion rings over top before serving.

Carol Gilbertson, Hawley, MN

CORNED BEEF AND CABBAGE
(Serves 4 to 6)

1 (4 lb.) corned beef brisket,
   soaked in cold water to
   cover for 2 hours to remove
   excess brine if necessary
1 bay leaf
6 peppercorns
1 onion, stuck with 2 cloves
1 carrot, sliced

1 celery rib, sliced
2 sprigs parsley
1 c. apple cider
6 carrots, halved crosswise
6 new potatoes
1 small head cabbage, cut into 4
   to 6 wedges

Combine all ingredients, except cabbage, with water to cover and cook on LOW, covered, for 8 to 10 hours. Remove corned beef and vegetables to a platter and keep warm. Add cabbage to pot; cover and cook on HIGH for 20 minutes. Place cabbage on platter with meat and vegetables. Serve with accompaniments.

Kathy Olsen, Duluth, MN

CORNED BEEF AND CABBAGE

3 lb. corned beef brisket
1 large onion, quartered
1 head cabbage, cut into small
    wedges
¼ tsp. pepper
2 Tbsp. vinegar
2 Tbsp. sugar
1 c. water

    Combine ingredients in cooker with cabbage on top. Cut meat in pieces, if necessary, to fit in cooker. Cook on LOW for 12 to 14 hours or on HIGH for 6 to 7 hours or on AUTOMATIC for 6 to 8 hours. Makes 4 servings.

Lenora Buck, Fargo, ND

STUFFED CABBAGE ROLLS

4 qt. water
8 large cabbage leaves
1 lb. ground beef or ham
½ c. instant rice
1 egg, slightly beaten
¼ c. milk
½ c. diced celery
⅓ c. diced onion
1 tsp. seasoned salt
¼ tsp. seasoned pepper
1 (8 oz.) can tomato sauce
1 c. water
½ tsp. oregano leaves

    1. Pour 4 quarts water in pot. Place pot, covered, on electric or gas rangetop heating unit over medium high heat until liquid reaches a boil (about 10 minutes). Place cabbage leaves in water; cover and remove from heat. Let stand for 10 minutes.

    2. Preheat a skillet over medium heat and brown meat. Remove from heat. Add rice, egg, milk, celery, onion, seasoned salt, and seasoned pepper; mix well.

    3. Remove cabbage leaves from water. Place ½ cup of meat mixture on each cabbage leaf. Roll and secure with toothpick.

    4. Pour water out of pot. In pot, mix tomato sauce, 1 cup water and oregano leaves. Place cabbage rolls in sauce. Place pot on base. Cover and simmer at Setting No. 3½ for 5 hours. Keep warm for serving at Setting No. 2. Makes 8 servings.

Betty Risse, Bismarck, ND

STUFFED GREEN PEPPERS WITH TOMATO SAUCE

6 large or 8 medium green
    peppers
1 lb. lean ground beef
⅓ c. chopped onion
½ c. chopped celery
1 c. instant rice
½ c. milk
1 egg
½ tsp. salt
¼ tsp. pepper
½ tsp. chili powder
1 (10½ oz.) can condensed
    tomato soup
1 soup can water

    1. Cut tops off peppers; remove stems and set tops aside. Clean out seeds.

    2. Preheat pot on electric or gas rangetop heating unit over medium

heat for 2 minutes. Brown ground beef; remove from heat. Add onion, celery, rice, milk, egg, salt, pepper, and chili powder to ground beef; mix. Stuff peppers with mixture.

3. In pot, combine tomato soup and water. Place pepper tops in bottom of pot; set stuffed peppers on tops to prevent peppers from spilling.

4. Place pot on base and simmer, covered, at Setting No. 5 for 2 hours. Spoon sauce over peppers when serving. Keep warm for serving at Setting No. 2. Makes 6 to 8 servings.

Betty Risse, Bismarck, ND

Notes

Notes

Cooking
for a
Crowd

Ways to use left-overs

If it's good food, don't throw it away. Little left-overs, or big ones, fit into many dishes. A switch in recipes here or a novel dessert there—and your left-overs are put to work in interesting ways. Egg yolks can substitute for whole eggs, for example. If bread is a bit dry, then it's just right for french toast. Other left-overs have a way of adding food value or a fresh new touch—such as fruit in muffins or vegetables in omelet.

Listed below are some of the dishes in which left-overs may be used.

Cooked snap beans, lima beans, corn peas, carrots, *In*
  Meat and vegetable pie
  Soup
  Stew
  Stuffed peppers
  Stuffed tomatoes
  Vegetables in cheese sauce

Cooked leafy vegetables, chopped, *In*
  Creamed vegetables
  Soup
  Meat loaf
  Meat patties
  Omelet
  Souffle

Cooked or canned fruits, *In*
  Fruit cup
  Fruit sauces
  Jellied fruit
  Quick breads
  Shortcake
  Upside-down cake
  Yeast breads

Cooked meats, poultry, fish, *In*
  Casserole dishes
  Hash
  Meat patties
  Meat pies
  Salads
  Sandwiches
  Stuffed vegetables

Cooked wheat, oat, or corn cereals, *In*
  Fried cereal
  Meat loaf or patties
  Sweet puddings

Cooked rice, noodles, macaroni, spaghetti, *In*
  Casseroles
  Meat or cheese loaf
  Timbales

Bread
  Slices *for*
    French toast
  Dry crumbs, *in*
    Brown betty
    Croquettes
    Fried chops
  Soft crumbs, *in*
    Meat loaf
    Stuffings

Cakes or cookies, *In*
  Brown betty
  Ice-box cake
  Toasted, with sweet topping, for dessert

Egg yolks, *In*
  Cakes
  Cornstarch pudding
  Custard or sauce
  Pie filling
  Salad dressing
  Scrambled eggs

Egg whites, *In*
  Custard
  Fruit whip
  Meringue
  Souffles

Hard-cooked egg or yolk, *In*
  Casserole dishes
  Garnish
  Salads
  Sandwiches

Sour cream, *In*
  Cakes, cookies
  Dessert sauce
  Meat stews
  Pie filling
  Salad dressing
  Sauce for vegetables

Sour milk, *In*
  Cakes, cookies
  Quick breads

Cooked potatoes, *In*
  Croquettes
  Fried or creamed potatoes
  Meat-pie crust
  Potatoes in cheese sauce
  Stew or chowder

COOKING FOR A CROWD

QUANTITIES TO SERVE 100

11 loaves bread
30 pounds meat to roast
2 quarts pickles
8 half pint glasses jelly
5 pounds butter
2 pounds coffee
200 rolls
10 dozen doughnuts
6 large, 9 small cakes
2 (16 pound) hams, baked
4 gallons baked beans
4 gallons ice cream
3 pecks potatoes
16 chickens (creamed chicken)
16 quarts cabbage salad
18 pies
1 quart coffee cream

Waldorf Salad: 8 quarts apples, 4 quarts celery, 4 cups nutmeats, 2 quarts salad dressing

Macaroni and Cheese: 10 pounds macaroni, 4 quarts medium white sauce, 2 cups cheese

Lemonade: 6 dozen lemons, 8 cups sugar, 18 quarts water

Canned vegetables: 4 No. 10 cans

Betty Risse, Bismarck, ND

QUANTITIES TO SERVE 50

25 pounds roast beef, lamb, or ham
25 pounds chicken
10 pounds meat loaf
20 pounds potatoes, mashed
5 large heads lettuce
10 heads cabbage
10 pounds carrots
2 (No. 10) cans tomatoes
2 (No. 10) cans wax or green beans
10 (No. 2) cans peas
1 quart salad dressing
1 quart whipping cream
2 pounds butter
1 pound coffee (80 cups)

1 pound rice, cooked (makes 2 quarts)
1 pound spaghetti, cooked (2¾ quarts)
1 quart coffee cream (75 servings)

COCOA OR HOT CHOCOLATE
(Quantity: Serves 50)

2½ c. cocoa or 5 sq. chocolate
2½ c. sugar
¼ tsp. salt
2 tsp. vanilla

1¼ qt. cold water
8½ qt. hot milk (or evaporated
    milk and water, 4¼ qt. each)

Make cocoa syrup by combining cocoa, sugar, and salt. Add water gradually and bring to a boil, stirring constantly. Boil for 3 minutes or until thickened. Add hot milk and blend. Add vanilla just before serving.

Betty Risse, Bismarck, ND

FESTIVE DAIRY PUNCH

1 (6 oz.) can frozen limeade

2 (6 oz.) cans frozen lemonade

Mix with 1 quart of water.

½ gal. cold milk
½ gal. vanilla ice cream

2 qt. 7-Up *or* ginger ale
½ gal. lime sherbet

Place ice cream and sherbet in container and break into small chunks. Add milk, juice, and pop (7-Up or ginger ale). Stir until ice cream is partially melted. Garnish with lime, orange, and lemon slices. Serves 40 to 50.

Lois Hulst, Sioux City, IA

COFFEE

1 c. coffee to 12 c. water

1 egg to each pound of coffee

Mix coffee with egg and a little water. When water boils, add coffee and boil for 5 to 8 minutes. Let stand to let coffee settle.

Betty Risse, Bismarck, ND

COFFEE

To make Coffee in electric percolator, always use cold water.

To make 25 cups, use 1½ cups of coffee. To make 50 cups, use 3 cups of coffee. To make 75 cups, use 4 cups of coffee. To make 100 cups, use 5½ cups of coffee.

Joan Lewis, Minneapolis, MN

BASIC WHITE SAUCE
(Yield: 2 gallons)

For thin sauce, use:

1 lb. butter
½ lb. flour
2 gal. hot milk

3 Tbsp. salt
½ tsp. pepper

For medium sauce, use:

2 lb. butter
1 lb. flour
2 gal. hot milk

3 Tbsp. salt
⅛ tsp. pepper

For thick sauce, use:

3 lb. butter
1½ lb. flour
2 gal. hot milk

3 Tbsp. salt
⅛ tsp. pepper

Melt butter; add flour, gradually blending to a smooth paste. Stir hot milk into butter and flour mixture. Cook until thickened, stirring constantly; season.

Joan Lewis, Minneapolis, MN

MASTER MIX FOR BISCUITS, MUFFINS, AND CORN BREAD

9 c. flour
⅓ c. baking powder
1 tsp. salt
¼ c. sugar

2 c. shortening
2 c. dry milk
2 tsp. cream of tartar

Mix and store in airtight can.

To make Biscuits, use:

3 c. mix

1 c. water

To make Muffins, use:

3 c. mix
1 egg

2 Tbsp. sugar
1 c. water

To make Corn Bread, use:

1½ c. mix
¾ c. corn meal
½ tsp. salt

2 Tbsp. sugar
¾ c. water
1 egg

Edie Raatz

THOUSAND ISLAND DRESSING
(Quantity: Serves 75 to 100)

3 or 4 dill pickles
1 (No. 2) can beets
1 green pepper

2 or 3 medium onions
Mayonnaise

Grind together the preceding ingredients. Drain and add mayonnaise to make about 2 gallons. Store in cool place.

Betty Risse, Bismarck, ND

MAYONNAISE
(Quantity: Serves 75 to 100)

12 eggs, well beaten
2 c. sugar
½ c. salt
1 Tbsp. mustard

6 qt. salad oil
2 c. vinegar
Juice of 2 lemons

Mix dry ingredients and add to eggs. Add salad oil, using electric beater at high speed. Add vinegar and lemon juice, then reduce speed to low. This can be stored for a long time in refrigerator. Use in Thousand Island Dressing.

Betty Risse, Bismarck, ND

FRENCH DRESSING
(Quantity: Banquet size)

8 (10½ oz.) cans tomato soup
4 c. salad oil
6 c. vinegar
6 c. sugar
12 tsp. salt

16 Tbsp. Worcestershire sauce
2 tsp. paprika
8 tsp. dry mustard
16 Tbsp. grated onion
16 Tbsp. finely cut green pepper

Mix dry ingredients. Add oil, a little at a time, and beat. Beat in soup and vinegar slowly. Add Worcestershire sauce, onion, and pepper.

Betty Risse, Bismarck, ND

FRENCH DRESSING
(Makes 1 quart)

Combine thoroughly in blender or mixer:

2 c. salad oil
¾ c. catsup
½ c. vinegar

1 c. sugar
1 Tbsp. salt
¼ c. finely chopped onions

Joan Lewis, Minneapolis, MN

CAULIFLOWER AND BROCCOLI SALAD

1 head cauliflower, broken into small pieces
1 head broccoli, broken into small pieces
⅓ c. chopped onion
½ c. green pepper, chopped into small pieces
1 (4 oz.) pkg. Cheddar cheese, shredded
½ lb. crisp fried bacon, broken into pieces
1 c. sour cream
1 c. Miracle Whip

Mix all vegetables together with cheese and bacon. Mix sour cream and Miracle Whip with ¼ cup sugar. Mix until creamy and well blended. Pour over vegetables. Let stand for several hours before serving.

Very good and keeps for several days. Makes a large salad, about 5 quarts.

Esther D. Lee, St. Paul, MN

FRUIT JELLO
(Quantity: Serves 50)

26 oz. (3¾ c.) jello
1 gal. water and/or fruit juice
3 qt. fruit, cut and drained

Heat ½ of the liquid; add to jello and stir until dissolved. Add the remaining cold liquid; chill. When the mixture begins to set, add fruit. Chill until ready to serve.

Betty Risse, Bismarck, ND

TUNA, EGG, AND MACARONI SALAD

For 8 servings, cook 1 (7 ounce) package macaroni or 7 ounces bulk macaroni according to package directions. Drain and rinse in cold water.

Add:

½ c. chopped celery
2 (7 oz.) cans tuna, drained
1 tsp. dehydrated onion or 4 tsp. sliced green onion
4 eggs, hard cooked and chopped
2 to 2½ c. seasoned salad dressing

For 50 servings, cook 6 (7 ounce) packages of macaroni or 2 pounds 10 ounces bulk macaroni according to package directions. Drain and rinse in cold water.

Add:

3 c. chopped celery
12 (7 oz.) cans tuna, drained
2 Tbsp. dehydrated onion or ½ c. sliced green onion
24 eggs, hard cooked and chopped
3 to 3½ qt. seasoned salad dressing

LETTUCE AND ORANGE SALAD

For 6 servings, use:

1 qt. chopped or torn lettuce
1 (11 oz.) can mandarin oranges
   or 1 c. oranges, drained

2 Tbsp. green onion, sliced

For 50 servings, use:

8 qt. chopped or torn lettuce
2 qt. mandarin oranges or 8 c.
   oranges, drained

1 c. green onion, sliced

Just before serving, top with Sweet Sour Dressing.

For 6 servings (yields ¾ cup), use:

½ c. vinegar
1 c. sugar

½ tsp. salt
Dash of pepper

For 50 servings (yields 1½ quarts), use:

1 qt. vinegar
4 lb. sugar

¼ c. salt
¾ tsp. pepper

Bring to a boil; thoroughly combine ingredients. Chill before putting over chopped vegetables or fruit.

Joan Lewis, Minneapolis, MN

CABBAGE WALDORF SALAD
(Quantity: Serves 50)

7 qt. cabbage, shredded
8 apples, cubed (unpeeled)
2 c. raisins

1 Tbsp. salt
4 Tbsp. sugar
½ tsp. pepper

Dressing:

1½ c. cream (sweet or sour)
½ c. vinegar

¼ c. sugar
1 tsp. salt

Toss all ingredients lightly; add the dressing just before serving.

Betty Risse, Bismarck, ND

POTATO SALAD TO SERVE 100

15 lb. potatoes, boiled and cut
5 doz. eggs, boiled and cut
1 bunch celery, cut fine
1 onion, chopped fine
1½ qt. mayonnaise

Can of milk (to thin mayonnaise)
A little mustard to taste
A little sugar to taste
Salt and pepper

Combine all. If more salad is needed, use 1½ dozen eggs for every 5 pounds of potatoes and 1 pint of dressing, seasoned to taste, with more celery added.

COLE SLAW

For 6 servings, use:

4 c. chopped or shredded cabbage

1 Tbsp. diced pimento
1 Tbsp. diced green pepper

For 50 servings, use:

8 qt. or 10 lb. chopped or shredded cabbage

¼ c. diced pimento
¼ c. diced green pepper

Mix with Sweet Sour Dressing.

Sweet Sour Dressing - For 6 servings (¾ cup), use:

½ c. vinegar
1 c. sugar

½ tsp. salt
Dash of pepper

For 50 servings (1½ quarts), use:

1 qt. vinegar
4 lb. sugar

¼ c. salt
¾ tsp. pepper

Bring to a boil to thoroughly combine ingredients. Chill before putting over vegetable or fruit.

Joan Lewis, Minneapolis, MN

POTATO SALAD

For 12 servings, use:

1 qt. diced potatoes
4 hard cooked eggs
1 c. diced celery

¼ c. chopped onion
2 Tbsp. diced pimento

For 50 servings, use:

4 qt. diced potatoes
16 hard cooked eggs
1 qt. diced celery

1 c. chopped onion
½ c. diced pimento

Cook potatoes the day of use and cool to room temperature. Mix all ingredients with Salad Dressing and chill.

Salad Dressing:

For 12 servings, use:

1 c. salad dressing
2¼ tsp. vinegar
¼ tsp. salt

Dash of pepper
½ tsp. salad mustard

For 50 servings, use:

1 qt. salad dressing
1 Tbsp. vinegar
1 tsp. salt

¼ tsp. pepper
2 tsp. salad mustard

Joan Lewis, Minneapolis, MN

EIGHT REUBEN SANDWICHES

2 c. drained sauerkraut
½ tsp. caraway seed
16 slices rye bread

½ c. bottled Russian dressing
Thinly sliced corned beef
Sliced cheese

Toast 2 cups drained sauerkraut with caraway seed. Spread 16 slices of rye bread with Russian dressing. Top 8 slices of bread with 2 ounces thinly sliced corned beef, ¼ cup sauerkraut, and 2 ounces sliced cheese on each. Cover with second slice of bread. Butter both sides and grill in skillet or electric sandwich toaster until cheese is melted.

Mrs. Goldie Mikish, Staples, MN

HAMBURGERS
(Quantity: 50)

10 lb. ground beef
5 eggs
4 Tbsp. salt

1 tsp. pepper
5 c. bread crumbs
6 c. water

Have beef ground twice. Mix ingredients well. Form into thin patties and fry.

Betty Risse, Bismarck, ND

BIG A'S MEAT LOAF

2 lb. hamburger
2 eggs
½ c. milk
2 c. croutons
2 c. cracker crumbs

1 tsp. Season-All seasoning
½ tsp. garlic salt
½ c. barbeque sauce
¼ c. honey

Mix together. Bake at 350° for 1 hour.

Mavis E. Dilts

HAM LOAF
(Quantity: Serves 50)

8 lb. fresh pork, ground
4 lb. smoked ham, ground
4 c. oatmeal
½ c. onion

8 eggs, slightly beaten
4 c. tomato juice
1 Tbsp. salt
½ tsp. pepper

Mix all ingredients; divide mixture into pans of similar size. Have pans well greased. Press mixture firmly into the corners. Bake at 350° for 1½ to 2 hours. Let stand in a warm place for 20 to 30 minutes before serving.

Betty Risse, Bismarck, ND

BBQ MEAT BALLS
(Serves 8 to 12)

Meat Balls:

1 lb. hamburger
½ c. milk

1 c. bread crumbs
¼ tsp. salt

Mix hamburger, milk, bread crumbs, and salt. Make into meat balls. For small ones, make 12 balls, for large ones, make 8 balls.

Sauce:

2 Tbsp. sugar
2 Tbsp. vinegar

1 Tbsp. Worcestershire sauce

Mix sugar, vinegar, and Worcestershire sauce. Put meat balls in pan and spoon sauce over meat balls. Bake for 1 hour at 375°.

Ruth and Bob Rensch, Wyoming, MN

MEAT BALLS
(Quantity: Serves 50)

8 lb. beef
4 lb. pork
8 eggs
1 qt. milk

2 c. dry bread crumbs
4 Tbsp. salt
¾ tsp. pepper
¾ tsp. allspice

Have meat ground 3 times. Combine all ingredients and mix until mixture rolls from side of bowl; form into balls. Brown balls in fat; place in baking pan. Cover with water or broth. Cover and bake for 1 hour at 350°. Thicken broth using 3 tablespoons cornstarch for each quart of broth. Boil until clear. Serve over Meat Balls. (Using cornstarch for thickening results in a glossy product.)

Betty Risse, Bismarck, ND

BARBEQUED HAMBURGER

For 6 servings, use:

1 lb. hamburger, browned
1½ tsp. lemon juice
2 tsp. vinegar
1½ Tbsp. water
⅔ c. catsup

1 Tbsp. brown sugar
1 Tbsp. dehydrated onion
1 tsp. dry mustard
1 tsp. salt
⅛ tsp. pepper

For 50 servings, use:

8 lb. hamburger, browned
¼ c. lemon juice
⅓ c. vinegar
¾ c. water
5 c. catsup

½ c. brown sugar
½ c. dehydrated onion
8 tsp. dry mustard
8 tsp. salt
1 tsp. pepper

After browning hamburger, add remaining ingredients; simmer for 15 or 20 minutes. Spoon into buns.

BARBECUED HAMBURGERS

4 lb. ground beef
2 c. ground or rolled crumbs
1 onion, grated

½ c. catsup
4 eggs, beaten
Season (salt and pepper)

Mix the following and let stand for ½ hour: Bread crumbs, onion, catsup, and beaten eggs. Add enough cold water so bread gets nice and moist. Add meat to this mixture and form patties; flour and brown.

Sauce for patties:

1 bottle catsup and 3 bottles
   water
3 Tbsp. prepared mustard

3 Tbsp. Worcestershire sauce
Onions, cut up (as much or little
   as you like)

Let simmer on top of stove. Pour over patties and bake at least ¾ hour.

Betty Michon, Detroit Lakes, MN

BARBECUED HAMBURGERS

10 lb. ground beef
3 c. bread crumbs
3 Tbsp. ground onion

2 eggs and ½ c. milk, beaten
4 to 5 tsp. salt and pepper

Mix well and form into patties; fry until brown. Put in roaster in layers with sliced onions. Add catsup and water (½ and ½) to cover. Bake for 1½ to 2 hours at 400°.

Betty Michon, Detroit Lakes, MN

RANCH BEANS

1 pkg. frozen Fordhook lima
    beans
1 lb. can pork and beans
1 lb. can dark red kidney beans
2 Tbsp. dry mustard
1½ c. brown sugar

¼ tsp. crushed red pepper
1 Tbsp. onion flakes
½ tsp. salt
1 Tbsp. white vinegar
6 to 8 slices thick bacon

In medium size baking dish, mix the beans together. Add dry ingredients and vinegar; stir to blend. Top with bacon strips. Bake in moderate oven until bacon is brown and sauce is bubbly. Serve hot from oven.

Yvonne Maddox, Duluth, MN

CHOW MEIN
(Quantity: Serves 20)

2 lb. veal, cut in 1 inch cubes
1 lb. lean pork, cut in 1 inch
    cubes
3 c. onions, coarsely cut
2 bunches celery, coarsely cut
2 (No. 2) cans mixed chow mein
    vegetables

1 (No. 2½) can tomatoes
1 small can mushrooms
4 Tbsp. bead molasses
8 Tbsp. soy sauce
1 c. flour (scant)
1 tsp. salt

Cover the veal with water. Add salt and boil ½ hour. Brown the pork, celery, and onions with enough fat to keep pork from sticking. While browning, add 4 tablespoons soy sauce. Put pork, onions, celery, and tomatoes in large kettle with veal. Add 4 tablespoons of brown sauce and cook slowly for 1½ to 2 hours.

Drain juice from mixed vegetables and save. Add vegetables and soy sauce to previously cooked ingredients. Cook slowly for about ½ hour and then thicken with the cup of flour, using the vegetable juice to moisten. Serve on Chinese fried noodles and with boiled rice.

Betty Risse, Bismarck, ND

SCALLOPED CHICKEN WITH RICE
(Quantity: 20 servings)

2 (5 lb.) chickens
2 c. uncooked rice
1 small onion

2 c. celery, chopped
1 green pepper or pimento
Salt and pepper to taste

Cook chicken until well done. Make sure you have 9 cups of broth. Chop chicken medium fine. Add following to slightly thickened broth: Skin of chicken (ground fine), 2 cups chopped celery, chopped onion, and pepper or pimento. Season with salt and pepper.

Cook rice for 20 minutes and rinse under hot water (6 cups cooked rice). Grease roaster well with butter. Put alternate layers of chopped chicken and rice in roaster with part of prepared gravy between until all is used. Top with buttered crumbs. Bake at 350° for 45 minutes.

Betty Risse, Bismarck, ND

CHICKEN HUNTINGTON
(Quantity: Serves 20)

1 (5 lb.) chicken, cooked and
   diced
1 pkg. elbow macaroni
1 large glass pimento

1 lb. cheese, cut
1 can peas
4 Tbsp. butter or margarine

Melt the shortening. Add flour enough to thicken, then the chicken broth; cook until thickened. Add remaining ingredients. Bake at 350° for 1 hour.

Betty Risse, Bismarck, ND

CREAMED CHICKEN WITH PIMENTO ON RICE
(Quantity: Serves 50)

6 chickens, cooked and diced
4 qt. milk
4 cans pimento, chopped
2 c. fat

2 c. flour
3 Tbsp. salt
1 Tbsp. pepper
8 c. rice (uncooked)

Melt fat. Add flour, salt, and pepper; cook until bubbly. Add milk slowly. Cook, stirring until thickened. Add the chicken and pimento. Serve hot over hot cooked rice. Chicken stock may be used in place of part of the milk. One 5 pound chicken equals 1 quart cooked diced meat.

Betty Risse, Bismarck, ND

CHICKEN HOT DISH
(Quantity: Serves 125 people)

5 lb. rice, cooked
5 large bunches celery, chopped
8 lb. carrots, chopped
2 lb. onions, chopped
30 lb. chicken, cooked and
   diced

6 cans mushroom soup
6 cans cream of chicken soup
16 c. milk and chicken broth
   combined

Cook vegetables until done in very little water. Layer first 5 ingredients as listed in long pans or casseroles. Pour soups, combined with milk and broth, over all. Cover with buttered crumbs. Bake until set. Cut in squares. (Six large chickens will be needed.)

Betty Risse, Bismarck, ND

SCALLOPED POTATOES
(Quantity: Serves 50)

20 lb. potatoes, sliced thin
2 Tbsp. salt
1 tsp. pepper

½ c. flour
1½ c. butter
2 qt. milk

Grease pans; put layer of potatoes in pans. Sprinkle with salt, pepper, and flour; dot with butter. Continue with layers until pans are ¾ full. Pour hot milk over to cover and bake at 350° for 1½ to 2 hours.

Betty Risse, Bismarck, ND

HAMBURGER AND CROUTON HOT DISH

2 lb. hamburger
1 pkg. Brownberry croutons
 (seasoned)
1 can cream of celery soup
1 can cream of chicken soup

1 can cream of mushroom soup
1 can milk
1 large can French fried onion
 rings

Put raw hamburger in an ungreased 9x13 inch pan (put in loosely - do not flatten down). Spread croutons over meat. Mix soups and milk; pour over meat and croutons. Sprinkle onion rings on top. Bake in 350° oven for 1 hour.

Esther D. Lee, St. Paul, MN

NOODLE PIZZA
(Serves 48 to 60)

A large recipe, suitable for church luncheon or family reunion.

3 (8 oz.) bags egg noodles,
 cooked and drained
8 eggs

1 qt. milk
Salt and pepper

Mix together well the eggs, milk, salt, and pepper. Divide noodles in 4 buttered baking pans, 9x13 inches. Pour milk mixture over noodles and bake in 400° oven until custard is set; remove from oven.

Cover with the following: Four (10¾ ounce) cans of tomato soup, seasoned well with onion salt, garlic salt, oregano, salt, and pepper. Be sure to season enough. This is really the pizza taste.

Partially brown 5 pounds hamburger and 2 medium onions. Divide this on top of each pan, then sprinkle grated cheese (about 1 cup per pan); return to oven for 10 to 15 minutes. Cut in squares and serve hot. Fry meat while noodle part is baking. Each pan will cut into 12 to 15 squares.

Edna Helberg, Sioux Falls, SD

TACOS

For 10 servings, use:

1 lb. hamburger, browned	1 tsp. Worcestershire sauce
1 Tbsp. dehydrated onion	1 tsp. Tabasco sauce
1 tsp. salt	½ lb. grated cheese
¾ c. catsup	20 taco shells

For 50 servings, use:

5 lb. hamburger, browned	5 tsp. Worcestershire sauce
⅓ c. dehydrated onion	5 tsp. Tabasco sauce
5 tsp. salt	2½ lb. grated cheese
3¾ c. catsup	100 taco shells

Brown hamburger, onion, and salt. Add catsup, Worcestershire sauce and Tabasco sauce. Mix and simmer for 10 minutes; cool. Add grated cheese. Fill each taco shell with 2 tablespoons filling. Bake at 350° for 10 to 15 minutes. Just before serving, top meat mixture with 2 tablespoons Salad.

Salad:

For 10 servings, use:

3 c. lettuce, cut fine	½ c. Sweet and Sour Dressing
¾ c. tomatoes, cut fine	½ tsp. Tabasco sauce

For 50 servings, use:

4 qt. lettuce, cut fine	2¼ c. Sweet and Sour Dressing
3¾ c. tomatoes, cut fine	2⅓ tsp. Tabasco sauce

Sweet and Sour Dressing:

½ c. vinegar	½ tsp. salt
1 c. sugar	Dash of pepper

Bring to a boil to combine ingredients and chill.

Joan Lewis, Minneapolis, MN

HARDY CHILI FOR HARDY APPETITES

2 lb. coarsely ground beef	1 c. chili powder
2 (1 lb.) cans dark kidney beans	1 Tbsp. cumin
2 (1 lb.) cans tomatoes	1 tsp. oregano
1 tsp. salt	1 tsp. celery flakes
1 tsp. crushed red pepper	2 Tbsp. vinegar
½ tsp. black pepper	2 (8 oz.) cans tomato sauce
1 large onion, finely chopped	3 Tbsp. virgin olive oil
3 jumbo cloves garlic, chopped	2 bay leaves

Saute onion, garlic, and ground beef in olive oil. Add chili powder and cumin, stirring until meat is done. Add tomatoes, tomato sauce, and beans (for very fine texture, puree tomatoes and beans in blender). Add remaining ingredients plus enough water to bring level to within 1½ inches of top of 5½ quart pot. Cover and simmer for 4 to 5 hours. Adjust pepper to your taste, but try original first. *Do not omit the vinegar.* Serve with rice or plain.

Especially good over scrambled eggs.

Yvonne Maddox, Duluth, MN

CHILI CON CARNE

For 8 servings, use:

1 lb. hamburger
2 Tbsp. dehydrated onion or ½
   c. fresh onion, chopped
2½ tsp. salt
¼ tsp. pepper
2 c. chopped celery
2 c. canned tomatoes, chopped
   (and juice)

¼ c. tomato paste
3 Tbsp. brown sugar
4 tsp. chili powder
1 (15½ oz.) can chili or kidney
   beans with liquid
3 Tbsp. cornstarch
3 Tbsp. water

For 50 servings, use:

6 lb. hamburger
¾ c. dehydrated onion or 3 c.
   fresh onion, chopped
⅓ c. salt
1½ tsp. pepper
3 qt. chopped celery
3 qt. canned tomatoes, chopped
   (and juice)

1½ c. tomato paste
1¼ c. brown sugar
½ c. chili powder
6 (15 oz.) cans chili or kidney
   beans with liquid
1¼ c. cornstarch
1¼ c. water

Brown hamburger, dehydrated or fresh onion, salt, and pepper. Add chopped celery; cook until celery is tender crisp. Add tomatoes, tomato paste, brown sugar, chili powder, and kidney beans with liquid. Simmer for about 20 minutes. If desired, thicken with cornstarch in water.

Notes

Ethnic Foods

COOKING WITH HERBS AND SPICES

Herbs and spices produce the great diversity of flavors in international cuisines. When using some that are unfamiliar to you, begin by adding small amounts so the flavoring is subtle. The best rule is season to taste! The following chart lists the favorite herbs and spices in twelve countries that represent some of the world's finest cuisine.

HERBS AND SPICES

CHINESE
Ginger
Anise Seed
Garlic
Onions
Red Pepper
Fennel Seed
Cloves
Cinnamon

FRENCH
Tarragon
Shallots
Chives
Fines Herbes
Marjoram
Thyme
Black Pepper
Rosemary

GERMAN
Caraway Seed
Dill Seed
Onion
Paprika
Ginger
Rosemary
Nutmeg
White Pepper

GREEK
Oregano
Mint
Bay Leaves
Garlic
Onion
Cinnamon
Fennel Seed
Black Pepper

HUNGARIAN
Paprika
Poppy Seed
Caraway Seed
Garlic
Dill Seed
Onion
Cinnamon
White Pepper

INDIAN
Curry
Cumin Seed
Coriander
Turmeric
Red Pepper
Black Pepper
Ginger
Cardamom Seed

INDONESIAN
Curry
Garlic
Red Pepper
Ginger
Cinnamon
Nutmeg
Cloves
Caraway Seed

ITALIAN
Garlic
Basil
Oregano
Onions
Sage
Fennel Seed
Red Pepper
Marjoram

MEXICAN
Chili Pepper
Cumin Seed
Oregano
Garlic
Onion
Coriander Seed
Sesame Seed
Cinnamon

SPANISH
Saffron
Paprika
Garlic
Onion
Parsley
Bay Leaves
Cumin Seed
Sweet Pepper

SWEDISH
Cardamom Seed
Nutmeg
Dill Seed
Bay Leaves
Allspice
Black Pepper
Mustard
Cinnamon

MOROCCAN
Red Pepper
Cumin Seed
Coriander
Mint
Saffron
Anise
Cardamom
Cinnamon

Chart Courtesy of American Spice Trade Association

ETHNIC FOODS

BREADS

NORWEGIAN STYLE FOODS - GRANDMA'S KUMLA

Vell, den yew tek as many potatoes as the crowd yew hev to cook fer. Den yew peel thee potatoes and grind dem, den yew tek one handfull of oatmeal and a small teaspoon of baking powder and flour to make dem stick together. Roll in balls and cook dem in ham juice. Shoo-er glad dat yew vill like dem. Tiss a special treat fer company.

Harlan Brekke, Fargo, ND

BIG BREAD ROUNDS

Start heating oven to 375°F. Meanwhile, unroll 1 package refrigerated crescent rolls on a cookie sheet. Cut off 2 (1 inch) strips of dough from short side. Place 1 strip at center of each lengthwise side. Roll out lightly with rolling pin into a 10 inch circle. Brush with slightly beaten egg yolk; sprinkle with 1 teaspoon sesame seed. Bake for 10 to 12 minutes or until done; remove. Serve warm or cold as bread of meal. Makes 1 (10 inch) round.

Helen May Johnson, Chanhassen, MN

HONEY DATE-WALNUT BREAD

1 c. water
1 c. coarsely cut pitted fresh
    dates
2 Tbsp. butter
¾ c. honey
1 egg
1¾ c. all-purpose flour
2 tsp. baking powder
½ tsp. salt
1 c. chopped walnuts

Heat water to boiling in saucepan. Add dates and cook for 3 minutes, stirring. Cool slightly. In mixing bowl, cream butter. Gradually beat in honey, then egg. Stir in date mixture. Sift flour, baking powder, and salt; add to creamed mixture with nuts. Stir to mix well. Pour into buttered 9x5x3 inch loaf pan. Bake in slow oven (300°F.) for 1 hour and 15 minutes or until done; cool. Do not slice until second day.

Helen May Johnson, Chanhassen, MN

APPLE KUCHEN

2 c. flour
¾ c. lard or butter (not
    margarine)
1 tsp. baking powder
½ tsp. salt
½ c. milk

Mix like pie crust in a 9x13 inch pan; pat down and build up sides about an inch. Slice baking apples ⅛ inch thick; arrange on dough single layered. (Peel apples first; do not use Delicious apples.)

Custard:

2 eggs	**1 tsp. vanilla**
1 c. sugar	**1 tsp. cinnamon**
2 Tbsp. flour	**1 c. half & half cream**

Beat eggs with sugar, flour, vanilla, and cinnamon; gradually add half & half cream. Mix well. Pour on top of sliced apples; try not to let cream mixture run over sides of dough (it will get soggy then). Sprinkle lightly with cinnamon. Bake at 375° for 30 to 40 minutes or until custard is set.

Peeled and sliced peaches can be used in place of apples.

Barb Fivecoate, Virginia, MN

MANNA BREAD

2 pkg. yeast	**¼ c. milk**
3¾ to 4 c. flour	**2 Tbsp. bacon drippings**
¼ pkg. onion soup mix	**1 Tbsp. sugar**
8 slices bacon	**2 Tbsp. corn meal**
1 (12 oz.) can beer	

Combine yeast, 1¾ cups flour, and soup mix in bowl. Cook and drain bacon (save oil); crumble. Heat beer, milk, sugar, and bacon drippings until warm (milk will curdle); add to preceding mixture. Beat at low speed for ½ minute, then at high speed for 3 minutes.

Stir in bacon and enough flour for stiff dough. Knead until smooth and elastic. Place in greased bowl. Turn once to grease dough; cover and let rise until double (40 to 45 minutes). Punch down; shape into 16 rolls and put in round pan. Brush with oleo and sprinkle with corn meal. Let rise for 25 minutes or until double. Bake at 375° for 20 minutes.

Barb Fivecoate, Virginia, MN

MOM'S KUCHEN

2 c. warm milk	**¾ c. sugar**
2 c. warm water	**2 pkg. dry yeast**
¾ c. oil	**10 c. flour (or more)**
1 Tbsp. salt	

Mix, knead, and let rise until double. Knead again; let rise, then roll out for crust.

Filling:

10 eggs, beaten	**6 c. liquid (I use 1 qt. farm cream**
2½ c. sugar	**and 2 c. milk)**
10 Tbsp. flour	**Fruit (any kind you wish)**

Cook filling until slightly thick; stir all the while cooking. Set aside to cool. Roll out thin crust. Put in the bottom of pie tins. Put in fruit; fill with custard and sprinkle with a mixture of sugar and cinnamon. Bake in oven at 350° until crust is golden brown.

Arlene Jewell, Bismarck, ND

FLAT BREAD

¾ c. buttermilk
¼ c. water
½ c. sugar
½ c. melted margarine

1 tsp. salt
¾ c. Malt-O-Meal
3 c. flour (or less)

Mix together. Roll thin and cut in triangles or squares. Bake until golden in a 400° oven.

Bonnie Sorby

FLAT BREAD - NORWEGIAN

1 box corn muffin mix
1 c. white flour
1 c. graham flour

3 Tbsp. sugar (little more)
1 c. buttermilk
1 tsp. soda

Stir the soda in the buttermilk, then mix it up with the rest of ingredients. Use pieces the size of a bun and roll them out. Add a little flour if hard to roll. Bake at 350° for 8 or 9 minutes (or until golden brown) on an ungreased cookie sheet.

Harlan Brekke, Fargo, ND

FRENCH BREAD

2½ c. hot water
1 Tbsp. salt
2 Tbsp. yeast

1 Tbsp. sugar
1 Tbsp. margarine
7 c. all-purpose flour

Knead, rise, and shape into 2 long loaves; let rise, then bake in 400° oven for about 30 minutes.

Rose Wendelbo, Grafton, ND

FRENCH SOURDOUGH BREAD

2 Tbsp. yeast
2½ c. water (warm)
6 c. unbleached flour
2 tsp. salt

Corn meal
Egg white wash (approx. 2 egg
    whites)

In mixing bowl, sprinkle yeast over water and let set for 10 minutes; stir to dissolve. Stir in 3 cups flour and beat at medium speed for 10 minutes; refrigerate mixture for approximately 45 minutes. Return to mixer and sprinkle in salt; beat for 1 minute. Gradually add enough flour to clean sides of bowl. During this process, you will have to stir by hand or use a dough hook. You will probably also have to add approximately 1 to 3 cups extra flour to clean sides of bowl. Dough should be just *slightly* sticky and rubbery.

Turn dough out onto floured board; knead for 5 minutes. Return dough to greased or oiled bowl; cover. Let rise until tripled. Punch down. Let rise again until tripled. Punch down and divide into 2 loaves. Let rest for 10 minutes. Use rolling pin to roll each loaf into ½ inch thick circle of dough (as in rolling out dough for sugar cookies).

Now use fingers and hands and tightly roll dough into "snake." Start at one side and roll away from you, keeping tight. When "snake" is formed, start in middle and tightly squeeze dough out to ends to elongate the "snake." Use slight pulling pressure. Repeat until air is removed.

Now use palms of hands to rub or roll back and forth to make "snake" skinnier and longer. Place on long narrow baking sheet, sprinkled with corn meal. Let rise until doubled. Slash diagonally down loaf, then brush with egg white wash. Bake for 15 minutes in 450° preheated oven. Mist loaves, then return for approximately 2 to 3 minutes. Repeat while watching bread carefully. Bread will be crisp and brown on top - done in center. Cut diagonally when cool. Yield: 2 loaves.

Janet Lozon, Owatonna, MN

GERMAN KUCHEN DOUGH AND FILLING

1 pkg. yeast	1 tsp. salt
¼ c. warm water	½ tsp. baking powder
1 tsp. sugar	3 Tbsp. melted shortening
2½ c. flour	1 egg
3 Tbsp. sugar	

Dissolve yeast in water. Melt shortening and add ⅓ cup cold water. Add egg, yeast, and flour mixture. Divide dough in 2 parts; press or roll dough and put into round cake pan. Add sliced peaches (canned or fresh).

Filling:

2 eggs, beaten	Dash of salt
⅔ c. sour cream	1 tsp. vanilla
2 level Tbsp. flour	

Pour over peaches. Bake in 350° oven for 25 to 30 minutes. Makes 2.

Rose Sauer, Grand Forks, ND

HONEY LEKUCHEN

1 c. honey
¾ c. sugar
3 eggs
½ c. ground almonds
¼ c. chopped citron
¼ c. orange peel

1 tsp. cinnamon
½ tsp. cloves, crushed
1 tsp. anise
1 c. black coffee or milk
4½ c. flour
1½ tsp. baking powder

Heat honey until thin and slightly darkened in color. Stir in sugar until dissolved; cool. Beat in eggs, nuts, and spices. Add coffee for dark or milk for light. Sift flour and baking powder; stir gradually into mixture until mixed thoroughly. Dough can be baked now or allowed to age, by placing dough in covered bowl and storing in a cool place for a day to a week.

Spread dough ½ inch thick on lightly buttered and floured cooky sheet. Bake in 400° oven till golden brown, about 12 to 15 minutes. Cut into oblongs, 2x3 inches.

Laila Schroeder

ITALIAN CHEESE TWISTS

¼ c. butter *or* margarine,
    softened
¼ tsp. basil, crushed
¼ tsp. oregano, crushed
¼ tsp. marjoram, crushed
¼ tsp. garlic powder
1 (16 oz.) loaf frozen bread
    dough, thawed

¾ c. shredded Mozzarella
    cheese (3 oz.)
1 slightly beaten egg
1 Tbsp. water
2 Tbsp. sesame seed

In a small bowl, combine butter or margarine, basil, oregano, marjoram, and garlic powder; set aside. On a lightly floured surface, roll bread dough into a 12 inch square. Spread butter mixture evenly over dough. Sprinkle with cheese. Fold dough into thirds. With a sharp knife, cut dough crosswise into 24 (½ inch) strips.

Twist each strip twice and pinch ends to seal. Place about 2 inches apart on a greased baking sheet. Cover and let rise in a warm place till almost double (about 30 minutes). Combine egg and water; brush over each twist. Sprinkle with sesame seed. Bake in a 375° oven for 10 to 12 minutes or till golden. Makes 24 twists.

Sonya Masset, Bismarck, ND

JAN'S PIZZA BUNS

1 lb. hamburger
1 medium chopped onion
10 to 12 oz. can pizza sauce
½ lb. sharp Cheddar cheese,
    shredded

½ c. mayonnaise
¾ tsp. Italian seasoning
Salt and pepper
2 doz. buns, split

Brown hamburger and onion; let cool. Stir in pizza sauce, cheese, mayonnaise, and spices. Spread mixture on split buns. Broil until bubbly.

Harlan Brekke, Fargo, ND

JULEKAKE

2 cakes compressed yeast
½ c. lukewarm water
3 c. milk, scalded
¾ c. sugar
½ c. butter
8½ c. flour
2 tsp. salt
2 eggs, beaten

½ c. chopped citron
½ c. candied cherries (or 1 c.
    mixed candied fruits)
½ c. currants
¾ c. chopped white and dark
    raisins
½ tsp. cardamom (if desired)

Dissolve yeast in lukewarm water. Pour scalded milk over sugar and butter. When lukewarm, add yeast mixture. Add salt and ½ of flour. Beat for 10 minutes. Add eggs, then fruit and remaining flour; knead well.

Place dough in greased bowl in warm place and let rise until double in bulk. Shape and place in greased loaf or round pans. When double in bulk, bake at 340°F. to 350°F. for 35 to 40 minutes. Remove from pan and brush with melted butter. Sprinkle with cinnamon and sugar.

Helen Johnson, Chanhassen, MN

KRINGLA - NORWAY

1 c. sugar
1 c. rich sour cream
½ tsp. salt

¾ tsp. soda
½ tsp. almond or other flavoring
3 c. flour

Mix sugar and cream together until all the sugar is dissolved. Add the rest of the ingredients (put the soda in the flour). Drop on a greased cookie sheet, or use a cookie press, and bake in a moderate oven for 10 minutes.

Helen May Johnson, Chanhassen, MN

SUGAR KRINGLES

4½ c. sifted flour
¾ c. light cream

1 lb. butter

Measure 4½ cups sifted flour into a large mixing bowl. Add ¾ cup light cream, mixing with a pastry blender. Add 1 pound of butter (firm but not hard) and knead until well mixed. Chill dough and divide into fourths for easier handling.

Roll dough out on a lightly floured board to ¼ inch thickness. Cut into 6 x ⅓ inch strips and form into loops, pretzel fashion. Dip top of each in sugar. Bake on ungreased cooky sheets in a moderate oven (350°) for 15 to 18 minutes.

Pearl Paulsrud, Montevideo, MN

NORWEGIAN COFFEE BREAD

2 pkg. dry yeast	**2 eggs, beaten**
½ c. lukewarm water	**1 lb. fruitcake mix**
3 c. milk, scalded	**1 c. raisins**
¾ c. sugar	**1 tsp. ground cardamon**
½ c. butter	**8 to 10 c. flour**
2 tsp. salt (or less)	

Dissolve yeast in ½ cup lukewarm water. Add butter to scalded milk; when lukewarm, add sugar and yeast mixture. Add ½ of flour; beat for about 10 minutes by hand or with mixer. Add eggs, 1 at a time, beating thoroughly after each addition. Add fruit and remaining flour; knead and place in bowl to rise.

When double in bulk, knead again. Let rise until light and shape into rounded loaves; place on greased pie tins. Brush tops with slightly beaten egg white. When double in size, bake at 350° for about 40 minutes. Cool loaves. Frost with powdered sugar glaze, if desired, and decorate with green and red candied cherries and almonds.

Eloise Hoff, Preston, MN

NORWEGIAN COFFEECAKE

1 tsp. cinnamon	**2½ c. flour**
¾ c. brown sugar	**½ tsp. salt**
¾ c. white sugar	**¾ c. melted shortening**

Mix all together; reserve 1 cup mixture for topping.

To remainder, add:

1 tsp. baking powder	**1 egg**
1 tsp. baking soda	**1 c. buttermilk**
1 tsp. vanilla	

Pour into 7x11 inch pan and sprinkle 1 cup topping over top. Bake in 350° oven for 25 to 30 minutes.

Luella Anderson, Bismarck, ND

OSLO KRINGLE - NORWEGIAN PASTRY

1 c. water	1 c. flour
½ c. butter	4 eggs

Melt butter in water. When it boils, remove from stove and quickly add all the flour at once. Blend to remove lumps. When smooth, add eggs, 1 at a time, beating well after each addition. Butter a cookie sheet and spoon dough on, making an oblong circle. Bake in 375° oven for ½ hour, then at 350° for 15 minutes and at 325° for 15 minutes.

When cool, frost with:

1 c. powdered sugar	½ tsp. almond extract
2 Tbsp. butter	

Add enough cream to spread easily. This should be a thin coat of frosting. Sprinkle on sliced almonds or walnut pieces.

Donna Krause, Detroit Lakes, MN

POTICA

8 c. flour (approx.)	½ c. sugar
1 c. lukewarm milk	1 tsp. salt
1½ c. lukewarm water	3 egg yolks
½ cake yeast (or 2 packets)	¼ lb. butter

Mix to a soft dough; let rise till double in bulk. After dough has raised and filling has been cooked, flour a white sheet that has been spread on a 40x60 inch table. Stretch dough very thin without breaking. Spread filling evenly over dough. Roll from widest side (jelly roll style); seal edge. Cut into loaves and seal ends. Grease bread pans. Bake at 350° for 10 minutes, then at 325° for 50 minutes. (Brush with glaze of 2 tablespoons coffee and 3 tablespoons sugar.)

Filling:

2 lb. walnuts, ground fine (4 c. equals 1 lb.)	2 to 3 c. sugar
	½ lb. butter
2 c. milk	3 egg whites

Mix all and heat over low heat.

Shirley Hill, Columbia Heights, MN

PULL-APART GARLIC BREAD

1 loaf frozen bread dough, thawed	½ c. margarine
	Garlic powder
¼ c. Parmesan cheese	Parsley flakes

Grease Bundt cake pan with extra margarine and dust with extra Parmesan cheese. Melt margarine and add cheese, garlic powder, and parsley flakes. Slice bread dough into ¼ inch pieces. Dip bread into margarine mixture and place in pan. Let rise and bake at 350° for ½ hour.

Harlan Brekke, Fargo, ND

RUSSIAN ZUCCHINI BREAD

3 eggs	1 tsp. baking powder
2 c. sugar	3 tsp. cinnamon
3 tsp. vanilla	3 c. grated zucchini (unpeeled)
1 c. oil	½ c. chopped maraschino
3 c. flour	cherries
1 tsp. soda	1 c. chopped nuts

Beat eggs. Add sugar, vanilla, and oil; beat. To this, add flour, soda, baking powder, and cinnamon, then beat. Add grated zucchini, maraschino cherries, and chopped nuts. Bake in 2 greased bread pans, 9½ x 5½ inches, at 350° for 1 hour. May be frozen.

Dorothy Willems, New London, MN

STROMBOLI

1 (1 lb.) loaf frozen bread dough	8 slices thinly sliced hard salami
½ c. canned mushrooms, sliced	(casing removed)
½ c. chopped green pepper	6 oz. thinly sliced pepperoni
½ c. chopped onion	(large round)
3 Tbsp. butter	¼ lb. thinly sliced Provolone
6 pieces thinly sliced ham	cheese

Allow dough to thaw according to package directions. Saute mushrooms, pepper, and onion in butter. Grease an 11x16 inch pan. Pat dough out in pan. Cover center third of dough with ham, salami, pepperoni, and cheese. Sprinkle with sauteed vegetables. Cut each side of dough into 8 equal strips, cutting just to the edge of the filling. Fold strips to center, alternating sides. Overlap ends of strips just enough to pinch together and seal.

Cover loosely and let rise in warm place until doubled in size, about 1½ hours. Bake, uncovered, in preheated 350° oven for 45 minutes or until golden brown. Cool to touch and cut into 8 slices. Serve hot. Number of servings: 8 sandwiches.

Sonya Masset, Bismarck, ND

GERMAN APPLE STRUDEL

3¼ c. flour	1 tsp. salt
2 Tbsp. oil	1 c. warm water
1 egg	

Place flour and salt in a bowl. Make a well in center and put the egg, oil, and warm water in it. Stir and turn onto a floured board to knead dough until smooth and elastic. Oil bowl and set aside in warm place for at least 45 minutes to rest.

Filling:

3 lb. apples
½ c. brown sugar
1½ c. white sugar

½ c. crumbs (bread or cracker)
Cinnamon

Peel and slice apples. Place dough, that has been resting, onto a floured cloth and stretch. Melt 1 stick of butter and sprinkle with pastry brush over entire stretched dough. Mix the apples and remaining ingredients just before spreading them on the dough. (This prevents weeping.)

Put the apples on ⅓ of the dough. Stretch dough that is hanging in excess and cut any that won't stretch out. Flip the dough over the apples on the sides and then roll with cloth. Coil into greased 13x9 inch pan (use aluminum foil, which has been greased). Bake at 350° for about 1 hour. Just before baking, spread strudel with melted butter.

Mary Patalas, Virginia, MN

SWEDISH BROWN BREAD

1 pkg. yeast
¼ c. warm water
¼ c. brown sugar
¼ c. molasses
1 Tbsp. salt

2 Tbsp. shortening
2½ c. hot water
2½ c. rye flour
3 Tbsp. caraway seed
3½ to 4 c. all-purpose flour

Soften yeast in warm water (110°). In a big bowl, combine brown sugar, molasses, salt, and shortening; add hot water and stir until sugar dissolves. Cool to lukewarm. Stir in rye flour; beat well. Add softened yeast and caraway seed; mix well. Reserving some of the all-purpose flour for kneading, add enough of remainder to make a soft dough.

Turn out on floured surface; cover and let rest for 10 minutes. Knead until smooth and satiny (about 10 minutes). Place dough in lightly greased bowl. Turn once to grease surface; cover and let rise until doubled. Punch down; turn out and divide into 2 portions.

Make dough into balls. Let rise for 10 minutes. Shape into loaves; place in greased pans. Cover and let rise until doubled. Bake at 375° for 25 to 30 minutes. Makes 2 (8½ x 4½ inch) loaves. Brush crust with butter.

"Patience is the art of concealing your impatience." - Franklin P. Jones.
Mildred Sjostrom, St. Peter, MN

SWEDISH COOKY RINGS - KRINGLOR

2 c. sifted all-purpose flour
2 tsp. double action baking
  powder
¼ tsp. salt
3 Tbsp. sugar
½ c. butter

1 egg, well beaten
6 Tbsp. milk
¼ tsp. lemon extract
¼ c. sugar (for dipping cookies,
  optional)

1. Sift flour, baking powder, salt, and 3 tablespoons sugar. Blend in butter with finger tips, knives, or pastry blender.

2. Add egg, milk, and extract; mix thoroughly. Chill in refrigerator overnight.

3. Cut dough into small balls. Roll these into slender strips, 8 to 9 inches long. Shape into rings or Kringlor. To shape Kringlor, bring ends of each strip together and twist. Form circle by bringing ends to the middle of the strip. Dip in sugar if desired.

4. Bake on ungreased cooky sheet in moderately hot oven (400°) for 12 to 15 minutes. Yield: 4 dozen cookies.

Helen H. Clark, Grand Forks, ND

SWEDISH POTATO PANCAKES - RÄRIVNA POTATISPLÄTTAR

1¾ c. grated raw potatoes
½ tsp. salt
1½ tsp. flour
1 tsp. cream

2 eggs, well beaten
¼ c. melted butter or fat (for
  frying)
Melted butter

1. Drain grated potatoes in sieve for a few minutes. Add salt, flour, cream, and beaten eggs; mix thoroughly.

2. Drop potato mixture into melted butter or fat in frying pan or griddle. Brown on one side; turn and brown on second side. Serve hot with melted butter. Yield: About 18 pancakes, 2½ inches across.

Helen H. Clark, Grand Forks, ND

SWEDISH TOAST

1 c. white sugar
½ c. brown sugar
1 c. shortening
2 eggs
1 c. sour cream
4½ c. flour, sifted

1 tsp. soda
1 tsp. baking powder
1 tsp. ground cardamon
1 tsp. cinnamon
½ tsp. salt

Sift together sifted flour, soda, and baking powder. Cream sugar and shortening. Add eggs and mix well, then add sour cream and flour, soda, baking powder, and seasoning. Divide into 3 parts and roll in flour into 3 long rolls to fit jelly roll pan.

Bake for 30 minutes in 350° oven. Slice right away in about ½ inch slices and place, cut side down, on 2 cookie sheets. Put back into oven and toast for about 15 minutes. Watch carefully - turn over if bottom is browning too fast. Ready to serve.

Bernice T. Eugenis, Saginaw, MN

BOHEMIAN RAISIN BISCUIT KOLACHY

1 c. raisins or currants
¼ c. firmly packed brown sugar
¼ c. water
1 to 2 tsp. lemon juice
1 (10 oz.) can refrigerated flaky
    biscuits

½ c. sugar
½ tsp. cinnamon
¼ c. margarine or butter, melted

In a small saucepan, combine raisins, brown sugar, water, and lemon juice; cook over medium heat for 7 minutes or until mixture thickens, stirring occasionally. Cool.

Separate dough into 10 biscuits. Combine sugar and cinnamon. Dip both sides of each biscuit in melted margarine, then in sugar mixture. Place rolls, sides touching, in greased 15x10 inch jelly roll pan or 13x9 inch pan. With thumb, make wide imprint in center of each roll. Fill with 1 rounded tablespoon raisin mixture. Bake in preheated 375° oven for 15 to 20 minutes or until golden brown.

Glaze:

½ c. powdered sugar
2 to 4 tsp. milk

½ tsp. vanilla

In small bowl, combine all glaze ingredients until smooth; drizzle over warm rolls. Makes 10 rolls.

Barb Fivecoate, Virginia, MN

IRISH SODA BREAD

4 c. flour
3 Tbsp. sugar
1 Tbsp. baking powder
1 tsp. salt
¾ tsp. baking soda

6 Tbsp. butter or margarine
1½ c. dark seedless raisins
1 Tbsp. caraway seed
2 eggs
1½ c. buttermilk

Preheat oven to 350°. Grease well a 2 quart round casserole. In large bowl with a fork, mix first 5 ingredients. With pastry blender or 2 knives, use scissor fashion and cut in butter until mixture resembles coarse crumbs. Stir in raisins and caraway seed.

In small bowl with fork, beat eggs slightly; remove 1 tablespoon and reserve. Stir buttermilk into remaining egg; stir into flour mixture just until flour is moistened. Dough will be sticky. Turn dough onto well floured surface. With floured hands, knead 10 strokes to mix thoroughly.

Shape dough into a ball. With sharp knife, cut a 4 inch cross about ¼ inch deep. Brush dough with reserved egg. Bake dough about 1 hour and 20 minutes or until toothpick inserted in center comes out clean. Cool in casserole on wire rack for 10 minutes. Remove from casserole and completely cool on rack. Makes 1 loaf.

Barb Fivecoate, Virginia, MN

SPAETZLE - DUMPLINGS

About 2¼ c. flour
1 medium egg, beaten

About ⅔ c. water
1 tsp. salt

Beat all ingredients together. Let the batter rest for 30 minutes. Have ready a large kettle full of rapidly boiling salted water. Put dough on a chopping board. With a knife, snip off small parts of the dough and flip them directly into the boiling water. The Spaetzle will rise to the surface when they are cooked. Drain them in a colander. Put them quickly into a deep, heated serving dish. Pour ¼ to ½ cup of melted butter over and serve with grated Parmesan cheese if desired.

Barb Fivecoate, Virginia, MN

GERMAN CHICKEN AND DUMPLINGS

Thaw 1 loaf frozen bread dough and shape into dumplings. Let rise until doubled. Fry chicken in large kettle. Add garlic, onion, and potatoes. Just barely cover with water, then cook on high temperature, uncovered, until boiling. Add dumplings; after 10 minutes, cover and reduce heat to low (or until cover doesn't jiggle) for about ½ hour.

Erna Ricker

BLUEBERRY PIEROGI - DUMPLINGS

1 medium potato (about 5 oz.)
1 large egg
1⅓ c. all-purpose flour (level)
2 to 3 Tbsp. water
1 c. fresh blueberries

2 Tbsp. granulated sugar
Butter
Superfine sugar
Sour cream

Scrub potato; boil until tender, then peel, mash, and cool. Mix potato with egg, flour, and enough water to form a dough; knead until smooth. Roll out on a prepared pastry cloth with a stockinet-covered rolling pin to a 12x9 inch rectangle. Cut into 3 inch squares.

Mix together blueberries and granulated sugar. Spoon 1 tablespoon of mixture onto each square of dough. Fold each square into a triangle, pressing edges together well to seal.

Bring a large saucepan of water to a boil. If you like, add salt to taste to the water. Drop pierogi into the boiling water and cook until they come to the surface; continue to cook for 2 minutes longer. With a slotted spoon, remove pierogi and drain.

Melt a generous amount of butter in a skillet. Add pierogi and lightly brown on both sides. Serve hot. Pass a bowl of superfine sugar and a bowl of sour cream. Makes 12, enough for 4 servings.

Instead of blueberries, you may use blue plums, mushrooms, or cabbage.

PIEROGI
(Basic dough)

2 c. flour	2 Tbsp. sour cream
½ c. warm milk or water	½ tsp. salt
1 whole egg and 1 yolk	1 tsp. butter (optional)

Mix ingredients and knead into soft pliable dough. Let rest for 10 minutes, covered with a warm bowl. Divide dough in halves and roll thin. Cut circles with large biscuit cutter. Place a small spoonful of filling a little to one side. Moisten edge with water; fold over and press edges together firmly. Be sure they are well sealed to prevent the filling from running out. Drop Pierogi into salted boiling water. Cook gently for 5 minutes. Lift out of water carefully with perforated spoon and serve with melted butter.

Cheese and Potato Filling:

1 heaping c. mashed potatoes	Salt and pepper to taste
1 small c. dry cottage cheese	Chives or onions, cut fine

Mix thoroughly but lightly and fill. Serve with melted butter and crumbs.
Barb Fivecoate, Virginia, MN

CASSEROLES

A FRENCH DINNER FOR 4

Hors d'oeuvres: Cucumbers hollowed out and filled with a tuna fish mixture of 1 small can tuna, 2 tablespoons salad dressing, and pepper. Slice into 1 to 2 inch cubes. Serve with French bread, either boughten or made - directions included, and white wine.

Salad: Tear at least 2 kinds of greens into 4 bowls. Top with dressing - 2 parts oil - 1 part vinegar and Pommery mustard to taste. Shake well and pour over greens. Serve with French bread and white wine.

Main Course - Beef Roll-Ups: Saute 6 green onions with a garlic clove (cut up) and ½ cup fresh mushrooms. Spoon onto 4 breakfast steaks. Roll and tie. Sprinkle with lemon pepper. Bake in 350° oven for 20 minutes or until brown. Serve with green beans, Cheese Souffle (see recipe from Julia Childs included), French bread, and a red wine.

Dessert: Chocolate Mousse (see recipe included) and coffee.

Janet Lozon, Owatonna, MN

IRISH CORNED BEEF CURED IN THE REFRIGERATOR
(Homemade)

2 c. rock salt or curing salt
2 c. dark brown sugar
10 cracked black peppercorns
1 tsp. whole allspice
2 bay leaves
2 whole garlic cloves
1 tsp. powdered sage
1 tsp. mace
1 tsp. paprika

1 Tbsp. pickling spices
(optional)
1 gal. lukewarm water
4 to 5 lb. piece of beef
(preferably brisket or
flanken; rump, chuck, eye
round roast, or bottom
round can also be used)

Wipe the meat with a damp cloth and pierce it deeply with a heavy fork or pick so that the brine will penetrate. Choose a container of enameled metal, glass, porcelain, or earthenware (never unlined metal), large enough to contain the meat and liquid.

Mix all ingredients in 1 quart of the water in container, and when blended and dissolved, add the meat and rest of the water. The liquid should completely immerse the meat and cover it by about 1½ inches. Cover the meat with a large inverted plate or board and weight down with canned goods or a heavy object such as a large axe head. Store beef in the refrigerator at a temperature of 37°F. (3°C.) for 8 to 12 days.

To cook the corned beef after the curing process is complete, discard brine; rinse beef with cold water and soak overnight. Place in a kettle of cold water; bring to a boil and simmer for 1 hour. Pour off water and add fresh boiling water to cover. Simmer until tender, about 4 to 4½ hours.

Barb Fivecoate, Virginia, MN

IRISH CORNED BEEF CURED IN A PLASTIC BAG
(Homemade)

1 c. coarse or kosher salt	½ tsp. paprika
¼ c. granulated sugar	½ tsp. bay leaf
1 Tbsp. cracked peppercorns	1 large garlic clove, minced
1 tsp. powdered allspice	1 medium onion, minced
1 tsp. powdered thyme	2 carrots, finely chopped
½ tsp. sage	5 lb. beef brisket

Trim meat of excess fat and wipe with a damp cloth. Cut meat into 2 or 3 pieces. In a mixing bowl, blend salt and spices. Rub the mixture into meat on all sides. Put each piece of meat in a sturdy plastic bag. Divide remaining salt and spice mixture, minced garlic, onion, and carrots among the bags. Close bags, squeezing out as much air as possible and pack the bags in a large bowl. The meat, salt, and spices begin developing their own juices within hours.

Cover with a large inverted plate or pie pan and weight down with canned goods or other similar weight. Store in the refrigerator for 18 to 25 days, turning the meat packages daily to be sure brine penetrates on all sides. Before cooking the corned beef after it is cured, remove beef from plastic bags, wash in cold water, and soak in large bowl of cold water for 8 hours or overnight.

Barb Fivecoate, Virginia, MN

IRISH BOILED CORNED BEEF DINNER

4 to 5 lb. home-cured corned beef (preferably brisket), rinsed, soaked, and ready to cook	4 or 5 small turnips
	6 to 8 small potatoes
	6 to 8 medium carrots
	1 head cabbage
6 to 8 medium whole white onions	6 to 8 small beets, cooked separately

Put the piece of corned beef in a large kettle of cold water and bring to a boil. Reduce heat and simmer for 2½ to 3 hours. Add the whole onions and turnips; cook for 30 minutes longer. Add carrots and potatoes; cook 15 minutes longer. Add the cabbage, cut in large wedges.

When meat and vegetables are tender, transfer meat to a hot platter and surround with vegetables. Serve with horseradish, mustard, and a pot of melted butter. Beets, cooked separately, are traditionally served with the boiled dinner.

I prefer the cabbage cooked separately, too. That way it retains its fresh taste and there is less risk of overcooking.

Barb Fivecoate, Virginia, MN

STUFFED CABBAGE ROLLS - A LA ITALIANO
(Or yum yum good)

10 large cabbage leaves
1 lb. ground beef
1 c. *cooked* rice
¼ c. chopped onion
1 egg, slightly beaten
¼ tsp. pepper

¼ tsp. red pepper
1 can condensed tomato soup
1 can condensed vegetable
  soup
2 Tbsp. dried Italian seasoning
  (Schilling)

Soak head of cabbage in warm water for 10 minutes (helps to loosen leaves). Cook cabbage leaves in boiling water for a few minutes to soften; drain. Combine beef, rice, onion, egg, and peppers with 2 tablespoons vegetable soup. Divide meat mixture among cabbage leaves; roll and serve with toothpicks. Place cabbage rolls in casserole; pour the soup on top. Bake at 250° for 2½ hours.

Jack Klebba, Anoka, MN

CABBAGE ROLLS

1 lb. ground beef
½ c. chopped onion
1 c. cooked rice

Salt and pepper (as you like it)
1 tsp. dry parsley
1 small head cabbage

Take heart out of cabbage; put in kettle with water and steam until leaves begin to fall apart. Drain. Combine remaining ingredients. Take cabbage leaf and put meat mixture into it; roll up. Place in casserole and cover with mushroom sauce or tomato sauce. Serves 4.

Barb Fivecoate, Virginia, MN

CABBAGE ROLLS

1 large head cabbage
1 lb. ground beef
2 Tbsp. salt
2 Tbsp. fat
½ c. hot water

¼ Tbsp. pepper
1 c. cooked rice
1 c. milk
2 Tbsp. brown sugar

Dip cabbage leaves in hot water. Combine meat, salt, pepper, rice, and milk; mix well. Place 1 tablespoon of meat mixture into each leaf; roll cabbage leaf around meat and fasten with toothpick (if necessary). Brown rolls lightly in hot fat. Sprinkle with brown sugar and add hot water. Bake in moderate oven (350°) until brown, or pressure cook for 10 minutes. If baked in oven, bake in covered pan until nearly done, then uncover to finish baking.

Barb Fivecoate, Virginia, MN

CABBAGE HOT DISH

1 lb. hamburger	½ head cabbage
1 c. raw rice	1 onion
1 egg	Celery to taste
1 onion	

Mix hamburger, raw rice, egg, and 1 onion; make balls. Put ½ of cabbage in bottom of small roaster. Add onion and meat, then add rest of cabbage. Mix 1 can stewed tomatoes, 1 can water, salt, pepper, and *Accent*. Pour over cabbage and meat. Bake for 2 hours in low oven (235°).

Mrs. Goldie Mikish, Staples, MN

HUNGARIAN CABBAGE BAKE

6 strips bacon	2 c. uncooked noodles
4 c. shredded cabbage	Sour cream
2 Tbsp. sugar	Paprika
1 tsp. salt	

Cut bacon into small pieces; saute. Remove bacon pieces, reserving drippings in pan. Add cabbage to bacon drippings. Sprinkle with sugar and cook, stirring until cabbage is tender. Sprinkle salt over cabbage as it cooks. Cook noodles in boiling water, salted, until tender; drain.

Blend bacon-cabbage mixture with noodles; arrange in greased casserole dish. Top with tablespoon size dollops of sour cream. Sprinkle with paprika. Bake at 350° for 20 minutes.

Barb Fivecoate, Virginia, MN

STIR-FRY BEEF AND VEGETABLES - CHINESE

Sauce:

2 tsp. beef bouillon	2 Tbsp. cider vinegar
⅓ c. water	2½ tsp. corn starch
¼ c. soy sauce	1 tsp. sugar

In small saucepan, heat and stir bouillon and water until dissolved. Stir together soy sauce, vinegar, corn starch, and sugar. Stir into bouillon mixture until thick; set aside.

¼ c. vegetable oil
2 cloves garlic, halved
1 to 2 lb. sirloin or round steak, cut into ⅛ inch diagonal slices

8 oz. can sliced and drained water chestnuts
2 green peppers, cut into strips
2 c. fresh mushrooms, sliced
1 large onion, sliced

In large heavy skillet or wok, heat 2 tablespoons oil over high heat. Add garlic and cook a few minutes. Add meat and stir-fry a couple of minutes. Remove meat and juices and set aside. Discard garlic. Wipe pan and heat 1 tablespoon oil. Add vegetables and stir-fry for about 5 minutes. Add remaining oil (1 tablespoon) around the edges of skillet or wok. Add meat and juices, then bouillon mixture. Stir, cover, and cook for 2 minutes. Stir to serve. Refrigerate leftovers.

Great the second time, too.

Harlan Brekke, Fargo, ND

CHOP SUEY

½ c. sliced pork
2 Tbsp. oil
2 onions, sliced
½ c. shelled shrimp
4 dried mushrooms, soaked
1 c. chopped cabbage

1 c. sliced ubod (coconut heart, used vegetable)
¼ c. sliced carrots
½ c. sliced green pepper
Soy
Cornstarch

Season pork and saute in oil. Add onions, shrimp, and mushrooms; cook for a few minutes, then add water to cover. When mixture boils, add vegetables. Cover and simmer until vegetables are cooked but still crisp. Season with soy and thicken with cornstarch.

Barb Fivecoate, Virginia, MN

LA TOURTIERE - FRENCH MEAT PIE

1 lb. ground beef
1 lb. ground pork
Salt and pepper

1 tsp. allspice
1 grated potato
Little onion

Cook meat and onion with a little water till it loses its red color. Add seasonings and cook a little longer.

Alma M. Callette, Grand Forks, ND

STIR-FRY CHICKEN LIVERS

1 ctn. chicken livers, cut up
2 Tbsp. onions, sliced
¼ c. cut up celery

⅓ c. green pepper, sliced thin
⅓ c. mushrooms, sliced

Spray a fry pan with Pam and heat to medium. Add all the ingredients; stir constantly while cooking. Soy sauce may be added for more flavor while cooking.

Whole raw shrimp or small pieces of raw chicken may be used instead of liver. Other vegetables may also be substituted.

Elizabeth Klug, Dickinson, ND

STIR-FRY WITH BEAN SPROUTS

¾ to 1 lb. bean sprouts
2 to 3 Tbsp. vegetable oil
6 sq. bean curd
Salt to taste

2 Tbsp. soy sauce
1 tsp. sugar
½ green or red pepper (for color)

1. Clean sprouts. Remove black skins and tails. Rinse under running cold water; drain well.

2. Towel dry bean curd squares; slice ¼ to ½ inch pieces.

3. With little oil, add as needed, lightly brown bean curd slices in batches, then add in soy sauce and sugar. Cook for a few seconds. Remove and set aside.

4. Rinse wok or skillet, or use a clean one. Over high heat, add oil; put in sprouts and pepper. Stir, cover, and cook for 2 to 3 minutes, depending on degree of tenderness required.

5. Uncover pan and put in the bean curd and pepper mixture. Mix well and cook for 1 to 2 minutes.

6. Serve hot or at room temperature.

Variations and additions: Pork, crabmeat, and shrimp may be added. Two scallions, finely sliced, to substitute for the red pepper. Lightly browned bean curd slices can be added to meatless cooked noodles. Bean curd - stir-fry with other vegetables like bamboo shoots, celery, and mushrooms.

Sammoy Knight, Minneapolis, MN

CHICKEN TETRAZZINI

2 slices bacon, finely cut
⅓ c. minced onions
½ c. minced green pepper
2 c. shredded American cheese
    (½ Cheddar)
¼ pimento, cut up
¼ c. toasted shaved almonds

1¾ c. peas
2 c. chicken, cooked and cut up
8 oz. macaroni, cooked and hot
    (2 c. uncooked)
Tomato slices
Ripe olives

Cook bacon until brown and crisp. Add and brown lightly in the bacon fat the minced onions and minced green pepper. Add shredded cheese, pimento, toasted shaved almonds, peas, and chicken. Mix lightly with macaroni. Heat, using chicken broth to moisten. Serve hot on a chop plate. Garnish with tomato slices and ripe olives. Serves 8.

This recipe was given to me by an aunt who was a very good cook.
Helen H. Clark, Grand Forks, ND

ENGLISH SAUSAGE ROLLS

1 beaten egg
⅓ c. fine dry bread crumbs
¼ c. finely chopped onion

1 lb. bulk pork sausage
1 (17½ oz.) pkg. (2 sheets)
frozen puff pastry, thawed

In a bowl, combine egg, bread crumbs, and onion. Add sausage; mix well. Shape mixture into 8 (5 inch) long rolls. Place sausage rolls in a shallow baking pan. Bake in a 400° oven for about 20 minutes or till done. Drain and cool on paper toweling.

Cut each puff pastry sheet into quarters. For each pastry roll, place 1 sausage roll near 1 long side of a pastry quarter. Roll up jellyroll style. Seal edges and ends. Place in an ungreased 15x10x1 inch baking pan. Repeat with remaining sausage and pastry. Bake in a 425° oven for about 20 minutes or till brown. To serve, cut each roll crosswise into 1 inch slices. Makes about 40.
Kathy Olsen, Duluth, MN

GERMAN-STYLE BRATWURST AND SAUERKRAUT

6 slices bacon
1 small onion, chopped
1 clove garlic, minced
1 (32 oz.) can sauerkraut, rinsed
    and well drained
2 medium potatoes, peeled and
    sliced
1 c. water
½ c. dry white wine or apple
    juice

1 Tbsp. brown sugar
1 Tbsp. instant chicken bouillon
    granules
1 tsp. caraway seed
1 bay leaf
1 lb. Bratwurst (6 or 7 links)
1 large apple, cored and sliced

In a large skillet, cook bacon over medium high heat until crisp; crumble and set aside. Reserve 2 tablespoons drippings in skillet. Cook onion and garlic in reserved drippings over medium heat until tender, stirring occasionally. Stir in sauerkraut, potatoes, water, white wine or apple juice, brown sugar, bouillon granules, caraway seed, and bay leaf. Add up to ½ cup more water, if necessary, to cover potatoes. Bring to boiling.

Score Bratwurst; add to sauerkraut mixture and reduce heat. Cover and simmer for 1 to 1¼ hours or until potatoes are just tender, stirring occasionally. Add the sliced apple; cover and cook for 5 to 10 minutes more or until apple is just tender. Remove bay leaf. Makes 5 servings.

One serving is 1½ high fat meat exchange, ½ bread exchange, 1 fruit exchange, and 1 vegetable.

Laila Schroeder, Shakopee, MN

TOMASO SELLENTINO LA SAGNA

1 (12 oz.) pkg. lasagna noodles
2 lb. hamburger
1 lb. small curd cottage cheese
2 cans Martha Gooch Italian
    spaghetti sauce

½ lb. Mozzarella cheese
6 Tbsp. Romano cheese
2 c. tomato sauce (6 oz. size)
½ c. Parmesan cheese

Saute hamburger. Add Martha Gooch sauce; simmer for 20 minutes. Cook lasagna in casserole (9x13 inches). Put layer of noodles, then sauce with meat, Mozzarella cheese, cottage cheese, and Romano cheese; repeat layers, ending with cheeses, Parmesan and Mozzarella. If it seems dry, add tomato sauce by pouring over top. Bake at 350° for 30 to 40 minutes.

Barb Fivecoate, Virginia, MN

WON TONS - CHINESE

¾ lb. ground pork (uncooked)
1½ tsp. salt
Dash of pepper
1 egg

2 mushrooms, minced
2 Tbsp. green onions, finely
    chopped
1 pkg. won ton skins

Mix well the first 6 ingredients. Put ½ teaspoon of filling just off center of each 4 inch won ton wrapper; fold over at center. Gently press the edges together. Fold in half again lengthwise. Pull the 2 corners, 1 over the other, and press them together with a little water to wet the edges. A properly wrapped won ton resembles a nurse's cap.

Heat 6 cups oil in a wok or deep-fryer until it reaches 350°. Fry the won tons for 2 minutes, a few at a time. Serve hot.

Won Ton Soup: Boil 6 cups chicken stock. Add 10 to 15 won tons and boil for 5 minutes. Add 2 tablespoons chopped green onion and 5 drops sesame oil.

Harlan Brekke, Fargo, ND

FRIED RICE ORIENTAL

2 bowls cooked rice
½ c. leftover chicken and pork
½ c. shrimp
1 Chinese sausage
3 Tbsp. oil

2 cloves crushed garlic
2 native onions, minced
¼ c. crabmeat
1 egg, beaten
Soy

Heat oil; saute garlic, onions, sausage, shrimp, and chicken. Add rice and continue cooking, stirring well, to heat rice. Add seasonings, then crabmeat and egg. Keep stirring until egg dries. Serve hot.

Barb Fivecoate, Virginia, MN

POLYNESIAN CHICKEN

1 (3 lb.) chicken or breasts
1 (8 oz.) can mushrooms,
   drained
1 (8 oz.) can pineapple chunks
   and juice

1 (4 oz.) apricot preserves
1 pkg. Lipton onion soup mix
1 (8 oz.) bottle oil base Russian
   dressing

Pour over chicken; cover and bake for 1 hour. Uncover and bake for ½ hour. Serve over rice.

Barb Fivecoate, Virginia, MN

POLISH GOEMPKI - PIGS IN BLANKETS

1 c. cooked rice
3 lb. hamburger
2 eggs
1 onion

Salt and pepper
1 large head cabbage, partially
   cooked to make leaves
   pliable

Mix first 5 ingredients; wrap in cabbage leaf and place in roaster pan. Cover with can of tomatoes. Sprinkle with a bit of flour. Bake approximately 1 hour at 350°.

Mrs. David Kosmatka, Forman, ND

ISABELLE'S OLLIE BOLLEN

3 c. flour
½ c. sugar
1 tsp. salt
2 tsp. baking powder
2 eggs

2 c. currants (can use raisins)
2 c. buttermilk
1 tsp. soda
1½ tsp. vinegar

Heat oil in deep-fryer to 350° to 400°. Mix eggs, sugar, buttermilk, flour, baking powder, and soda. Add vinegar, salt, and currants. Use 2 spoons or ice cream scoop to form balls. Drop balls into hot oil and cook till golden brown. Sprinkle with powdered sugar.

Mrs. David Kosmatka, Forman, ND

PAUL'S SWEET AND SOUR CHICKEN WINGS

2 pkg. chicken wings (about 20)
2 eggs

¾ c. cornstarch
½ tsp. salt

Cut each wing in 3 parts. Put wing tips in water and bring to a boil. Rinse and re-cover with water. Add ½ stalk celery, ½ carrot, ¼ onion, and salt and pepper to taste. Cook. Save stock for sauce.

Mix eggs, cornstarch, and salt. Dip remaining 2 wing sections in mixture; coat well. Fry in ¼ inch oil over medium heat till brown. Place in roaster pan and cover with sauce. Bake at 350° for 30 to 45 minutes, turning at least once.

Sweet and Sour Sauce:

1 tsp. salt
¼ c. vinegar
3 Tbsp. catsup
1 c. sugar

1 Tbsp. soy sauce
¼ c. chicken stock
2 tsp. Accent or MSG

Mix well.

Mrs. David Kosmatka, Forman, ND

CHICKEN ADOBO - PHILLIPPINE ISLANDS

About 3 lb. chicken, cut up
3 tsp. salt
1 tsp. black pepper
2 bay leaves

4 to 6 cloves garlic, crushed
¾ c. white vinegar
3 Tbsp. salad oil

Wash chicken and wipe dry. Sprinkle with salt and pepper. Place in Dutch oven. Add bay leaves and garlic. Pour vinegar over and marinate for 30 minutes to 1 hour. Cook over moderate heat until chicken is tender, adding a little water as liquid evaporates, to keep chicken moist. When chicken is done, turn up heat to dry up remaining liquid. Add oil to pan and fry until brown and crisp on surface. Lift out and drain oil. Serve with rice and your choice of green vegetables.

Yvonne Maddox

ITALIAN CHICKEN PARMESAN

3 whole chicken breasts, boned
   and skinned
2 eggs, slightly beaten
1 tsp. salt
⅛ tsp. pepper
¾ c. bread crumbs
½ c. oil
2 c. tomato sauce

¼ tsp. basil
⅛ tsp. pepper
½ tsp. oregano
¼ tsp. garlic powder
1 Tbsp. margarine
½ c. Parmesan cheese
8 oz. sliced Mozzarella
Spaghetti

Pound chicken until ¼ inch thick. Combine eggs, salt, and pepper. Dip chicken in bread; brown quickly in oil. Drain on paper towel. Put in shallow pan; stir in tomato sauce, basil, oregano, and garlic powder. Heat to boiling and simmer for 10 minutes. Stir in margarine; pour over chicken. Sprinkle on Parmesan cheese. Cover and bake for 30 minutes at 325°F. (preheated oven). Put Mozzarella on top and return to oven, uncovered, for 10 minutes. Serve with spaghetti.

Judy Altman, St. Paul, MN

CHICKEN STIR-FRY WITH VEGETABLES

2 whole breasts of chicken
15 oz. can bean sprouts
15 oz. can bamboo shoots
1 ctn. pea pods
¼ c. chopped green onions
Couple chunks of garlic, minced
1 c. chopped celery
1 can water chestnuts
½ c. carrots, julienned
1 c. broccoli (frozen works best)

½ c. + 2 Tbsp. beef broth
3 Tbsp. soy sauce (more if like)
1 Tbsp. cornstarch
1 Tbsp. ginger, sprinkled around
Rice
Additional vegetables (if desired such as fresh mushrooms, slivered almonds, green peppers)

Spray wok with Pam. Saute onions and garlic. Add remaining vegetables; stir-fry till tender. (You may pick and choose which vegetables you want to use.) Reserve vegetables. Brown chicken, adding 1 tablespoon soy sauce in wok. Return vegetables to wok. Add ginger and remaining soy sauce. Add beef broth. With the 2 tablespoons of broth, add cornstarch.

Tracy Lozon, Owatonna, MN

ENCHILADAS

1½ lb. ground beef
1 small onion
Italian seasoning to taste
    (approx. ½ tsp.)
1 large can Old El Paso mild
    enchilada sauce

1 can cream of mushroom soup
¾ can beer
Lots of grated Cheddar cheese
1 pkg. flour tortilla shells

Brown ground beef with onion and Italian seasoning; drain. Heat enchilada sauce, beer, and cream of mushroom soup. Place tortilla on counter and put 1 large tablespoon of meat in 1 end of tortilla; roll up. Place, seam side down, in a 9x13 inch pan. When all meat and tortillas are used up, pour the sauce over all Enchiladas. Put lots of grated Cheddar cheese on top. Bake at 350° for about 30 minutes.

Mavis Ann Hjulberg, Minneapolis, MN

GRILLED CHICKEN TACOS

2 lb. green peppers or podlano
    peppers
Vegetable oil
4 whole chicken breasts, boned
    and skinned
Salt and pepper

2 Tbsp. butter or margarine
12 flour tortillas
1½ c. (6 oz.) shredded Monterey
    Jack cheese
1½ c. picante sauce

Brush peppers with oil. Bake on cookie sheet at 450°F. for 20 minutes or until skin blisters, turning once. Remove from oven; place in plastic bag. Close bag and let stand for 15 minutes. Peel peppers; cut into thin strips.

Pound chicken to even thickness. Brush with oil; season with salt and pepper. Place on grill over hot coals for 6 to 8 minutes or until cooked through, turning once. Cut into ¼ inch slices.

Melt butter in skillet. Add peppers and chicken; heat through. Spoon ½ cup chicken mixture down center of each tortilla. Top with 2 tablespoons each cheese and picante sauce. Makes 6 servings.

Tammy Weight, Anoka, MN

CRISPY OVEN-FRIED MEXICAN CHICKEN

1 c. mixed vegetable juice
¼ tsp. hot sauce
2¼ lb. chicken parts, skinned
2 oz. sharp Cheddar cheese,
    finely shredded
1½ c. corn flake crumbs
1 tsp. garlic powder

½ tsp. salt
½ tsp. pepper
½ tsp. chili powder
½ tsp. paprika
½ tsp. oregano leaves
½ tsp. ground cumin

In shallow pan (not aluminum), combine vegetable juice and hot sauce. Add chicken parts and marinate for 30 minutes at room temperature, turning chicken frequently. Drain chicken and discard marinade.

In large plastic bag, combine rest of ingredients. Place chicken pieces in bag and shake to coat chicken. Place chicken on baking sheet, sprayed with nonstick cooking spray. Bake in oven at 350° until tender and crisp, about 1 hour.

Arlene Jewell, Bismarck, ND

PENNSYLVANIA DUTCH SWEET AND SOUR TURKEY
(Bernadette Stankard)

1 turkey, cut up
2 onions, chopped
1 clove garlic, minced
1 bay leaf
2 whole cloves
1 to 2 tsp. mustard seed

2 Tbsp. cornstarch
1 to 4 c. sugar
1 to 2 c. vinegar
2 tsp. salt
10 peppercorns

Place turkey in large pot or Dutch oven with 4 cups water. Add onions, garlic, bay leaf, cloves, mustard seed, salt, and peppercorns. Cover and simmer for 2 hours. Remove turkey and strain broth. Return broth to pot and add cornstarch, combined with sugar and vinegar. Cook, stirring constantly, until sauce thickens. Add turkey and simmer for 15 minutes more. Serves 6.

Barb Fivecoate, Virginia, MN

FLEISCH KEICKLIN

Dough:

1 c. sour cream and 1 c. milk or 1 pt. half & half	**7 c. flour**
	1 Tbsp. sugar
6 eggs	**½ tsp. salt**

Mix ingredients. Let dough set for 30 minutes. Roll out pieces about the size of a walnut.

Filling:

3 eggs	**2 medium chopped onions**
2 lb. ground beef	**Garlic salt**
4 Tbsp. water	

Deep-fry at 375°. Yield: 20 servings.

Betty Risse, Bismarck, ND

STUFFED TOFU

Use 4 to 5 squares of bean curd, firm ones of 3 inch squares preferred. Towel dry and cut into 4 triangles.

Stuffing:

5 oz. ground pork	**1 to 2 tsp. soy sauce**
1 Tbsp. dried shrimp	**Freshly ground pepper**
1 small tsp. fresh ginger, finely minced	**1 Tbsp. Chinese wine or sherry**
	Some cornstarch
1 small tsp. green onion, finely minced	

1. Mix all the ingredients for the filling together.

2. Make a slit in each bean curd triangle on the wide side.

3. Stuff carefully each triangle without breaking them. Smooth the outer edges.

4. Heat a skillet with oil. Put in the triangles with the meat side down. Fry for 2 to 3 minutes till brown. Turn to brown the 2 flat sides, too, for a few more minutes.

These can be served 2 ways:

1. Drain on towels. Arrange on serving platter with sprigs of cilantro or parsley.

2. Serve with tomato or any chillie sauce. Simmer it with a cup of unsalted stock, a few pieces of finely chopped scallions, and ginger until a little liquid is left. Put tofu pieces onto serving plate. Thicken sauce with cornstarch and pour over the tofu; garnish.

Sammoy Knight, Minneapolis, MN

AS A SALAD OR BUFFET DISH

4 to 5 sq. bean curd, fried till brown, then cut into squares (little bite-size)
Some bean sprouts, scalded (clean off tails and skins)
Shredded cucumber

Shredded yam bean (jicama)
Sliced pineapple (fresh, not canned, bite-size)
Sliced tomato (bite size)
3 to 4 hard-boiled eggs (in wedges)

All these ingredients may be arranged on a serving platter with the sauce on the side, or toss with the sauce and serve individually or in a big bowl for self-service.

Sauce - Mix well:

3 Tbsp. brown sugar
5 Tbsp. crunchy peanut butter
1/4 to 1/2 c. chillie sauce (as per taste)

Some thick soy sauce
Vinegar to taste
Sugar to taste
Salt to taste

Add some water, if needed, for more smoothness.

Sammoy Knight, Minneapolis, MN

GERMAN STUFFED PORK CHOPS

1/4 c. finely chopped onion
1 medium clove garlic, minced
2 Tbsp. butter or margarine
1 c. dry rye bread cubes
1/4 c. chopped parsley
4 thick pork chops

1 (10 3/4 oz.) can condensed golden mushroom soup
1/2 c. sour cream
1/4 c. water
1/8 tsp. caraway seed
1 medium apple, cut in eighths

To make stuffing, in saucepan, cook onion with garlic in butter till tender. Add bread and parsley. Trim excess fat from chops. Slit each chop from outer edge toward bone; stuff with bread mixture and fasten with skewers.

In skillet, brown chops; pour off fat. Blend in soup, sour cream, water, and caraway. Cover and cook over low heat for 1 hour and 15 minutes; stir occasionally. Add apple; heat.

Barb Fivecoate, Virginia, MN

SAUERBRATEN

A famous German dish. A sweet sour beef to be served with boiled potatoes and red cabbage.

1 (3½ to 4 lb.) chuck roast or
   oxtail
2 onions
2 bay leaves
6 whole cloves

12 peppercorns
12 juniper berries
2 tsp. salt
1 pt. red wine vinegar

Place roast in an earthenware bowl with onions, seasonings, vinegar, and ½ cup water (heated to boiling); marinate for 3 days or more. Turn meat twice a day with 2 wooden spoons - never pierce with a fork. Keep in a cool place.

To cook, drain meat and brown thoroughly on all sides in hot fat in a heavy skillet. Add marinade; cover pan and simmer slowly for 3 or 4 hours or until tender. Serve meat with Gingersnap Gravy. Makes 6 to 8 servings.

Gingersnap Gravy:

2 Tbsp. sugar
8 crumbled gingersnaps

Flour and water paste (1 Tbsp.
   flour to 1 c. liquid)

When meat is done, remove to platter. Pour off excess fat. Add sugar and gingersnaps; cook for 10 minutes longer. Thicken with flour and water paste. Bring to a boil; season and serve.

Laila Schroeder, Shakopee, MN

QUESADILLAS WITH PICADILLO FILLING

2 Tbsp. cooking oil
1 lb. beef round steak, finely
   chopped

½ c. chopped onion
1 clove garlic, minced

In a large skillet, heat 2 tablespoons oil; cook beef, onion, and garlic till beef is brown and onion is tender.

2 medium tomatoes, peeled and
   chopped
1 medium apple, peeled, cored,
   and chopped
½ c. raisins
1 to 3 canned jalapeno peppers,
   drained and chopped

2 Tbsp. vinegar
1 tsp. sugar
1 tsp. salt
½ tsp. ground cinnamon
⅛ tsp. ground cloves
⅛ tsp. ground cumin

Stir in tomatoes, apple, raisins, jalapeno peppers, vinegar, sugar, salt, cinnamon, cloves, and cumin; simmer, covered, for 20 minutes.

½ c. toasted slivered almonds	Dairy sour cream
12 (6 inch) flour or corn tortillas	Sliced green onions
2 Tbsp. cooking oil	Radish roses
2 c. shredded lettuce	

Stir in almonds; cook, uncovered, for 2 minutes more. Remove from heat. Place about ¼ *cup* filling on each tortilla. Fold tortillas in halves; secure each with a wooden toothpick if desired.

In a skillet, heat 2 tablespoons cooking oil; cook filled tortillas, a few at a time, in the hot oil about 2 minutes per side or till light brown. Keep warm in a 300° oven while frying remaining tortillas.

To serve, place 2 quesadillas atop some of the shredded lettuce on a plate. Garnish with sour cream, green onions, and radish roses. Makes 6 servings.

Don't let the big words in the title put you off. Quesadillas (kay-sah-DEE-yahs) are made with flour or corn tortillas and are something between a turnover and a grilled sandwich. Picadillo (pee-kah-DEE-yoh) is a beef mixture made with tomato, onion, apple, raisins, nuts, and sweet spices. If you're not up to the heat of 3 jalapenos, use fewer jalapenos and remove the fiery ribs to which the pepper seeds are attached.

Karen Thompson, W. ST. Paul, MN

CHOW MEIN

1 lb. leftover pork or 1 lb. cubed uncooked pork	2 beef bouillon cubes
2 Tbsp. onion	1 can bean sprouts
2 to 3 c. chopped celery	1 can mushrooms
2 c. finely sliced cabbage	2½ Tbsp. soy sauce
¾ c. water	2½ Tbsp. cornstarch
	¼ c. water

If using uncooked pork, fry till done or leftover pork just until brown. Add onion and chopped celery; fry until soft. Add cabbage, water, and beef bouillon cubes; simmer until cabbage is cooked. Add bean sprouts, mushrooms and juice, and soy sauce; simmer for 10 minutes.

Mix cornstarch and water; add to mixture. Stir to thicken. Serve over chow mein noodles or rice.

Marie Burt, Owatonna, MN

EASY PORK AND VEGETABLE WOK

2 lb. pork steak, cut in strips	2 Tbsp. corn starch
½ c. soy sauce	

Coat meat and let set for 4 hours. Heat 3 ounces peanut oil in wok till smoking starts, then add meat and cook until done. Remove meat. Add frozen Chinese and Japanese vegetables and cook until done. Place meat back in wok and let simmer until hot. Serve on rice.

May add ½ to 1 cup light wine to meat.

Janet Lozon, Owatonna, MN

MAHNDU - KOREAN EGG ROLL
(Mŏn-dū)

½ lb. beef, ground
½ lb. ground pork
¼ c. onion, chopped fine
1 c. cabbage, shredded, cooked,
    and then measured after
    cooked
1 regular size can bean sprouts,
    drained, rinsed, and
    chopped

⅓ c. celery, chopped
1 green onion, chopped
1 tsp. salt
1 Tbsp. soy sauce
1 tsp. sesame oil
½ tsp. black pepper
½ Tbsp. corn starch

Brown meat. Add all ingredients. Use store bought egg rolls. Makes 18 large rolls.

Patty Senger, Fargo, ND

BULGOGI - KOREAN BBQ BEEF
(Bull-gō-gēe)

1 lb. round steak (family steak)
2 Tbsp. sugar
2 Tbsp. sesame oil
4 Tbsp. soy sauce

1 tsp. ground sesame seed
4 Tbsp. chopped green onion
½ to ¾ tsp. garlic powder
½ to ¾ tsp. black pepper

Cut beef in strips (3 inches square). Mix all ingredients; marinate beef for 3 to 4 hours. Barbecue on grill or in oven.

Patty Senger, Fargo, ND

EGG ROLLS

2 pkg. egg rolls
4 chicken breasts
2 cans water chestnuts
1 bunch celery
2 bunches green onions
15 fresh mushrooms

1 can bean sprouts
1 bottle cooking oil
2 heaping tsp. ginger
¼ c. soy sauce
2 eggs, beaten with small
    amount of water

Cook chicken breasts until tender; cool and dice in very small pieces. Dice other vegetables into small pieces. Drain and rinse bean sprouts and water chestnuts, then dice water chestnuts. Toss all together. Add ginger and soy sauce.

Put all rolls in pan to heat. Lay wraps out, 1 at a time. Paint wrap with egg and water mixture. Spoon 1 very heaping tablespoon on each wrap in corner. Roll and seal. Paint seal with egg mixture and firm up. Cook 3 Egg Rolls at a time. Brown on both sides. Drain on Scot towels.

Janet Lozon, Owatonna, MN

KLUSKAS - POLISH RAW POTATO DUMPLINGS

5 or 6 large potatoes	About 1 c. flour
2 tsp. salt	½ tsp. baking powder
1½ lb. loin pork steak	⅓ c. butter
1 large onion	

Peel large potatoes. Wash and grate on fine holes on box grater. Drain off all liquid from grated potatoes. Add salt, baking powder, and flour. Add enough flour to make a thick dumpling dough. Drop by spoonfuls into boiling water. Boil for about 25 minutes; drain.

Add to the following: Cut loin pork steak into small cubes. Melt butter and add finely diced onion and pork cubes. Saute until pork is nice and brown. Add drained dumplings and continue sauteing for about 20 minutes more. If dumplings and meat become dry, add a little bit of water and a little bit more butter or oleo.

Annette Zubinski, Duluth, MN

SCRAMBLED EGGS WITH TOMATOES
(Costa Rican style)

3 eggs, beaten	Salt and pepper to your taste
1 diced up small tomato	

Combine eggs with tomato, salt, and pepper. Cook in frying pan with no oil, shortening, or grease. The tomato will keep the egg from sticking to the pan. Makes enough for 2 people.

Kathy Hanson, Owatonna, MN

KNISHES

Dough:

2½ c. all-purpose sifted flour	1 tsp. baking powder
½ tsp. salt	2 eggs
⅔ c. salad oil	2 Tbsp. water

Sift the flour, baking powder, and salt into a bowl. Make a well in the center and drop the eggs, oil, and water into it. Work into a flour mixture with the hand and knead until smooth.

Roll dough into 3 inch circles, paper thin. Place tablespoon of filling on each. Draw the edges together and pinch firmly. Place on an oiled baking sheet, pinched edges up. Bake in a 375° oven for 35 minutes or until browned.

Filling:

½ c. minced onions
1½ c. ground cooked meat
1 egg
¼ tsp. pepper

2 Tbsp. salad oil
2 c. mashed potatoes
1 tsp. salt

Lightly brown the onions in oil. Add the cooked meat, potatoes, egg, salt, and pepper, mixing until smooth.

Annette Zubinski, Duluth, MN

FRIED RICE - CHINESE

3 c. cold cooked rice
½ to 1 c. ham, shrimp, chicken, turkey, cooked pork, or cooked beef
2 stalks celery, diced
1 medium onion, diced

3 green onions, diced (optional)
2 Tbsp. soy sauce
2 Tbsp. oil
2 beaten eggs (scramble and cook before using)

Heat oil in wok or Teflon pan. Add rice, meat, celery, onions, and soy sauce; stir-fry until hot. Add precooked scrambled eggs. Serve.

Renee Ulberg, Bismarck, ND

FETTUCCINE ALFREDO - ITALIAN

8 oz. uncooked wide egg noodles
½ c. margarine or butter
½ c. whipping cream

¾ c. grated Parmesan cheese
½ tsp. salt
Dash of pepper
2 tsp. snipped parsley

Cook noodles as directed on package; drain. Heat margarine and cream over low heat until margarine is melted. Stir in cheese, salt, and pepper. Pour sauce over hot noodles, stirring until noodles are coated. Sprinkle with parsley. May also crumble fried bacon over before serving.

Note: Put cheese in only to melt.

Renee Ulberg, Bismarck, ND

DENMARK FRIKADELLER MEATBALLS

¾ lb. ground beef
¼ lb. pork, ground
⅔ c. milk
½ c. flour

1 egg
1¼ tsp. salt
1¼ tsp. grated onion
¼ c. margarine

Mix all ingredients and shape into small round cakes. Melt some shortening and place cakes in pan; brown first on one side, then the other. Cover and let steam until done.

Barb Fivecoate, Virginia, MN

McGREW KRAUTBURGERS

Dough:

2 c. warm water
1 pkg. yeast (dry)
½ c. warm water
Flour

5 Tbsp. sugar
1 Tbsp. salt
6 Tbsp. melted shortening

Dissolve yeast in ½ cup water and combine with 2 cups warm water. Add sugar, salt, and slightly cooled shortening. Mix in enough flour to make a light dough. Roll dough to ¼ inch thickness; cut into squares.

Place filling on each square and seal. Place each square (seam side down) on a greased pan and bake for 20 minutes in a hot oven (375°) or until brown. Brush top with butter when krautburgers are removed from oven.

Filling:

1 medium size cabbage
4 medium onions
1 c. shortening

4 lb. hamburger
1 Tbsp. pepper
1 Tbsp. salt

Chop cabbage and onions fine. Cook in ½ of shortening over low heat until done. Do not brown. Cook, covered to steam, stirring often until done. Drain off excess fat; season. Add cabbage and onion to hamburger in a frying pan and cook over low heat for 20 minutes.

Barb Fivecoate, Virginia, MN

GREEK MOUSSAKA - LAMB AND BEEF DISH

1 c. milk
½ c. grated Cheddar cheese
Onion powder
½ tsp. French mustard
1 egg
1 Tbsp. dried bread crumbs or
   crushed biscuits
1 lb. ground beef
4 to 5 lean lamb shoulder cuts
1 large or 2 small eggplants
5 Tbsp. oil

1 clove garlic
1 Tbsp. Worcestershire sauce or
   ketchup
2 Tbsp. chopped parsley
1 Tbsp. tomato puree
4 to 5 ripe tomatoes or small can
   tomatoes
3 medium potatoes
2 Tbsp. butter
1¾ Tbsp. flour

Preheat oven to 400°. Slice eggplants. Sprinkle well with salt and leave for 30 minutes. Cook chopped and crushed garlic in 2 tablespoons oil until soft. Add meat and cook until changes color. Add Worcestershire sauce, parsley, and tomato puree. Put into baking dish to keep warm.

Skin tomatoes by dipping in boiling water for 10 seconds and then into cold; peel and slice. Peel and slice potatoes. Drain liquid from eggplants; wash in cold water and dry. Heat 2 tablespoons oil. Fry eggplant slices until brown on both sides. Drain on kitchen paper. Put tomato slices on top of eggplants and season. Fry potato slices in remaining oil until brown and place over top of tomatoes.

Make cheese sauce: Heat butter and stir in flour. Add milk; stir until it boils. Add seasoning, mustard, and ½ the cheese. When dissolved, cool slightly and mix in egg yolk. Beat egg white and fold into sauce. Pour sauce over top of Moussaka. Sprinkle top with grated cheese and dried bread crumbs; cook for 20 to 25 minutes in oven until top is well browned.

Barb Fivecoate, Virginia, MN

INDONESIAN-STYLE BEEF AND BANANAS

Lois tells us that everyone who has tried this dish likes it. Serve cooked red peppers with a sprig of coriander alongside.

¼ c. soy sauce
2 Tbsp. lemon juice
1 Tbsp. molasses
1 clove garlic, minced
½ tsp. ground ginger
¼ tsp. ground red pepper
1 lb. boneless beef top-round
    steak (bias-sliced in
    bite-size strips)

2 Tbsp. cooking oil
⅓ c. water
⅓ c. creamy peanut butter
3 large bananas, cut into 1 inch
    chunks
Hot cooked rice
Chopped peanuts

Combine soy sauce, lemon juice, molasses, garlic, ginger, and red pepper. Place beef in a plastic bag set in a bowl. Pour soy mixture over meat; seal bag. Marinate in refrigerator for several hours or overnight, turning occasionally. Drain, reserving marinade.

Heat oil in wok or 12 inch skillet. Stir-fry meat, ½ at a time, for 3 minutes or till done. Return all meat to skillet; push to sides of pan. Add reserved marinade, water, and peanut butter to center of skillet, stirring till peanut butter is melted and mixture is smooth. Add bananas; heat through for 1 to 2 minutes. Serve over rice. Sprinkle with peanuts. Makes 4 servings.

Per serving: 626 calories, 33 grams protein, 52 grams carbohydrates, 33 grams fat, 74 milligrams cholesterol, 1,921 milligrams sodium. USRDA: 18% vitamin C, 18% thiamine, 18% riboflavin, 51% niacin, 32% iron, 37% phosphorus.

Sonya Masset, Bismarck, ND

CHILI RELLENOS

1 large can evaporated milk
4 eggs
4 Tbsp. flour
½ lb. Monterey Jack cheese,
    grated

½ lb. sharp Cheddar cheese,
    grated
2 (4 oz.) cans whole green chiles
1 (8 oz.) can tomato sauce
    (optional)

Beat evaporated milk, eggs, and flour. Alternate chiles and cheese. Pour batter over this mixture and add tomato sauce. Bake at 350° for 30 minutes.

Bernice T. Eugenis, Saginaw, MN

TOAD-IN-THE-HOLE - ENGLISH

1 Tbsp. bacon drippings or
    vegetable oil
½ lb. link pork sausages
¾ c. all-purpose flour
Pinch of salt
¼ c. grated very sharp Cheddar
    cheese

1¼ c. milk
2 eggs
2 Tbsp. minced fresh parsley
Salt and freshly ground pepper

Preheat oven to 425°F. Melt bacon drippings in 9 inch ovenproof glass pie plate in oven. Add sausages and bake until browned, 15 to 20 minutes, turning frequently, to prevent sticking.

Meanwhile, sift flour and salt into medium bowl. Stir in cheese. Beat milk, eggs, and parsley in small bowl. Season with salt and pepper. Stir enough of milk mixture into flour to make smooth stiff batter. Let stand for 5 minutes. Stir in remaining milk mixture. Pour batter over sausages. Reduce oven temperature to 400°F. Bake sausages until batter is puffed and brown, about 30 minutes.

Kathy Olsen, Duluth, MN

OLD-FASHIONED IRISH STEW
(Makes 6 servings)

3 lb. (1 inch thick slices) lamb
    neck, fat trimmed and
    reserved
4 medium onions, thinly sliced
1 medium onion, chopped
1 lb. medium carrots, peeled,
    halved crosswise, and
    quartered lengthwise

1 lb. medium boiling potatoes, 1
    sliced thinly, remainder
    quartered
3 c. lamb stock or beef broth
4 Tbsp. minced fresh parsley
Salt and freshly ground pepper

Mince lamb fat. Cook in heavy Dutch oven over high heat until fat renders, stirring frequently, about 5 minutes. Strain drippings and return to Dutch oven. Heat over medium high heat. Pat lamb dry; add in batches (do not crowd) and cook until brown, about 5 minutes per side. Transfer to large bowl using slotted spoon. Add sliced and chopped onions, carrots, and sliced potato to pan; cook until light brown, stirring frequently, about 5 minutes. Return lamb to pan, spooning vegetables on top. Add stock.

Reduce heat; cover and simmer gently for 1 hour. Add quartered potatoes, pushing into liquid. Cover and simmer until potatoes and lamb are tender when pierced with fork, about 35 minutes. Drain liquid from pan into heavy large skillet; degrease cooking liquid. Boil until reduced by half, about 15 minutes. Return to stew. Mix in 2 tablespoons parsley. Season with salt and pepper. Ladle stew onto heated platter. Sprinkle with remaining parsley.

Kathy Olsen, Duluth, MN

IRISH LAMB OR MUTTON STEW

3 lb. lamb, cut from the neck or breast into ½ inch cubes
6 large potatoes
3 medium onions
1 tsp. thyme
1 tsp. salt

Black pepper
2 c. chicken broth
2 Tbsp. butter
1½ Tbsp. flour
Finely chopped parsley

Peel and slice potatoes and onions thickly. Combine thyme, parsley, salt, pepper, and flour. Butter a casserole and place a layer of potato slices, a layer of onions, and a layer lamb cubes. Sprinkle with the spice and flour mixture. Continue layering the casserole until all ingredients are used, sprinkling each layer with the spice and flour mixture. Add chicken broth; cover and cook in a 350° oven for 1½ hours or until lamb is tender, adding more chicken broth or hot water if the stew becomes too dry.

Kathy Olsen, Duluth, MN

ORIENTAL EGG FOO YONG

6 eggs
1½ c. drained bean sprouts
¼ c. instant onion or 1 c. chopped onion

2 Tbsp. chopped green pepper
½ tsp. salt
Dash of pepper

Beat eggs; combine with rest of ingredients. Fry in fry pan like patties; drain on paper towel if desired. Serve hot with soy sauce. Sliced water chestnuts and diced cooked pork or shrimp can be added.

Sauce - Combine in saucepan:

1 c. chicken broth or bouillon
2 Tbsp. soy sauce (I use the light kind)

1 Tbsp. cornstarch

Cook and stir over low heat until thickened. *A budget stretcher!*

Jane Klein, Bellevue, WA

ORIENTAL PORK FRIED RICE

2 eggs, beaten
4 c. cold cooked rice
1 c. diced leftover pork
3 Tbsp. salad oil

½ c. chopped green onions and tops
½ pkg. dry onion soup mix
2 Tbsp. soy sauce

Heat oil in wok or large frying pan. Cook eggs, scrambling until small pieces. Add rice, soy sauce, and soup mix. Fry until thoroughly mixed and brown. Add meat and onions; stir. Serves 6.

Also good with leftover chicken, beef, ham, bacon, or shrimp. Also can add water chestnuts, bean sprouts, mushrooms, etc.

Jane Klein, Bellevue, WA

ORIENTAL STEW

Fresh mushrooms
Pineapple tidbits
Green and red bell peppers
Onions
Water chestnuts

Celery
Thin sliced beef (round steak,
    breakfast steaks, flank
    steak)

Cut all vegetables oriental style. Tenderize steak up to ½ hour, then cut into ½ inch strips.

Make sauce of:

1 beef bouillon cube
1½ c. water or pineapple juice
2 Tbsp. cornstarch

¾ tsp. powdered ginger (or less)
2 tsp. sugar
3 Tbsp. soy sauce

Mix the cornstarch with juice or water and bouillon. Add other ingredients in saucepan. Bring to a boil to thicken. Brown meat for 1 to 3 minutes in hot oil. Return to serving dish. Cover and cook vegetables in hot oil no longer than 3 minutes. Crispness of vegetables is important. Return meat to skillet; blend hot sauce through and serve.

To accompany: All you need is rice and my Chinese Green Salad (included).

Chinese Green Salad:

Crisp greens
1 can mandarin oranges
Onion rings or chopped
    scallions

Shrimp (optional)
Almonds (optional)

Jane Klein, Bellevue, WA

IRISH LAMB STEW

1½ lb. lamb, cut into 2 inch
   cubes
1 Tbsp. shortening
2 medium onions, chopped
4 c. beef broth
3 medium potatoes, peeled and
   thinly sliced
½ tsp. salt

¼ tsp. pepper
⅛ tsp. thyme leaves, crushed
6 Tbsp. flour
1 (10 oz.) pkg. frozen peas,
   partially thawed
¼ tsp. celery seed
¼ tsp. marjoram leaves,
   crushed

In large skillet or crock pot with browning unit, brown meat in shortening. Combine browned meat in slow cooker with remaining ingredients, except peas and flour. Cover and cook on LOW for 8 to 10 hours or until meat and potatoes are done. Add peas, then flour, dissolved in ½ cup cold water. Turn control to HIGH; cover and cook for 15 to 20 minutes. Makes 5 to 6 servings.

Betty Michon, Detroit Lakes, MN

SPANISH RICE

½ c. bacon, diced
4 Tbsp. chopped celery
2 Tbsp. chopped green pepper

2 c. boiled rice
2 c. tomatoes
¼ tsp. salt and pepper

Heat bacon and when brown and edges are curled, add rice and cook slowly until brown. Stir constantly. Add rest of ingredients and cook slowly for 15 minutes; stir frequently.

SPAETZLE

3 eggs
½ tsp. salt
½ c. water

1¾ c. all-purpose flour
2 Tbsp. butter or margarine
Boiling salted water

In a bowl, beat together the eggs, salt, water, and flour until very well blended. Melt butter in a wide pan and keep near cooking area. Bring a large kettle of boiling salted water to a boil. Place a colander with large holes over the boiling water so that bottom of colander is about 2 inches above water level. Ladle about ¼ cup batter into colander, then force the batter through the holes with a rubber spatula so that the batter falls in droplets into the water.

When Spaetzle float to surface, stir, if necessary. Cook an additional 10 seconds, then skim Spaetzle from water; drain and place in the pan of melted butter. Shake pan to completely coat Spaetzle. Repeat procedure until all butter is used. Serve buttered Spaetzle immediately. Makes 4 to 6 servings.

To make Spaetzle ahead of time: Cool, cover, and refrigerate up to 3 days or freeze up to 2 months.

Laila Schroeder, Shakopee, MN

EGG FOO YONG

A good recipe for a meal on the table in less than 30 minutes!

4 eggs, beaten
1 Tbsp. instant onion (or small onion, minced)
1 c. flaked shrimp, chicken, or pork pieces

Salt and pepper to taste
Garlic powder to taste
1 can drained bean sprouts (or fresh)

Mix together and fry in small amount of oil in pan. Turn only once. Serve with sauce and rice.

Sauce:

1 c. chicken broth (bouillon cube can be used)
2 Tbsp. corn starch

2 Tbsp. sugar
2 Tbsp. soy sauce
2 Tbsp. vinegar

Stir constantly till thick and clear over low heat.

Pat and Don Jensen, Minneapolis, MN

SOUR CREAM ENCHILADAS
(Makes 1 dozen)

1 lb. Longhorn cheese

1 lb. Monterey Jack cheese

Sauce:

1 can cream of chicken soup (condensed)
1 pt. sour cream
1 small can chopped green chiles (make sure you don't grab "hot" flavor)

1 pkg. tortillas (corn)
1 bunch green onions

1. Fry tortillas (only till pliable) and drain.
2. Combine soup, sour cream, and chiles to make sauce.
3. Grate both cheeses and chop onions.
4. Fill tortillas with grated cheese, 1 large tablespoon of sauce and sprinkle with onion; roll up.

Repeat until all tortillas are filled, leaving small amount of sauce, cheese, and onion for topping. Bake in cake pan at 325° for 20 minutes.

Jane Klein, Bellevue, WA

SWEET-SOUR RED CABBAGE

1 head red cabbage (5 c. shredded)	1 tsp. salt
2 bay leaves	1/8 tsp. pepper
6 cloves	2 c. water
1 onion (whole)	1/3 c. vinegar (or red wine)
2 apples, peeled and sliced	1 Tbsp. bacon fat
	2 Tbsp. brown sugar

Cook cabbage in 2 cups salted water. Add seasoning and onion, picked with cloves. Add apple slices in covered pan and cook for 25 to 30 minutes until tender. Add fat, vinegar, and brown sugar. Thicken with a little flour if necessary. Makes 6 servings.

Laila Schroeder, Shakopee, MN

WILD RICE/WHITE RICE GROUND BEEF CASSEROLE

1/2 c. wild rice (see cooking directions)	1 c. boiling water with 2 beef bouillon cubes
1/2 c. white rice (raw)	2 lb. lean ground beef
1 can cream of chicken soup	3/4 c. chopped celery
1 can cream of mushroom soup	3/4 c. chopped onion

Saute celery and onion; add beef and brown. Season with celery salt, garlic salt, pepper, onion salt, and paprika (about 1/4 teaspoon each). If recipe seems dry, add either water or broth.

The original recipe uses all wild rice. This recipe can be used either way - very good for freezing and frozen in small quantities for small meals. I cook wild rice on top of stove for 15 minutes before adding to mixture. Insurance for a well done casserole.

Lucille Y. Wickham, Minneapolis, MN

ROUMANIAN NOODLE CHARLOTTE

Pudding:

1 lb. broad noodles	1 c. sour cream
3 eggs	1 1/4 c. cottage cheese
1 c. sugar	

To make the pudding, boil the noodles until they are tender and drain them completely. Place in a large bowl and add eggs with sugar. Mix until foamy, then add the sour cream and mix until smooth. Add the cottage cheese and mix well. Place in a greased pudding pan and level off.

Topping:

1 c. corn flake crumbs	1/2 grated orange rind
1/8 c. sugar	1/2 c. grated lemon rind
1/4 c. cinnamon	1/2 c. melted butter

Prepare the topping by mixing the corn flake crumbs, orange and lemon peels, sugar, and cinnamon in a bowl; mix well. Sprinkle on top of the pudding until completely covered. Sprinkle melted butter over the topping. Bake for 35 minutes in a preheated 325° oven.

Sauce:

1 c. fruit cocktail
½ c. grenadine

1 pt. pineapple juice
⅛ c. cornstarch

To make the fruit sauce, place the fruit cocktail in a strainer and reserve the juice. In a saucepan, place the pineapple juice, grenadine, and reserved fruit cocktail juice. Bring to a light boil and add the cornstarch (which has been dissolved in water). Add the fruit and serve with Roumanian Noodle Charlotte. Serves 6 to 8.

Mary Patalas, Virginia, MN

SOUFFLE DEMOULE, MOUSSELINE
(For 6 to 8 people)

The noncollapsible unmolded cheese souffle.

Preliminaries:

A baking dish to hold the souffle dish
A 2 qt. straight sided baking dish (4 to 5 inches deep for the souffle)

½ Tbsp. softened butter
2 Tbsp. finely grated Swiss cheese

Preheat oven to 350°. Put enough water in the baking dish so it will come at least halfway up the souffle dish. Place dish of water in lower third of oven. Spread butter inside souffle dish, being sure bottom is especially well coated. Roll cheese around in dish to cover bottom and sides.

The souffle sauce base:

2½ Tbsp. butter
A heavy bottomed 2½ qt. saucepan
A wooden spoon
3 Tbsp. flour

¾ c. hot milk
A wire whip
½ tsp. salt
⅛ tsp. pepper
Pinch of nutmeg

Melt the butter in the saucepan. Stir in flour with a wooden spoon and cook slowly, stirring, for 2 minutes without browning. Remove from heat. Let cool a moment, then beat in all the hot milk, stirring vigorously with a wire whip. Boil, stirring, for ½ minute. Remove from heat and beat in the salt, pepper, and nutmeg.

Adding eggs to sauce base:

3 eggs (U.S. graded "large")	**Pinch of salt**
A clean dry bowl	**¼ tsp. cream of tartar**
3 extra egg whites (6 to 7 Tbsp.)	**1 c. (4 oz.) coarsely grated Swiss**
A balloon whip or electric mixer	**cheese**

Break the eggs, 1 by 1, dropping the whites into the clean bowl and beating yolks into hot sauce. Add the 3 extra egg whites to those in the bowl, and with a clean dry whip or electric mixer, beat them for a moment at moderate speed until they begin to foam. Add the salt and cream of tartar; beat at top speed until egg whites hold in a mass in the beater and when beater is lifted the egg whites form stiff peaks with slightly drooping points.

Stir ¼ of the egg whites into the hot sauce to lighten it. Stir in the cheese; scoop the rest of the egg whites on top. Fold egg whites into the sauce, using a rubber spatula and plunging it down through the center of the mixture, drawing it to the sides of the pan, turning it, and lifting it out. You will thus bring a bit of the sauce up over the egg whites and prevent the whites from collapsing. Fold rapidly, turning the pan as you go. The whole operation should not take more than ½ minute.

Baking: Scoop the souffle mixture into the prepared dish, which the mixture should fill by no more than about ⅔. Set in the dish of hot water in preheated oven and bake for about 1¼ hours. The souffle should cook slowly, which is why it is set in hot water; regulate oven heat so water in dish never quite simmers.

Souffle is done when it has risen about ½ inch over the top of its dish. The top will be brown and the sides will show the faintest line of shrinkage from the dish. If you are not ready to serve, leave souffle in hot turned off oven. It will gradually sink about 2 inches as it cooks - which is why you want a deep dish.

Unmolding: When you are ready to serve, turn a warm lightly buttered serving dish over the souffle. Reverse the 2, giving a sharp downward jerk and the souffle will drop onto the plate. If the baking dish was properly buttered and the souffle sufficiently cooked, it will unmold perfectly.

Janet Lozon, Owatonna, MN

COOKIES, BARS, CAKES

ANISE DROPS - GERMANY

3 eggs
1 c. sugar

1 c. flour
1½ Tbsp. anise seed

Stir the sugar and eggs for ½ hour (10 minutes with an electric beater). Add flour and anise seed. Drop on a greased cookie sheet and let them stand until a hard crust forms on top (about 8 hours). Bake in a moderate oven for about 10 minutes. The tops will puff up to resemble icing.

These are popular with those who like the anise flavor. In a covered tin, they will keep fresh a long time.

Helen May Johnson, Chanhassen, MN

ANISE DROPS - GERMAN

4 eggs
1¼ c. sugar

3 c. flour
1¼ Tbsp. crushed anise seeds

Beat eggs with sugar until thick and white. Add flour and stir in anise seeds. Drop by teaspoon on cooky sheet 1 inch apart. Let dry, uncovered, overnight. Bake at 300° for 20 minutes until pale golden.

Laila Schroeder, Shakopee, MN

LES MADELEINES

1½ c. flour
3 eggs
¾ c. sugar

¼ lb. butter
Lemon juice

Beat eggs with sugar till they are light yellow and form a ribbon when dropped from a spoon. Add flour; beat well. Add lemon juice (just a few drops) and finally fold in the melted butter. Bake for 20 to 25 minutes in 375° oven.

Janet Lozon, Owatonna, MN

MEXICO WEDDING CAKES

Mix together thoroughly:

1 c. soft shortening (½ butter)
⅓ c. sugar

⅔ c. ground almonds, filberts,
or walnuts

Sift together and work in:

1⅔ c. sifted all-purpose flour

¼ tsp. salt

Chill dough. Roll with hands into round balls; place on ungreased cookie sheets about 2 inches apart. Flatten slightly with bottom of a glass. Bake until set - not brown, at 325°F. for about 12 minutes. Cool in pan. While slightly warm, carefully dip in 1 cup confectioners sugar.

Helen May Johnson, Chanhassen, MN

ISRAEL

2¼ c. sifted all-purpose flour
2 tsp. double acting baking
   powder
¼ tsp. salt
3 Tbsp. salad oil
3 whole eggs

1 c. sugar
1 tsp. almond extract
1 tsp. grated lemon peel
1 c. chopped blanched almonds
½ c. snipped pitted dates
⅓ c. snipped raisins

Make early in the day or day before. Set oven for 350°F. Sift flour, baking powder, and salt. In large bowl with electric mixer at medium speed, beat salad oil with eggs and sugar until fluffy. At low speed, blend in flour mixture, almond extract, and lemon peel, then with spoon, fold in almonds, dates, and raisins.

Grease and flour a jelly roll pan (15½ x 10½ x 1 inch). In jelly roll pan with 2 spoons, form dough into 2 long strips, each 3½ inches wide and about 3 inches apart. Now make 2 strips of foil of same length as loaves; lay against center side of each loaf to keep them from spreading.

Bake for 30 minutes, then remove from pan to wire rack and cool about 15 minutes. Increase oven temperature to 400°F. Now cut loaves into ½ inch crosswise slices; place slices on ungreased cookie sheet and bake for 10 minutes, turning once or until lightly toasted. Makes 3 dozen.

Serve with stewed or canned fruit at dessert time or with your favorite beverage.

Helen May Johnson, Chanhassen, MN

COCONUT BALLS - SWITZERLAND

4 egg whites
1 c. confectioners sugar
2 c. coconut

½ c. flour
1 tsp. vanilla

Beat egg whites until stiff. Add vanilla and sugar gradually. Add flour and the coconut. Drop an inch apart on a greased and floured cookie sheet. Bake in moderate oven for 15 minutes.

Helen May Johnson, Chanhassen, MN

CREAMY PUFF KISSES - HUNGARY

5 egg whites
2½ c. sugar

½ tsp. vanilla
Few grains of salt

Beat egg whites and salt until very stiff. Add sugar gradually. Fill small greased muffin tins ⅔ full and bake in slow oven for 30 minutes.

Helen May Johnson, Chanhassen, MN

SHORTBREAD - DENMARK

½ c. butter
¾ c. brown sugar
1 egg
½ tsp. vanilla

⅛ tsp. salt
¾ c. chopped nuts
½ tsp. baking powder
1½ to 2 c. flour (all-purpose)

Cream the butter and sugar. Add unbeaten egg and beat well. Add vanilla, the sifted together dry ingredients, and nuts. Form little balls (using more flour if necessary) and place on a cookie sheet to bake in a hot oven for 8 to 10 minutes.

You may substitute coconut for nuts if you wish.

Helen May Johnson, Chanhassen, MN

ABERGAVENNY NUTS - ENGLISH

1 c. molasses (Orleans)
1 c. sugar
1 c. shortening (½ butter - ½ lard)

1 tsp. salt
1 Tbsp. ginger
2 tsp. soda
½ c. water (warm)

Mix in order given. Add enough flour to form a stiff dough. Mold with the hands into small balls. Press into the top of each ball a strip of preserved ginger. Bake on greased cookie sheet, 1 inch apart in moderate oven for 10 to 15 minutes.

Helen May Johnson, Chanhassen, MN

NEW YEAR CAKES (GALETTES) - BELGIUM

1 lb. butter (2 c.)
1 lb. sugar (2 c.)

1 lb. flour (4 c.)
8 eggs

Melt butter. Add the sugar, flour, and last, the eggs; mix well. Add flavoring if desired. Bake on a waffle or galette iron. Cut in small cookies. These keep well and are very fine served with tea.

Helen May Johnson, Chanhassen, MN

BOUREKAKIA - GREEK WALNUT ROLL

Strussel sheets
1 lb. ground walnuts
2 Tbsp. sugar

½ tsp. cinnamon
½ tsp. ground cloves
½ lb. melted butter

Cut pastry sheets in 3 inch strips; use 2 for each nut roll. Brush each strip with the melted butter. Mix walnuts, sugar, and spices. Sprinkle 1 tablespoon mixture over strips and roll like jelly roll. Place rolls on cookie sheets and brush again with melted butter. Bake at 350° until golden brown.

Prepare a syrup, using:

2 c. sugar
1 c. water

1 slice lemon

Boil until thin syrup is formed. Pour cooled syrup over hot pastry.

Pastry sheets called "phyllo" are available ready made at Greek grocery stores or bakeries. In non-Greek shops, ask for "Strussel sheets."

Helen May Johnson, Chanhassen, MN

COFFEE KISSES - FRENCH

¼ c. strong clear coffee
1¼ c. sugar

3 egg whites
3 Tbsp. confectioners sugar

Boil the coffee and sugar to the "soft ball" stage. Pour on the stiffly beaten egg whites, gradually beating all the time. Stir in confectioners sugar. Drop on a greased and floured cookie sheet; sprinkle the top of each kiss with a little pulverized or very finely ground (instant) coffee and bake in a very slow oven until brown. *Remove* carefully.

Helen May Johnson, Chanhassen, MN

ROSQUITAS PARA TE - LITTLE WREATHS FOR TEA
(Mexico)

¼ c. sugar
½ c. butter or margarine
1 tsp. grated orange rind
3 egg yolks, beaten

2 c. sifted all-purpose flour
2 tsp. baking powder
1 egg white (unbeaten)

Measure sugar, butter, and orange rind into a mixing bowl. Cream together until light and fluffy. Add egg yolks. Mix until thoroughly combined, then sift flour and baking powder together into mixture. Stir, forming moderately stiff dough. Turn out on a lightly floured board and roll ½ inch thick.

Cut with a 2½ inch doughnut cutter. Place cookies on a lightly greased baking sheet and brush with egg white. Bake in a 375°F. oven for 20 minutes until lightly browned. Makes 8 large cookies or 16 smaller ones.

These are especially good served with a cup of Mexican chocolate about 3 o'clock in the afternoon.

Helen May Johnson, Chanhassen, MN

TEA COOKIES - RUSSIA

1 c. sugar
3 eggs
1 c. sour cream
⅘ c. flour (enough to roll)
1 c. chopped almonds

¾ c. butter
½ tsp. baking powder
½ tsp. salt
Sugar and cinnamon (for top)

Mix the slightly beaten eggs, sour cream, flour, baking powder, and salt. Toss on a floured board. Spread with a layer of butter. Place dough in bowl; cover and chill (do not freeze) for ½ hour.

Roll as thin as possible. Strew with chopped almonds, sugar, and cinnamon. Roll like a jelly roll and cut in ¼ inch rounds. Bake on a greased cookie sheet in moderately hot oven for 10 to 12 minutes. This is like a puff paste dough.

Helen May Johnson, Chanhassen, MN

POLISH WAFERS - POLAND

⅓ c. sugar
3 Tbsp. butter
2 Tbsp. fruit juice or brandy

1 egg
2 c. flour
Few grains of salt

Cream the butter and sugar and add unbeaten egg and salt; beat well, then add brandy. Mix in flour using more, if needed, for rolling; cut. Prick with a fork as for a cracker. Bake on a greased cookie sheet in a moderate oven for 8 minutes and watch to prevent burning. These are very much like a sweet cracker.

Helen May Johnson, Chanhassen, MN

GERMAN COOKIES

4 eggs
1 lb. brown sugar
2½ c. flour
1 tsp. cinnamon

½ tsp. cloves
1 tsp. vanilla
1 c. nuts

Beat eggs well, then add sugar and beat some more. Add flour and spices; mix well. Add vanilla and nuts. These cookies are also good with raisins, dates, or citrus fruit mix added with the nuts. Bake on greased baking sheet for 20 minutes at 350°.

Carol Gilbertson, Hawley, MN

SPRITZ

1 c. butter
1 c. powdered sugar
2 egg yolks

½ tsp. almond flavoring
2½ c. flour
½ tsp. baking powder

Cream butter and sugar. Add egg yolks and flavoring. Sift together flour and baking powder; add to creamed mixture. Put dough through a cookie press, making S or wreath shapes. Bake on ungreased cookie sheet in a 400°F. oven for about 10 minutes or until delicately browned.

Helen Johnson, Chanhassen, MN

CARDAMOM COOKIES - SWEDISH

1¾ c. flour
2 tsp. baking powder
¼ tsp. salt
2 eggs
¼ tsp. crushed cardamom
    seeds

⅓ c. butter
¾ c. sugar
Almonds

Sift together flour, baking powder, and salt. Add cardamom. Cream butter and sugar; add unbeaten eggs, 1 at a time, beating well after each addition. Add flour mixture until stiff enough to roll out. Cut in fancy shapes. Place on ungreased cookie sheet; decorate with almonds and bake in 350° oven until light brown.

Sigrid Johnson, Hibbing, MN

SANDBAKKELSE
(Brown sugar)

1 c. brown sugar
1 c. shortening

2 c. flour

Cream shortening. Add sugar and cream well. Add flour. Pinch off a small ball of dough. Place it in the center of tin and, with thumb, press dough evenly on inside of sandbakkelse tin, spreading it as thin as possible on the bottom and sides of tin. Place filled tins on cookie sheet. Bake in moderate oven at 350° to 375° for 15 minutes or until golden brown.

Pearl Paulsrud, Montevideo, MN

SANDBAKKELSE

1 c. sugar
1 c. butter
1 egg

3 Tbsp. cream
1 tsp. almond extract
Flour (about 2 c.)

Cream sugar and butter. Add egg, cream, and extract. Add enough flour so batter can be molded into tins. Bake until lightly brown at 350°.

Luella Anderson, Bismarck, ND

CHINESE COOKIES

½ c. shortening
½ tsp. soda
1 c. coconut
1 c. walnuts, cut fine

1 c. dates, cut fine
1 c. sugar
1½ c. flour
1 egg

Mix in order. Roll in balls the size of walnuts with part of cherry on top. Bake at 375° for 12 minutes.

Marie Capen, Duluth, MN

CZECHOSLOVAKIAN COOKIES

1 c. softened butter
1 c. sugar
2 egg yolks
1 tsp. vanilla

2 c. flour
1 c. chopped walnuts
¾ c. jam

Cream butter and sugar. Add egg yolks and vanilla; cream well. Blend in flour and walnuts. Spread ½ dough into a greased 8 inch square pan. Spread jam over dough. Spread remaining dough over top. Bake at 325° for 1 hour.

Barb Fivecoate, Virginia, MN

IRISH DROP COOKIES

1½ c. raisins
1 tsp. soda
⅔ c. shortening
1 c. sugar
1 c. brown sugar

1 tsp. nutmeg
1 tsp. cinnamon
½ tsp. salt
2 eggs
3½ c. flour

Boil raisins in water. When cooked, take from stove and pour ½ cup juice in cup; throw rest out. To raisin juice, add the rest of the ingredients. Bake at 350° for about 10 minutes. Frost.

Barb Fivecoate, Virginia, MN

SWEDISH HEIRLOOM COOKIES

1 c. shortening (½ butter)
1 c. confectioners sugar
1¼ c. ground almonds

2 c. flour
1 Tbsp. water
1 Tbsp. vanilla

Cream shortening and butter with confectioners sugar. Add almonds. Blend in flour. Add water and vanilla. Shape into balls using 1 level tablespoon of dough for each cookie. Place on ungreased baking sheet and flatten slightly. Bake at 325° for 12 to 15 minutes. Roll in powdered sugar while still warm. Makes 4½ dozen.

Carol Gilbertson, Hawley, MN

CANADIAN BARS

½ c. butter, melted
5 Tbsp. sugar
5 Tbsp. cocoa

1 tsp. vanilla
1 egg

Mix well.

Add:

2 c. graham cracker crumbs
½ c. coconut

½ c. chopped nuts

Put in 9 inch square pan and pack firmly.

Mix together:

4 Tbsp. butter
3 Tbsp. milk

2 Tbsp. instant vanilla pudding

Mix well. Add 2 cups confectioners sugar; mix well until smooth. Spread over first layer. Cool at least 1 hour in refrigerator. Top with chocolate frosting and cut in squares.

Lorraine Long, Grand Rapids, MN

ORIENTAL RICE KRISPY BARS

¾ c. brown rice syrup
1 to 2 tsp. tahini (optional)

5 c. crispy brown rice cereal

Heat brown rice syrup for about 1 minute in small saucepan. Add tahini (optional). Mix in crispy brown rice cereal. Put in oiled pan. Wet hands and pack; let set. Can refrigerate for 15 to 20 minutes.

Dee Millard, Edina, MN

KRUMBAKA

4 eggs, beaten
1 c. sugar
½ c. butter (be sure to use butter)

2 Tbsp. cornstarch
1½ c. flour
1 tsp. vanilla

Heat krumbaka iron for about 20 minutes, turning often to heat both sides. Drop about a teaspoonful on iron and squeeze, cooking until slightly browned. Remove and roll in cone while hot.

Rosalie Wendelbo, Grafton, ND

KRUM BAKER

6 eggs
1 scant c. melted butter
1 c. flour
¼ tsp. salt

1 tsp. cardamon (vanilla can be used)
1¼ c. sugar

Divide eggs and beat separately. Add yolks to whites and mix. Beat in sugar. Measure flour before sifting. Add cardamon and salt; sift twice and add to egg mixture. Add melted butter. Drop from teaspoon and bake for 1 minute or until light brown. Roll in stick (I use a wooden cone). Let cool for 1 minute before removing from stick. Bake in hot krumbaka iron without greasing iron.

Helen H. Clark, Grand Forks, ND

KRUM BAKE

6 eggs, well beaten
1 c. sugar
1 c. melted butter

1½ c. sifted flour
Cardamon or vanilla

Beat eggs well. Add sugar and beat well. Add melted butter and sifted flour. Add a little cardamon or vanilla for flavor. To bake, follow directions on krum bake iron.

Tina Knudsen, Owatonna, MN

KRUM BAKE - NORWEGIAN

4 eggs, beaten well
1 c. white sugar
½ c. melted butter, cooled
1½ c. flour
½ tsp. salt

1 tsp. vanilla
2 Tbsp. corn starch, mixed with the flour
Scant ½ tsp. ground cardamon

Mix all ingredients. Pour a small amount on heated krum bake iron. Bake on medium high on small burner (a few seconds); turn over and bake other side. Roll immediately.

Harlan Brekke, Fargo, ND

LARGE RAISIN BUTTERMILK SCONES - ENGLISH

2¾ c. unbleached flour
1 Tbsp. double acting baking
   powder
½ tsp. baking soda
¾ tsp. salt
½ tsp. cinnamon
⅓ c. sugar

½ stick (¼ c.) cold unsalted
   butter, cut into bits
¼ c. chilled vegetable
   shortening
½ c. raisins
2 large eggs
¾ c. buttermilk

In a bowl or food processor, blend the flour, baking powder, baking soda, salt, cinnamon, sugar, butter, and shortening until the mixture resembles meal. (If using a food processor, transfer the mixture to a bowl.) Stir in the raisins and make a well in the center of the mixture.

In a small bowl, beat the eggs lightly with buttermilk. Pour the mixture into well and stir flour mixture together gently with egg mixture to form a dough. Drop the dough by slightly rounded ¼ cup measures, 2 inches apart, onto buttered baking sheets; smooth the tops slightly with moistened hands and bake the scones in a preheated 425°F. oven for 20 minutes or until they are golden. Serve the scones warm. Makes about 10 scones.

Kathy Olsen, Duluth, MN

RAISIN SCONES - ENGLISH
(Makes about 25)

All-purpose flour
3¼ c. all-purpose flour
4 tsp. cream of tartar
2 tsp. baking soda
1 tsp. salt
6 Tbsp. (¾ stick) well chilled
   butter or margarine

1 c. golden raisins
5 Tbsp. sugar
1 c. (about) milk
Unsalted butter
Strawberry jam

Preheat oven to 425°F. Lightly flour baking sheet. Combine 3¼ cups flour, cream of tartar, baking soda, and salt in large bowl. Cut in butter using pastry blender or 2 knives until mixture resembles coarse meal. Stir in raisins and sugar. Mix in enough milk to form soft, but not sticky, dough.

Turn dough out onto lightly floured surface and knead gently until dough holds together. Roll dough out to thickness of ½ inch. Cut out rounds using 2 inch cutter (push straight down, do not twist). Arrange rounds on prepared sheet. Dust tops lightly with flour. Bake scones until puffed and golden, about 10 minutes. Serve immediately with butter and jam.

Kathy Olsen, Duluth, MN

ROSETTES - NORWAY

2 eggs, slightly beaten
1 Tbsp. sugar
¼ tsp. salt

1 tsp. vanilla
1 c. milk
1 c. flour

Add all other ingredients to eggs, beating until smooth. If full of air bubbles, strain and let stand an hour. Set rosette iron in at least 4 inches of deep fat and heat to 360°F. to 370°F. Drain iron slightly and dip into batter, covering only sides of the iron. If batter does not cling to iron, fat is too hot or too cool. Lower iron into fat and fry for about 1 minute or until delicately browned. Loosen Rosette from iron with a fork and drain, inverted, on paper towels. Sprinkle with powdered or granulated sugar with flour sifter. Keep iron hot during frying.

Helen Johnson, Chanhassen, MN

GORO - NORWAY

3 eggs
1 c. sugar
1 c. heavy cream
2½ c. flour

1 c. melted butter
¼ tsp. ground cardamon
1 Tbsp. brandy or cognac
1 tsp. vanilla

Beat eggs until lemon colored. Add sugar, beating well. Add remaining ingredients. Roll out like cookies and cut to fit goro iron. Place cookie in heated iron; hold over heat, turning until golden brown on both sides. Cut in sections while still warm.

Note: Goro irons can be purchased at most department stores in housewares or at Maid of Scandinavia.

Helen Johnson, Chanhassen, MN

FATTIGMAND

3 egg yolks
1 whole egg
4 tsp. sugar
¼ tsp. ground cardamom

¼ c. heavy cream
1 Tbsp. melted butter
1 tsp. vanilla
About 1¼ c. flour

Beat eggs until lemon colored (up to 15 minutes). Combine sugar and cardamom; add gradually to eggs, beating until light. Add butter, cream, and vanilla. Gradually stir in flour until dough is just stiff enough to handle; chill.

Roll about ⅓ of dough at a time on floured board until very thin. Cut in 2 inch long strips with fluted wheel or a knife, then cut crosswise at a slant to form diamonds. Slit dough at one point of diamond and bring opposite point through the slit. Fry in deep fat at 365°F. for about 1 minute or until light brown, turning once; drain. May be dusted with powdered sugar.

Helen Johnson, Chanhassen, MN

KRUMBAKE

1 egg
½ c. sugar
1 c. whipping cream
1¼ c. flour

½ tsp. baking powder
¼ tsp. salt
1 tsp. vanilla

Beat egg well. Add sugar and vanilla. Add whipping cream, then dry ingredients and beat until smooth. When krumbake iron is hot on both sides, put 1 teaspoon batter on the greased iron and bake over low heat until light brown. Roll on stick immediately, shaping into cones.

Helen Johnson, Chanhassen, MN

SANDBAKKELS

1½ c. sugar
1½ c. butter
½ c. oleomargarine
1 egg

Pinch of salt
1 tsp. vanilla
About 4 c. flour

Cream sugar and shortening. Add beaten egg, salt, and flavoring. Use flour, enough to handle easily. Make a ball in palm of hand and press or shape into sandbakkel tins (special fluted tins of muffin type). Bake in moderate oven (325°F. to 350°F.) until golden brown, about 12 to 15 minutes.

Helen Johnson, Chanhassen, MN

WAR CAKE

1½ c. raisins
1 c. sugar
2 Tbsp. lard or shortening
Pinch of salt

1½ c. cold water
2 tsp. cinnamon
¼ tsp. nutmeg
¼ tsp. cloves

Cook preceding ingredients about 5 minutes, then set aside to cool.

1 tsp. soda
1 tsp. vanilla

2 c. flour
1 tsp. baking powder

When mixture is cool, add soda and vanilla. Sift together flour and baking powder; add this to the preceding mixture and bake for about 30 to 35 minutes or until done, in a 350° oven.

Barb Fivecoate, Virginia, MN

SZARLOTKA - APPLE CAKE

3 lb. apples
1 c. sugar
½ tsp. vanilla
2 raw yolks
½ tsp. vanilla
½ lb. butter

3 c. flour
½ c. powdered sugar
½ c. sour cream
½ c. dried unseasoned bread
   crumbs

Cook peeled, sliced, tart apples with cup of sugar, a sprinkle of water, and ½ teaspoon vanilla until a jamlike filling forms; set aside.

Cut butter into flour. Add powdered sugar, yolks, sour cream, and vanilla; work into a dough. Wrap it in foil and refrigerate for 1 hour. Divide in 2. Roll out and line rectangular pan with 1 portion.

Evenly sprinkle dough in pan with bread crumbs and then add apple filling. Roll out other portion of dough and cover apple filling, making sure it stretches to all 4 sides of the pan, but does not overhang its ring. Bake in preheated 350° oven for 30 minutes or until done. When cooled, cut into squares. Before cutting cake, it can be dusted with powdered sugar, or you can top each square with a dollop of whipped cream just before serving.

Barb Fivecoate, Virginia, MN

DANISH APPLE CAKE

½ c. melted butter
2 c. dry bread crumbs
½ c. sugar
1 tsp. vanilla
3 c. applesauce (sweetened)
1 c. whipping cream

Melt butter; add bread crumbs and sugar. Stir until crumbs are light brown in heavy skillet over low heat. Into a buttered dish, press a layer of crumbs. Add vanilla to applesauce and put a layer on bread crumbs, then a layer of crumbs and applesauce until all is used. Chill and unmold; frost with whipped cream.

Barb Fivecoate, Virginia, MN

ITALIAN COFFEE CAKE

2 cubes oleo
1½ c. sugar
4 well beaten eggs
2 c. sour cream
2 tsp. soda
3 c. flour
2 tsp. vanilla
2 tsp. baking powder
¼ c. brown sugar
¼ c. white sugar
1 c. chopped nuts
2 tsp. vanilla

Mix together first 8 ingredients. Combine brown and white sugars, nuts, and vanilla; cut into batter. Bake in a 9x13 inch greased cake pan. Bake at 325° for 45 to 60 minutes.

Barb Fivecoate, Virginia, MN

JABLKA NA SZARLOTKE - APPLE CAKE FILLING

4 lb. tart apples
1¼ c. sugar
1 tsp. lemon juice

Peel apples; slice and place in pot. Add ¾ cup boiling water and cook gently until apples are tender. Add sugar and lemon juice and cook until a thick filling forms. Pour mixture into sterilized, dry 1 pint or ½ pint jars, leaving about 1 inch head space.

Place in water bath with water reaching no more than ¾ of the way up. Place lids on jars loosely; gently bring to boil and keep at a slow rolling boil for 20 minutes. Tighten the lids; remove from bath. Dry, cool, and store in cool dark fruit cellar.

Barb Fivecoate, Virginia, MN

CREPES AND PANCAKES

CREPES

2 c. flour
3 eggs
2 c. milk

2 Tbsp. sugar
2 Tbsp. vanilla
2 Tbsp. oil

Mix flour and eggs in a large bowl. Slowly add 2 cups of milk and then the other ingredients. Butter a pan and heat it. Pour a little batter in the pan, turning it to cover the bottom. As soon as the crepe begins to brown, turn it. Crepes are eaten cold or warm, sprinkled with sugar or spread with jam. You can also eat them with ham and cheese.

Janet Lozon, Owatonna, MN

SMOREN - PANCAKE CRUMBLES

1 c. flour
½ tsp. salt
1 c. milk
¼ c. butter

½ tsp. baking powder
2 egg yolks
2 egg whites, stiffly beaten

Sift flour, salt, and baking powder. Add well beaten egg yolks and milk; mix well. Fold in stiffly beaten egg whites. Melt butter in heavy skillet. Pour batter in hot butter. When it begins to thicken on the bottom, turn with pancake turner. Keep turning and chopping until lightly browned and little balls of crumbles are formed. These may be dusted with powdered sugar or served with syrup. *Also good plain.*

Annette Zubinski, Duluth, MN

POTATO PANCAKES - PLACKI KARTOFLANE

4 lb. potatoes
1 small onion
2 tsp. salt

2 beaten eggs
5 Tbsp. flour

Using grater blade of food processor, grate peeled potatoes and onion. Combine with salt, eggs, and flour. Spoon batter into hot lard and fry until golden brown and crispy on both sides. Serve immediately.

Barb Fivecoate, Virginia, MN

POTATO PANCAKES

2 qt. grated potatoes
2 eggs
1 heaping Tbsp. flour
6 slices finely chopped fresh
    bread

1 minced onion
3 tsp. baking powder
Parsley (optional)
1½ tsp. salt
1½ tsp. pepper

Mix well. Fry until golden brown on both sides. I prefer oil for the frying.

Annette Zubinski, Duluth, MN

SWEDISH PANCAKES

6 eggs
½ c. sugar (scant)
3½ c. milk
1 tsp. salt

4 Tbsp. melted butter
2 c. flour with ½ tsp. baking
    powder

Beat eggs well, but not foamy. Add milk. Sift dry ingredients and add; beat until smooth. Add melted butter. Let stand for 1 hour, then beat well and brown on hot skillet until nicely browned. Serve with syrup, sugar, blueberry sauce, or lingonberries.

Annette Zubinski, Duluth, MN

WELSH PARSLEY PANCAKES - CREMPOG LAS
(Makes about 18 (3 inch) pancakes)

1 c. sifted all-purpose flour
1 c. finely chopped onions
1 c. coarsely chopped parsley
    (about 1 large bunch)
¾ c. plus 1½ Tbsp. whole wheat
    flour
½ tsp. salt

¼ tsp. freshly ground pepper
1 c. (or more) milk
2 eggs, beaten to blend
¼ lb. mushrooms, thinly sliced
    (about 1½ c.)
Vegetable oil (for frying)

Mix first 6 ingredients in medium bowl. Make well in center. Add 1 cup milk and eggs; blend until smooth, adding more milk if batter is too thick. Stir in mushrooms.

Heat ⅛ inch oil in heavy large skillet over medium high heat. Ladle batter into skillet using 2 tablespoons for each pancake. Cook until bottom side is golden brown, about 3 minutes. Turn and cook until second side is golden brown and pancake is cooked through, about 3 minutes.

Kathy Olsen, Duluth, MN

SWEDISH PANCAKES - PLÄTTER

2 c. milk
4 beaten eggs
1 tsp. salt

2 Tbsp. sugar
1 tsp. cinnamon
1½ c. flour

Put margarine in pan; get pan hot. Make size of pan by tilting to spread batter. Make cakes very thin; turn once and roll up.

Mary Kleven

PAUUUKAKKO
"Pan" Cake

3 eggs
¾ qt. milk
1¼ c. flour

1 tsp. salt
¼ lb. butter

Beat eggs and add about ½ milk. Gradually add the remaining milk, flour and salt and beat hard with a spoon until smooth. Melt butter in a 9x13 inch cake pan. Pour batter over melted butter. Bake at 450° for about 30 minutes. Sprinkle sugar on to while warm.

Rose V. Johnson, Virginia, MN

DESSERTS

RICE CUSTARD PUDDING - RISGRYNSKAKA
(Swedish)

½ c. rice
1½ c. boiling water
2 eggs
½ c. sugar

½ tsp. salt
¼ tsp. nutmeg
2 c. milk
¼ c. raisins

1. Wash rice and drain thoroughly; add to boiling water. Cover and cook gently until all water is absorbed and rice is tender, about 20 minutes.

2. Beat eggs slightly. Add sugar, salt, and nutmeg; stir in milk. Add cooked rice and raisins.

3. Turn into 1 quart casserole. Bake in slow oven (325°) for 1½ to 2 hours. Yield: 6 servings.

Helen H. Clark, Grand Forks, ND

TOSCAS - SWEDISH TARTS

6 Tbsp. butter
¼ c. sugar
1 c. flour
⅓ c. nuts

¼ c. sugar
1½ Tbsp. cream
2 tsp. flour

Mix butter, sugar, and flour. Put into tart pans or muffin tins to make cups. Put the rest of ingredients in pan; bring to a boil. Put in tart cups. Bake for 15 minutes in 350° oven.

Edie Raatz

APPLE CAKE WITH VANILLA SAUCE - SWEDISH
(Äppelkaka Med Vaniljsäs)

6 Tbsp. butter
2¾ c. finely crushed Swedish
toast or Zwieback crumbs

2 c. sweetened applesauce (No.
303 can)
Vanilla Sauce

1. Melt butter in saucepan. Add crumbs and stir until all crumbs are mixed with butter and slightly browned.

2. Sprinkle ⅓ crumb mixture over bottom of shallow buttered 6 cup casserole or baking dish. Cover with 1 cup applesauce. Add another ⅓ crumb mixture; cover with remaining applesauce and sprinkle top with remaining ⅓ crumb mixture.

3. Bake, uncovered, in moderate oven (350°) for 25 to 30 minutes.

4. Chill Apple Cake in refrigerator. Unmold and serve with Vanilla Sauce. Yields 6 servings.

Vanilla Sauce - Vaniljsås:

1 c. light cream	3 Tbsp. sugar
1 egg yolk	2 tsp. vanilla
1 egg	1 c. whipping cream, whipped

1. Scald light cream. Mix egg, egg yolk, and sugar. Add scalded cream and stir until well mixed.
2. Cook in top of double boiler until sauce coats a metal spoon. Remove from heat and add vanilla. Cool, stirring occasionally.
3. When cold, fold in whipped cream. Yields about 2½ cups.

Note: One 6 ounce package of Zwieback yields 2¾ cups crushed crumbs.

Helen H. Clark, Grand Forks, ND

BEIGNET AUX POMMES

Batter:

1 c. sifted flour	1 c. milk
1 large egg, separated	5 large apples
Pinch of salt	Granulated sugar
2 Tbsp. oil	Oil (for frying)

Put the flour in a bowl; make a well in it and add egg yolk, salt, and oil to the well. Using a whisk, slowly bring flour into the egg yolk. Add milk as you go along. Beat the mixture well; there should not be any lumps. Strain the batter into another bowl and let stand for at least 30 minutes.

Peel the apples; core and cut into ¼ inch slices. Sprinkle with sugar. Heat the oil to 375° to 400°. Beat egg white until it is a not-too-stiff foam and fold into batter. Dip apple slices; add to oil. When golden brown on each side, drain on paper toweling. Sprinkle with sugar.

Janet Lozon, Owatonna, MN

KULTA - VELLIS
Finnish Fruit Sauce

1 qt. water	1 stick cinnamon or ½ tsp.
¼ lb. prunes	ground cinnamon
¾ c. seedless raisins	Pinch of salt
½ c. sugar	2 tsp. cornstarch
1 Tbsp. lemon juice	1 tsp. rice (optional)

Cook prunes and raisins in water slowly for 1 hour or until prunes are soft. Add sugar, lemon juice, cinnamon, salt and rice. Continue cooking until rice is done, about 10 minutes. Add cornstarch, which has been mixed with ¼ c. cold water, and cook a few minutes longer. For thicker sauce, add more cornstarch. Serves about 6.

Rose V. Johnson, Virginia, MN

MOUSSE AU CHOCOLAT
(Very good!)

6 oz. dark chocolate
½ oz. butter (1 Tbsp.)

4 eggs
¼ pt. whipping cream

Melt chocolate in saucepan. Add butter. Beat the cream. Add egg yolks to the melted chocolate; mix well. Beat well the egg whites. Add whites to chocolate mixture. Add beaten cream very gently; put in the refrigerator.

Janet Lozon, Owatonna, MN

ROMMEGRAT
(Without cream)

1 stick margarine
½ tsp. salt

4 c. scalded milk
¾ c. flour

Melt butter or margarine in heavy kettle (save a small amount to pour over when done). Add flour; stir until smooth. Bring to a boil and add scalded milk. Stir to prevent lumping. Boil again and add salt. Sprinkle with sugar and cinnamon. Add reserved melted margarine. Makes 8 servings.

Pearl Paulsrud, Montevideo, MN

ROMMEGROT - NORWEGIAN CREAM MUSH

¼ lb. butter, melted
½ c. flour
1 qt. milk
⅓ c. sugar

Salt
Sugar
Cinnamon
Melted butter

Mix butter and flour together. Gradually add 1 quart of milk and bring to a boil. Add sugar and salt; cook until thickened, stirring constantly. Put into serving dish; top with melted butter. Sprinkle with sugar and cinnamon.

Eloise Hoff, Preston, MN

BREAD AND BUTTER PUDDING - ENGLISH
(Makes 10 servings)

½ c. (1 stick) butter (room
   temperature)
5 (¾ inch thick) firm white bread
   slices
½ c. firmly packed light brown
   sugar
½ c. raisins

1 Tbsp. grated orange peel
4 c. half & half
5 eggs
Brandy
Additional light brown sugar
1 c. whipping cream, whipped to
   soft peaks

Preheat oven to 300°F. Generously butter bread. Cut each slice diagonally into 2 triangles. Arrange bread, butter side up, in 9x13 inch baking dish. Sprinkle with ½ cup brown sugar, raisins, and peel. Beat half & half and eggs to blend. Pour into dish. Bake until firm, 40 to 50 minutes. Spoon into bowls.

Drizzle with brandy. Sprinkle with additional brown sugar. Serve immediately with whipped cream.

Kathy Olsen, Duluth, MN

TRIFLE - ENGLISH
(Makes 8 servings)

1 (8 inch) sponge cake
1 c. raspberry jam
¾ c. sherry
¾ c. raspberry juice (from
    frozen raspberries)
2 c. Custard (recipe follows)
Fresh fruits (2 c. diced or sliced
    pineapple, 2 sliced

bananas, two 10 oz. pkg.
frozen raspberries, 2 or 3 c.
sliced or diced peaches, or
whatever fruit is in season)
1 c. whipping cream
Walnuts, angelica, chocolate
    curls, or other decoration

Cut sponge cake into 3 layers. Line an 8 inch bowl with 1 layer of cake. Spread cake with ¼ cup raspberry jam. Combine sherry and raspberry juice. Pour ⅓ of mixture over cake. Spread with ¼ of Custard. Add layer of pineapple. Repeat with cake layer, jam, sherry and juice, Custard, bananas, and raspberries. Repeat with layer of cake, jam, sherry and juice, Custard, and peaches, ending with a fourth layer of Custard. Cover with a thick layer of stiffly beaten whipped cream. Garnish with remaining jam and decorate as desired.

Custard:

4 egg yolks
¼ c. sugar
Pinch of salt

2 c. milk
1 tsp. vanilla

Beat egg yolks. Add sugar and salt. Scald milk and add slowly to egg mixture in top of double boiler. Cook over hot water, stirring constantly, until Custard thickens. Cool. Add vanilla. Chill thoroughly.

Note: Raspberries and bananas are important to the flavor of this dessert.

Kathy Olsen, Duluth, MN

SWEDISH RICE PUDDING

1 qt. milk

½ c. medium grain rice

Cook in double boiler over medium heat until still milky, but rice is poofed (approximately 45 to 50 minutes) or when rice tastes cooked through. Beat 2 eggs. Add some of rice mixture to eggs so as not to curdle. Add 1 teaspoon vanilla, pinch of salt, and ⅓ cup sugar. Makes approximately 1½ quarts.

Marie Burt, Owatonna, MN

RASPBERRY SYLLABUB - ENGLISH
(Makes 6 to 8 servings)

1 to 1½ lb. fresh raspberries
½ c. superfine sugar
¼ c. brandy

1½ c. well chilled whipping
   cream
Rolled wafer cookies

Set aside 12 to 16 raspberries. Combine remaining raspberries, sugar, and brandy in bowl; cover and refrigerate for 2 to 3 hours. Drain raspberries, reserving liquid. Mash raspberries gently. Drain berries again, reserving liquid. Beat cream to stiff peaks. Fold in mashed raspberries. Divide reserved liquids among goblets. Spoon or pipe raspberry cream over top. Decorate with reserved raspberries; refrigerate until firm. Serve with rolled wafer cookies.

Kathy Olsen, Duluth, MN

SWEDISH RICE PUDDING

1 c. raw rice
2 qt. whole milk
¼ tsp. salt
¾ c. sugar

1 tsp. vanilla
1 tsp. almond flavoring
4 egg yolks

Rinse rice in warm water. Cook in milk over low heat until somewhat thickened (about 1 hour); stir quite often. Add salt, sugar, and flavorings. Beat egg yolks. Pour a little of the hot rice mixture into eggs, then add all to rice. Cook for 1 minute more, stirring. Pour into serving dish and let cool. Sprinkle with cinnamon and sugar.

Beat 4 egg whites until stiff. Add ¼ teaspoon cream of tartar and 8 tablespoons sugar gradually, beating until mixture will stand in stiff peaks. Put on top of cooled rice and brown in oven at 400° for 10 to 15 minutes.

Joyce Bonawitz, Moorhead, MN

NANA'S HOLIDAY RAISIN PUDDING

1 c. flour
1 tsp. baking powder
½ tsp. baking soda
¼ tsp. nutmeg
¼ tsp. salt
½ c. milk

½ c. sugar
1 Tbsp. butter
¼ tsp. vanilla
½ c. raisins
½ c. walnuts (optional)

Sift together first 5 ingredients and put in a separate bowl. Put sugar and butter in separate bowl and mix well. Alternate putting flour mixture and milk into sugar and butter bowl. Finally, add vanilla and raisins. Pour into large greased loaf pan.

Sauce:

1 c. brown sugar
2 c. boiling water

2 Tbsp. butter

Pour over dough mixture and bake at 350° for 40 to 45 minutes. (Place loaf pan on cookie sheet so doesn't boil over in oven!) Serve with whipped cream if desired.

Marian Hughes

SERNIK - CHEESECAKE

⅓ c. butter
3 raw egg yolks
2 c. powdered sugar
2 lb. Farmers cheese
2 tsp. Cream of Wheat
3 beaten egg whites

⅓ c. raisins
1 Tbsp. chopped candied
   orange rind
1 tsp. vanilla
½ tsp. salt

Cream room temperature butter in mixer; gradually add egg yolks, powdered sugar, and Farmers cheese (ground or pulverized in food processor). Add beaten egg whites, raisins, orange rind, vanilla, Cream of Wheat, and salt. Mix well and transfer to greased cake pan, sprinkled with bread crumbs. Bake in 350° oven for 60 minutes.

Barb Fivecoate, Virginia, MN

CARAMEL PECAN PUMPKIN PIE - IRISH

Unbaked 9 inch pie shell
1 c. sugar
1 Tbsp. all-purpose flour
½ tsp. salt
¼ tsp. cinnamon
¼ tsp. nutmeg

¼ tsp. allspice
¼ c. top milk
2 slightly beaten eggs
½ tsp. lemon extract
½ tsp. vanilla
2½ c. cooked pumpkin

Line a 9 inch pie plate with pastry. Combine sugar, flour, salt, and spices. Add top milk to slightly beaten eggs. Add extracts and pumpkin; mix well. Add sugar mixture; combine.

Pour into unbaked pie shell. Bake at 425° for about 10 minutes. Reduce temperature to 350° and bake for about 40 minutes longer. Sprinkle Caramel Topping on pie.

Caramel Topping:

1 c. brown sugar
¼ tsp. salt

¼ c. melted butter
1 c. whole pecans

Combine all ingredients; sprinkle on top of pie. Place 4 or 5 inches below broiler unit. Broil until pecans are toasted and sugar is melted (5 to 8 minutes). Serve only a small wedge as it is quite rich.

Barb Fivecoate, Virginia, MN

FISH

TUNA ZUCCHINI SUISSE - FRENCH

2 c. shredded unpared zucchini
(about 3 zucchini)
¾ tsp. salt, divided
4 eggs
1½ c. milk
2 (6 or 7 oz.) cans tuna, drained
and flaked

1 c. (4 oz.) shredded Swiss
cheese
½ c. finely chopped onion
1 Tbsp. lemon juice
¼ tsp. pepper
¼ tsp. dried dill weed
2 Tbsp. packaged bread crumbs

Mix zucchini with ½ teaspoon salt; let stand for 15 minutes. Drain and pat dry. Combine prepared zucchini with remaining ¼ teaspoon salt and all other ingredients, except bread crumbs. Mix thoroughly.

Sprinkle greased 10 inch pie plate with bread crumbs, then turn mixture into dish. Bake at 350° for 40 minutes or until knife inserted comes out clean. Let stand for 5 minutes. Garnish with pepper rings if desired.

Barb Fivecoate, Virginia, MN

BAKED LUTEFISH

Lutefish

Salt

Soak fish in water until ready to bake; drain and salt. Wrap fish in cheesecloth and put in covered roaster, or line 9x13 inch cake pan with foil and place fish in pan, then cover with foil. Bake at 400° for 20 minutes for about 3 to 4 pounds of fish. Increase baking time for larger amount.

Eloise Hoff, Preston, MN

PICKLED FISH - GERMAN

Bring 2 quarts of water to boil with 1 tablespoon of salt. Drop fish in and bring to a boil, then take fish out and cover with brine.

Brine:

1 c. vinegar
2 c. water
½ c. sugar

Pickling spices
1 onion

Boil about 10 minutes and pour over fish; refrigerate till they jell.

Donna Krause, Detroit Lakes, MN

LAKSLOOTA - FINNISH

Potatoes (about 2 qt.)
½ lb. red salt salmon
1 medium onion

2 Tbsp. flour
Milk

Do not add any salt. Peel and slice the potatoes. Put a heavy layer of potatoes in buttered casserole. Cut fish in small pieces. Add a layer of fish, onion, and a little flour. Continue layers until ingredients are used up and casserole is full. Add milk to almost cover; top with buttered crumbs. Bake in moderate oven until potatoes are done, about 1½ hours.

Barb Fivecoate, Virginia, MN

LASAGNA AND PIZZA

ESKIMO PIZZAS

1 pkg. English muffins
½ lb. grated sharp Cheddar
   cheese
1 sliced medium onion
Several slices bacon, cut into 1
   inch pieces

½ tsp. chervil
Mayonnaise
Pepper

Separate 4 muffins so you have 8 pieces. Spread with mayonnaise. Lay several rings of onion on top. Sprinkle some pepper on. Heap with grated cheese. Put 4 to 6 small pieces bacon on top. Sprinkle with chervil. Place on broiler pan and broil until bacon is crisp, about 15 minutes. Watch so cheese doesn't burn.

Carol Reynolds, Hibbing, MN

FEISTA LASAGNA
(Serves 10 to 12)

6 chicken breast halves, cooked
2 (10 oz.) cans tomatoes with
   jalapeno chiles
1 (2¼ oz.) can sliced olives
8 (8 inch) flour tortillas

2 large avocados, peeled and
   sliced
2 c. sour cream
1½ lb. Jack cheese, shredded

Remove skin and bone; shred meat with fingers. Combine tomatoes and olives, lightly crushing tomatoes with back of spoon. Spread thin layer of tomato mixture in bottom of 9x13 inch baking dish. Arrange 4 tortillas over tomatoes, overlapping as needed to cover dish.

Add another layer of about ½ the tomato mixture. Add a layer of ½ the chicken, then ½ the avocado slices. Spread 1 cup of sour cream evenly over avocado using rubber spatula or back of spoon. Sprinkle about ½ the cheese; repeat layers. Bake, uncovered, at 325° for 35 to 45 minutes. Cut into squares to serve.

Jane Klein, Bellevue, WA

BEEFY MEXICAN LASAGNA

1 lb. ground beef
1 (16 oz.) can whole tomatoes,
   cut up
1 (1⅛ oz.) pkg. Durkee taco
   seasoning
1 (2.8 oz.) can Durkee French
   fried onions

1 (12 oz.) ctn. cottage cheese
1½ c. (6 oz.) shredded Cheddar
   cheese
2 eggs, slightly beaten
12 (6 inch) flour or corn tortillas
1 tomato, chopped
Shredded lettuce

In large skillet, brown beef; drain. Add canned tomatoes and taco seasoning; simmer, uncovered, for 5 minutes. In bowl, stir ½ can French fried onions, cottage cheese, 1 cup Cheddar cheese, and eggs. Place 3 tortillas on bottom of greased 8x12 inch baking dish. Overlap 6 tortillas around side of the dish.

Spoon meat mixture evenly in dish. Top with 3 tortillas, then with cheese mixture. Bake, covered, at 350° for 45 minutes. Sprinkle with remaining cheese. Place remaining onions in center of casserole. Bake, uncovered, for 5 minutes longer. Before serving, arrange tomatoes and lettuce around edge of casserole.

Hint: Casserole is better if the tortillas are broken into pieces rather than put in whole.

Rose Wendelbo, Grafton, ND

SPAGHETTI PIE

6 oz. spaghetti
2 Tbsp. butter or margarine
⅓ c. grated Parmesan cheese
2 well beaten eggs
1 c. cottage cheese (8 oz.)
1 lb. ground beef *or* bulk pork
    sausage
½ c. chopped onion
¼ c. chopped green pepper

1 (8 oz.) can (1 c.) tomatoes, cut
    up
1 (6 oz.) can tomato paste
1 tsp. sugar
1 tsp. dried oregano, crushed
½ tsp. garlic salt
½ c. shredded Mozzarella
    cheese (2 oz.)

Cook the spaghetti according to package directions; drain (should have about 3 cups spaghetti). Stir butter or margarine into hot spaghetti. Stir in Parmesan cheese and eggs. Form spaghetti mixture into a "crust" in a buttered 10 inch pie plate. Spread cottage cheese over bottom of spaghetti crust.

In skillet, cook ground beef or pork sausage, onion, and green pepper till vegetables are tender and meat is browned; drain off excess fat. Stir in *undrained* tomatoes, tomato paste, sugar, oregano, and garlic salt; heat through. Turn meat mixture into spaghetti crust. Bake, uncovered, in 350° oven for 20 minutes. Sprinkle the Mozzarella cheese atop. Bake for 5 minutes longer or till cheese melts. Makes 6 servings.

Sonya Masset, Bismarck, ND

MEXICAN PIZZAS

1 lb. ground beef
1 c. chopped onion
1 clove garlic, minced
1½ tsp. chili powder
1 tsp. salt
1 (8 oz.) can tomato sauce
½ c. water

6 (8 inch diameter) flour tortillas
Salad oil
1 (4 oz.) can diced green chilies
½ c. chopped green onions
3 c. (12 oz.) Jack cheese, grated
2 medium tomatoes, diced
1 avocado, diced (optional)

Brown beef in skillet; drain fat. Add onion and garlic; saute until onion becomes transparent. Add chili powder, salt, tomato sauce, and water; mix well. Bring mixture to a boil and simmer for 15 minutes.

Brush each tortilla lightly with oil; place on a lightly greased cookie sheet and brown by placing under broiler 3 inches from heat source for 2 minutes. Top each tortilla with approximately ½ cup meat mixture, 1 tablespoon diced green chilies, 1 tablespoon chopped green onion, and ½ cup grated cheese.

Bake in 400° oven for 8 to 10 minutes or until cheese is melted. Garnish with tomatoes and avocado if desired. These may be cut into 6 to 8 wedges and served as an appetizer.

Jane Klein, Bellevue, WA

MARIE'S EASY LASAGNA

1 lb. ground beef
1 (32 oz.) jar Ragu spaghetti
    sauce
1 jar Prego

Garlic salt to taste
Cooked lasagna noodles
Shredded Mozzarella cheese
Sliced Swiss cheese

Brown meat; drain fat. Add sauces, garlic, and salt. Boil noodles for 25 minutes. Place layer of noodles in 9x11 inch pan, then add a layer of meat sauce and layer of cheese. Repeat; cover and bake for 30 minutes and uncovered for 30 minutes in 350° oven.

Marie Burt, Owatonna, MN

LEFSE

TINA'S FAVORITE LEFSE

10 lb. russet potatoes
Salt
¾ lb. butter

½ c. half & half
½ c. whipping cream

Cook and mash potatoes with salt. Add butter, half & half, and whipping cream. When cool, rice potatoes. Mix 3 cups riced potatoes and 1 cup flour; do not overmix. Make into balls and roll out. Use pastry cloth and cover on rolling pin for best results.

Tina Knudsen, Owatonna, MN

POTATO LEFSE

10 large potatoes
1 c. heavy cream

½ c. melted butter
1 Tbsp. salt

Use ½ cup sifted flour for each cup of mashed potatoes. Do not add flour until you are ready to roll.

Donna Krause, Detroit Lakes, MN

LEFSE - SCANDINAVIAN

5 large boiled potatoes
5 Tbsp. butter
½ c. heavy cream

1 tsp. salt
About 1 c. flour

Mash potatoes while hot. Add butter, cream, and salt, beating until light and fluffy; cool. Work in just enough flour to handle (about 1 cup). Dough may be a little sticky. Shape on very well floured board into cylinder, 2½ inches in diameter, then cut into slices, 1 inch thick, rolling each as thin as possible and using flour lavishly.

Carry Lefse with a long flat stick to hot ungreased pancake griddle, lefse griddle, or top of kitchen range. Bake until light brown on both sides. Remove from pan with stick and pile on a towel, keeping covered with another towel. Serve rolled up with butter, brown sugar, or other fillings. Store in refrigerator or freezer.

Note: A lefse stick can be purchased or made from the stick of a discarded window shade by filing one end very flat and rubbing it well with flour.

Helen Johnson, Chanhassen, MN

LEFSE

5 c. cooked russet potatoes, riced
½ c. half & half
½ c. butter or margarine
4 tsp. sugar
1 tsp. salt
2 c. all-purpose flour

Cook and rice potatoes. While still hot, add half & half, butter, sugar, and salt. Cool completely; cover and refrigerate. Divide mixture in half. In mixing bowl, mix 1 cup of flour into first ½ of potato mixture. Shape into 9 balls. On floured board, roll out each ball with stocking covered lefse rolling pin to a very thin circle.

Bake on moderately hot lefse griddle until flecked with brown; turn and bake other side. Cool between wax paper and dish towels. Add remaining flour to second half. Makes 18 Lefse. Serve with sugar and butter or brown sugar, butter, and cinnamon.

Eloise Hoff, Preston, MN

LEFSE

8 c. mashed or riced potatoes
½ c. whipping cream (can use half & half)
8 Tbsp. (heaping) butter
1 Tbsp. salt
4 scant c. flour

Put butter, cream, and salt with hot potatoes. Be sure to let get cool. Put in flour and roll out as thin as possible. Fry on grill (no grease); turn once. Let cool slightly and cover so it doesn't dry out.

Mary Kleven

MEATS

SUNDAY BEEF ROAST - SÖNDAGSSTEK

4 lb. rump roast in 1 piece
1 Tbsp. butter, melted
2 tsp. salt
1 bay leaf
6 whole allspice
3 whole white peppers
1½ tsp. dark corn syrup

1 Tbsp. vinegar
1 onion, sliced
3 whole anchovies, cleaned, or 6
    anchovy fillets
1 c. hot water
6 Tbsp. flour
½ c. cold water

1. Brown meat on all sides in melted butter, allowing 10 to 15 minutes for browning each side. Sprinkle browned side with salt as the meat is turned.

2. Add bay leaf, whole allspice, and whole peppers. Mix syrup and vinegar and spoon over top of meat. Cover with sliced onion and anchovies. Add 1 cup hot water.

3. Cover kettle tightly and simmer for 3 hours or until meat is tender.

4. Remove meat to serving platter. Strain liquid in kettle. Measure liquid and add sufficient water to make 3 cups. Return to kettle and heat to boiling point.

5. Mix flour and ½ cup cold water into a smooth paste. Stir into hot liquid in kettle. Stir constantly until gravy thickens. Turn heat very low and cook gravy for 10 minutes. Serve with roast. Yields 12 servings.

Helen H. Clark, Grand Forks, ND

POTAGE A LA RUSSE
(Makes 8 to 10 servings)

1 small chicken (about 2½ lb.) or
    ½ large stewing chicken,
    trimmed of fat
6 c. water
1 c. finely chopped celery
1 c. finely chopped onion
½ c. finely chopped carrot
4 chicken bouillon cubes
1½ c. whipping cream

¼ c. (½ stick) unsalted butter
¼ c. all-purpose flour
1 c. sauerkraut (preferably
    fresh), rinsed, drained,
    sqeezed dry, and finely
    chopped
Salt and freshly ground white
    pepper

Combine chicken and water in Dutch oven and bring to boil over medium high heat. Reduce heat to medium low and simmer until chicken is cooked, about 45 minutes. Remove chicken and set aside until cool enough to handle. Set aside 1 cup cooking liquid. Add celery, onion, carrot, and bouillon cubes to liquid remaining in Dutch oven. Place over medium low heat and simmer until vegetables are tender, about 12 minutes. Reduce heat to low; stir in cream and bring mixture to gentle simmer.

Meanwhile, melt butter in small saucepan over low heat. Add flour and whisk constantly for 3 minutes. Blend in reserved 1 cup cooking liquid. Increase heat to medium and cook until thickened. Gradually whisk into vegetable mixture and simmer until slightly thickened. Keep warm.

Discard skin and bones from chicken. Cut meat into bite-size pieces; add to soup. Stir in sauerkraut. Season to taste with salt and white pepper. Ladle into bowls and serve.

Diane Haan

PIGS FEET SULTANA

2 pigs feet or oxtail
1 large onion
2 ripe tomatoes, skinned
2 pimentos
2 cloves garlic

Parsley
1 c. boiled garbanzos, chickpeas
2 boiled potatoes
Salt and pepper

Boil pigs feet in salted water with 1 bay leaf and some peppercorns. When tender, remove from bones and cut in pieces. Make a sauce of garlic, onion, and tomatoes in a little oil. Add pigs feet, garbanzos, and potatoes; cook a few minutes. Add parsley.

Barb Fivecoate, Virginia, MN

PORK CHOPS - HUNGARIAN STYLE

6 pork chops
1½ c. onion slices
2 cloves garlic, finely cut (or ¼
    tsp. garlic powder)
1 tsp. caraway seed
1 tsp. salt

1 c. sour cream
1 Tbsp. cooking oil
1 tsp. dill seed
2 tsp. paprika
1 c. water

Brown pork chops on both sides in hot oil. Add onion, garlic, seasonings, and water; bring to a boil. Reduce heat. Cover tightly and simmer for about 1 hour or until chops are tender. Slowly stir in the sour cream. Heat gently for 5 minutes. Do not boil. Serves 5 to 6.

Delicious with buttered noodles or mashed potatoes.

Annette Zubinski, Duluth, MN

DANISH MEAT BALLS

2 lb. beef
2 lb. veal
2 tsp. salt
5 eggs
½ tsp. white pepper

½ tsp. black pepper
3 Tbsp. onion juice
7 Tbsp. flour
2½ c. milk

Grind beef and veal together, then add all other ingredients at once. Mix real well. Add more milk if necessary. Fry in butter, carefully browning on all sides.

Carol Gilbertson, Hawley, MN

POLYNESIAN MEAT BALLS

This is the all time favorite at our holiday glogg open house.

6 slices white bread	**1 tsp. MSG**
Milk	**1 Tbsp. parsley**
2 lb. ground round steak	**½ c. soy sauce**
½ lb. ground pork sausage	**1 tsp. hot pepper sauce**
1 tsp. onion powder	**Water chestnuts**
1 tsp. garlic salt	

In a large bowl, crumble well the white bread; moisten with milk. Add ground round steak and ground pork sausage. Combine well. Add onion powder, garlic salt, MSG, parsley, soy sauce, and hot pepper sauce.

Shape into medium size balls around cut up water chestnuts. Brown well in hot oil, shaking pan frequently. Freeze in coffee cans. Before serving, wrap in foil paper and bake in moderate oven until piping hot. Serve in chafing dish with sauce made by melting together equal parts of grape jelly and chili sauce.

Annette Zubinski, Duluth, MN

NORWEGIAN MEAT BALLS - KJÖD KAGER

1 lb. ground round steak	**¼ lb. fresh pork**
1 egg	**1 Tbsp. cornstarch**
1 medium minced onion	**½ c. milk, scalded**
Salt and pepper	**⅛ tsp. nutmeg**
⅛ tsp. allspice	**⅛ tsp. ginger (optional)**

Grind meat very fine. Beat egg slightly and add with milk and cornstarch to meat mixture; mix well. Add rest of ingredients. Beat thoroughly until very light, then form into small balls; brown in butter. Simmer slowly until done, adding a little water if necessary.

When done, remove meat balls. Add more butter to drippings. Add flour and brown. Add enough water to make a medium thick gravy. Season with salt and pepper and add meat balls. These meat balls may be prepared several hours before serving as they are just as delicious when reheated.

Annette Zubinski, Duluth, MN

VIENNESE HAMBURGER

2 lb. ground beef
1 egg
¼ c. bread crumbs
¼ c. milk
2 tsp. salt
1½ c. sliced onions
½ c. butter or margarine,
   divided

3 Tbsp. flour
2 beef bouillon cubes
2 c. boiling water
2 Tbsp. tomato paste
1 c. sour cream
8 oz. broad noodles, cooked
½ tsp. poppy seeds

Combine beef, egg, bread crumbs, milk, and salt; mix well. Shape into 24 small patties. Cook onions in ¼ cup butter or margarine until light golden in color and tender; remove from pan. Add patties; brown on both sides; remove from pan.

Stir flour into drippings in pan. Dissolve bouillon cubes in paste; mix. Stir gently over low heat until thickened; return patties to pan and simmer gently for 20 minutes. Just before serving, stir in sour cream; heat carefully. After rinsing noodles in hot water, sprinkle in poppy seeds. Serve beef mixture on noodles. Serves 8.

Carol Gilbertson, Hawley, MN

HUNGARIAN VENISON ROAST

3 lb. venison roast
3 medium peeled potatoes
3 medium peeled carrots
3 small peeled onions
2 tsp. salt

1 tsp. pepper
1 tsp. caraway seeds
5 strips bacon
1 c. water

Place venison in roaster in proportion with size of roast. Add 1 cup water and encircle roast with vegetables. Salt and pepper roast and vegetables at same time, then sprinkle with caraway seeds. Place bacon to cover roast completely, lapping over. Place cover on roast and bake at 325° for 3 hours.

For a nice appearing browned effect, raise temperature to 350° for last 30 minutes with cover off or just enough to brown top.

Carol Gilbertson, Hawley, MN

POLISH EASTER BROTH

2 Polish sausages, smoked
2 qt. water
2 Tbsp. vinegar
2 heaping Tbsp. plain
   horseradish

3 heaping Tbsp. flour
2 heaping Tbsp. sour cream
3 c. water
2 hard-boiled eggs
2 slices hard crust rye bread

Cook the 2 sausages in a large enough pot in 2 quarts of water for at least 45 minutes. Remove from heat. Remove the sausages and let the water chill. Strain or skim fat from water and add salt to taste, about 1 teaspoon.

Using a separate 2 quart pot, pour in 3 cups of water and while stirring, add the flour through a sifter slowly to avoid lumps. Add horseradish, vinegar, and sour cream, stirring thoroughly. Add this mixture to the preceding water from sausage and cook to a boil. Add more salt or horseradish to suit taste.

Serve with croutons made from slices of the cooked sausage, hard-boiled eggs, and hard crust rye bread. Other sliced meats, such as ham, veal, beef, and pork may also be added.

Barb Fivecoate, Virginia, MN

PORK CHOW MEIN

12 oz. pork tenderloin
1 green pepper
4 slices pineapple
10 slices carrot
3 tsp. corn starch (mix with
    water)

3 Tbsp. corn starch (for coating)
3 egg whites
3 Tbsp. flour
$\frac{1}{5}$ tsp. salt
2 green onions, cut into 1½ inch
    long pieces

To marinate pork:

¾ tsp. salt
$\frac{1}{5}$ tsp. pepper
½ tsp. wine or wine vinegar
2 Tbsp. soy sauce

1 Tbsp. corn starch
1 Tbsp. cold water
1 egg yolk
1 tsp. baking soda

Seasoning Sauce:

4 Tbsp. white vinegar
6½ Tbsp. sugar
6½ Tbsp. catsup

6½ Tbsp. pineapple juice
¾ tsp. salt

1. Pound the pork (this is to tenderize it), then cut into 1 to 1½ inch squares. Marinate for at least 3 hours.

2. Cut green pepper into halves; remove seeds and membranes and cut into 1½ inch squares. Next, cut 4 slices of pineapple into the same size squares; set aside.

3. Heat 6 cups oil. While oil is heating, coat each piece of pork in corn starch (for coating). When oil is ready, fry pork until brown and done (about 2 minutes). Take out and reheat oil, then fry once more until crispy. Remove pork and drain off oil from frying pan.

4. Put all the ingredients for Seasoning Sauce in a saucepan. When boiling, add 3 teaspoons corn starch (mixed with water).

5. Put into frying pan, 2 tablespoons oil; fry the green pepper, green onions, pineapple, and carrot, stirring constantly. Add the Seasoning Sauce, continuing to stir-fry, until thickened. Add the pork; mix well and serve immediately.

Harlan Brekke, Fargo, ND

CHORIZO

6 to 7 feet pork casings (optional)

1 (3 lb.) boneless pork shoulder roast, well chilled

Trim fat from chilled roast. Chop enough fat to make 1 cup; set aside. Discard any remaining fat. Cut meat into ½ inch cubes. With coarse blade of food grinder, grind together pork and reserved pork fat.

½ c. white vinegar
3 Tbsp. water
3 cloves garlic, minced
2 Tbsp. paprika
1 Tbsp. chili powder
2½ tsp. crushed red pepper
2 tsp. salt

2 tsp. ground red pepper
1 tsp. sugar
1 tsp. black pepper
½ tsp. coriander seed
½ tsp. dried oregano, crushed
¼ tsp. ground cumin

In a blender container, combine vinegar, water, garlic, paprika, chili powder, crushed red pepper, salt, ground red pepper, sugar, black pepper, coriander seed, oregano, and ground cumin; cover and blend till spices are ground. Sprinkle spice mixture evenly over pork; mix thoroughly. Shape sausage into patties, or, if desired, fill casings for links.

Karen Thompson, W. St. Paul, MN

NORWEGIAN SYLTA

1 small veal shank
1 lean pork shoulder or loin roast (2 lb. or so)

1 small handful whole allspice
2 to 3 bay leaves (laurel)
Salt and pepper

Cover meat with water; cook until meat falls from the bone. Cool and cut up meat. Strain juice. Add cut up meat and let come to boil. Pour into a glass loaf pan. Let stand for 24 hours or until set.

Barb Fivecoate, Virginia, MN

PASTA

GNOCCHI - ITALIAN DUMPLINGS

5 c. flour
1 egg
5 heaping c. boiled riced
  potatoes (warm)

1 tsp. salt

Place flour on board. Make a well in the flour; add egg, riced potatoes, and salt. Mix all ingredients together in same manner as making bread. Work quickly. Do not work too long or dough will be too soft. After completely mixing, shape dough in form, 8 x 10 inches and 1½ inches wide. Roll, then cut into pieces of 1¼ inches long. Put on slightly floured board and make small indentation on each piece with your index finger so it shall absorb sauce more readily.

Cook: Add 2 large heaping tablespoons salt to large kettle of water and bring to a brisk boil. Add Gnocchis and boil for about 2 minutes. Drain and serve with spaghetti sauce. Sprinkle with Romano cheese.

ITALIAN SAUCE WITH MEATBALLS

¾ lb. ground beef
¼ lb. ground pork
1 c. fine dry bread crumbs
½ c. grated Romano cheese
1 Tbsp. minced parsley

1 clove garlic, cut fine
¼ c. milk
2 eggs
1½ tsp. salt
½ tsp. pepper (black)

Mix thoroughly and shape into medium balls. Brown well in hot fat or oil. Add No. 2 can tomatoes (put through sieve) and 1 can of tomato paste; simmer for a few hours slowly.

Barb Fivecoate, Virginia, MN

AFRO-ITALIAN-AMERICAN SPAGHETTI SAUCE

Original recipe from Restaurant Romano, Tripoli, Lybia.

2 lb. ground beef (lean)
1 large onion, finely chopped
3 to 5 cloves (jumbo) garlic,
  chopped
1 tsp. celery flakes
1 tsp. basil
1 tsp. marjoram
1 tsp. oregano
3 bay leaves
1 generous pinch of rosemary

1 (6 oz.) can tomato paste
2 (8 oz.) cans tomato sauce
2 (16 oz.) cans plum tomatoes
¾ to 1 c. flour
8 oz. can mushrooms, chopped
  with liquid
3 to 4 Tbsp. virgin olive oil
1½ tsp. salt
½ tsp. crushed red pepper
½ tsp. white pepper

In a large heavy pot, saute onion and garlic in olive oil. Add meat and cook until most of the pink is gone. Add flour and blend with oil and meat juices; stir continuously until flour begins to brown. All cans of tomatoes, sauce, paste, and mushrooms are added now, while stirring to blend. Add enough water to bring mixture level to within 1 inch of top of pot, stirring until well blended.

Bring to boil; reduce heat to lowest point that will allow liquid to continue to bubble. Cover and simmer at least 5 hours. Longer simmering improves flavor. Amount of flour may be adjusted to make sauce as thin or thick as you like it.

Yvonne G. Maddox, Duluth, MN

ITALIAN SPAGHETTI SAUCE

1 lb. ground beef
1 (16 oz.) can stewed tomatoes
1 (8 oz.) can tomato sauce
1 (6 oz.) can tomato paste
½ lb. mushrooms (or 1 small
    can)

1 medium onion, chopped
¼ tsp. minced garlic
½ tsp. dry basil leaves
2 pinches oregano
Salt to taste

This makes enough sauce for 1 pound of dry spaghetti.

Joyce McCann, St. Cloud, MN

SPAGHETTI SAUCE

Brown in 2 tablespoons of shortening:

1 c. minced onion

1 lb. hamburger

Add:

2 cloves garlic, minced
2 tsp. parsley flakes
1 pt. tomatoes
2 (6 oz.) cans tomato paste
1½ c. water

1 Tbsp. salt
½ tsp. pepper
1 tsp. sage
¼ tsp. thyme
2 bay leaves

Simmer over low heat for 3 to 4 hours.

Renee Ulberg, Bismarck, ND

PASTA VAZZOO

¼ c. oil
½ tsp. oregano
½ tsp. basil

½ tsp. parsley
¼ tsp. bay leaf (optional)

Crush seasonings and brown in the oil. Add ½ clove of garlic, chopped. Add one 8 ounce can tomato sauce; *simmer.*

On a separate burner, boil 4 ounces small egg pasta shells according to instructions on box (12 ounces). *Do not drain.* Drain a 12 to 15 ounce can Northern beans and add. Add first mixture to tomato sauce and simmer for 5 to 10 minutes. Serve in bowls. Makes 5 to 6 servings.

Dan Ferullo, Margaret Hulst, Austin, MN

SALADS

SLOVENIAN POTATO SALAD

6 medium potatoes
¼ c. cider vinegar
½ tsp. salt

1 medium thinly sliced onion
3 Tbsp. salad oil
⅛ tsp. pepper

Boil potatoes in jackets until cooked. Drain and let stand until cool; remove skins. Slice thin into a salad bowl. Add salt, pepper, sliced onion, oil, and vinegar. Toss gently and serve.

Annette Zubinski, Duluth, MN

HOT GERMAN POTATO SALAD

4 potatoes
2 hard-boiled eggs (optional)
½ c. vinegar
½ c. water
1 Tbsp. sugar
½ tsp. dry mustard
2 tsp. salt (or to taste)

¼ tsp. pepper
1 Tbsp. flour
1 medium onion, finely chopped
2 Tbsp. chopped parsley (to
  taste)
½ lb. bacon

Wash potatoes and cook, covered, about 40 minutes. Place eggs in water halfway through cooking time. Peel potatoes while hot and slice; keep warm. Cook bacon until crisp and set aside. Fry onion in grease and set aside.

Crumble bacon and mix with onion and potatoes. To bacon drippings, add flour and brown on high heat, stirring constantly. Slowly add, stirring constantly, the vinegar, water, sugar, mustard, salt, and pepper. Bring to a boil so flour thickens to thin gravy consistency. Pour dressing over potatoes. Add parsley. Mix well with wooden spoon so as not to mash potatoes. Serve warm.

Heat in 200° oven for 30 minutes. Sprinkle with parsley and sliced hard eggs on top. May be reheated in 200° oven or in microwave on ROAST to warm.

Barb Fivecoate, Virginia, MN

GERMAN POTATO SALAD

6 large potatoes
1 c. chopped onion
½ lb. diced bacon
2 Tbsp. cornstarch
½ c. sugar

½ c. vinegar
1 c. water
½ tsp. salt
¼ tsp. celery seed

Boil large potatoes in salted water. Peel while hot; cool and dice to bite-size. Saute chopped onion and diced bacon in large skillet (good idea to drain off all but ⅓ to ½ grease before adding onion, then cook till bacon is crisp and onion soft). Add cornstarch and mix until smooth. Add sugar and allow to caramelize.

Prepare mixture of vinegar, 1 cup water, salt, and celery seed and add to bacon when caramelized. Stir over low heat till thickens. Pour over potatoes and toss.

Jean Marquette

SIENISALAATLE - FINNISH FRESH MUSHROOM SALAD

½ lb. thin sliced fresh
   mushrooms
1 c. water
1 Tbsp. lemon juice
¼ c. sour cream

2 Tbsp. grated onion
½ tsp. salt
Dash of pepper
Romaine

Boil water and lemon juice. Add mushrooms; cover and simmer for 2 to 3 minutes. Remove and drain. Combine sour cream, onion, salt, and pepper. Toss mushrooms carefully in sauce. Serve on crisped romaine leaves.

Annette Zubinski, Duluth, MN

SAUCES

SWEET AND SOUR SAUCE - CHINESE STYLE

5 Tbsp. white vinegar
6½ Tbsp. sugar
6½ Tbsp. catsup

6½ Tbsp. pineapple juice
½ tsp. salt
1 Tbsp. corn starch

Mix first 5 ingredients in kettle and bring to a boil. Add the corn starch (mixed with a little water) slowly. Boil until clear.

Harlan Brekke, Fargo, ND

QUICK PLUM SAUCE - CHINESE

1 c. plum jelly or preserves
2 Tbsp. brown sugar

2 Tbsp. vinegar

Combine all ingredients and heat on stove or microwave until mixture boils; refrigerate.

Renee Ulberg, Bismarck, ND

SOUPS

TOFU SOUP

2 sq. bean curd
5 oz. minced pork
1 oz. minced shrimp
½ to 1 egg (depending on size)
1 Tbsp. oil
2 to 3 Chinese mushrooms, sliced

1 clove garlic, minced
½ can bamboo shoots
1 stalk spring onion, chopped up coarsely
Salt and pepper to taste
1 to 2 tsp. soy sauce (to taste)
2 c. stock

1. Mash the bean cakes and mix with minced pork, prawns, and ½ of the egg. Add a little salt and pepper. Form the mixture into balls (1 teaspoon size).
2. Heat oil and fry garlic till brown; remove.
3. Add the stock; bring to boil.
4. Add bamboo shoots; simmer for 15 minutes.
5. Add the tofu balls, mushrooms, pepper, salt, and soy sauce to taste.
6. Serve in bowls. Garnish with spring onions.

Sammoy Knight, Minneapolis, MN

WILD RICE SOUP

1 qt. chicken broth
2 cans cream of chicken soup
¼ c. grated carrots
1 c. diced celery
1 large onion, diced

4 green onions, sliced (for garnish, optional)
2 to 3 c. cooked wild rice
2 tsp. granulated chicken flavor

Simmer all for 1 to 1½ hours. Can cut up small pieces of cooked chicken and add to soup.

Mary Kleven, Grand Rapids, MN

CHEESE SOUP - GERMAN DISH

1½ c. diced potatoes
1 c. chopped onions
1 tsp. salt
2 beef bouillon cubes

2 c. water
1 c. beer
¼ lb. grated cheese

Combine first 5 ingredients; simmer for 10 minutes. Blend-puree; return to pan and add cheese, stirring over low heat until cheese melts. Gradually whisk in the beer and stir until mixed into cheese. Serve hot.

Janet Lozon, Owatonna, MN

CABBAGE-KRAUT STUFFING FOR PIEROGI

1 head cabbage (6 inches in
    diameter)
1 (16 oz.) can sauerkraut
2 onions (3 inches in diameter)

½ lb. mushrooms
2 Tbsp. caraway seeds (whole)
Salt
Black pepper

Slice cabbage or shred cabbage in thin strips. Place in a gallon pot and add water to just cover the cabbage. Add 1 heaping teaspoon of salt. Cover and cook for ½ hour. Strain the liquid from sauerkraut and add to the cooking cabbage and cook for at least 15 minutes more. Take from heat and drain the cabbage-sauerkraut through colander.

Slice or shred the 2 onions thinly and saute in butter, margarine, or oil until slightly golden brown. Slice the mushrooms and saute in butter, margarine, or oil until they stop steaming. Mix onions, mushrooms, and caraway seeds with cabbage-sauerkraut mixture. Add salt and pepper to taste and let steam in covered pot over low heat for ½ hour, mixing occasionally. Makes about 2 quarts of stuffing.

Barb Fivecoate, Virginia, MN

SAUERKRAUT SOUP - KAPUSNIAK

1 qt. sauerkraut
1 qt. meat stock
4 slices bacon

2 Tbsp. or more flour
Salt and pepper

Drain sauerkraut, reserving liquid. Rinse sauerkraut in cold water; drain and squeeze out all moisture. Chop and add to meat stock. Cook for 60 minutes. Dice bacon and fry until crumbly. Remove from heat.

Stir in flour and ½ cup Sauerkraut Soup liquid to a smooth paste; simmer until thick and bubbly and return to soup. Season to taste with salt and pepper (optional, a dash of caraway) and simmer awhile longer. If not as tart as you like, add a little of the reserved sauerkraut juice.

Barb Fivecoate, Virginia, MN

CLEAR BEET SOUP - CZYSTY BARSZCZ CZERWONY

3 c. stock
2 to 3 c. beet liquid
1 Tbsp. vinegar (more or less)
Dash of mushroom powder
1 Tbsp. dry red wine

Salt and pepper
Garlic powder
1 tsp. Maggi extract or soy
    sauce
MSG (monosodium glutamate)

To stock, add beet liquid from canned beets; bring to boil. Reduce heat and simmer briefly. Season to taste with salt, pepper, and garlic powder. Add vinegar, extract, mushroom powder, and MSG. Dry red wine may be added. The barszcz should be sweet, tart, and tangy.

Barb Fivecoate, Virginia, MN

VEGETABLES

CABBAGE MARINARA - GERMAN

1 lb. ground beef
1 large onion
¼ tsp. thyme
¼ tsp. oregano
¼ tsp. garlic powder

¼ tsp. pepper
1 tsp. salt
6 c. coarsely shredded cabbage
2 cans tomato soup

Brown hamburger with onion and seasoning. Butter cake pan; spread 3 cups of cabbage on the bottom, then the hamburger, then the other layer of cabbage. Cover with 2 cans of tomato soup, undiluted. Bake for 1 hour, covered, at 350°.

Florence Schovanec, St. Paul, MN

RED CABBAGE

1 head red cabbage
1 small onion
1 Tbsp. flour
1 Tbsp. sugar
1 Tbsp. oil

1 Tbsp. caraway seeds
2 Tbsp. vinegar
1 tsp. salt
1 tsp. pepper
Small amount of water (optional)

Saute cabbage and onion in oil after chopping to desired size; cook until limp. Add flour to thicken. Add water for desired consistency, then by small amounts, add sugar, vinegar, caraway seeds, salt, and pepper; simmer until softened and rich in gravylike sauce. Cook about 1 hour and 15 minutes.

Barb Fivecoate, Virginia, MN

STUFFED VEGETABLES - GREEK STYLE

10 large tomatoes, eggplant, or
   green peppers
2 lb. ground round
2 large onions
½ c. rice
1 can tomato sauce

1 c. water
1 Tbsp. mint, chopped
2 Tbsp. parsley, chopped
1 clove garlic, chopped
Salt and pepper

Brown ground round and chopped onions. Add the rest of the ingredients and simmer for about 20 minutes, then stuff scooped out vegetables. (Pepper should be dipped into boiling water previously.) Place in baking pan with 1 cup water and bake until light brown. Cover and bake in 350° oven for 30 minutes. Serves 4 to 6 people.

Barb Fivecoate, Virginia, MN

TERIYAKI-SAUCED VEGETABLES - ORIENTAL

1 Tbsp. brown sugar
1/4 tsp. garlic powder
2 Tbsp. dry sherry
2 Tbsp. oil
1 c. sliced water chestnuts,
    drained

1/2 tsp. ginger
1/8 tsp. pepper
2 Tbsp. soy sauce
1 c. thinly sliced carrots
6 oz. pkg. frozen pea pods,
    thawed and drained

In small bowl, combine brown sugar, ginger, garlic powder, pepper, sherry, and soy sauce; mix well and set aside. In large skillet or wok, heat oil over high heat. Add vegetables and sauce; stir-fry for 5 to 7 minutes or until carrots are crisp tender. Serve immediately. Makes 4 servings at 140 calories per serving.

Peggy Mielke, Chisholm, MN

COLCANNON - IRISH
(Makes 6 servings)

2 lb. baking potatoes, peeled
    and thinly sliced
8 oz. parsnips, peeled and thinly
    sliced
2 medium onions, thinly sliced
1/2 medium cabbage (coarse
    outer leaves removed and
    reserved), finely shredded

2 1/2 c. boiling water
1/4 c. (1/2 stick) unsalted butter
1 1/2 tsp. salt
1/4 tsp. freshly ground pepper
1 to 2 Tbsp. milk (optional)

Arrange 1/3 of potatoes over bottom of heavy medium saucepan. Layer on 1/3 of parsnips, 1/3 of onions, and 1/3 of shredded cabbage; repeat layers twice more. Pour in water. Cover tightly with reserved cabbage leaves. Cover and simmer until vegetables are very tender, about 1 hour.

Discard whole cabbage leaves. Drain mixture in large sieve. Return vegetables to saucepan. Add butter, salt, and pepper. Mash until fluffy, adding milk if dry.

Kathy Olsen, Duluth, MN

CANTONESE VEGETABLES

1 (10 oz.) pkg. frozen peas
1 (9 1/2 oz.) pkg. frozen French
    style green beans
1/4 lb. bacon, cut in 1 inch pieces
1/2 c. chopped onions

1 can sliced water chestnuts
1 (4 oz.) can sliced mushrooms
1/4 c. slivered almonds
1 1/2 tsp. soy sauce

Cook vegetables according to directions on package. Fry bacon in large skillet. Remove bacon and saute onions in bacon grease. Drain grease and add all other ingredients, except bacon and almonds. Heat through. Before serving, toss with bacon and almonds.

Barb Fivecoate, Virginia, MN

PIECZARKI MARYNOWANE - PICKLED MUSHROOMS

1 lb. or more fresh mushrooms
1 c. 6% distilled vinegar
1 c. water
1 quartered onion
1 thinly sliced carrot
1 bay leaf

10 peppercorns
3 grains allspice
5 cloves
1 tsp. salt
1 to 5 Tbsp. sugar (depending
   on tartness)

Wash mushrooms of medium size and cook in large amount of salted water for 20 minutes. In pot, combine vinegar, water, onion, carrot, bay leaves, peppercorns, allspice, cloves, salt, and sugar; simmer under cover for 10 minutes. With slotted spoon, transfer mushrooms to clean twist off jars and cover with marinade, evenly distributing vegetables and spices. When cool, refrigerate. Prepare several days before serving.

Barb Fivecoate, Virginia, MN

PIECZARKI NADZIEWANE - BAKED STUFFED MUSHROOMS

1 lb. large store bought
   mushrooms
3 Tbsp. butter
2 minced onions

2 Tbsp. bread crumbs
1 Tbsp. chopped dill and/or
   parsley
Salt and pepper to taste

Remove the stems from mushrooms. Chop the stems very fine and fry in butter with onions until tender. Add rest of ingredients; mix well. Fill each mushroom cap with mixture; place in baking pan. Top with grated yellow cheese. Sprinkle with melted butter and bake in 375° oven for 20 minutes or until caps are fully cooked.

Barb Fivecoate, Virginia, MN

STIR-FRIED MIXED VEGETABLES

1½ c. bok choy, sliced in 1 inch
   pieces (looks like celery)
¼ lb. fresh snow peas, stringed
   and cut in thirds
4 oz. fresh mushrooms, sliced
3 green onions, sliced in ½ inch
   pieces
1½ c. broccoli, sliced, peeled,
   and blanched for 1½
   minutes

½ green pepper, sliced
3 oz. water chestnuts, sliced
3 oz. bamboo shoots, sliced
   (right from can)
1 clove garlic, crushed
1 slice fresh ginger, crushed
2 Tbsp. cooking oil

Seasoning Sauce:

⅓ c. chicken stock
1 tsp. sugar
1 Tbsp. light soy

2 Tbsp. vodka
1 Tbsp. oyster sauce

Thickening:

1 Tbsp. corn starch

2 Tbsp. cold water

Combine corn starch and water in small bowl and set aside.

Heat 2 tablespoons cooking oil in wok till smoking. Add green onions, garlic, and ginger. Be careful not to burn garlic and ginger (peel first, then smash). Add fresh mushrooms and water chestnuts; stir-fry for 30 seconds. Add bamboo shoots and stir-fry for 30 seconds. Add broccoli and green pepper; stir-fry for 30 seconds. Add bok choy and snow peas; stir fry for 1½ minutes.

Add Seasoning Sauce and mix thoroughly; bring to boil. Add thickener to boiling liquid and stir till thickened. Mix thoroughly. Serve immediately. Serves 6 to 8.

Janet Lozon, Owatonna, MN

Notes

Notes

Dressings
& Salads

APPROXIMATE 100 CALORIE PORTIONS

Almonds (shelled)—12 to 15 nuts
Angel cake—1¾ inch cube
Apple—1 large
Apple pie—⅓ normal piece
Apricots—5 large
Asparagus—20 large stalks
Bananas—1 medium
Beans—⅓ cup canned baked
Beans—green string—2½ cups
Beets—1⅓ cups sliced
Bread—all kinds—slice ½ inch thick
Butter—1 tablespoon
Buttermilk—1⅛ cups
Cabbage—4 to 5 cups shredded
Cake—1¾ inch cube
Candy—1 inch cube
Cantaloupe—1 medium
Carrots—1⅔ cups
Cauliflower—1 small head
Celery—4 cups
Cereal—uncooked—¾ cup
Cheese—1⅛ inch cube
Cottage cheese—5 tablespoons
Cherries—sweet fresh—20 cherries
Cookies—1 to 3 inches in diameter
Corn—⅓ cup
Crackers—4 soda crackers
Crackers—graham—2½ crackers
Cream—thick—1 tablespoon
Cream—thin—4 tablespoons
Cream sauce—4 tablespoons
Dates—3 to 4
Doughnuts—½ doughnut
Eggs—1⅓ eggs
Fish—fat—size of 1 chop
Fish—lean—size of 2 chops
Flour—4 tablespoons
Frankfurter—1 small
French dressing—1½ tablespoons
Grapefruit—½ large
Grape juice—½ cup
Grapes—20 grapes
Gravy—2 tablespoons
Ice cream—½ cup
Lard—1 tablespoon
Lemons—3 large
Lettuce—2 large heads

Macaroni—¾ cup cooked
Malted milk—3 tablespoons
Marmalade and jelly—1 tablespoon
Marshmallows—5 marshmallows
Mayonnaise—1 tablespoon
Meat—cold sliced—⅛ inch slice
Meat—fat—size ½ chop
Meat—lean—size 1 chop
Milk—⅝ cup (regular)
Molasses—1½ tablespoons
Onions—3 to 4 Medium
Oranges—1 large
Orange juice—1 cup
Peaches—3 medium fresh
Peanut butter—1 tablespoon
Pears—2 medium fresh
Peas—¾ cup canned
Pecans—12 meats
Pie—¼ ordinary serving
Pineapple—2 slices 1 inch thick
Plums—3 to 4 large
Popcorn—1½ cups
Potatoes—sweet—½ medium
Potatoes—white—1 medium
Potato salad—1 cup
Prunes—dried 4 medium
Radishes—3 dozen red button
Raisins—¼ cup seeded or
    2 tablespoons seeded
Rhubarb—stewed and sweetened
    —½ cup
Rice—cooked ¾ cup
Rolls—1 medium
Rutabagas—1⅔ cups
Sauerkraut—2½ cups
Sherbet—4 tablespoons
Spinach—2½ cups
Squash—1 cup
Strawberries—1⅓ cups
Sugar—brown—3 tablespoons
Sugar—white—2 tablespoons
Tomatoes—canned—2 cups
Tomatoes—fresh—2 to 3 medium
Turnips—2 cups
Walnuts—8 to 16 meats
Watermelon—¾ slice 6 inches
    diameter

DRESSINGS AND SALADS

BONNIE'S FRENCH DRESSING

1 large onion, sliced and
   chopped
1/4 c. lemon juice
1/2 c. brown vinegar

1 c. sugar
2/3 c. ketchup
1/2 tsp. salt
1 Tbsp. paprika

Blend preceding ingredients together and add 3/4 cup oil and reblend. Makes 1 quart.

Marie Burt, Owatonna, MN

COLESLAW DRESSING

1/3 c. sugar
1/8 tsp. pepper
1/2 tsp. salt
1 Tbsp. grated onion
1 Tbsp. vinegar

1/2 tsp. celery seed
1 tsp. prepared mustard with
   horseradish
1 1/2 c. Miracle Whip
Cabbage, shredded

Mix all together and chill.

Vivian Van Esch, Owatonna, MN

DEE'S THOUSAND ISLAND DRESSING

2 c. mayonnaise
1/4 c. chili sauce
1 tsp. paprika
1 Tbsp. ground parsley

1 Tbsp. Worcestershire sauce
1/2 c. ripe olives
4 hard cooked chopped eggs
1 c. chopped celery

Blend and store in refrigerator.

Marie Burt, Owatonna, MN

FRENCH DRESSING

1 c. Mazola oil (Wesson oil
   separates)
1/2 c. sugar or honey
1/4 c. vinegar
2/3 c. catsup

Juice of 1 lemon
1 tsp. salt
Some coarse pepper
1 small onion, grated
1 small clove garlic (optional)

Put in lots of paprika too. Put all ingredients in a quart jar and shake well.
Lorraine Long, Grand Rapids, MN

FRENCH DRESSING

1 c. salad oil
1 c. white sugar
⅓ c. catsup
⅓ c. vinegar

1 small onion
1 tsp. celery seed
1 tsp. salt (optional)

Put all ingredients in blender. Blend on medium until well mixed. Store in glass container.

Evelyn Pedersen

SESAME SOY DRESSING

¼ c. salad oil
2 Tbsp. vinegar
2 Tbsp. sherry

2 Tbsp. lemon juice
2 tsp. soy sauce
2 tsp. sesame seeds

Jane Klein, Bellevue, WA

APRICOT SALAD

1 small box orange jello
1 (No. 2) can crushed pineapple
   and juice
¾ c. sugar
1 medium size ctn. Cool Whip

2 small jars apricot baby food
   with tapioca
1 (8 oz.) pkg. cream cheese,
   softened

Put jello and pineapple with juice in pan and heat until mixture simmers. Add sugar, baby food, and cut up cream cheese. Dissolve and mix well. Do not beat. Chill real well. Add Cool Whip slowly. Do not beat. Put into bowl and garnish with chopped nuts if you wish.

Diane Kemmetmueller, Anoka, MN

BEEF-POTATO SALAD

2 lb. potatoes
½ c. dry white wine or chicken
   broth
2 Tbsp. wine vinegar
⅓ c. vegetable or olive oil (or
   combination)
½ tsp. dry mustard
½ c. chopped parsley
1 tsp. leaf oregano, crumbled
1 tsp. salt

¼ tsp. pepper
1 large red onion, thinly sliced
2 green peppers, seeded and cut
   into thin strips
1½ lb. cooked roast beef, cut
   into thin strips
1 head lettuce, washed, dried,
   and chilled
2 tomatoes, cut into wedges

Cook potatoes in boiling salted water to cover in a large saucepan until tender, about 25 minutes. Drain, peel, and slice in a large bowl. Combine wine, vinegar, oil, mustard, parsley, oregano, salt, and pepper in a small bowl. Pour over warm potato slices; toss gently and let stand at room temperature for 20 minutes. Add onion, peppers, and roast beef; toss. Line salad bowl with lettuce; mound potato-beef mixture into center. Arrange tomato wedges around top of salad.

Bernice T. Eugenis, Saginaw, MN

BUTTERMILK COOKIE SALAD

1 c. buttermilk
2 pkg. instant vanilla pudding
2 (8 oz.) Cool Whip
2 cans drained mandarin
   oranges
1 pkg. striped chocolate cookies

Mix buttermilk and instant vanilla pudding together. Add Cool Whip. Fold in drained mandarin oranges. Crush chocolate cookies and stir in just before serving. This can also be frozen and served as a dessert.

CABBAGE-FRUIT SALAD
(Serves 6)

2 c. finely shredded green
   cabbage
1 (8 oz.) can crushed pineapple,
   drained
2 medium apples, chopped
   (about 2 c.)
1 c. seedless red or green
   grapes
1 c. plain yogurt
⅓ c. salad dressing
1 Tbsp. packed brown sugar
¼ tsp. salt

Mix cabbage, pineapple, apples, and grapes. Mix remaining ingredients; toss with cabbage mixture.

Millie Monte, Chisholm, MN

CHERRY JELLO SALAD

1 (3 oz.) pkg. cherry jello
1 c. hot water
1 can cherry pie filling
2 c. miniature marshmallows
1 (9 oz.) ctn. Cool Whip

Dissolve cherry jello in hot water. Stir in cherry pie filling. Cool until syrupy in texture. Add miniature marshmallows and Cool Whip. Makes a large salad.

Patricia Larson, Grafton, ND

CHICKEN SALAD

½ c. cut chicken
½ c. cut grapes
2 Tbsp. chopped celery
2 Tbsp. mayonnaise

Mix together; garnish with toasted slivered almonds. Serve on lettuce. Makes 2 servings.

Sandi Erickson, Montevideo, MN

CHICKEN SALAD

3 c. cooked chicken, cut up*
8 oz. pkg. Chinese pea pods, chopped
½ c. sliced water chestnuts

⅓ c. chives, chopped
2½ c. red seedless grapes, cut up
½ c. slivered almonds

Toss and refrigerate.

Before serving, add *dressing:*

⅓ c. vegetable oil
3 Tbsp. soy sauce
3 Tbsp. lemon juice

2 Tbsp. sugar
¼ tsp. pepper
⅛ tsp. ginger

* To cook chicken for salad, cook whole chicken for *1 minute* in heavy boiling water. Turn off heat. Lift chicken completely out of water. Return to the pot. Cover and let set for 1 hour.

Jean Loh, Minneapolis, MN

CHICKEN SALAD

1 c. grated carrots
2 c. cooked diced chicken breast
1 Tbsp. chopped onion

1 c. chopped celery
½ c. salad dressing
Salt and pepper to taste

Fold in shoestring potatoes or chow mein noodles just before serving.
Peggy Mielke, Chisholm, MN

CHICKEN AND CELERY SALAD

2½ c. cooked chicken chunks
2 c. sliced celery
1 c. orange sections, halved
½ c. coarsely chopped walnuts
3 Tbsp. vegetable oil

3 Tbsp. lemon juice
2 tsp. sugar
1 tsp. ginger
1 tsp. basil leaves, crushed
1/16 tsp. ground white pepper

In large bowl, combine chicken, celery, oranges, and walnuts; set aside. In small bowl, blend remaining ingredients; pour over chicken mixture. Toss until well coated. Refrigerate for about 20 minutes. Serve on lettuce leaves if desired.

Bernice T. Eugenis, Saginaw, MN

CHICKEN-ORANGE SALAD

4 c. diced cooked chicken
¼ c. diced water chestnuts
½ c. diced celery
¼ c. pitted black olives
½ c. olive oil
3 navel oranges, peeled and
  sliced

Juice of 1 lemon
Juice of 1 lime
3 red onions, sliced or diced
2 Tbsp. chopped chives
1 tsp. salt
1 tsp. paprika
Bite-size salad greens

Combine chicken, water chestnuts, celery, and olives. Pour ½ of olive oil over chicken mixture and toss. Place orange and onion slices in single layer in shallow pan. Pour remaining olive oil evenly over slices. Chill for 1 hour.

Combine lemon juice, lime juice, chives, salt, and paprika. Pour ½ of mixture over chicken and ½ over orange and onion slices. Toss lightly. Line platter with bite-size greens. Heap chicken mixture in center. Surround salad with alternating orange and onion slices. Chill until ready to serve. Serves 6.

Bernice Eugenis, Saginaw, MN

CHICKEN SALAD SUPREME

4 c. cubed cooked chicken
1 c. seedless white grape halves
¾ c. chopped celery
1 (11 oz.) can mandarin orange
  segments, drained *or* 1 (8
  oz.) can pineapple chunks,
  drained

½ c. slivered almonds, toasted
1 c. mayonnaise or salad
  dressing
¼ c. real lemon juice (frozen
  concentrate)
1 tsp. salt
¼ tsp. ground nutmeg

In large bowl, combine first 5 ingredients and set aside. In another bowl, mix next 4 ingredients and pour over chicken mixture. Refrigerate for ½ hour or more. Serve on lettuce leaf and use additional grapes and almonds for garnish.

Bernice T. Eugenis, Saginaw, MN

CHOCOLATE PUDDING SALAD

1 large pkg. *instant* chocolate
  pudding
½ c. slivered almonds
½ c. mini chocolate chips

½ c. maraschino cherries
1 c. miniature marshmallows
1 large (8 oz.) container Cool
  Whip

Make chocolate pudding according to the package directions. Add almonds, chocolate chips, maraschino cherries, miniature marshmallows, and Cool Whip. Decorate top with some mini chocolate chips, cherries, or almonds.

Diane Kemmetmueller, Anoka, MN

CORNED BEEF SALAD

1 pkg. lemon jello
3 c. boiling water

1 c. corned beef (12 oz.)

Let set a little.

4 hard-boiled eggs, chopped
    fine
1 c. celery
1 c. Miracle Whip

2 Tbsp. chopped onion
½ c. chopped pepper
1 Tbsp. pickle relish

Combine Miracle Whip with jello mixture and add remaining ingredients; refrigerate overnight.

Bernice T. Eugenis, Saginaw, MN

EASY SALAD

1 (3 oz.) pkg. lime jello (dry)
1 (9 oz.) cottage cheese
1 (8 oz.) can crushed pineapple,
    drained

1 (8 oz.) Cool Whip
1 c. miniature marshmallows
¼ to ½ c. chopped walnuts

Mix dry jello and pineapple until well dissolved. Add cottage cheese and mix well. Add Cool Whip and mix. Add marshmallows and fold in. Sprinkle chopped nuts on top; refrigerate overnight.

Alma M. Collatte, Grand Forks, ND

SALAD

1 can tuna or chicken
1 c. chopped celery

1 c. grated carrots
1 Tbsp. minced onion

Mix together preceding ingredients and refrigerate.

When ready to serve, mix in:

1 c. mayonnaise (or more)

1 (4 oz.) can shoestring potatoes

Serve on lettuce leaf or just plain. Serves 6.

Bonnie Gunderson, Fargo, ND

FLORENTINE SALAD

1½ lb. spinach
1 clove garlic, slivered
¾ c. salad oil
½ c. red wine vinegar
½ tsp. salt

Dash of pepper
3 hard cooked eggs, chopped
4 slices bacon, crisply fried and
    crumbled

Wash spinach; remove stems and tear leaves into bite-size pieces. Dry and chill for 2 hours. Let garlic stand in oil for 1 hour; remove garlic. Just before serving, mix oil, vinegar, salt, and pepper in large salad bowl. Add spinach and toss with dressing until leaves are well coated. Sprinkle with chopped eggs and crumbled bacon; toss. Makes 10 servings.

Variation - Hot Florentine Salad: Heat oil, vinegar, salt, and pepper in small chafing dish or saucepan over low heat, stirring constantly. Toss hot dressing with spinach until leaves are well coated. Toss with chopped eggs and bacon. Serve immediately.

Janet Lozon, Owatonna, MN

FRUIT SALAD

1 can chunky fruit cocktail　　　**1 can chunky pineapple**
1 can mandarin oranges

Add any other fruits such as grapes, strawberries, banana (banana added after all mixed together). Drain the canned fruit and save the juice. Use 1 cup of combined juices and add 2 tablespoons Tang and 1 package vanilla instant pudding. Mix with mixer or blender to get smooth.

Note: Pour some of saved juice over the fruit; let set a little while for flavor.

Sandi Erickson, Montevideo, MN

FRUIT SALAD

1 (16 oz.) can crushed pineapple　　**1 (3 oz.) pkg. instant pistachio**
**　　in own juice**　　　　　　　　　　**　　pudding**

Combine preceding ingredients overnight. Add carton of Cool Whip and as many colored miniature marshmallows as you like (nuts are optional).

Mrs. Goldie Mikish, Staples, MN

FRUIT SALAD

1 (3 oz.) pkg. vanilla instant　　　**1 (8 oz.) Cool Whip**
**　　pudding**　　　　　　　　　　　　**1 (16 oz.) fruit cocktail**
1 c. buttermilk　　　　　　　　　　**1 (15 oz.) crushed pineapple**

Mix pudding with buttermilk. Fold in Cool Whip, then add drained fruit. Just before serving, add Keebler's fudge stripe cookies and mix together. If you like, you can add mandarin oranges and cherries.

Marion Nelson, Dickinson, ND

JELLO-APPLESAUCE SALAD

⅓ c. red hots
1 c. water
2 c. applesauce

1 small pkg. jello (I use
    strawberry)
Whipped topping

Bring red hots and water to a boil. Add applesauce and jello; mix and let set. You can top with whipped topping or serve plain.

Irene McDonald, Owatonna, MN

HOLIDAY SALAD

2 pkg. orange jello
2 c. boiling water

1 pt. orange sherbet
1 can drained mandarin oranges

Mix jello and boiling water; cool. Dissolve orange sherbet. Combine jello and sherbet; beat until smooth. Add drained mandarin oranges and let set. Ready to eat.

Edie Raatz, Dickinson, ND

MEDITERRANEAN RICE SALAD

1 pkg. chicken Rice-A-Roni,
    cooked and chilled
2 small jars marinated artichoke
    hearts
½ green pepper, finely chopped

10 to 12 black olives, sliced
10 to 12 stuffed olives, sliced
Green onion, chopped
½ c. mayonnaise (Best Foods)
⅓ tsp. curry powder

Drain artichokes and save marinade. Add rest of ingredients (except mayonnaise, curry, and marinade). Mix the mayonnaise, curry, and marinade together and add to salad. Chill. Serves 6 to 8.

Jane Klein, Bellevue, WA

MID-EAST SALAD

1 head cauliflower
1 bunch broccoli
1 cucumber, sliced
1 bunch green onions, sliced
1 green pepper

1 c. fresh mushrooms, sliced
1 can pitted black olives (add
    whole)
1 (16 oz.) bottle Italian dressing
    (any oil base brand)

Wash and thoroughly drain ingredients. Cut into bite-size pieces. Pour dressing over vegetables. Keep in a leakproof container and turn over occasionally to marinate overnight or at least 8 hours before serving.

Note: Quick, easy salad to take to a picnic.

Sonya Masset, Bismarck, ND

PASTA SALAD

1 large box colored spiral pasta	2 cucumbers, diced
2 green peppers, diced	2 tomatoes, diced

Cook pasta as directed on package. Add remaining ingredients.

Dressing:

1 large bottle Italian dressing	1 bottle Salad Supreme

Mix Italian dressing and Salad Supreme; pour over salad mixture. Chill before serving.

Joyce Bell, Golden Valley, MN

PASTA VEGETABLE SALAD

1 lb. spiral noodles	1 head broccoli
2 pkg. herb Hidden Valley dressing	1 red onion, sliced thin
	Cherry tomatoes, cut in halves
1 head cauliflower	

Cook noodles according to directions on package. Mix herb dressing according to directions on package, preferably a few hours earlier. Break cauliflower and broccoli into small pieces. Mix everything together, except tomatoes, and marinate overnight. Fold tomatoes in before serving.

Hard-boiled eggs or diced ham, chicken, or turkey may be added for variety.

Bonnie Sorby

POTATO SALAD
(Hot)

8 large potatoes, cooked and grated	1 c. grated cheese (Cheddar)
	1/4 c. melted butter
1 c. green onions, chopped	2 c. diced ham
2 c. sour cream	Salt and pepper

Mix well. Bake in buttered 9x13 inch pan for 35 to 40 minutes. May top with crushed potato chips before baking if desired.

Renee Ulberg, Bismarck, ND

QUICK MIX SALAD

1 can blueberry pie mix	2 c. miniature marshmallows
1 (16 oz.) can fruit cocktail, drained well	1 (8 oz.) ctn. Cool Whip

Patricia Larson, Grafton, ND

SEVEN-UP SALAD

2 (3 oz.) pkg. lemon jello
2 c. boiling water
2 c. Seven-Up
1 (20 oz.) can crushed
    pineapple, drained (save
    juice)

1 c. miniature marshmallows
2 large bananas, sliced

Use 9x13 inch pan. Dissolve jello in boiling water. Add Seven-Up. Chill until it starts to set. Add pineapple, marshmallows, and bananas; chill until firm.

Topping:

½ c. sugar
2 Tbsp. flour
1 c. pineapple juice
1 egg, beaten

2 Tbsp. butter
1 c. whipped cream
¼ c. shredded American cheese
3 Tbsp. Parmesan cheese

Combine sugar and flour. Stir in juice and beaten egg. Cook over low heat until thickened; remove from heat and add butter. Cool. Fold in whipped cream. Spread over set jello mixture and sprinkle on cheese.

Evelyn Pedersen

SAUERKRAUT SALAD

1 large can sauerkraut
1 onion, diced
1 c. celery, diced

1 green pepper, diced
½ tsp. celery seed

Drain sauerkraut and squeeze juice out. Mix all together.

Add:

¾ c. sugar
½ c. vinegar

½ c. salad oil

Mix and pour over sauerkraut and refrigerate for a few hours. Will keep well if kept in refrigerator.

Marlys Wendorf, St. Cloud, MN

SHRIMP MACARONI SALAD

1 (7 oz.) pkg. ring or spiral
    macaroni
¾ c. chopped ripe olives
¾ c. chopped green olives
2 cans shrimp (or 1 c. sliced crab
    sticks)

1 c. chopped celery
1 small onion, chopped
4 hard-boiled eggs, chopped

Mix together and add dressing.

Dressing:

½ c. catsup
½ c. French dressing

1 c. mayonnaise or Miracle Whip

Renee Ulberg, Bismarck, ND

TUNA LUNCHEON SALAD

2 cans tuna
⅓ c. ripe olives
⅓ c. chopped onion
½ c. minced dill pickle

3 Tbsp. pickle juice
¼ c. chopped celery
½ c. mayonnaise

Mix all ingredients and chill. Before serving, add 1½ cups crushed Fritos. Serves 4 or 5.

Elynor Pederson, Montevideo, MN

SUMMER SALAD

Dressing:

2 c. real mayonnaise
1 c. sugar
¾ c. vinegar

1 can Eagle Brand condensed
    milk (not evaporated)

Blend and pour over:

1 (16 oz.) pkg. shell macaroni,
    cooked and drained
3 large carrots, grated
1 large green pepper, diced

1 small diced onion
1 red pepper, diced
1 cucumber, diced
1 c. celery, diced

Let stand for several hours or overnight.

Barb Nyborg, Fort Collins, CO

WILTED LETTUCE SALAD

Wilted lettuce won't wait. Serve immediately to enjoy its peak flavor.

2 bunches leaf lettuce, washed
4 slices bacon, diced
¼ c. vinegar
⅓ c. chopped green onions

¼ tsp. salt
⅛ tsp. pepper
2 tsp. sugar

Just before serving, shred lettuce with knife (about 4 cups). In large skillet, fry bacon until crisp. Add vinegar; heat through. Remove skillet from heat. Add lettuce.

Janet Lozon, Owatonna, MN

Notes

Microwave

MICROWAVE HINTS

1. Place an open box of hardened brown sugar in the microwave oven with 1 cup hot water. Microwave at high for 1½ to 2 minutes for ½ pound or 2 to 3 minutes for 1 pound.
2. Soften hard ice cream by microwaving at 30% power. One pint will take 15 to 30 seconds; one quart, 30 to 45 seconds; and one-half gallon 45 seconds to one minute.
3. One stick of butter or margarine will soften in 1 minute when microwaved at 20% power.
4. Soften one 8-ounce package of cream cheese by microwaving at 30% power for 2 to 2½ minutes. One 3-ounce package of cream cheese will soften in 1½ to 2 minutes.
5. Thaw frozen orange juice right in the container. Remove the top metal lid. Place the opened container in the microwave and heat on high power 30 seconds for 6 ounces and 45 seconds for 12 ounces.
6. Thaw whipped topping...a 4½ ounce carton will thaw in 1 minute on the defrost setting. Whipped topping should be slightly firm in the center but it will blend well when stirred. Do not overthaw!
7. Soften jello that has set up too hard—perhaps you were to chill it until slightly thickened and forgot it. Heat on a low power setting for a very short time.
8. Dissolve gelatin in the microwave. Measure liquid in a measuring cup, add jello and heat. There will be less stirring to dissolve the gelatin.
9. Heat hot packs in a microwave oven. A wet finger tip towel will take about 25 seconds. It depends on the temperature of the water used to wet the towel.
10. To scald milk, cook 1 cup milk for 2-2½ minutes, stirring once each minute.
11. To make dry bread crumbs, cut 6 slices bread into ½-inch cubes. Microwave in 3-quart casserole 6-7 minutes, or until dry, stirring after 3 minutes. Crush in blender.
12. Refresh stale potato chips, crackers or other snacks of such type by putting a plateful in the microwave oven for about 30-45 seconds. Let stand for 1 minute to crisp. Cereals can also be crisped.
13. Melt almond bark for candy or dipping pretzels. One pound will take about 2 minutes, stirring twice. If it hardens while dipping candy, microwave for a few seconds longer.
14. Nuts will be easier to shell if you place 2 cups of nuts in a 1-quart casserole with 1 cup of water. Cook for 4 to 5 minutes and the nut meats will slip out whole after cracking the shell.
15. When thawing hamburger meat, the outside will many times begin cooking before the meat is completely thawed. Defrost for 3 minutes, then remove the outside portions that have defrosted. Continue defrosting the hamburger, taking off the defrosted outside portions at short intervals.
16. To drain the fat from hamburger while it is cooking in the microwave oven (one pound cooks in 5 minutes on high), cook it in a plastic colander placed inside a casserole dish.
17. Cubed meat and chopped vegetables will cook more evenly if cut uniformly.
18. When baking large cakes, brownies, or moist bars, place a juice glass in the center of the baking dish to prevent a soggy middle and ensure uniform baking throughout.
19. Since cakes and quick breads rise higher in a microwave oven, fill pans just half full of batter.
20. For stamp collectors: place a few drops of water on stamp to be removed from envelope. Heat in the microwave for 20 seconds and the stamp will come right off.
21. Using a round dish instead of a square one eliminates overcooked corners in baking cakes.
22. When preparing chicken in a dish, place meaty pieces around the edges and the bony pieces in the center of the dish.
23. Shaping meatloaf into a ring eliminates undercooked center. A glass set in the center of a dish can serve as the mold.
24. Treat fresh meat cuts for 15 to 20 seconds on high in the microwave oven. This cuts down on meat-spoiling types of bacteria.
25. A crusty coating of chopped walnuts surrounding many microwave-cooked cakes and quick breads enhances the looks and eating quality. Sprinkle a layer of medium finely chopped walnuts evenly onto the bottom and sides of a ring pan or Bundt cake pan. Pour in batter and microwave as recipe directs.
26. Do not salt foods on the surface as it causes dehydration (meats and vegetables) and toughens the food. Salt the meat after you remove it from the oven unless the recipe calls for using salt in the mixture.
27. Heat left-over custard and use it as frosting for a cake.
28. Melt marshmallow creme in the microwave oven. Half of a 7-ounce jar will melt in 35-40 seconds on high. Stir to blend.
29. Toast coconut in the microwave. Watch closely as it browns quickly once it begins to brown. Spread ½ cup coconut in a pie plate and cook for 3-4 minutes, stirring every 30 seconds after 2 minutes.
30. Place a cake dish up on another dish or on a roasting rack if you have difficulty getting the bottom of the cake done. This also works for potatoes and other foods that don't quite get done on the bottom.

MICROWAVE

HOW TO GET THE BEST FROM YOUR MICROWAVE

General Tips:

1. To test whether a dish is microwave-safe or not, place it in the microwave oven next to a glass measuring cup half full of water. Heat at FULL (100%) power for 1 minute. If dish is hot, it should not be used in the microwave oven. If it is warm, use only for reheating. If dish is room temperature, it is safe to use for all microwave cooking.

2. Pay attention to standing times in recipes! Internal heat finishes the cooking after the dish is removed from the oven.

3. Make sure the cooking utensil rests on a solid heatproof surface during the standing or resting time specified in the recipe.

4. Set a timer for the minimum cooking time called for in a recipe. Check the doneness of food, then microwave for the additional time, if necessary.

5. When frequent stirring is necessary for a dish, leave a wooden spoon or microwave-safe utensil in the dish in the microwave oven.

6. To prevent messy boil-overs, use a cooking container 2 to 3 times larger than the volume of the sauce, soup, drink, or other liquid dish you are preparing.

7. If cooking uniform pieces of food, such as meatballs or chicken wings, arrange in a circle in the cooking utensil for even cooking.

8. Place tougher or thicker parts of food toward the outside edges of cooking pan or tray.

9. Do not use gold or silver trimmed dishes in a microwave oven; arcing may occur. Arcing is an electrical current that flows from the oven wall to metal in the oven, causing a light flash and popping sound. This may cause damage to the magnetron tube, the interior oven wall, or the cooking utensil.

10. If arcing occurs, turn power off immediately.

11. If there are small children in your house who might reach the controls and accidentally turn the microwave oven on, keep a glass measure or bowl containing about 1 cup of water in the oven to prevent damage to it.

12. A microwave oven works especially well with foods that have a naturally high moisture content, such as fish, poultry, fruits, and vegetables.

13. Dense foods, such as a potato, will take longer to cook in a microwave oven than lighter-textured foods, such as cake.

Meats and Fish:

14. Cook clams and mussels right in their shells for an easy-to-prepare appetizer. Arrange on pie plate, hinged-side toward the outside of plate and cover loosely with wax paper. For 3 (5 ounce) clams, microwave at FULL (100%) power for 3 to 5 minutes or until shells open.

15. If your roast beef is too rare, microwave slices right on dinner plate until desired doneness.

16. For one-step cooking and draining of excess fat, crumble ground meat into microwave-safe plastic colander set in a casserole. The fat will drain

into the casserole during cooking.

17. No-fuss, fancy hors d'oeuvres: Wrap pineapple chunks or water chestnuts in bacon and fasten with wooden pick. Place on paper toweling and microwave at FULL (100%) power until the bacon is thoroughly cooked.

18. For an instant hot dog in a warm bun, lightly score a fully cooked frankfurter and place in the bun. Wrap loosely in paper toweling and microwave at FULL (100%) power for 30 to 45 seconds.

19. For barbecued spareribs and chicken, microwave until tender, then grill long enough for a charcoal flavor and a crisp exterior.

20. Remember: Boneless meats cook more evenly than meats on the bone, because bones attract more microwave energy than meat.

Fruits and Vegetables:

21. To get the maximum amount of juice from citrus fruits, microwave at FULL (100%) power for 15 to 30 seconds before squeezing.

22. Peel, core, or pierce whole fruit, such as apples, before microwaving to allow steam to escape and avoid spattering.

23. When microwaving cabbage-family vegetables, such as fresh broccoli or cauliflower, cover loosely with wax paper for better flavor and color.

24. For an easy, quick single serving of frozen vegetables: Put ½ cup frozen vegetables with 1 tablespoon of water in custard cup. Cover with wax paper. Microwave at FULL (100%) power for 1½ to 2 minutes.

25. Here's how to cook crisp frozen hash brown or French fried potatoes in half the time! Partially thaw first in microwave oven following package directions, then fry or bake conventionally to finish.

26. To plump raisins and other dried fruits, place in a small bowl and sprinkle with a few drops of water. Microwave at full (100%) power for 15 to 30 seconds.

27. Use your microwave to dry fresh herbs. Wash and pat herbs dry on paper toweling. Measure 1½ cups leaves (without stems). Spread on double thickness of paper toweling and microwave at FULL (100%) power for 4 to 5 minutes, stirring several times.

28. Shortcut acorn squash: Pierce the skin of medium size (1¼ pounds) squash and microwave at FULL (100%) power for 4 minutes. Cut in half; remove seeds and microwave another 4 minutes. Let squash stand for 5 minutes.

29. Cook broccoli or asparagus with tender flower ends pointing toward center and with tougher stem ends pointing out.

Kitchen Helps:

30. Separate cold bacon in its packaging by microwaving the package at FULL (100%) power for 30 to 45 seconds.

31. To soften solidly frozen ice cream for easier scooping, microwave container at LOW (30%) power for 20 to 40 seconds.

32. Soften 1 stick butter at HALF (50%) power for 45 to 55 seconds. Remove any foil wrapping before microwaving.

33. To soften cream cheese, remove metallic wrapper and loosely wrap

in wax paper. Microwave on LOW (30%) power for 1½ to 2 minutes for the 3 ounce size and 3 to 4 minutes for 8 ounce size.

34. Use doubled muffin paper liners for microwaving muffins; the liners will help absorb any excess moisture.

35. Loosen hard brown sugar by adding an apple slice or a few drops of water to box; microwave at FULL (100%) power for a few seconds.

36. To melt chocolate, microwave in a microwave-safe cup at FULL (100%) power for 45 to 60 seconds per ounce of chocolate.

37. To make chocolate curls, place unwrapped block of chocolate on microwave-safe plate. Heat at HALF (50%) power for 8 to 12 seconds. Scrape off curls with swivel-bladed vegetable peeler.

38. "Toasted" coconut: To brown 1 cup shredded coconut, spread out on microwave-safe pie plate. Microwave at FULL (100%) power for 2 to 3 minutes, stirring several times.

39. Make your own chocolate syrup for milk: Combine 1¼ cups granulated sugar, 1 cup unsweetened cocoa powder, ¾ cup water, and ⅛ teaspoon salt in 1 quart measuring cup. Microwave at FULL (100%) power for 2 minutes or until mixture boils; stir. Continue cooking for 2 minutes longer, stirring every 30 seconds. Don't let mixture boil over. Stir in ½ teaspoon vanilla. To serve, stir 2 tablespoons of the syrup into 8 ounce glass of milk. Syrup will keep for up to 1 month when tightly covered in refrigerator.

40. For fried or poached eggs, always pierce yolks with a wooden pick *before* microwaving to prevent bursting.

41. Quick cup of tea, instant coffee, or cocoa: Heat the water directly in the cup instead of boiling a large tea kettle of water conventionally. A cup with 6 ounces of water microwaved at FULL (100%) power will be steaming after 1¼ to 2 minutes. Two cups will take 2½ to 3 minutes.

42. Speedy toasted cheese sandwich: Toast 2 slices bread (white or whole wheat) in a toaster or toaster oven. Place slice of cheese on one piece of toast. Spread with mustard, if you wish, then top with remaining piece of toast. Place sandwich on paper plate and microwave at MEDIUM HIGH (70%) power for 15 to 20 seconds or until the cheese melts.

Warming Up Foods:

43. Microwave dinner rolls in napkin lined straw serving basket at FULL (100%) power for 15 to 30 seconds, depending on number and size of rolls.

44. Wrap sandwich in paper toweling and microwave - the paper absorbs excess moisture.

45. Heat pancake syrup in its own container, cap removed, or in serving pitcher at FULL (100%) power.

46. Heat gravy in serving bowl or gravy boat at FULL (100%) power for 1 minute per cup.

47. To warm a 12 ounce jar of sundae or fruit sauce topping, remove the lid and microwave at FULL (100%) power for 45 to 60 seconds.

48. Reheat take-out fast food in its own paper wrapping at FULL (100%) power. If a container has a foil top, remove and cover loosely with wax paper.

49. Reheat fast food double-decker hamburger in its plastic package at

FULL (100%) power for 20 to 40 seconds.

50. To crisp and renew fresh flavor of day old cookies, crackers, or potato chips, microwave at FULL (100%) power for 5 to 15 seconds.

51. Warm a slice of apple pie with "melty" cheese on top by microwaving at FULL (100%) power for 15 to 20 seconds.

52. Popped corn can be reheated at FULL (100%) power for 15 to 20 seconds per cup.

53. As a general rule, to reheat foods, allow 1½ to 2 minutes for each cup of refrigerated mixture.

54. Hot pancakes: Arrange 3 already cooked pancakes, overlapping on microwave-safe plate. Cover loosely with wax paper and microwave at FULL (100%) power for 20 to 30 seconds.

Defrosting:

55. Defrost and heat food in boilable plastic bags right in the bag. Place the bag in a microwave-safe pie plate and cut an "X" in the bag above the liquid line for venting.

56. Frozen juice concentrate can be defrosted in its container. Remove lid from one end. Defrost at HALF (50%) power for 2 to 2½ minutes for 6 ounce can, and 4½ to 5 minutes for 12 ounce can.

57. Thaw frozen fish fillets right in its own packaging at LOW (30%) power.

Janet Lozon, Owatonna, MN

MICROWAVE HINTS

1. If chocolate or coating becomes too thick, thin with a little cooking oil in microwave.

2. Melt semi-sweet or milk chocolate in micro oven in a zipper type plastic bag. Cut off a corner of bag and squeeze out to decorate cookies, candy, or cakes.

3. To peel a tomato, microwave enough water to immerse tomatoes in a microwave-safe container until boiling. Plunge tomatoes into water and allow to stand for 30 to 60 seconds; remove to cold water and peel.

4. Increase juice from lemons or oranges by microwaving for 15 to 20 seconds before squeezing.

5. Ordinary Hint: After peeling and cutting onions or garlic; to remove any unpleasant odor, just rinse hands in cold water immediately and all onion or garlic odors disappear.

Lorraine Follsath, Anoka, MN

APPETIZERS, SNACKS, AND CANDIES

GRANOLA

8 c. rolled oats
1⅓ c. shredded or flaked
   coconut
½ c. wheat germ
½ c. sunflower seeds or
   chopped nuts

½ c. packed brown sugar
½ c. honey
½ c. cooking oil
½ tsp. salt
1 tsp. vanilla

Combine all ingredients in 4 quart glass mixing bowl; mix well. Microwave, uncovered, for 14 to 16 minutes or until toasted, stirring every 4 to 5 minutes. Cool. Serve as a cereal with milk or use as a topping for ice cream, yogurt, or pudding. Makes about 10 cups.

Mary Ann Ohman, Fargo, ND

CARAMEL CORN

Place 16 cups popped corn in a large paper bag.

Coating:

1 c. brown sugar
¼ c. light corn syrup
½ tsp. baking soda

1 stick butter
½ tsp. salt
1 tsp. vanilla

Combine in 8 cup batter bowl, the brown sugar, butter, corn syrup, and salt; microwave on FULL power for 1 to 2 minutes or until mixture bubbles. Boil for 3 minutes, stirring after each minute. Add soda and vanilla; stir well as this will foam up and pour over popcorn in bag. Shake very well.

Fold bag down and microwave on FULL power for 1 minute. Shake well. Microwave on FULL power for 1 minute. Shake well. Microwave on FULL power for 30 seconds. Shake well. Microwave on FULL power for 30 seconds. Shake well. Pour onto 2 cookie sheets. Let cool. Store in airtight container.

Sandi Erickson, Montevideo, MN

ELAINE'S MICROWAVE CARAMEL CORN

1 c. brown sugar
½ c. butter
¼ c. white syrup

½ tsp. salt
½ tsp. soda

Pop 2 batches of popcorn in air popper. Combine the brown sugar, butter, syrup, and salt. Microwave for 2 minutes or until boiling, then add ½ teaspoon soda. Pour over popcorn in a brown bag. Microwave on HIGH for 1½ minutes. Remove bag and shake. Microwave for another 1½ minutes.

Harlan Brekke, Fargo, ND

MICROWAVE CARAMEL CORN

Combine in 2 or 3 quart Ultra 21 casserole:

1 c. brown sugar
1 stick butter or margarine

¼ c. white Karo syrup
½ tsp. salt

Heat in microwave on HIGH for 4 minutes; remove and stir. Heat for 2 minutes on HIGH. Remove and stir. Add ½ teaspoon baking soda; stir until fluffy. Put 12 cups popped popcorn in Ultra 21 deep roasting pan. Pour caramel mixture over popped corn and cover with Ultra 21 medium roasting pan. Microwave on HIGH for 1½ minutes. Shake and return for 1 minute. Shake and return for 30 seconds. Pour on a cookie sheet to cool. Two batches fits in a Modular Mate Square 4.

Diane Rueb, Owatonna, MN

TASTES LIKE MORE PRETZELS
(Makes about 8 cups)

1 (12 oz.) pkg. mini twist pretzels
¼ tsp. garlic powder

¼ c. butter or margarine
¼ c. Parmesan cheese, grated

1. Place pretzels in large microwave-safe bowl; set aside. Combine butter and garlic powder in 1 cup glass measure.
2. Microwave (HIGH), uncovered, for 30 to 45 seconds or until melted. Stir to combine. Drizzle mixture over pretzels; mix lightly. Sprinkle with grated cheese; mix lightly again.
3. Microwave (HIGH), uncovered, for 3 to 4 minutes or until mixture starts to toast, stirring once or twice. Cool. Store in tightly covered container.

Lorraine Follsath, Anoka, MN

POTATO STICKS

2 Tbsp. Parmesan cheese
¼ tsp. paprika
Dash of pepper, salt, or other seasonings

⅛ tsp. onion powder or salt
1 medium potato, scrubbed
2 tsp. butter or margarine, melted

In small flat dish, combine Parmesan, paprika, onion powder, and other seasonings; set aside. Cut potato in half lengthwise; put cut sides down and cut in half lengthwise again, cutting each quarter into about three ¾ inch thick strips. Dip strips in melted butter, then in Parmesan mixture, coating all sides of potato strips.

Place strips in single layer in microwave-safe pie plate or square baking dish. Microwave on HIGH, uncovered, for 3 minutes; turn strips over and rearrange. Continue microwaving on HIGH for 3 minutes or until barely tender. Makes 1 serving. For 4 potatoes, 2 times the recipe.

Each serving: 211 calories, 7 grams protein, 12 grams fat, 23 grams carbohydrate, 167 milligrams sodium, 39 milligrams cholesterol.

Janet Lozon, Owatonna, MN

MICROWAVE CHEX PARTY MIX
(Watch, it burns)

6 Tbsp. butter or margarine	**2 c. Corn Chex cereal**
1 tsp. seasoned salt	**2 c. Rice Chex cereal**
4 tsp. Worcestershire sauce	**¾ c. salted mixed nuts or**
2 c. Wheat Chex cereal	**miniature pretzel twists**

Microwave butter in shallow 2 quart glass baking dish until melted. Stir in seasoned salt and Worcestershire sauce. Add Chex and nuts. Mix until all pieces are coated. Microwave on HIGH setting for 7 minutes or until crisp, stirring every 2 minutes. Spread on absorbent paper towels to cool. Store tightly covered. Makes 6¾ cups.

Janet Lozon, Owatonna, MN

NO-FUSS CARAMEL CORN

3 qt. popped corn	**¼ c. light corn syrup**
1½ c. peanuts	**½ tsp. salt**
1 c. packed brown sugar	**½ tsp. baking soda**
½ c. butter	

Place popped corn and peanuts in a large brown paper bag; set aside. Combine brown sugar, butter, corn syrup, and salt in 2 quart glass bowl or casserole. Microwave (HIGH) for 3 to 4 minutes, stirring after each minute, until mixture comes to a boil. Microwave for 2 minutes more. Stir in baking soda.

Pour syrup mixture over popped corn and peanuts in bag. Close bag and shake well. Microwave (HIGH) for 1½ minutes. Shake bag well. Microwave for 1½ minutes more. Shake bag and pour caramelized popcorn into large roasting pan. Cool and stir to separate caramel corn kernels. Makes about 3 quarts.

Make sure all popcorn gets well coated.

Janet Lozon, Owatonna, MN

CHEESE AND ZUCCHINI SNACKS
(Very good)

½ c. shredded Cheddar cheese
½ c. shredded zucchini
   (unpeeled)
¼ tsp. garlic salt
¼ tsp. onion salt

2 Tbsp. grated Parmesan
   cheese
2 Tbsp. salad dressing
8 to 10 pieces Melba toast

Combine all ingredients and mix well; spread on Melba toast. For 1 serving: Microwave, uncovered, for 20 seconds on MEDIUM (50%) power or until the cheese is melted. Serve immediately.

This mixture can be stored in the refrigerator for 2 to 3 days to prepare a quick snack as desired.

Helpful Hint: Length of microwave time varies with the amount of topping on toast. Try this mixture on toasted English muffins topped with cooked crumbled bacon. This mixture can also be used on a dry type cracker. If time is a factor, use ½ the time recommended previously and HIGH (100%) power.

Janet Lozon, Owatonna, MN

SPICY FRANKS

1 (10 oz.) jar currant jelly
3 Tbsp. prepared mustard

1 lb. skinless franks (about 10)

Combine jelly and mustard in 1½ quart glass casserole. Microwave for about 4 to 5 minutes on MEDIUM HIGH (ROAST) or until jelly melts. Beat well with rotary beater to blend in mustard. Cut each frank crosswise into 6 pieces. Stir into jelly mixture and continue cooking for 3 to 4 minutes on HIGH or until franks are hot. Serve in chafing dish with toothpicks. Makes about 60 appetizers.

Tip: Substitute 2 packages (8 ounce each) cocktail franks for skinless franks.

Janet Lozon, Owatonna, MN

GARLIC WALNUT NIBBLERS

2 Tbsp. butter
½ tsp. garlic salt

1 c. walnuts or almonds

Combine all ingredients in a small bowl or 2 cup glass measure. Microwave, uncovered, for 5 minutes on HIGH (100%) power, stirring twice during last 3 minutes. Cool walnuts on a paper towel. Store in a covered jar. Use as a snack or as croutons.

Janet Lozon, Owatonna, MN

SUGARED SPICED NUTS

Will keep for 6 to 8 weeks in a metal or airtight container in a cool place. Nice to serve with sherry or punch.

¾ c. brown sugar
¾ tsp. salt
1 tsp. cinnamon
½ tsp. ground cloves or
   coriander
¼ tsp. allspice
¼ tsp. nutmeg or cardamom

2½ Tbsp. water
1 c. walnut halves
1 c. pecan halves
1 c. Brazil nuts (or replace
   variety of nuts with 3 c. of
   one type like walnuts)

In a 1 quart glass casserole, combine brown sugar, salt, spices, and water; cook, uncovered, for 2 minutes, stirring once. Add ½ cup nuts to syrup mixture; stir with a fork until coated, then lift out nuts with fork to drain excess syrup and place in a single layer in oblong glass dish.

Prepare another ½ cup nuts as before; add to those in the dish. Cook, uncovered, for 4 minutes or until syrup on nuts begins to harden slightly. Transfer nuts to waxed paper to cool until crisp. Finish the remaining nuts in the same manner.

These are also delicious used as a topping for ice cream.

Janet Lozon, Owatonna, MN

CREATE-A-HOT-DIP

1 (8 oz.) pkg. cream cheese
½ c. mayonnaise or salad
   dressing

2 green onions, sliced
1 Tbsp. dried parsley flakes

Place cream cheese in medium glass mixing bowl. Microwave about 2 to 2½ minutes on MEDIUM HIGH (ROAST) or until softened. Add mayonnaise, onions, and parsley *plus ingredients from one of the variations.*

Variations:

Hot Crab Dip - Add:

1 (6 oz.) can crabmeat, drained
   and flaked
½ c. slivered almonds

2 Tbsp. dry white wine
1 Tbsp. horseradish
¼ tsp. Worcestershire sauce

Microwave for 4 to 6 minutes on MEDIUM HIGH (ROAST) or until hot (about 120°F.).

Hot Spinach Dip - Add:

1 (10 oz.) pkg. frozen chopped
    spinach, thawed and
    drained well
6 slices bacon, crisply fried and
    crumbled

⅓ c. grated Parmesan cheese
2 tsp. lemon juice

Microwave for 3 to 5 minutes on MEDIUM HIGH (ROAST) or until hot (about 120°F.).

Janet Lozon, Owatonna, MN

ORIENTAL MEATBALLS
(Excellent!!!)

Meatballs:

1 lb. ground beef
½ lb. ground pork
⅓ c. finely chopped canned
    water chestnuts (½ of 8 oz.
    can)
¼ c. finely chopped green
    pepper

3 to 4 green onions, chopped
½ tsp. salt
2 Tbsp. soy sauce
2 Tbsp. juice from pineapple

Sauce:

1 Tbsp. instant beef bouillon
¼ c. packed brown sugar
2 Tbsp. cornstarch
1 (20 oz.) can chunk pineapple in
    natural juice

1 Tbsp. soy sauce
2 Tbsp. vinegar
¼ c. water

1. Combine meatball ingredients in large mixing bowl; mix well. Shape into 1 inch meatballs. Arrange in 12x8 inch glass baking dish, stacking any extra meatballs along outer edge; cover with paper towel.
2. Microwave (HIGH) for 6 minutes. Carefully rearrange meatballs; cover.
3. Microwave (HIGH) for 2 to 3 minutes or until no longer pink.
4. Combine beef bouillon, brown sugar, cornstarch, soy sauce, vinegar, and water in 4 cup glass measure. Stir in juice from pineapple.
5. Microwave (HIGH), uncovered, for 3 to 4 minutes or until mixture boils and thickens. Stir in pineapple. Drain meatballs; pour sauce over meatballs.
6. Microwave (HIGH), uncovered, for 2 to 3 minutes or until heated through. Serve with toothpicks. Makes 45 to 50 meatballs.

Tips: Meatballs can be prepared ahead through step 5. Increase time in step 6 to 3 to 4 minutes if at room temperature and 5 to 6 minutes if mixture has been refrigerated. For ease in shaping meatballs, occasionally wet hands with cold water.

Janet Lozon, Owatonna, MN

BACON WANDS
(Very good)

12 thin bread sticks   **6 slices bacon, cut in halves**

Wrap bread stick with bacon; cook for 5 to 6 minutes on HIGH. May also wrap oysters, shrimp, or olives.

Janet Lozon, Owatonna, MN

MINI PIZZAS

4 English muffins
1 (8 oz.) can tomato sauce
½ tsp. oregano leaves
Dash of garlic powder
1 c. (4 oz.) shredded Mozzarella
cheese
Optional ingredients (green
pepper strips, pepperoni,

sliced small mushrooms,
grated Parmesan cheese,
Italian sausage, cooked,
pimiento-green olives,
sliced, onion, chopped)

Split English muffins in halves and toast. Mix tomato sauce, oregano, and garlic powder. Spread on toasted muffin halves. Sprinkle with shredded cheese. Top with optional ingredients. Cut each muffin half into 4 pieces. Place 8 pieces in a circle on 2 paper plates. For each plate, cook, uncovered, in microwave for 1 minute at HIGH or until cheese is melted. Makes 32 appetizers.

Millie Perrault, Duluth, MN

MUSHROOM-CHEESE CANAPES

1 Tbsp. butter or margarine
1 drop liquid pepper sauce
1 Tbsp. all-purpose flour
1 (4 oz.) can chopped
mushrooms, drained
(reserve liquid)
1 c. (4 oz.) shredded sharp
Cheddar cheese

48 Melba toast rounds or
crackers
1 Tbsp. chopped parsley
1 (2 oz.) jar pimientos, drained
and thinly sliced

Melt butter with liquid pepper sauce in a 1 quart glass measuring pitcher in microwave oven (30 seconds on HIGH). Blend in flour and mushroom liquid. Stir cheese into sauce. Cook, uncovered, for 1½ to 2 minutes at HIGH; stir once.

Stir chopped mushrooms into cheese sauce. Spread mixture on toast rounds or crackers and garnish with parsley and pimiento. To reheat, put 6 canapes in a circle on a paper plate. For each plate, cook, uncovered, for 30 seconds on HIGH. Makes 48 canapes.

Millie Perrault, Duluth, MN

CARAMEL NUT ROLLS

2 tsp. unflavored gelatin
3 Tbsp. water
¼ c. sugar
⅓ c. light corn syrup
1½ tsp. vanilla
3 to 3½ c. unsifted powdered
    sugar

1 (14 oz.) pkg. caramels
    (unwrapped)
2 Tbsp. water
3 c. (12 oz.) chopped dry roasted
    peanuts

1. Combine gelatin and water in small glass mixing bowl; let stand for 5 minutes. Stir in sugar and corn syrup.

2. Microwave (HIGH), uncovered, for 2 to 3 minutes or until mixture boils, stirring once. Cool for 5 minutes.

3. Add vanilla. Beat on high speed for 6 to 8 minutes or until mixture forms soft peaks. Gradually beat in 1 cup powdered sugar. Gradually stir in additional powdered sugar until very stiff. Turn onto powdered sugar-coated counter. Knead until easy to handle, adding additional powdered sugar as needed; set aside.

4. Grease two 22 inch long pieces of waxed paper. Sprinkle chopped nuts down center of each paper, about 4 inches wide by 18 inches long. Place caramels in 4 cup glass measure; add water.

5. Microwave (HIGH), uncovered, for 2 to 2½ minutes or until softened, stirring once. Stir until smooth. Let stand for 5 minutes. Pour melted caramels evenly over chopped nuts.

6. Divide marshmallow mixture in half. Roll each with hands to form roll 18 inches long. Place each roll on caramel mixture. Using waxed paper, lift caramel-nut mixture and roll around center to cover marshmallow. Wrap in waxed paper. Repeat with remaining roll. Refrigerate to set. Slice crosswise into 1 inch slices with knife dipped in hot water. Makes 36 pieces of candy, 165 calories each.

Joan Cooney, St. Cloud, MN

MICROWAVE DIVINITY

4 c. sugar
1 c. light corn syrup
¾ c. water
¼ tsp. salt

3 egg whites
1 tsp. vanilla
1 c. chopped pecans

1. Mix together sugar, corn syrup, water, and salt in 1½ to 2 quart casserole or mixing bowl with pouring spout. Cook in microwave on FULL power for 7 minutes and stir. Cook for 7 more minutes and stir. Cook for 7 more minutes.

2. While sugar cooks, beat egg whites until stiff peaks form in large mixing bowl. Gradually pour hot syrup over egg whites while beating at high speed until mixture is thickened and candy starts to lose its gloss.

3. Add vanilla and nuts to beaten mixture. Drop by teaspoon onto waxed paper, or pour in 15x9 inch pan and cut in squares when cool. Yields 6 to 7 dozen pieces.

Barb Fivecoate, Virginia, MN

MICROWAVE PEANUT BRITTLE

2 c. sugar
1 c. white corn syrup
⅓ c. water
1 lb. raw peanuts

1 Tbsp. butter or margarine
1 Tbsp. soda
1 tsp. vanilla

1. Grease two 15½ x 12 inch cookie sheets; keep warm.
2. Place sugar, corn syrup, water, and peanuts in a 3 quart casserole. Cook in microwave on FULL power for 5 minutes; stir. Cook for 5 minutes longer.
3. Quickly add butter and vanilla. Cook 5 minutes and stir. Cook for 5 minutes longer.
4. Remove from oven; stir in soda. Pour ½ of candy onto each sheet, spreading to ¼ inch thickness. Cool. Break into pieces. Store in tins. Put wax paper between each layer. Put a paper towel between wax paper and place in top of tin. This keeps candy from getting sticky and tough.

Barb Fivecoate, Virginia, MN

MICROWAVE PEANUT BRITTLE

1 c. white sugar
1 c. peanuts
½ c. white syrup

1 tsp. vanilla
1 Tbsp. butter or margarine
1 tsp. baking soda

Combine sugar, peanuts, and syrup in 4 cup glass bowl; microwave on HIGH for 3 ½ minutes. Add vanilla and margarine; cook for 30 seconds. Remove and stir in soda. Spread on Teflon cookie sheet.

Marlys Swehla, Albert Lea, MN

PEANUT BRITTLE

1 c. sugar
½ c. water
½ c. light corn syrup
1 (7 oz.) jar dry roasted peanuts

1 tsp. vanilla
¾ c. coconut (optional)
1 tsp. baking soda

Stir together sugar, water, and syrup in a 2 quart casserole. Microwave on HIGH (100%) for 12 to 14 minutes or until bubbly. Stir in nuts. Microwave on HIGH (100%) for 4 to 6 minutes or until light brown. Stir coconut and vanilla into syrup. Microwave on HIGH (100%) for an additional 1 or 2 minutes or until hard crack stage is reached. Add baking soda; stir until light and foamy. Pour mixture onto a lightly greased cookie sheet. Spread to ¼ inch thickness; cool. Break into pieces. Makes 1 pound.

Carol Gilbertson, Hawley, MN

SPECIAL FUDGE SAUCE

2 c. packed brown sugar
⅔ c. light corn syrup
⅓ c. unsweetened cocoa
½ c. whipping cream or half & half

¼ c. liqueur, 2½ tsp. liqueur flavoring, or 1 tsp. vanilla

1. Combine brown sugar, corn syrup, cocoa, and whipping cream in 2 quart glass mix 'n pour bowl; stir until smooth.
2. Microwave (HIGH), uncovered, for 6 to 7 minutes or until mixture boils and thickens, stirring once or twice (sauce continues to thicken with standing).
3. Stir in liqueur; pour into desired containers. Refrigerate until served. Best served warm. Makes about 2½ cups, 160 calories per 2 tablespoons.

Joan Cooney, St. Cloud, MN

NO-FAIL FUDGE

3 c. sugar
¾ c. margarine
1 (5 oz.) can evaporated milk
1 (12 oz.) pkg. chocolate chips
1 pkg. miniature marshmallows
    or use 2 c. (7 oz. jar)
    marshmallow creme

1 c. chopped nuts
1 tsp. vanilla

Combine sugar, margarine, and milk in large glass mixing bowl. Cover with plastic wrap. Microwave for 8 to 10 minutes, stirring occasionally, until dissolved. Continue for 5 minutes more or until soft ball stage (236°). Stir in chocolate chips and marshmallows until melted. Add nuts and vanilla; beat. Pour into buttered 9x13 inch pan; chill and cut into squares.

Bonnie Sooby

VELVEETA FUDGE

½ lb. butter
½ lb. Velveeta cheese
½ c. cocoa

½ tsp. vanilla
2 lb. powdered sugar
Nuts (optional)

Combine butter and cheese in glass bowl and microwave until melted, about 2½ minutes. Using a mixer, blend in vanilla, cocoa, and powdered sugar. Turn into buttered 9x13 inch pan. Press in place and cool. Cut into ½ inch squares to serve.

Marlys Swehla, Albert Lea, MN

TWO-LAYER FUDGE IN THE MICROWAVE

Here's an easy recipe that makes a great holiday treat. Make ahead and store in the freezer.

2 sq. (2 oz.) unsweetened
  baking chocolate
1 (8 oz.) pkg. cream cheese,
  halved
½ tsp. vanilla

2¼ c. unsalted powdered sugar
¼ tsp. almond extract
2½ c. unsifted powdered sugar
⅓ c. sliced almonds

1. Microwave (HIGH) chocolate in uncovered small glass dish for 1 to 1¼ minutes or until melted, stirring once; set aside. Place ½ of cream cheese in 1 quart glass mix 'n pour bowl.

2. Microwave (HIGH), uncovered, for 30 to 45 seconds or until softened; stir until smooth. Mix in chocolate and vanilla. Add 2¼ cups powdered sugar; beat until smooth. Spread evenly in buttered 10x6 inch pan. Refrigerate to set, about 10 minutes.

3. Microwave (HIGH) remaining cream cheese in uncovered 1 quart glass mix 'n pour bowl for 30 to 45 seconds or until softened. Blend in extract. Add 2½ cups powdered sugar; beat until smooth. Mix in almonds. Spoon mixture over chocolate layer; spread evenly. Refrigerate until set, about 2 hours. Cut into 1 inch squares. Store, covered, in refrigerator. Makes about 60 squares, 60 calories each.

Mary Hocking, Fargo, ND

NO FAIL FUDGE

3 c. sugar
¾ c. butter or margarine
1 (5 oz.) can evaporated milk
1 (12 oz.) pkg. semi-sweet
  chocolate pieces

1 (10 oz.) jar marshmallow
  creme
1 c. chopped nuts
1 tsp. vanilla

1. Combine sugar, butter, and milk in buttered large glass mixing bowl; cover with plastic wrap.

2. Microwave on ROAST for 10 minutes. Stir and continue cooking on ROAST for 5 to 6 minutes or until mixture forms a soft ball in cold water. Stir in chocolate pieces until melted. Fold in marshmallow creme, nuts, and vanilla.

3. Pour into buttered 3 quart (13x9 inch) pan. Chill until firm; cut into squares. Makes 72 fudge squares.

Eileen Rekowski, St. Cloud, MN

TOFFEE PIECES

10 graham crackers
½ c. butter or margarine
¾ c. packed brown sugar

¼ c. chopped nuts
1 (6 oz.) pkg. semi-sweet
  chocolate pieces

1. Place crackers on bottom of buttered 2 quart (12x7 inch) glass baking dish; set aside. Combine butter and brown sugar in 4 cup glass measure.

2. Microwave on ROAST for about 2 minutes or until butter is melted. Stir in nuts. Pour syrup over crackers.

3. Microwave on ROAST for 4 to 5 minutes or until bubbly. Top with chocolate pieces and continue cooking on ROAST for about 1½ minutes or until chocolate is softened. Spread chocolate evenly over top. Chill for about 30 minutes or until cool; cut into bars. Makes about 24 bars.

Eileen Rekowski, St. Cloud, MN

CRUNCHY TOFFEE IN THE MICROWAVE

Here's an easy and delicious recipe for holiday candy.

¾ c. butter
1¼ c. granulated sugar
1 tsp. salt
¼ c. water

1 c. unblanched almonds, slivered
½ tsp. baking soda
½ c. chocolate chips

Combine butter, sugar, salt, water, and almonds in a buttered 2 quart glass measure. Microwave, uncovered, on HIGH for 4 minutes. Stir well and microwave, uncovered, on HIGH about 8 minutes or until candy is light brown (290°F.). Add soda and pour onto a cookie sheet.

Microwave chocolate chips in a 1 cup glass measure on HIGH for 1½ minutes or until soft. Stir and spread over candy. Cool at room temperature and break into pieces.

Place toffee in fancy tins and give as gifts.

Dessa Clafton

CREAM CHEESE MINTS

1 (3 oz.) pkg. cream cheese
3½ c. unsifted powdered sugar
¼ tsp. mint, lemon, cherry, or almond extract

½ tsp. butter flavoring
3 drops food coloring
2 Tbsp. sugar

1. Microwave (HIGH) cream cheese in small mixing bowl for ¼ to ½ minute or until softened. Beat at medium speed until smooth. Gradually beat in powdered sugar. Add extract, flavoring, and food coloring; mix well.

2. Roll about 1 teaspoon of mixture into a ball. Dip in sugar and place, sugar side down, in candy mold. Press lightly to fill mold. Invert to remove from mold. Store mints in cool dry place.

Mints can be rolled into balls and flattened slightly instead of using molds. Makes about 50 mints.

Dessa Clafton

SOUPS, SALADS, SANDWICHES, MISCELLANEOUS

BROCCOLI AND HAM SOUP

1 medium onion, chopped
1 clove garlic, minced
2 Tbsp. butter or margarine
2 c. (10 oz.) diced fully cooked
   ham
2 (13 oz.) cans chicken broth
2 c. chopped fresh broccoli (or
   frozen)

1 (7½ oz.) can tomatoes, cut up
½ c. water
½ c. elbow macaroni
¼ tsp. ground nutmeg
Grated Parmesan cheese
   (optional)

In 3 quart casserole, combine onion, garlic, and butter. Place in microwave; cook for 3 minutes on HIGH till tender. Stir in ham, broth, broccoli, undrained tomatoes, water, macaroni, and nutmeg; cover. Cook for 15 minutes at HIGH; stir once. Cook for 8 minutes on medium till broccoli and macaroni are tender. Season to taste with salt and pepper. If desired, sprinkle individual servings with Parmesan cheese. Makes 6 servings.

Marlys Swehla, Albert Lea, MN

CLAM CHOWDER

3 slices raw bacon, diced
1 (8 oz.) can minced clams
   (undrained)
1½ c. peeled and cubed
   potatoes
⅓ c. finely chopped onion
1 medium size carrot, diced

2 Tbsp. flour
1 c. milk
½ c. light cream
1 tsp. salt
⅛ tsp. pepper
¼ tsp. thyme

Place bacon in a deep 2 quart nonmetallic casserole. Heat, covered with a paper towel, in microwave oven for 2 to 3 minutes or until bacon is crisp. Remove cooked bacon with a slotted spoon. Crumble bacon and set aside. Reserve drippings in casserole. Drain liquid from clams and add to bacon drippings. Set clams aside.

Add potatoes, onion, and carrot to casserole. Heat, covered, in microwave oven for 8 to 10 minutes or until vegetables are tender; stir occasionally. Blend flour into vegetable mixture. Gradually, stir in milk until smooth. Heat, uncovered, in microwave for 2 to 3 minutes or until thickened and smooth.

Stir in cream, salt, pepper, thyme, and reserved clams. Heat, uncovered, in microwave for 2 to 3 minutes or until heated through. Garnish with crumbled bacon before serving. Serves 4.

Clayone Carlson (Roy B.), Fargo, ND

MICROWAVE TOMATO SOUP

In *separate* 2 quart microwave bowls, put:

2 c. milk   **2 c. tomatoes**

Heat each bowl to the same degree of heat. With my microwave it takes 2½ to 3 minutes on HIGH (microwaves vary in heat, so time what is best for your microwave). Put a pinch of soda into the hot milk (be careful not to curdle it while heating it). Stir.

Put a pinch of soda into the hot tomatoes and stir. Next, slowly pour and stir the tomatoes into the milk (the red into the white). Salt, pepper, and butter may be added. *Enjoy.*

Elizabeth Millard, Grand Rapids, MN

BROCCOLI SALAD
(Serves 6)

1 head broccoli   **6 slices bacon**
½ c. raisins

Cut 1 head broccoli to bite-size. "Plump" ½ cup raisins in micro with 1 tablespoon water; drain. Fry 6 slices bacon until crisp, then crumble.

Dressing:

¾ c. *real* mayonnaise   **1½ Tbsp. cider vinegar**
2 Tbsp. sugar   **Onion to taste, diced tiny**

Put dressing on and toss ½ hour before serving.

Linda Hamann, Golden Valley, MN

TACO SALAD

1 lb. lean beef or pork   **½ to 1 c. thinly sliced onion**
1 (1¼ oz.) pkg. taco seasoning   **½ to 1 c. thinly sliced green**
** mix**   ** pepper**
1 (16 oz.) can kidney beans   **1 c. shredded Cheddar cheese**
** (undrained)**   **4 c. coarsely broken corn chips**
1 medium head lettuce   **1 (8 oz.) bottle Western style**
2 large tomatoes, coarsely   ** salad dressing**
** chopped**

Place ground meat in micro-safe 2 quart casserole. Microwave on HIGH for 5 minutes, stirring halfway through to break up meat. Add taco seasoning mix and undrained kidney beans. Microwave on HIGH for 10 minutes, stirring twice. Let stand for 10 minutes to cool slightly.

Break lettuce into bite-size pieces and place in large serving bowl. Add tomatoes, onion, green pepper, and cheese; toss lightly. Add meat mixture, chips, and salad dressing; toss. Serve immediately. Makes 6 to 8 main dish servings.

Ruth Weis, Bemidji, MN

EASY REUBEN SANDWICHES

6 oz. sliced corned beef,
    chopped
½ c. sauerkraut, drained and
    chopped
2 Tbsp. salad dressing
½ tsp. horseradish

¼ tsp. salt
Dash of hot pepper sauce
2 Tbsp. butter, melted
4 slices rye bread, toasted
4 slices Swiss cheese

Mix together corned beef, sauerkraut, salad dressing, horseradish, salt, and hot pepper sauce. Butter one side of bread. Spread buttered side of bread with 3 tablespoons of corned beef mixture and a slice of cheese. Place on paper towel or paper plate. Microwave on HIGH (100%) for 1 or 2 minutes or until cheese begins to melt. Makes 4.

Carol Gilbertson, Hawley, MN

DELUXE SCRAMBLED EGGS
(Yield: 4 to 6 servings)

6 eggs
⅓ c. dairy sour cream
Dash of pepper
1 Tbsp. butter or margarine

⅓ c. shredded Cheddar cheese
¼ tsp. salt
6 slices bacon, cooked and
    crumbled (optional)

Beat eggs with fork in medium mixing bowl. Add cheese, sour cream, salt, pepper, and bacon if desired; blend well. Set aside. Place butter in 1 quart casserole. Heat in microwave oven on FULL power for 20 to 40 seconds or until melted. Tilt casserole until butter evenly coats bottom. Pour egg mixture into casserole. Cook in microwave oven on FULL power for 4 to 5 minutes or until eggs are set, but still moist. Stir 1 to 2 times during cooking time.

Peggy Mielke, Chisholm, MN

OATMEAL

¾ c. hot water
⅓ c. quick oats

Dash of salt

Microwave on HIGH for 1 minute. Take out and stir. Put in for 45 seconds. Let set for 1 to 2 minutes before serving. Serves 1. Use 4 cup Pyrex pitcher.

Bonnie Sorby

FISH, POULTRY, MEATS

CREAM SAUCE

2 Tbsp. butter or margarine
2 Tbsp. flour
1 tsp. instant chicken bouillon

1 c. milk
1 Tbsp. Parmesan cheese (if desired)

1. Microwave (HIGH) butter in 2 cup glass measure for ¼ to ½ minute or until melted. Blend in flour and bouillon. Gradually stir in milk.
2. Microwave (HIGH), uncovered, for 2 to 3 minutes or until mixture boils and thickens, stirring once or twice. Stir in cheese. Serve sauce over fish. Makes about 1 cup, 2 calories per 2 tablespoons.

Joan Cooney, St. Cloud, MN

FISH AND SEAFOOD

The microwave cooks fish better than any other way. Texture of fish is ideal. Fish cooks almost as fast as it heats, so overcooking must be carefully avoided! I prefer to defrost fish on HIGH power for 2 to 3 minutes per pound. Rest 10 minutes. Cook on HIGH. Generally when fish flakes, it's done. For microwave fish, it should flake easily with fork *after* "carry-over cooking" time. Four to 6 minutes per pound is very accurate timing for fish as a "rule of thumb." Add more time if foods are added to fish. Arrange in dish with thick portions to outside or fold under small ends of fillets.

Cover fish to cook. Poaching or steaming are conventional fish cooking techniques very adaptable in the microwave. Wax paper is a good cover for 12x8 inch dish. Parchment paper may be wrapped around each fillet in lieu of covering. A favorite of mine is to wrap fish in lettuce leaves during cooking. This traps steam and helps baste fish.

Salmon fillets and roasts are excellent when cooked this way. Covering fish exceptions are those with crumb coatings which you wish to remain dry. When placed on rack, uncovered, breaded fish sticks, etc., cook very nicely and coating remains dry.

For more browning, place under hot broiler element or infra-red element in microwave, if you have one, a few minutes. Overcooked fish is dehydrated, leaving a dry texture and strong flavor. To eliminate a fishy odor, brush with white wine after purchasing. This does not change taste when cooking. If fish is frozen, it must be defrosted before cooking. Be very careful not to overdefrost. Shield small sides.

Jane Klein, Bellevue, WA

BAKED FISH
(An easy, quick dinner!)

This is a favorite fish recipe of mine from "Let's Cook Microwave!" by Barbara Harris.

1 lb. fish fillets	2 Tbsp. butter
½ tsp. salt	1 large sliced tomato
¼ tsp. pepper	½ thinly sliced green pepper
1 small thinly sliced onion	1 Tbsp. Worcestershire sauce
⅓ c. sauterne wine (optional)	

In a 12x8 inch dish, arrange fish; sprinkle with salt and pepper. Cover with onion. Pour wine over fish; marinate for 30 minutes, turning fish over after 15 minutes. In 1 cup glass measure, melt butter. Pour over fish. Cover with tomatoes and green pepper. Sprinkle with Worcestershire; microwave (HIGH), covered, for 6 to 7 minutes, rotating dish ¼ turn halfway through cooking. Rest for 5 minutes. Serves 4. *Looks pretty.*

Jane Klein, Bellevue, WA

TUNA CASHEW CASSEROLE

1 (6½ oz.) can tuna, drained	½ soup can water
1 c. chow mein noodles	½ c. cashew nuts
2 Tbsp. finely chopped onion	1 (6 oz.) pkg. potato chips,
1 c. celery, diced	squashed in bag
1 Tbsp. oleo	
1 (10¾ oz.) can cream of mushroom soup	

Melt oleo in 1½ quart casserole for 30 seconds on HIGH. Add celery and onion. Cook, covered, on HIGH for 2 to 3 minutes until tender. Add remaining ingredients, except potato chips. Stir until well blended. Cook, covered, on HIGH for 7 minutes, stirring halfway through. Stir and sprinkle potato chips on top. Cook for 3 to 5 minutes more until heated through or 170° on temperature probe.

Dessa Clafton

SUMMER LASAGNA
(Microwave on diet)

1 (8 oz.) can tomato sauce	1 tsp. parsley flakes
1 medium onion, chopped	3 medium zucchini (about 9
¼ tsp. basil leaves	inches long)
¼ tsp. salt	1 large tomato, sliced
Dash of pepper	2 Tbsp. grated Parmesan
¼ tsp. oregano leaves	cheese
1 c. Ricotta cheese	
½ c. shredded Mozzarella cheese	

Combine tomato sauce, onion, basil, salt, pepper, and oregano in small mixing bowl; set aside. In medium bowl, combine Ricotta, Mozzarella, and parsley; set aside. Peel zucchini and cut off ends. Slice zucchini lengthwise into strips. Arrange strips in 8x8 inch baking dish; cover with wax paper. Microwave at HIGH for 6 to 8 minutes or until fork tender. Drain liquid. Place zucchini on paper towels to absorb excess moisture; cool slightly.

Layer 4 to 6 strips in bottom of baking dish; reserve 6 strips for second layer. Spread Ricotta mixture over zucchini. Layer with sliced tomatoes. Spread ½ of tomato sauce mixture over tomatoes. Top with zucchini slices. Pour remaining sauce over zucchini and sprinkle with Parmesan. Reduce power to 50% (MEDIUM) and microwave, uncovered, for 20 to 25 minutes or until zucchini is tender and mixture is hot in center. Let stand for 5 minutes before serving. Serves 6. Calories per serving: 129.

Lois Haworth, Fargo, ND

BAKED CHICKEN A LA KING

½ c. butter or margarine
½ c. unsifted all-purpose flour
3 c. milk
6 c. cubed cooked chicken
1 (4 oz.) can mushroom stems
  and pieces (undrained)

2 Tbsp. chopped pimento
1 tsp. salt
¼ tsp. pepper
1 c. packaged seasoned
  croutons

1. Place butter in 3 quart glass casserole.
2. Microwave on ROAST for 2 to 2½ minutes or until melted. Blend in flour. Gradually stir in milk; mix well.
3. Microwave on HIGH for 4 minutes. Beat with rotary beater and continue cooking on HIGH for about 4 minutes or until thickened. Beat with rotary beater until smooth. Stir in remaining ingredients, except croutons. Cover with glass lid or plastic wrap.
4. Microwave on REHEAT for 10 to 12 minutes or until hot. Let stand, covered, for 5 minutes. Sprinkle croutons on top and serve. Makes 6 to 8 servings.

Eileen Rekowski, St. Cloud, MN

QUICK CHICKEN DINNER

1 (10 oz.) pkg. frozen mixed
  vegetables
1 can cream of mushroom soup
1 can mushrooms (undrained)

1 medium onion, chopped
1½ c. cut up cooked chicken
1 c. crushed potato chips

Rinse frozen vegetables under cold water to separate; drain. Mix all ingredients, except potato chips, in 2 quart casserole. Cover tightly and microwave on HIGH for 5 minutes; stir. Cover and microwave until hot for 5 to 7 minutes longer. Sprinkle with crushed chips.

Diane Rueb, Owatonna, MN

TURKEY NOODLE BAKE

1 (10¾ oz.) can condensed
    cream of chicken soup
¼ c. water
2 c. cooked turkey
1 c. chopped celery

½ c. coarsely chopped nuts
¼ c. chopped onion
1 Tbsp. chopped pimento
1 (3 oz.) can chow mein noodles

1. Combine all ingredients, including 1 cup chow mein noodles, in 2 quart casserole; mix well. Cover with glass lid or plastic wrap.

2. Microwave on REHEAT for 8 to 10 minutes or until hot. Let stand, covered, for 5 minutes. Sprinkle top with remaining noodles and serve. Makes about 4 servings.

Eileen Rekowski, St. Cloud, MN

EASY CHICKEN RICE

1 (10½ oz.) can condensed
    chicken broth
1 tsp. soy sauce
⅓ c. finely chopped onion
1 c. quick cooking rice

1 c. cubed cooked chicken
1 (7 oz.) can cut green beans,
    drained
1 (5 oz.) can water chestnuts,
    drained and sliced

1. Combine all ingredients in 2 quart glass casserole. Cover with glass lid or plastic wrap.

2. Microwave on HIGH for 8 to 10 minutes or until hot. Let stand, covered, for 5 minutes before serving. Makes about 4 servings.

Eileen Rekowski, St. Cloud, MN

SWEET AND SOUR TURKEY

1 (6 oz.) pkg. frozen pea pods
2 Tbsp. water
1 small onion, thinly sliced
¼ c. chopped green pepper
1 large stalk celery, sliced
    diagonally
2 c. cooked cubed turkey
1 (15½ oz.) can pineapple
    chunks packed in own juice
    (juice reserved)

4 tsp. cornstarch
1 tsp. instant chicken bouillon
    granules
Dash of ground ginger
¼ tsp. salt (optional)
1 tsp. brown sugar
1½ Tbsp. soy sauce
1 Tbsp. vinegar

Place pea pods and water in 2 quart casserole; cover. Microwave at HIGH for 2 to 3 minutes or until defrosted. Break apart and drain. Stir in onion, green pepper, celery, turkey, and pineapple chunks; set aside.

In 4 cup measure, combine cornstarch, bouillon, ginger, salt, and brown sugar. Stir in soy sauce, vinegar, and pineapple juice. Microwave at HIGH for 2 to 3 ½ minutes or until sauce is clear and thickened, stirring every minute. Fold sauce into turkey mixture; cover. Microwave at HIGH for 4 to 6 minutes or until heated through. Serves 4.

Note: For low sodium diet, substitute low-salt soy sauce and bouillon. Per serving: Calories: 188. Sodium: 534 milligrams. Cholesterol: 35 milligrams. Exchanges: 1 vegetable, 2 fruit, 1½ lowfat meat.

David Janz, Dickinson, ND

ROAST TURKEY

12 to 15 lb. turkey, thawed
Salt

Favorite stuffing or onion and
celery

1. Remove giblets and neck from turkey; set aside and use as desired. Wash turkey; pat dry. Sprinkle cavity with salt. Stuff turkey, if desired, or place pieces of onion and celery in cavity.

2. Place turkey, breast side up, in large baking dish. Cover loosely with waxed paper.

3. Microwave (HIGH) for 30 minutes. Turn turkey, breast side down; cover with waxed paper.

4. Microwave (HIGH) for 30 to 45 minutes or until just about done.

5. Transfer turkey, breast side up, to clean baking pan.

6. Bake, uncovered, at 375° for 30 to 60 minutes or until golden brown and meat thermometer registers 165° in inner thigh area. Let stand for 15 minutes before carving. Makes about 20 servings, 395 calories each.

Joan Cooney, St. Cloud, MN

SAUSAGE-BREAD STUFFING

2 c. chopped celery
1 c. chopped onion
1 Tbsp. water
12 oz. mild pork sausage
1 (12 oz.) pkg. unseasoned
bread cubes (about 8 c.)

2 eggs
1 (14½ oz.) can chicken broth
1½ Tbsp. poultry seasoning

1. Combine celery, onion, and water in 1 quart glass casserole. Cover with casserole lid.

2. Microwave (HIGH) for 6 to 7 minutes or until partially cooked; stir. Crumble pork sausage into casserole; cover.

3. Microwave (HIGH) for 5 to 6 minutes or until sausage is no longer pink and celery and onion are tender; drain.

4. In large bowl, combine sausage mixture with remaining ingredients, mixing lightly. Transfer mixture to 3 quart glass casserole. Cover with casserole lid.

5. Microwave (HIGH) for 9 to 10 minutes or until heated (150°), stirring once. Makes about 15 servings, 215 calories each.

Joan Cooney, St. Cloud, MN

GLAZED CHRISTMAS HAM

1 c. apple jelly
1 Tbsp. cornstarch
⅛ tsp. dry mustard
2 Tbsp. butter or margarine
1 Tbsp. brandy or bourbon (if
    desired)

8 to 10 lb. semi-boneless ham
Whole cloves (if desired)
1 c. apple juice

1. Mix together jelly, cornstarch, and mustard in 4 cup glass measure until cornstarch is blended.

2. Microwave (HIGH), uncovered, for 3 to 3½ minutes or until mixture boils and thickens, stirring once or twice. Stir in butter and brandy; set aside.

3. Score ham and insert cloves in every other diamond-shape if desired. Place in 3 to 4 quart glass casserole. Pour apple juice over ham. Cover with waxed paper or casserole cover.

4. Microwave (HIGH) for 5 minutes, then microwave (MEDIUM - 50%) for 40 minutes, rotating dish once and basting with juices. Turn ham over; baste. Insert microwave meat thermometer; cover.

5. Microwave (HIGH) for 5 minutes, then microwave (MEDIUM - 50%) for 40 to 50 minutes or until ham reaches internal temperature of 140°, rotating dish once and basting with juices. Spoon ½ of glaze over ham.

6. Microwave (HIGH), uncovered, for 3 to 3½ minutes or until glaze melts and coats ham. Allow to stand for 10 minutes, covered with foil. Remove ham from dish and place on serving platter. Spoon on additional glaze. Carve and serve. Makes about 24 servings, 465 calories each.

Joan Cooney, St. Cloud, MN

PORK CHOPS WITH STUFFING

Combine in bowl:

2 Tbsp. margarine
1 rib celery

2 Tbsp. onion

Microwave for 1½ to 2 minutes on FULL power; stir once. Add ⅔ cup milk and 3 cups dry stuffing; mix well. Sprinkle ½ package dry brown gravy mix in bottom of 8x8 inch glass baking dish. Cover with 3 or 4 thin pork chops. Put stuffing on top of chops. Cover with 2 or 3 more thin chops and top with the rest of the gravy mix. Cover with Saran Wrap, leaving open one corner as a vent. Microwave at 80% or MEDIUM HIGH for 14 to 16 minutes. Let stand, covered, for 5 minutes.

Barbara Kaste, Fargo, ND

FIVE MINUTE PORK CHOP

1 boneless loin pork chop (½
    inch thick)

½ tsp. barbeque seasoning

Sprinkle pork chop with seasoning. Place pork chop in microwave-safe dish; cover with plastic (leave a corner of the wrap open a little). Microwave on MEDIUM LOW or 30% power (200 watts) for 2 minutes. Turn pork chop over and cover; continue microwaving for 2 to 2½ minutes. Contains 198 calories.

Two pork chops need 4 minutes per side. Four pork chops need 9 minutes per side.

Jane Klein, Bellevue, WA

PORK BARBEQUE SEASONING

2½ Tbsp. salt
2 Tbsp. paprika
1½ Tbsp. flour or garlic powder

1½ Tbsp. onion powder
1 Tbsp. chili powder

Combine ingredients and store in shaker. Makes ½ cup. One teaspoon seasoning contains ¼ teaspoon salt (500 milligrams sodium).

Jane Klein, Bellevue, WA

SWEET AND SOUR PORK

¼ c. brown sugar
2 Tbsp. cornstarch
¼ c. cider vinegar
2 Tbsp. soy sauce
1 (8¼ oz.) can pineapple
   chunks, drained (juice
   reserved)

1 lb. boneless pork, cut in ½ to
   ¾ inch cubes
1 (5 oz.) can water chestnuts,
   drained and sliced
1 medium green pepper, cut in
   ¼ inch strips
½ chopped onion

Combine sugar and cornstarch in 1½ to 2 quart casserole. Stir in vinegar, soy sauce, and pineapple juice. Add pork; cover. Microwave at HIGH for 2 minutes. Reduce power to 50% (MEDIUM). Microwave for 10 to 15 minutes or until pork is no longer pink in center, stirring once or twice. Add water chestnuts, green pepper, and onion; cover. Microwave for 4 to 6 minutes until pepper is tender crisp, stirring once during cooking. Mix in pineapple chunks. Serve over rice or fried noodles. Serves 4.

David Janz, Dickinson, ND

SWEET-SOUR MEAT BALLS

1 finely chopped onion
¾ tsp. season salt
1 can tomato soup
3 Tbsp. lemon juice

¼ c. firmly packed brown sugar
1 lb. ground beef
1 (13 to 14 oz.) can drained
   pineapple chunks

Combine first 5 ingredients in 1½ quart casserole and microwave, covered, for 7 minutes, stirring occasionally. Meanwhile, make small meat balls out of the ground beef. Place them in the sauce, spooning some sauce over them. Microwave for 7 minutes; stir once at 3½ minutes. Stir in pineapple and microwave for 1 minute. Serve on toothpicks as an appetizer or serve with rice as a main dish.

Mary Ann Ohman, Fargo, ND

SWEET AND SOUR MEATBALLS

1 lb. lean ground beef	1 Tbsp. oil
1 c. soft bread crumbs	1 clove garlic, peeled and
1 egg, slightly beaten	crushed
¼ tsp. salt	¼ c. chopped onion
¼ tsp. ground coriander	1 (8½ oz.) can water chestnuts
2 Tbsp. prepared horseradish	1 (15½ oz.) can unsweetened
Cornstarch	pineapple chunks, drained
½ c. oil (if preparing in wok)	(reserve ½ c. juice)
1 (10 oz.) pkg. frozen Brussels	Sweet and Sour Sauce
sprouts	2 c. hot cooked rice

Combine first 6 ingredients; mix thoroughly and shape into about 8 small balls. Roll each ball in cornstarch. (If using wok, heat ½ cup oil to 375°F. Fry few meatballs until browned; set aside.) Cook meatballs in microwave for about 5 minutes on MEDIUM HIGH power; set aside.

Cook Brussels sprouts in covered casserole dish on HIGH for about 4 to 5 minutes till tender; set aside. In serving dish, cook 1 tablespoon oil and clove of garlic till browned, 15 to 20 seconds (approximately) on HIGH. Remove and discard garlic. Add onion and cook about 15 to 20 seconds on HIGH. Add Brussels sprouts, meatballs, water chestnuts, and pineapple chunks. Pour on Sweet and Sour Sauce; stir. Cook till heated through, about 5 minutes on MEDIUM HIGH power. Serve over hot cooked rice. Makes 4 servings.

Sweet and Sour Sauce:

⅓ c. sugar	2 Tbsp. cornstarch, dissolved in
⅓ c. cider vinegar	½ c. reserved pineapple
2 Tbsp. soy sauce	juice (from canned
2 Tbsp. sherry	pineapple chunks)
¼ c. tomato sauce or catsup	

Combine all ingredients; cook on MEDIUM power, stirring occasionally, till sauce is thickened.

Clayone Carlson (Roy B.), Fargo, ND

MOCK CHOW MEIN
(Microwave or conventional oven)

1 lb. ground lean beef *or* pork (or combination)
1 medium onion, chopped
1 c. thinly sliced celery
4 c. shredded unpeeled zucchini
2 tsp. instant beef bouillon granules or bouillon cubes
1 (4 oz.) can mushrooms, drained *or* 1 (8 oz.) can

sliced water chestnuts *or* bamboo shoots, drained
3 to 4 Tbsp. soy sauce
½ c. instant rice
¾ c. water
⅛ tsp. black pepper
Chow mein noodles

Place meat and onion in microwave-safe 2 to 2½ quart casserole. Microwave (HIGH) for 4½ to 5½ minutes or until meat is no longer pink, stirring once. Stir in remaining ingredients, except chow mein noodles. Cover with lid; microwave (HIGH) for 10 to 15 minutes, stirring once. Let stand, covered, for 5 minutes. Serve on chow mein noodles. Makes 8 servings.

Conventional oven: Bake at 350° for 30 minutes.

Each serving: 185 calories, 15 grams protein, 8 grams fat, 15 grams carbohydrates, 661 milligrams sodium, 43 milligrams cholesterol.

Margaret Hulst, Waltham, MN

STUFFED GREEN PEPPERS

4 large green peppers
1 lb. ground beef
1 medium onion, finely chopped
1 tsp. salt

¼ tsp. pepper
1½ c. cooked rice
1 (16 oz.) can tomato sauce

Wash peppers; cut in halves lengthwise and remove seeds and white membrane. Crumble beef into a 1½ quart casserole. Add onion; cook, uncovered, on HIGH for about 5 minutes, stirring once during cooking period. Cook until meat loses its red color.

Stir in salt, pepper, rice, and ½ of the tomato sauce. Fill green pepper halves with mixture, mounding mixture on top. Place in a glass baking dish. Top each pepper with a dribble of remaining tomato sauce. Cook, covered, on HIGH for 8 to 10 minutes or just until peppers are tender.

Bonnie Gunderson, Fargo, ND

STUFFED PEPPER POT
(Serves 4)

4 large green peppers
1 lb. lean ground beef
1 small chopped onion
2 c. cooked rice

1 (8 oz.) can tomato sauce
2 Tbsp. chopped celery
1 tsp. salt
Dash of pepper

To be prepared on *baking sheet.* Cut thin slice from stem end of pepper. Remove seeds with teaspoon; discard. In 1½ quart glass casserole, combine onion and ground beef; place in microwave oven and cook for 2 to 3 minutes on FULL power or until onion becomes transparent and beef slightly brown.

Add remaining ingredients, except peppers; mix well. Stuff peppers with mixture and place on baking sheet. Cover with plastic wrap and microwave for 12 to 15 minutes on ⅔ power (MEDIUM HIGH).

For conventional oven: Combine onion and hamburger in skillet; brown lightly on stove top at medium high heat. Assemble as directed. Bake at 350°F. for 45 minutes.

Betty Risse, Bismarck, ND

GOLD NUGGET BEEF LOAF

1½ lb. ground beef
½ c. applesauce
1¼ tsp. salt
¼ tsp. nutmeg
⅛ tsp. pepper

1 c. coarse soft bread crumbs
1 small onion, finely chopped
1 egg
4 oz. Cheddar cheese

Combine applesauce, salt, nutmeg, and pepper. Add ground beef, bread crumbs, onion, and egg, mixing lightly but thoroughly. Cut cheese into ½ inch cubes and fold into meat mixture. Place in 9 inch round microwave-safe baking dish, pressing lightly to flatten top. Form a hole about 1 inch in diameter in center of loaf. Cover with waxed paper; microwave at HIGH for 8 minutes or MEDIUM for 12 minutes. Rotate dish ½ turn and continue cooking at HIGH for 6½ minutes or at MEDIUM for 12 minutes. Let stand for 10 minutes before serving. Cut in wedges. Makes 6 servings.

Marlys Swehla, Albert Lea, MN

FOUR BEAN HOTDISH

½ lb. ground beef
½ tsp. salt
½ lb. bacon, cut up
1 onion
1 can butter beans, drained
1 can lima beans, drained
1 can kidney beans, drained

1 large can pork and beans
½ c. brown sugar
½ tsp. mustard
2 Tbsp. molasses
¼ c. white sugar
¼ c. catsup

Brown ground beef, onion, and bacon in a 2½ quart casserole. Add remaining ingredients and stir thoroughly. Microwave on HIGH for 10 to 15 minutes till boiling. Turn to simmer and cook for 30 to 40 minutes longer.

Ruth Weis, Bemidji, MN

LASAGNA

1 lb. hamburger
2 cloves minced garlic
1 (6 oz.) can tomato paste
2 Tbsp. olive oil

1 can tomatoes
½ tsp. pepper
½ tsp. oregano
1 tsp. salt

Brown hamburger and garlic. Add other ingredients and simmer for 20 minutes. Meanwhile, boil lasagna noodles with salt and olive oil added to water. When done, drain and alternate layers of noodles, sauce, and cheese for 3 layers as follows: Sparingly with Kraft cheese on first layer, Mozzarella on second layer, and sparingly with Kraft topped with Mozzarella on top layer. Be generous with the Mozzarella. Bake for about ½ hour in moderate (350°) oven.

Bonnie Gunderson, Fargo, ND

MICROWAVE MEAT BALL STEW

1½ lb. hamburger
1 egg, beaten
¼ c. chopped onion
1 c. bread crumbs

2 Tbsp. shortening
1 tsp. salt
¼ tsp. pepper

Mix together all but the shortening. Make into 24 meat balls; brown in shortening. Pour off excess fat.

Add:

1 can tomato soup
1 c. beef broth
1 c. diced carrots

1 c. potatoes, cut in medium
chunks
1 large onion, cut in chunks

Cook all vegetables first. Put in casserole and place in the microwave with plastic on top for 12 minutes.

Emma Buhl, Long Prairie, MN

EASY BEEF STEW
(Microwave)

2 Tbsp. beef drippings
1 medium onion, peeled and
finely chopped
1 bay leaf
1 c. cooked carrots
1 c. cooked potatoes

½ tsp. salt
½ tsp. celery seed
2 c. gravy, *made in roasting pan*
2 c. cubed cooked roast beef
Paprika

1. Heat drippings in 8 inch glass baking dish in microwave oven until hot, 20 to 30 seconds.
2. Add onion; cook for 3 minutes on HIGH.

3. Add remaining ingredients, except paprika, to onion. Mix and cover with wax paper. Cook for about 8 minutes at HIGH. Stir a couple times. Sprinkle paprika before serving. Makes 4 servings.

Mrs. Goldie Mikish, Staples, MN

MUSHROOM BEEF RICE

3 c. cooked rice
8 slices cooked beef roast
1 (10¾ oz.) can condensed
   cream of mushroom soup

¼ c. milk
1 tsp. leaf basil
½ tsp. salt
½ tsp. dried parsley flakes

1. Place rice in a 2 quart (8x8 inch) glass baking dish. Top with beef slices. Combine soup, milk, and seasonings in a 4 cup measure. Pour over meat and rice. Cover with plastic wrap.

2. Microwave on REHEAT for 10 to 12 minutes. Let stand, covered, for 5 minutes before serving. This layered casserole does not need stirring. Makes 3 to 4 servings.

Eileen Rekowski, St. Cloud, MN

STIR-FRY TOMATO BEEF
(Microwave)

A cooking school favorite and picture pretty!

2 lb. sirloin, round, flank, or
   chuck steak
2 Tbsp. sugar
½ c. soy sauce
1 clove minced garlic
¼ tsp. ginger
3 Tbsp. salad oil

2 large green peppers, cut in
   strips
3 green onions (1 inch slices
   with tops)
2 large tomatoes, cut in wedges
1 Tbsp. cornstarch
¼ c. water

Slice steak diagonally across grain in ⅛ inch thick slices. (Freeze for 30 minutes to slice easier.) In 2 cup glass measure, combine sugar, soy sauce, garlic, and ginger. Pour over meat in medium bowl; marinate for 30 minutes, turning meat after 15 minutes.

Preheat browning skillet (HIGH) for 6 minutes or fry pan on range until very hot. Remove meat from marinade, reserving extra. Add oil and meat. Microwave (HIGH) for 5 to 6 minutes, stirring halfway through cooking. Add green peppers and onions. Microwave (HIGH) for 3 to 4 minutes, stirring halfway through cooking.

Top with tomato wedges. In 1 cup glass measure, combine cornstarch, water, and remaining marinade. Microwave (HIGH) for 1 to 2 minutes, stirring once or twice until thick. Pour over stir-fry. Microwave (HIGH) for 1 to 2 minutes more. Rest for 5 minutes. Serve on cooked rice. Serves 6 to 8.

This is a favorite from "Let's Cook Microwave" by Barbara Harris.

Jane Klein, Bellevue, WA

MICROWAVE COOKING
(Makes 4 servings)

2 Tbsp. butter
1 lb. boneless round steak, cut
    into thin strips
½ c. finely chopped onion
Salt and pepper to taste
1 (¾ oz.) pkg. mushroom gravy
    mix

1 c. water
1 (4½ oz.) jar mushrooms,
    drained
½ c. sour cream

In 8 inch round baking dish, heat butter on HIGH for 1 to 2 minutes. Stir in steak, onion, salt, and pepper; cover. Heat on HIGH for 8 to 9 minutes, stirring occasionally. Let stand, covered, for 5 minutes.

Meanwhile, in a glass bowl, combine gravy mix, water, and mushrooms. Heat at HIGH for 4 to 5 minutes or until thickened, stirring twice. Stir in sour cream until smooth. Blend gravy with steak. If necessary, heat at LOW for 2 to 3 minutes just before serving.

Patricia Gingerelli

VEGETABLES

HARVARD BEETS
(Serves 4)

2 tsp. cornstarch
¼ tsp. salt (optional)
Dash of pepper
Dash of ground cloves
2 Tbsp. cider vinegar

1 (16 oz.) can sliced beets,
   drained (⅓ c. liquid
   reserved)
1 Tbsp. orange juice

In 1 quart casserole, combine cornstarch, salt, pepper, and cloves. Blend in vinegar, beet liquid, and orange juice. Microwave at HIGH for 1 to 2 minutes or until clear and thickened, stirring every minute. Add beets. Microwave at HIGH for 1 to 4 minutes or until beets are thoroughly heated. Calories per serving: 40.

Lois Haworth, Fargo, ND

CHEESY BROCCOLI CASSEROLE

2 (10 oz.) pkg. frozen chopped
   broccoli
1 (10¾ oz.) can condensed
   cream of mushroom soup
1 (5 oz.) can water chestnuts,
   drained and sliced

½ tsp. seasoned salt
4 oz. process cheese spread,
   sliced
2 Tbsp. oleo
⅓ c. dry bread crumbs

1. Place broccoli in fluted baking dish; cover with waxed paper.
2. Microwave for 10 to 12 minutes or until thawed; drain. Stir in soup, chestnuts, and salt. Arrange evenly in dish. Top with cheese slices.
3. Microwave oleo in glass dish for ½ minute or until melted. Stir in crumbs; sprinkle over cheese.
4. Microwave, uncovered, for 10 to 12 minutes or until heated through, rotating dish once or twice. Makes 6 to 8 servings.

Dessa Clafton

CHEESY BROCCOLI ONION CASSEROLE

2 (10 oz.) pkg. frozen chopped
   broccoli
1 can condensed cream of
   mushroom soup
1 (16 oz.) can whole onions,
   drained

½ tsp. seasoned salt
4 oz. process cheese spread,
   sliced
2 Tbsp. butter
⅓ c. dry bread crumbs

Microwave broccoli in covered 1½ quart glass casserole for 10 to 12 minutes or until thawed; drain. Stir in soup, onions, and salt. Top with cheese slices. Microwave butter in glass dish for ½ minute or until melted. Stir in crumbs. Sprinkle over cheese. Microwave, uncovered, for 10 to 12 minutes, rotating dish twice. Makes 6 to 8 servings.

Mary Ann Ohman, Fargo, ND

CREAMY CABBAGE

1 medium head cabbage
2 Tbsp. water
1 (3 oz.) pkg. cream cheese
2 Tbsp. milk
½ tsp. salt
½ tsp. celery seed
Dash of pepper

Shred cabbage into 1½ quart glass casserole. Add water. Microwave, covered, for 7 to 9 minutes, stirring once. Add remaining ingredients. Microwave, covered, for 1 minute or until cheese is softened. Stir lightly to mix. Garnish with paprika. Serves 5 to 6.

Mary Ann Ohman, Fargo, ND

CARROT CASSEROLE
(Makes about 5 servings)

3 c. (about 6 medium) shredded
   carrots
1 egg, slightly beaten
½ c. crushed soda crackers
   (about 12 sq.)
¾ c. milk
½ c. (2 oz.) shredded Cheddar
   cheese
¼ c. water
2 tsp. instant onions, minced
½ tsp. salt
Dash of pepper

1. Combine carrots and water in 1 quart microwave-safe casserole. Cover with casserole lid.
2. Microwave (HIGH) for 4½ to 5 minutes or until tender, stirring once. Mix in remaining ingredients, except cheese. Cover with casserole lid.
3. Microwave (HIGH) for 4 minutes. Stir to move cooked portion to center.
4. Microwave (MEDIUM - 50%) for 4 to 5 minutes or until center is set, rotating dish once. Sprinkle with cheese. Let stand, covered, until melted.

Note: Dry bread crumbs can be substituted for cracker crumbs.

Lorraine Follsath, Anoka, MN

FROSTED CAULIFLOWER

1 medium head cauliflower (1¼
   to 1½ lb.)
2 Tbsp. water
½ tsp. salt
½ c. mayonnaise
1 tsp. finely chopped onion
1 to 2 tsp. prepared mustard
3 oz. shredded Cheddar cheese
   (about ¾ c.)
Paprika

Remove outer leaves of cauliflower; cut out core, leaving head whole. Place cauliflower in a 1½ quart casserole. Add water and salt. Microwave, covered, on HIGH for 6 to 7 minutes per pound; rotate dish ¼ turn halfway through cooking time. Let stand, covered, for 5 minutes; drain.

Combine mayonnaise, mustard, and onion; spread over cooked cauliflower. Sprinkle with cheese. Microwave at 50% power for 1 minute till cheese melts. Sprinkle lightly with paprika. Makes 4 to 6 servings.

Diane Kemmetmueller, Anoka, MN

AU GRATIN POTATOES

10 medium potatoes, peeled and cut into small cubes
2 Tbsp. water
2 c. (8 oz.) shredded Cheddar cheese
1 tsp. salt

2 c. (1 pt.) half & half or whipping cream
2 Tbsp. butter or margarine
½ c. dry bread crumbs
½ tsp. paprika

1. Combine potatoes and water in 3 quart glass casserole. Cover with casserole lid.
2. Microwave (HIGH) for 18 to 22 minutes or until potatoes are just about tender, stirring twice.
3. Stir cheese and salt into potatoes. Pour half & half over all.
4. Microwave (HIGH), uncovered, for 10 to 12 minutes or until cheese melts and sauce thickens, stirring once or twice; set aside.
5. Microwave (HIGH) butter in 1 cup glass measure for 15 to 30 seconds or until melted. Stir in bread crumbs and paprika. Sprinkle over potatoes.
6. Microwave (HIGH) for 1 to 2 minutes or until heated through. Makes about 10 servings, 320 calories each.

Tip: Casserole can be prepared ahead through step 3. Refrigerate and increase time in step 4 to 20 to 22 minutes.

Joan Cooney, St. Cloud, MN

BAKED POTATOES
(Serves 2)

2 baking potatoes
Chopped cooked bacon

Sour cream or butter

Unwrap potatoes and prick all over with knife or fork. Set in oven and microwave for 15 minutes on HIGH setting. Turn potatoes over once during cooking (about halfway through). Cut potatoes open and dress as desired.

Arlene Byrne, Rochester, MN

CHILI POTATOES

Bake potatoes in microwave, sliced in a dish, on HIGH. Take Hormel chili and Cheddar cheese; put on top. Heat for 2 minutes on top of potatoes on MEDIUM, covered, in microwave. Garnish with sour cream and chives.

Karla Oeltjenbruns, Owatonna, MN

POTATO LASAGNA
(Serves 6 to 8)

Raw potatoes, sliced
Onion
2 (8 oz.) cans tomato sauce
Mozzarella cheese

2 lb. hamburger
1 can Cheddar cheese soup
Oregano

Line a 9x13 inch cake pan with 2 layers of potatoes. Brown hamburger and onion; drain. Add soup with onion and hamburger. Pour over potatoes. Spread tomato sauce over mixture and sprinkle with oregano. Bake for 1 to 1¼ hours or until done, at 350°, covered with foil. Sprinkle cheese over the potatoes the last 5 minutes.

Note: Cooking size depends on the size of pan used. Freezes well. Good for quick warm ups in microwave.

Elaine Majerus

DELUXE POTATOES

1 (24 oz.) pkg. frozen hash
   brown potatoes
2 Tbsp. chopped green onion
2 Tbsp. chopped green pepper
1 (10¾ oz.) can condensed
   cream of potato soup

1 (10¾ oz.) can condensed
   cream of celery soup
1 c. (8 oz.) sour cream
⅛ tsp. paprika
½ tsp. parsley flakes

1. Combine hash browns, onion, and green pepper in 1½ quart glass casserole. Cover with casserole lid.
2. Microwave (HIGH) for 9 to 10 minutes or until steaming hot, stirring once. Add soups and sour cream; mix well. Cover.
3. Microwave (HIGH) for 10 to 12 minutes or until heated through, stirring once. Sprinkle with paprika and parsley flakes. Makes about 8 servings.

Dessa Clafton

POTATOES-PARMESAN CHEESE

3 medium potatoes

Parmesan cheese

Melt butter in microwave pie plate. Wash potatoes (do not peel); cut in halves. Coat potatoes with melted butter on all sides. Put cut side up on plate. Sprinkle with Parmesan cheese and cover with waxed paper. Cook on HIGH for 10 minutes or until done.

Harlan Brekke, Fargo, ND

PARMESAN POTATOES

Dice raw potatoes into bite-size chunks; place in microwave casserole. Sprinkle with:

Parmesan cheese **Lemon pepper**
Garlic powder

Dot with butter. Cover with Saran Wrap. Micro on HIGH for 10 minutes or until tender.

Bonnie Gunderson, Fargo, ND

MICROWAVE SCALLOPED POTATOES

1¼ c. sliced potatoes **Pepper**
Nonfat dry milk **Paprika**
Onion

Peel and slice potatoes and place slices into cold water. Butter a small casserole. Place a layer of drained sliced potatoes in bottom of casserole. Sprinkle with nonfat dry milk. Add a thin slice of onion and sprinkle on some pepper. Continue layering until you use all the potato slices. Top with butter and paprika. Cook, covered, for 6 to 7 minutes (cover with wax paper).

Barbara Kaste, Fargo, ND

FANTASTIC POTATO SALAD

7 c. cubed cooked potatoes **½ c. cubed cooked ham**
2 c. chopped celery **½ c. chopped onion**
1 c. commercial sour cream **2 Tbsp. sugar (optional)**
1 Tbsp. prepared mustard **1 Tbsp. salt (may be omitted)**
2 env. unflavored gelatin **½ c. chopped green pepper**
Strips of green pepper **8 hard cooked eggs**
1 c. buttermilk **2 c. mayonnaise**
4 radishes, sliced

Oil 12 cup Bundt pan. Slice 2 of hard cooked eggs into 8 slices; place 1 slice in large flutes in bottom of pan. Lay strips of green pepper in narrow flutes. Place radish slices on sides in larger flutes.

In saucepan, combine gelatin and buttermilk; heat over medium heat, stirring until gelatin is dissolved; *cool.* In large bowl, combine all ingredients and gelatin mixture. Heap the salad into Bundt pan; press firmly into place. Cover and refrigerate until set, preferably overnight.

To unmold, use a thin narrow plastic knife or spatula and loosen center core of salad. Unmold on serving plate and serve with additional mayonnaise if desired.

Lorraine Follsath, Anoka, MN

HOT GERMAN POTATO SALAD

6 strips bacon
4 medium potatoes
½ c. sugar
2 Tbsp. flour
1½ tsp. salt
½ tsp. celery salt

¼ tsp. dry mustard
Dash of pepper
1 c. water
½ c. vinegar
¼ c. chopped onion
¼ c. chopped celery

Place bacon in a 2 quart casserole; cover with a paper towel. Microwave on HIGH (100%) for 4 to 5 minutes. Remove bacon from drippings. Crumble and set aside. Wash and pierce surface of potatoes. Microwave on HIGH (100%) for 8 to 10 minutes. Wrap in foil and allow to stand for 5 minutes.

While potatoes are standing, stir sugar, flour, and seasonings into bacon fat until smooth. Add water, vinegar, onion, and celery; microwave on HIGH (100%) for 4 to 6 minutes or until thickened. Peel and slice potatoes ⅛ inch thick or dice into ½ inch cubes. Toss gently into sauce. Sprinkle top with crumbled bacon. Microwave on HIGH (100%) for 2 to 3 minutes or until hot and bubbly. Makes 4 to 6 servings.

Carol Gilbertson, Hawley, MN

HOT GERMAN POTATO SALAD
(Microwave)

4 slices bacon, diced
¼ c. finely chopped onion
3 tsp. flour
⅓ c. cider vinegar
2 Tbsp. brown sugar

¼ tsp. celery seed
Salt and pepper to taste
4 medium potatoes, baked,
    peeled, and sliced

Set power select at HIGH. In oblong baking dish, heat bacon and onion for 3½ to 5 minutes, stirring occasionally. Stir in flour, vinegar, sugar, celery seed, salt, and pepper; heat for 1 to 1½ minutes or until slightly thickened, stirring once. Add potatoes and heat for 3 to 4 minutes or until heated through, stirring once. Serve warm.

May substitute 2 (16 ounce) cans sliced potatoes, drained, for the baked potatoes.

Clayone Carlson (Roy B.), Fargo, ND

VEGETARIANS DINNER
(Serves 4)

1 large eggplant, sliced
    lengthwise into 8 pieces, ¼
    inch thick
3 ripe tomatoes, sliced

1½ c. spaghetti sauce
½ c. grated Mozzarella cheese
Salt and pepper

Arrange eggplant slices in dish. Top with tomato and season generously. Cover with remaining eggplant slices. Pour spaghetti sauce over and cover with Saran Wrap. Microwave on HIGH setting for 15 minutes. Add cheese and microwave for 3 minutes, uncovered. Calories: 188 per serving. Utensils: 2 quart rectangular dish.

Arlene Byrne, Rochester, MN

SUMMER GARDEN TREAT

1½ lb. fresh broccoli
2 to 3 small zucchini
3 Tbsp. margarine or butter
½ tsp. garlic salt

½ head cauliflower
2 tomatoes, cut into wedges
¼ c. Parmesan cheese
¼ tsp. thyme

Wash broccoli and cut into pieces about 2½ inches long. Trim stalks to about ¼ inch thick. Place toward the edge of a 12 inch glass serving plate or glass pizza dish with flower ends toward center of dish. Cut the cauliflower into flowerets. Place between broccoli. Slice zucchini and mound in center of plate. Cover with plastic wrap.

In a measuring cup, combine margarine, garlic salt, and thyme; set aside. Microwave vegetables at FULL power for 9 to 11 minutes or until tender. Microwave margarine mixture till melted (about 1 minute). Drain excess liquid from vegetables. Remove plastic wrap.

Arrange tomato wedges over other vegetables. Drizzle margarine mixture over top and sprinkle with Parmesan cheese. Microwave (FULL power), uncovered, an additional 1½ to 2 minutes or until tomatoes are heated.

Note: This works with any assortment of vegetables with a similar cooking time. If you are using a vegetable that requires a longer cooking time, just partially cook before assembling.

Absolutely delicious - even as a leftover - cold.

Peggy Mielke, Chisholm, MN

DILLED ZUCCHINI

In 1½ quart casserole, combine:

6 c. sliced zucchini
¼ c. water

½ tsp. salt

Cover and micro-cook until almost done (about 10 minutes), stirring twice. Keep hot while preparing Dill Sauce.

2 Tbsp. butter
1 Tbsp. flour
1 tsp. lemon juice
½ tsp. salt

½ tsp. paprika
½ tsp. dried dill weed
½ c. milk

In 2 cup micro dish, melt butter (about 30 seconds). Blend in flour, lemon juice, salt, paprika, and dill weed. Stir in milk; cook, uncovered, in microwave until sauce is thick and bubbly, stirring every 30 seconds. Drain cooked zucchini. Pour Dill Sauce over zucchini and mix. If necessary, micro till hot. Makes 6 servings.

Bonnie Gunderson, Fargo, ND

GARDEN VEGETABLE CASSEROLE
(Makes 4 servings)

2 small yellow summer squash,
    sliced
1 medium zucchini, sliced
1 small white onion, sliced
1 tomato, sliced

2 Tbsp. grated Parmesan
    cheese
½ tsp. seasoned salt
½ tsp. basil
½ tsp. thyme

To be prepared in *Versatility pan.* Place all sliced vegetables in Versatility pan and mix all other ingredients. Toss lightly. Cover and microwave on FULL power for 8 to 10 minutes.

For conventional oven: Place in oven for 20 to 25 minutes at 350°F.

Betty Risse, Bismarck, ND

DESSERTS

BAKED APPLES

4 apples
Brown sugar replacement

Margarine (diet)
Cinnamon

Core apples and place in 1 quart casserole. Place 1 tablespoon brown sugar replacement in core of each apple. Sprinkle with cinnamon and top with 1 teaspoon diet margarine. Cover with plastic wrap (venting opposite corners) and bake on FULL power for 5 to 8 minutes until apples are tender. Serves 4.

Elaine Rolerat, East Grand Forks, MN

BAKED APPLES
(Microwave on diet)

4 medium apples
⅓ c. diet raspberry soda

¼ tsp. cinnamon

Core apples, leaving ½ inch of bottom intact. Place in custard cups. Combine soda and cinnamon in 1 cup measure. Spoon mixture into centers of apples. Cover each apple loosely with plastic wrap. Microwave at HIGH for 4 to 5½ minutes or until apples are fork tender, rearranging and rotating apples after ½ the time. Let stand for 2 minutes. Serve warm. Serves 4.

Variations - Rum Baked Apples: Combine ⅓ cup diet cream soda, ½ teaspoon rum extract, ¼ teaspoon cinnamon, and ⅛ teaspoon ginger for filling.

Maple Baked Apples: Combine ⅓ cup diet cream soda, ½ teaspoon maple extract, ¼ teaspoon nutmeg, and ¼ teaspoon allspice for filling. Calories: 88.

Lois Haworth, Fargo, ND

APPLE DESSERT

6 c. apples, peeled, cored, and
　　sliced
3 Tbsp. honey
1 Tbsp. lemon juice
¼ tsp. salt
¼ tsp. nutmeg
1 Tbsp. grated orange rind

1 c. Wheat Chex cereal, crushed
½ c. unsifted all-purpose flour
1 tsp. cinnamon
½ c. firmly packed brown sugar
½ c. chopped roasted salted
　　almonds
¼ c. butter

Place apple slices in 2 quart glass baking dish. Combine in a small bowl the honey, lemon juice, salt, nutmeg, and orange rind. Pour over apple slices and mix into apples with fork. Combine crushed cereal, flour, cinnamon, brown sugar, and almonds in a medium bowl. Cut in butter until crumbly. Sprinkle evenly over apples. Microwave on HIGH for 14 to 16 minutes or until apples are tender. Serves 6 to 8.

Mary Ann Ohman, Fargo, ND

SPICED PEACHES

1 (29 oz.) can peach halves
½ c. packed brown sugar
½ c. white vinegar

1 cinnamon stick, broken
Whole cloves

1. Drain peach syrup into 2 cup glass measure. Add brown sugar, vinegar, and cinnamon, stirring until smooth.
2. Microwave (HIGH), uncovered, for 3 to 4 minutes or until mixture boils, stirring once.
3. Stud each peach half with 3 cloves. Divide peaches between 2 pint jars. Pour hot syrup over peaches; cover and refrigerate. Makes 2 pints, 80 calories/peach.

Joan Cooney, St. Cloud, MN

PEACH CRISP
(Microwave dessert)

3 (16 oz.) cans peach halves,
    drained and cut in halves
⅓ c. butter or margarine
⅓ c. all-purpose flour
1 c. uncooked oats (quick or
    old-fashioned)

½ c. packed brown sugar
½ tsp. salt
¼ tsp. ground cinnamon
¼ tsp. ground nutmeg

Arrange peaches in an 8 inch square glass baking dish. Melt butter in small glass bowl in micro oven for 45 to 60 seconds on HIGH. Mix flour, oats, brown sugar, salt, cinnamon, and nutmeg in a bowl. Add melted butter and mix until crumbly. Sprinkle crumb mixture over peaches. Cook, uncovered, in micro oven for 7 to 8 minutes on HIGH; rotate dish 1 quarter turn once. Makes 8 servings.

Millie Perrault, Duluth, MN

EASY RICE PUDDING

2¼ c. milk
½ c. Minute rice
⅔ c. raisins

1 regular pkg. vanilla pudding
    mix

Combine all ingredients and cook on HIGH for 7 to 10 minutes. Stir twice. Butterscotch pudding can be used instead of vanilla.

Harlan Brekke, Fargo, ND

EASY RICE PUDDING

1 (2¾ oz.) pkg. egg custard mix
2 c. milk
1½ c. cooked rice

½ c. raisins
Nutmeg

Pour egg custard mix into bowl; gradually stir in milk until smooth. Add rice and raisins; mix well. Cook, uncovered, in 1 quart glass casserole in microwave oven for 4 minutes; stir well. Cook for 3 minutes longer. Stir again. Sprinkle nutmeg over top of pudding (may want to stick it in a little longer). Serves 4.

Bonnie Sorby

SWIRLED AMARETTO CHEESECAKE

Crust:

¼ c. butter or margarine
1 c. graham cracker crumbs
   (about 12 sq.)

2 Tbsp. sugar
¼ tsp. cinnamon

Filling:

2 (8 oz.) pkg. cream cheese
⅔ c. sugar
3 eggs
1 c. (8 oz.) sour cream
1 tsp. vanilla

2 Tbsp. unsweetened cocoa
2 Tbsp. sugar
3 Tbsp. Amaretto liqueur or 1
   Tbsp. liqueur flavoring

1. Microwave (HIGH) butter in 8 inch round glass baking dish for 30 to 60 seconds or until melted. Stir in crumbs, sugar, and cinnamon until thoroughly combined. Press into bottom and up sides of dish; set aside.

2. Microwave (HIGH) cream cheese in 2 quart glass mix 'n pour bowl for 1 to 1 ½ minutes or until softened; beat until creamy. Mix in ⅔ cup sugar until smooth. Add eggs, 1 at a time, beating well after each. Blend in sour cream and vanilla. Pour ½ (about 2 cups) of mixture into crust. Combine cocoa and 2 tablespoons sugar; mix well. Add to remaining mixture along with Amaretto; mix well. Pour over vanilla filling, allowing chocolate to swirl through vanilla.

3. Microwave (MEDIUM - 50%), uncovered, for 15 to 18 minutes or until center is almost set, rotating dish twice. Cool and refrigerate at least 6 hours before serving. Store, covered, in refrigerator. Makes about 10 servings, 395 calories each.

Joan Cooney, St. Cloud, MN

EASY RHUBARB CRISP

4 c. sliced rhubarb
1 c. sugar

2 Tbsp. flour
1 egg, slightly beaten

Combine rhubarb, sugar, 2 tablespoons flour, and egg in 8 inch round glass baking dish; mix until evenly combined.

Topping:

½ c. unsifted all-purpose flour
½ c. rolled oats
⅓ c. packed brown sugar

¼ tsp. nutmeg
¼ c. oleo or butter

Combine flour, oats, brown sugar, and nutmeg. Cut in oleo until crumbly. Sprinkle over rhubarb. Microwave (HIGH), uncovered, for 12 to 14 minutes or until rhubarb is tender, rotating dish once or twice. For a crisp topping, put under broiler for a few minutes.

Dessa Clafton

RHUBARB CRISP

4 c. rhubarb, cut in ½ inch
    pieces
1 c. sugar
1¼ c. flour
½ tsp. cinnamon

½ c. water
½ c. rolled oats
1 c. firmly packed brown sugar
½ c. butter

Combine rhubarb, sugar, ¼ cup of the flour, cinnamon, and water in an 8x8 inch glass baking dish; stir to mix well. Cover tightly with plastic wrap; microwave for 5 minutes on HIGH.

Mix together the remaining 1 cup of flour, oats, and brown sugar in large bowl. Cut in butter with pastry blender to make a crumb mixture. Sprinkle topping evenly over cooked rhubarb mixture. *Do not* cover. Microwave for 10 minutes on HIGH, turning dish ¼ turn after 5 minutes. Topping should be golden brown and rhubarb tender when finished.

Sandi Erickson, Montevideo, MN

MICROWAVE PUMPKIN

Don't throw away those Halloween pumpkins - use for bars, cakes, cookies, and pies.

Remove skin; cut in chunks and put into microwave casserole dish. Pour in ¼ cup of water and cover with Saran Wrap. Poke 3 or 4 holes in Saran Wrap; cover casserole dish and microwave for about 10 to 15 minutes (until tender). Drain, mash, and freeze in 2 cup containers. Take any pumpkin recipe and use this pumpkin instead of canned.

It makes the most delicious pumpkin Bundt cake.

Marylou Wallner, Plymouth, MN

HOW TO MICROWAVE PUMPKIN

First, microwave it on HIGH for 2 minutes. Pierce the skin for steam to vent. Use an ice pick and make 4 holes in different areas of the pumpkin. Complete microwaving on HIGH, turning the pumpkin over after ½ the cooking time. Let stand until cool enough to handle. Cut pumpkin open, remove seeds, and scrape pulp from shell. Puree pulp in blender. Takes 6 to 7 minutes per pound, so weigh the pumpkin. Two pounds of fresh pumpkin yields 2 cups of cooked pumpkin.

Maryls Swehla, Albert Lea, MN

FROSTING

1 (3 oz.) pkg. cream cheese
1 Tbsp. butter or margarine
2 c. powdered sugar

1 or 2 Tbsp. milk
¼ tsp. vanilla

Mix all ingredients together.

MaryLou Wallner, Plymouth, MN

DELUXE RICE CEREAL BARS
(Easy and good)

6 oz. (about 3 sq.) white
   chocolate coating
1 c. crunchy peanut butter

4 c. crisp rice cereal
1 c. salted peanuts

Combine coating and peanut butter in 2 quart glass mix 'n pour bowl. Microwave on HIGH, uncovered, for 2½ to 3 minutes or until coating is melted, stirring twice. Add cereal and peanuts; mix until coated. Press into buttered 12x8 inch or 13x9 inch pan. Refrigerate until set, about 1 hour. Cut into squares. Makes about 24 bars.

Lorraine Follsath, Anoka, MN

BRAN BARS
(For fiber)

¼ c. margarine (or butter)
5 c. miniature marshmallows (or
   40 large marshmallows)
3 c. raisin bran cereal

2 c. Fiber One (or any 100% bran
   cereal, or any other cereal
   as desired)
½ c. nuts (optional)

In a 3 quart microwave dish, melt the margarine (or butter) on HIGH for 1 minute. Add marshmallows and cook, covered, on HIGH (MAXIMUM power) for 2 to 2 ½ minutes until soft. Stir and mix in cereals. Press into a Pam sprayed 9x13 inch pan. Cool and cut into bars.

MICROWAVE LEMON BARS

1 c. all-purpose flour
½ c. butter or margarine
⅓ c. powdered sugar
2 eggs
1 c. sugar

2 Tbsp. flour
2 Tbsp. lemon juice
1 tsp. grated lemon rind
½ tsp. baking powder
Powdered sugar

Mix flour, butter, and ⅓ cup powdered sugar until crumbly. Press into bottom of 8 inch square micro-pan. Cook on HIGH for 5 minutes. Combine remaining ingredients, except last addition of powdered sugar. Beat with electric mixer until smooth. Pour over baked crust. Cook on HIGH for 6 to 8 minutes or until center tests done, rotating dish if bars are rising unevenly. Let stand, covered, with waxed paper. Cool and cut into bars. Sprinkle with powdered sugar. Total cooking time: 11 to 13 minutes. *Very good.*

Gertie Helm, Bismarck, ND

FIVE MINUTE CHEESE CAKE

¼ c. butter
⅔ c. graham cracker crumbs
2 Tbsp. flour
2 Tbsp. sugar
½ tsp. cinnamon

1 (8 oz.) pkg. cream cheese
⅓ c. sugar
1 egg
1 Tbsp. lemon juice

Microwave butter in an 8 inch pie plate till melted. Mix in remaining crust ingredients (graham cracker crumbs, flour, sugar, and cinnamon) and press into pan.

For filling, microwave cream cheese for 1 minute or until soft. Beat in remaining ingredients and pour into crust. Microwave on HIGH for 4 to 5 minutes. Spoon topping over cheesecake (use cherry, blueberry, or raspberry).

Marlys Swehla, Albert Lea, MN

CHEESECAKE FONDUE

1 (8 oz.) pkg. cream cheese
⅓ c. sugar

1 egg
1 tsp. vanilla

Microwave (HIGH) cream cheese in 2 to 3 cup glass serving dish for 1 to 1¼ minutes or until softened, stirring once. Blend in sugar. Beat in egg. Microwave (HIGH), uncovered, for 1½ to 2 minutes or until thickened, stirring every ½ minute. Stir in vanilla.

Dippers:

Assorted fruits
Angel food cake cubes

Sugar cookies or wafers

Arrange fruits, cake cubes, and cookies on large tray with sauce. Have guests dip the items in the sauce.

Dessa Clafton

PEACHY BUTTER BRICKLE CAKE

1 (1 lb. 13 oz.) can sliced
   peaches

1 pkg. butter brickle cake mix
½ c. softened butter

Empty peaches and syrup into 2 quart utility dish. Blend dry cake mix with butter. Sprinkle over peaches. Microwave on FULL power for 17 to 20 minutes, turning every 5 minutes. Serve warm or cold. Good with whipped cream or ice cream.

Mary Ann Ohman, Fargo, ND

PINEAPPLE DOWNSIDE-UP CAKE

¼ c. margarine
⅓ c. packed light brown sugar
1 (16 oz.) can pineapple slices, drained (reserve juice)
4 maraschino cherries, cut in halves
1¼ c. flour
¾ c. sugar

2 tsp. baking powder
½ tsp. salt
1 egg
⅓ c. oil
½ c. reserved pineapple juice
½ tsp. vanilla
½ tsp. almond extract

Cut 2 circles of waxed paper to fit bottom of 8 inch round layer cake pan. Place paper in pan. Place margarine on top of waxed paper liner and microwave on HIGH for 45 seconds or until melted. Sprinkle brown sugar over margarine. Arrange 7 pineapple slices on top of sugar mixture. Decorate centers of slices with cherries.

Place flour, sugar, baking powder, and salt in a medium bowl. Blend together egg, oil, pineapple juice, and flavorings. Pour into dry ingredients and use a wooden spoon to combine. Pour batter over pineapple slices. Microwave on MEDIUM for 5 minutes; rotate dish once. Microwave on HIGH for 4 to 4½ minutes; rotate twice. When done, toothpick will come out clean. Let cake stand in pan for 5 minutes. Invert on serving platter. Makes 7 servings.

Marlys Swehla, Albert Lea, MN

ORANGE ZUCCHINI CAKE
(Makes 16 servings)

1 c. cooking oil
4 eggs
⅓ c. orange juice
2 tsp. baking powder
1 tsp. cinnamon
½ tsp. nutmeg
1 Tbsp. sugar

2 c. packed brown sugar
1 to 3 tsp. grated orange peel
2 c. shredded zucchini
2⅔ c. unsifted flour
½ tsp. salt
¼ tsp. cloves
¼ tsp. cinnamon

1. Beat together oil, brown sugar, and orange peel. Add eggs, 1 at a time, beating well after each. Blend in juice and zucchini. Add flour, baking powder, 1 teaspoon cinnamon, salt, nutmeg, and cloves. Mix just until blended.

2. Grease 10 to 12 cup fluted *microwave-safe* tube pan. Combine sugar and ¼ teaspoon cinnamon. Sprinkle pan with mixture, coating all surfaces; shake out excess. Spoon batter evenly into pan.

3. Microwave (MEDIUM HIGH - 70%), uncovered, for 15 minutes, rotat-

ing pan once, *then* microwave (HIGH) for 4 to 5 minutes or until no longer doughy, rotating pan once. Remove from oven and let stand for 10 minutes; invert onto serving plate.

Lorraine Follsath, Anoka, MN

MICROWAVE PIE CRUST

Combine in food processor bowl:

1¼ c. flour
⅓ tsp. salt

⅓ c. shortening

Press pulse 4 times. Add ¼ cup ice water. Blend until it just forms a ball. Let dough rest for 10 to 20 minutes, covered with the bowl or plastic bag. (Yes, it can rest much longer, if necessary; do not refrigerate!) Roll out on pastry cloth with stockingette covered rolling pin to insure success. Put into pie pan; pierce 3 dozen times. Microwave on FULL power for 6 to 7 minutes.

Barbara Kaste, Fargo, ND

IMPOSSIBLE FRENCH APPLE PIE

6 c. tart apples, peeled and
    sliced
1¼ tsp. cinnamon
¼ tsp. nutmeg
1 c. sugar

¾ c. milk
½ c. Bisquick
2 eggs
2 Tbsp. butter or margarine,
    softened

Grease 10 inch micro-safe pie plate or quiche dish (better as it has higher sides). Mix apples and spices; place in plate. Beat remaining ingredients till smooth (15 seconds on high in blender or 1 minute with hand mixer); pour over apples.

Streusel:

1 c. Bisquick
½ c. chopped nuts

⅓ c. brown sugar
3 Tbsp. firm butter or margarine

Combine Streusel until crumbly. Sprinkle apples with Streusel. Bake until knife comes out clean. Cook on FULL power for 10 to 12 minutes.

Elaine Rolerat, East Grand Forks, MN

FUDGE BROWNIE PIE

2 eggs
1 c. sugar
½ c. butter or margarine, melted
½ cup unsifted all-purpose flour
⅓ c. cocoa

¼ tsp. salt
1 tsp. vanilla
½ c. chopped nuts
Ice cream
Hot Fudge Sauce

Beat eggs in small mixer bowl; blend in sugar and melted butter or margarine. Combine flour, cocoa, and salt. Add to butter mixture. Stir in vanilla and nuts. Pour into lightly greased 8 inch pie pan. Bake at 350° for 25 to 30 minutes or until almost set (pie will not test done). Cool and cut into wedges. Serve topped with ice cream and Hot Fudge Sauce. Makes 6 to 8 servings.

Hot Fudge Sauce:

¾ c. sugar
½ c. cocoa
1 (5 oz.) can evaporated milk

⅓ c. light corn syrup
⅓ c. butter or margarine
1 tsp. vanilla

Combine sugar and cocoa in small saucepan; blend in evaporated milk and corn syrup. Cook over medium heat, stirring constantly, until mixture boils. Boil and stir for 1 minute. Remove from heat. Stir in butter or margarine and vanilla. Serve warm.

Bonnie Gunderson, Fargo, ND

LEMON MERINGUE PIE

1 c. sugar
⅓ c. cornstarch
⅛ tsp. salt

2 c. cold water
1 to 2 drops yellow food color

In 2 quart casserole, mix together sugar, cornstarch, and salt. Blend in water and food color; stir until smooth. Microwave at HIGH for 6 to 8 minutes, stirring after 3 minutes until slightly thickened. In medium bowl, beat 3 egg yolks well. Add hot sauce. Mix well. Microwave at MEDIUM HIGH for 4 to 6 minutes, stirring after 2 minutes until thick.

3 Tbsp. butter
¼ c. fresh lemon juice
2 tsp. grated lemon rind

1 microwaved pastry shell (or any other)

Stir butter, juice, and rind into mixture. Pour into pastry; finish with meringue, or if desired, cool and decorate pie with whipped cream.

Meringue: Beat 3 egg whites with ½ teaspoon cream of tartar until stiff peaks form. Gradually beat in 6 tablespoons sugar to make glossy meringue; spread over pie. Microwave at MEDIUM for 3 to 4 minutes until meringue is set.

Power level: HIGH (10), MEDIUM HIGH (7), and MEDIUM (5). Microwave time: 13 to 18 minutes total.

Donna Krause, Detroit Lakes, MN

PUMPKIN PIE

2 eggs
1 c. packed brown sugar
1 Tbsp. flour
1 tsp. cinnamon
½ tsp. salt
½ tsp. nutmeg

¼ tsp. ginger
⅛ tsp. allspice or cloves
1 can (about 16 oz.) pumpkin (2 c.)
1 (13 oz.) can evaporated milk
9 inch unbaked pastry shell

1. Combine all ingredients, except pastry shell; beat until smooth. Pour into unbaked pastry shell (use glass pie plate).

2. Microwave (HIGH), uncovered, for 7 to 8 minutes or until filling is set around edge, rotating pie once or twice. Meanwhile, preheat oven to 450°.

3. Bake for 15 to 20 minutes or until knife inserted near center comes out clean. Cool. Serve with whipped cream if desired. Makes about 8 servings, 330 calories each.

Tip: With combination oven, microwave-bake in preheated 450° oven for 9 minutes, then bake for 7 to 9 minutes.

Joan Cooney, St. Cloud, MN

Notes

Notes

Potpourri

HANDY CHART OF KITCHEN MATH
(Size of Pans and Baking Dishes)

Cooking need never become a crisis, when you use our handy charts. Need a 4 or 6-cup baking dish? Will your fancy mold be the right size for the recipe? See below for the answers.

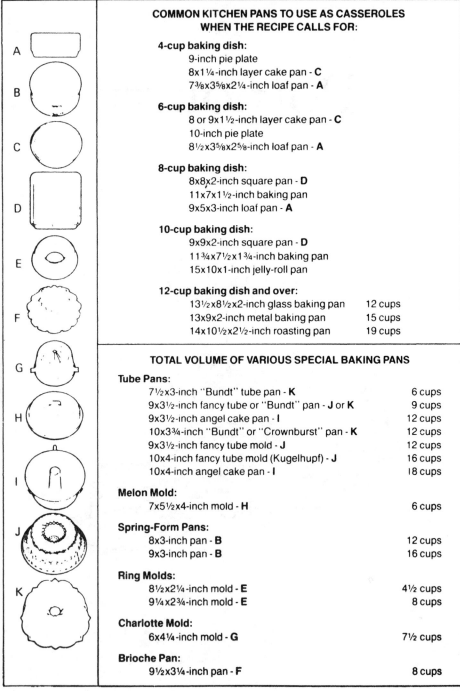

COMMON KITCHEN PANS TO USE AS CASSEROLES WHEN THE RECIPE CALLS FOR:

4-cup baking dish:
9-inch pie plate
8x1¼-inch layer cake pan - **C**
7⅜x3⅝x2¼-inch loaf pan - **A**

6-cup baking dish:
8 or 9x1½-inch layer cake pan - **C**
10-inch pie plate
8½x3⅝x2⅝-inch loaf pan - **A**

8-cup baking dish:
8x8x2-inch square pan - **D**
11x7x1½-inch baking pan
9x5x3-inch loaf pan - **A**

10-cup baking dish:
9x9x2-inch square pan - **D**
11¾x7½x1¾-inch baking pan
15x10x1-inch jelly-roll pan

12-cup baking dish and over:

13½x8½x2-inch glass baking pan	12 cups
13x9x2-inch metal baking pan	15 cups
14x10½x2½-inch roasting pan	19 cups

TOTAL VOLUME OF VARIOUS SPECIAL BAKING PANS

Tube Pans:

7½x3-inch "Bundt" tube pan - **K**	6 cups
9x3½-inch fancy tube or "Bundt" pan - **J** or **K**	9 cups
9x3½-inch angel cake pan - **I**	12 cups
10x3¾-inch "Bundt" or "Crownburst" pan - **K**	12 cups
9x3½-inch fancy tube mold - **J**	12 cups
10x4-inch fancy tube mold (Kugelhupf) - **J**	16 cups
10x4-inch angel cake pan - **I**	18 cups

Melon Mold:

7x5½x4-inch mold - **H**	6 cups

Spring-Form Pans:

8x3-inch pan - **B**	12 cups
9x3-inch pan - **B**	16 cups

Ring Molds:

8½x2¼-inch mold - **E**	4½ cups
9¼x2¾-inch mold - **E**	8 cups

Charlotte Mold:

6x4¼-inch mold - **G**	7½ cups

Brioche Pan:

9½x3¼-inch pan - **F**	8 cups

POTPOURRI

DIPS AND HORS D'OEUVRES

VEGETABLE DIP

1 c. Miracle Whip
1 pt. sour cream
2½ tsp. Salad Supreme
   (seasoning)

½ tsp. dill weed
Juice from ½ lemon
1 pkg. Hidden Valley Ranch
   dressing

Mix all together and let stand overnight.

Eleanor Baerboom, Coon Rapids, MN

SHRIMP AND CRAB DIP

8 oz. cream cheese
6 heaping Tbsp. mayonnaise
6 Tbsp. chili sauce
½ tsp. lemon juice

½ tsp. Worcestershire sauce
2 tsp. grated onion
2 cans shrimp
2 cans crabmeat

Make 1 hour ahead and chill.

Tammy Weight

DIP

1 c. Parmesan cheese
1 c. Mozzarella cheese
12 oz. artichoke hearts, cut up

1 c. mayonnaise
½ to 1 clove garlic, chopped and
   smashed

Mix all together and refrigerate until ready to use. You can make up to 2 days ahead. Just before serving, bake at 350° for 25 minutes in an 8x8 inch pan or glass dish. Serve with chips or crackers. If baked in glass pan, lower heat to 325°.

Dorothy Willems, New London, MN

GALA SOUR CREAM DIP
(Yield: 3½ cups)

2 c. dairy sour cream
½ c. chopped onion
¼ c. chopped green pepper
2 Tbsp. chopped pimento
1 Tbsp. horseradish

2 tsp. dill weed
1 tsp. Worcestershire sauce
1 tsp. seasoned salt
⅛ tsp. garlic powder
⅛ tsp. pepper

Combine all ingredients in a small bowl; cover for 2 or 3 hours or overnight.

1 lb. round rye bread (unsliced)
Assorted vegetable dippers

Bread cubes

Meanwhile, preheat oven to 400°. Cut a thin slice from top of bread. Carefully hollow out bread, leaving 1 inch shell on sides and bottom. Cut inside pieces into 1 inch cubes. Place bread shell and cubes on baking sheet. Bake about 10 minutes or until toasted. Cool completely on wire rack.

To serve, spoon sour cream mixture into shell. Serve with vegetables and bread cubes as dippers. As bread is consumed, slice top of bread and cut into cubes as additional dippers. Dip can also be served with crackers or chips.

Yogurt can be substituted for the sour cream (less calories).

Rita Bible, Minneapolis, MN

MEXICAN DIP

Layer:

1 can refried beans
1 (8 oz.) container sour cream
   (mix in taco seasoning)
1 small onion, chopped
1 small can black olives,
   chopped

1 (8 oz.) container guacamole
   dip
1 medium tomato, chopped
1 small can chopped chilie
   peppers
Shredded Monterey Jack cheese

Marlys Wendorf, St. Cloud, MN

CHICKEN NIBLETS

2 tsp. Worcestershire sauce
2 egg whites, slightly beaten
¼ c. flour
2 Tbsp. cornstarch
1 tsp. salt

½ tsp. white pepper
1 c. corn oil
2 whole fryer chicken breasts,
   skinned, boned, and cut
   into 1½ to 2 inch pieces

Stir Worcestershire sauce into egg whites. Mix together flour, corn-starch, salt, and pepper. Dip each piece in egg whites, then in flour; shake off excess. Fry for 5 to 7 minutes or until golden brown; drain. Makes about 3 dozen pieces.

Donna Krause, Detroit Lakes, MN

CHICKEN CANAPES

15 oz. can chicken
2 tsp. mayonnaise
½ c. chopped salted almonds,
   toasted

2 Tbsp. sweet pickle relish

Mix and serve on crackers.

Anne La Fleur, Duluth, MN

HOT CRAB SPREAD

½ lb. crabmeat (or canned
    crabmeat), drained
1 tsp. dry mustard
½ c. crushed onion
Garlic croutons

2 tsp. onion juice
1 tsp. Worcestershire sauce
4 hard-boiled eggs, cut up fine
1½ c. mayonnaise

Mix all together. Put into 1 quart baking dish. Sprinkle with Parmesan cheese. Bake at 350° for 30 minutes. Serve with crackers.

Ann Strandemo, Bismarck, ND

SUPER SEAFOOD SPREAD

1 (7 oz.) can water packed
    albacore tuna, drained, or 7
    oz. shrimp or crabmeat
1½ c. (12 oz.) sour cream
⅓ c. picante sauce
1 (7 oz.) env. Italian salad
    dressing mix

2 tsp. lemon juice
1 hard-boiled egg, finely
    chopped
¼ c. ripe olive slices

Place seafood of your choice in mixing bowl; break up finely with fork. Add remaining ingredients, except olives; mix well. Chill. Garnish with olives and additional picante sauce if desired. Serve with crackers, chips, or raw vegetables. Makes about 2½ cups of dip.

Heidi Weight, Anoka, MN

JALAPENO CHIP DIP

2 (8 oz.) pkg. Philadelphia cream
    cheese
1 jar jalapeno pepper Cheez
    Whiz

1 Tbsp. hot sauce

Beat until well mixed. Use with various chips.

TERESA'S CORNED BEEF CHEESE BALL

2 (8 oz.) cream cheese
3 pkg. Buddig wafer corned
    beef, shredded in blender or
    food processor

1 Tbsp. chopped onion
1 Tbsp. Worcestershire sauce

Form into ball and refrigerate. May roll in chopped nuts.

Diane Kemmetmueller, Anoka, MN

CHEESE BALL

2 (8 oz.) pkg. cream cheese
1 (8 oz.) can crushed pineapple,
   drained
¼ c. chopped green peppers

2 Tbsp. chopped onions
1 Tbsp. salt
2 c. chopped pecans

Mix and roll in the *chopped* pecans.

Schelly, Owatonna, MN

TERIYAKI BEEF STRIPS APPETIZER

1 lb. beef sirloin or tenderloin,
   cut in 4x2 inch strips
1 c. sherry
⅔ c. soy sauce

2 cloves garlic, crushed
1 Tbsp. chopped fresh or
   candied ginger

Lace strips on skewers. Combine remaining ingredients. Add beef and marinate in refrigerator for 12 to 18 hours. Place on preheated grill, keeping end of skewers on outside edge of grill for easier handling. Grill quickly on high flame, turning once. Makes 3 to 4 dozen.

Elynor Pederson, Montevideo, MN

GARLIC MUSHROOMS

2 lb. fresh mushrooms
4 cloves garlic, minced
⅓ c. olive oil
⅔ c. white wine vinegar
⅓ c. dry red or white wine

2 Tbsp. soy sauce
2 Tbsp. honey
2 Tbsp. chopped parsley
1 Tbsp. salt

Saute garlic in oil. Add vinegar, wine, honey, soy sauce, parsley, and salt. Stir until mixture is well blended and hot. Place mushrooms in container that has a tightly fitted lid. Pour hot mixture over mushrooms; allow to marinate from 1 to 3 hours or more, turning container over several times. Marinade can be used as a salad dressing.

Rose Sauer, Grand Forks, ND

CRAB PUFFS

Puffs:

1 c. water

1 stick oleo

Melt and add 1 cup flour. Use a wooden spoon and mix together fast until it forms a ball. Add 4 eggs, 1 at a time; mix well. Drop by teaspoon on an ungreased cookie sheet. Bake in 400° oven for 30 to 35 minutes (until browned).

**Few drops of Tabasco sauce
Mayonnaise (approx. ½ c.,
enough to moisten)**

crab, in mixer and then fold in crabmeat. Cut ttle filling in each one.

Lorraine Sojka, Duluth, MN

SOUPS

SOUP COMBINATIONS

Tomato soup and clam chowder.
Green pea and tomato soup.
Cream of mushroom soup and cream of celery soup.
Clam chowder and cream of celery soup.

Anne La Fleur, Duluth, MN

HURRY-HEARTY SOUPS

Split pea soup with ham strips.
Vegetable soup with tiny cooked meat balls.
Cream of mushroom soup with can of shrimp.
Tomato soup with can of minced clams.

Anne La Fleur, Duluth, MN

SOUP TRICKS

Cream of Corn Soup - Combine:

1 (10½ oz.) can cream of chicken soup (or cream of mushroom or cream of celery)

½ c. mayonnaise
1½ to 2½ c. milk
2 c. whole kernel corn

Heat thoroughly.

Anne La Fleur, Duluth, MN

POTATO SOUP

1 medium size potato (per person), cubed
3 stalks celery, cubed
1 small onion, cubed
½ lb. bacon, diced and fried crisp

3 beef bouillon cubes (takes care of salt)
2 c. milk

Put potatoes, celery, onion, and bouillon cubes in a large kettle with water enough to cover. Cook until tender. Add bacon and milk; cook for about 5 minutes or until hot. Serves 7 people.

Kim Moyer, Thief River Falls, MN

GOLDEN CREAM SOUP

3 c. chopped potatoes
1 c. water
½ c. celery slices
½ c. carrot slices
¼ c. chopped onion
1 tsp. parsley flakes
1 chicken bouillon cube
½ tsp. salt
Dash of pepper
1½ c. milk
2 Tbsp. flour
½ lb. (or less) Velveeta process
    cheese, cubed

In large saucepan, combine potatoes, water, celery, carrot, onion, parsley flakes, bouillon cube, and seasonings; mix well. Cover and simmer for 15 to 20 minutes or until vegetables are tender. Gradually add milk to flour, mixing until well blended. Add milk mixture to vegetables; cook until thickened. Add process cheese spread; stir until melted. Makes 6 to 8 servings.

Mayabelle Morganson, Bemidji, MN

CORN AND CHEESE SOUP

1 pkg. frozen kernel corn
4 russet potatoes, pared and
    diced
1 c. sliced celery
½ c. chopped onions
½ can (14½ oz.) chicken broth
½ can water
2 c. milk
3 Tbsp. flour
1½ c. shredded cheese
⅛ tsp. pepper

Combine corn, potatoes, celery, onions, broth, and water; bring to boil. Simmer, covered, for 15 to 20 minutes or until vegetables are tender. Combine milk and flour; gradually blend into vegetable mixture. Cook until slightly thickened. Add cheese and pepper; stir until cheese melts. Add dumplings.

Dumplings:

1½ c. flour
½ c. milk
1 egg
1 tsp. salt

Ten minutes before serving, drop by teaspoonfuls into soup and cook, covered.

Gloria Smith, Jackson, MN

E-Z CHEESE BROCCOLI SOUP

1 (15 oz.) can chicken broth
1 can water
1 (10½ oz.) pkg. frozen chopped
    broccoli
1 can cream of chicken soup
1 can cream of potato soup
8 oz. cubed American cheese
6 Tbsp. (or more) Cheez Whiz
    (jalapeno or plain)

Bring to a boil the chicken broth and 1 can water. Add frozen chopped broccoli. When broccoli breaks apart, add cream of chicken soup, cream of potato soup, American cheese, and Cheez Whiz. Heat until cheese is melted and soup is hot. *Do not* boil.

Margaret Hulst, Waltham, MN

VEGETABLES

CALIFORNIA POTATOES

6 to 8 medium size potatoes
3 slices bacon

1 pkg. dry onion soup

Clean 6 to 8 medium size potatoes. Do *not* peel them. Cut them in eighths or slice thick. Place in a 9x9 inch pan. Cut 3 slices of bacon into small pieces and place on top. *Note:* ½ stick of oleo or butter may be used in place of bacon.

Sprinkle 1 package of dry onion soup on top. *Do not* add any liquid. Cover with foil and bake for 1½ hours at 350°.

Edna Helberg, Sioux Falls, SD

CARROT PENNIES
(Makes 2 (½ cup) servings)

1 c. carrots, sliced (2 medium
**   size carrots)**
¼ c. water
1 tsp. butter or margarine

1 tsp. brown sugar
1 tsp. water
Few grains of salt

Cook carrots in ¼ cup water until tender, about 10 minutes. Add remaining ingredients and mix lightly. Cook for 3 minutes to blend flavors.

Helen H. Clark, Grand Forks, ND

BEETS IN ORANGE SAUCE
(Makes 2 servings, about ½ cup each)

1 Tbsp. sugar
Few grains of salt
1 tsp. cornstarch
¼ c. orange juice

2 tsp. lemon juice
1 tsp. butter or margarine
¾ c. or 8 oz. can beets, cooked
**   or canned**

Combine sugar, salt, and cornstarch; mix well. Stir in orange juice. Cook and stir until thickened; remove from heat. Blend in lemon juice and fat. Add beets and reheat.

Helen H. Clark, Grand Forks, ND

HEALTH DRESSING

This is an easy dressing to make, will keep fresh indefinitely and is suitable for all kinds of green salads.

Put 1 large, peeled clove garlic in a pint jar. Add in order - ½ cup of each: chili sauce, sugar, olive oil or cooking oil, and vinegar. Add ½ teaspoon salt, 1 teaspoon paprika, and ½ teaspoon pepper. Shake thoroughly.

Rose V. Johnson, Virginia, MN

CREOLE CORN

2 c. cooked corn
3 Tbsp. bacon fat
3 Tbsp. chopped onion

3 Tbsp. chopped green pepper
¼ tsp. salt
⅛ tsp. paprika

Heat fat in frying pan. Add onion and green pepper; brown. Add rest of ingredients and cook slowly for 5 minutes; stir frequently. Leftover fresh corn may be used.

Marie Capen, Duluth, MN

PAM'S YUMMY CORN

1 can whole kernel corn (don't
    drain)
1 can cream style corn

1 box Jiffy corn bread mix
8 oz. sour cream
½ c. chopped onion

Mix all together and bake at 350° for about 1½ hours or till set.

It's almost like a corn pudding.

Karen Berg, Owatonna, MN

TWICE-BAKED YAMS

2 lb. (about 6 medium) yams or
    sweet potatoes
1 Tbsp. salad oil
¼ c. sour cream
¼ c. milk

2 Tbsp. packed brown sugar
2 Tbsp. butter or margarine
⅛ tsp. salt
2 Tbsp. coarsely chopped
    pecans

Preheat oven to 375°F. Rub yams with oil; prick with fork to let steam escape. Bake until tender, 35 to 45 minutes. Cut a thin slice lengthwise from each yam and discard. Scoop out pulp, leaving a thin shell. Mash pulp until very smooth.

Beat in sour cream and milk. Beat in brown sugar, butter, and salt until light and fluffy. Stir in pecans. Increase oven temperature to 400°F. Place shells in an ungreased 13x9 inch baking dish and fill with yam mixture. Bake until filling is golden, about 20 minutes. Makes 6 servings, 310 calories each.

Phylliss Mae Johnson, Winona, MN

SWEET POTATO PIE
(Makes 9 inch pie)

2 c. cooked mashed sweet
    potatoes
⅔ c. brown sugar
3 eggs, beaten
¾ tsp. salt

1 c. whole milk
½ tsp. cinnamon
1½ Tbsp. melted butter
⅛ tsp. nutmeg
⅛ tsp. cloves

Combine potatoes, sugar, salt, and spices. Mix together eggs, milk, and butter; stir into sweet potato mixture. Pour in chilled unbaked pastry shell. Bake for 45 minutes in 375° oven or until tests done.

Millie Monte, Chisholm, MN

SWISS VEGETABLE

1 (16 oz.) bag frozen broccoli, carrots, and cauliflower combination, thawed and drained
1 (10¾ oz.) can condensed cream of mushroom soup
1 c. (4 oz.) shredded Swiss cheese
⅓ c. sour cream
¼ tsp. pepper (black)
1 (4 oz.) jar pimiento, chopped and drained
1 (2.8 oz.) can French fried onions

Combine vegetables, soup, ½ cup cheese, sour cream, pepper, pimiento, and ½ can French fried onions. Pour into a 1 quart casserole. Bake, covered, at 350° for 30 minutes. Top with remaining cheese and onions. Bake, uncovered, for 5 minutes longer. Makes 6 servings.

Mary Weight

SPINACH CHEESE BAKE
(Serves 4)

1 (10 oz.) pkg. frozen chopped spinach
2 Tbsp. flour
2 eggs, beaten
1 (3 oz.) pkg. cream cheese, softened and cubed
¾ c. American cheese, shredded or cubed
¼ c. butter, cubed
1½ tsp. instant minced onion
½ tsp. salt
½ c. fine bread crumbs, mixed with ¼ c. melted butter
⅓ c. Parmesan cheese

In 1½ quart covered dish, cook spinach till tender. Stir in flour, eggs, first 2 cheeses, cubed butter, onion, and salt; mix well. Bake for 30 minutes at 350°. Top with bread crumbs and ¼ cup butter. Top this with Parmesan cheese; brown and serve.

Mary Hocking, Fargo, ND

BROCCOLI SOUFFLE

A dish that rises to the occasion - a guest luncheon special.

3 Tbsp. butter or regular
   margarine
3 Tbsp. flour
1 c. milk
¼ tsp. salt
⅛ tsp. pepper

½ lb. (about 2½ c.) grated
   process cheese
1 (10 oz.) pkg. frozen chopped
   broccoli, partially thawed
½ c. finely chopped onion
3 eggs, separated

Melt butter in saucepan. Stir in flour to make smooth paste. Add milk, salt, and pepper; cook for 5 minutes. Add cheese; stir until melted. Fold in broccoli and onion. Fold in well beaten egg yolks. Lightly fold in egg whites, beaten until stiff but not dry (you'll still see some white pieces). Pour into 2 quart baking dish with straight sides. Set in pan of hot water in moderate oven (350°F.) for 1 hour.

Margaret Riley, Duluth, MN

BROCCOLI BAKE

2 frozen broccoli, chopped
2 eggs
½ c. salad dressing

1 can mushroom soup
1 small onion, grated

Cook broccoli according to directions on box. Top with grated cheese and cracker crumbs. Bake at 325° for 1 hour.

Marcy Weight

POTATO ONION BAKE

2½ lb. potatoes, peeled and
   sliced
1 c. thinly sliced onion
¼ c. oleo

½ tsp. salt
¼ tsp. pepper
¼ tsp. oregano, crushed
⅛ tsp. thyme, crushed

Preheat oven to 350°. Layer potatoes and onion in greased 2½ quart casserole. Pour oleo and seasoning mixture over vegetables. Cover and bake for 50 to 60 minutes until vegetables are tender.

Mayabelle Morganson, Bemidji, MN

GREEN ONION PIE

2 c. flour
⅔ c. boiling water
4 Tbsp. shortening

4 Tbsp. chopped green onion
2 tsp. salt
Oil (for frying)

Place flour in bowl. Add the boiling water and mix; let cool. After 3 minutes, add a little cold water if dough is too dry. Knead the dough thoroughly until it is smooth. Cover and let rest for 15 minutes. Remove dough to floured board; divide dough into 8 pieces. Knead and roll each piece of dough into 10 inch round as in making pie crust. Rub ½ tablespoon shortening on dough and sprinkle the whole top with ¼ teaspoon salt and ½ tablespoon chopped green onion.

Roll dough up as for jelly roll, making sure ends are tightly closed. Now form into a round snail shape, tucking the final end into the center of the bun, then press down and roll out until ¼ inch thick.

Heat ¼ inch peanut oil in frying pan. Place the pie in and fry about 2 minutes. Use low heat (375°) and cover the pan. Flip over and continue frying until this side is golden brown and crispy. Shake the pan often while frying as this makes a flaky pastry. Cut into small pieces to serve.

Janet Lozon, Owatonna, MN

BBQ POTATOES

Take 6 to 8 potatoes and cook till just barely done. Peel and slice them while still hot.

1 c. oil　　　　　　　　　　　**1 tsp. salt**
⅓ c. red vinegar　　　　　　　**1 tsp. pepper**

Bring to boiling point and pour over potatoes.

Add:

½ tsp. celery seed　　　　　　**½ tsp. mustard seed**
¼ c. chopped celery　　　　　**½ c. onions**

Cover and chill.

Norma Amundson, Morris, MN

CASEROLES

BAKED BEANS

1 green pepper, chopped
1 medium onion, chopped
2 (No. 2) cans pork and beans
1 (No. 2) can pork and beans
    with brown sugar

1 c. catsup *or* tomato soup
½ c. brown sugar
1 lb. bacon, chopped in 1 inch
    pieces

Fry pepper, onion, and bacon all together. Drain; add beans, brown sugar, and catsup. Bake in large casserole, uncovered, for 1 hour at 375°.

Evelyn Pedersen

HURRY-UP BAKED BEANS

2 (1 lb.) cans baked beans
¼ c. chopped onion
½ tsp. dry mustard

⅓ c. molasses
Grated rind of 1 orange

Empty baked beans into a large saucepan. Add chopped onion, dry mustard, molasses, and grated rind of 1 orange; heat thoroughly. Serves 6.

Rita J. Bible, Minneapolis, MN

SPECIAL IDEAS

Try adding 1 cup diced unpeeled apple to 1 can baked beans after heating - for variety.

Anne La Fleur, Duluth, MN

FLUFFY WILD RICE

2 c. wild rice (uncooked) or 1 c.
    wild and 1 c. white

4 c. boiling water

Preheat oven to 500°. Shut off oven. Put rice and boiling water in a covered Dutch oven; leave in oven overnight. Next morning, rinse thoroughly in cold water. Rice is ready for hot dish recipe.

Margaret Riley, Duluth, MN

CELERY HOT DISH

1 stalk celery (bunch)

1 can cream of chicken soup

Clean and cut whole stalk of celery in 1 inch pieces. Cook in very small amount of water for about 5 minutes. Try to have no cooking water left ... otherwise drain. Add soup. Put in casserole. Heat for 30 minutes in moderate oven.

Anne La Fleur, Duluth, MN

CHICKEN-WILD RICE CASSEROLE

5 c. cooked wild rice
2 c. diced chicken
½ c. green pepper, diced
1 can mushrooms, diced

1 can cream of mushroom soup
1 can cream of chicken soup
Celery

Bake at 300° for 1 hour.

Diane Haan, Bismarck, ND

WILD RICE CASSEROLE

1 small pkg. cubed Velveeta
cheese
1 can (2½ c.) stewed tomatoes
½ c. diced onions
1 c. wild rice, washed

1½ c. boiling water
1 can sliced green olives
1 can mushrooms, drained
½ c. olive oil
1½ tsp. salt

Mix and put in a 3 quart casserole. Bake, uncovered, for 1½ hours at 350°. Stir once or twice so rice on top doesn't get hard.

Diane Haan, Bismarck, ND

WILD RICE CASSEROLE

2 c. wild rice (uncooked) or 1 c.
wild and 1 c. white

4 c. boiling water

Preheat oven to 500°. Shut oven off. Put rice and boiling water in Dutch oven (covered). Leave in oven overnight. Next morning, rinse thoroughly in cold water. Drain well. Put rice in casserole.

½ c. butter
1 c. cream of celery soup
1 can cream of mushroom soup
Few slivered almonds

½ medium onion, chopped
Dash of salt
1½ Tbsp. dry onion soup
¼ tsp. pepper

Melt butter. Add cream of celery soup, cream of mushroom soup, almonds, onion, salt, dry onion soup, and pepper. Mix together. Heat this mixture, then pour ½ of soup mixture over the rice. Mix in crumbled bacon. Pour the rest of the mixture on the rice. Sprinkle crumbled potato chips on top. Bake in 350° oven for 45 minutes to 1 hour. Good to serve with chicken. Serves 16.

Margaret Riley, Duluth, MN

TURKEY WILD RICE CASSEROLE

6 green onions, chopped
½ c. chopped green pepper (or more)
1 c. slivered almonds
1 c. mushrooms (I'd use drained canned mushrooms)
1 c. wild rice or combination of wild and white (about 3 c. cooked)

2 Tbsp. butter
2 Tbsp. flour
2 c. half & half (1 pt.)
1 small (8 oz.) jar Cheez Whiz
2 or 3 c. cooked turkey or chicken, cut up

Saute the onions, pepper, almonds, and mushrooms; set aside. Cook the rice in boiling salted water until just tender. Drain and set aside.

To prepare a thin white sauce, melt the butter. Remove saucepan from burner and stir in the butter until smooth. Now add the half & half; return to burner and cook until mixture slightly thickens, stirring constantly. (I have found this to be the best way to make a smooth white sauce.) To this thin white sauce, add the Cheez Whiz and stir well. Now combine all of the ingredients and bake in a casserole at 300° for 45 minutes or a little longer if necessary.

Mary Patalas, Virginia, MN

WILD RICE FISH CASSEROLE

1 small can mushrooms (or more)
3 c. drained cooked wild rice (1 c. uncooked)

1 small (6½ oz.) can tuna or salmon (or more)
10¾ oz. can mushroom soup
1 soup can milk

Saute the drained mushrooms in butter. Add the rest of the ingredients. Place in a buttered casserole and bake at 300° for 45 minutes. Do not cover the casserole.

Mary Patalas, Virginia, MN

WILD RICE PATTIES

3 c. cooked wild rice (about 1 c. uncooked)
½ c. grated sharp cheese or your favorite cheese

¼ c. fine cracker crumbs
1 tsp. salt
Dash of pepper
2 eggs, slightly beaten

Combine all the ingredients; mix well. Shape into cakes or patties, using more cracker crumbs, if necessary, to make the mixture firm. Brown each lightly in butter in a hot skillet.

Mary Patalas, Virginia, MN

WILD RICE CASSEROLE

1 c. wild rice
1 lb. chop suey meat
⅓ c. diced green pepper (or more)
2 c. chopped celery
½ c. shredded raw carrot

1 (10¾ oz.) can mushroom soup
1 (No. 2) can bean sprouts plus liquid
1 Tbsp. Worcestershire sauce
1 Tbsp. soy sauce
Salt and pepper to taste

Soak the wild rice for 2 hours in warm water. Brown meat, then add diced pepper, celery, and shredded carrot. Cover and cook for about 5 minutes. Drain the wild rice; add to the meat mixture. Add soup, bean sprouts with liquid, Worcestershire sauce, soy sauce, and seasonings to taste.

Pour into a buttered casserole or roaster and add some water if necessary. Cover and bake at least 1 hour at 375°. This should make about 12 average servings, however, 4 or 5 hungry people could eat all of it!!

Mary Patalas, Virginia, MN

CHOW MEIN HOT DISH

1 lb. ground beef
2 c. celery, chopped fine
1 large onion
1 tsp. salt
⅓ c. soy sauce (or less)

3 c. boiling water
1 can mushroom soup and ½ can water
1 c. raw rice, washed

Bake for 1 to 2 hours at 375°. Stir often.

Tammy Weight

CHICKEN CHOW MEIN

1 stewing chicken
1 or 2 large onions
½ bunch celery
1 can drained chow mein vegetables

⅓ bottle soy sauce
3 Tbsp. corn starch with 4 Tbsp. cold water

Cook chicken till tender (about 3 hours). Remove from broth and cool. Add onions and celery to broth and cook till tender. Add 1 can drained chow mein vegetables. Add ⅓ (small) bottle soy sauce until broth is nice and brown. Salt and pepper to taste. Add cut up chicken and bring to simmer. Add corn starch thickening.

Mayabelle Morganson, Bemidji, MN

TURKEY STRATA

6 slices day old bread
2 c. cubed cooked turkey
½ c. chopped onion
½ c. chopped celery
¼ c. chopped green pepper
½ c. mayonnaise

¾ tsp. salt
1 can cream of mushroom soup
½ c. American cheese,
   shredded
1¼ c. milk
2 beaten eggs

Butter 2 slices of bread; cut into ½ inch cubes and set aside. Cut rest of bread into 1 inch cubes. Place ½ of the *unbuttered* cubes into an 8x8x2 inch baking dish. Combine turkey, vegetables, mayonnaise, salt, and pepper to taste. Spoon mixture over bread cubes in the baking dish. Put other ½ of unbuttered bread cubes on top.

Combine milk and eggs; pour over. Cover and chill in refrigerator. Next day, spoon soup over the top. Top with buttered bread cubes. Bake at 350° for 1 hour. Sprinkle the shredded cheese on the last 10 minutes of baking. Let stand a few minutes after removing from oven before cutting.

Margaret Hulst, Waltham, MN

TURKEY LOAF

1 lb. ground turkey
¾ c. tomato juice
½ to ¾ c. Quaker Oats
1 egg or ¼ c. Egg Beaters

3 Tbsp. onion
1 tsp. celery salt
1 tsp. Worcestershire sauce

Mix and place in greased baking pan. Bake for 1 hour at 350°.

Dode Desch, St. Paul, MN

IMPOSSIBLE TURKEY PIE

2 c. cut up cooked turkey or
   chicken
1 (4½ oz.) jar sliced mushrooms,
   drained
½ c. sliced green onions
½ tsp. salt

1 c. shredded Swiss cheese (4
   oz.)
1½ c. milk
¾ c. Bisquick baking mix
3 eggs

Heat oven to 400°. Lightly grease 10 inch pie plate. Sprinkle turkey (or chicken), mushrooms, onions, salt, and cheese into pie plate. Beat remaining ingredients till smooth; pour into pie plate. Bake until golden brown and knife inserted comes out clean, 30 to 35 minutes. Let stand for 5 minutes before cutting. Garnish with parsley if desired. Refrigerate any leftover pie. Makes 6 to 8 servings.

Evelyn Pedersen

COUNTRY GARDEN DINNER

2 c. sliced raw potatoes
1 tsp. salt
1 Tbsp. butter or margarine
1 c. diced celery
1 c. diced carrots

¼ c. butter or margarine
1 lb. ground beef
½ c. chopped onion
½ c. sliced green pepper
1 c. canned tomatoes

In a greased baking dish (1½ quarts), arrange the sliced potatoes. Sprinkle with ½ teaspoon of salt and dot with 1 tablespoon of butter. Cover with the celery and carrots. Heat 2 tablespoons of the butter in a skillet. Brown the beef lightly (cooking time - 5 minutes), breaking in small pieces and sprinkling the remaining salt. Arrange beef over carots.

Cook the onion and pepper in remaining butter until tender and transparent (cooking time - 5 minutes); arrange over meat. Pour the tomatoes over the top. Bake, covered, for 30 minutes in 350° oven. Remove cover and bake another 30 minutes. Total baking time: 1 hour. Servings: 6.

Marie Capen, Duluth, MN

TEN MINUTE DINNER

1 lb. ground beef
1 onion, chopped
1 can mushroom soup
1 can cream of chicken soup

1 can frozen mixed vegetables,
   drained
1 bag chow mein noodles

Brown beef and onion. Add soups, drained mixed vegetables, and ¾ chow mein noodles. Pour into casserole; top with remaining noodles. Bake at 400° for about 10 minutes in 1½ quart casserole. Makes 6 servings.

Emma Buhl, Long Prairie, MN

SIX SOUP HOT DISH

1 lb. wide noodles
2 lb. hamburger, browned
1 can onion soup
1 can chicken rice soup

1 can cream of chicken soup
1 can mushroom soup
2 cans cream of celery soup
1 can whole kernel corn

Bake for 1 hour at 350°.

Irene L. Moe, Fargo, ND

BEEF TOMATO RICE STEW

2 large onions
2 Tbsp. fat or oil
½ lb. ground beef
4 c. cooked or canned tomatoes

½ c. uncooked rice
1 c. water
Salt and pepper as you like

Chop onions. Put onions, fat or oil, and ground beef in pan. Cook until meat is browned and onions are tender. Add rest of the ingredients; cover and cook slowly for about 25 minutes until rice is tender. Makes 6 servings, 1 cup each.

Mrs. Emma Buhl, Long Prairie, MN

HAMBURGER HASH BROWN HOT DISH

8 oz. frozen shredded hash
   browns, thawed
1 lb. hamburger
1 medium onion, chopped
1 (10 oz.) pkg. frozen peas,
   thawed

1 (10¾ oz.) can cream of
   mushroom soup
6 slices American cheese
1 (3 oz.) can French fried onion
   rings

Butter 9x13 inch glass pan on bottom and sides. Cover with hash browns. Brown meat, and onion in fry pan. Place both on top of potatoes. Salt and pepper, then sprinkle with peas. Mix soup and milk in a bowl and pour over mixture. Place cheese slices on top and cover with foil. Bake at 350° for 45 to 60 minutes. Remove foil and sprinkle onion rings on top and return to oven for 15 minutes. Makes 8 to 10 servings.

Virginia Fyhsen, Duluth, MN

SURPRISE HOT DISH

½ lb. veal
½ lb. pork
¼ lb. noodles
¼ lb. grated American cheese

1 small can pimentos
1 can mushrooms and juice
1 can whole kernel corn
Buttered crumbs

Dice and brown veal and pork. Cook noodles for 10 minutes and drain. Combine with meat and add American cheese, pimentos, and mushrooms with juice. Mix together and cook for about 10 minutes. Add whole kernel corn; season to taste. Cover with buttered crumbs and bake for 1 hour at 350°.

Marie Capen, Duluth, MN

POTATO HOTDISH

1 lb. hamburger
4 c. sliced potatoes (raw)
1 can Cheddar cheese soup
½ c. milk
1 small onion

1 can tomato soup
½ tsp. oregano
½ tsp. pepper
1 pkg. Mozzarella cheese

Brown hamburger and onion. Mix potatoes, hamburger, milk, and cheese soup into 9x13 inch pan. Cover with tomato soup and spices. Bake for 1 hour at 375°. Add Mozzarella cheese and bake for 15 minutes longer.

Jo Ann Stuckel, St. Cloud, MN

208

HEARTY BEEF 'N POTATO CASSEROLE

This is ready to cook in just 15 minutes.

4 c. (½ of 30 oz. bag) frozen
potato rounds
1 lb. ground beef
1 (10 oz.) pkg. frozen chopped
broccoli, thawed
1 (2.8 oz.) can Durkee French
fried onion
1 medium tomato, chopped
(optional)

1 (10¾ oz.) can cream of celery
soup
⅓ c. milk
1 c. (4 oz.) shredded Cheddar
cheese
¼ tsp. garlic powder
⅛ tsp. pepper

Place potatoes on bottom and up sides of 8x12 inch casserole. Bake, uncovered, at 400° for 10 minutes. Brown beef in large chunks; drain. Place beef, broccoli, ½ can onions, and tomato in potato shell. Combine soup, milk, ½ cup cheese, and seasonings; pour over mixture. Bake, covered, at 400° for 20 minutes. Top with remaining cheese and onions. Bake, uncovered, for 2 to 3 minutes longer. Makes 6 servings.

Microwave directions: Crumble beef in large bowl. Cook on HIGH for 4 to 5 minutes. Stir halfway through cooking time. Drain well. Stir in broccoli, ½ can onions, soup, milk, ½ cup cheese, and seasonings. Cook on HIGH, uncovered, for 6 minutes. Stir halfway through. Add tomato and spoon into potato shell. Cook, uncovered, on HIGH for 8 minutes. Top with remaining cheese and onions. Cook on HIGH for 1 minute.

Kim Moyer, Thief River Falls, MN

SANDY'S LAZY DAY LASAGNE

6 oz. pkg. lasagne or wide
noodles
¼ tsp. oregano
1 (15½ oz.) can spaghetti sauce
1 lb. extra lean ground beef,
browned

1 c. cream style cottage cheese
1 (6 oz.) pkg. sliced Mozzarella
cheese

Cook noodles as per package; drain. Combine oregano with spaghetti sauce. In greased 10x11 inch baking dish, alternate layers of noodles, cottage cheese, Mozzarella cheese, and sauce, using sauce for top layer. Bake at 375° for about 30 minutes. Makes 4 servings.

Gloria Smith, Jackson, MN

PIZZA CASSEROLE

12 oz. enriched wide noodles
1½ lb. ground beef
3 c. pizza sauce

2 tsp. salt
2 c. shredded Mozzarella or
American cheese

Cook noodles in salted water for 2 to 3 minutes. Brown beef; drain fat. Add pizza sauce, salt, and pepper; stir to blend. Layer noodles, sauce, and cheese. Bake at 350° for 30 minutes.

Marian Nelson, Dickinson, ND

SPAGHETTI PIZZA

12 oz. spaghetti, broken in 2
    inch pieces and cooked
2 eggs, beaten
½ c. milk

1 c. Mozzarella cheese
¾ tsp. garlic powder
1 tsp. salt

Mix preceding ingredients and pour into greased cookie sheet. (Use jelly roll pan with higher sides.) Bake at 400° for 15 minutes.

Remove and top with:

1 medium jar Ragu or Prego
    spaghetti sauce
3 c. Mozzarella cheese
1 pkg. hamburger, browned and
    drained

1 pkg. pepperoni (or sausage)
Chopped mushrooms
Chopped olives

Return to oven at 350°. Bake for ½ hour. Let stand for 5 minutes before cutting.

Mary Hocking, Fargo, ND

BEEF BURGER SUPPER

2 lb. lean ground beef
¾ c. soft bread crumbs
1 (5¾ oz.) can mushroom steak
    sauce

½ c. diced green peppers
¼ c. finely chopped onion
2 eggs, well beaten
½ tsp. salt

Lightly but thoroughly blend ingredients. Press into a 1½ quart ring mold. Bake at 350° for about 50 minutes. Drain meat juices off; unmold on serving platter. Fill center with mashed potatoes and top with additional hot mushroom steak sauce if desired. Yield: 6 to 8 servings.

Anne La Fleur, Duluth, MN

SOUPER STROGANOFF

1½ lb. round steak, cut in strips
    and pounded
¼ c. flour
Dash of pepper
¼ c. butter

4 Tbsp. onion
Garlic salt to taste
1 (10½ oz.) can beef broth
1 c. sour cream
3 c. cooked noodles

Dust meat with flour and pepper. In skillet, brown meat in butter. Add mushrooms, onion, and garlic; brown lightly. Stir in soup. Cover and cook for 1 hour or so until meat is tender. Stir often. Gradually blend in sour cream. Cook over low heat for 5 minutes longer. Serve over cooked noodles. Serves 7.

Marie Burt, Owatonna, MN

BEEFY BUMWICHES

5 to 6 lb. boneless bottom or rump roast	1 Tbsp. sugar
2 c. water	¼ tsp. cinnamon
2 cloves garlic, minced	1 can beef consomme
2 env. onion soup mix	2 bouillon cubes
	1 Tbsp. vinegar

Put all the ingredients in a covered roasting pan. Roast in a 300° oven until very tender (4 to 5 hours). Remove meat from juice; cool. Skim fat from juice. Pull meat apart (shred) and return to juice.

To serve, reheat either in oven or microwave. Serve on hard rolls or buns. Can be made well in advance of use.

Bobbi Westerbur

SAUSAGE FILLED CREPES

Crepes:

2 c. Bisquick	1½ c. milk
4 eggs	

Mix ingredients and beat until smooth. Make crepes using crepe maker or small saute fry pan.

Filling:

4 Jimmy Dean sausages (3 regular and 1 hot)	1 medium Velveeta cheese
1 large (8 oz.) Philadelphia cream cheese	1 onion, chopped

Remove sausage from casing; brown and drain grease. Add cream cheese, Velveeta, and onion. Heat until cheese melts. Fill crepes and roll (amount of filling depends on size of crepes you want). I trim the ends of crepes after they're filled to make them more uniform. Bake at 350° for about 20 minutes. (If desired, can be made ahead, frozen, and baked just before serving.)

Marge D.

BROCCOLI AND HAM QUICHE

1 c. shredded Cheddar
1 c. shredded Swiss
1 c. milk

4 eggs, whipped
½ c. shredded broccoli
½ c. diced ham

Pour into a pie shell and bake at 350° for 1 hour.

Diane Kemmetmueller, Anoka, MN

EGG HOTDISH

1½ doz. eggs
¼ c. milk, mixed with eggs
1 can mushroom soup
1 tsp. salt

1 can mushrooms
2 c. ham
1¼ c. cheese

Add milk and salt to eggs; scramble. Cook until soft. Combine mushrooms to soup. Layer eggs, ham, mushrooms, soup, and cheese; repeat. Cover and bake at 250° for 60 minutes. Take cover off last 10 minutes. (Sprinkle with paprika.)

Marlys Wendorf, St. Cloud, MN

OVEN OMELET

¼ c. butter or margarine
1½ doz. eggs
1 c. dairy sour cream

1 c. milk
2 tsp. salt
¼ c. chopped green onion

In oven, melt butter in a 13x9x2 inch baking dish. Tilt dish to coat sides. In a large bowl, beat eggs, sour cream, milk, and salt until blended. Stir in onion. Pour into buttered pan. Bake until eggs are set and still moist, about 35 minutes. Serves 10 to 12. Recipe can easily be cut in half. You may add ½ cup crumbled cooked bacon and ½ cup cubed cheese.

Marlys Wendorf, St. Cloud, MN

MEATS

BEEF POT ROAST
(Makes 6 servings, about 4 ounces each)

2 lb. beef chuck roast (boneless)
1 medium size carrot (whole)
1 medium size onion (whole)
¼ c. cooking sherry (if desired;
   can use water instead)

¼ c. water
Few grains of salt
Few grains of pepper

Brown beef on both sides in heavy pans or Dutch oven. Add remaining ingredients; cover and cook slowly on top of the range until tender, about 2 ½ to 3 hours. Add more water if needed.

Helen H. Clark, Grand Forks, ND

CALIFORNIA ROAST
(Serves 8)

5 to 6 lb. roast

Salt and pepper

Brown roast in Dutch oven at 275°; salt and pepper lightly.

Mix together:

1 pkg. onion soup mix
10 oz. cottage cheese
1 can mushroom soup (can use
   1 pkg. dehydrated beef

mushroom soup mix instead
of can)

Spread mixture over roast. Bake at 275° for 4 or more hours, covered (this makes its own gravy).

I use only ½ of the onion soup. It makes it less salty. If the roast is juicy enough you won't have to add water to the gravy.

Mary Hocking

LEMON-MARINATED CHUCK ROAST

1 (4 lb.) beef chuck roast
1 tsp. grated lemon peel
½ c. lemon juice
⅓ c. cooking oil
2 Tbsp. sliced green onion with
   tops

4 tsp. sugar
1½ tsp. salt
1 tsp. Worcestershire sauce
1 tsp. prepared mustard
⅛ tsp. pepper

Combine all ingredients and pour over roast. Cover and let stand for 3 hours at room temperature or overnight, turning several times. Remove roast from marinade. Reserve marinade. Pat excess moisture from roast with paper towel.

Grill roast over *medium* hot coals for 17 to 20 minutes. Turn and cook for 17 to 20 minutes more for rare to medium rare. Heat reserved marinade. Remove meat from grill and carve across the grain into thin slices. Serves 6 to 8.

Kathy Tischler, Woodbury, MN

MEAT BALLS

1 lb. ground meat
3 slices dry bread, crumbled

1 small can Carnation milk

Mix together. Make Meat Balls and place in casserole raw.

Pour over:

1 can chicken gumbo soup

1 can onion soup

Bake for 2 hours, covered, at 350°; uncover last ½ hour.

Sadie Lobland, Hibbing, MN

CUBED STEAK HAYSTACKS

1 pkg. frozen hash browns with
    onion
6 beef cubed steaks
2 Tbsp. oil

Salt
Catsup
Shredded Cheddar cheese

Prepare frozen hash browns with onion. Set hash browns aside. Cook cubed steaks in oil. Take skillet from heat; season steaks with salt. Spread 2 teaspoons of catsup on each steak, then top each steak with ½ cup hash browns and 1 tablespoon shredded Cheddar cheese. Return to skillet and cover; cook till cheese melts.

Marion Nelson, Dickinson, ND

PORCUPINES
(Oven supper dish)

½ c. uncooked rice
1 lb. ground round (beef)
1 tsp. minced onion

½ tsp. salt
1½ to 2 c. solid canned
    tomatoes

Mix all ingredients, except tomatoes; shape into balls. Place in baking dish. Pour tomatoes over all. Bake at 350° for 1 hour and 20 minutes. Makes 2 casseroles.

Anne La Fleur, Duluth, MN

LIVER STEAK

2 pieces cut up bacon
Liver
1 onion

1 c. chicken broth
1 can cream of mushroom,
    chicken, or celery soup

Fry bacon. Season flour; dip liver in it and brown liver in bacon fat on both sides. Slice onion on top, then add chicken broth and soup. Bake at 350° for 30 to 45 minutes - 1 hour if thick.

Janet Lozon, Owatonna, MN

LAZY DAY STROGANOFF

2 lb. round steak, cubed
1 env. Lipton onion soup
1 can cream of mushroom soup

1 can cream of celery soup
⅓ can water

Mix preceding ingredients together and place in crock pot set on HIGH temperature until mixture is hot, then reduce temperature to MEDIUM setting for about 8 hours. When ready to serve, add 1 can mushrooms and ½ cup sour cream if desired. Serve over wet noodles or cooked rice.

Eloise Hoff, Preston, MN

BROILED HAMBURGER

1 lb. lean chopped round beef
1 Tbsp. onion

3 Tbsp. toasted wheat germ

Mix chopped round beef with onion and toasted wheat germ. Form into 1 inch thick patties and broil for 4 minutes per side. Yield: 4 servings.

Pat Johnson, Battle Lake, MN

RYP'S MOCK-FILLET MIGNON

1½ lb. hamburger
3 to 4 slices Canadian bacon, minced

1 *small* jar mushrooms, minced
Pepper

Combine ingredients; shape into patties. Grill until desired doneness. Serve on buns.

Peggy Rypka, Owatonna, MN

SUPER BOWL SUNDAY SANDWICHES

Shaved ham (amount desired)
Cheez Whiz (amount desired)

Pepper to taste

Put in crock pot. Warm thoroughly on LOW setting, stirring occasionally. Serve on buns.

Optional: A few drops of Tabasco sauce may be added.

Peggy Rypka, Owatonna, MN

215

SAUCE FOR CHICKEN OR PORK CHOPS

1 lb. fresh mushrooms
¼ c. butter or margarine
2 Tbsp. soy sauce
1 can cream of mushroom soup

½ c. milk or water
2 cloves minced garlic
2 Tbsp. fresh parsley

Saute mushrooms in butter or margarine. Add soy sauce, cream of mushroom soup, milk or water, minced garlic, and fresh parsley. If using chops, brown first and pour over; bake in 350° oven for 1½ hours. Add more liquid if required. If using chicken breasts, skin and lay in pan. Pour over and bake as with the chops.

Rose Sauer, Grand Forks, ND

TERIYAKI MARINADE FOR BEEF, CHICKEN, OR PORK

This recipe received from the Banyon Inn at Lahaina - Maui, Hawaii.

1 c. soy sauce
1 c. white sugar

1 Tbsp. fresh crushed garlic
1 Tbsp. fresh grated ginger root

Mix together. Marinate meat for 8 to 12 hours. (I use a Tupperware bowl and turn it over every 3 to 4 hours.)

GIBLET GRAVY
(Makes about 5 cups)

Turkey neck and giblets
1 medium size onion, chopped
 (½ c.)
Few celery tops
1 tsp. salt

Dash of pepper
1 bay leaf
Water
½ c. flour

1. Combine turkey neck, giblets (except liver) with onion, celery tops, salt, pepper, bay leaf, and 4 cups water in a medium size saucepan.

2. Heat to boiling; lower heat, cover, and simmer for 20 minutes longer or until tender.

3. Strain broth; measure. Add more water, if necessary, to make 4 cups. Chop giblets; reserve.

4. After turkey is removed from roasting pan; remove rack. Tilt pan and pour off all fat.

5. Add the 4 cups giblet broth to pan; stir and scrape over low heat until all browned bits are dissolved. Stir the 1 cup cold water into the flour; blend well. Add mixture to liquid in pan. Cook, stirring constantly, until gravy thickens and boils. Lower heat; simmer for 5 minutes. Stir in chopped giblets. Taste; add additional salt and pepper if needed.

Janet Lozon, Owatonna, MN

HOMEMADE SHAKE AND BAKE FOR CHICKEN

1 c. fine bread crumbs
1 tsp. poultry seasoning
1/4 tsp. onion salt
1/4 c. flour
1 Tbsp. paprika

1/2 tsp. pepper
1 tsp. salt
1 tsp. garlic salt
1/2 tsp. marjoram

Mix all together well. Dip chicken in melted butter. Roll in preceding ingredients. Lay in foil covered pan. Bake at 350° for approximately 1 hour. Do not turn chicken.

Ann Strandemo, Bismarck, ND

HOMEMADE TACO SEASONING MIX

2 tsp. chili powder
1 1/2 tsp. paprika
1 1/2 tsp. cumin
1 tsp. onion powder

3/4 tsp. garlic salt
1/2 tsp. salt
Dash of cayenne

Combine all ingredients. Use instead of 1 (1 1/4 or 1.25 ounce) package of taco seasoning mix. If not using entire amount, store tightly covered in cool dry place. Makes 3 tablespoons.

Ruth Weis, Bemidji, MN

SPAGHETTI SAUCE

2 onions, diced fine
1 lb. ground beef and veal (if you like)
1 tsp. salt
1/4 tsp. garlic powder
1 tsp. oregano
1/2 tsp. cumin powder
1 tsp. sugar
1 bay leaf

1 bouillon cube
1 tsp. Worcestershire sauce
1/2 tsp. chili powder
1/4 tsp. Tabasco sauce
2 cans tomato paste
2 cans water
2 cans tomatoes
1 can mushrooms, drained

Brown beef and onions together. Add remaining ingredients. Simmer for 2 hours or more, adding more water and salt if needed.

"Mike" Skaret, Austin, MN

SPAGHETTI SAUCE

¼ c. olive oil
3 sections thinly sliced garlic
   buds
½ fresh green pepper, sliced
2 medium size onions, chopped
   or sliced
1 lb. hamburger
1 (No. 303) can tomatoes

1 can tomato soup
1 can mushroom soup
½ Tbsp. salt
½ tsp. pepper
2 dashes Tabasco sauce
2 dashes oregano
1 bay leaf

In olive oil, brown and simmer thinly sliced garlic buds, sliced green pepper, and chopped or sliced onions. Into this mixture, crumble and brown hamburger. Add tomatoes, tomato soup, and mushroom soup. Season with salt, pepper, Tabasco sauce, oregano, and crumbled bay leaf. Simmer for 2 hours or more. Serve over hot pasta.

Bonnie Gunderson, Fargo, ND

SPAGHETTI SAUCE

1½ lb. veal and ground beef
½ c. chopped onion
2 c. diced celery
½ c. chopped green pepper
1 whole fresh garlic
46 oz. can tomato juice
No. 3 can tomatoes
1 can tomato paste or tomato
   sauce

1 Tbsp. salt
1 tsp. curry powder
1 Tbsp. chili powder
¼ tsp. cayenne pepper
½ tsp. oregano
Paprika (to color)
Mushroom (if you like)

Brown veal, ground beef, onion, celery, green pepper, and garlic. Add remaining ingredients.

"Mike" Skaret, Austin, MN

SKILLET-GLAZED HAM FOR TWO

½ c. packed brown sugar
1½ tsp. flour
½ tsp. dry mustard

1 Tbsp. vinegar
2 Tbsp. ginger ale or beer
4 slices ready-to-eat ham

Mix first 3 ingredients in skillet. Blend in vinegar and ginger ale or beer. Cook over low heat, stirring until sugar is dissolved. Add ham; heat thoroughly. Spoon sauce over ham slices.

Betty Case, Hibbing, MN

COUNTRY HAM WITH RED EYE GRAVY

1 (8 to 12 oz.) slice country ham
    (¼ to ½ inch thick)
Small piece of ham fat
1 Tbsp. brown sugar

¾ c. water
¼ c. strong black coffee
1 tsp. French's Worcestershire
    sauce

Slash fat edge of ham to prevent curling. Heat skillet with ham fat in it. Add ham and cook over low heat until lightly browned on one side. Turn and sprinkle with ½ the sugar. Brown second side; turn and sprinkle with remaining sugar. Turn ham in pan quickly to caramelize sugar on both sides. Remove ham to serving dish and keep warm. Add water, coffee, and Worcestershire sauce to skillet; simmer for 5 minutes, stirring occasionally. Serve hot gravy over ham. Makes 2 to 3 servings.

Janet Lozon, Owatonna, MN

BREAKFAST SAUSAGE

6 to 7 feet pork casings
    (optional)

1 (3 lb.) boneless pork shoulder
    roast, well chilled

Trim fat on chilled pork roast to ¼ inch; discard trimmed fat. Cut meat into ½ inch cubes. With coarse blade of food grinder, grind pork.

1 egg white
1 Tbsp. ground sage
2 tsp. salt

1½ tsp. black pepper
1 tsp. ground red pepper
½ tsp. dried savory, crushed

In a small bowl, beat egg white slightly with a fork. Stir in ground sage, salt, black pepper, ground red pepper, and savory. Add egg white mixture to ground pork; mix thoroughly. Shape sausage into patties, or, if desired, fill casings for links. To shape patties easily, form sausage into 2½ inch diameter logs. Wrap and freeze. To use, thaw sausage till still icy. Cut partially frozen log into ½ inch thick slices. Thaw completely and cook. Makes about 3 pounds.

Karen Thompson, West St. Paul, MN

BAKED HAM-POTATO CASSEROLE
(Makes 2 (1 cup) servings)

1 c. potato, mashed
⅔ c. smoked ham, cooked and
    chopped

2 tsp. onion, finely chopped
2 tsp. butter or margarine
¼ c. cheese, shredded

Mix potato and ham. Cook onion in the fat until onion is clear but not brown. Place the mixture in a small casserole and top with cheese. Bake at 375°F. (moderate oven) until top begins to brown and cheese is melted, about 25 minutes.

Note: Dehydrated mashed potatoes may be used. Prepare potatoes according to directions on package.

Helen H. Clark, Grand Forks, ND

DOWN SOUTH BARBEQUE

2 onions, sliced
4 to 5 lb. pork roast or picnic
  ham

5 whole cloves
2 c. water

Put ½ of the onions on the bottom of the crock pot, then add meat and other ingredients with remaining onions on top. Cover and cook for 8 hours on LOW heat. Add 1 (16 ounce) bottle of barbeque sauce and chopped onion. Cover and cook for 1½ hours more on HIGH heat, stirring so it won't stick. Serve in big bowls.

Marian Nelson, Dickinson, ND

ORANGE GLAZED SPARERIBS

4 lb. pork spareribs
1 (6 oz.) can frozen orange
  concentrate, thawed

1½ tsp. Worcestershire sauce
½ tsp. garlic salt
⅛ tsp. pepper

In large kettle, cover ribs with salted water. Cover and simmer until ribs are almost tender (about 1 hour); drain thoroughly. Meanwhile, in a bowl, combine remaining ingredients. Place ribs in a shallow roasting pan; brush with sauce. Roast at 350° until ribs are glazed and brown, 30 to 40 minutes. Baste occasionally with sauce. Makes 4 servings.

Karen Miller

SLOPPY RIBS

3 to 3½ lb. pork ribs
1 env. Sloppy Joes seasoning
  mix
1 c. water
¾ c. barbeque sauce
3 Tbsp. brown sugar

2 Tbsp. vinegar
1 Tbsp. Worcestershire sauce
1 Tbsp. chili powder
½ tsp. salt
1 medium onion, chopped

Cut spareribs into serving pieces. Place into shallow pan. Cover with foil and bake in 350° oven for 60 minutes. Pour off excess fat. Combine rest of ingredients in a saucepan and bring to a boil. Pour over ribs and bake, uncovered, at 350° for 1 hour or until tender; baste occasionally.

Karen Miller

PORK CHOPS AND POTATOES

¾ c. Carnation milk
1¼ c. water
6 potatoes
1½ tsp. salt
Few grains of pepper

2 Tbsp. flour
1 Tbsp. butter
Bread crumbs
6 pork chops
1 egg, beaten

Scald milk and water in a double boiler. Pare and slice potatoes in ¼ inch slices. Place a layer in a buttered baking dish. Sprinkle with salt and pepper; dredge with flour. Dot with bits of butter. Repeat and add scalded milk until it can be seen through the top layer.

Dip pork chops in beaten egg and roll in bread crumbs. Place on top of potatoes and bake in moderate oven at 350°F. until potatoes are soft. Yields 6 servings.

Helen H. Clark, Grand Forks, MN

PORK CHOPS WITH CHICKEN RICE SOUP

Spread chops with prepared mustard; dip in flour and brown on both sides. Pour 1 can chicken rice soup over and simmer about 30 minutes or until tender.

Mrs. Goldie Mikish, Staples, MN

BARB E. QUE PORK CHOPS

1 can tomato soup	2 Tbsp. honey
¼ c. water	½ tsp. cinnamon
1 Tbsp. instant onion (or leave out)	½ tsp. ginger
	½ tsp. salt
3 Tbsp. soy sauce	⅛ tsp. clove

Combine ingredients; mix well. Pierce chops; marinate for 15 minutes, turning once. Place on grill. Brush with remaining marinade while cooking.

Kathy Fischler, Woodbury, MN

GOURMET PORK CHOPS

6 rib pork chops (¾ to 1 inch thick)	¾ c. chopped celery
	1 (6 oz.) can mushrooms
2 Tbsp. butter	3 Tbsp. butter
1 tsp. salt	¼ tsp. salt
⅛ tsp. pepper	2 c. wild rice, cooked
⅓ c. chopped onion	⅓ c. light cream

Grease 12x8 inch covered baking dish. Brown seasoned pork chops in 2 tablespoons butter. (Season chops with salt and pepper.) Cook onion and celery in 3 tablespoons of butter until tender. Add mushrooms and bouillon cubes, crushed; stir until dissolved. Add ¼ teaspoon salt, rice, and cream. Pat mixture in baking dish. Place chops on top; cover tightly. Bake in moderate oven at 350° for 30 minutes. Uncover and continue baking for 15 minutes or until chops are done.

Irene L. Moe, Fargo, ND

TWICE-COOKED NOODLES WITH PORK

Noodles in a stir-fry dish? The Chinese have been doing it for years. To use noodles in a stir-fry such as this one, cook the noodles in water first, then stir-fry them till slightly crisp. Add them to the other stir-fried ingredients at the end.

1 lb. boneless pork	1 Tbsp. catsup
6 oz. fine noodles or spaghetti	1 tsp. sugar
1 medium cucumber, halved lengthwise and seeded	3 to 4 Tbsp. cooking oil
3 Tbsp. soy sauce	2 Tbsp. red pepper oil or chili oil
2 tsp. cornstarch	2 cloves garlic, minced
1/3 c. water	1 tsp. grated ginger root

Partially freeze pork; thinly slice into bite-size strips. In a saucepan, cook noodles according to package directions. Rinse in cold water and drain well. Meanwhile, cut halved cucumber crosswise into thin slices; set aside.

In a bowl, stir soy sauce into cornstarch; stir in water, catsup, and sugar; set aside. In a large skillet or wok, heat 2 tablespoons cooking oil over medium heat. Add ½ of the cooked noodles. Cook and stir for 7 to 9 minutes or till slightly crisp. Transfer to a plate. Repeat with remaining 1 to 2 tablespoons cooking oil and the remaining noodles.

In the skillet or wok, heat 1 tablespoon red pepper oil or chili oil. Add garlic and ginger root; stir-fry for 30 seconds. Add cucumber; stir-fry for 30 seconds. Remove cucumber, leaving any oil in the skillet. Add remaining 1 tablespoon red pepper oil or chili oil to skillet; add pork and stir-fry for 2 to 3 minutes or till brown.

Stir the cornstarch mixture; stir into pork in skillet. Cook and stir till thickened and bubbly. Cook and stir 2 minutes more. Stir in cucumber and noodles; heat through. Makes 4 servings.

The mouth-tingling heat in this dish comes from chili oil. This pungent seasoning is sesame oil that has been infused with fiery crushed red pepper. Buy it in an oriental market or make your own.

Karen Thompson, West St. Paul, MN

POULTRY

MRS. HOVIS' FRIED CHICKEN

2 chickens (each about 3 lb.)
2 tsp. coarse salt (such as
    kosher salt)
1 Tbsp. freshly ground black
    pepper
1 tsp. poultry seasoning
1 Tbsp. paprika

Pinch of cayenne pepper
2 c. unbleached flour
1 lb. solid white shortening
1 lb. pure lard (or increase the
    quantity of white shortening
    by 1 lb.)
¼ c. bacon fat

Carefully cut each chicken into 8 pieces: 2 legs, 2 thighs, 2 breast pieces, 2 wings (with wing tips removed if desired). Use the carcasses for soups and stock. Combine the salt, black pepper, poultry seasoning, paprika, and cayenne and blend well. Coat chicken pieces with this mixture. Coat the pieces with flour.

The Southern technique calls for putting the flour in a large heavy brown paper bag, adding the chicken pieces, a few at a time, and tossing. Remove and shake off excess flour. Heat ½ the white shortening, ½ the lard, and ½ the bacon fat in each of 2 large skillets, preferably black iron.

Heat the fat until it is lightly smoking. Put the chicken pieces in, skin side up, and cook until crisp and golden brown on one side, about 12 to 14 minutes. Turn the pieces and continue cooking for 12 to 14 minutes on the second side, taking care not to burn the pieces. Yield: 8 or more servings.

Janet Lozon, Owatonna, MN

BROILED CHICKEN BREASTS

Wash and dry 2 large chicken breasts. Split them down the middle. Rub juice of 1 lime on breasts. Broil, skin side up, on lightly oiled grill (well pre-heated) for 5 minutes on 1 side and 10 minutes on the other. Sprinkle with fresh, chopped, or dried tarragon. Makes 4 servings.

Pat Johnson, Battle Lake, MN

BAKED CHICKEN BREAST

4 to 6 chicken breasts, skinned
Cajun-Creole seasoning

Margarine

Place skinned chicken in shallow pan; spread each breast with margarine. Sprinkle to taste each breast with cajun seasoning. Bake with enough water in pan so as not to burn. Bake at 350° for 45 minutes. After 40 minutes, remove from oven and sprinkle a dash of sugar over each breast. Return to oven for 5 minutes.

Joyce Bell, Golden Valley, MN

BAKED CHICKEN WITH SAUCE

1 c. sour cream
½ c. dry sherry

1 c. mushrooms
1 can cream of mushroom soup

Combine preceding ingredients and pour over raw chicken pieces in a shallow pan. Bake for 1½ to 2 hours at 350°.

Anne La Fleur, Duluth, MN

BARBEQUE CHICKEN

½ c. vinegar
⅓ c. oil
2 Tbsp. ketchup
2 tsp. salt
2 tsp. Worcestershire sauce
1 tsp. paprika

1 tsp. minced onion
1 clove minced garlic
½ tsp. hot pepper sauce
¼ tsp. dry mustard
1 (2½ to 3½ lb.) chicken

Combine all ingredients, except chicken, in a large shallow plastic or glass container. Add chicken; cover tightly and marinate for at least 2 hours at room temperature or overnight in the refrigerator. Turn at least once. Cook 5 to 6 inches from heat; baste frequently with leftover sauce. Barbecue for 30 to 45 minutes; turn often until tender.

Karen Miller

UNFORGETTABLE CHICKEN WINGS

12 chicken wings (2 lb.)
Cooking oil or shortening (for deep fat frying)
3 Tbsp. butter or margarine
1 (2 oz.) bottle (¼ c.) hot pepper sauce

½ c. dairy sour cream
¼ c. mayonnaise or salad dressing
1 Tbsp. lime juice
Celery sticks (optional)

Cut off and discard tips of chicken wings. Cut wings at joints to form 24 pieces. Fry wing pieces, a few at a time, in deep hot cooking oil or shortening (375°) for 8 to 10 minutes or till golden brown. Drain on paper towels. Transfer wings to a serving dish.

In a saucepan, melt butter or margarine. Stir in hot pepper sauce. Pour over wings. Turn wings to coat. For dipping sauce, in a bowl, stir together sour cream, mayonnaise or salad dressing, and lime juice. Serve wings with dipping sauce and, if desired, celery sticks. Makes 24.

Karen Thompson, West St. Paul, MN

CHICKEN HOT DISH

2 cans chicken ala king (Swanson)
2 cans boned chicken (5 oz.)

2 c. cooked macaroni
1 can mushroom bits
½ c. sliced stuffed olives

Mix preceding ingredients together.

Add on top:

1 can chow mein noodles
½ c. slivered almonds

½ c. shredded Cheddar cheese
1 stick butter, melted

Cover and bake at 350° for 30 to 45 minutes; remove cover and let brown.

Mary Hocking

BAKED CHICKEN DRUMMIES
(Makes 32 wings)

Combine:

⅔ c. melted butter
1 tsp. salt

½ tsp. garlic powder

Mix:

1½ c. bread crumbs

½ c. Parmesan cheese

Dip wings in butter mixture, then roll in crumb mixture. Place on jelly roll sheet and bake for 30 minutes at 400°.

Mary Hocking

DUCK

Clean 2 (4 pound) ducks. Brush with soy sauce; sprinkle lightly with celery salt and garlic powder. Sprinkle garlic powder in cavities. Grill over a drip pan - duck is very greasy. (Two ducks will fit on 1 Weber turkey rack.) Bake approximately 3 hours.

Peggy Rypka, Owatonna, MN

TOMATO SAUCE AND CHICKEN - ITALIAN

Onions
Celery
2 (8 oz.) cans tomato sauce

4 cans water
1 chicken
Salt and pepper

Fry onions and celery (amount depends on you, or 1 medium onion and 2 celery stalks). Add tomato sauce plus 4 cans of water. Cut up chicken; salt and pepper well. Brown in skillet. After all the chicken has been browned, add to the sauce that has been simmering.

When chicken and sauce has simmered for about ½ hour, add potatoes and whatever else you may like. After potatoes are half done (I always use green beans), bake or cook on top of stove.

Marcy Weight, Anoka, MN

CHICKEN LASAGNA MADE WITH UNCOOKED NOODLES

Step-saving discovery! The lasagna noodles go into this layered casserole uncooked; then cheese, sauce, and noodles all cook at once. You can use any brand of regular whole wheat or spinach noodles.

1 c. cream style cottage cheese
3 oz. pkg. cream cheese,
   softened and cut up
10¾ oz. can condensed cream
   of mushroom soup
1 c. loose pack frozen cut
   broccoli
⅓ c. sliced celery
¼ c. milk

1 tsp. minced dried onion
¼ tsp. dried oregano, crushed
⅛ tsp. ground sage
6 lasagna noodles
1 c. chopped cooked chicken or
   turkey
½ c. shredded Cheddar cheese
   (2 oz.)
⅔ c. boiling water

In a mixing bowl, stir together cottage cheese and cream cheese; set aside. In a mixing bowl, combine soup, broccoli, celery, milk, dried onion, oregano, and sage; set aside. Place 2 uncooked lasagna noodles in a greased 10x6x2 inch baking dish. Layer with ½ the cottage cheese mixture and ⅓ of the soup mixture. Repeat layers of noodles, cottage cheese, and soup.

Top with remaining noodles, chicken, and remaining soup mixture. Sprinkle with Cheddar cheese. Slowly pour boiling water into dish around entire inside edge. Cover tightly with foil. Bake in 350° oven for 60 to 65 minutes or until done. Let stand, covered, for 10 minutes. Makes 6 servings.

Janet Lozon, Owatonna, MN

GRILLED CHICKEN TACOS

2 lb. green peppers or podlano
   peppers
Vegetable oil
4 whole chicken breasts, boned
   and skinned
Salt and pepper

2 Tbsp. butter or margarine
12 flour tortillas
1½ c. (6 oz.) shredded Monterey
   Jack cheese
1½ c. picante sauce

Brush peppers with oil; bake on cookie sheet at 450°F. for 20 minutes or until skin blisters, turning once. Remove from oven; place in plastic bag. Close; let stand for 15 minutes. Peel peppers; cut into thin strips.

Pound chicken to even thickness. Brush with oil; season with salt and pepper. Place on grill over hot coals for 6 to 8 minutes or until cooked through, turning once. Cut into ¼ inch slices.

Melt butter in skillet. Add peppers and chicken; heat through. Spoon ½ cup chicken mixture down center of each tortilla; top with 2 tablespoons each cheese and picante sauce. Makes 6 servings.

Tammy Weight

FISH

LOBSTER TAILS ON THE GRILL

Using kitchen shears, cut down both sides of membrane; peel back and cut off. Brush with garlic-butter. Grill, shell side down, until just flaky (will start to curl). *Do not overcook.* Serve with garlic-butter.

Peggy Rypka, Owatonna, MN

GARY'S SALMON FILLETS

On each fillet, sprinkle:

Lemon juice
Garlic powder

Dry mustard
Celery salt

With skin side down, wrap individually in heavy-duty foil. Grill, turning frequently, until flaky. Meat will fall off skin very easy.

Peggy Rypka, Owatonna, MN

SALMON STEAKS

6 salmon steaks
⅓ c. butter
½ tsp. salt

¼ tsp. paprika
1 tsp. Worcestershire sauce
2 Tbsp. grated onion

Place steaks in a greased shallow baking pan. Melt butter; add seasonings and sauce. Spread over salmon. Sprinkle 1 teaspoon onion over each steak. Bake in moderate oven at 350° for 25 to 30 minutes. Makes 6 servings.

Ruth Dandeweerd, Preston, MN

RICE AND SALMON BALLS

1 lb. can salmon
1 c. cooked rice (not instant)
2 beaten eggs

1 tsp. minced onion
1 tsp. salt
½ c. bread crumbs

Mix. Form balls and place in shallow pan.

Combine:

1 can mushroom soup
½ can water

2 tsp. chopped green pepper

Pour this mixture over salmon balls. Bake in 350° oven for 30 minutes.

Anne La Fleur, Duluth, MN

SALMON CUSTARD CASSEROLE
(Serves 2)

Preheat oven to 350°. Grease two 10 ounce casserole dishes. In medium bowl with fork, beat 2 eggs slightly.

Stir in:

½ c. undiluted evaporated milk	¼ tsp. salt
1 (7¾ oz.) can salmon, drained	½ tsp. dry mustard
1 Tbsp. chopped chives	Dash of pepper

Mix well to flake salmon. Pour into casseroles; sprinkle with paprika. Set casseroles in shallow baking pan. Fill pan with hot water to come halfway up casseroles. Bake for 25 to 30 minutes until knife inserted in center comes out clean.

ESCALLOPED SALMON OR SALMON LOAF

1 can salmon	½ c. cracker crumbs
Salt and pepper	½ c. milk
2 tsp. lemon juice	2 egg whites, stiffly beaten
2 egg yolks	

Mix milk, crumbs, yolks, lemon juice, salmon, salt, and pepper. Fold in stiffly beaten whites. Bake for ¾ hour at 375°.

Betty Michon, Detroit Lakes, MN

SALMON LOAF

1 can red salmon	1 Tbsp. butter
2 eggs	1 tsp. salt
1 c. milk	1 Tbsp. parsley

Pour into buttered dish and bake for 1 hour. Serve with white sauce into which parsley has been added, or peas and hard cooked eggs may be used instead of parsley.

Marie Capen, Duluth, MN

SALMON LOAF

1 can salmon, drained (save oil)	½ c. milk
1 Tbsp. butter	1 c. cracker crumbs
3 eggs, beaten light	Salt and pepper to taste

Mix all the preceding ingredients together and put in buttered loaf pan. Bake at 325° to 350° for ½ hour.

Dressing for loaf:

1 c. hot milk	1 egg, beaten
Salmon oil	1 Tbsp. cornstarch
1 Tbsp. butter	

Cook until it thickens and add 1 tablespoon catsup. Remove Salmon Loaf from pan. Cover with dressing and serve.

Betty Case, Hibbing, MN

FISH MARINADE

½ c. butter
½ c. soy sauce
1 tsp. garlic salt

1 Tbsp. Worcestershire sauc
1 tsp. Chinese oil

Combine all ingredients and bring to a boil. As you are barbecuing or baking fish, baste often. *Especially delicious on salmon.*

Lorraine Sojka, Duluth, MN

CRAB LASAGNA

½ lb. lasagna noodles (9
   noodles)
1 Tbsp. oil

2 cans cream of shrimp soup
2 cans king crab

Cook lasagna noodles in boiling salted water with oil added. Heat cream of shrimp soup and king crab; set aside.

Mix together:

1 (8 oz.) pkg. cream cheese
2 c. cream style cottage cheese
1 c. chopped onion

1 beaten egg
1 tsp. salt
¼ tsp. pepper

Grease 9x13 inch pan. Layer as follows: 3 noodles, ½ of cheese mixture, 3 noodles, *all* of crab mixture, 3 noodles, and remaining cheese mixture. Place 12 slices of tomato on top. Sprinkle each with a little sugar. Bake in 350° oven for 45 minutes.

Sprinkle with 1 cup sharp Cheddar cheese and bake for 45 minutes longer. Let stand for 5 to 10 minutes before cutting. Can be made day before but do not put tomatoes on till ready to serve.

Sonya Masset, Bismarck, ND

BREADS

use olive oil instead of butter

GARLIC CROUTONS

to 400°. Trim crusts from 4 slices white bread. Generously
of bread slices; sprinkle with ¼ teaspoon garlic powder. Cut
into ½ ...   s; place in baking pan. Bake for 10 to 15 minutes, stirring occasionally, until golden brown and crisp. ✓ *more*

Leave in oven or not Janet Lozon, Owatonna, MN
or several hrs to "dry"

HOMEMADE CROUTONS

Cut leftover bread into small squares. Lay out squares on a cookie
sheet. Add lots of melted butter to lightly saturate bread squares. Sprinkle paprika, seasoned salt, garlic powder, and parsley over buttered bread. Bake at
375° for 10 minutes or till quite dry and toasted, stirring occasionally. *Enjoy on
salads, etc.*

Diane Kemmetmueller, Anoka, MN

BUTTERED BREAD CRUMBS

1 to 3 Tbsp. butter or other fat   **1 c. bread crumbs**

Melt the fat; don't brown. Add the bread crumbs and mix with a fork until
all crumbs are covered. Use to top au gratin dishes.

Anne La Fleur, Duluth, MN

POTATO PANCAKES

2 qt. grated raw potatoes   **1 tsp. salt**
3 beaten eggs   **½ c. flour**
½ c. half & half cream   **½ tsp. baking powder**

Mix and fry. *Easy and very good.*

Mrs. Goldie Mikish, Staples, MN

BAKED FRENCH TOAST

1 c. corn flakes, crushed   **¼ stick margarine**
2 eggs   **6 slices bread**
¼ c. milk

Mix preceding ingredients, except corn flakes and margarine. Dip
bread first in mixture, then in corn flake crumbs. Lay single on cookie sheet.
Pour melted margarine over top and bake for 10 to 15 minutes at 400°.

Mrs. Goldie Mikish, Staples, MN

KANIP - STRIPS OF DUMPLINGS

3 eggs
½ tsp. salt

6 Tbsp. milk
Flour

Beat eggs. Add salt and milk. Add flour until bread dough consistency. Cut dough by small strips into lightly salted boiling water. Strips will float to top when done; remove from water. Use in your favorite soups and stew recipes instead of dumplings.

Gretchen Marquart, Red River Valley

PERFECT PASTA

3 c. durum flour *(not* semolina)
Approx. ¾ c. water

1 egg (optional)

Combine flour (egg) and enough water to make a very stiff dough. (You may refrigerate the dough at this time for an hour or more if desired. It seems to make for easier handling.) Roll out to ⅛ inch thickness by hand or with a pasta machine. Let air dry on flour about 1 hour, turning after 30 minutes. Cut according to desired width and let dry on a floured surface. Cook immediately or store in an airtight container after pasta is thoroughly dry. (Fresh pasta cooks in considerably less time than commercial pasta. *Do not overcook.)*

Variations:

Tomato Pasta: Add one 6 ounce can of tomato paste to 3 cups durum flour and enough water to make a stiff dough.

Spinach Pasta: Add ½ cup cooked pureed spinach to 3 cups durum flour and enough water to make a stiff dough. Canned spinach will work, but frozen or fresh spinach makes a prettier product.

Herb Pasta: Use herbs of your choice *or* ¼ cup chopped fresh parsley and 1 teaspoon dill weed to 3 cups durum flour and enough water to make a stiff dough.

Lemon-Dill Pasta: Add ½ cup lemon juice, 1 teaspoon lemon peel, and 1 tablespoon dill weed to 3 cups durum flour and enough water to make a stiff dough. Excellent as a side dish with fish.

Note: A touch of butter and grated Parmesan cheese is all any of these pastas need. Bon Appetit!!!

Mary Hocking, Fargo, ND

POPOVERS THAT POP

1 c. sifted flour
¼ tsp. salt
2 eggs

1 c. milk
1 Tbsp. melted shortening

Sift flour and salt together. Beat eggs and add milk, shortening, and sifted dry ingredients. Beat until smooth with rotary beater. Fill greased muffin tins ½ full and bake at 450° for 20 minutes. Reduce heat to 350° and bake for 15 minutes longer. Makes 8.

Marie Burt, Owatonna, MN

BRAN MUFFINS APLENTY

2 c. boiling water
5 tsp. baking soda
6 c. wheat bran flakes cereal
2 c. sugar
1 c. shortening

4 eggs
1 qt. buttermilk
5 c. flour
1 tsp. salt

Mix boiling water and baking soda. Add bran cereal and set aside to cool. Cream sugar and shortening in a large bowl. Stir in eggs, 1 at a time; beat well. Stir in buttermilk. Stir in flour and salt. Add bran mixture and mix well. Tightly cover and store in the refrigerator. When ready to bake, drop by spoonfuls (don't stir) into greased muffin tins. Bake at 375° for 20 minutes. Makes 5½ dozen muffins.

Lenora Buck, Fargo, ND

MUFFINS

1 c. sugar or 1½ c. honey
2¼ c. flour
½ tsp. salt
2½ tsp. soda
2 eggs
½ c. oil (sunflower oil is best)

1 c. boiling water
1 c. raisins or dates
2 c. buttermilk
3 to 4 c. unprocessed hard red
   spring wheat bran

Pour boiling water over dates or raisins and add soda. Mix together lightly. Pour in muffin tins. Bake at 375° for 20 minutes.

Sonya Masset, Bismarck, ND

FLAT BREAD
(All-Bran cereal)

1½ c. All-Bran
½ c. lard, melted
½ c. sugar
1 c. buttermilk
1 c. warm water

1 tsp. soda
2 tsp. baking powder
1½ tsp. salt
Scant 5 c. flour

232

Pour warm water on All-Bran; let stand for 5 minutes. Mix rest of ingredients into All-Bran mixture; roll thin. Cut in desired pieces and bake on cookie sheet at 325°. Can also be baked on lefse grill at 325° to 350° and then finished in oven at 250° for about 10 minutes.

Use rolling pin with stocking on.

Pearl Paulsrud, Montevideo, MN

SOUTHERN GAL BISCUITS

2 c. flour
4 tsp. baking powder
½ tsp. cream of tartar
½ tsp. salt

2 Tbsp. sugar
½ c. shortening
1 egg (unbeaten)
⅔ c. milk

Stir to a stiff dough. Knead 5 times. Roll or pat to ½ inch thickness and cut with biscuit cutter. Bake for 10 to 15 minutes at 450°.

Can be used for shortcake.

Edna Helberg, Sioux Falls, SD

BUTTERHORNS

1 c. butter (no oleo)
½ c. sugar
2 c. sifted flour
1 c. ground almonds or 1 tsp.
    almond flavor

¼ tsp. baking powder
1 tsp. vanilla
Pinch of salt

Cream butter and sugar. Stir in flour, baking powder, salt, and flavor. Make into rolls and chill overnight. Cut in slices and bake. Roll in sugar while hot. Bake at 375°.

These can be rolled in green and red sugar at Christmastime.

Mildred Sjostrom, St. Peter, MN

CINNAMON ROLLS

1 pkg. active dry yeast   ¼ c. water

Soften yeast in warm water (110°).

1 c. milk, scalded
¼ c. margarine
¼ c. sugar

1 tsp. salt
1 egg
3½ c. flour (all-purpose)

Combine first 4 ingredients. Add 1 cup of flour; beat well, then beat in softened yeast and egg. Gradually add remaining flour; beat well. Cover and let rise in warm place till double (about 2 hours). On lightly floured surface, roll out the dough. Spread ½ cup softened margarine on dough. Sprinkle 1 cup sugar and 1 tablespoon cinnamon over dough. Roll lengthwise as for jelly roll; seal edge.

Cut in 1 inch slices. Place, cut sides down, in greased 13x9 inch pan. Cover and let rise till double (about 1 hour). Bake at 375° for 20 to 25 minutes; remove from pan. Frost with confectioners icing.

Gretchen Marquart

GOLDEN CROWN ROLLS

1 c. scalded milk	1½ pkg. yeast (dry)
½ c. melted butter or oleo	2 eggs, beaten
¼ c. sugar	4½ c. flour
1 tsp. salt	

Combine milk, shortening, sugar, and salt. Scald and let cool. Dissolve yeast in ¼ cup warm water and beat eggs; add yeast and eggs. Mix. Add flour to make a soft dough; let rise until double. Knead; let rise another 10 minutes. Shape into golf size balls.

½ c. melted butter	½ c. chopped nuts
¾ c. sugar and cinnamon	

Roll balls in a mixture of first butter, then sugar and cinnamon, and then chopped nuts. Arrange in a greased angel food cake pan; *let rise.* Bake at 350° for 40 to 45 minutes.

Sadie Labland, Hibbing, MN

RHUBARB ROLLS

3 c. rhubarb, diced small	4 tsp. baking powder
2¼ c. sifted flour	⅔ c. milk
½ tsp. salt	⅓ c. half & half

Sift flour, baking powder, and salt together. Mix milk and cream. Gradually add this to flour mixture, stirring to stiff batter. Turn mixture onto floured board and knead lightly. Roll to about ¼ inch thick and arrange rhubarb on it. Roll up and cut in 1½ inch slices.

Make thin syrup from 1½ cups sugar and 1½ cups cold water. Pour into large baking pan (9x13 inches). Add 2 to 3 teaspoons red food coloring to make bright red. Arrange cut rolls in pan, side by side (like cinnamon rolls). Bake at 400° for about 30 minutes. Serve warm with cream. Serves 12.

Evelyn Pedersen

SOUR CREAM COFFEE CAKE

Blend together and set aside (topping):

⅓ c. brown sugar	2 tsp. cinnamon
¼ c. sugar	1 c. crushed pecans

Blend together and set aside (flour mixture):

2 c. flour	1 tsp. baking powder
1 tsp. baking soda	1 tsp. salt

Cream together:

½ c. margarine	3 eggs (1 at a time)
1 c. sugar	1 tsp. vanilla

To the preceding creamed mixture, blend 1 cup sour cream and the flour mixture, alternating between the two. Grease and flour angel food cake pan. Pour ½ batter into pan and sprinkle with ½ topping mixture. Add rest of batter and follow with rest of topping. Cut back and forth with knife to give swirl effect. Bake at 325° for 45 to 50 minutes.

Connie Jeske, Owatonna, MN

JAM AND CHEESE LOAF MORNING BREAD

1 pkg. active dry yeast (quick-rising yeast will not work for this recipe because it rises too rapidly in the refrigerator)	1 beaten egg
	1 Tbsp. sugar
	8 oz. pkg. cream cheese, softened
½ c. warm water (110° to 115°)	½ c. sugar
2½ c. packaged biscuit mix	1 Tbsp. lemon juice
	¼ c. desired jam or preserves

1. In a bowl, dissolve yeast in warm water. Stir in biscuit mix, egg, and 1 tablespoon sugar; mix well. Turn out onto surface dusted with additional biscuit mix. Knead gently for 20 strokes. Place dough on center of greased 15 ½ x 12 inch baking sheet. Roll to 14 x 9 inches.

2. In a mixing bowl, combine cream cheese, ½ cup sugar, and juice; spread mixture lengthwise down center third of rectangle. Make 3 inch cuts at 1 inch intervals on both long sides. Fold strips at an angle over filling; cover. Chill for 2 to 24 hours. Bake in a 350° oven for 20 minutes. Spoon jam down center of loaf. Bake for 5 minutes more. Cool for 10 minutes. Makes 12 servings. There are 230 calories per serving.

Beth Thelen, Fargo, ND

CHEESE BUBBLE BREAD

2 loaves frozen white bread, thawed	½ tsp. dried parsley
	½ tsp. onion powder
32 (¾ inch) cubes of Cheddar cheese	½ tsp. garlic powder
	½ c. butter, melted
½ tsp. thyme	1 c. Parmesan cheese
½ tsp. oregano	

Divide each loaf into 16 pieces. Shape into balls around cheese cubes. Dip into melted butter with spices. Roll in Parmesan cheese and place into well greased Bundt pan. Cover and let rise in warm place until bread rises above the top of the pan. Bake at 375° for 40+ minutes, depending on oven. Remove from pan immediately.

I use onion powder and garlic powder instead of salts.

Georgine Isakson, Fargo, ND

COWBOY BREAD

2 c. brown sugar
1 tsp. nutmeg
1 tsp. cinnamon
1 c. shortening
3 c. flour

2 eggs
1 c. sour milk
½ tsp. baking soda
1 tsp. baking powder

Mix together first 5 ingredients. Put aside 1 cup for topping. Mix with remaining ingredients and pour into greased and floured pan. Top with 1 cup of the saved mixture. Bake in 9x13 inch pan at 350° for 35 minutes.

Good served with chili or as a snack.

Bonnie Gunderson, Fargo, ND

MANDARIN ORANGE BREAD

4 eggs
1½ c. sugar
2½ c. flour
2 tsp. salt
2 tsp. soda
1½ c. quick oats

2 (11 oz.) undrained mandarin
  oranges
3 oz. pkg. orange flavored
  gelatin
1 c. chopped pecans

Combine eggs and sugar. Beat until light, about 2 minutes. Sift flour, salt, and soda; add to egg mixture and blend until smooth, about 2 minutes longer. Add remaining ingredients and mix very well. Spoon into 2 greased and floured 9x5 inch loaf pans. Bake at 325° for 1 hour. Remove from pans immediately. Allow to stand for 24 hours before slicing. Makes 2 loaves.

Marie Capen, Duluth, MN

CRANBERRY NUT BREAD

Juice and grated rind of 1
  orange
2 Tbsp. melted butter
1 well beaten egg
½ c. chopped nuts
2 c. cut up fresh cranberries

1 c. sugar
2 c. flour
½ tsp. soda
½ tsp. baking powder
½ tsp. salt

Sift together all dry ingredients. Combine juice, rind, and butter with enough water to make ¾ cup juice. Stir in egg. Pour mixture into dry ingredients to which cranberries and nuts have been added. Bake in greased 9x5 inch pan for 1 hour at 350°.

Anne La Fleur, Duluth, MN

STRAWBERRY BREAD

3 c. flour
1 tsp. salt
1 tsp. soda
2 c. sugar
3 tsp. cinnamon (or more, up to 8, depending on taste)

4 eggs
1¼ c. oil
1 tsp. vanilla
2 (10 oz.) pkg. frozen strawberries
Nuts (optional)

Mix all dry ingredients in a bowl. Make a well. Add eggs, oil, and vanilla; stir. Add thawed strawberries and nuts. Don't mix too much. Bake at 350° for 1 hour and 10 minutes in 2 loaf pans.

Sue Christenson, Egan, MN

DATE LOAF

3 c. white sugar
1 Tbsp. butter
1 c. chopped pecans

1 c. dates, cut fine
1 c. cream
1 tsp. vanilla

Mix all together, except nuts. Cook in heavy saucepan until mixture reaches soft ball stage, stirring constantly. Cool, then add nuts and vanilla; beat until cold. Pour into cold wet cloth and roll about 2 inches in diameter and let set until firm. Cut in about ¼ inch thick slices.

Barb Fivecoate, Virginia, MN

BATTER RHUBARB BREAD
(Prize winner)

1½ c. brown sugar
⅔ c. liquid shortening
1 egg
1 c. sour milk (or cream)
1 tsp. salt

1 tsp. soda
1 tsp. vanilla
2½ c. flour
1½ c. finely diced rhubarb
½ c. chopped nuts

Combine brown sugar and shortening. Stir in egg and sour milk with vanilla. Add sifted dry ingredients. Stir in rhubarb and nuts. Pour into 2 well greased loaf pans. Combine topping ingredients and sprinkle on top. Bake at 325° for about 40 minutes. Do not overbake. Remove from pans after 2 or 3 minutes; cool.

Topping:

½ c. sugar   1 Tbsp. butter
½ tsp. cinnamon

Lucille Engstrom, St. Paul, MN

HONEY WHOLE WHEAT BREAD
(Prize winner)

2 pkg. active dry yeast   ⅓ c. soft margarine or other
3¾ c. whole wheat flour   shortening
4 to 4½ c. all-purpose flour   ⅓ c. honey
1 Tbsp. salt   2¼ c. water
¼ c. Saco buttermilk powder

In large mixer bowl, combine 2 packages yeast, 1 cup of whole wheat flour, 1 cup all-purpose flour, salt, Saco buttermilk powder, soft margarine, and honey. Add very warm (120° to 130°) tap water to flour mixture. Blend at low speed until moistened. Beat for 3 minutes at medium speed. By hand, gradually stir in remaining 1¾ cups flour to make a soft dough.

Turn dough out on lightly floured board and knead until smooth and elastic (8 to 10 minutes). Place in greased bowl, turning to grease all sides. Cover; let rise in warm place free from drafts until double in bulk (about 1 hour or more). (Do not shortcut here.)

Punch dough down; divide dough into 2 parts. Mold into balls. Allow to rest, covered with inverted bowl, for 10 minutes. Shape into loaves. Place in 2 greased 8½ x 4½ x 2½ or two 9 x 5 x 3 inch pans. Let rise until double (about 1 hour or more). Bake at 400° for 25 to 30 minutes or until golden brown and loaves sound hollow when tapped. Cover with foil towards last to prevent burning. Remove from pans and cool on racks. Makes 2 loaves.

Lucille Engstrom, St. Paul, MN

BARS

HELPFUL HINT

Hard brown sugar or raisins may be softened by placing a damp paper towel in the bag or box and closing it tightly. Microwave for 20 to 30 seconds. Let stand for 1 minute. Sugar or raisins should now be softened and ready for use.

RICE KRISPIES CARAMEL BARS

Make Rice Krispies mixture according to box directions and spread ½ in pan.

Melt:

1 pkg. caramels
1 can sweetened condensed
  milk

¼ c. butter

Spread on Rice Krispies mixture and spread on remaining ½ rice Krispies mixture.

Mary Hocking, Fargo, ND

COCA-COLA BARS

2 c. flour
2 c. sugar
3 Tbsp. cocoa
2 sticks margarine
1 c. Coca-cola

1½ c. mini marshmallows
½ c. buttermilk
1 tsp. soda
2 beaten eggs
1 tsp. vanilla

Combine flour, sugar, and cocoa in a bowl. In a saucepan, combine margarine, Coke, and marshmallows. Heat to boiling point and pour over dry ingredients, then beat. Add buttermilk, soda, eggs, and vanilla; mix well. Put in greased 10x15 inch pan at 350° for 30 minutes.

Frosting:

1 stick margarine
6 Tbsp. Coke

3 Tbsp. cocoa

Heat to boiling point. Pour over 4 cups powdered sugar and chopped nuts; mix well. Spread on warm bars.

Alma M. Collette, Grand Forks, ND

NO BAKE GRAHAM CRACKER BARS

1 lb. graham crackers
1 c. brown sugar
1 c. coconut
½ c. butter
½ c. chopped nuts

½ c. cut up maraschino cherries
½ c. milk
Powdered sugar
Cherry juice

Line pan with whole graham crackers. Bring to a boil and cook for 1 minute the milk, brown sugar, and butter. Let cool and spread over crackers. Sprinkle over the top the coconut, chopped nuts, and maraschino cherries. Crush enough graham crackers to make a cup and sprinkle over the top. Cover all with whole graham crackers.

Frost with powdered sugar frosting made with cherry juice. Chill in refrigerator till you wish to cut into squares.

Edna Olson, Duluth, MN

PECAN PIE BARS

1 c. shortening
2 c. flour
3 eggs
1 tsp. vanilla
½ tsp. salt

1 c. brown sugar
½ tsp. salt
1 c. sugar
1 c. dark corn syrup
1½ c. pecans

Mix shortening (can use ½ butter), brown sugar, flour, and ½ teaspoon salt. Mix as for pie crust and pat into 9x13 inch pan. Bake at 350° for 10 minutes. Beat eggs gently. Add sugar, vanilla, corn syrup, and ½ teaspoon salt. Add pecans. Pour over crust and bake for 15 minutes at 350°. Reduce heat to 275° and bake until set (about 20 minutes). Cool and cut into bars.

Diane Kemmetmueller, Anoka, MN

SUPER GOOD APPLE BARS

2 c. sugar
1 c. vegetable oil
2 eggs
1 tsp. vanilla
2 c. all-purpose flour
1 tsp. soda

1 tsp. cinnamon
¼ tsp. salt
3 c. peeled chopped apples
1 c. chopped nuts
Frosting (follows)

Heat oven to 350°. Combine sugar, oil, eggs, and vanilla; beat until light. Add flour, soda, cinnamon, and salt; mix well. Stir in apples and nuts. Spread in greased 13x9 inch pan. Bake for 45 minutes or until apples are tender; cool. Frost and cut into bars. Makes 24 to 30 bars.

Frosting:

2 (3 oz.) pkg. cream cheese
1½ c. powdered sugar

3 Tbsp. butter or margarine,
softened

Combine all ingredients; blend until smooth and of spreading consistency.

Diane Kemmetmueller, Anoka, MN

APPLESAUCE BARS

1¼ c. flour
½ tsp. soda
½ tsp. cinnamon
¼ tsp. nutmeg
Dash of ground cloves

½ c. shortening
¾ c. sugar
1 egg
½ c. applesauce
½ tsp. vanilla

Sift together flour, soda, salt, and spices. Cream together shortening and sugar. Add egg, beating until light and fluffy. Add applesauce and vanilla; mix well. Add flour mixture; mix well. Spread into greased and floured 8x8 inch pan. Bake at 350° for 50 minutes.

Mix ½ cup confectioners sugar and 1 tablespoon hot milk. Spread on bars while warm. Yield: 18 bars.

One half cup chopped nuts and ½ cup raisins can be added with flour mixture.

Anne La Fleur, Duluth, MN

APPLE OATMEAL BARS

½ c. margarine
2 eggs
1 c. oatmeal
1 c. diced apples, cored and
**   pared**
½ c. walnuts, broken
½ tsp. nutmeg

1 c. sugar
1 c. flour
1 tsp. baking powder
½ tsp. soda
½ tsp. salt
½ tsp. ground cloves
½ tsp. cinnamon

Cream sugar, shortening, and eggs. Add flour with dry ingredients; mix well. Add oatmeal, apples, and nuts, mixing thoroughly. Bake in greased jellyroll pan at 375° for 25 minutes.

Anne La Fleur, Duluth, MN

APPLE ROLY POLY
(Basic recipe)

Baking Powder Biscuit Dough:

2 c. all-purpose flour
3 tsp. baking powder
1 tsp. salt
2 to 4 Tbsp. shortening

About ⅔ c. bottle milk or ⅓ c.
evaporated milk and ⅓ c.
water

Sift dry ingredients together. Cut in shortening as for pie crust until mixture is crumbly. Add enough milk while stirring with fork to make a soft dough that can be easily handled. Roll into a rectangle, 12x8 inches. Spread with 1 tablespoon soft butter.

3 c. cored, pared, and chopped
tart apples (about 4 apples)
3 Tbsp. butter or margarine
¼ c. brown sugar, firmly packed
½ c. granulated sugar

½ tsp. cinnamon
1 c. water
2 Tbsp. lemon juice
2 tsp. grated lemon rind
(optional)

Prepare apples. Cover within ½ inch of the edge of rectangle. Sprinkle with mixture of brown sugar and cinnamon; roll up from lengthwise side like a jelly roll, then cut the roll into 1 to 1½ inch crosswise slices.

Now boil granulated sugar, 2 tablespoons butter, water, and lemon juice for 10 minutes. Pour this syrup into a shallow baking dish, 10x6x2 inches. Place the rolls, cut side down, in the syrup. Spread them with remaining tablespoon of butter. Bake in a hot oven at 425° for 35 minutes. Serve warm with cream. Serves 9.

Note: Two cups packaged prepared biscuit mixture may be substituted for the Baking Powder Biscuit Dough recipe. Substitute 2 cups blueberries or 2 cups chopped peaches for the apples.

Anne La Fleur, Duluth, MN

RYAN'S FAVORITE CHOCOLATE MINT BROWNIES

¾ c. sugar
½ c. butter
3 eggs, beaten
1 c. flour

½ tsp. salt
1 (16 oz.) can Hershey's
chocolate syrup
Chopped nuts (if desired)

Combine all ingredients. Pour into 9x13 inch pan. Bake at 350° for 30 minutes. Cool.

Frost with the following:

2 c. powdered sugar
½ c. butter
2 Tbsp. milk
½ tsp. peppermint extract

Green food coloring
1 c. chocolate chips
6 Tbsp. butter

Mix sugar, ½ cup butter, milk, extract, and food coloring together; spread over cooled bars. Refrigerate for 30 minutes. Melt chocolate chips and 6 tablespoons butter in double boiler and pour over brownies; refrigerate.

Diane Kemmetmueller, Anoka, MN

CHOCO-WALNUT BARS

Crumb base:

¾ c. margarine, cut up
2 c. oatmeal
1¼ c. flour

¾ c. firmly packed brown sugar
½ tsp. salt
½ tsp. soda

For crumb base, add butter to combined oats, sugar, salt, and soda. Beat on low speed until mixture is crumbly. Press firmly into bottom of well greased 13x9 inch pan.

Topping:

1 c. chopped walnuts
1 (6 oz.) pkg. chocolate chips

1 (14 oz.) can sweetened
   condensed milk

For topping, sprinkle walnuts and chocolate chips evenly over crust. Pour condensed milk over nuts and chips. Bake in preheated oven at 350° for 25 minutes or until lightly golden brown; cool. Chill to set chocolate; cut into bars.

Evelyn Pedersen

CRISPY DATE BARS

1 c. flour
½ c. packed brown sugar

½ c. margarine or butter,
   softened

Combine and mix until crumbly; press into ungreased 10x15 inch cookie sheet. Bake at 375° for 10 to 12 minutes.

In a medium saucepan, combine:

1 c. dates, chopped
½ c. sugar

½ c. margarine

Cook over medium heat until mixture boils, stirring constantly; simmer for 3 minutes. Beat 1 egg well. Put about ½ cup of your date filling in with the egg and stir up real good. Return this into the date filling in saucepan. Cook just until mixture bubbles, stirring constantly. Take off fire and stir in 1 teaspoon vanilla.

Pour this filling over:

2 c. Rice Krispies

1 c. chopped walnuts

Mix well. Spread this over your baked crust. Cool completely. Frost with cream cheese frosting (using browned butter in frosting). Refrigerate leftovers. A double batch will make an 11½ x 7½ inch jelly roll pan *and* a 9 x 13 inch cake pan!!!

Marlys Wendorf, St. Cloud, MN

BROWNIES

Right in your 9x13 inch cake pan, melt 1 cup margarine and 4 squares unsweetened chocolate!!! Take off fire.

Add:

2 c. sugar	**1½ c. flour**
4 eggs	**1 tsp. vanilla**

Stir this all well with a fork. Add chopped nuts; stir well. Bake at 400° for 20 to 25 minutes. Cool and frost!! Frost with either cream cheese frosting or chocolate frosting.

Marlys Wendorf, St. Cloud, MN

CREAM CHEESE BARS

1 pkg. yellow cake mix	**8 oz. cream cheese**
½ c. margarine	**2 c. sugar (cut down to 1½ c.)**
3 eggs	**1½ tsp. vanilla**
½ c. pecans, chopped	

Combine cake mix, margarine, 1 egg, and ¼ cup pecans. It will be crumbly. Pat into jelly roll pan. Mix cream cheese, 2 eggs, vanilla, and sugar together; pour over cake mixture. Top with ¼ cup pecans. Bake at 350° for 30 to 35 minutes.

Karla Oeltyenbruns, Owatonna, MN

BUTTERSCOTCH BARS

1½ c. sifted flour	**½ c. soft butter**
¾ c. brown sugar	**¼ tsp. salt**

Mix until crumbly. Put in a 9x13 inch pan. Bake at 375° for 10 minutes.

In the meantime, melt over hot boiling water:

1 (6 oz.) pkg. butterscotch chips	**1 Tbsp. water**
¼ c. white syrup	**¼ tsp. salt**
2 Tbsp. butter	

Melt together. Add 2 cups broken walnuts and spread on top of baked layer. Bake at 375° for 8 minutes. Watch closely.

Pearl Paulsrud, Montevideo, MN

RUM RAISIN CUSTARD BARS

1 c. raisins
½ c. water
1 c. firmly packed brown sugar
¾ c. margarine or butter,
   softened
1¼ c. flour
2 c. quick cooking rolled oats
½ tsp. baking soda

½ c. sugar
½ c. firmly packed brown sugar
2½ tsp. cornstarch
1½ c. sour cream
3 egg yolks
½ tsp. vanilla
½ tsp. rum extract

Heat oven to 350°F. Grease a 9x13 inch pan. In small saucepan, combine raisins and water; bring to boil. Drain; set aside. In large bowl, beat 1 cup brown sugar and margarine until light and fluffy. Lightly spoon flour into measuring cup and level off. Add flour, oats, and baking soda to margarine mixture. Mix at low speed until crumbly. Press ½ of crumb mixture in bottom of prepared pan. Bake at 350° for 8 minutes.

In medium size heavy saucepan, combine sugar, ½ cup brown sugar, and cornstarch. Stir in sour cream and egg yolks. Cook this mixture over medium heat until mixture thickens, stirring constantly. *Do not boil.* Stir in raisins, vanilla, and rum extract. Pour mixture evenly over crumb crust. Sprinkle remaining crumb mixture over filling. Return to oven and bake for 30 to 40 minutes or until golden brown. Cool completely. Cut into bars. Store in refrigerator. Makes about 36 bars.

Owatonna, MN

ORANGE-FROSTED WALNUT-SPICE BARS

½ c. butter or margarine
1 c. sugar
2 large eggs
1½ c. unsifted flour
1 tsp. baking powder
2 tsp. grated orange rind

½ tsp. salt
¼ tsp. pumpkin pie spice
1 c. coarsely shredded yellow
   squash
½ c. chopped walnuts
⅛ tsp. ground cardamom

Grease 9 inch square baking pan. Heat oven to 350°F. In 2 quart saucepan, melt butter over low heat. Remove from heat. With spoon or wire whisk, stir in sugar and eggs until blended. Add flour, orange rind, pumpkin spice, cardamom, baking powder, and salt; beat until smooth. Batter will be quite stiff at this point. Squash will add moisture.

Stir in squash and walnuts. Pour mixture into pan. Bake for 35 minutes or until toothpick inserted into center comes out clean. Cool in pan on wire rack.

For frosting, combine:

3 oz. pkg. cream cheese
½ tsp. vanilla
2 c. powdered sugar

½ stick butter or margarine
2 Tbsp. orange juice

Frost and cut into bars. You may also cut the bars first and place frosting into a pastry bag with a large star tip. Pipe a star of frosting in the center of each bar and top with a walnut half. Store in airtight container.

Owatonna, MN

PEANUT BUTTER BARS

1¼ c. creamy peanut butter
½ c. softened butter or
  margarine
4 c. honey graham cereal,
  crushed

2 c. powdered sugar
1 Tbsp. shortening
1 (6 oz.) pkg. milk chocolate
  chips

Mix peanut butter and margarine or butter in a 2½ quart mixing bowl. Stir in crushed cereal. Stir in the powdered sugar, ⅓ cup at a time. Press firmly into an ungreased 9x9 inch square pan. Heat shortening and chocolate chips over very low heat, stirring constantly, until melted and smooth. Spread over peanut butter mixture in pan; refrigerate for 1 hour till firm. Remove 10 minutes before serving. Cut into bars; refrigerate remaining bars. Makes 24 bars.

Diane Kemmetmueller, Anoka, MN

PRIZE BUTTER BARS

¾ c. butter (or margarine)
½ c. sugar
2 c. flour
½ tsp. vanilla
¼ tsp. salt

⅓ c. (3 oz.) cream cheese
¼ c. butter
¾ c. packed brown sugar
1 c. coconut or chopped nuts

Beat together the first 5 ingredients until particles are fine. (With mixer, use low speed.) Press all but 1 cup firmly into bottom of ungreased 13x9 inch pan. Combine remaining ingredients; beat well. Spoon here and there over mixture in pan. Bake at 375° for 5 minutes. Spread topping to cover. Sprinkle with remaining crumbs. Bake for 25 to 30 minutes or until light golden brown.

Dee Rieker

PEANUT BUTTER-CHOCOLATE BARS

½ c. sugar
⅓ c. brown sugar, packed
⅓ c. peanut butter
¼ c. margarine, softened
1 tsp. vanilla
2 Tbsp. water
1 egg

1¼ c. all-purpose flour
½ tsp. baking soda
½ tsp. salt
½ c. chopped peanuts
1 c. M&M's plain chocolate
  candies

Heat oven to 375°. Grease and flour rectangular pan, 13 x 9 x 2 inches. Mix sugars, peanut butter, margarine, and vanilla. Beat in water and egg. Mix in flour, baking soda, and salt. Stir in peanuts and M&M's. Spread dough in pan. Bake until light brown, 22 to 25 minutes. Cool; cut into bars, about 2 x 1½ inches. Makes 36 bars. *Tasty and easy!*

Dee Rieker

BROWN SUGAR CHEWS

1 egg
1 c. firmly packed brown sugar
1 tsp. vanilla
½ c. sifted flour
¼ tsp. soda
¼ tsp. salt
¼ c. flaked coconut
1 c. raisins

Grease an 8 inch square pan. Stir together (do not beat) egg, sugar, and vanilla. Quickly stir in flour, soda, and salt. Blend in coconut and raisins. Spread in pan and bake in moderate oven (350°) for 18 to 20 minutes. Cookies will be soft in center. Makes 16 square cookies or 32 bars.

Pearl Paulsrud, Montevideo, MN

CHOCOLATE CHIP SPICE BARS

¾ c. shortening
¾ c. sugar
¾ c. brown sugar
2 eggs
1 tsp. vanilla
2 c. flour
1 tsp. soda
1 tsp. salt
2 tsp. cinnamon
½ tsp. ground cloves
½ tsp. nutmeg
1 c. chocolate chips

Mix in order given. Bake at 375° for 20 to 25 minutes in 9x13 inch pan.

Janet Lozon, Owatonna, MN

GOOEY CLUSTERS BARS

1½ c. Gold Medal all-purpose
    flour
1½ c. quick cooking oats
1 c. packed brown sugar
¾ tsp. baking soda
¼ tsp. salt
1 egg
½ c. margarine or butter,
    softened
1 c. flaked coconut
1 (6 oz.) pkg. semi-sweet
    chocolate chips
1 (12.25 oz.) jar caramel flavored
    topping
2 c. Clusters cereal
2 Tbsp. margarine or butter,
    softened

Heat oven to 350°. Grease rectangular pan, 13x9x2 inches. Mix flour, oats, brown sugar, baking soda, salt, and egg. Stir in ½ cup margarine with fork until mixture is crumbly. Press 3½ cups of the crumbly mixture in pan. Bake for 15 minutes.

Sprinkle with coconut, then with chocolate chips; drizzle with caramel topping. Mix remaining crumbly mixture and the cereal; cut in 2 tablespoons margarine. Sprinkle over top; press with fork. Bake until golden brown, 20 to 25 minutes. Cool for 30 minutes. Loosen edges from sides of pan; cool completely. Cut into bars, about 2x1 inch. Makes 54 bars.

High altitude directions (3500 to 6500 feet): Increase first baking time to 17 minutes and second baking time to about 25 minutes.

Joyce Goodeski, Hibbing, MN

FROSTINGS AND CAKES

BEST RUM CAKE EVER

1 or 2 qt. rum	1 tsp. soda
1 c. butter	Lemon juice
1 tsp. sugar	Brown sugar
2 large eggs	Nuts
1 c. dried fruit	Baking powder

Before you start, sample the rum to check for quality (good, isn't it?). Now go ahead. Select a large mixing bowl, measuring cup, etc. Check the rum again. It must be just right. To be sure rum is of the highest quality, pour 1 level cup of rum into a glass and drink it as fast as you can. Repeat.

With an electric mixer, beat 1 cup of butter in a large fluffy bowl. Add 1 seaspoon on thugar and beat again. Meanwhile, make sure that the rum is of the finest quality. Try another cup. Open second quart of necessary. Add 2 arge leggs, 2 cups fried druit and beat till high. If druit gets stuck in beaters, just pry it loose with a drewscriver. Sample the rum again, checking for tonscisticity.

Next, sift 3 cups peppar or salt (it really dosen't matter which). Sample the rum again. Sift ½ pint of lemon juice. Fold in chipped butter and strained nuts. Add 1 babblespoon of brown thugar, or whatever color you can find. Wix mel. Grease oven and turn cake pan to 350 gredees. Now pour the whole mess into the coven and ake. Check the rum again and go to bed.

Carol Reynolds, Hibbing, MN

CHOCOLATE CHIP FROSTING

1½ c. sugar	6 Tbsp. oleo or butter
6 Tbsp. milk	

Bring to rolling boil, then boil for 30 seconds. Remove from heat. Add ½ cup chocolate chips. Cool until right thickness. Spread on cake or brownies.

Heidi Weight

QUICK CHOCOLATE FROSTING

1 (6 oz.) pkg. chocolate chips
1 (15 oz.) can sweetened
    condensed milk

Microwave until mixture bubbles, about 2 minutes and 15 seconds in a 4 cup glass measuring cup. Beat until smooth and add ½ teaspoon vanilla.

Betty Ratzlaff, Fargo, ND

CHOCOLATE ZUCCHINI CAKE

½ c. margarine
½ c. oil
1¾ c. sugar
2 eggs
1 tsp. vanilla
½ c. sour milk

2½ c. flour
4 Tbsp. cocoa
½ tsp. baking powder
1 tsp. soda
1 tsp. salt
2 c. grated zucchini

Mix the preceding ingredients together. One fourth cup chocolate chips and ¼ cup nuts may be sprinkled on top for frosting before baking. Bake in a 9x13 inch pan for 40 to 45 minutes at 325°.

Note: Add 1 teaspoon lemon juice to sweet milk to sour it.
Mildred Kennedy, Grand Forks, ND

NUTRITIOUS DATE CAKE

1 c. rolled oats
1 c. buttermilk
½ c. brown sugar
1 egg
½ c. oil
½ c. graham *and* ½ c. whole
    wheat flour *or* 1 c. white
    flour

1 tsp. baking soda
½ tsp. baking powder
½ tsp. salt
¾ c. chopped dates

Combine oats and buttermilk in small bowl; set aside to soak. Beat eggs. Add brown sugar and oil. Mix flours with soda, baking powder, and salt. Blend dry ingredients into sugar-oil mixture. Add oats and buttermilk mixture and chopped nuts.

Topping - Blend with fork:

1 Tbsp. sugar
¼ tsp. cinnamon

¼ c. chopped nuts

Bake at 325° for 30 minutes in 8x8 inch pan.
Tina Knudsen, Owatonna, MN

LAZY DAISY CAKE
(With frosting)

1 c. sugar
2 eggs
½ c. milk
1 Tbsp. butter

1 c. flour
1 tsp. baking powder
¼ tsp. salt

Beat sugar and eggs. Sift flour, baking powder, and salt; add to sugar and egg mixture. Heat milk and butter to boiling point and add to mixture. Bake in 8x8 inch pan for 30 minutes at 375°.

Frosting:

5 Tbsp. brown sugar   **Cocoanut (optional)**
2 Tbsp. cream

Mix brown sugar and cream; spread over hot cake. Sprinkle with cocoanut and brown under broiler (or in oven for a few minutes longer).

Anne La Fleur, Duluth, MN

OLD COUNTRY BUFFETS HOT FUDGE PUDDING CAKE

1 c. flour   **½ tsp. salt**
¾ c. sugar   **½ c. milk**
2 Tbsp. unsweetened cocoa   **2 Tbsp. melted shortening**
2 tsp. baking powder   **1 tsp. vanilla**

Preheat oven to 350°. In a large mixing bowl, combine flour, sugar, cocoa, baking powder, salt, milk, shortening, and vanilla. Blend until smooth. Pour cake mixture into ungreased 9 inch square pan.

Topping:

¾ c. brown sugar   **1¾ c. hot water**
¼ c. unsweetened cocoa

In a small mixing bowl, mix together brown sugar, cocoa, and hot water, making sure the brown sugar is dissolved. Pour over batter. Bake at 350° for 40 to 45 minutes or until cake is set. Best if served warm. Makes 6 to 8 servings.

Diane Kemmetmueller, Anoka, MN

SUPER GERMAN CHOCOLATE AND COCONUT CAKE

1 box German chocolate cake   **1½ c. flaked coconut**
    mix   **¾ can cream of coconut**

Mix cake mix as per directions on box. Add flaked coconut. Bake as per directions on box. When baked, take from oven and punch holes in cake with meat fork. Over cake, pour ¾ can of cream of coconut.

Cool and frost cake with 8 ounce carton Cool Whip (beat). To this, add remaining cream of coconut (beat into Cool Whip). Frost. Refrigerate; it keeps for several days.

Dorothy Benson, Jackson, MN

BLACKBERRY CAKE

3 c. all-purpose flour
½ tsp. baking powder
1 tsp. soda
1 c. sugar
½ tsp. cloves
½ tsp. nutmeg
1 (15 oz.) can blackberries with
    juice

½ tsp. salt
2 tsp. cinnamon
1 c. raisins
1 c. chopped pecans
2 sticks margarine
3 eggs

Mix all dry ingredients; set aside. Cream margarine and sugar. Add eggs, 1 at a time, then add milk and berries. Add mixture to dry ingredients and bake in a Bundt pan at 300° for an hour or until done. Sprinkle with confectioners sugar or dribble icing on top. Frost or leave it plain.

Edna Olson, Duluth, MN

BANANA NUT CAKE
(Prize winner)

2 c. sifted flour
1 tsp. baking powder
1 tsp. soda
½ tsp. salt
½ c. shortening
1½ c. sugar

2 eggs
1 c. mashed bananas
¾ c. sour milk
1 tsp. vanilla
½ c. chopped nuts

Cream shortening. Add sugar gradually. Add eggs and vanilla; beat till light. Add remaining ingredients, alternating with sour milk, bananas, and nuts; beat well. Grease and flour 3 (3x8 inch) pans. Bake at 375° for 25 to 30 minutes and bake till tests done. Frost when cool.

Frosting:

½ c. milk
2 Tbsp. flour
¼ c. butter
¼ c. Crisco

½ c. sugar
1 tsp. vanilla
¼ c. chopped nuts

Combine milk and flour; boil until thick. Beat butter and Crisco for 4 minutes. Slowly add sugar; beat for 4 minutes. Add milk and flour mixture; beat for 4 minutes. (A very fluffy frosting and not overly sweet.) Dust chopped nuts on top.

Lucille Engstrom, St. Paul, MN

MILLIER NO-BAKE FRUIT CAKE

1 c. grape juice
1 lb. graham crackers
1 (8 oz.) pkg. candied cherries
3 c. nutmeats

1 lb. marshmallows
1 lb. dates, diced
1 (8 oz.) pkg. candied pineapple
¼ tsp. salt

Heat juice in pan over low heat. Add marshmallows and salt; stir until smooth. Set aside to cool. Crush graham crackers very fine. Mix crumbs, dates, fruit, and nuts. Add marshmallow mixture and mix again.

Line a 2 quart glass dish with wax paper and pour in mixture. Press down firmly and wrap with foil; chill.

Emma P. Buhl, Long Prairie, MN

GINGERBREAD WITH CHOCOLATE CHIPS

½ c. shortening	1½ c. flour
½ c. sugar	¾ tsp. salt
1 egg	¾ tsp. soda
½ c. molasses	½ tsp. ginger
½ c. boiling water	½ tsp. cinnamon

Cream shortening and sugar. *Add* eggs and molasses; *beat. Add* dry mixture to the creamed mixture, alternately with water, beating after each addition. *Add* a handful of chocolate chips to batter before baking. *Bake* in greased 8x8x2 inch pan at 350° for 35 to 40 minutes or until done. Serve warm. *Delicious with whipped cream.*

Mildred Kennedy, Grand Forks, MN

FROSTED CHIFFON CAKE

Custard:

5 Tbsp. cake flour	3 Tbsp. lemon juice
1 c. sugar	¼ c. water
Rind of 1 orange	1 egg, slightly beaten
½ c. orange juice	

1. Buy or bake large chiffon cake.
2. Make custard; cook and *cool!!*
3. Whip 1 pint of whipping cream.
4. Cut cake in 3 layers.
5. Combine whipped cream and custard.
6. Frost cake between layers, then top and sides; refrigerate for several hours before serving. Keeps well refrigerated for 2 or 3 days.

Sigrid Johnson, Hibbing, MN

COOKIES

CREAM WAFERS

1 c. butter   2 c. flour
⅓ c. whipping cream

Mix together; chill for ½ to 1 hour. Roll ⅛ inch thickness. Cut with 1½ inch cutter or middle of donut cutter. Dab each with sugar; prick with fork. Bake for 7 to 9 minutes at 375°. Let cool completely; frost.

Frosting:

¼ c. butter   ¾ c. powdered sugar

Thin with milk. Frost between 2 cookies.

100 GOOD COOKIES

1 c. white sugar   1 tsp. cream of tartar
1 c. brown sugar   1 tsp. baking soda
1 c. margarine   1 c. Rice Krispies
1 c. oil   1 c. oatmeal
1 egg   1 c. flake coconut
1 tsp. vanilla   1 c. nutmeats
½ tsp. salt   3½ c. flour

Mix all together. Roll in balls that equal a heaping teaspoon, then flatten with fork. Bake at 350° for 12 to 15 minutes. Makes about 100 cookies!

Evelyn Pedersen

SALTED PEANUT CRISPS

1 c. shortening (part butter or   3 c. flour
   margarine)   ½ tsp. soda
1½ c. brown sugar   1 tsp. salt (optional)
2 eggs   2 c. salted peanuts
2 tsp. vanilla

Mix first 4 ingredients thoroughly. Blend together flour, soda, and salt; stir in. Mix in peanuts. Drop by teaspoon onto lightly greased cookie sheet. Flatten with bottom of greased glass dipped in sugar. Place cookies 2 inches apart. Bake at 375° for 8 to 10 minutes. Yield: 6 dozen 2 inch cookies.

Evelyn Pedersen

POWDERED SUGAR SPRITZ

1 c. powdered sugar
1 c. butter
1 beaten egg
1 tsp. vanilla

2 c. flour
1 tsp. cream of tartar
½ tsp. soda

Cream sugar and butter; add egg and vanilla. Add flour, cream of tartar, and soda. Put through a cookie press. Bake at 350° for 10 to 12 minutes.

Pearl Paulsrud, Montevideo, MN

GUMDROP OATMEAL COOKIES

1 c. sifted flour
½ tsp. baking powder
½ tsp. soda
½ c. soft shortening
½ c. granulated sugar
½ c. brown sugar
1½ c. oatmeal (uncooked)

½ c. gumdrops, fine cut
1 Tbsp. water
¼ tsp. salt
Shredded coconut (to suit)
1 egg
1 tsp. vanilla

Sift together flour, baking powder, and salt into bowl. Add shortening, sugar, egg, water, and vanilla. Beat until smooth, about 2 minutes. Lightly stir in rolled oats and gumdrops. Shape dough into small balls; roll each in coconut. Bake on greased cookie sheet in 350° oven for 12 to 15 minutes. This yields about 3 dozen cookies.

Edna Olson, Duluth, MN

SOFT PUMPKIN COOKIES

½ c. softened butter
1½ c. brown sugar
1 c. pumpkin (can)
1 egg
1 tsp. vanilla
2½ c. flour

1 tsp. baking powder
1 tsp. baking soda
1 tsp. cinnamon
½ tsp. nutmeg
¼ tsp. salt

Cream butter and sugar in a large mixing bowl. Add egg and stir. Add vanilla; beat until fluffy. Combine flour, baking powder, baking soda, cinnamon, nutmeg, and salt; add to butter mixture alternating with the pumpkin, beating after each addition.

Drop by rounded tablespoon on a slightly greased cookie sheet. Smooth tops and bake at 350° for 15 to 20 minutes or until lightly browned; cool.

Frost with:

2 c. powdered sugar
1 tsp. vanilla

3 Tbsp. milk
1 Tbsp. melted butter

Edna V. Olson, Duluth, MN

BITS 'O BRICKLE COOKIES

6 oz. pkg. (1 c.) Bits 'O Brickle
    chips by Heath
1½ Tbsp. liquid shortening
6 Tbsp. unsifted flour
½ c. butter
6 Tbsp. sugar

6 Tbsp. packed brown sugar
½ tsp. vanilla
1 egg
½ tsp. salt
½ tsp. baking soda
1¼ c. plus 2 Tbsp. unsifted flour

Preheat oven to 325°. In a small bowl, mix Bits 'O Brickle chips with liquid shortening until evenly coated, then stir in 6 tablespoons flour until well coated; set aside.

In a large bowl, combine butter, sugar, brown sugar, and vanilla; beat until creamy. Beat in egg. Gradually add salt, baking soda, and flour. Mix well. Stir in coated chips. Drop by rounded teaspoons onto greased cookie sheets. Bake at 325° for 10 to 12 minutes. Makes 50 (2 inch) cookies.

Diane Kemmetmueller, Anoka, MN

PINEAPPLE-COCONUT DROPS

½ c. butter or margarine,
    softened
½ c. granulated sugar
½ c. brown sugar
1 (8¼ oz.) can crushed
    pineapple, well drained
1 egg

1 tsp. vanilla
2 c. flour
1 tsp. baking powder
¼ tsp. baking soda
¼ tsp. salt
½ c. shredded coconut

Cream butter and sugars till fluffy. Beat in pineapple, egg, and vanilla. Stir together flour, baking powder, soda, and salt. Stir into creamed mixture. Blend in coconut. Drop from teaspoon on greased cookie sheet. Bake at 375° for about 8 minutes. Makes about 42 cookies.

Patricia Larson, Grafton, ND

DATE NUT BALLS

1 lb. dates
1 c. black walnuts
2 Tbsp. orange juice (fresh or
    frozen)

Powdered sugar

Grind dates and black walnuts. Add orange juice; mix well. Roll into 1 inch balls. Roll in powdered sugar.

Helen May Johnson, Chanhassen, MN

COCONUT AND DATE COOKIES

1 c. white sugar	2 eggs
1 c. brown sugar	2 tsp. vanilla
1 c. shortening	½ c. coconut
1 c. dates, chopped	2 c. flour
2 c. oatmeal	½ tsp. salt
1 tsp. soda	

Cream sugar and shortening. Add eggs. Combine dry ingredients; add to first mixture and roll into balls. Roll in sugar and press down with fork. Bake at 350°.

Dorothy Willems, New London, MN

DEVILS FOOD DROP COOKIES

½ c. butter	2 c. sifted flour
1 c. brown sugar	½ tsp. soda
1 egg	¼ tsp. salt
1 tsp. vanilla	¾ c. sour cream
2 sq. melted chocolate	½ c. chopped nuts

Cream butter and sugar. Beat egg and vanilla. Stir in chocolate. Sift together dry ingredients; add to chocolate mixture alternating with the sour cream. Mix well. Stir in nuts. Drop on greased sheet. Bake at 350° for 10 minutes; cool and frost.

Frosting:

2 c. powdered sugar	1 tsp. vanilla
2 Tbsp. butter	2 Tbsp. cocoa

Liquid coffee to make frosting of spreading consistency (2 or 3 tablespoons).

Marie Burt, Owatonna, MN

XMAS COOKIES

1 c. margarine	1 tsp. salt
1½ c. brown sugar	1 tsp. cinnamon
2 eggs	1 c. flour
1 tsp. soda	

Mix all together and set aside.

2 lb. dates	3 slices candied pineapple
About 1 c. packaged candied red cherries	1 c. walnuts, cut up
About 1 c. packaged candied green cherries	1 c. pecans, cut up

After preceding ingredients are mixed, add 1½ cups flour, then add to first part. Bake at 350° for 15 minutes or until light brown. Drop by spoon. *Very good.*

Goldie Mikish, Staples, MN
Betty Ratzlaff, Fargo, ND

DATE DROP COOKIES

1 c. butter or oleo, softened
1½ c. white sugar
3 eggs
3 c. sifted all-purpose flour
1 tsp. baking soda
1 tsp. ground cinnamon

⅛ tsp. salt
1 Tbsp. water
1 (8 oz.) pkg. pitted dates, snipped
1 c. coarsely chopped walnuts

Beat butter or oleo and sugar together in large mixing bowl until creamy. Add eggs, 1 at a time. Sift together next 4 ingredients; beat into sugar mixture. Add water to dates; stir into batter with nuts. Chill for 1 hour. Drop heaping teaspoon about 2 inches apart on greased cookie sheet. Bake at 350° for 10 to 12 minutes. Makes 5 dozen.

Irma Schuler, Valley City, ND

NO ROLL SUGAR COOKIES

1 c. sugar
1 c. powdered sugar
1 c. butter
1 c. oil
2 eggs

4¼ c. flour
1 tsp. soda
1 tsp. cream of tartar
1 tsp. salt
1 tsp. vanilla

Chill about 2 hours or overnight. Roll in 1 inch balls; flatten with glass dipped in sugar. Bake at 375°. Makes 9 dozen.

Rose Wendelbo, Grafton, ND

SWIRLED LEMON COOKIES

1 c. (2 sticks) butter or margarine
1 (3 oz.) pkg. cream cheese
1 c. sugar
1 large egg, beaten
1 Tbsp. finely grated lemon rind

1 Tbsp. lemon juice
2½ to 2¾ c. unsifted all-purpose flour
1 tsp. baking powder
About 6 maraschino cherries

Beat butter and cream cheese in bowl until fluffy. Add sugar gradually; beat well. Add egg, lemon rind, and juice. Stir in 2½ cups flour and the baking powder. If necessary, add additional flour to make a soft dough.

Pat cherries dry with paper toweling; cut into ¼ inch pieces. Heat oven to 375°F. Spoon small amount of dough into pastry bag fitted with large star tip. Pipe swirls of dough into 1¾ inch muffin pan cups. Put a piece of cherry in the center of each swirl. Bake for 15 minutes or until light golden brown. Remove from pans; transfer to wire racks and allow to cool. Makes 4½ dozen.

Owatonna, MN

PUMPKIN COOKIES

2 c. white sugar
1 c. shortening
1 egg
1 can pumpkin
1½ tsp. cinnamon
1 c. ground walnuts

2 tsp. vanilla
2 tsp. soda
2 tsp. baking powder
Dash of salt
4 c. flour
1 c. raisins

Mix well. Drop on cookie sheet. Bake for 8 to 10 minutes in 375° oven. Frost with maple flavoring frosting.

K. Lauks, Owatonna, MN

PUMPKIN COOKIES

2 c. brown sugar
1 c. lard
2 eggs
1 can pumpkin
2 c. dates or raisins
½ c. nuts
2 tsp. vanilla

4 c. flour
2 tsp. soda
4 tsp. baking powder
2 tsp. cinnamon
½ tsp. ginger
1 tsp. allspice
Dash of salt

Bake at 350°. Frost while warm with browned butter icing.

K. Stoltz

ORANGE CHEESE CHOCOLATE CHIP COOKIES

1 c. shortening
1 c. sugar (white)
1 (3 oz.) pkg. cream cheese
2 eggs
2 Tbsp. grated orange peel

2 tsp. vanilla
2 c. sifted flour
Dash of salt
1 (6 oz.) pkg. chocolate chips

Grease cookie sheet. Bake for 12 minutes at 350°.

CHOCOLATE ROCKIES

1 (12 oz.) pkg. chocolate chips
2 eggs
1 c. powdered sugar

1 tsp. vanilla
2 c. miniature marshmallows
1 c. chopped nuts

Melt chocolate chips in double boiler. Beat slightly the 2 eggs. Add powdered sugar and vanilla. Add to chocolate chips. Fold in miniature marshmallows and chopped nuts. Drop by spoonful onto waxed paper; cool.

Evelyn Pedersen

OATMEAL SNACKS
(Cookies)

1 egg
½ c. melted butter (margarine)
½ c. honey
1 c. whole wheat flour
½ tsp. baking soda

½ tsp. cinnamon
1½ c. rolled *(not* quick cooking) oats
½ c. chopped walnuts or almonds

Beat egg. Add butter and honey; blend well. Stir in flour, baking soda, and cinnamon. Add to liquid mixture and mix well, making sure there are no lumps. Stir in oats and nuts. Bake at 325° for 12 to 15 minutes letting cookies cool on rack for 5 minutes. Move to cake rack.

These cookies are chewy and not too sweet.

Pat Johnson, Battle Lake, MN

CRISPY SUGAR COOKIES
(Never fail)

1 c. butter
2 c. sugar
¼ c. cream
4 c. sifted flour
2 eggs, well beaten

1 tsp. baking powder
1 tsp. salt
2 tsp. vanilla
½ tsp. soda

Cream butter until soft. Add sugar; gradually cream until fluffy. Add eggs, 1 at a time. Stir in dry ingredients and mix well. Chill for 2 hours. Roll on floured board.

Dee Bach, Owatonna, MN

MY MOST FAVORITE COOKIE
(No-roll powdered sugar cookies)

1 c. powdered sugar
1 c. margarine
1 egg
1 tsp. vanilla

2 c. flour
½ tsp. cream of tartar
½ tsp. soda
¼ tsp. salt (optional)

Sift together flour, cream of tartar, soda, and salt. Cream sugar and shortening. Add egg and vanilla. Sift dry ingredients and beat well. Roll into balls; press down with glass dipped in sugar. May be chilled overnight or less. Bake at 350° for about 12 minutes. Yield: 3½ dozen.

Lucille Wickha, Minneapolis, MN

GINGER COOKIES

¼ c. brown sugar
¼ c. unsalted margarine
1 egg, lightly beaten
¼ tsp. vanilla extract
1 tsp. ground ginger

¼ tsp. allspice
¼ tsp. cinnamon
¼ tsp. ground cloves
½ c. + 1 Tbsp. flour

1. Combine sugar and margarine in bowl and cream well with electric mixer. Beat in egg and vanilla. Stir in ½ cup flour and spices.

2. Lightly grease cookie sheet and sprinkle with 1 tablespoon flour. Shake off excess. Spoon small amounts of dough on cookie sheet, leaving 2 inches between each drop. Bake at 375° for 6 to 7 minutes. Cool on cake rack. Yield: 3 dozen.

Pat Johnson, Battle Lake, MN

AUNT SARAH'S GINGER BALLS

¾ c. shortening
1 c. sugar
1 egg
6 tsp. molasses
2 c. flour

2 tsp. soda
1 large rounded tsp. ginger
1 tsp. cinnamon
½ tsp. cloves

Cream shortening and sugar. Add beaten egg and molasses. Sift soda and spices with flour. Add to creamed mixture until well blended. Roll into balls (size of walnut) and roll in sugar. Place on cookie sheet. Space well apart. Bake at 350° for 12 to 15 minutes. Makes 3 dozen.

Marcy Weight

AUNT ROSE'S GINGER COOKIES
(Makes 2 dozen)

⅔ c. margarine
1 c. sugar
4 Tbsp. molasses
1 tsp. cinnamon
1 tsp. ginger
1 egg

2 tsp. soda
2 c. flour
¼ tsp. salt
⅛ c. black walnuts (fine, optional)

Mix well (dough will be very stiff). Shape into balls the size of half an egg. Roll in sugar and put on cookie sheet (greased). Bake at 400° for 10 to 12 minutes.

Carol Broten, Owatonna, MN

MOLASSES COOKIES

¾ c. shortening
1 egg
1 c. sugar
¼ c. molasses
2¼ c. flour (or little less if want chewier)

¼ tsp. salt
1 tsp. cinnamon
2 tsp. soda
½ tsp. cloves
1 tsp. ginger

Cream together shortening, egg, and sugar, then add molasses. Blend, then add flour, salt, cinnamon, soda, cloves, and ginger. Roll in ball; roll in sugar. Bake at 350° for 8 to 10 minutes.

Mary Hocking, Fargo, ND

PIES

CREAM CHEESE PIE CRUST

1 (8 oz.) pkg. cream cheese   4 c. flour
1 lb. butter (or margarine)

Let cream cheese and butter reach room temperature. Combine ingredients; mix well. Divide dough into 6 or 7 portions. Roll each portion into a circle large enough to fit an 8 inch foil pie tin. Place them in foil pans; cover them with plastic wrap and freeze. This easy-to-work dough recipe makes 6 to 7 pie crusts.

Lenora Buck, Fargo, ND

PIE CRUST

1 c. lard   1 tsp. baking powder
3 c. flour   ⅓ c. cold water

Makes 1 (9 inch) pie.

Alma M. Collette, Grand Forks, ND

COTTAGE CHEESE TARTS

1 small container cottage   1 c. lard
     cheese   2 c. flour
1 tsp. salt   1 can favorite canned pie filling

Mix all the preceding ingredients, except pie filling, together and let stand, covered, in refrigerator overnight. Roll dough thin like pie crust. Dough is sticky and some flour will be needed on rolling surface. Cut dough in 3 inch squares. Place 1 tablespoon of favorite canned pie filling in center of each square. Fold 4 corners to center; pinch together firmly. Place tarts on ungreased cookie sheet. Bake for 15 minutes in a 400° oven. Remove from pan to wax paper and frost with Powdered Sugar Frosting.

1 c. powdered sugar   1 tsp. butter
1 Tbsp. milk

Bobbi Westerbur

CRUSTLESS CUSTARD PIE

Mix together:

4 Tbsp. flour   2 whole eggs and 2 egg yolks
½ c. sugar

Add:

2 c. milk (skim)   Vanilla (as desired)
Dash of nutmeg

Beat together well. Pour into greased 9 inch pie pan. Bake at 350° for 60 minutes or until done. Use 2 spare egg whites to make meringue or use all 4 eggs in pie and garnish top with nutmeg.

Pat Johnson, Battle Lake, MN

RASPBERRY, GOOSEBERRY, BLACKBERRY, OR CURRANT PIE
(You'll use this all summer)

Pastry for 2 crust, 9 inch pie
4 c. fresh or frozen fruit
3 Tbsp. cornstarch
⅔ to 1 c. sugar
⅛ tsp. salt
1½ Tbsp. lemon juice or ½ tsp. cinnamon
2 Tbsp. butter

Line 9 inch pie pan with pastry. Defrost frozen berries just enough to separate. Combine cornstarch, sugar, cinnamon, and salt; mix with fruit and let stand about 15 minutes. Place berry mixture in unbaked pie shell; dot with butter and top with lattice crust. Bake in preheated 425° F. oven for 35 to 45 minutes. Yields 6 servings.

Strawberry Pie: Use 4 cups sliced strawberries and 1 teaspoon grated orange rind in place of raspberries and lemon juice.

Helen H. Clark, Grand Forks, ND

RHUBARB PIE

3 c. rhubarb (4 c. can be used if all can be covered with egg mixture)
1 egg white
1 c. sugar
1 egg yolk
½ c. soda crackers, crushed

Beat egg white with a pinch of salt. Add sugar and egg yolk and beat. Add crackers; mix, then add rhubarb. Be sure all is covered with egg white mixture. Bake for 40 minutes at 350° or until done.

Mildred Sjostrom, St. Peter, MN

MOM'S SOUR CREAM APPLE PIE

2 Tbsp. flour
⅛ tsp. salt
¾ c. sugar
1 egg
1 c. sour cream
½ tsp. vanilla
2 c. chopped apples

Sift flour, salt, and sugar together. Add slightly beaten egg, sour cream, and vanilla; beat until smooth. Add chopped apples. Pour mixture in pastry lined 9 inch pie pan. Bake in 400° oven for 15 minutes. Reduce heat to 350° and bake for 30 minutes longer. Remove from oven and add the following Crumb Topping.
Crumb Topping:

⅓ c. sugar
⅓ c. flour

1 tsp. cinnamon
¼ c. butter

Blend together and sprinkle over filling. Bake in hot oven for 10 minutes.

Arlene Jewell, Bismarck, ND

SOUR CREAM PIE

1 c. thick sour cream
½ c. raisins
½ tsp. cinnamon
1 c. sugar

1 Tbsp. cornstarch
¼ tsp. cloves
4 egg yolks
1 egg white

Combine dry ingredients. Stir in sour cream, beaten egg yolks, and the 1 egg white. Cook until thick, stirring. Remove from heat and stir in raisins. When cool, pour into baked pie shell.

Make meringue of the other:

3 egg whites
6 Tbsp. sugar

½ tsp. vanilla

Spread on filling and bake till meringue is slightly browned.

Elizabeth Klug, Dickinson, ND

DESSERTS

CHRISTMAS APPLE SLICES

30 caramels	1 stick margarine
1 can Borden's milk	

Melt in microwave (watch, this is very hot). Slice red and green Delicious apples; dip in pineapple juice. Arrange slices in a wreath shape (½ a batch makes a lot). Dip apples in caramel mixture for a delicious holiday dessert.

Gayle

SPEEDY APPLESAUCE DESSERT

The kids will make this for you.

1 c. fine graham cracker crumbs (about 15 sq.)	¼ c. butter, melted
½ tsp. cinnamon	1¼ c. thick applesauce
¼ c. sugar	Whipped cream

Mix cracker crumbs, cinnamon, sugar, and butter. Place 3 tablespoons crumb mixture in the bottom of a sauce dish or sherbet dish (fix 5). Place ¼ cup applesauce on top of crumbs in each dish. Divide remaining crumbs and sprinkle over applesauce; chill. Top with a daub of whipped cream just before serving. Yields 5 servings.

Helen H. Clark, Grand Forks, ND

APPLE CRISP

Place in greased 8 inch square pan, 4 cups sliced, pared, cored baking apples.

Blend until crumbly, then spread over apples:

¾ c. brown sugar, packed	¾ tsp. cinnamon
½ c. sifted flour	¾ tsp. nutmeg
½ c. rolled oats	⅓ c. soft butter (or margarine)

Bake until apples are tender and topping is golden brown. Serve warm with cream, ice cream, or hard sauce. Temperature: 375° (or glass at 350°). Time: 30 to 35 minutes. Serves 6 to 8 people.

Anne La Fleur, Duluth, MN

APPLE FLAKE CRUNCH

6 c. cored, pared, sliced apples
2 Tbsp. brown or granulated
sugar
⅓ c. orange juice
⅓ c. brown sugar
3 Tbsp. butter or margarine

½ c. crushed corn flakes
½ c. all-purpose flour
¼ tsp. nutmeg
¼ tsp. cinnamon
1 Tbsp. grated orange rind
(optional)

Arrange apples in a greased 10x6x2 inch baking dish. Sprinkle the 2 tablespoons sugar on top, then pour about ½ of the orange juice over this. Now work the ⅓ cup brown sugar and 2 tablespoons butter together with a spoon until creamy.

Add corn flakes, flour, spices, and orange rind; mix until crumbly. Spread on top of apples. Sprinkle rest of orange juice over top, then dot on remaining butter. Bake at 375° for 45 minutes. Serve warm or cold with cream or ice cream.

Anne La Fleur, Duluth, MN

APPLE COBBLER

2 apples, peeled and sliced
(about 2 c.)
3 Tbsp. firmly packed brown
sugar
1 tsp. lemon juice
¼ tsp. cinnamon

⅓ c. flour
1 Tbsp. sugar
1 tsp. baking powder
2 Tbsp. milk
1 Tbsp. corn oil

In small bowl, toss together apples, brown sugar, lemon juice, and cinnamon. Spoon into 2 (10 ounce) custard cups. Stir together flour, white sugar, and baking powder. Stir in milk and corn oil until moistened. Drop by teaspoon into apple mixture. Bake in 400° oven for 20 to 25 minutes or until browned. Serve warm. Makes 2 servings.

Helen Rasmussen, St. Germain, WI

COUNTRY APPLE DESSERT

1 pkg. Pillsbury Plus yellow cake
mix
⅓ c. oleo or butter
1 egg
20 oz. can apple pie filling
½ c. packed brown sugar

½ c. chopped nuts
1 tsp. cinnamon
1 c. dairy sour cream
1 egg
1 tsp. vanilla

In large bowl, combine cake mixture, oleo, and egg at low speed until crumbly. Press into ungreased 9x13 inch pan. Spread with pie filling. Combine brown sugar, nuts, and cinnamon; sprinkle over apples.

In a small bowl, blend sour cream, egg, and vanilla; pour over mixture. Bake at 350° for 40 to 50 minutes or until topping is golden. Serve warm and be sure and refrigerate any leftovers.

Tip: To use fresh apples instead of pie filling, combine ¼ cup packaged brown sugar and 2 tablespoons cornstarch. Stir in 1 cup water and 1 tablespoon lemon juice. Add 4 cups thinly sliced peeled apples. Heat to boiling and simmer for 5 minutes.

Diane Haan

RHUBARB STRAWBERRY CRUNCH

2 c. flour	1 c. granulated sugar
2 c. packed brown sugar	2 Tbsp. cornstarch
1 c. butter or margarine	1 c. cold water
2 c. rolled oats (uncooked)	1 tsp. vanilla
6 c. rhubarb (½ inch slices)	1 (3 oz.) pkg. strawberry gelatin

Mix flour and brown sugar in a large bowl. Cut in butter. Mix in rolled oats. Gently pat ½ the mixture into bottom of a 9x13 inch baking pan. Save remaining ½ for topping. Spoon rhubarb evenly over the crust.

Mix sugar and cornstarch in a saucepan. Stir in water and cook over medium heat until mixture comes to a boil and is clear and thickened. Add vanilla. Spoon over rhubarb. Sprinkle dry gelatin over the top. Top with remaining crumbs. Bake at 350° for 40 to 45 minutes. Serve either warm or cold, topped with whipped cream or ice cream. Makes 12 to 15 servings.

Diane Kemmetmueller, Dayton, MN

RHUBARB COBBLER

2 eggs, beaten	¾ c. sugar
2 Tbsp. flour	3 c. rhubarb, chopped

Mix and pour into a greased casserole dish.

Topping - Mix until crumbly and pat on top of first mixture:

⅔ c. flour	4 Tbsp. butter
⅓ c. brown sugar	

Bake at 350° for 30 minutes.

Marie Burt, Owatonna, MN

AMAZING RHUBARB COBBLER

½ c. (1 stick) margarine	½ c. milk
1 c. flour	2 c. (¼ inch pieces) rhubarb
½ c. sugar	1 c. hot water
2 tsp. baking powder	1 c. sugar
Cinnamon	

Melt margarine in 9 inch round pan. Make a batter of flour, ½ cup sugar, baking powder, and milk; spoon over melted margarine. Place rhubarb over the batter. Stir the 1 cup sugar into hot water until dissolved. Pour over rhubarb; sprinkle with cinnamon. Bake at 350° for 40 minutes. Makes 4 to 6 servings.

Virginia Fyksen, Duluth, MN

RHUBARB TORTE

Make a crust of:

1 c. flour
5 Tbsp. powdered sugar

½ c. margarine

Mix with a fork until crumbly. Line this in an 8x10 inch pan (saving a few crumbs for top). Bake this for 10 minutes at 350°. While crust is baking, beat 2 eggs.

Add:

1½ c. sugar
¼ c. flour
¼ tsp. salt

¾ tsp. vanilla
2 to 3 c. rhubarb, finely cut
½ c. slivered almonds (optional)

Add this to baked crust. Top with saved crumbs and bake at 350° until golden brown. This serves 8.

Patricia Larson, Grafton, ND

BUTTERFINGER DESSERT

1 stick and 2 Tbsp. oleo
15 soda crackers (sq.)

15 graham crackers (sq.)

Crush crackers and oleo; press ¾ in 9x13 inch pan.

Blend together:

2 small pkg. instant vanilla
    pudding

2 c. skim milk

Add 2 cups vanilla ice cream. Pour over cracker layer; refrigerate until set. Add to layer 1 carton Cool Whip (8 ounces). Put remainder of crackers on top. Crush 3 large Butterfinger bars for topping; refrigerate.

Mary Hocking, Fargo, ND

CUPCAKE CUSTARD

1 c. sugar
⅓ c. flour
¼ c. lemon juice
3 egg whites, beaten stiff

3 Tbsp. butter
3 egg yolks, well beaten
1 c. milk

Cream sugar and butter. Add flour, egg yolks, lemon juice, and milk. Fold in egg whites. Pour or spoon into custard cups. Place custard cups in a shallow pan of water. Bake at 350° for 35 minutes or until custard is set.

Edna Helberg, Sioux Falls, SD

CHOCOLATE DE CREME DESSERT

6 oz. chocolate chips
2 eggs
1 Tbsp. sugar

1 Tbsp. brandy
¾ c. milk, heated

Put all preceding ingredients into a blender; blend for 2 minutes. Pour into dessert glasses; chill until firm (about 2 hours). Serve with whipped cream or Cool Whip.

Ann Strandemo, Bismarck, ND

FROZEN PUMPKIN DESSERT

1 (8 oz.) pkg. Philadelphia Brand
   cream cheese, softened
¾ c. sugar
1 (16 oz.) can pumpkin

3 Tbsp. brandy (optional)
1 tsp. pumpkin pie spice
1 (8 oz.) container Cool Whip
1 c. chopped almonds

Combine cream cheese and sugar, mixing until well blended. Add pumpkin, brandy, and spice; mix well. Reserve ½ cup of Cool Whip. Fold remaining Cool Whip and almonds into pumpkin mixture. Pour into 9 inch square pan; freeze. Top with reserved Cool Whip.

Patricia Larson, Grafton, ND

KIWI DELIGHT

1 angel food cake, torn in pieces
1 box instant vanilla pudding
1 (8 to 12 oz.) frozen whipped
   topping

1 lb. strawberries, sliced
1 kiwi fruit, sliced

Mix instant vanilla pudding as directed on package. Add whipped topping. In glass bowl, place ⅓ angel food, ⅓ pudding mixture, and ⅓ strawberries. Repeat, lining outside of bowl with kiwi (second layer). Repeat third layer. Refrigerate for 4 or more hours. Serves 12. Contains 1600 calories.

Arlene Byine, Rochester, MN

ORANGE FLUFF
(Makes 3 (½ cup) servings)

3⅓ Tbsp. orange flavored
   gelatin
¼ c. hot water
½ c. buttermilk

2 Tbsp. orange juice
1 Tbsp. lemon juice
1 egg white, stiffly beaten

Dissolve gelatin in hot water. Add buttermilk and juices. Chill until slightly thickened. Fold egg white into gelatin mixture. Pour into 3 custard cups or a mold; chill until firm. Remove from mold and serve with custard sauce.

Helen Clark, Grand Forks, ND

LEMON DESSERT

3 egg yolks, beaten
1 c. Eagle Brand milk

Juice and rind of 2 lemons

Beat. Spread graham cracker crumbs on bottom. Add dessert. Spread with 1 cup whipped cream on top and rest of crumbs.

Betty Ratzlaff, Fargo, ND

LEMON FRUIT FREEZE

⅔ c. oleo
⅓ c. sugar

3 c. crushed Rice Krispies

Melt oleo; stir in sugar and then add Rice Krispies (reserve ⅓ cup for top). Press into a 9x13 inch pan. Bake at 300° for 12 minutes; cool.

Mix:

1 (14 oz.) Eagle Brand milk
½ c. lemon juice
1 (21 oz.) can lemon pie filling

1 (17 oz.) can fruit cocktail, well drained

Pour into shell and freeze.

Elizabeth Klug

FRUIT DELIGHT

1 (11 oz.) can mandarin orange
   segments
2 (16 oz.) cans or jars fruit for
   salad

¾ c. coconut
1 c. miniature marshmallows
¾ c. dairy sour cream

Combine drained chilled fruits, coconut, and marshmallows. Fold in sour cream and chill 1 hour. Makes 6 to 8 servings.

Pearl Paulsrud, Montevideo, MN

CHERRY DELIGHT

1 c. flour
2 Tbsp. sugar
3 oz. cream cheese
1 tsp. vanilla
¼ tsp. salt
1 tsp. baking powder

½ c. confectioners sugar
½ c. chopped walnuts
1 egg, slightly beaten
4 Tbsp. butter or margarine
½ pt. whipping cream
1 can cherry pie filling

Combine the flour, butter or margarine, sugar, egg, baking powder, and nuts. Press into a 9x9 inch baking pan. Bake in 350° oven for 15 minutes; cool. Blend the softened cream cheese with confectioners sugar and vanilla. Fold in the whipped whipping cream; spread on crust. Top the cream layer with the cherry pie filling; refrigerate for 4 or more hours before serving. Garnish with whipped cream.

Edna V. Olson, Duluth, MN

CHERRY CHEESECAKE

1 thawed (8 oz.) ctn. Cool Whip
1 can cherry pie filling
⅓ c. reconstituted lemon juice

1 (8 oz.) pkg. cream cheese
1 ready made (9 inch) graham
   cracker pie crust

In a bowl, mix room temperature cream cheese and lemon juice. When blended, hand fold in Cool Whip. Put this into pie crust. Top with cherry pie filling. Put in refrigerator for about 2 hours before serving.

Carol Reynolds, Hibbing, MN

ORANGE SAUCE - DESSERT

3 egg yolks, beaten
½ c. sugar

½ c. orange juice (frozen)

Cook in double boiler. Stir until thick; cool. Fold into whipped cream or Dream Whip. Serve on angel or chiffon cake, or your own favorite cake. *A very good dessert.*

Sadie Lobland, Hibbing, MN

PEANUT BUTTER PARFAIT DESSERT

1 pkg. (pudding included) devils
   food cake mix
½ c. butter, melted

¼ c. milk
1 egg
¾ c. peanuts

Combine all ingredients in large bowl until well blended. Spread in 13x9 inch pan, greased and floured. Bake at 350° for 20 to 25 minutes; cool.

¾ peanut butter

1½ c. powdered sugar

In small bowl, combine peanut butter and powdered sugar until crumbly; set aside.

8 oz. cream cheese, softened
2½ c. milk
8 oz. container Cool Whip,
   thawed

5¼ oz. pkg. instant pudding
   (vanilla)

In large bowl, beat cream cheese until smooth. Add milk, Cool Whip, and pudding mix. Beat for 2 minutes until well blended. Alternate mixtures by pouring pudding mixture over cake first, crumbly mixture, then pudding, and crumbly. Sprinkle with ½ cup peanuts and grate 1 large milk chocolate bar on top.

This dessert is so good, it's like dying and going to heaven.

Shirley Dukart, Bloomington, MN

PINEAPPLE MACADAMIA CHEESE PIE

Crust:

1 c. chopped macadamia nuts	**6 Tbsp. melted butter**
¾ c. graham cracker crumbs	**2 Tbsp. sugar**

For crust, combine all ingredients and press into an 8 inch pie pan to cover bottom and sides; refrigerate.

Filling:

1 (8 oz.) can crushed pineapple in juice	**¾ c. plain yogurt**
	½ c. sugar
12 oz. softened cream cheese	**1 tsp. vanilla**
1 egg	

For filling, drain pineapple well, pressing out excess juice with back of spoon. Combine remaining ingredients. Spread pineapple over crust, reserving 2 tablespoons for garnish. Pour filling over pineapple. Bake in 350° oven for 20 minutes; cool. Refrigerate at least 2 hours. Before serving, garnish with reserved pineapple. Makes 6 servings.

Diane Kemmetmueller, Anoka, MN

JAMS AND JELLIES

CHOKECHERRY SYRUP

4 c. chokecherry juice
4 c. white sugar

2 c. light Karo syrup

Place all ingredients into a 5 quart preserving kettle; bring to the boiling point over high heat, stirring to dissolve sugar. When syrup comes to a boil, turn heat to medium and continue boiling for 10 to 15 minutes or until foam starts climbing sides of the kettle. *Watch closely.* Remove from heat and pour into sterilized jars. Use on pancakes, waffles, and ice cream.

Helen H. Clark, Grand Forks, ND

ZUCCHINI ORANGE JAM

6 c. zucchini
6 c. sugar
1 c. crushed pineapple and juice

½ c. real lemon
1 (6 oz.) pkg. orange jello

Cook zucchini for 6 minutes. Add sugar, lemon juice, and pineapple; cook for 6 minutes more. Remove from heat; add jello. Stir till dissolved, then put in jars and seal.

Marion Nelson, Dickinson, ND

PEACH CONSERVE

12 peaches
4 oranges

1 lemon
8 c. sugar

Prepare fruit as follows: Peel and pit peaches. Grate rind from oranges and lemon. Peel oranges. Put all fruit through a food grinder, or put in blender for a minute. Add sugar and let stand for 1 hour. Cook slowly for about 1 hour or until mixture is right consistency. Watch carefully so it doesn't scorch. Place in hot sterilized jars and seal with paraffin while still hot.

Sonya Masset, Bismarck, ND

RHUBARB JELLY

When you freeze rhubarb, do not use sugar. In the spring when the new crop is ready, do this: Place all the rhubarb from the freezer (from the year before) in a large juice bag, or a colander with a cheesecloth lining. Let stand overnight. The next morning, use this juice and make jelly following the Sure-Jell recipe.

This makes a beautiful, tasty jelly.

Mavis Holmberg, Fargo, ND

RHUBARB JAM

5 c. cut rhubarb   ½ c. water
4 c. sugar

    Cook for 15 minutes; stir to dissolve sugar. Add 1 can blueberry pie mix. Cook for 5 minutes more. Remove from heat and add 1 (6 ounce) raspberry jello; stir well. Cool in jars and freeze.

Mary Weight

BAKED CRANBERRIES

1 lb. cranberries   ½ c. water
2 c. sugar

    Set over low flame long enough to melt sugar, then bake for 1 hour at 350°. Serve cold or hot with turkey or chicken.

Marie Capen, Duluth, MN

CRANBERRY BUTTER

1 (12 oz.) pkg. (about 3 c.)   1½ Tbsp. lemon juice
   cranberries   1 tsp. grated lemon peel
1½ c. water   ½ tsp. thyme
1¾ c. brown sugar   ¼ tsp. salt

    Bring cranberries and water to a boil over high heat in a large covered saucepan. Boil for 5 minutes or until cranberries are soft. In a blender, blend the mixture until smooth. Press through a strainer to remove cranberry skins and return pulp to pan. Stir in sugar, lemon juice and peel, thyme, and salt. Cook over medium heat, stirring often for about 30 minutes or until mixture thickens to the consistency of thin applesauce. Cool and refrigerate. Makes about 2½ cups.

Lenora Buck, Fargo, ND

PICKLES

PICKLED EGGS

2 c. white vinegar
½ c. water

2 Tbsp. sugar
1 tsp. salt

Mix and pour over the following:

10 to 12 hard-boiled, peeled
   eggs
1 sliced onion

1 tsp. pickling spice (in small
   cheesecloth)

Put in large peanut butter jar.

Mrs. Goldie Mikish, Staples, MN

MARINATED CUCUMBERS
(The best ever)

5 to 6 cukes

1 Tbsp. *canning* salt

Slice cukes and sprinkle with salt. Let stand for 10 minutes or more. Drain and rinse.

Combine:

2 c. mayonnaise (not salad
   dressing)
½ c. vinegar
¾ c. sour cream
2 tsp. salt
Pepper (we use 1 tsp.)

1 tsp. sugar
Dill weed to taste
Chopped green onion (tops and
   all) to taste
Fried bacon, crumbled, or bacon
   bits

Combine cukes and sauce. *Enjoy.*

Peggy Mielke, Chisholm, MN

REFRIGERATED PICKLES
(Crisp and crunchy)

2 c. sugar (white)
1 c. vinegar (dark)

1 tsp. mustard seed
1 tsp. celery seed

Boil all together, then cool.

7 c. cucumber, peeled and sliced
1 c. sliced onions

½ c. green peppers

Sprinkle 1 tablespoon of canning salt; let stand for 1 hour, then pour off liquid. Put in container and put brine over. (Store in refrigerator.)

Joyce McCann, St. Cloud, MN

see also
S+H church cookbook
Pg. 249

276

OVERNIGHT PICKLES
(For sodium controlled diets)

Although pickles made without salt are never quite as crunchy as the usual product, these are very close, providing you choose your cucumbers carefully. Avoid those that are waxed because the flavors can not easily penetrate the wax coating.

4 very firm, medium size
   pickling cucumbers,
   scrubbed and thinly sliced
3 tsp. whole pickling spices
2 tsp. honey (more if sweeter
   pickles are preferred)

2 tsp. fresh dill, finely chopped
6 Tbsp. white vinegar
2 Tbsp. red wine vinegar
⅛ tsp. cayenne (or more to
   taste)

1. Place cucumbers in a bowl.

2. Combine the remaining ingredients in a saucepan; bring to a boil and simmer for 1 minute.

3. Pour hot mixture over cucumbers and let stand for an hour or until cucumbers have become slightly limp.

4. Empty the cucumbers and juice into a jar; cover. Let chill in refrigerator overnight. Yield: 1 pint.

The pickles can be safely stored in refrigerator for several months. This same recipe can be used for pickling beets. Cook, peel, and slice 6 medium beets and mix with a few thin slices of Bermuda onion if desired. Continue as for cucumbers, omitting dill.

Pat Johnson, Battle Lake, MN

DRINKS

APPLE JUICE

Take out stem and blossom ends of crab or regular apples; cut in halves. Larger apples need to be quartered. To each ice cream pail full of apples, add the same amount of boiling water and 2 tablespoons of cream of tartar. Let set for 24 hours.

Drain off juice and bring to boil. Discard the apples. Sweeten the juice to taste with ½ to 1 cup sugar. (Note: ½ cup for regular apples and a good ¾ cup for crab apples.) Makes more than ½ gallon of juice. Crab apples make a nice color and good flavor. The juice can be sealed while hot. Also can add red cinnamon candy for taste and color.

Frances Schwartzbaver

HOT MULLED CIDER

½ c. brown sugar
¼ tsp. salt
2 qt. Speas apple cider
1 tsp. whole allspice

1 tsp. whole cloves
3 inch stick cinnamon
Dash of nutmeg

Combine brown sugar, salt, and cider. Tie spices in cheesecloth bag. Add slowly. Bring to boil; simmer, covered, for 20 minutes. Serve hot with cinnamon stick.

Corrine Schjollegerdes, Owatonna, MN

HOT APPLE CIDER

Mix and heat in a large kettle:

8 c. water
8 c. apple cider
1 presweetened Kool-Aid
   (cherry punch)

½ tsp. cinnamon
¼ tsp. nutmeg
¼ tsp. cloves

Elizabeth Klug, Dickinson, ND

A HEALTH DRINK

4 Tbsp. honey
1 qt. warm water

8 Tbsp. lemon juice

Dissolve honey in warm water. Add lemon juice. Cool and drink a small cupful every morning.

Elizabeth Klug, Dickinson, ND

TOMATO JUICE

Peel, core, and quarter tomatoes; simmer until pulpy. Strain 12 cups of juice.

Add:

1 tsp. salt	1 tsp. dried sweet basil
⅛ tsp. pepper	1 Tbsp. sugar
1 tsp. celery salt	2 Tbsp. lemon juice
1 tsp. onion salt (optional)	

Also cook until tender:

Onion	2 sticks celery
2 carrots	A little parsley

Strain and add to tomato juice. Bring juice to boil again; simmer for 5 minutes. Put in cartons; set cartons in ice water. When cooled, put in freezer.

Donna Krause, Detroit Lakes, MN

RHUBARB SLUSH
(Makes 5 quarts)

8 c. rhubarb, cut small	8 c. water

Boil together until soft. Strain and cool.

1 (3 oz.) strawberry jello	2 c. vodka
4 c. sugar	7-Up or ginger ale
½ c. lemon juice	

After cooling (but still a little warm), dissolve strawberry jello. Add sugar, lemon juice, and vodka. Freeze for 24 hours. Serve with 7-Up or ginger ale.

Diane Kemmetmueller, Anoka, MN

SUNSHINE WEDDING PUNCH

3 cans (6 oz.) frozen orange juice concentrate	1 qt. ginger ale
1 (6 oz.) can frozen grapefruit juice concentrate	2 limes or oranges, thinly sliced

Reconstitute fruit juices according to directions on can. Pour into punch bowl. When ready to serve, add ginger ale and ice. Float lime or orange slices in punch. Makes about 30 (½ cup) servings.

Anne La Fleur, Duluth, MN

FLAVORED MILK DRINKS

For each serving, add 1 of the following syrups, fruits, or flavorings to a tall glass. Fill glass with cold milk and stir thoroughly. Serve.

Banana: Add ½ banana, mashed.

Chocolate: Add 1½ to 2 tablespoons cocoa syrup or canned chocolate syrup.

Peanut Butter: Add 1 tablespoon peanut butter, 2 tablespoons sugar, and dash of maple flavoring.

Orange Blossom: Add ¼ to ⅓ cup orange juice, 1 teaspoon sugar, and about 2 drops of almond flavoring.

Coffee: Add 1½ to 2 teaspoons powdered instant coffee and 2 tablespoons sugar, dissolved in 2 teaspoons water.

Berry: Add 2 teaspoons strawberry or raspberry jam or ice cream topping, or thawed frozen berries and 2 to 3 drops red food coloring.

Anne La Fleur, Duluth, MN

MELON COOLER
(Or summertime soup)

1 small cantaloupe, honeydew,
   or watermelon
1 (20 oz.) can crushed
   pineapple, packed in its own
   juice

1 c. crushed ice
Unsweetened pineapple juice
Mint sprigs (optional)

1. Peel and seed melon; cut into chunks
2. In electric blender or food processor, combine ½ of melon, all of crushed pineapple, and ice. Blend on high speed, gradually adding remaining melon cubes. Blend till smooth.
3. Thin mixture with unsweetened pineapple juice to drinking consistency desired. Garnish glass with mint sprigs.

Pat Johnson, Battle Lake, MN

MEXICAN HOT CHOCOLATE

Mix together:

¼ c. cocoa
¾ c. sugar
⅛ tsp. salt

3 to 4 tsp. cinnamon
1 tsp. nutmeg

Heat 1 quart milk (hot). Add dry ingredients; beat with wire whip or mixer (2 minutes). Add 1 teaspoon vanilla. Serve with whipped topping.

Renee Ulberg, Bismarck, ND

CANDY

SPICED PEANUTS SNACK

3 c. dry roasted peanuts (16 oz. jar)
¾ c. sugar

1 Tbsp. pumpkin spice
1 egg white, slightly beaten

Toss peanuts with the egg white. Add sugar and pumpkin pie spice; spread on pan. Bake at 300° for 20 minutes.

Mildred Sjostrom, St. Peter, MN

TRIPLE TREATS CANDY

1 (11½ oz.) pkg. (2 c.) Nestle milk chocolate morsels
2 Tbsp. vegetable shortening
1 (14 oz.) pkg. Kraft caramels

3 Tbsp. butter or margarine
2 Tbsp. water
1 c. Planters walnut pieces

Melt over hot (not boiling) water, Nestle milk chocolate morsels and vegetable shortening. Stir until morsels melt and mixture is smooth. Remove from heat. Pour ½ of melted chocolate into an 8 inch greased foil lined square pan; spread evenly. Refrigerate until firm (about 15 minutes).

Return remaining chocolate mixture to low heat. Melt caramels and butter or margarine with water over low heat, stirring until smooth. Stir in Planters walnut pieces until well blended. Pour into the chocolate lined pan. Spread evenly. Refrigerate until tacky, about 15 minutes.

Top with remaining melted chocolate; spread evenly to cover caramel filling. Return to refrigerator and chill until firm (about 1 hour). Cut into 1x2 inch rectangles. Refrigerate until ready to serve. Makes about 2½ dozen candies. Preparation time: 45 minutes.

Variation: One cup coarsely chopped Planters peanuts may be substituted for walnut pieces.

Diane Haan

CLUB SODA CRACKER'S CANDY

Club crackers
1 c. butter

½ c. sugar
1 pkg. slivered almonds

Line a cookie sheet with aluminum foil, then line it with club crackers. Boil butter and sugar just until it boils. Pour over the crackers and sprinkle with almonds. Bake at 350° for 10 minutes.

Helen H. Clark, Grand Forks, ND

CARAMELS

2 c. white sugar
1½ c. corn syrup

1 c. butter
1½ c. thin cream

On medium low, cook ½ cup of cream with sugar, syrup, and butter until smooth. Add rest of cream and cook to hard ball stage. Pour in buttered pan and cut before completely set.

Pat Palmer, Fargo, ND

CARAMELS

1 c. sugar
¾ c. dark corn syrup
½ c. butter

1 c. light cream (half & half)
½ c. chopped nuts
½ tsp. vanilla

Combine sugar, syrup, butter, and ½ of the cream; bring to boil, stirring constantly. Add remaining cream and cook slowly (medium low) to hard ball (260°). Remove from heat. Add nuts and vanilla. Pour into greased 8 inch square pan. Mark in squares when partially cool. Cut when cold. Wrap caramels into squares of waxed paper (or Saran). Keep in airtight container. Makes 36.

Evelyn Pedersen

ENGLISH BUTTER TOFFEE
(Makes 1 pound, 6 ounces)

1 c. sugar
1 c. (2 sticks) unsalted butter
¼ c. water
½ tsp. salt
1 tsp. vanilla

4 oz. milk chocolate
4 oz. sweet cooking chocolate
(best quality)
¼ c. finely chopped toasted
pecans or walnuts

Butter 10x15 inch baking sheet. Combine sugar, butter, water, and salt in heavy saucepan. Place over medium high heat and bring to boil, stirring until sugar is dissolved. Continue boiling, shaking pan occasionally, until candy thermometer registers 305°F. (hard crack stage). Remove from heat and stir in vanilla. Pour onto baking sheet in 10x10 inch square. Let stand until cool and hardened.

Melt 2 ounces of each chocolate in small pan over very low heat. Spread evenly with spatula on top side of toffee. Immediately sprinkle with ½ of nuts; refrigerate for 30 minutes.

Using spatula, carefully turn toffee over. Repeat with remaining chocolate and nuts. Return to refrigerator and chill for at least 30 minutes. When firm enough to handle, break toffee into pieces. Store in airtight container in cool dry place.

Instead of combining chocolates, toffee can be coated with 8 ounces of either type.

Kathy Olsen, Duluth, MN

ENGLISH TOFFEE

1 c. white sugar
1 c. butter or oleo

3 Tbsp. water

Put in saucepan and heat, stirring, till butter melts. Cook and stir till bubbles up thick and turns amber in color, 20 to 30 minutes. Pour onto ungreased pizza pan or cookie sheet. While still hot, cut.

Sherry Kuns, Owatonna, MN

PECAN FUDGE

4 c. pecans

½ c. butter

Toast this mixture in slow oven for 30 to 40 minutes and stir.

Boil for 5 minutes:

4½ c. white sugar
1 large can evaporated milk
3 (6 oz.) pkg. chocolate chips

3 (4½ oz.) milk chocolate bars
1 pt. marshmallow cream

Add pecans and pour into pans (large cookie sheet or two 9x13 inch pans).

Diane Rueb, Owatonna, MN

HOT FUDGE SAUCE

1 c. sugar
2 Tbsp. flour

2 Tbsp. cocoa
1 c. boiling water

In saucepan, mix dry ingredients. Add boiling water. Bring mixture to a boil. Boil for 4 minutes.

Delicious served over ice cream, chocolate roll, or sponge cake.

Bobbi Westerbur

BUTTER CRUNCH CANDY

1 c. butter or margarine
1 c. sugar

¼ c. water

Grease 8x11 inch pan. In a large iron skillet, mix butter or margarine, sugar, and water. Cook over medium flame, stirring constantly with a wooden spoon. After coming to a boil, cook for 7 minutes or until it becomes a light caramel color. Cover bottom of pan with nuts and pour caramel mixture over nuts (pecans preferred). Let cool and break into pieces.

You may also melt chocolate bits and spread on one side before breaking.

Helen May Johnson, Chanhassen, MN

SOUR CREAM CANDY

2 c. sugar
1 c. sour cream

1 tsp. vanilla
Chopped nuts

Boil sugar and sour cream gently until a soft ball is formed in cold water. Take off stove and cool until cold. Beat until creamy. Add nuts and pour into well greased pan. Cut into squares.

Ann Strandemo, Bismarck, ND

CHOCOLATE MINTS

3 c. sugar
1 stick margarine

1 c. half & half cream

Boil to soft ball stage. Take off stove.

Add:

1 tsp. mint flavoring

1 (6 oz.) pkg. chocolate chips

Mix well. Drop by teaspoonful on waxed paper.

Ann Strandemo, Bismarck, ND

DIVINITY

4 c. sugar
1 c. white syrup

¾ c. water

Place in saucepan over low heat. Stir until sugar is dissolved, then cook, without stirring, to 255° (hard ball stage). Remove from heat and pour (beating constantly) in a fine stream into 3 egg whites, stiffly beaten. Continue beating until it holds its shape and loses its gloss. Add 1 teaspoon vanilla and 1 cup nutmeats. Drop quickly onto waxed paper.

Gloria Smith, Jackson, MN

PEANUT BUTTER FUDGE

2 cans Eagle Brand milk
1 (12 oz.) pkg. peanut butter
   chips
1 (6 oz.) pkg. semi-sweet
   chocolate

1 (12 oz.) pkg. milk chocolate
   chips
5 Tbsp. butter or margarine

Heat 1 can Eagle Brand milk, 2 tablespoons butter, and package of peanut butter chips until chips are melted. Line an oblong casserole dish with 2 layers of waxed paper. Spread peanut butter mixture over paper.

In same pan, heat both chocolates, 3 tablespoons butter, and 1 can Eagle Brand; spread over other layer. Sprinkle top with ½ cup finely chopped pecans and pat in. Chill about 2 hours. Cut in small squares.

Barb Fivecoate, Virginia, MN

PENUCHE CANDY

2 c. brown sugar
½ c. condensed milk
2 Tbsp. corn syrup (white)
2 Tbsp. butter
1 c. chopped nuts

1 c. white sugar
½ c. water
¼ tsp. salt
1 tsp. vanilla

Mix sugars, syrup, salt, milk, and water; cook until it forms a soft ball in water, 235°. Remove from heat; add butter and let cool to lukewarm before heating. Add vanilla and beat until creamy. Add nuts. Pour on buttered Pyrex dish. When cool, cut in squares.

Barb Fivecoate, Virginia, MN

QUICK AND MILD CHOCOLATE CANDY

12 oz. pkg. Nestle's chocolate
   chips
12 oz. pkg. Nestle's
   butterscotch chips

1 can Borden's Eagle Brand milk
1 c. walnut nutmeats
1 tsp. vanilla

In saucepan, melt chocolate, butterscotch chips, and milk together. Do not boil. Add nutmeats and vanilla. Pour into 9x9 inch pan that you line with foil. Cut into squares while warm.

Dorothy Benson, Jackson, MN

HUNGARY MAPLE CANDIED WALNUTS

1 c. sugar
1 Tbsp. light corn syrup
⅓ c. water
½ tsp. salt

½ tsp. maple flavoring
1 Tbsp. butter
2 c. walnut halves

Mix first 4 ingredients in heavy saucepan, stirring over low heat, until sugar is dissolved. Boil to soft ball stage, 238°. Remove from heat and blend in flavoring and butter. Add nuts. Stir gently to coat nuts until creamy. Turn out on waxed paper or foil and separate nuts.

Helen May Johnson, Chanhassen, MN

SUGAR AND SPICE PECANS

¼ c. (½ stick) butter
1 lb. pecan halves
1 tsp. salt
2 Tbsp. 10X (confectioners)
   sugar

½ tsp. ground cinnamon
10X (confectioners) sugar

Preheat oven to moderate (350°). Melt butter in 13x9x2 inch baking pan in oven. Add pecans; sprinkle with salt and mix well. Return to oven for 20 minutes, stirring occasionally. Remove ½ the nuts to sheet of aluminum foil to cool.

Stir together 2 tablespoons 10X sugar and cinnamon in small bowl. Sprinkle mixture over remaining nuts in pan; toss well to coat. Cool nuts in pan. Store pecans separately in 2 airtight containers at room temperature. Just before serving sugared pecans, lightly dust with 10X sugar.

Fran Toler, Minneapolis, MN

POPCORN BALLS

8 c. popped corn
½ c. brown sugar
½ c. corn syrup (use light if
   adding coloring)

¼ c. butter or margarine
½ tsp. salt

Cook in Dutch oven pan. Bring to a boil and boil for 2 minutes. Pour over corn.

Owatonna, MN

ENGLISH CHRISTMAS LOAF CANDY

6 c. white sugar
1 pt. white Karo syrup

1½ pt. cream (do not use
   canned milk)

Mix together and cook until it forms a firm ball in cold water. Remove from stove and beat. Add 1½ cups chopped English walnuts. Makes about 5 pounds.

Prepare pan: Well grease loaf pan and line with wax paper, then grease paper. Let stand until cold. Turn pan upside-down to remove candy. Wrap in wax paper and let stand at least 12 hours, then it may be sliced or cubed.

Helen May Johnson, Chanhassen, MN

Notes

Notes

Helpful Hints

EQUIVALENT CHART

3 tsp. . . . . .1 tbsp.	¼ lb. crumbled Bleu cheese . . . . .1 c.
2 tbsp. . . . . .⅛ c.	1 lemon . . . . .3 tbsp. juice
4 tbsp. . . . . .¼ c.	1 orange .⅓ c. juice
8 tbsp. . . . . .½ c.	1 lb. unshelled walnuts . . . .1½ to1¾ c. shelled
16 tbsp.. .1 c.	2 c. fat . . . . .1 lb.
5 tbsp. + 1 tsp. . . . . .⅓ c.	1 lb. butter . . . . .2 c. or 4 sticks
12 tbsp. .¾ c.	2 c. granulated sugar. . . . . .1 lb.
4 oz. . . . . .½c.	3½ - 4 c. unsifted powdered sugar . . . . . . .1 lb.
8 oz. . . . . .1 c.	2¼ c. packed brown sugar . . . . .1 lb.
16 oz.. . . . . .1 lb.	4 c. sifted flour. . . . . .1 lb.
1 oz. . . . . .2 tbsp. fat or liquid	4½ c. cake flour. . . . . .1 lb.
2 c. . . . . .1 pt.	3½ c. unsifted whole wheat flour. . . . . . . .1 lb.
2 pt. . . . . .1 qt.	4 oz. (1 to 1¼ c.) uncooked
1 qt. . . . . .4 c.	macaroni. . . . . .2¼ c. cooked
⅝ c. . . . . .½ c. + 2 tbsp.	7 oz. spaghetti . . . . .4 c. cooked
⅞ c. . . . . .¾ c. + 2 tbsp.	4 oz. (1½ to 2 c.) uncooked
1 jigger. . . . . .1½ fl. oz. (3 tbsp.)	noodles . . . . .2 c. cooked
8 to 10 egg whites. . . . . .1 c.	28 saltine crackers . . . . .1 c. crumbs
12 to 14 egg yolks. . . . . .1 c.	4 slices bread . . . . .1 c. crumbs
1 c. unwhipped cream . . . . .2 c. whipped	14 square graham crackers. . . . . . .1 c. crumbs
1 lb. shredded American cheese . . . . .4 c.	22 vanilla wafers . . . . .1 c. crumbs

SUBSTITUTIONS FOR A MISSING INGREDIENT

1 square **chocolate** (1 ounce) = 3 or 4 tablespoons cocoa plus ½ tablespoon fat.
1 tablespoon **cornstarch** (for thickening) = 2 tablespoons flour.
1 cup sifted **all-purpose flour** = 1 cup plus 2 tablespoons sifted cake flour.
1 cup sifted **cake flour** = 1 cup minus 2 tablespoons sifted all-purpose flour.
1 teaspoon **baking powder** = ¼ teaspoon baking soda plus ½ teaspoon cream of tartar.
1 cup **sour milk** = 1 cup sweet milk into which 1 tablespoon vinegar or lemon juice has been
    stirred; or 1 cup buttermilk (let stand for 5 minutes).
1 cup **sweet milk** = 1 cup sour milk or buttermilk plus ½ teaspoon baking soda.
¾ cup **cracker crumbs** = 1 cup bread crumbs.
1 cup **cream, sour, heavy** = ⅓ cup butter and ⅔ cup milk in any sour milk recipe.
1 teaspoon **dried herbs** = 1 tablespoon fresh herbs.
1 cup **whole milk** = ½ cup evaporated milk and ½ cup water or 1 cup reconstituted nonfat dry
    milk and 1 tablespoon butter.
1 package **active dry yeast** = 1 cake compressed yeast.
1 tablespoon **instant minced onion, rehydrated** = 1 small fresh onion.
1 tablespoon **prepared mustard** = 1 teaspoon dry mustard.
⅛ teaspoon **garlic powder** = 1 small pressed clove of garlic.
1 lb. **whole dates** = 1½ c. pitted and cut.
3 medium **bananas** = 1 c. mashed.
3 c. **dry corn flakes** = 1 c. crushed.
10 **miniature marshmallows** = 1 large marshmallow.

GENERAL OVEN CHART

Very slow oven . . . . .250° to 300° F.	
Slow oven . . . . .300° to 325° F.	
Moderate oven . . . . .325° to 375° F.	
Medium hot oven . . . . .375° to 400° F.	
Hot oven . . . . .400° to 450° F.	
Very hot oven . . . . .450° to 500° F.	

CONTENTS OF CANS

Of the different sizes of cans used by commercial canners, the most common are:

Size:	Average Contents
8-oz. . . . . .1 cup
picnic . . . . .1¼ cups
No. 300 . . . . .1¾ cups
No. 1 tall .2 cups
No. 303 . . . . .2 cups
No. 2 . . . . .2½ cups
No. 2½ . . . . .3½ cups
No. 3 . . . . .4 cups
No. 10 . . . . .12 to 13 cups

HELPFUL HINTS

THE CODED LOAD

With list in hand, my husband left
To buy the grocery load,
But soon returned to shout at me:
"You've written it in code!"

What's this you mean, Product 19?
And 1 tube large QT?
Six small V-8's, the ones on sale?
And 2 bars pink Phase III?

You want a jug of 409?
Two Jell-O 1-2-3?
One K2r, the 4 ounce size?
A small jar MSG?

Two S.O.S., 1 VO5?
And Colgate MFP?
Six 7-Up and 1 A.1.?
Four cans of Grape Hi-C?

One half & half and 2 whole wheat,
From off the day-old shelf?
"If this is what you want, my dear,
You'll have to go yourself!"

HOUSEHOLD HINTS

Box cakes usually make 3 layers. Put together 2 layers and serve. Wrap third layer for freezing. Days later you may need a quick dessert.

For a flaky crust, be sure you do not roll crust too many times. Always flour the rolling pin and roll away from you.

As a rule a full cooky jar means a happy and healthy family.

If you want to make cupcakes for a picnic, just remember that any cake mix filling an 8 inch round pan will make 12 cupcakes if baked in muffin tins.

When scalding milk, grease inside bottom of pan and it will not scorch.

Never carve a roast until it has cooled, so juices can go back into the roast.

When recipe calls for buttermilk instead of milk, add to milk, 1 teaspoon baking powder and same amount of soda.

When cookies are baked, save out 10 or 12 in a plastic bag and freeze. Next time cookies are baked, add 10 more, etc. When guests drop in, or school or church groups want a donation of cookies, you will be ready.

Emma Buhl, Long Prairie, MN

SUBSTITUTIONS FOR COOKING

Baking that will pitch-hit for you in an emergency (cooking tips).

Biscuit mix: For 1 cup, substitute 1 cup flour plus 1½ teaspoons baking powder, ½ teaspoon salt, and 1 tablespoon shortening.

Corn syrup: For 1 cup, use 1 cup sugar plus ¼ cup more of the liquid called for in the recipe.

Butter: For 1 cup, use 1 cup margarine, or ⅞ cup salad, nut, or vegetable oil, or 14 tablespoons salad shortening plus ½ teaspoon salt.

Heavy cream: For 1 cup (not for whipping), substitute ¾ cup milk plus ⅓ cup melted butter.

Garlic: For 1 clove, use ¼ teaspoon garlic powder, or use 1 teaspoon garlic salt and reduce regular salt by ½ teaspoon.

Honey: For 1 cup, mix 1 cup sugar with ¼ cup more of the liquid used in recipe.

Ruth Weis, Bemidji, MN

COOKING TIPS

1. Peel garlic cloves and put in small jar in refrigerator with cooking oil to cover. Use oil in stir-fry (small amount) or for seasoning and crush garlic when needed. Replenish oil if necessary.

2. Store fresh ginger root in aluminum foil in freezer. Peel just amount needed and grate; rewrap and pop back into freezer. Keeps a *long* time.

Ruth Weis, Bemidji, MN

TABASCO

For a few drops, use a dash of cayenne or red pepper.

Ruth Weis, Bemidji, MN

HINTS

1. Wild rice can be added to all meat or poultry soups.

2. Boiled wild rice can be served with cream and sugar for breakfast. I prefer to skip the sugar and cream and just add a big "dab" of butter.

3. Cubed baked ham can be used in wild rice casseroles. I have substituted it for chop suey meat or chicken with good results!

4. To make pink frosting or pink whipped toppings, add some dry fruit gelatin (cherry, strawberry, or raspberry). Sprinkle it over the whipped cream or whipped topping and beat in just enough to blend.

Mary Patalas, Virginia, MN

COOKING TIPS SUBSTITUTES

Here are some commonly used substitutes. Remember that if you have the "substitute" and not the first ingredients that you can use this table backwards.

One teaspoon double acting baking powder: Substitute 1½ teaspoons single acting baking powder or ¼ teaspoon baking soda plus ½ cup sour milk.

One cup butter: Substitute 1 cup margarine or ⅞ cup (14 tablespoons) lard or solid shortening plus ½ teaspoon salt.

One square unsweetened chocolate: Substitute 3 tablespoons cocoa plus 1 tablespoon shortening.

One cup coffee cream: Substitute 3 tablespoons butter plus ⅞ cup (14 tablespoons) milk.

One cup heavy cream: Substitute ⅓ cup butter plus ¾ cup milk.

One whole egg: Substitute 2 egg yolks.

One tablespoon flour for thickening: Substitute ½ tablespoon cornstarch or 2 teaspoons quick cooking tapioca.

One cup all-purpose flour: Substitute 1 cup plus 2 tablespoons cake flour.

One cup cake flour: Substitute ⅞ cup (14 tablespoons) all-purpose flour.

One cup sifted flour: Substitute 1 cup minus 2 tablespoons unsifted flour.

One tablespoon fresh herbs: Substitute 1 teaspoon dried herbs.

One cup honey: Substitute 1¼ cups sugar plus ¼ cup liquid.

One cup fresh whole milk: Substitute 1 cup reconstituted nonfat dry milk plus 2 tablespoons butter or ½ cup evaporated milk plus ½ cup water.

One cup sour milk or buttermilk: Substitute 1 tablespoon lemon juice or vinegar plus enough sweet milk to make 1 cup.

One cup solid shortening: Substitute ⅞ cup (14 tablespoons) salad or vegetable oil.

Wally Littlefield, Fargo, ND

COOKING SUGGESTIONS

Whipped cream stays fluffy if you add 3 tablespoons of unsifted powdered sugar to each pint of whipping cream before you whip it. Add ½ teaspoon of vanilla or other flavoring at the same time.

Grease a pan in which you wish to melt chocolate. It won't stick to the pan and is easy to remove with a rubber spatula.

To measure butter without packing into cup, fill a glass measuring cup with water, leaving just enough space for the specified measure of shortening. Push shortening down until water rises to the 1 cup mark.

When making cupcakes and you run out of muffin tins in which to place the paper baking cups, just make yourself more cup holders from the bands of two-piece jar lids. Set the rows of bands on a cooky sheet or cake pan and put the paper cups inside, then fill and bake.

When making banana bread or cake, substitute banana baby food for mashed bananas. Two small jars of baby food equal 1 cup mashed bananas. Baby food is easy to store and always handy.

Freezing peas from the garden? To shell more easily, cover with hot water until pods turn bright green; drain. Cool with cold water. Peas will pop out by pressing on the back side of pods. Do a large quanity in the sink with hot water from the tap.

When making rolled cookies, cut the ends from small fruit juice cans and use to cut out cookies, then while cutter is in place, sprinkle sugar, nuts, or candies inside the can. This avoids waste.

To avoid a crumbly cake, freeze, then cut and frost. This prevents crumbs from getting into frosting and is easy to cut and frost.

Dust doughnuts with instant cocoa mix for a nice flavor treat.

Before turning an angel food or layer cake onto a plate, sprinkle the plate with powdered sugar. The cake won't stick.

To fix bacon for a crowd, lay strips on rack in roasting pan so fat edge overlaps lean side of next slice. Bake in hot oven (400°) for 12 to 15 minutes or till done. No need to turn, drain, or watch.

If soup or stew is too salty, you can add cut raw potato to the pot, discarding the potato once it's boiled.

Marlys Swehla, Albert Lea, MN

HELPFUL HINTS

Buff away water marks on furniture with a clean cloth and a little toothpaste.

Thaw frozen fish in milk for a fresh caught flavor.

Water hanging plants with ice cubes. They won't drip through before being absorbed.

Remove bumper stickers by rubbing with nail polish remover.

To make rolling dough for pies easier, place dough between 2 sheets of wax paper and roll. This prevents dough from tearing and sticking to rolling pin.

To improve salad dressing, mix a chopped boiled egg in commercial salad dressing the next time you have a salad. The family will think it's homemade dressing. It's different and special.

Try giving your children pancakes in their favorite colors. Simply add *food coloring* and they'll love them.

Decrease the salty taste in oversalted soup by adding a pinch of brown sugar. *Amazing, but it works!*

Betty Case, Hibbing, MN

BURNT AND SCORCHED PANS

Sprinkle burnt pots liberally with baking soda, adding just enough water to moisten. Let stand for several hours. You can generally lift the burned portion right out of the pan.

Stubborn stains on nonstick cookware can be removed by boiling 2 tablespoons of baking soda, ½ cup vinegar, and 1 cup water for 10 minutes. Re-season pan with salad oil.

Always place a jar lid or marbles in the bottom part of your double boiler. The rattling sound will signal if the water has boiled away.

Betty Case, Hibbing, MN

TO AVOID SCRAPING CARROTS

Scrub carrots, then boil. When tender, rinse in cold water and the skins may be rubbed off easily, just like the skins on beets.

Carol Gilbertson, Hawley, MN

REMOVE STAIN FROM HANDS

When cooking a numerous amount of apples - to remove stain, put lemon juice on hands and rub in sugar.

Margaret Riley, Duluth, MN

A BISCUIT TIP

Making a batch of biscuits to serve with fried chicken? Add a few tablespoons of minced parsley and a few teaspoons of minced onion to the 2 cup flour recipe of biscuits.

Bernice T. Eugenis, Saginaw, MN

PREPARING BEANS TO COOK FOR A RECIPE

Using 9 cups of water for every 1 cup beans, soak the beans for 4 to 5 hours or overnight. Discard the water. Add fresh water. Cook beans for ½ hour. Throw out water and use as your recipe directs.

Janet Lozon, Owatonna, MN

NAVY BEANS FOR SOUP

Rinse beans and then cover with water; bring to boil and cook for 10 minutes. Remove from stove and set pan in sink. Add 1 teaspoon baking soda and stir. This will foam and take the gas out of beans for eating later. Rinse beans again with cold water. Add ham bone, 1 medium onion, 1 cup celery, salt, and pepper; bring to boil. Lower heat to simmer and cook for 2 hours.

Barb Fivecoate, Virginia, MN

BASIC SEASONINGS

1 (10 oz.) box table salt (I use ½ box of salt)
1 Tbsp. onion salt
2 Tbsp. celery salt
1 Tbsp. garlic salt
2 Tbsp. paprika

4 Tbsp. black pepper
4 Tbsp. white pepper
2 Tbsp. dill seed (or weed)
3 Tbsp. monosodium glutamate
4 Tbsp. white sugar

Mix all together.

Note: For hotter mixture, add 1 tablespoon curry powder or dry mustard.

Mrs. Cara Mueller, St. Paul, MN

FREEZING HERBS

Freeze a supply of fresh herbs if you want to have them for winter cooking. Process them immediately after picking. Run the herbs under cool tap water; shake off the excess moisture. Gently pat dry between towels. Lift several stalks with tongs and swish them in boiling water for a few seconds. Cool and air dry on toweling. Package them in freezer bags; remove excess air and seal. Package some as herb combinations - for instance, bay leaf and thyme or dill and chives.

NUTRITION TIP

More starch in the diet and less sugar and fat is recommended by Iowa State University Nutritionist, Betsy Schafer. She suggests that 55 to 60% of the day's calories come from carbohydrates. That would mean eating 6 to 8 servings daily of rice, legumes, potatoes, and corn. "As long as you go easy on the high-fat accompaniments, this would be a low calorie way to eat," she says. For example, 1 large potato equals 145 calories; 1 medium, 90; ½ cup cooked rice equals 95 calories. Instead of topping with butter (100 calories per tablespoon), use 2 tablespoons of grated Parmesan cheese (50 calories), or stewed tomatoes mixed with grated cheese, or a mixture of chopped parsley, chives, basil, and dill.

HELPFUL HINTS

Substitute 1 tablespoon dehydrated onion for ¼ cup fresh chopped onion.

Substitute 2 tablespoons dehydrated onion for ½ cup fresh chopped onion.

Substitute ¼ cup dehydrated onion for 1 cup fresh chopped onion.

Betty Risse, Bismarck, ND

COFFEE FILTERS

To separate coffee filters, stick a 2 inch piece of masking tape on the outside of the stack of coffee filters and, *"pull."* One filter will come loose at a time. Stick the same piece of masking tape onto the next filter and it's ready to use for the next time you make coffee.

Elizabeth Millard, Grand Rapids, MN

COOK WITH HONEY

Use low as temperature as possible to avoid scorching.
Decrease oven temperature 25° when baking.
Substitute ⅔ cup honey for 1 cup sugar.
Baking: Substitute honey for sugar, cup for cup.
Reduce liquid by ¼ for each cup honey used and add ¼ teaspoon soda

if soda is not in recipe.

Use ⅓ cup honey and juice of 1 lemon or orange for fruit salad dressing.

Add a little honey to stewed tomatoes or rutabagas to curb bitter taste. *Amazing!!*

Glaze carrots with 1 tablespoon melted butter, 3 tablespoons honey, and sprinkle of ginger. Mix in skillet. Add cooked carrots and cook over low heat, turning carrots until glazed.

Add ¼ cup honey to cake mix batter during last 2 minutes of beating for moister cake.

Substitute honey for sugar in meringue, spoon for spoon.

Honey Chicken: Combine ⅓ cup honey, 1 tablespoon mustard, juice of 1 lemon, ⅛ teaspoon garlic powder, basil, or cinnamon. Baste chicken when baking or barbecuing.

Laila Schroeder, Shakopee, MN

TERMS USED IN RECIPES

Bake: To cook covered or uncovered, in an oven or oven-type appliance. For meats cooked uncovered, it's called roasting.

Baste: To moisten foods during cooking with pan drippings or special sauce to add flavor and prevent drying.

Beat: To make mixture smooth by adding air with a brisk whipping or stirring motion using spoon or electric mixer.

Blend: To thoroughly mix two or more ingredients until smooth and uniform.

Boil: To cook in liquid at boiling temperature (212° at sea level) where bubbles rise to the surface and break. For a full rolling boil, bubbles form rapidly throughout the mixture.

Braise: To cook slowly with a small amount of liquid in tightly covered pan on top of range or in oven.

Broil: To cook by direct heat, usually in broiler or over coals.

Candied: To cook in sugar or syrup when applied to sweet potatoes and carrots. For fruit or fruit peel, to cook in heavy syrup till transparent and well coated.

Chill: To place in refrigerator to reduce temperature.

Chop: To cut in pieces about the size of peas with knife, chopper, or blender.

Cool: To remove from heat and let stand at room temperature.

Cream: To beat with spoon or electric mixer till mixture is soft and smooth. When applied to blending shortening and sugar, mixture is beaten till light and fluffy.

Cut in: To mix shortening with dry ingredients using pastry blender or knives.

Dice: To cut food in small cubes of uniform size and shape.

Dissolve: To disperse a dry substance in a liquid to form a solution.

Glaze: A mixture applied to food which hardens or becomes firm and adds flavor and a glossy appearance.

Grate: To rub on a grater that separates the food into very fine particles.

Marinate: To allow food to stand in a liquid to tenderize or to add flavor.

Mince: To cut or finely chop food into very small pieces.

Mix: To combine ingredients, usually by stirring, till evenly distributed.

Poach: To cook in hot liquid, being careful that food holds its shape while cooking.

Precook: To cook food partially or completely before final cooking or reheating.

Roast: To cook, uncovered, without water added, usually in an oven.

Saute: To brown or cook in a small amount of hot shortening.

Scald: To bring to a temperature just before the boiling point where tiny bubbles form at the edge of the pan.

Scallop: To bake food, usually in a casserole, with sauce or other liquid. Crumbs are often sprinkled atop.

Steam: To cook in steam with or without pressure. A small amount of boiling water is used, more water being added during steaming process if necessary.

Stir: To mix ingredients with a circular motion until well blended or of uniform consistency.

Toss: To mix ingredients lightly.

Truss: To secure fowl or other meat with skewers to hold its shape during cooking.

Whip: To beat rapidly to incorporate air and produce expansion, as in heavy cream or egg whites.

MEDICINAL
(For stuffed up heads)

Boil onion; strain off onion pieces. Add honey and lemon to taste; drink. This definitely loosens everything up.

Janet Lozon, Owatonna, MN

TEMPTING MAIN DISH IDEAS

When broiling meats or bacon on a rack, place a piece or two of dry bread in the broiler pan to soak up the dripped fat. This not only helps to eliminate smoking of the fat but reduces the chances of the fat catching fire.

Tenderizing meat - Mechanical methods: Grinding, cubing, and pounding meat breaks down the connective tissue and makes meat tender. Marinating: Soaking meat in acid mixtures such as lemon juice or vinegar tenderizes meat and adds flavor. Often herbs and spices are included in commercial marinades. Meat tenderizers: These are derivatives of natural food-tenderizing agents found in some tropical fruits (such as papaya) which soften meat tissue only while meat is cooking.

For juicier burgers, add a stiffly beaten egg white to each pound of hamburger, or make patties with one tablespoon of cottage cheese in the center.

Marbled beef, which has intermingling of fat with lean, indicates tenderness and rich flavor.

Pork chops which are light in color are corn fed.

If you rub the skin of a chicken with mayonnaise before baking, the skin will get crisp and brown.

A half teaspoon of dry mustard added to a flour mix for frying chicken adds great flavor.

The darker the flesh of a fish, the higher it is in calories.

Rule of thumb for cooking fish: Cook 10 minutes for each inch of thickness.

To keep raw fish fresh and odorless, rinse them with fresh lemon juice and water, then dry thoroughly, wrap, and refrigerate.

For fluffier omelets, add a pinch of cornstarch before beating.

Bacon will lie flat in the pan if you prick it thoroughly with a fork as it fries.

Tenderize tough meat by rubbing both sides with vinegar and olive oil. Let it stand for 2 hours before cooking.

To shape meatballs, use an ice cream scoop to make uniform balls.

Mildred Sjostrom, St. Peter, MN

"Our wisdom comes from our experience, and our experience comes from our foolishness."

Mildred Sjostrom, St. Peter, MN

FRESH FROM THE OVEN

Water or milk (whole, skimmed, evaporated, or reconstituted nonfat dry) are most often used for breads. Water makes the crust crisp, while milk produces a soft crust and a creamy-white crumb. The liquid must be at the correct temperature; if it is too hot, it will kill the yeast; if it is too cold, the dough will take longer to rise.

Many different kinds of fat (butter, margarine, shortening, salad oil, or lard) can be added to bread dough to improve flavor and make the dough stretch more easily. The bread will have a tender crumb and stays soft longer.

Eggs added to a yeast dough add flavor, color, and nutrition. They soften the crust and give the interior a fine crumb.

Do not try to speed up the yeast in bread dough by increasing the amount of flour, sweetener, or salt, or by adding ingredients. These will only make the bread heavier.

To test the rising of yeast dough: The dough is doubled when 2 finger tips pressed ½ inch into it leaves dents that remain. If dents fill in quickly, let rise 15 minutes longer and test again.

Ways to glaze bread before baking are: For a dark, shiny glaze, brush on 1 beaten egg yolk. For a light shiny glaze, beat the whole egg or brush on melted butter or margarine. For shine with no color, brush on 1 egg white beaten with 1 tablespoon water.

How can I test the vitality of yeast? Just before using the yeast, mix some into ¼ cup of lukewarm water that has been enriched with ¼ teaspoon of sugar, the food for the yeast. If the yeast mixture does not start to bubble within 5 to 10 minutes, your microorganisms are dead or enervated and will not leaven your dough or batter.

When baking bread, if tops brown too quickly, cover loosely with foil. To test for doneness - tap top of loaf lightly with your finger tips. If it sounds hollow and is well browned on top, the bread is ready. Remove loaves from pans immediately so bottoms don't become soggy; cool on wire racks.

If you roll out dough between 2 sheets of waxed paper, dab some water under the bottom sheet and it won't skid away.

All ingredients for bread making should be at room temperature. It's important to use the right size pan.

Bread stores in a cool, dry place best. It may be kept in the refrigerator but will go stale more quickly. Bread keeps in the freezer for 3 months if tightly wrapped and you make sure to press out as much air as possible.

DEFINITELY DESSERT

Fudge won't "sugar" if you add a dash of cream of tartar.

Soften "hard as a rock" brown sugar by placing a slice of soft bread or ½ an apple in the package and closing tightly. In a couple hours the brown sugar will be soft again.

Too much sugar in a recipe? Add a few drops of lemon juice or vinegar.

Use a pizza cutter to cut bars or bar cookies into nice, smooth squares in half the time.

The more egg yolks in doughnut dough, the less grease they will absorb when fried.

A few potato slices added to the oil will keep doughnuts from burning.

After mixing the dough for doughnuts, put in refrigerator at least 1 hour to make it easier to handle.

Sweetened condensed milk and evaporated milk are entirely different products and *cannot* be used interchangeably in recipes. Sweetened condensed milk is fresh, whole milk with 60% of the water removed and 45% cane sugar added (sugar acts as a preservative). Evaporated milk is whole milk from which water is removed but no sugar added. Sweetened condensed milk has a much thicker consistency and is great for desserts because it will not get "sugary" when heated and will not form ice crystals in frozen desserts. Also, it thickens without heat when combined with an acid such as lemon, orange, pineapple, or apple juices.

If you are melting chocolate in a double boiler or a custard cup set in a pan of water, do not boil the water as this will only thicken or curdle the chocolate.

To keep granulated sugar from lumping, place a couple of salt crackers in container and cover tightly.

Before measuring honey or other syrup, oil the cup with cooking oil and rinse in hot water.

The key to successful custard preparation is low heat; high heat causes the eggs to curdle, resulting in lumpy, thin mixtures. Either cook custard in a double boiler or if cooking over direct heat, always use a heavy saucepan. Stir the mixture constantly with a whisk. Check thickness by lifting the spoon from custard and holding it for 15 to 20 seconds. If the spoon does not show through mixture, the custard has thickened to the correct consistency.

PERFECT PARTY PLEASERS

Cheese and fruit tasting is an easy, conversation-making way to entertain friends before dinner. Seasonal varieties of fruit include peaches, nectarines, sweet cherries, figs, grapes, apricots, pineapple, strawberries, plums, and melons. Or try fruits such as papaya and mangoes. Dried fruits such as prunes and raisins also team nicely with cheese and fresh fruits.

Some cheese and fruit combinations: Cheddar, Provolone, and Camembert with pineapple, grapes, pears, and walnuts. Brie, Monterey Jack, and Feta with tangerines, strawberries, and dried prunes. Colby, Gjetost, Emmenthaler, and Roquefort with apricots, pineapple, and plums.

Remember, if cooking the cheese for your appetizers, that excessive heat and prolonged cooking turns it stringy and leathery. When making a sauce, stir in the cheese toward the end of cooking time just until totally melted.

To keep egg yolks from crumbling when slicing hard cooked eggs, wet the knife before each cut.

The pointed end of a beer can opener is an excellent tool for deveining shrimp.

Out of ginger ale? Mix equal parts of Coke and 7-Up.

Use styrofoam egg cartons as trays when you need extra ice cubes for parties.

If the carbonation fizzes out of your champagne, add one raisin to the bottle. The raisin won't affect the taste but it's raw sugar will start the bubbling up again.

Christmas Starter, dinner or breakfast: Serve cranberry juice topped with lime sherbet.

You can use frozen dough to make flaky crusts for appetizers. Thaw, cut into desired shapes, put in filling, brush with butter, bake for 10 to 15 minutes at 375°. Fillings can be chopped up chicken, roast beef, or any cooked seafood, or any cooked vegetables as mushrooms, broccoli, or cauliflower.

Place bay leaves (which are never to be eaten) in a tea ball for easy removal from sauces (or stews).

For instant white sauce: Blend together 1 cup soft butter and 1 cup flour. Spread in an ice cube tray; chill well. Cut into 16 cubes before storing in a plastic bag in the freezer. For medium thick sauce, drop 1 cube into 1 cup of milk and heat slowly, stirring as it thickens.

Store carton of cottage cheese upside-down. It will keep twice as long.

Try a new spice for your appetizers in place of salt. Blend together 2½ teaspoons each of paprika, dry mustard, and garlic powder, 5 teaspoons onion powder, ½ teaspoon ground black pepper, and ¼ teaspoon celery seed. Put all in a shaker and pass up the salt.

Mildred Sjostrom, St. Peter, MN

"There is a difference between not thinking of someone and forgetting him."

Mildred Sjostrom, St. Peter, MN

POTPOURRI

To determine whether an egg is fresh without breaking the shell, immerse the egg in a pan of cool salted water. If it sinks to the bottom, it is fresh. If it rises to the surface, throw it away.

Vinegar brought to a boil in a new frying pan will prevent food from sticking.

When frying, turn a metal colander upside-down over the skillet. This allows steam to escape, but keeps the fat from spattering.

Club soda cleans and polishes kitchen appliances at the same time.

When a drain is clogged with grease, pour a cup of salt and a cup of baking soda into the drain followed by a kettle of boiling water. The grease will usually dissolve immediately and open the drain.

Rub stainless steel sinks with lighter fluid if rust marks appear. After the rust disappears, wipe with your regular kitchen cleaner.

Once an onion has been cut in half, rub the leftover side with butter and it will keep fresh longer.

Popcorn: It should always be kept in the freezer. Not only will it stay fresh, but freezing helps eliminate "old maids." "Old maids" can also be eliminated by running ice cold water over the kernels before throwing into the popper.

Pinch of rosemary to water cooking rice will add an interesting flavor.

Cook wild meats with onions; cuts down wild flavor.

Do you substitute ingredients? This is always risky - don't do it! For example, sifted flour is not interchangeable with unsifted.

Food will keep hot up to 1 hour if taken somewhere, by wrapping hot food in double thickness of aluminum foil.

Garlic helps to prevent cholesterol build up. Helps prevent heart disease by slashing cholesterol levels in the blood and lowering dangerous blood fat levels.

Don't let spilled wine spoil your prettiest tablecloth. While the stain is still wet, cover it with a mound of ordinary table salt; when dry, just brush away. The salt will absorb the wine so completely you won't even have to wash the cloth.

Shaving cream is one of the most useful upholstery cleaners.

To remove water rings and stains from inside small glass or crystal vases, dampen the inside and add any toilet bowl cleaner. Let stand for 10 minutes; rinse thoroughly.

To clean and shine copper pots, rub with Worcestershire sauce or catsup. The tarnish will disappear.

To get cotton white socks white again, boil in water to which a slice of lemon has been added.

SUPER SOUPS AND SCRUMPTIOUS SALADS

Did you know? Cooking in cast iron definitely boosts iron intake. Soup simmered for a few hours in an iron pot has almost 30 times more iron than soup cooked in another pan.

Thickeners for soups can be either flour or cornstarch. It is a good idea to add the thickener with the pan off the heat to avoid the danger of lumping. Flour is good for soups to be served hot. Cornstarch is better for cold soups.

Most important of all, remember that hot soups should be served *hot* and cold soups *cold* - none benefit from being served lukewarm.

If delayed in tossing salads, greens will stay fresh under a drape of paper towels wrung out of ice water.

Always shake an oil and vinegar dressing just before using.

When unmolding a salad, always sprinkle a few drops of water on the serving plate. It will be easy to move the salad around to position it correctly.

For a stay, put garnish in a molded salad, arrange design, pour over thin layer of partially set gelatin. Chill.

To test freshness of dried herbs, rub them between your hands. Oil of your hand extracts the essence of the herb. If there is no smell, they are no good.

Season with seeds to add flavors: Caraway - Tangy and slightly sweet. Cardomon - Spicy. Celery - Strong, use sparingly. Cumin - Slightly bitter. Dill - Pungent and strong in flavor. Fennel - Licorice flavor. Mustard - Dry mustard is a mixture of ground seeds of several mustard varieties. Sesame - Sweet, nutty flavor.

For crunchy cole slaw, cut cabbage in half and soak in salted water for an hour. Drain well, then proceed with recipe.

Add a small amount of beet vinegar to mayonnaise to give it a pretty color for salads.

EVERYBODY'S FAVORITES

To improve an inexpensive cake mix, add 1 tablespoon butter to the batter for a richer-tasting cake.

Discover baking with mayonnaise. Try substituting mayonnaise as a shortening or oil - it blends easily, adds moistness, and contributes toward a tender texture.

Throwaway Cake Plate: Save bottom cardboards from pizza and cover with aluminum foil. Great if you are donating a cake or pie to a cake sale.

Dip spoon in hot water before measuring lard, butter, etc. - it will slip off the spoon more easily.

Put flour in a large salt shaker and use for dusting cake pans, meat, etc. It is less messy and doesn't waste flour.

For recipes using beaten egg whites, the eggs should be separated when cold and the whites allowed to come to room temperature (egg whites reach their highest volume if beaten at room temperature). Cream of tartar or sugar added to the egg whites will increase the stability of the foam ... the sugar should be added a little at a time. Be careful not to overbeat egg whites or they will become stiff and dry, having lost their elasticity, and will almost certainly collapse as soon as heat is applied. Be sure beaters and bowl, etc. are completely free of oil - any trace of oil will prevent the egg whites to fluff up.

Don't grease cookie sheets or cookies will tend to spread too much. When baking several batches in succession, let sheets cool before placing more dough on them or the dough will soften and spread and finished cookies will be misshapen. If you don't have enough spare cookie sheets, use inverted baking pans.

Any recipe which says, "and add one egg," can be made better by separating the white and yolk. This white, when beaten separately, adds bubbles, tenderness, and makes the finished product lighter. This is true for nearly all boxed items.

Child's Party: Push animal shaped cookie cutters lightly into icing. Fill depressed outlines with chocolate icing. *Also,* fill ice cream cones (flat bottoms) with cake batter half full and bake. Decorate with icing topped with colored sugar.

If your layer cakes stick to the bottom of their pans, return them to a warm oven briefly. The layers will come out intact in just a short time.

For baking cakes, use shiny metal pans or pans with a nonstick finish. Avoid dull, dark or enamel pans which can cause uneven and excessive browning. If using glass or porcelain-coated aluminum pans, reduce the oven temperature 25°F. If baking more than 1 at a time, arrange the pans in the oven so that you get the best air flow - stagger them from one shelf to another, not one directly on top of another. And do not have a pan touching the walls of the oven or touching another pan. Good air flow is very important to proper baking. (This is true for trays of cookies also.)

"A rumor is like a check - never endorse it till you're sure it's genuine."

HOW TO CORRECT MISTAKES IN COOKING

Too sweet:

Add salt.
If it's a main dish or vegetable, add a teaspoon of cider vinegar.

Pale gravy:
Color with a few drops of Kitchen Bouquet (available at grocery stores).
To avoid the problem in the first place, brown the flour well before adding the liquid. This also helps prevent lumpy gravy.
A different way of browning flour is to put some flour into a custard cup and place beside meat in the oven. Once the meat is done the flour will be nice and brown, ready to make a rich, brown gravy.

Thin gravy:
Mix water and flour or cornstarch into a smooth paste. Add gradually, stirring constantly, and bring to a boil.

Try instant potato flakes instead of flour.

Gravy - smooth as silk:
Keep a jar with a mixture of equal parts of flour and cornstarch. Put 3 or 4 tablespoons of this mixture in another jar and add some water. Shake, and in a few minutes you will have a smooth paste for gravy.

Greasy gravy:
Add a small amount of baking soda if it is quite greasy.

See Removing the Excess Fat, Kitchen Hints.

Wilted vegetables:
If fresh vegetables are wilted or blemished, pick off the brown edges. Sprinkle with cool water, wrap in towel, and refrigerate for an hour or so.

Perk up soggy lettuce by adding lemon juice to a bowl of cold water and soak for an hour in the refrigerator.

Douse quickly in hot and then ice water with a little apple cider vinegar added.

Lettuce and celery will crisp up fast if you place it in a pan of cold water and add a few raw sliced potatoes.

Cream that will not whip:
Chill cream, bowl, and beater well.

Set bowl of cream into a bowl of ice while you're whipping.

Add the white of an egg. Chill and then whip.

If the cream still does not stiffen, gradually whip in 3 or 4 drops of lemon juice.

Cream whipped ahead of time will not separate if you add a touch of unflavored gelatin (¼ teaspoon per cup of cream).

To eliminate a lot of mess when whipping cream with an electric beater, try this: Cut 2 small holes in the middle of a piece of waxed paper, then slip the stems of the beaters through the holes and attach the beaters to the machine. Simply place paper and beaters over the bowl and whip away.

Soggy mashed potatoes:
Overcooked potatoes can become soggy when the milk is added. Sprinkle with dry powdered milk for the fluffiest mashed potatoes ever.

Soggy potato chips, cereal, and crackers:
If potato chips lose their freshness, place under the broiler for a few moments. Care must be taken not to brown them.

You can crisp soggy cereal and crackers by putting them on a cookie sheet and heating for a few minutes in the oven.

Brown sugar "hard as a rock":
If you need it in a hurry, simply grate the amount called for with a hand grater.

Soften by placing a slice of soft bread in the package and closing tightly. In a couple hours the brown sugar will be soft again.

Put brown sugar and a cup of water (do not add to the sugar, set it alongside of

it) in a covered pan. Place in the oven (low heat) for awhile.
Or, buy liquid brown sugar.

Frozen bread loaves and rolls:
Place in brown paper bag and put in 325° oven for 5 minutes to thaw completely.

To keep the salt shaking:
Wrap a small piece of aluminum foil tightly around the shaker. The foil is moistureproof and it will keep dampness out of the salt.
To prevent clogging, keep 5 to 10 grains of rice inside your shaker.

No corkscrew for the wine bottle:
Run hot water on the neck of the bottle. Heat expands the glass, causing the cork to pop out.

SHORTCUTS IN THE KITCHEN

Baked potatoes in a hurry:
Boil them in salted water for about 10 minutes before popping into a very hot oven.
Cut a thin slice from each end before popping into the oven.
Insert a nail to shorten the baking time by 15 minutes.

Chopping onions without tears:
You'll shed less tears if you cut the root end of the onion off last.
Freeze or refrigerate before chopping.
Peel under cold running water.
Or, periodically rinse hands under cold water while chopping.

Peeling thin-skinned fruit:
Refrigerate tomatoes. Hold tomato firmly and scrape with a paring knife from the bottom to the top several times. Prick the skin with the point of the knife. The peeling will remove easily.
Place thin-skinned fruits into a bowl; cover with boiling water and let set for 1 minute. Peel with a paring knife.
Or, spear the fruit on a fork and hold over a gas flame until the skin cracks, then peel.

Ripe ideas:
Instead of using a fruit ripening bowl, place green fruits in a perforated plastic bag. The holes allow air movement, yet retain the odorless ethylene gas which fruits produce to promote ripening.
Exposure to direct sunlight softens tomatoes instead of ripening them. Leave the tomatoes, stem up, in any spot where they will be out of direct sunlight.
Ripen green bananas or green tomatoes by wrapping them in a wet dish towel and placing them in a paper sack.
Bury avocados in a bowl of flour.

Removing the excess fat:

If time allows, the best method is refrigeration until the fat hardens on the top.

Eliminate fat from soup and stew by dropping ice cubes into the pot. As you stir, the fat will cling to the cubes. Discard the cubes before they melt. Or, wrap ice cubes in a piece of cheesecloth or paper towel and skim over the top.

Lettuce leaves absorb fat also. Place a few into the pot and watch the fat cling to them.

If you prop up one leg of your electric fry pan (set it on a knife handle) you can make relatively grease free hamburgers or bacon by frying on the elevated side of the pan.

When broiling meats on a rack, place a piece of bread in the broiler pan to soak up the dripping fat. This not only eliminates smoking fat, but reduces the chances of the fat catching fire.

Add 1 tablespoon of vinegar to the fat in which you are going to deep fry. If will keep the food from absorbing too much fat and eliminate the greasy taste.

Eliminating the spattering and sticking:

When pan-frying or sauteing, always heat your pan before adding the butter or oil. Not even eggs stick with this method.

Sprinkle a little salt into the frying pan to prevent spattering.

Vinegar brought to a boil in a new frying pan will prevent foods from sticking.

When frying, turn a metal colander upside-down over the skillet. This allows steam to escape, but keeps the fat from spattering.

Meat loaf will not stick if you place a slice of bacon on the bottom of the pan.

If muffins are sticking to the tin pan, place the hot pan on a wet towel. They will slide right out.

Non-smoke broiling:

Add a cup of water to the bottom portion of the broiling pan before sliding into the oven. The water absorbs smoke and grease.

Vanishing unpleasant cooking odors:

While cooking vegetables that give off unpleasant odors, simmer a small pan of vinegar on top of the stove.

Or, add vinegar to the cooking water.

Add a few teaspoons of sugar and cinnamon to an empty pie tin and slowly burn over the stove. Your family will think you have been baking all day.

Tenderizing meat:

Boiled meat: Add a tablespoon of vinegar to the cooking water.

Tough meat or game: Make a marinade of equal parts cooking vinegar and heated bouillon. Marinate for 2 hours.

Steak: Simply rub in a mixture of cooking vinegar and oil. Allow to stand for 2 hours.

And if you want to stew an old hen, soak it in vinegar for several hours before cooking. It will taste like a spring chicken!

Don't "clam up":

Clams and oysters will be simple to open if washed with cold water, then placed in a plastic bag and put in the freezer for an hour.

Preventing boil-overs:
Add a lump of butter or a few teaspoons of cooking oil to the water. Rice, noodles, or spaghetti will not boil over or stick together.

Preventing skin on sauces and jellies:
Spread a thin layer of melted butter or cream over jellies, puddings, and other sauces right after cooking. Stir and all the skin and foam will disappear.

Preparing cut fruit ahead of time:
Toss the freshly cut fruit in lemon juice and it will not darken. The juice of ½ a lemon is enough for a quart or 2 of cut fruits.

Or, cover with 1 cup syrup made of equal parts of water and sugar cooked until syrupy.

Softening butter:
Grating a stick of butter softens it quickly.

Soften for spreading by inverting a small heated pan over the butter dish for a while.

Measuring sticky liquids:
Before measuring honey or other syrup, oil the cup with cooking oil and rinse in hot water.

Instant white sauce:
Blend together 1 cup soft butter and 1 cup flour. Spread in an ice cube tray; chill well. Cut into 16 cubes before storing in a plastic bag in the freezer. For medium thick sauce, drop 1 cube into 1 cup of milk and heat slowly, stirring as it thickens.

Getting the catsup out of the bottle:
Insert a drinking straw; push it to the bottom of the bottle and then remove. Enough air will be admitted to start an even flow.

Unmolding gelatin:
Rinse the mold pan in cold water and then coat with salad oil. Your mold will drop out easily and will have an appealing luster.

Hamburgers in a hurry:
Poke a hole in their centers when shaping. The center will cook quickly and when the hamburgers are done, the holes are gone.

Shrinkless sausage:
Sausages will shrink less and not break at all if they are boiled about 8 minutes before being fried.

Or, you can roll them lightly in flour before frying.

Removing the corn silk:
Dampen a paper towel or terry cloth and brush downward on the cob of corn. Every strand should come off.

Cutting sticky foods:
Before chopping, flour the pieces in a paper bag.

Or, dip your shears or knife in hot water while cutting.

What a ham!
Ridding the ham of the rind: Slit the rind lengthwise on the underside before placing it in the roasting pan. As the ham bakes, the rind will pull away and can be removed easily without lifting the ham.

A good cup of coffee:
One pinch of salt in the basket will remove some of the acid taste. For clear coffee, put egg shells in after perking. And remember, always start with cold water.

Your own mini "Mr. Coffee":
Put a teaspoon of "drip" coffee into a small strainer (2½ inch diameter) and place in a cup. Pour boiling water over grounds until cup is full. Let steep to desired strength. It's not a bad idea to place mini coffee filters (make your own) in the strainer before adding coffee.

Two "flavorite" hints:
A different flavoring for tea: Instead of using sugar, dissolve old-fashioned lemon drops or hard mint candy in your tea. They melt quickly and keep the tea clean and brisk.

Iced tea:
Add a small amount of very hot water to instant tea before adding cold water. The crystals will dissolve completely for better flavor.

How to prepare a hard-boiled egg:
Don't laugh, there is more to it than you think. Place eggs in a pan; cover with cold water and pour in some vinegar or salt. The vinegar will keep the eggs from oozing out if the shells crack while cooking. Bring to a boil and remove from heat. Let set in covered pan for 15 minutes. Drain off hot water. Now shake the pan back and forth, causing the eggs to crack against the side. Cool with cold water and peel.

Here are some more "eggscellent" hints:
To determine whether an egg is fresh without breaking the shell, immerse the egg in a pan of cool salted water. If it sinks to the bottom, it is fresh. If it rises to the surface, throw it away.

Fresh eggs are rough and chalky in appearance. Old eggs are smooth and shiny.

To determine whether an egg is hard-boiled, spin it. If it spins round and round, it is hard-boiled. If it wobbles and will not spin, it is raw.

Pierce the end of an egg with a pin and it will not break when placed in boiling water.

A few drops of vinegar will keep poached eggs from running all over the pan.

Eggs beat up fluffier when not too cold. They should be at cool room temperature for best results.

By adding vinegar to the water, you can boil cracked eggs without having the white run out of the shell.

When eggs are stuck to the carton, just wet the box and the eggs can be easily removed without cracking the shells.

Beaten egg whites will be more stable if you add 1 teaspoon cream of tartar to each cup of egg whites (7 or 8 eggs).

A small funnel is handy for separating egg whites from yolks. Open the egg over the funnel and the white will run through and the yolk will remain.

For baking, it's best to use medium to large eggs. Extra large eggs may cause cakes to fall when cooled.

Brown and white shelled eggs are of the same quality.

Egg shells can be removed easily from hot hard-boiled eggs if they are quickly rinsed in cold water first.

To keep egg yolks fresh for several days, cover them with cold water and store in the refrigerator.

Egg whites can be kept frozen up to 1 year. Add them to a plastic container as you "collect them" for use in meringues, angel food cake ... 1 cup equals 7 or 8 egg whites. You can also refreeze defrosted egg whites.

For fluffier omelets, add a pinch of cornstarch before beating.

KITCHEN CLEAN-ER-UPERS

Appliances:
To rid yellowing from white appliances try this: Mix together ½ cup bleach, ¼ cup baking soda, and 4 cups warm water. Apply with a sponge and let set for 10 minutes. Rinse and dry thoroughly.

Instead of using commercial waxes, shine with rubbing alcohol.

For quick clean-ups, rub with equal parts water and household ammonia.

Or, try club soda. It cleans and polishes at the same time.

Blender:
Fill part way with hot water and add a drop of detergent. Cover and turn it on for a few seconds. Rinse and drain dry.

Breadboards:
To rid cutting board of onion, garlic, or fish smell, cut a lime or lemon in two and rub the surface with the cut side of fruit.

Or, make a paste of baking soda and water and apply generously; rinse.

Broiler pan:
Sprinkle the hot pan heavily with dry laundry detergent. Cover with a dampened paper towel and let the burned food set for awhile. The pan should require little scouring.

Can opener:
Loosen grime by brushing with an old toothbrush. To thoroughly clean blades, run a paper towel through the cutting process.

Cast iron skillets:
Clean the outside of the pan with commercial oven cleaner. Let set for 2 hours and the accumulated black stains can be removed with vinegar and water.

After cleaning pan, take a piece of waxed paper and while skillet is still warm, wipe around the inside to prevent rusting.

Or, when clean rub a small amount of oil on the inside of the pan to keep it seasoned.

Did you know? Cooking in cast iron definitely boosts iron intake. Soup simmered for a few hours in an iron pot has almost 30 times more iron than soup cooked in another pan.

Copper pots:

Fill a spray bottle with vinegar and add 3 tablespoons of salt. Spray solution liberally on copper pot. Let set for awhile, then simply rub clean.

Dip lemon halves in salt and rub.

Or, rub with Worcestershire sauce or catsup. The tarnish will disappear.

Dishes:

Save time and money by using the cheapest brand of dishwashing detergent available, but add a few tablespoons of vinegar to the dishwater. The vinegar will cut the grease and leave your dishes sparkling clean.

Before washing fine china and crystal, place a towel on the bottom of the sink to act as a cushion.

To remove coffee or tea stains and cigarette burns from fine china, rub with a damp cloth dipped in baking soda.

To quickly remove food that is stuck to a casserole dish, fill with boiling water and add 2 tablespoons of baking soda or salt.

Dishwasher film:

Fill dishwasher with all your dirty dishes. However, never put any silver, aluminum, or brass in the washer when this method is used or you will have a mess. Put a bowl in the bottom of the dishwasher. Pour 1 cup of household bleach into the bowl. Run through washing cycle but do not dry. This is important. Fill bowl again with 1 cup white vinegar and let the dishwasher go through entire cycle. This will remove all film not only from your glasses but from your dishwasher too.

Drains:

When a drain is clogged with grease, pour a cup of salt and a cup of baking soda into the drain followed by a kettle of boiling water. The grease will usually dissolve immediately and open the drain.

Coffee grounds are a no-no. They do a nice job of clogging, especially if they get mixed with grease.

Garbage disposal:

Grind a ½ lemon or orange rinds in the disposal to remove any unpleasant odor.

Glassware:

Never put a delicate glass in hot water bottom side first; it will crack from sudden expansion. The most delicate glassware will be safe if it is slipped in edgewise.

Vinegar is a must when washing crystal. Rinse in 1 part vinegar to 3 parts warm water. Air dry.

When one glass is stuck inside another, do not force them apart. Fill the top glass with cold water and dip the lower one in hot water. They will come apart without breaking.

A small nick in the rim of a glass can be smoothed out by using an emery board.

Scratches on glassware will disappear if polished with toothpaste.

Grater:
For a fast and simple clean-up, rub salad oil on the grater before using.

Use a toothbrush to brush lemon rind, cheese, onion, or whatever out of the grater before washing it.

Meat grinder:
Before washing, run a piece of bread through it.

Oven:
Following a spill, sprinkle with salt immediately. When oven is cool, brush off burnt food and wipe with a damp sponge.

Sprinkle bottom of oven with automatic dishwasher soap and cover with wet paper towels. Let stand for a few hours.

A quick way to clean oven parts is to place a bath towel in the bathtub and pile all removable parts from the oven onto it. Draw enough hot water to just cover the parts and sprinkle a cup of dishwasher soap over them. While you are cleaning the inside of the oven, the rest will be cleaning itself.

An inexpensive oven cleaner: Set oven on warm for about 20 minutes, then turn off. Place a small dish of full strength ammonia on the top shelf. Put a large pan of boiling water on the bottom shelf and let it set overnight. In the morning, open oven and let it air awhile before washing off with soap and water. Even the hard baked-on grease will wash off easily.

Plastic cups, dishes, and containers:
Coffee or tea stains can be scoured out with baking soda.

Or, fill the stained cup with hot water and drop in a few denture cleanser tablets. Let soak for 1 hour.

To rid foul odors from plastic containers, place crumpled-up newspaper (black and white only) into the container; cover tightly and leave overnight.

Refrigerator:
To help eliminate odors, fill a small bowl with charcoal (the kind used for potted plants) and place it on a shelf in the refrigerator. It absorbs odors rapidly.

An open box of baking soda will absorb food odors for at least a month or two.

A little vanilla poured on a piece of cotton and placed in the refrigerator will eliminate odors.

To prevent mildew from forming, wipe with vinegar. The acid effectively kills the mildew fungus.

Use a glycerine-soaked cloth to wipe sides and shelves. Future spills wipe up easier. And after the freezer has been defrosted, coat the inside coils with glycerine. The next time you defrost, the ice will loosen quickly and drop off in sheets.

Sinks:

For a sparkling white sink, place paper towels across the bottom of your sink and saturate with household bleach. Let set for ½ hour or so.

Rub stainless steel sinks with lighter fluid if rust marks appear. After the rust disappears, wipe with your regular kitchen cleaner.

Use a cloth dampened with rubbing alcohol to remove water spots from stainless steel.

Spots on stainless steel can also be removed with white vinegar.

Club soda will shine up stainless steel in a jiffy.

See Bathroom cleaners, Bathroom Hints.

Sponge:

To renew and freshen, soak overnight in salt or baking soda water.

Wash in dishwasher.

Teakettle:

To remove lime deposits, fill with equal parts vinegar and water. Bring to a boil and allow to stand overnight.

Thermos bottle:

Put a few tablespoons of baking soda in bottle and fill with warm water.

Or, drop in a few denture cleanser tablets and let soak for an hour or so.

Tin pie pans:

Remove rust by dipping a raw potato in cleaning powder and scouring.

FOOD FRESHNESS

Bacon and sausage:

To prevent bacon from curling, dip the strips in cold water before frying.

Bacon will lie flat in the pan if you prick it thoroughly with a fork as it fries.

Keep bacon slices from sticking together; roll the package into a tube shape and secure with rubber bands.

A quick way to separate frozen bacon: Heat a spatula over the stove burner, then slide it under each slice to separate it from the others.

Have you ever tried to get roll sausage out of a package, only to find that half of it is stuck to the surrounding paper? Try running cold water over the paper before you remove the contents. Or, let it set in cold ice water for awhile.

Bananas:

Toss freshly peeled bananas in lemon juice and they will not darken.

Freeze bananas that are on the verge of going bad. They also make delicious popsicles.

If they've darkened, peel and beat slightly. Put into a plastic container and freeze until it's time to bake bread or cake.

Bread:

A rib of celery in your bread bag will keep the bread fresh for a longer time.

Freshen dried bread by wrapping in a damp towel and placing it in the refrigerator for 24 hours. Remove towel and heat in oven for a few minutes.

Broccoli:
Broccoli stems can be cooked in the same length of time as the flowers if you
    make X incisions from top to bottom through stems.

Brown sugar:
Store in plastic bag. Wrap tightly. Place in coffee can with snap-on lid.
Or, store in refrigerator.

Butter:
A butter stretcher: To make 2 pounds of butter, slowly beat in 2 cups of evapora-
    ted milk (a little at a time) to 1 pound of butter. Pour into pan and chill.

Cake:
Place ½ apple in the cake box.
Or, a slice of fresh bread fastened with toothpicks to the cut edge of a cake will
    keep the cake from drying out and getting stale.

Cheese:
To keep cheese from drying out, wrap in a cloth dampened with vinegar.

Cookies:
Place crushed tissue paper on the bottom of your cookie jar.

Corn:
To keep sweet corn yellow, add 1 teaspoon lemon juice to the cooking water a
    minute before you remove it from the stove.
Salted cooking water only toughens corn.

Cottage cheese:
Store carton upside-down. It will keep twice as long.

Crackers:
Can be kept crisp in the most humid weather by storing in the refrigerator. Be
    sure they are wrapped securely.

Cranberries:
Cranberries will grind very neatly when frozen. Wash the berries, pat dry, and
    freeze in plastic bag until ready for use.

Fish and shrimp:
Thaw fish in milk. The milk draws out the frozen taste and provides a fresh-
    caught flavor.
Or, try soaking fish in vinegar and water before cooking it for a sweet tender
    taste.
The fishy smell can be removed from your hands by washing with vinegar and
    water or salt and water.
To get rid of the "canned taste" in canned shrimp, soak them in a little sherry
    and 2 tablespoons of vinegar for about 15 minutes.

Garlic:
Garlic cloves can be kept in the freezer. When ready to use, peel and chop be-
    fore thawing.
Or, garlic cloves will never dry out if you store them in a bottle of cooking oil.

310

After the garlic is used up, you can use the garlic-flavored oil for salad dressing.

Honey:
Put honey in small plastic freezer containers to prevent sugaring. It also thaws out in a short time.

If it has sugared, simply place the jar in a boiling pot of water.

Ice cream:
Ice cream that has been opened and returned to the freezer sometimes forms a waxlike film on the top. To prevent this, after part of the ice cream has been removed, press a piece of waxed paper against the surface and reseal the carton.

Lemons:
Store whole lemons in a tightly sealed jar of water in the refrigerator. They will yield much more juice than when first purchased.

After you've squeezed a lemon for its juice, wrap and freeze the rind. When a recipe calls for lemon rind, you will not have to grate a fresh lemon.

Submerging a lemon in hot water for 15 minutes before squeezing will yield almost twice the amount of juice.

Or, warm them in your oven for a few minutes before squeezing.

Lettuce and celery:
They keep longer if you store them in the refrigerator in paper bags instead of cellophane ones. Do not remove the outside leaves of either until ready to use.

Lettuce will not rust as quickly if you place a paper towel or napkin in the storage container.

Line the bottom of the vegetable compartment with paper toweling. This absorbs the excess moisture and keeps all vegetables and fruits fresher for a longer period of time.

Or, put a few dry sponges in the vegetable compartment to absorb moisture.

Marshmallows:
They will not dry out if stored in the freezer. Simply cut with scissors when ready to use.

Meat:
When browning any piece of meat, the job will be done more quickly and effectively if the meat is perfectly dry and the fat is very hot.

Olive oil:
You can lengthen the life of olive oil by adding a cube of sugar to the bottle.

Onions:
To keep dry onions from sprouting and becoming soft, wrap individually in foil. They will stay firm for some time.

Once an onion has been cut in half, rub the leftover side with butter and it will keep fresh longer.

Parsley:
Keep fresh and crisp by storing in a wide-mouth jar with a tight lid.
Parsley can also be frozen.

Too many peeled potatoes:
Cover them with cold water to which a few drops of vinegar have been added.
Keep refrigerated and they will last for 3 or 4 days.

Popcorn:
It should always be kept in the freezer. Not only will it stay fresh, but freezing
helps eliminate "old maids."
"Old maids" can also be eliminated by running ice cold water over the kernels
before throwing into the popper.

Potatoes:
A leftover baked potato can be rebaked if you dip it in water and bake in a 350°
oven for about 20 minutes.

Poultry:
After flouring chicken, chill for 1 hour. The coating adheres better during frying.
For golden brown chicken every time, put a few drops of yellow food coloring in
the shortening after it has heated.
Wear rubber gloves to transfer a turkey from roasting pan to platter.
Truss the bird with dental floss when grilling. Dental floss does not burn and is
very strong.

Salad:
To remove the core from a head of lettuce, hit the core end once against the
countertop sharply. The core will then twist out. This method prevents un-
sightly brown spots which result when you cut into the core end.
If salad greens are wet and you need them right away, place in a pillow case
and spin dry in your washing machine for a few seconds. This hint is especially good to know if you are serving salad to a large crowd.

Salt:
Since most recipes call for both salt and pepper, keep a large shaker filled with
a mixture of both; ¾ salt and ¼ pepper is a good combination.
When to add salt: Soups and stews - add early. Meats - sprinkle just before
taking off the stove. Vegetables - cook in salted water.

Soup:
Before opening a can of soup, shake well and open it at the bottom end instead
of the top. The soup will slide out nicely.

Vegetables:
To restore a fresh flavor to frozen vegetables, pour boiling hot water over them,
rinsing away all traces of the frozen water.
Try cooking in broth for a nice flavor.

CLEANING HINTS

Cleaning the bathtub:

For an extremely stained tub, use a mixture of peroxide and cream of tartar. Make a paste and scrub vigorously with a small brush; rinse thoroughly.

If stains persist, spread the preceding mixture over stains and apply a drop or 2 of household ammonia. Allow to set for 2 hours before scrubbing.

Very old porcelain stains: Shave a bar of naphtha soap into a bucket of hot water and add ½ cup of mineral spirits. Stir to dissolve the soap, then brush on stain vigorously.

More tub and sink cleaners:

Light stains can often be removed by simply rubbing with a cut lemon.

For dark stains, and especially rust, rub with a paste of borax and lemon juice.

To brighten up a bathtub which has yellowed, rub with a solution of salt and turpentine.

A sure way to remove bathtub decals:

Soak decals in mineral spirits, then scrape away. Spray down with Fantastik spray cleanser and rub with the abrasive side of a sponge. Now, wax the entire tub, tiles, and faucets with Turtle Wax. It will shine like new. Turtle Wax is an excellent cleaner and refinisher.

Rub in Turtle Wax well with a soft cloth and let stand for a few minutes. Do not let it dry. Polish with a clean cloth or buff with an electric buffer. Your bathroom will gleam.

Clogged shower heads:

If your shower head is clogged, try boiling it in ½ cup vinegar and 1 quart water for 15 minutes.

For plastic shower heads, soak in equal amounts of hot vinegar and water.

Ceramic tile:

Before you start cleaning the walls or tiles, run your shower a while with the hottest tap water available. Dirt loosened by steam will come off faster.

For light jobs, wash with a solution of ½ cup ammonia, ½ cup white vinegar, ¼ cup washing soda, and 1 gallon warm water.

For extensive stains, make a paste of baking soda and bleach, then scrub with a small brush; rinse thoroughly.

Or, try a product by the name of Chrome & Tile Cleaner by Santeen products (available at hardware stores). It does a fantastic job of cleaning the recessed spaces between tiles.

Heavy shower stall film:

Rub lightly with a plain piece of dry fine steel wool (not the soap filled variety). Try a patch first to be sure it isn't scratching your tile. If it is, you should use a finer piece of steel wool. As you scour the tile, you will see the scum coming right off. Wash down after the job is completed.

Washing shower curtains:

Fill the washing machine with warm water and add 2 large bath towels. Add ½ cup each of detergent and baking soda. Run through entire wash cycle.

However, add 1 cup vinegar to the rinse water. Do not spin dry or wash vinegar out. This method will not work without the bath towels. Hang immediately. Wrinkles will disappear after curtain has thoroughly dried.

Removing mildew from shower curtains:
To prevent mildew, soak in a solution of salt water before hanging them for use.
Use baking soda to remove mildew from small areas.
For stubborn stains on light colored curtains, wash in preceding manner, followed by a rub-down with lemon juice.

Two excellent fixture cleaners:
To save time and money while providing the best shine possible to bathroom fixtures, use an old cloth which has been dunked in kerosene. Kerosene removes scum quickly and the odor will only remain for awhile.
Spray fixtures liberally with Spray & Wash laundry soil and stain remover. Rub with cloth for an excellent shine.

Toilet rings:
Flush toilet to wet sides. Apply paste of borax and lemon juice. Let set for 2 hours and then scrub thoroughly.
Or, rub with a fine grade of sandpaper. If the rings are years old, try wet sandpaper (available at hardware stores).

Glass shower doors:
For a quick shine, rub with a sponge dampened in white vinegar.

What to do with your basic drip:
If the drip occurs during the night and you can't sleep, simply wrap a cloth around the opening of the faucet.
Or, tie a string to the faucet, long enough to reach the drain. Water will run down the string noiselessly until you have time to fix it.

Sweet smells in the bathroom:
For a nice aroma, place a fabric softener sheet in the wastepaper basket.
Or, add a touch of fragrance by dabbing your favorite perfume on a light bulb. When the light is on, the heat releases the aroma.

Stopping marred floors:
When moving furniture, slip old heavy socks over their legs.

Floor cover-up:
Renovate floors which have become faded in spots by mixing brown shoe polish with floor wax and applying to spots. It will give the floor an antique look.

Remove squeaks forever:
Quiet floor squeaks by dusting talcum powder or dripping glue into the cracks.

Rub those scratches away:
Use a piece of very fine steel wool dipped in floor wax.

Rocking without worries:

Your rocker will not scratch waxed floors if you line the rocker arcs with adhesive tape.

Or, wax the arcs of your rocker at the same time you do the floors.

Removing heel marks:

Remove the spots with kerosene or turpentine.

Or, try an ordinary pencil eraser.

Removing tar spots:

Use paste wax. This also works on shoes.

Nail polish spills:

To remove nail polish from waxed floors or tile, let it solidify before attempting removal. When the polish is barely solid and pliable it can be peeled off. Smears are removed by wiping up the polish before it has dried, or by using a solvent on completely hardened polish.

Removing crayon marks:

Remove from vinyl tile or linoleum with silver polish.

A quick shine between waxings:

Mop with a piece of waxed paper under your mop. The dirt will also stick to the waxed paper.

Nylon stockings for dusting:

Place a nylon stocking over your dust mop. Discard the stocking and you will have a clean mop.

Did you know?

The basic ingredients of many commercial spot removers is 2 parts water to 1 part rubbing alcohol.

Cleaning your machine:

Fill the washer with warm water and pour a gallon of distilled vinegar into it. Run the machine through an entire cycle. The vinegar will cleanse the hoses and unclog soap scrum from them.

Ring around the collar:

Use a small paint brush and brush hair shampoo into soiled shirt collars before laundering. Shampoo is made to dissolve body oils.

Mark heavily with chalk. The chalk will absorb the oils and once the oil is removed, the dirt will come off easily. This method may require a few applications if the yellow line has been there for some time. If the shirt is new, one application should do it.

Or, apply a paste of vinegar and baking soda. Rub in and wash as usual. This method also removes dirt and mildew.

No more lint:

To remove lint from corduroy, wash and allow to dry very slowly. While clothing is still damp, brush with a clothes brush. All the lint will come off, but remember, the clothing must be damp.

You will eliminate the lint problem by adding 1 cup white vinegar to the final rinse cycle.

Or, put a yard of nylon netting into the dryer with wet clothes to act as a lint catcher.

If the lint, under and around the filter of dryer seems damp, it means the outside vent is clogged. You better clean it out before the machine breaks down.

The final rinse cycle:

To make sure clothes receive a thorough rinsing, add 1 cup white vinegar to the rinse cycle. This will help dissolve the alkalines in soaps and detergents. Plus, it will give you soft and sweet smelling clothing for just pennies.

The vinegar is a must for hand washing. It cuts down soap so fast you will only have to rinse 2 times.

A teaspoon of Epsom salts to a gallon of rinse water will help keep most materials from fading or running.

Creme rinse your sweaters:

For the best results when hand washing sweaters, put a capful of creme hair rinse in the final rinse water.

Or, rinse wool garments in lukewarm water and a few tablespoons of glycerine. This will keep them soft and will also help prevent itching when they are worn.

Accidentally washed woolen item:

Soak in tepid water to which you have added a good hair shampoo. Sometimes this will soften the wool fibers enough to allow for a reshaping. It's worth a try.

Washing feather pillows:

First check for any open or weak seams. Place the pillow in a pillowcase. Wash 2 pillows at a time for a balanced load or add towels for balance. Fill your washer with warm water and push pillows down to saturate them completely before turning on the gentle cycle. Stop the wash halfway through the washing and turn pillows over. To dry, put feather pillows (not foam rubber) into dryer along with a clean tennis shoe. Drying will take up to 2 hours.

Renovating feather pillows:

Set dryer on air setting and let pillows tumble for 15 minutes. However, make sure there are no holes in the pillows or the feathers will work through.

Make your own fabric softener sheets:

Pour a few capfuls of any fabric softener into a small bowl of water. Swish a washcloth in the solution. Ring it out and toss into the dryer along with the wet clothes. It's that simple. But best of all, it is a lot less expensive than using the tear-off sheet brands.

Machine washing dainty garments:

Drop you dainty garments into a pillowcase and fasten the loose end with a plastic bag tie. Place in washer and wash on a gentle cycle.

Too many suds:
Anytime your washing machine overflows from too many suds, sprinkle with salt. Suds will disappear.

Procedure for cleaning velvet:
To clean, raise nap and remove wrinkles. Hold garment (pile side up) over steaming water to which a little ammonia has been added. Finish by brushing well and ironing lightly on the wrong side.

Renovating stiffened chamois:
Soak in warm water to which a spoonful or so of olive oil has been added.

When the red wine spills:
Sprinkle the spill immediately with lots of salt. Dunk into cold water and rub the stain out before washing.

Cleanest work clothes ever:
Add ½ cup of household ammonia to the wash water.

Removing grease from suede:
Sponge with a cloth dipped in vinegar or club soda. Restore nap of suede by brushing with a suede brush.

Getting white socks white again:
Boil in water to which a slice of lemon has been added.

A fast way to dampen clothes:
Place clothes in dryer and add 2 thoroughly wet bath towels. Set dryer on a no heat setting and let clothing tumble until desired dampness.
If you have dampened ironing that you can't finish, stick it in the freezer until you are ready to catch up.

Faster ironing:
Place a strip of heavy-duty aluminum foil over the entire length of the ironing board and cover with pad. As you iron, heat will reflect through to the underside of the garment.
Starch your ironing board cover. This also helps the cover stay clean longer.

Ironing embroidery:
Lay the embroidery piece upside-down on a turkish towel before ironing. All the little spaces between the embroidery will be smooth when you are finished.

STAIN REMOVAL HINTS

Removing alcoholic beverages:
Soak fresh stains in cold water and a few tablespoons of glycerine (available at drugstores). Rinse with white vinegar and water. These stains turn brown with age so treat immediately.

Blood:
Cover area with meat tenderizer. Apply cool water to make a paste. Wait 15 to 30 minutes, sponge with cool water.

Chewing gum:
Place garment in plastic bag and put in freezer. Scrape off frozen gum.

Or, loosen gum by soaking in white vinegar or rubbing with egg white before laundering.

Candle wax or crayon:
Place the stained area between clean paper towels or pieces of a brown paper bag and press with a warm iron.

Grease on double knit:
Club soda works wonders for removing grease from double knit fabrics.

Fruit stains:
Remove stain by stretching the stained area over a bowl and pouring boiling water, from a height of several feet, through the stain.

Ballpoint ink:
Apply hairspray liberally to stain. Rub with a clean dry cloth and the ink usually disappears. This works exceptionally well on polyester fabrics.

Or, try rubbing alcohol on the spot before laundering.

Rust:
Apply lemon juice and salt, then place in the sun.

Rust can also be removed from white washables by covering the stains with cream of tartar, then gathering up the ends of the article so that the powder stays on the spot. Dip the entire spot into hot water for about 5 minutes. Ordinary laundering will complete the job.

A commercial rust remover by the name of Barkeeper's Friend may be used.

Mildew:
Dry in the sun after moistening with lemon juice and salt.

Treat by adding ½ cup of liquid Lysol to the wash water.

On leather, sponge with equal amounts of water and rubbing alcohol.

Perspiration:
Soak the garment in warm vinegar water.

Scorch:
On whites, sponge with a piece of cotton which has been soaked in peroxide. Use the 3% solution sold as a mild antiseptic.

For linen and cotton, dampen a cloth with peroxide, lay it on the scorched area, and iron with a warm iron.

Shoe polish:
Remove with rubbing alcohol. Use 1 part alcohol and 2 parts water on colored fabric. Use it straight on whites.

Tar:
Rub the tar spot with kerosene until removed, then wash with detergent and
water. The kerosene will not take the color out of most fabrics, but you better test it first.

CLEVER CLOTHING HINTS

An easy way to hem a dress:
A sink plunger is a handy gadget to use when marking a skirt for hemming.
Mark the handle at the desired length, then move the plunger around the
hem. It stands by itself, leaving your hands free to mark or pin.

Threading a needle:
Spray a bit of hair spray or spray starch on you finger when threading a needle
and apply it to the end of the thread. The thread stiffens just enough to
ease the job of finding the eye.

Sharpening a machine needle:
Stitch through a piece of sandpaper.

Make heavy seams "seam" easy:
Rub seams with a piece of hard bar soap. The machine needle will go through
the material with ease.

Storage for sewing tools:
Use an empty thermometer case as a holder for extra long and fine needles
that are hard to store in a sewing box.
Use plastic pill bottles with snap-on tops to hold the extra small buttons.

Pins and needles all over the place:
Safety pins can be gathered and threaded onto a pipe cleaner, then, bend the
pipe cleaner into a circle and twist the ends together.
Keep a small magnet in your sewing basket and use it to pick up pins and needles that drop to the floor while you are sewing.

Reusing a zipper:
Spray it heavily with spray starch and it will sew like new. Zippo! It works.

Buttons and buttonholes:
Here's a tip for keeping those 4 hole buttons on longer. Sew through only 2
holes at a time, breaking the thread and knotting it for each pair of holes.
This way, should one set break loose, the other side will still hold the button.
Use dental floss or elastic thread to sew buttons on children's clothing. The
bottons will take a lot of wear before falling off.
If you have trouble removing a button from a garment, slide a comb under the
button and cut with a razor blade.
To make a straight cut for a buttonhole on heavy fabric, lay buttonhole section
over a bar of soap and cut with a razor blade.

A red hot idea for belt holes:
Poke with a red hot steel knitting needle.

"Snappy" ideas:
Sew the snap point on first, then take a piece of chalk and touch this little point. Turn the material over, rub it with your finger, and you will find that you have marked the exact place where the snap should be sewed on.

A quick trick for sewing on emblems:
Use a few dabs of any good white glue on the back of the emblem and press it in position on the clothing, then let it set for a few minutes. The emblem can then be stitched by hand or machine without any worry that it will turn out lopsided. The glue subsequently washes out.

Creeping machine foot pedal:
Glue a piece of foam rubber to the bottom of a portable sewing machine foot control and it will not creep on the floor.

Worn elastic:
Whenever elastic that is sewed on a garment becomes worn or stretched, just baste cord elastic through the worn elastic. Pull it up and knot.

Eliminating the knot:
When sewing with a single thread, does it constantly knot? If so, try this: After you thread the needle, be sure to knot the end that was cut off closest to the spool.

After oiling the sewing machine:
Stitch through a blotter several times to avoid surplus oil from damaging your fabrics.

"Darn it" - Two different ways:
Use a glass marble as a darning egg when mending fingers of a glove.
One of the easiest ways to mend a hole in a garment is to place a thin sheet of paper under the hole and darn back and forth with the sewing machine. When the garment is washed the paper will dissolve. This is ideal for bedsheets with big tears or rips.

A handy pin cushion:
A bar of soap makes an ideal place to stick needles and pins. It lubricates them so that they will go through stiff fabrics with ease.

Great balls of yarn:
When you are working with more than 1 ball of yarn, put the balls in a plastic bag with small holes, like the bag potatoes come in. Thread the different yarns through various holes in the bag. The yarn will stay clean and untangled throughout the project.

Sewing on plastic:
Put wax paper over the seam and the sewing machine will not stick to the plastic nor pucker. The wax paper will tear off easily after the job is done.

Avoiding the slips and slides when sewing on nylon:
When repairing seams on nylon jackets or lingerie, make the job a lot simpler
by placing a piece of paper underneath the section you are going to sew.
Stich through the fabric and paper. When finished, tear the paper off.

HELPFUL HINTS

Loose linoleum edges are easy to fix:
Work linoleum cement (available at hardware stores) under the loosened edge
of the corner, using a dull knife. Put a few heavy books over the area and
let dry for 24 hours.

To seal linoleum seams:
Run a strip of cellophane tape down the full length of the crack. Shellac over
the tape and the surface will hold up indefinitely.

A faster working carpet sweeper:
Dampen the brushes of your carpet sweeper before using and it will do a much
better job of picking up lint and string.

Cleaning your floor polisher:
If wax has built up on the felt pads of your floor polisher, place the pads between
several thicknesses of paper toweling and press with a warm iron. The
towels will quickly absorb the old wax.

Fantastic furniture polish:
Use ⅓ cup each boiled linseed oil, turpentine, and vinegar. Mix together and
shake well. Apply with a soft cloth and wipe completely dry. Wipe again
with another soft cloth. Do not try to boil your own linseed oil - it is not the
same. Buy it at a hardware or paint store.
Or, add a teaspoon of apple cider vinegar to your favorite liquid furniture polish.

To remove polish build-up:
Mix ½ cup vinegar and ½ cup water. Rub with a soft cloth that has been moistened with solution, but wrung out. Dry immediately with another soft
cloth.

Polishing carved furniture:
Dip an old soft toothbrush into furniture polish and brush lightly.

Is your seat sagging?
Tighten a drooping cane chair seat by giving it a hot water bath and placing it
outside in the sunlight to dry and shrink. After it has dried thoroughly, apply
either lemon or cedar oil to prevent cracking and splitting.
Sagging springs in chair: Turn the chair upside-down. Make a pattern of the
upper-structure frame. Transfer the pattern either to a piece of scrap ma-
sonite or plywood (⅛ inch). Nail to the upper structure. By doing this, the
springs are pushed back into the chair, eliminating the sag.

Cigarette burns:

For small minor burns, try rubbing mayonnaise into the burn. Let set for awhile before wiping off with a soft cloth.

Burns can be repaired with a wax stick (available in all colors at paint and hardware stores). Gently scrape away the charred finish. Heat a knife blade and melt the shellac stick against the heated blade. Smooth over damaged area with your finger. But always consider the value of the furniture. It might be better to have a professional make the repair.

Or, make a paste of rottenstone (available at hardware stores) and salad oil. Rub into the burned spot only, following the grain of the wood. Wipe clean with a cloth that has been dampened in oil. Wipe dry and apply your favorite furniture polish.

WHAT CAUSES RINGS

1. The garment is soiled all over. Removing the spot leaves a conspicuous clean area.
2. Wrong cleaning methods. For example, failing to "feather out" the cleaning fluid so there is no definite edge or saturating the spot with cleaning fluid.
3. The fabric water spots because it contains sizing. With a spot made by a substance which contains both water and grease, the cleaning fluid removes the grease but not the water ring. Water rings occur most often on silk and rayon. To remove water rings, rub the material against itself, then with a coin or your fingernail rub the ring lightly. If it still remains, hold the spot above the spout of a steaming tea kettle.

HOW TO USE CLEANING FLUID

1. If the colorfastness of the garment is doubtful, test a hidden part, such as an inside seam, with the cleaning fluid. Energine Fireproof Cleaning Fluid will not injure the color of any colorfast material.
2. Brush fabric to remove loose soil.
3. Place an absorbent cloth or clean white blotter under the spot.
4. Moisten a clean cloth, dark if the garment is dark, with cleaning fluid.
5. With quick, light strokes brush the moistened cloth over the spot, covering a larger area than the spot. "Feather out" the cleaning fluid so there is no definite edge. Rub lightly until there is no clear line between the spot and the area around it. Change the cleaning cloth and pad under the spot if they become soiled.
6. If the spot has not come out, repeat the process. It is better to apply cleaning fluid sparingly several times than to saturate a spot with it.

THE STEPS

When more than one step is listed, use them consecutively. When you sponge with water, then Energine Fireproof Cleaning Fluid - or the other way around - let the fabric dry in between the two steps. You won't need to carry out all the steps listed after every spot unless it proves stubborn.

Step 1. Sponge with Energine Fireproof Cleaning Fluid.

Step 2. Sponge with cold or lukewarm, not hot, water. Use cold water on soft drink, egg, blood, ice cream, and meat juice stains.

Step 3. Rub in petroleum jelly to soften the stain.

Step 4. Wash in warm water with a synthetic detergent or soap.

Step 5. Moisten spot with cold or lukewarm water. Rub in some pepsin powder and allow to remain for ½ hour. Sponge with water.

Step 6. Soak for a short while in a bowl of Energine Fireproof Cleaning Fluid.

Step 7. If color remains, sponge with denatured alcohol. On acetate and colored materials use a mixture of 1 part alcohol, 2 parts water.

Step 8. Apply glycerine and rub lightly between hands. Let stand ½ hour. Sponge with lukewarm water. For fruit stains, allow the glycerine to remain for several hours.

Step 9. Place stained part of article over bowl. Fasten with string. Pour boiling water on stain from height of 2 or 3 feet.

Step 10. Sponge with hydrogen peroxide to which sodium perborate has been added (1 teaspoon per pint). Rinse well. Don't use on colored material without testing colorfastness of hidden part of garment.

Step 11. Sponge with nail polish remover unless the fabric is acetate. Do not use nail polish remover on acetate. It may cause a hole.

Step 12. Sponge with turpentine.

THREE SOLUTIONS TO REMOVE WHITE WATER RINGS AND SPOTS

Dampen a soft cloth with water and put a dab of toothpaste on it. For stubborn stains, add baking soda to the toothpaste.

Make a paste of butter or mayonnaise and cigarette ashes. Apply to spot and buff away with a slightly damp cloth. Polish as usual.

Apply a paste of salad oil and salt. Let stand briefly. Wipe and polish.

HELPFUL HINTS

Removing paper that is stuck to a wood surface:

Do not scrape with a knife. Pour any salad oil, a few drops at a time, on the paper. Let set for awhile and rub with a soft cloth. Repeat the procedure until the paper is completely gone.

Old decals can be removed easily by painting them with several coats of white vinegar. Give the vinegar time to soak in, then gently scrape off.

Scratches:

Make sure you always rub with the grain of the wood when repairing a scratch.

Walnut: Remove the meat from a fresh, unsalted walnut or pecan nut. Break it in half and rub the scratch with the broken side of the nut.

Mahogany: You can either rub the scratch with a dark brown crayon or buff with brown paste wax.

Red Mahogany: Apply ordinary iodine with a number 0 artist's brush.

Maple: Combine equal amounts of iodine and denatured alcohol. Apply with a Q-tip, then dry, wax, and buff.

Ebony: Use black shoe polish, black eyebrow pencil, or black crayon.

Teakwood: Rub very gently with 0000 steel wool. Rub in equal amounts of linseed oil and turpentine.

Light finished furniture: Scratches can be hidden by using tan shoe polish. However, use only on shiny finishes.

For all minor scratches: Cover each scratch with a generous amount of white petroleum jelly. Allow it to remain on for 24 hours. Rub into wood. Remove excess and polish as usual. Or, apply a product called Liquid Gold (available at grocery stores).

For larger scratches: Fill by rubbing with a wax stick (available in all colors at your hardware or paint store) or a crayon that matches the finish of the wood.

Marble table-top stains:

Sprinkle salt on a fresh cut lemon. Rub very lightly over stain. Do not rub hard or you will ruin the polished surface. Wash off with soap and water.

Scour with a water and baking soda paste. Let stand for a few minutes before rinsing with warm water.

For horrible marble stains, try this: Place the marble table in hot sunlight. If this is not possible, heat the marble for 1 hour or more under a hot spotlight (never a sun lamp), then, swab on white household bleach. Continue this every hour or so until discoloration is gone. (Sometimes this may take a couple of days.) Rinse with water and dry. Move to shade and polish with paste carnauba wax. Never use oil polish or soft waxes on marble; they can cause discoloration.

Removing candle wax from wooden finishes:

Soften the wax with a hair dryer. Remove wax with paper toweling and wash down with a solution of vinegar and water.

Proper cleaning and care for leather table tops:

Remove all wax build-up with a vinegar and water solution (¼ cup vinegar and ½ cup water). To raise any indentations such as pressure points from lamps or ash trays, apply lemon oil to the leather twice a day for a week. To maintain results, use lemon oil monthly.

Damp closets:

To help prevent dampness in a closet, fill a coffee can with charcoal briquets. Punch holes in the cover and place the container on the floor. For larger closets, use 2 or 3 (1 pound) coffee cans.

You can also cut down on dampness by wrapping and tying together 12 pieces of chalk and hanging them in your closet.

Musty smells:
For sweet smelling closets, hang an old nylon stocking filled with cedar chips in the closet. This also serves as an excellent moth repellant.

To remove musty odors from a trunk, place a coffee can filled with kitty litter deodorizer inside the trunk overnight.

Helping prevent moth damage:
In addition to mothballs, put whole cloves in pockets of woolen coats or in bags with sweaters when storing for the off season. They help prevent moth damage and have a nice spicy odor.

Before storing blankets for the summer, wash them and add 2 cups of mothballs to the rinse water.

This hint "can" solve your problem:
Store out of season clothes in large plastic lidded trash cans. Not only will your clothes be mothproof, they will stay dry in damp basements.

Storing fine china plates:
Insert paper plates or paper napkins between fine china plates as you stack to prevent scratching.

Before applying contact paper:
Make patterns of the shelves and drawers with newspaper. Transfer the patterns to the contact paper before cutting and you will have an excellent fit.

Tips for storing jewelry, belts, and handbags:
Egg cartons serve as excellent storage containers for jewelry.

Place a piece of chalk in your jewelry box to prevent costume jewelry from tarnishing.

To avoid tangled chains and necklaces, screw cup hooks to the inside of your closet door for tangle-free hanging.

Hook large shower curtain hooks over the clothes rod for hanging handbags and belts.

No spills:
Tack a piece of sewing elastic across the inside of a drawer to keep small bottles (nail polish, ink ...) upright in your desk or dresser drawers.

How to preserve a favorite news clipping:
Dissolve a milk of magnesia tablet in a quart of club soda overnight. Pour into a pan large enough to accommodate the flattened newspaper. Soak clipping for 1 hour; remove and pat dry. Do not move until completely dry. Estimated life: 200 years.

Wrapping packages:
To premeasure the length of gift wrapping paper from a large roll, wrap a string around the package first, then cut off the desired length and use it as a measuring guide.

Before tying a package for mailing, wet the string or cord with water. This method prevents the string from slipping and when dry it will hold extra tight.

Here's more:
Keep clear plastic wrap in the refrigerator to prevent it from ever sticking together.

When mailing cookies, pack in popcorn to help keep them from crumbling.

Sometimes mildew can be removed from papers and book pages by a good dusting with cornstarch. Allow the powder to remain on for several days before giving it the brush-off.

Your favorite photo negatives can be stored behind the actual print in your scrapbook for safekeeping.

Empty soft drink cartons are ideal for storing light bulbs.

When postage stamps are stuck together, place them in the freezer. They will usually come apart and the glue will still be usable.

Extension cords can be conveniently stored without tangling, by simply winding the cord loosely and slipping it into a cardboard tube (from paper towels or tissue paper).

Grease spots on wallpaper:
Make a paste of cornstarch and water. Let it remain on the spot until dry, then brush off. If the stain persists, try, try again.

If the preceding method fails, try a paste of Fuller's Earth and carbon tetrachloride (both available at hardware stores) and use it in the same way.

Or, apply a piece of clean blotting paper to the grease spot and press with a warm iron. Do more than once, using a fresh blotter each time. Remove any lingering traces by rubbing with a cloth dipped in borax.

Removing crayon marks:
Treat as a greasy spot.

Rub lightly with a dry soap-filled steel wool pad. Do not wet.

Or, rub very gently with baking soda sprinkled on a damp cloth.

Crayon marks on vinyl can be removed with silver polish.

To remove everyday smudges:
Erase away light marks (pencil, fingerprints, dirt) with art-gum squares (available at stationery stores).

Removing cellophane tape:
Put a blotter against the tape and press with a warm iron.

An easy tip to avoid expensive plastering bills:
If the plaster is cracking on the ceiling, try this: Mix some Elmer's glue with baking soda, making a paste. Apply to cracks with fingers. If the ceiling is colored, add food coloring to match. This trick could help postpone replastering for months.

Plaster with no lumps:
If you add plaster to water, instead of water to plaster, the mixture will be lump free.

Another plaster tip:
You can slow the hardening of plaster by adding a little vinegar to the mixture.

How to hide nail holes from the landlady:
Rub toothpaste into the hole and smooth with a damp sponge.

Cleaning rough plastered walls:
Instead of using a cloth or sponge, try using nylon or Banlon socks. No small pieces will be left behind as you work.

A crack filler:
Fill cracks with steel wool or newspaper before finishing off with plaster.

The best wall cleaner:
Combine ½ cup ammonia, ¼ cup white vinegar, ¼ cup washing soda, and 1 gallon warm water for the perfect solution for cleaning walls.

Brushing away cobwebs:
Slip a sock or two over the end of a yardstick. Secure with a rubber band. Also good for cleaning under the refrigerator and radiators.

Take the "pane" out of washing your windows:
Never wash windows on sunny days. They will dry too fast and show streaks. Never use soap.

Add ½ cup ammonia, ½ cup white vinegar, and 2 tablespoons of cornstarch to a bucket of warm water for a perfect window washing solution.

For fast clean-ups, wash with a cloth soaked in white vinegar. This method is great when washing only a few indoor windows.

Shine with newspaper instead of paper towels. It is cheaper and some feel easier. Be sure you have read the papers or the project could take all day.

No more guess work when drying the inside panes with vertical strokes and the outside panes with horizontal strokes, or vice versa - you will notice quickly which side has the smudges.

After windows have dried, rub a clean blackboard eraser over them for a really fine shine.

Before washing the inside windows:
To avoid taking down drapes, drape them through a clothes hanger and hang from the curtain rod. Drapes will be safely out of the way.

Keeping Jack Frost off windows:
The problem of ice covered windows can be solved by adding ½ cup rubbing alcohol or anti-freeze to each quart of water used.

Rub the inside of windows with a sponge that has been dipped in rubbing alcohol or anti-freeze. Polish with paper towels or newspaper.

Try a cloth moistened with glycerine, rub on, leaving a little of the glycerine on the inside of the glass.

Or, head south.

Window and mirror cleaner:
Duplicate the "blue kind" by filling a spray bottle with 3 tablespoons of ammonia, 1 tablespoon vinegar, and cool water. Add a drop or 2 of food coloring.

Spotted window sills:
Pour a little diluted rubbing alcohol on a soft cloth and rub the entire surface. The spots will not only disappear, but the sills will look freshly painted.

Some rather "shady" ideas:
Rub unwashable window shades with a rough flannel cloth which has been dipped in flour or corn meal.
A soft eraser may remove spots and stains.
Keep parchment shades clean by waxing them.

Are your tiebacks straight?
A foolproof way to get tiebacks straight across from each other when hanging curtains is to use your window shade as a measuring guide.

Window shade tears:
Repair with colorless nail polish. This works wonders on small tears.

Cleaning screens:
For a thorough job, brush on both sides with kerosene. Wipe with a clean cloth. This method will also prevent rust from forming. Be sure to dust the screens with a small paint brush before you begin.
For small jobs, rub a brush-type hair roller lightly over the screen and see how easily it picks up all the lint and dust.

Cleaning sliding door tracks:
Generally, the tracks of sliding glass doors are very hard to clean. Try wrapping a small cloth around an eraser and rub dirt away.

Cleaning aluminum window frames:
Try a cream silver polish.

Venetian blinds:
To repair a venetian blind tape that has broken, simply tape the side that faces the wall with heavy-duty packing tape. Apply white canvas shoe polish.

HELPFUL HINTS

Plastic table tops:
You will find that a coat of Turtle Wax is a quick pick-up for dulled plastic table tops and counters.
Or, rub in toothpaste and buff.

Glass table tops:
Rub in a little lemon juice. Dry with paper towels and shine with newspaper for a sparkling table.
Toothpaste will remove small scratches from glass.

Chrome cleaning:
For sparkling clean chrome without streaks, use a cloth dampened in ammonia.

Storing leftover paint:

To prevent scum forming on leftover paint, lace a disc of aluminum foil directly on the paint surface. To make the disc the correct size, set the can on the foil and cut around it.

Keep oil base paint fresh by adding 4 tablespoons of mineral spirits only to the top layer of the paint. Do not mix until the next paint job.

Tightly fit the lids of paint containers and store upside down. Scum will not form on paint.

Always mark the paint level and color on each can before storing.

Use nail polish or shoe polish bottles for leftover paint and label. They are excellent for small touch-ups.

When tiny touch-ups are necessary, use throw away Q-tips instead of soiling a dry paint brush.

Cleaning paint brushes:

A new paint brush will last longer and be much easier to clean if it soaks in a can of linseed oil for 12 hours before it is ever used.

To soften hard paint on brushes, soak in hot vinegar. Follow with a wash in warm, sudsy water.

After washing brushes and rollers, use a fabric softener in the final rinse water. It helps them stay soft and pliable.

Use a coffee can when cleaning paint brushes with paint thinner. After the brushes have been cleaned, cover the can and let stand for a few days. The paint will settle to the bottom and you can pour the clean thinner into a can and reuse.

Fast clean-ups:

When working on a paint job which takes a couple of days, save time by wrapping brushes in foil and freezing (stick them right into the freezer compartment of your refrigerator). Let brushes defrost an hour or more before returning to the job.

Put a large plastic bag over your roller pan before putting the paint in. When you are through, throw the bag away.

Banishing paint odor:

Add 2 teaspoons of vanilla extract per quart of paint.

Place a large pan of water which contains a tablespoon of ammonia in the freshly painted room. Leave overnight.

Or, place a large cut onion into a big pan of cold water. Paint odors will sponge into the onion within a very short time.

Lumpy paint:

The best strainer of all is an old nylon stocking.

An old eggbeater is excellent for stirring paint.

Cut a circle from an old screen slightly smaller than the can lid. As the screen settles, it will carry all lumps to the bottom.

Stick it!

After painting, apply some of the paint to a popsicle stick. It is a handy color guide to matching colors when shopping.

Preventing white paint from yellowing:
Stir a drop of black paint into any good white paint.

Paint removers for face and hands:
Cooking oil or baby oil is a better way to remove paint because it will not burn the skin.
For easy removal, rub Vaseline on exposed skin.
Before painting, give fingernails a good coating of bar soap for the fastest wash-up ever.

Before puttying windows:
Mix putty with the paint that matches the woodwork.

Antiquing furniture:
Try using a small piece of carpet to work in the glaze. It gives a beautifully grained effect.

FANTASTIC FURNITURE HINTS

Removing glue from furniture:
Airplane or cement glue can be removed by rubbing with cold cream, peanut butter, or salad oil.

Tips for wicker:
To keep wicker furniture from turning yellow, wash with a solution of warm salt water.
To prevent drying out, apply lemon oil once in awhile.
Never let wicker freeze. This will cause cracking and splitting.
Wicker needs moisture, so use a humidifier in the winter.

Removing rust on metal furniture:
A good scrubbing with turpentine should accomplish the job.

Proper cleaning and care of vinyl upholstery:
Never oil vinyls because oil will make the vinyl hard. If this happens it is almost impossible to soften it again. For proper cleaning, sprinkle baking soda or vinegar on a rough damp cloth, then wash with a very mild dishwashing soap. Body oil will cause vinyl to become hard so it should be cleaned once in awhile.

Leather upholstery:
Clean with a damp cloth and saddle soap.
Prevent leather from cracking by polishing regularly with a cream made of 1 part vinegar and 2 parts linseed oil.

Removing blood stains from upholstery:
Cover the spot immediately with a paste of cornstarch and cold water. Rub lightly and place object in the sun to dry. The sun will draw the blood out into the cornstarch. Brush off. If the stain is not completely gone, try, try again.

330

Grease and oil stains:
Pour salt on grease spill immediately. The salt will absorb the grease and prevent staining.
Or, sprinkle talcum, cornstarch, or Fullers Earth on a fresh stain. Rub in well and let stand until the stain is absorbed. Brush off and wipe with a damp cloth.

Wobbly chair legs:
Secure a loose chair leg by wrapping the loose end with a small strip of nylon hose or thread before applying the glue, then reinsert.
A few drops of wood expander will achieve the same results.

Wobbly table:
If your table wobbles because of a short leg, put a small amount of Plastic Wood on waxed paper. Set the short leg on it and allow to dry. Trim down with a sharp knife and smooth with sandpaper.

Not just another screwy idea:
Should metal screws on your home appliances keep coming loose, a dab of shellac placed under the heads before tightening them, holds them securely in place.

To loosen joints:
Put vinegar in a small oil can and apply liberally to joints to loosen old glue.

Longer lasting sandpaper and easier sanding:
Sandpaper will last longer, work better, and resist cracking if the paper backing is dampened slightly, then wrapped around a block of wood.

Mending a leaking vase:
Coat the inside with a thick layer of paraffin and allow it to harden. The paraffin will last indefinitely and the vase will not leak.

Cutting plywood:
Prevent plywood from splitting by putting a strip of masking tape at the point where you plan to start sawing.

How to find a wall stud:
Hold a pocket compass level with the floor and at a right angle to the wall. Slowly move it along the surface of the wall. Movement of the compass needle will indicate the presence of nails and reveal the stud location. Wall studs are usually 16 inches apart, center to center.

Preventing nylon cord and rope from fraying:
Shellac the ends of the rope and it will not unravel.
To prevent nylon cord or twine from fraying at a cut end, heat the end over a small flame. The strands will bond into a solid unit. Knots can be prevented from working loose by this same method.

Preventing rust on tools:
Place a piece of charcoal, chalk, or several mothballs in your toolbox to attract any moisture.

Sticky dresser drawers:
They will slide easily again if you rub candle wax or soap on the runner of the side that seems to be sticking.

Is your screw loose?
Stick a wooden kitchen match in the screw hole and break it off, then put the screw back in.

Wind a few strands of steel wool around the threads of the screw before screwing it in.

Paint the screw of a wobbly drawer knob with fingernail polish before inserting it. When the polish dries, it will hold the screw tightly.

Or, dip in glue or putty and it will hold tight.

Difficulty loosening a tight screw:
Heat the edge of a screwdriver to its hottest point before loosening a screw.

Or, put a few drops of peroxide on the tight screw and soak for a few minutes.

Remember this:
Left is loose and right is tight.

Loosening a rusted bolt:
You can often loosen a rusted bolt by applying a cloth soaked in any carbonated beverage.

A drop or two of ammonia will loosen it right up.

Before screwing it back in, wrap thread around it and coat with Vaseline to avoid future rusting.

Wax tools with an automobile paste wax. A light coat will ward off corrosion for quite some time.

Or, store small tools in a bucket of sand.

Preventing a screwdriver from slipping:
Rub chalk on the blade.

Stop squeaks:
Use nonstick vegetable spray to lubricate squeaky hinges, sticky locks, bicycle chains, roller skate wheels, and so on.

After sanding a surface:
Pull an old nylon stocking over your hand and rub lightly over the wood. You will be able to locate the slightest rough spot.

Finding a gas leak:
Lather the pipes with soapy water. The escaping gas will cause the soapy water to bubble, revealing the damaged areas. You can make a temporary plug by moistening a cake of soap and pressing it over the spot. When the soap hardens it will effectively close the leak until the gas man comes.

More hints for the handy person:
Just a speck of nail polish remover will splice cassette tapes.

For accuracy in drilling metal, use a small drill first.

When drilling hard metal, add a drop or 2 of turpentine to the drill point instead of oil for lubrication.

A small quantity of kerosene will help ease a hand saw through a tight cut.

Thaw a frozen water pipe with a hair dryer.

To prevent snow from sticking to a shovel, cover shovel with spray wax.

For cockeyed pictures try these:

Wind some adhesive tape around the center of the picture wire. The wire will be less likely to slip on the hanger.

Place masking tape on the back 4 corners of your picture and press against the wall.

Or, wrap masking tape (sticky side out) around the middle of a rounded toothpick and place a few near the bottom, back side of the frame.

Preventing experimental holes when hanging pictures:

Cut a paper pattern of each picture or mirror that you plan to hang and pin to the wall. After you've found the correct positions for the hangers, perforate the paper with a sharp pencil to mark the wall.

Before you drive nails into the wall, mark spot with an X of cellophane tape. This trick will keep the plaster from cracking when you start hammering.

When the landlady says, "no nails in the wall," hang pictures with sewing machine needles. They hold up to 30 pounds.

A wet fingerprint shows the exact spot for the hanger. The print dries without a mark.

Finishing unfinished picture frames:

Stain them beautifully with ordinary liquid shoe polish. Apply one coat and let dry. Follow with another coating, then wax with a good paste wax. Brown polish gives the wood a walnut glow and oxblood polish emulates a rich mahogany. Tan polish will appear as a light maple color.

SKIN AND BODY CARE HINTS

The fastest way to dry up a blemish:

Dab it with lemon juice a few times a day.

The best deep pore cleanser around:

Bring a quart of water to a boil and take it to a table. Add the juice or peel of ½ a lemon and a handful of any herbs (rosemary, basil, thyme, mint ...). Cover your hair with a shower cap and drape another towel over your head and the pot, holding your face about 12 inches above the water. With closed eyes, let your face steam for 15 minutes. Afterward, rinse with very cold water to close pores. Note: Do not use more than once a week or you will deplete your skin of too many natural oils.

A cheap but terrific facial scrub:

Make a paste of oatmeal and water. Apply to face and allow to dry until it feels tight. Rub off with your fingers, using lots of back and forth motion. This scrub sloughs off dead skin, gets rid of blackheads.

Sweeten your complexion with sugar:

Mix a teaspoon of sugar with soap lather and use the same as cleansing grains.

Treat yourself to a hot oil treatment:

For a professional hot oil treatment, saturate hair with olive, sesame, or corn oil. Run the hottest water possible over 2 towels in your washing machine. After towels are wet, turn machine to spin cycle. Wrap head in plastic or aluminum foil before applying hot towels. Wait 20 minutes for best results. By using this method, your towels will be hot without the mess of dripping water.

Setting lotion:

A teaspoon of sugar or gelatin dissolved in a cup of warm water makes a handy setting lotion.

Or, for an extra firm set, use your favorite flavor of jello. That's right, fully prepared and ready to eat. Use as you would any jellied type of setting lotion.

Also, try witch hazel or stale beer.

Hair conditioner:

Mayonnaise gives dry hair a good conditioning. Apply ½ cup mayonnaise to dry, unwashed hair. Cover with a plastic bag and wait for 15 minutes. Rinse a few times before shampooing thoroughly.

Final rinse:

For blondes, rinse hair with water containing a few tablespoons of lemon juice. For brunettes and redheads, rinse with water containing several tablespoons of apple cider vinegar. Both will remove soapy film and give the hair a beautiful shine.

Brunettes and redheads can also rinse their hair with coffee. Do not rinse it out. You will be amazed at how rich and shiny your hair will appear.

Homemade dry shampoo:

If regular shampooing is impossible, make your own dry shampoo by mixing together 1 tablespoon salt and ½ cup cornmeal. Transfer to a large holed salt shaker; sprinkle it on oily hair lightly and brush out dirt and grime.

Baby powder or cornstarch can also be used as dry shampoos.

A quick hair set:

Instead of using electric rollers everyday, try the following tip: Roll hair completely dry and cover with a warm damp towel for a few minutes. Allow hair to dry for a perfect quick set.

Terrific eye cream:

Before retiring, apply castor oil around your eyes. Make sure it is the odorless form. Plastic surgeons use it on their patients following surgery.

Manicure:

Mix 1 cup warm water and juice of ½ lemon. Soak finger tips for 5 minutes. Rinse and pat dry, pushing back cuticles. Rub lemon peel against nail, back and forth, vigorously. Finish by buffing with a soft cloth.

Quick drying nail polish:
For faster drying nail polish, set hands in a bowl of very cold water when nails are partially dry.

Or, stick your hands in the freezer.

Nonstick nail polish bottle:
Treat a new bottle of nail polish by rubbing petroleum jelly inside the cover and on the grooves of the bottle. You will never have any trouble opening it, even after months.

You'll never have to throw away nail polish again:
Your nail polish will always be smooth and easy to apply if you store it in the refrigerator. Frosted nail polish will not separate either.

However, if it has hardened or gotten to the gummy stage, place the bottle in a pan of boiling water. In no time the polish will be good as new.

Longer lasting perfume:
Oily skin holds perfume scents longer than dry skin. So, before applying perfume, rub a very thin layer of Vaseline on your skin and you will smell delicious for hours.

Cucumber for tired eyes:
Place fresh cold cucumbers on your eyelids to rid them of redness and puffiness.

Make your own deodorant - two different ways:
Mix 2 tablespoons alum (available at drugstores) into 1 pint warm water; stir well. Add a small amount of your favorite cologne or after-shave lotion. Transfer to spray bottle.

Or, mix 2 teaspoons of baking soda, 2 teaspoons of petroleum jelly, and 2 teaspoons of talcum powder. Heat in a double boiler over low heat and stir until smooth cream forms. Put cream in a small container with a tight lid and use as you would regular cream deodorant.

A "berry" good treatment for teeth:
Dip a toothbrush in a mashed strawberry and brush vigorously to remove yellowing and stains.

Or, brush with plain baking soda until you see the difference.

Mending broken lipstick:
Heat the broken ends over a match until they melt enough to adhere when pressed together. Cool in refrigerator.

Sunburn relievers:
To cool down affected areas, rub with apple cider vinegar.

Pat with a wet tea bag.

Or, apply a paste of baking soda and water.

TERRIFIC CAR HINTS

Quick cleaning windows:
Baking soda quickly cleans spatters and traffic grime from windshields, headlights, chrome, and enamel. Wipe with soda sprinkled onto a damp sponge; rinse.
Use plastic net bags (the kind onions come in) to wash windshields when insects have accumulated. Simply tie a few bags into one bag and rub away.

Removing bumper stickers:
Use nail polish remover or lighter fluid. Gently scrape away with a razor blade or knife.

Removing rust spots:
Briskly scrub the rust spots on your bumpers with a piece of foil which has been crumbled, or use fine steel wool.
Use a soap filled steel wool pad.
Kerosene helps too.

Scratches:
Take a matching color crayon and work into the scratch well.

Tar removers:
Soak tar spots with raw linseed oil. Allow to stand until soft, then wipe with a soft cloth which has been dampened with the oil.

To remove price tag sheets:
Sponge hot vinegar onto the price sheets liberally. Scrape gently. Continue applying vinegar until sheet is gone.
Lemon extract works also.
Or, apply salad oil. Let set for awhile and scrape away.

Two parking hints:
On cold days and evenings, back your car into the garage. If needed, your car will be in good position for using jumper cables.
If you have bumped the front fender of your car into the back wall of your garage, try this: Suspend a small rubber ball on a string from the ceiling of the garage so that when the ball strikes your windshield you will know the car is far enough in to close the garage door.

Ways to identify your car or bike:
Drop a business card or file card with your name and address down the window slot. Just in case you have to prove the car is yours some day.
To identify a stolen bicycle, even though the serial number may have been filed off, roll the file card around a pencil, remove the bicycle's seatpost and drop the card into the bicycle frame. It can easily be removed as proof of ownership.

Cigarette ashes:
Ashes that continue to burn in the car ashtray are a nuisance. Prevent this by placing an inch of baking soda (or gravel) in the bottom of the tray.

Battery corrosion-proofer:
Scub battery terminals and holder with a strong solution of baking soda water, then smear with petroleum jelly.

Preventing doors and trunk from freezing:
Wipe or spray the rubber gaskets with a heavy coating of vegetable oil. The oil will seal out water, but will not harm the gasket. This is especially good before having your car washed in the winter.
Spray "lock tight" graphite into key hole and move with key for several turns to work through lock. Will keep water out in winter and lock won't freeze up.

Opening a frozen lock:
Heat the key with a cigarette lighter or match. Never force the key. Turn very gently.

Would you believe, a hair dryer will start your car?
Before you call the car starting service on cold mornings, remember this: Your car will probably start if you blow hot air on the carburetor from a hair dryer. It works ... it honestly does.

Salt remover for carpeting:
Combine equal amounts of vinegar and water to remove salt residue left behind from winter.

To eliminate windshield freeze-ups when parked outdoors:
Place your rubber floor mats over the windshields. Secure the mat with windshield wipers. You will save yourself the chore of scraping.

Make your own washer solvent that won't freeze:
Combine 1 quart rubbing alcohol, 1 cup water, and 2 tablespoons liquid detergent. This formula is guaranteed not to freeze down to 35° below zero.

Before you get stuck:
Place a bag of kitty litter in your car trunk, just in case you get stuck in the ice or snow. It provides excellent traction.

If you are stuck:
And there is no kitty litter, sand, or shovel available, remove the rubber mats from your car and place them in front of the rear wheels. You just might get out all by yourself.

CARPET CARE HINTS

Stains be gone:
For fresh stains: Plain club soda is an instant spot remover and it is fantastic. Pour a little on the spot, let it set for a few seconds, and sponge up thoroughly.
For older stains: Combine 2 tablespoons detergent, 3 tablespoons vinegar, and 1 quart of warm water. Work into stain and blot as dry as possible.
Tide is the best stain remover for stubborn spots: Make a sudsy solution of Tide laundry detergent and warm water. Brush the suds into the stain vertically

and horizontally with a soft brush. Blot up excess. If the stain persists, repeat process. This works 9¾ times out of 10.

The last step is important too!
After you've completed one of the preceding methods, cover the spot with a clean towel and place a heavy book on top of it. When the towel becomes damp replace it with a dry one.

An instant spot remover:
Try shaving cream. Foam is a good spot remover and it is ready instantly. Wash up with water or club soda.

Repairing a burn:
Remove some fuzz from the carpet, either by shaving or pulling out with a tweezer. Roll into the shape of the burn. Apply a good cement glue to the backing of the rug and press the fuzz down into the burned spot. Cover with a piece of cleansing tissue and place a heavy book on top. This will cause the glue to dry very slowly and you will get the best results.

Flattened carpet:
If heavy furniture has flattened the pile of your rugs, raise it with a steam iron. Build up good steam and hold your iron over the damaged spot. Do not touch the carpet with the iron. Brush briskly.

Removing candle wax drippings:
Place a blotter or brown paper bag over the spot and put a hot iron over the blotter. After a few minutes, the wax will be absorbed into the blotter. Repeat if necessary.

Repairing braided rugs:
Braided rugs often rip apart. Instead of sewing them, use clear fabric glue to repair. It's that fast and easy.

Spot remover for indoor-outdoor carpeting:
Spray spots liberally with a prewash commercial spray. Let it set for several minutes, then hose down and watch the spots disappear.

A carpet brightener:
Sprinkle a generous amount of salt on your carpet. Let stand for an hour before vacuuming. You will be amazed at the results.

Before you shampoo:
To prevent rust marks from forming on a wet carpet, put little plastic bags or small glass jars on each furniture leg. This also eliminates the dreadful job of moving furniture from one end of the room to the other.

Who tracked the mud in?
Sprinkle salt on damp mud spots. Give the salt at least 15 minutes to soak up the mud, then vacuum up and away.

Sooty footmarks:
Try an artgum eraser on light colored carpets.
Or, sprinkle soiled areas with salt. Wait ½ hour and then vacuum.

Opposites attract:
Ever wanted to be a genius? Then, next time red wine spills on your carpet, remove it with white wine.

Removing chewing gum:
Press ice cubes against the gum until it becomes brittle and breaks off, then use a spot remover to vanish last traces.

Glue:
Glue can be loosened by saturating the spot with a cloth soaked in vinegar.

Ballpoint ink marks:
Saturate the spot with hairspray. Allow to dry. Brush lightly with a solution of water and vinegar.

GENERAL CLEANING TIPS

Artificial flowers:
Pour some salt into a large paper bag with the flowers. Shake vigorously. The salt won't look soiled at first, but wait until you see its color when you run water on it.

Ballpoint pens:
If your ballpoint becomes clogged with excessive ink and fuzz, insert it in the filter portion of a cigarette. Just a few quick turns and it's ready for use.

Candles:
Sponge with a piece of cotton dampened with rubbing alcohol.
Did you know? Candles burn more slowly and evenly with minimum wax drippings if you place them in the freezer for several hours before using.

Candle holders:
If your candle holders are coated with wax, place in the freezer for an hour or so. The wax will peel off in a jiffy with absolutely no injury to the silver.
Or, run under very hot water and dry with a paper towel.

Grills:
Barbecue grill: Tear off a sheet of heavy-duty aluminum foil large enough to completely cover your grill. Press foil shiny side down on grill and fold sides under, covering as tightly as possible. When coals have nearly reached their hottest point, place grill over coals for 10 minutes. Remove foil and any charred grease or food on your grill should drop off leaving your grill clean and shiny.
Before ever using your barbecue grill, spray it heavily with vegetable oil.
Restaurant grills: A fast and effective way to clean a grill is to use leftover brewed coffee. Pour it on a hot or cold grill. Wipe off and you will be amazed at the results.

Guitar:
Rub toothpaste on your guitar. Let it dry, then buff for a super shine.

Household odors:
Here's a way to kill household odors and always have a fresh smelling house for just pennies. Put a few drops of wintergreen oil (available at drugstores) on a cotton ball and place out of sight in each room. It will last for months and is as effective as room sprays.

Toss dried orange and lemon rinds into your fireplace for a spicy aroma.

Iron:
To remove mineral deposits from the inside of a steam iron, fill it with equal part of water and white vinegar. Let it steam for several minutes, then disconnect and let set for 1 hour. Empty and rinse out with clear water.

Remove brown or burned-on spots by rubbing with a heated solution of vinegar and salt.

Remove wax build-up by rubbing with very fine sandpaper. Next, polish with a piece of fine soapless steel wool, then wipe off with a damp cloth.

Or, clean the outside of your iron with toothpaste or silver polish.

Jewelry:
Clean with a soft cloth dabbed in toothpaste.

Pewter:
One of the best ways to clean pewter is to rub with cabbage leaves.

Or, try a homemade mixture of wood ashes moistened with water.

Piano keys:
Apply toothpaste to a well dampened cloth. Rub the keys well, wipe dry, and buff with a dry soft cloth.

Radiator:
Hang a damp cloth behind the radiator, then blow with the blower end of your vacuum cleaner. The dust and dirt will be blown into the damp cloth.

Telephone:
Clean your telephone with rubbing alcohol to keep it new looking.

Vases with small openings:
Dampen the inside of vase and add any toilet bowl cleaner. Let stand for 10 minutes and stains will disappear.

Longer lasting panty hose:
Before you ever wear a new pair of hose they should be frozen first. No kidding, they will last longer if you wet them thoroughly, ring out gently, place in a plastic bag, and toss in the freezer. Once frozen, thaw in bathtub and then hang to dry. It's a wild and crazy hint, but it's true!

Or, starch them very, very lightly. This helps resist runs and they will also go on easily.

Stopping a run:
Apply hair spray or rub with a wet bar of soap. Of course, the old standby, clear nail polish, is still a good run stopper.

Before ever wearing a new garment:
Touch the center of each button (front and back) with clear nail polish. This will seal the threads and buttons will stay on much longer.

A wrinkle-free idea:
Hang your wrinkled garment on the curtain rod in your bathroom and run the hottest water possible from your shower. Close the bathroom door and let the water run for awhile. This allows the steam to penetrate the material, thus eliminating the wrinkles. When traveling, this hint should be remembered.

A great cover-up:
If you are in a hurry and notice a stain on your white suit, cover it up by rubbing baby powder into the stain.

Shave away fuzz balls:
Remove those little balls of fuzz from an old shirt collar by going over the surface with a clean shaver. It will not harm the fabric.

The preceding trick works on sweaters too!
Remove knots and balls from sweater by shaving with a regular razor (very gently) or an electric shaver.
Or, remove by rubbing with a very fine piece of sandpaper.

Sticky zippers:
They will slide easily if rubbed with a lead pencil.

Removing hem creases:
White vinegar will help remove a permanent crease. Sponge the material liberally with the vinegar and press with a warm iron.
Try this trick when lengthening old jeans: The white hem lines will disappear if you mix permanent blue ink with a little water (keep adding water until you get the perfect shade), then apply with a small brush. Let dry and no more telltale hemline.

A quick pair of ski jeans:
Convert regular jeans into ski pants by spraying with a waterproof fabric protector.

Some hints you should know about canvas shoes:
Spray new canvas or rope trimmed shoes with a fabric protector to keep them looking new.
To clean rope trimmed canvas shoes, rub with a toothbrush that has been dipped in rug shampoo.
Keep new white tennis shoes looking new by spraying heavily with starch.

AMAZING ANIMAL HINTS

Keeping the cat off your favorite chair:
Stuff a few mothballs in the cushion of a chair or sofa and your cat will stay clear.

Cats hate plastic coverings! Cover your chair until your cat realizes the chair is a no-no.

Fleas will "flee":
If you place some fresh pine needles in his doghouse or underneath his bed pad.
Or, salt the crevices of his doghouse and wash him periodically with salt water.

A safety tip for "Rover":
Tape reflector tape on your dog's or cat's collar to help cut down the danger of its being struck by a car at night.

When the ants come marching in:
Place small sponges soaked in sugar sweetened water wherever ants have been seen. Collect the sponges periodically and plunge into hot water.
Rid red ants from your pantry by putting a small quantity of green sage on the cupboard shelves.
Ant hills outside the home can be destroyed by pouring a kettle of boiling water down each opening.

There's a bee in the house:
If a wasp or bee gets into the house, reach for the hairspray. Most insect sprays only infuriate them, but the hairspray stiffens their wings, immobilizing them immediately. This works on all winged insects.

How to treat bug bites:
Treat insect bites with a poultice of either cornstarch or baking soda, mixed with vinegar, fresh lemon juice, or witch hazel.
Apply a paste made of meat tenderizer and water.
Or, rub bites with wet bar soap to help relieve itching.

Bee stings:
Apply a poultice of baking soda and water.
Or, try applying a fresh cut slice of raw onion to the sting to help draw out the poison. Hold the onion in place with tape.

FOR THE BIRDS

It's hard to give up the trappings of Christmas, but evergreen needles get dry and the pretty tree has to go.
Some families think it's fun to turn their Christmas tree into a bird feeder. Stringing food for the birds is a pleasant way to spend an afternoon when the weather is blustery.
Cheese cubes give the feathered visitors necessary protein. They like raisins, peanuts in the shell, and dried fruit, which are all easy to string. Leftover donuts can perch on the tips of branches. Popcorn is fun to take turns stringing and eating.
One of my New Year's resolutions is to keep the bird feeders full. I ran across some recipes for holiday treats for birds.

Cardinal Christmas Crunch:

Raw beef suet
2 c. bread crumbs
¼ c. bird seed mixture

1 c. green grapes, cut in pieces
½ tsp. sand

Place bread crumbs, bird seed, and grapes in medium size bowl; set aside. Put
suet through meat grinder, then into double boiler to melt. Remove from
heat; allow to cool and harden slightly. Reheat and pour 1½ cups over dry
mixture. Add sand. Mix well with fork. Turn into foil loaf pan, 5x3x1 inch.
Refrigerate until firm. Place on feeder tray and enjoy watching the lovely
red visitors.

Chickadee Cones:

Raw beef suet
Sunflower seeds

Pine cones
Millet seeds

Put suet through meat grinder, then melt it in a double boiler; set aside to
harden slightly. Reheat. Use pine cones with string or wire attached.
Spoon warm suet over until well coated. Sprinkle immediately with millet.
Push sunflower seeds under scales. Spoon suet over cones again to build
up suet and make seeds secure. Refrigerate until firm and hang from tree
branches.

Sparrow Specialty:

Raw beef suet
1½ c. wild bird seed
1 c. bread crumbs

1 c. graham crackers, crumbled
½ tsp. sand

Put seed, crumbs, and crackers in medium size bowl; set aside. Put suet
through meat grinder, then melt in double boiler. Allow suet to cool and
harden slightly. Reheat and pour 1 cup over dry ingredients. Add sand for
grit. Mix well and spoon into foil loaf pan, 5x3x1 inch. Refrigerate until firm.
Place on feeder tray.

Helen H. Clark, Grand Forks, ND

HINTS - FOR THE BIRDS

They'll love you for it!
Help make their nesting easier and provide building materials. Collect lint from
your dryer, bits of string, yarn from your sewing basket and hair from your
brush. Fasten together very lightly and attach to a tree branch.

A "pine" treat for the birds in the winter:
Cover pine cones with hardened bacon grease or other type of fat. Roll in bird
seed or bread crumbs. Hang from a tree branch or tuck into bushes.

More ideas for the birds:
To attract birds to an outdoor birdbath, drop in a few colored marbles.
When you cannot find a funnel to put bird seed in the feeder, use the cut-off top
of a bleach jug or an old milk carton.

GARDENING - GREEN THUMB HINTS

A perfect seed row marker:
Mark the planting date on each seed packet, then slip small plastic bags over
each seed packet and secure with a twist-tie. You will never have doubts
about which plants are which if you follow this procedure.

Aid tomato plants with panty hose:
To avoid cutting into your prize winning tomato plants, tie the stalks with panty
hose that have been cut lengthwise.

Assuring baby tomatoes a good start:
Mix fireplace ashes into the surrounding soil. Remove the top and bottom lids
from coffee cans and set a can over each plant. (Step firmly on the can to
set it into the ground.) Remove cans when plants are a few weeks old.

The know-hows of organic gardening:
Herbs are nature's insecticides. Include a variety of them in your garden.
Basil near tomatoes repels worms and flies.
Mint, sage, dill, and thyme protect cabbage, cauliflower, broccoli, and Brussels
sprouts from the cabbage moth.

Ailing houseplants - "They'll reflect all the love you give them":
Your houseplant will come out of its slump if you cover it with a plastic bag,
along with a pest strip. Make sure the entire plant is under the bag. Remove the bag in a few days and you will find it in good health. This is excellent to do when transferring plants from outside into the house.
Give your plant a shot of Geritol on a regular basis for 3 months. Within a
month, you will notice new leaves have begun to appear.
Or, feed your plant a tablespoon of castor oil, followed by a good drink of water.

Bug beaters:
Aphids and spiders: Wash total plant off with mild detergent and water.
Black flies: Combine 2 tablespoons of plain ammonia and 1 quart of water. Wa-
ter soil.
White flies: Mix 2 tablespoons of dishwashing liquid in 1 gallon of water and
spray on leaves.
Scales: For instant removal of slugs, place plant in pot of water.
Pests of all kinds: Plant a garlic clove along with your plant. As it grows, simply
keep cutting it down so it will not disturb the appearance of the plant. Gar-
lic will not harm the plant, but the bugs hate it.

Houseplant on the mend:
A tiny splint made of toothpicks and tape will often save the broken stem of a
plant.

Cleaning plant leaves:

Dust with a feather duster.

Glycerine is one of the best substances to use if you wish to put a gloss on the leaves of your plants. Put a few drops of glycerine on a cloth and swab the leaves with it. It is much better than olive oil or mayonnaise, since it is not a dust collector.

A half and half mixture of milk and water also makes a fine solution for glossing leaves.

Homemade trellises:

Snip off the hook of a wire coat hanger; bend remaining wire into a fun, creative shape, such as a heart or a star, then push ends into the pot to make a miniature trellis for your ivy to grow on.

Support tall plants with old adjustable brasslike curtain rods.

Eliminating the scratches:

Corn pads are terrific coasters for plant pots. Simply stick them on and you will be able to use that pot that has been scratching your table for years.

Another planting hint:

For good drainage use broken clay pot, cracked walnut shells, fruit pits, marbles, charcoal, or stones on the bottom of the pots.

Ferns love tea parties too!

A good tonic for ferns is to water them with weak tea. In addition to their tea break, plant a wet soggy tea bag along with your fern.

Let worm infested ferns meet their "match." Stick matches into the soil with the sulphur end down. For an ordinary size plant, use 4 matches and for a large one use 6. Ferns enjoy the nitrogen content in a very weak solution of ammonia and water.

Ways to help your cut flowers last longer:

Always cut stems at an angle with a very sharp scissors or knife.

Split the ends of thick stems before putting them in a vase. Split ends give stems a better chance to absorb moisture.

Always cut stems under water. That way, no air bubbles can form to stop the free flow of water into the stem.

Remove leaves below the waterline, as decaying vegetable matter poisons the water.

Aspirin tablets, pennies, and ice cubes are all said to lengthen the lives of fresh cut flowers. However, the best preservation is 2 tablespoons of white vinegar and 2 tablespoons of cane sugar in a quart of water. The vinegar inhibits the growth of organisms and the sugar serves as food.

Refrigerate each night. This alone can double their lives.

Flowers will last longer if not crowded in the vase.

Reviving wilted flowers:

Cut stems and place in hot water. Let them rest in a dark place until water cools, then transfer into cold water.

WEIGHTS AND MEASURES IN THE METRIC SYSTEM

1 bushel = 35.24 liters
1 bushel = 4 pecks
1 peck = 8.81 liters
1 peck = 8 quarts
1 quart (dry) = 1.101 liters
1 quart (liquid) = .946 liters
1 quart = 2 pints = 4 cups
1 pint (dry) = .551 liters
1 pint (liquid) = .473 liters
1 pint = 2 cups
1 cup (dry) = .275 liters
1 cup (liquid) = .236 liters
1 cup = 8 ounces
1 cup (dry) = .275 liters = 275. milliliters
1 cup (liquid) = .236 liters = 236. milliliters
1 ounce (liquid) = .0296 liters = 29.6 milliliters
1 ounce (liquid) = 2 tablespoons
1 tablespoon = 3 teaspoons = 180 drops
1 tablespoon = .0148 liters = 14.8 milliliters = 4 drams
1 teaspoon = .00493 liters = 4.93 milliliters = 1⅓ drams
1 ounce (dry) = 28.35 grams
1 pound = 453.6 grams = 16 ounces
1000 milliliters = 1 liter
1 kiloliter = 2.25 pounds
1 bushel = 40 pounds
1 bushel = 7.45 kiloliters
1 kilogram = 2.25 pounds

Annette Zabinski, Duluth, MN

WEIGHTS AND MEASURES
(Standard abbreviations)

t. - teaspoon
T. - tablespoon
c. - cup
f.g. - few grains
pt. - pint
qt. - quart
d.b. - double boiler

B.P. - baking powder
B.S. - baking soda
oz. - ounce
lb. - pound
pk. - peck
bu. - bushel

1 ounce (liquid) = .0296 liters = 29.6 milliliters
1 ounce (liquid) = 2 tablespoons
1 tablespoon = 3 teaspoons = 180 drops
1 tablespoon = .0148 liters = 14.8 milliliters = 4 drams
1 teaspoon = .00493 liters = 4.93 milliliters = 1⅓ drams
1 ounce (dry) = 28.35 grams
1 pound = 453.6 grams = 16 ounces
1000 milliliters = 1 liter
1 kiloliter = 2.25 pounds
1 bushel = 40 pounds
1 bushel = 7.45 kiloliters
1 kilogram = 2.25 pounds

Annette Zabinski, Duluth, MN

WEIGHTS AND MEASURES
(Standard abbreviations)

t. - teaspoon
T. - tablespoon
c. - cup
f.g. - few grains
pt. - pint
qt. - quart
d.b. - double boiler

B.P. - baking powder
B.S. - baking soda
oz. - ounce
lb. - pound
pk. - peck
bu. - bushel

(Guide to weights and measures)

1 teaspoon - 60 drops
3 teaspoons - 1 tablespoon
2 tablespoons - 1 fluid ounce
4 tablespoons - ¼ cup
5⅓ tablespoons - ⅓ cup
8 tablespoons - ½ cup
16 tablespoons - 1 cup

1 pound - 16 ounces
1 cup - ½ pint
2 cups - 1 pint
4 cups - 1 quart
4 quarts - 1 gallon
8 quarts - 1 peck
4 pecks - 1 bushel

Annette Zabinski, Duluth, MN

CROWD PLEASERS
Quantities to Serve 100 People

COFFEE	— 3 lb.
LOAF SUGAR	— 3 lb.
CREAM	— 3 quarts
WHIPPING CREAM	— 4 pt.
MILK	— 6 gallons
FRUIT COCKTAIL	— 2½ gallons
FRUIT JUICE	— 4 #10 cans (26 lb.)
TOMATO JUICE	— 4 #10 cans (26 lb.)
SOUP	— 5 gallons
OYSTERS	— 18 quarts
WIENERS	— 25 lb.
MEAT LOAF	— 24 lb.
HAM	— 40 lb.
BEEF	— 40 lb.
ROAST PORK	— 40 lb.
HAMBURGER	— 30-36 lb.
CHICKEN FOR PIE	— 40 lb.
POTATOES	— 35 lb.
SCALLOPED POTATOES	— 5 gallons
VEGETABLES	— 4 #10 cans (26 lb.)
BAKED BEANS	— 5 gallons
BEETS	— 30 lb.
CAULIFLOWER	— 18 lb.
CABBAGE FOR SLAW	— 20 lb.
CARROTS	— 33 lb.
BREAD	— 10 loaves
ROLLS	— 200
BUTTER	— 3 lb.
POTATO SALAD	— 12 quarts
FRUIT SALAD	— 20 quarts
VEGETABLE SALAD	— 20 quarts
LETTUCE	— 20 heads
SALAD DRESSING	— 3 quarts
PIES	— 18
CAKES	— 8
ICE CREAM	— 4 gallons
CHEESE	— 3 lb.
OLIVES	— 1¾ lb.
PICKLES	— 2 quarts
NUTS	— 3 lb. sorted

To serve 50 people, divide by 2.
To serve 25 people, divide by 4.

Jane Klein
Bellevue, Washington

Continued on next page.

PLANNING FOR A CROWD

Foods	*Servings*	*Serving Unit*	*Amt. to Purchase*
BEVERAGES			
Coffee, ground	40-50	¾ c.	1 lb. (5 c.)
Cream for coffee	25	1 Tbsp.	1 pt.
Milk	24	1 c.	1½ gal.
Tea leaves	50	¾ c.	1 c.
DESSERTS			
Cake	24	2½" squares	(1) 15½ x 10½ x 1 in. sheet cake
Ice cream	24	½ c. or 1 slice	3 qt.
Pie	30	⅙ of pie	(5) 9 inch pies
Whipped cream	25	2 Tbsp.	1 pt.
FRUIT			
Canned	24	½ c.	(1) 6½ or 7¼ lb. can
MEAT			
Beef roast, chuck	25	4 oz.	12¼ lb., bone in
Ground beef	25	3 oz. pattie	6¾ lb.
Ham, baked, sliced	25	4 oz.	10 lb., boneless
Chicken	24	¼ chicken	6 chickens
Turkey	25	3 oz.	15 lb.
Turkey, roll, precooked	25	3 oz.	6-7 lb.
PASTA, RICE			
Rice, long-grain	24	½ c., cooked	1½ lb., uncooked
Spaghetti and noodles	25	¾ c., cooked	2½ lb., uncooked
RELISHES (combine several)			
Carrot strips	25	2-3 strips	1 lb.
Celery	25	1 (2-3") piece	1 lb.
Olives	25	3-4 olives	1 qt.
Pickles	25	1 oz.	1 qt.
SALADS			
Fruit	24	⅓ c.	2 qt.
Potato	24	½ c.	3 qt.
Tossed vegetable	25	¾ c.	5 qt.
Salad dressing	32	1 Tbsp.	1 pt.
SOUP	25	1 c. (main course)	1½ gal. or (2) 50 oz. cans, condensed
VEGETABLES			
Canned	25	½ c.	(1) 6½-7¼ lb. can
Fresh:			
Lettuce, for salad (Iceberg)	24	⅙ head, raw	4 heads
Potatoes, mashed	25	½ c., mashed	6¾ lb., raw
Potatoes, baked	25	1 medium	8½ lb., raw
Frozen:			
Beans, green or wax	25	⅓ c.	5¼ lb.
Carrots	25	⅓ c., sliced	5 lb.
Corn, whole kernel	25	⅓ c.	5 lb.
Peas	25	⅓ c.	5 lb.
Potatoes, French fried	25	10 pieces	3¼ lb.
MISCELLANEOUS			
Butter	32	1 pat	½ lb.
Juice	23	½ c.	(2) 46 oz. cans
Potato chips	25	¾-1 oz.	1-1½ lb.
French bread	24	¾ inch slice	(1) 18 inch loaf

Jane Klein
Bellevue, WA

TIMETABLE FOR ROASTING TURKEYS

WEIGHT (unstuffed)	ROASTING TIME (unstuffed turkey)	ROASTING TIME (stuffed turkey)
6 lb.	2 hr.	2 hr. 30 min.
7 lb.	2 hr. 5 min.	2 hr. 40 min.
8 lb.	2 hr. 10 min.	2 hr. 50 min.
9 lb.	2 hr. 15 min.	3 hr.
10 lb.	2 hr. 30 min.	3 hr. 20 min.
11 lb.	2 hr. 45 min.	3 hr. 40 min.
12 lb.	3 hr.	4 hr.
13 lb.	3 hr. 15 min.	4 hr. 20 min.
14 lb.	3 hr. 30 min.	4 hr. 40 min.
15 lb.	3 hr. 45 min.	5 hr.
16 lb.	4 hr.	5 hr. 20 min.
17 lb.	4 hr. 15 min.	5 hr. 40 min.
18 lb.	4 hr. 30 min.	6 hr.
19 lb.	4 hr. 45 min.	6 hr. 20 min.
20 lb.	5 hr.	6 hr. 40 min.
21 lb.	5 hr. 15 min.	7 hr.
22 lb.	5 hr. 30 min.	7 hr. 20 min.

TO DEFROST A TURKEY IN THE REFRIGERATOR

WEIGHT OF TURKEY	DEFROSTING TIME
4 to 10 pounds	1 to 2 days
10 to 20 pounds	2 to 3 days
20 to 24 pounds	3 to 4 days

SEASONING GUIDE

Get acquainted with spices and herbs. Add in small amounts, ¼ teaspoon for each 4 servings. Taste before adding more. Crush dried herbs or snip fresh herbs before using. If substituting fresh for dried, use 3 times more fresh herbs.

Freeze fresh herbs and enjoy them all winter long. Wash, then blanch the herbs in boiling water for 10 seconds. Chill in ice water 1 minute; pat dry. Package in small moisture-vaporproof bags or foil; seal; label. Freeze. Use while frosty.

Appetizers, Soups

CRANBERRY JUICE: Add cinnamon, allspice, and/or cloves. Serve hot or chilled.

FRUIT COCKTAIL: Try adding mint or rosemary.

STUFFED CELERY: Mix caraway seed with cream cheese; fill celery. Dash with paprika.

TOMATO COCKTAIL: Add ¼ teaspoon dried basil, per cup.

CHICKEN SOUP: Add a dash of rosemary, tarragon or nutmeg. Sprinkle paprika atop for color.

CLAM CHOWDER: Add a dash of caraway seed, sage, or thyme.

CONSOMME: Dash in basil, marjoram, savory, or tarragon.

FISH CHOWDER: Add bay leaves, curry powder, or dill.

MUSHROOM SOUP: Season with curry, oregano, or marjoram.

ONION SOUP: Add marjoram.

OYSTER STEW: Lightly add cayenne, mace, or marjoram.

POTATO SOUP: Dash with mustard or basil. Top with snipped chives or parsley.

SPLIT-PEA SOUP: Add dash basil, chili powder, or rosemary.

TOMATO SOUP: Dash in basil, dill, oregano, sage, or tarragon.

VEGETABLE SOUP: Try allspice, oregano, sage, or thyme.

Breads, Pasta

BISCUITS: Add caraway seed, thyme, or savory to flour. Serve with meat.

BREAD: Make each loaf a surprise by adding caraway seed, cardamom, or poppy seed.

COFFEE CAKE: Mix crushed aniseed in batter. For variety, sprinkle cinnamon-sugar mixture atop or add poppy seed filling.

CORN BREAD: Add poultry seasoning or caraway seed to dry ingredients. Be adventuresome, add ½ teaspoon rosemary to batter.

CROUTONS: Toss toast cubes in melted butter, seasoned with basil, marjoram, or onion salt.

DOUGHNUTS: Add mace or nutmeg to dry ingredients. After frying, roll in cinnamon sugar.

DUMPLINGS: Add thyme or parsley (fresh or flakes) to batter.

MUFFINS: Blueberry — add dash of nutmeg to dry ingredients. Season plain muffins with caraway seed or cinnamon.

NOODLES: Butter, then sprinkle with poppy seed.

ROLLS: Add caraway seed. Or, sprinkle with sesame seed.

SPAGHETTI: Toss with butter, Parmesan, and snipped chives.

WAFFLES: Add poultry seasoning to batter, serve with creamed chicken. Or add cardamom to honey; pour over waffles.

Eggs, Cheese

BAKED EGGS: Sprinkle dash of thyme or paprika over the top.

CREAMED EGGS: Add mace.

DEVILED EGGS: Add celery seed, cumin, mustard, savory, chili powder, or curry powder.

OMELET: Try with dash of marjoram or rosemary (go easy!).

SCRAMBLED EGGS: Sprinkle lightly with basil, thyme, rosemary, or marjoram. Add seasonings near the end of cooking.

SOUFFLE: Add ¼ teaspoon marjoram to 4-egg souffle. To cheese souffle, add basil or savory.

CHEESE CASSEROLES: Spark with dash sage or marjoram.

CHEESE FONDUE: Try adding a dash of basil or nutmeg.

CHEESE RABBIT (rarebit): Try with mace or mustard.

CHEESE SAUCE: Add mustard or a dash of marjoram or thyme.

CHEESE SPREAD: Blend sage, caraway seed, thyme, or celery seed into melted process cheese.

COTTAGE CHEESE: Blend in chives, or a dash of sage, caraway seed, dill, anise, or cumin. Prepare several hours ahead of time.

CREAM CHEESE: Blend in curry powder, marjoram, caraway seed, or dill. Sprinkle paprika or cayenne atop. Use as celery filling or appetizer spread.

YIELDS, EQUIVALENTS & SUBSTITUTIONS

Food	If Your Recipe States	You Will Need Approximately
Apples	1 cup chopped or sliced	1 medium
Apricots	3 cups dried or 5 cups cooked	1 pound
Bacon	½ cup crumbled	8 slices crisply fried
Baking powder	1 tsp.	⅝ tsp. cream of tartar plus ¼ tsp. baking soda OR ¼ tsp. baking powder plus ½ c. buttermilk, yogurt or molasses
Bananas	1 cup sliced	2 small or 1 medium
	2 cups mashed	3 medium
Beans, green or wax	3 cups 1-inch pieces, uncooked OR 2½ cups cooked	1 pound
dried	2½ cups uncooked or 6 cups cooked	1 pound
Beef	1 cup ½-inch pieces	5 ounces
ground	2 cups	1 pound
Blueberries, fresh	2½ cups	1 pint
Bread	12 slices (⅝ inch thick)	1 pound
	1 cup soft crumbs or ½ cup dry	2 slices
Broccoli	1½ cups cooked	1 pound
Brussels sprouts	2 cups cooked	1 pound
Butter or margarine	2 cups	1 pound
Buttermilk	1 cup	1 Tbsp. white vinegar or lemon juice plus sweet milk to make 1 cup; let stand 5 minutes OR 1 cup plain yogurt
Cabbage	3½ to 4½ cups shredded	1-pound head
Carrots	1 cup ¼-inch slices	2 medium
	1 cup shredded	1½ medium
	1 cup ¼-inch diagonally sliced	2½ medium
	2½ cups sliced	1 pound
Catsup	1 cup	8 oz. tomato sauce plus ½ cup brown sugar and 2 Tbsp. vinegar
Cauliflower	3 cups flowerets	1 pound
Celery	1 cup ¼-inch slices	2 medium stalks
	1 cup ¼-inch diagonally sliced	2 medium stalks
	1 cup thin sliced	1¾ medium stalks
Cheese, American or Cheddar, Swiss, etc.	1 cup shredded	4 ounces
cottage	2 cups	16 ounces
cream	6 tablespoons	3 ounces
	1 cup (16 tablespoons)	8 ounces
Cherries, sour	7 cups whole or 3½ cups pitted	1 quart or 1¾ pounds
sweet	2½ cups whole	1 pound

Continued on next page.

Food	If Your Recipe States	You Will Need Approximately
Chicken	3-4 cups cooked pieces	3 pound fryer
Chocolate, chips	1 cup	6 ounces
unsweetened	8 squares (1 ounce each)	8 ounces
unsweetened	1 ounce	3 Tbsp. cocoa plus 1 Tbsp. butter
semi-sweet	2 (1 ounce) squares	⅓ cup semi-sweet chips
semi-sweet	5 (1 ounce) squares	3 (1 ounce) squares unsweetened plus ¼ cup sugar
grated	¼ cup	1 ounce square
Coconut	1⅓ cups shredded	4 ounces
	1⅓ cups flaked	4 ounces
Coffee, ground	80 tablespoons or 5 cups	1 pound
Corn	1 cup kernels	2 medium ears
Cornmeal	3 cups uncooked or 12 cups cooked	1 pound
Crab	¾ to 1 cup flaked	1 pound raw (in shells)
Crackers, round butter	125	1 pound
Cranberries	4 cups uncooked or 3 cups cooked	1 pound fresh
Cream, dairy sour	1 cup	8 ounces
	1 cup	1 Tbsp. lemon juice plus evaporated milk to make 1 cup
whipping	1 cup (2 cups whipped)	½ pint
Crumbs, chocolate wafer	1 cup finely crushed	19
graham cracker	1¼ cups finely crushed	16 squares
saltine cracker	1 cup finely crushed	28
vanilla wafer	1 cup finely crushed	22
Cucumber	1 cup chopped	¾ medium
Dates	2½ cups pitted	1 pound pitted dates
Eggs, whites	1 cup	8 to 10
whole	1 cup	4 to 6
	1 egg	2 yolks plus 1 Tbsp. water (for thickening sauces and custards) OR 2 yolks only (for baking)
yolks	1 cup	12 to 14
Eggplant	4 cups diced	1 pound
Escarole	10 cups bite-size pieces	1 medium head
Flour, all purpose	3½ cups	1 pound
all-purpose (for thickening)	2 Tbsp.	1 Tbsp. cornstarch, potato starch, rice starch or arrowroot, OR 4 tsp. quick cooking tapioca
cake	1 cup	1 cup minus 2 Tbsp. all-purpose
Garlic	1 clove	⅛ tsp. garlic powder
Gelatin, unflavored	1 Tbsp.	¼-ounce envelope
sweetened with sugar	⅓ cup	3-ounce package
Ginger	1 Tbsp. grated raw	⅛ tsp. ground dry spice
Grapefruit	1 cup fresh juice	1 (20 ounce) fresh grapefruit
Grapes	2 cups	1 pound
Green pepper	1 cup chopped	1 medium
Ham	3 cups ground	1 pound boneless
Herbs	1 Tbsp. fresh	1 tsp. dried leaves or ½ tsp. ground

Continued on next page.

Food	If Your Recipe States	You Will Need Approximately
Honey	1 cup	12 ounces
Horseradish	1 Tbsp. fresh grated	2 Tbsp. bottled
Lemon, juice	2 to 3 tablespoons	1 medium lemon
peel	1½ to 3 teaspoons grated	1 medium lemon
Lentils	2¼ cups uncooked or 5 cups cooked	1 pound
Lettuce	6 cups bite-size pieces	1 pound head
Macaroni	4 cups cooked	2 cups uncooked
Marshmallow creme	7 ounces	2 cups
	1 cup	16 large marshmallows
Marshmallows	10 miniature	1 large
	1 cup	11 large or 110 miniature
Melon, canteloupe or honeydew	3-4 cups	3 pound melon
watermelon	16 cups	18 pound melon
Milk, evaporated	1½ cups	12 ounces
whole	1 cup	1 c. skim plus 2 tsp. butter (for cooking)
skim	1 cup	⅓ cup nonfat dry milk plus about ¾ cup water
Molasses	1 cup	12 ounces
Mushrooms	3 c. ¼-inch slices or 1 c. cooked slices or 6 ounce can	8 ounces fresh
	3 ounces dried	1 pound fresh
Mustard	1 Tbsp. prepared	1 tsp. dry
Noodles, egg	4 to 5 cups cooked	4 to 5 cups uncooked (8 ounces)
Nuts (without shells), almonds	3½ cups	1 pound
peanuts	3 cups	1 pound
pecans	4 cups	1 pound
walnuts	4 cups	1 pound
nuts in shell	½ pound nutmeats	1 pound in shell
Oats, quick-cooking	1¾ cups cooked	1 cup uncooked
Olives, pimiento-stuffed	1 cup sliced	15 large or 36 small
ripe	1 cup sliced	48 medium
Onions, green	1 cup sliced	9 (with tops)
white	½ cup chopped	1 medium
Orange, juice	⅓ to ½ cup	1 medium orange
peel	1 to 2 tablespoons grated	1 medium orange
Parsley	½ cup chopped	1 bunch
Peaches	2 cups sliced or diced	1 pound or 4 medium
Pears	2 cups sliced or diced	1 pound or 4 medium
Peas, dried split	2 cups uncooked or 5 cups cooked	1 pound
fresh	1 cup cooked	1 pound pea pods
Pineapple	3½ cups diced	2½ pound pineapple
Potatoes	1 cup ½-inch pieces	1 medium
	1 cup ¼-inch pieces	1 medium
	1 cup grated	1 medium
	3 medium	1 pound
	2 cups cooked, mashed	1 pound uncooked

Continued on next page.

Food	If Your Recipe States	You Will Need Approximately
Prunes	2 cups dried (about 50)	1 pound
Radishes	1 cup sliced	12
Raisins	3 cups	1 pound
Raspberries	2½ cups	1 pint
Rhubarb	2 cups cooked	1 pound uncooked
Rice, converted		
(parboiled)	3 to 4 cups cooked	1 cup uncooked
precooked (instant)	3 cups cooked	1½ cups uncooked
regular (white)	3 cups cooked	1 cup uncooked
	2 cups uncooked or 6 cups cooked	1 pound uncooked
wild	3 cups cooked	1 cup uncooked
Shortening	2 cups	1 pound
	1 cup	⅞ cup lard or oil plus ½ tsp. salt OR 1⅛ cup butter or margarine
Shrimp	2 cups (¾ pound) cooked	1½ pounds raw (in shells)
Spaghetti	4 cups cooked	7 to 8 ounces uncooked
Strawberries	4 cups sliced	1 quart
Sugar, brown	2¼ cups (firmly packed)	1 pound
granulated	2 cups	1 pound
	1 cup	1 cup honey plus a pinch of baking soda OR 1 cup Karo syrup (reduce liquid in recipe by ¼ cup for either)
powdered	4 cups	1 pound
Tomato juice	1 cup	½ cup tomato sauce plus ½ cup water
Tomato sauce	2 cups	¾ cup tomato paste plus 1 cup water
Tomatoes	1 cup chopped	1 medium tomato
Turkey	6 pounds boneless, cooked meat	12 pound whole turkey
	1 cup cooked	1 pound whole turkey
Yeast	⅗ oz. compressed cake yeast	1 pkg. active dry or 1 Tbsp. active dry
Zucchini	2 cups sliced	1 medium

The yields, equivalents and substitutions listed on this chart are approximations. Not all substitutions may be made with successful results. If in doubt, call the Barlow Home Economists.

COMMON CAN SIZES

No. 1 (Picnic)	=	10½ to 12 oz. or 1¼ cups
No. 300	=	14 to 16 oz. or 1¾ cups
No. 303	=	16 to 17 oz. or 2 cups
No. 2	=	20 oz. or 2½ cups
No. 2½	=	29 oz. or 3½ cups
No. 3	=	46 oz. or 5¾ cups
No. 10	=	6½ to 7 lb., 5 oz. or 12 to 13 cups It also equals 7 No. 303 cans or 5 No. 2 cans

Helen Clark, Jackie Novak, Grand Forks N.D.

CHEESE GUIDE

Cheese	How it looks and tastes	How to serve
American, Cheddar	Favorite all-around cheeses. Flavor varies from mild to sharp. Color ranges from natural to yellow-orange; texture firm to crumbly.	In sandwiches, casseroles, souffles, and creamy sauces. With fruit pie or crisp crackers; on a snack or dessert tray with fruit.
Blue, Gorgonzola, Roquefort	Compact, creamy cheeses veined with blue or blue-green mold. Sometimes crumbly. Mild to sharp salty flavor. (Stilton is similar, but like a blue-veined Cheddar.)	Crumble in salads, salad dressings, dips. Delicious with fresh pears or apples for dessert. Blend with butter for steak topper. Spread on crackers or crusty French or Italian bread.
Brick	Medium firm; creamy yellow color, tiny holes. Flavor very mild to medium sharp.	Good for appetizers, sandwiches, or desserts. Great with fresh peaches, cherries, or melons.
Brie *(bree)*	Similar to Camembert, but slightly firmer. Distinctive sharp flavor, pronounced odor.	Serve as dessert with fresh fruit. Be sure to eat the thin brown and white crust.
Camembert *(kam' em bear)*	Creamy yellow with thin gray-white crust. When ripe, it softens to the consistency of thick cream. Full, rich, mildly pungent.	Classic dessert cheese— serve at room temperature with fresh peaches, pears, or apples, or with toasted walnuts and crackers.
Cottage	Soft, mild, unripened cheese; large or small curd. May have cream added.	Used in salads, dips, main dishes. Popular with fresh and canned fruits.
Cream	Very mild-flavored soft cheese with buttery texture. Rich and smooth. Available whipped and in flavored spreads.	Adds richness and body to molded and frozen salads, cheesecake, dips, frostings, sandwich spreads. Serve whipped with dessert.
Edam, Gouda	Round, red-coated cheeses; creamy yellow to yellow-orange inside; firm and smooth. Mild nutlike flavor.	Bright hub for dessert or snack tray. Good in sandwiches or crunchy salads, or with crackers. Great with grapes and oranges.
Liederkranz, Limburger	Robust flavor and highly aromatic. Soft and smooth when ripe. Liederkranz is milder in flavor and golden yellow in color. Limburger is creamy white.	Spread on pumpernickel, rye, or crackers. Team with apples, pears, and Tokay grapes. Serve as snack with salty pretzels and coffee.

Cheese	How it looks and tastes	How to serve
Mozzarella, Scamorze	Unripened. Mild-flavored and slightly frim. Creamy white to pale yellow.	Cooking cheese. A "must" for pizza, lasagne; good in toasted sandwiches, hot snacks.
Muenster (mun' stir)	Between Brick and Limburger. Mild to mellow flavor, creamy white. Medium hard, tiny holes.	Use in sandwiches or on snack or dessert tray. Good with fresh sweet cherries and melon wedges.
Parmesan, Romano	Sharp, piquant, very hard cheese. Come in shakers grated. (Parmesan is also available shredded.) Or grate your own.	Sprinkle on pizza, main dishes, breads, salads, soups. Shake over buttered popcorn!
Port du Salut (por du sa lu')	Semisoft, smooth, and buttery. Mellow to robust flavor between Cheddar and Limburger.	Dessert cheese—delicious with fresh fruit; great with apple pie. Good for snack tray.
Provolone (pro vo lo' nee)	Usually smoked; mild to sharp flavor. Hard, compact and flaky. Pear or sausage shaped.	Use in Italian dishes, in sandwiches, on snack and appetizer trays.
Swiss	Firm pale yellow cheese, with large round holes. Sweet nutlike flavor.	First choice for ham-cheese sandwiches, fondue. Good in salads, sauces, as a snack.
Process cheeses	A blend of fresh and aged natural cheeses, pasteurized and packaged. Smooth and creamy, melts easily. May be flavored.	Ideal for cheese sauces, souffles, grilled cheese sandwiches, in casseroles. Handy for the snack tray, too.

Measure of Food Per Purchasing Unit

Food	Purchasing Unit	Measure in Unit
Almonds (shelled)	1 lb.	about 2½ cups
Almonds (unshelled)	1 lb.	about ½ lb. meats
Apples (fresh)	1 lb.	about 2-3
Apricots (fresh)	1 lb.	about 5-6
Bacon	1 lb.	about 28-30 slices
Bananas	1 lb.	about 3 bananas
Beans (dried)	1 lb.	about 2 cups double or triple in bulk when cooked
Beans, lima (dried)	1 lb.	about 2½ cups double or triple in bulk when cooked
Bread	1½ lb. loaf	about 22 slices
Bread (sandwich)	1 loaf	about 30-35 slices
Butter	1 lb.	2 cups
Carrots	1 lb.	about 3-5 carrots
Cheese (cottage)	1 lb.	2 cups
Cheese (American)	1 lb.	4 cups grated
Chocolate	1 lb.	16 squares
Cocoa	1 lb.	4 cups (4 Tbsp. cocoa = 1 sq. chocolate)
Coconut	1 lb.	6 cups
Coffee	1 lb.	5½ cups
Cornmeal	1 lb.	3 cups
Cornstarch	1 lb.	3 cups
Crackers	1 lb.	about 38-40 crackers
Crackers (saltines)	1 lb.	about 125 crackers
Cranberries	1 lb.	4 cups
Dates	7½ oz. pkg.	about 35 dates
Egg whites	. . . .	8 to a cup
		1 egg white equals 2 Tbsp.
Egg yolks	. . . .	10-12 to a cup
		1 egg yolk equals 1 Tbsp.
Eggs, whole	. . . .	4-6 eggs to a cup
Marshmallows	1 lb.	80-90
Oats (rolled)	1 lb.	4 cups
Oils	1 lb.	2 cups
Onions	1 lb.	4-6 onions
Orange (one)	. . . .	⅓-½ cups juice
Parsnips	1 lb.	3-5 parsnips
Peaches	1 lb.	3-5 peaches
Peanuts (shelled)	1 lb.	2¾ cups
Pears	1 lb.	3-4 pears
Peas (in the pod)	1 lb.	2-3 servings
Pecans (shelled)	1 lb.	3-4 cups
Potatoes (Irish)	1 lb.	2-4 potatoes
Potatoes (sweet)	1 lb.	2-3 potatoes
Prunes (average size)	1 lb.	40-60

Continued on next page.

Raisins	1 lb.	2¾ cups
Rice	1 lb.	2 cups
Shortening	1 lb.	2⅓ cups
Spinach	1 lb.	3-4 servings
Sugar (granulated)	1 lb.	2 cups
Sugar (brown)	1 lb.	2⅔ cups
Sugar (powdered)	1 lb.	3½ cups
Tea	1 lb.	6½ cups
Tomatoes	1 lb.	2-5 tomatoes
Walnuts (shelled)	1 lb.	3 cups (broken pieces)
Walnuts (soft shell)	1 lb.	1½ cups meats
Squash	1 lb.	1 cup mashed
Cabbage (shredded)	1 lb.	3 cups
Cabbage (cooked)	1 lb.	2 cups
Cheese (grated)	1 lb.	2-4 cups (more if very dry)
Cranberries (sauce)	1 lb.	3 plus cups
Lemons (juice)	1 dozen	2 plus cups
		1 egg equals 3 Tbsp.
Evaporated milk	1 tall can	1⅔ cups
Flour (white)	1 lb.	4 cups
Flour (whole wheat)	1 lb.	4½ cups
Lard	1 lb.	2 cups
Lemons	1 lb.	3-5 lemons (1 lemon has about 3-4 Tbsp. juice)

THIS HANDY CHART MAKES SELECTING YOUR
STORAGE CONTAINERS TO FIT YOUR PURCHASE
QUANTITIES EASY!!!

Diane Rueb
Owatonna, MN

NEW DESIRABLE WEIGHTS

DESIRABLE WEIGHTS FOR MEN AND WOMEN

WEIGHTS FOR WOMEN

HEIGHT (with shoes on) 2-inch heels	SMALL FRAME	MEDIUM FRAME	LARGE FRAME
4' 10"	92-98	96-107	104-119
11"	94-101	98-110	106-122
5' 0"	96-104	101-113	109-125
1"	99-107	104-116	112-128
2"	102-110	107-119	115-131
3"	105-113	110-122	118-134
4"	108-116	113-126	121-138
5"	111-119	116-130	125-142
6"	114-123	120-135	129-146
7"	118-127	124-139	133-150
8"	122-131	128-143	137-154
9"	126-135	132-147	141-158
10"	130-140	136-151	145-163
11"	134-144	140-155	149-168
6' 0"	138-148	144-159	153-173

WEIGHTS FOR MEN

HEIGHT (with shoes on) 1-inch heels	SMALL FRAME	MEDIUM FRAME	LARGE FRAME
5' 2"	112-120	118-129	126-141
3"	115-123	121-133	129-144
4"	118-126	124-136	132-148
5"	121-129	127-139	135-152
6"	124-133	130-143	138-156
7"	128-137	134-147	142-161
8"	132-141	138-152	147-166
9"	136-145	142-156	151-170
10"	140-150	146-160	155-174
11"	144-154	150-165	159-179
6' 0"	148-158	154-170	164-184
1"	152-162	158-175	168-189
2"	156-167	162-180	173-194
3"	160-171	167-185	178-199
4"	164-175	172-190	182-204

Weight in Pounds According to Frame (In Indoor Clothing)

Continued on next page.

DAILY CALORIE NEEDS FOR WOMEN

HEIGHT	SMALL FRAME	MEDIUM FRAME	LARGE FRAME
4' 11"	1635	1725	1845
5' 0"	1665	1770	1890
5' 1"	1695	1800	1935
5' 2"	1740	1845	1995
5' 3"	1785	1875	2040
5' 4"	1845	1950	2100
5' 5"	1890	1995	2145
5' 6"	1950	2040	2220
5' 7"	2010	2130	2280
5' 8"	2055	2175	2340
5' 9"	2115	2235	2400
5' 10"	2175	2295	2460
5' 11"	2220	2340	2505
6' 0"	2265	2415	2580

DAILY CALORIE NEEDS FOR MEN

HEIGHT	SMALL FRAME	MEDIUM FRAME	LARGE FRAME
5' 2"	1845	1965	2085
5' 3"	1890	2010	2130
5' 4"	1950	2070	2205
5' 5"	2010	2130	2265
5' 6"	2045	2175	2325
5' 7"	2115	2235	2400
5' 8"	2175	2310	2460
5' 9"	2235	2370	2520
5' 10"	2295	2430	2595
5' 11"	2355	2490	2670
6' 0"	2430	2565	2745
6' 1"	2505	2640	2820
6' 2"	2595	2730	2910
6' 3"	2670	2805	3000

These charts based on the average calorie needs for individuals of specific height and frame. Your individual calorie needs may fluctuate 10% below these averages depending on your metabolism and activity (or inactivity).

It takes a loss of 3500 calories to lose one pound. If you eat 500 calories less a day than your body requires, you should lose a pound every seven days. The reverse also applies for gaining one pound. Adding 3500 calories over caloric needs will add one pound of weight.

THE TWENTY-THIRD POUND

My appetite is my shepherd
    I shall not want
It makes me to sit down and stuff myself
    It leadeth me to my refrigerator repeatedly
It leadeth me in the path of Burger King for a Whopper
    It destroyeth my shape
Yea, though I knoweth I gaineth, I will not stop eating
    For the Food tasteth so good
The ice cream and cookies, they comfort me
    When the table is spread before me, it exciteth me,
    for I knoweth that soon I shall dig in.
As I fillith my plate continuously, my clothes runneth smaller
    Surely bulges and excess weight shall follow me
    all the days of my life and -
I will be fat forever.

Notes

Notes

Notes

Notes

Heart Health

CALORIES OF COMMON SNACK FOODS

Foods	Calories	Foods	Calories
Cheest twists, 1 oz.	153	M & M's, 1 pkg.	172
Cheese crackers with		Oatmeal cookie	63
peanut butter, 1	34	Oreo cookie	48
Chocolate chip cookie, 1	57	Peanuts, 1 Tbsp.	85
Corn chips, 1 oz.	154	Peanut butter cookie	57
Doughnut (sugar)	144	Pizza, a slice	150
French fries, 1 serving	151	Popcorn, popped, 1 cup	54
Frozen yogurt, ½ cup	211	Popsicle	65
Granola bar, 1	108	Potato chips, 10	113
Graham crackers, 2 squares	210	Pretzel, 3 ring	11
Hard candy, 6 pieces	54	Raisinets	119
Hershey bar	108	Ritz crackers, 3	54
Hershey kisses, 6	302	Snickers bar	159
Hostess twinkie	154	Soft serve ice cream, ½ cup	164
Jelly beans, 10 pieces	152	Vanilla ice cream, ½ cup	145
Life savers, 5 pieces	66	Vanilla Shake	324

Here are the lowest calorie selections at some of the popular fast food restaurants:

* ARBY's: junior roast beef (250); turkey without dressing (323).

* BURGER KING: hamburger (290); Whopper Junior (370).

* KENTUCKY FRIED chicken: breast with rib (241); thigh (276); coleslaw (122); cheeseburger (300).

* McDONALDS: chicken McNuggets (290); cheeseburger (300).

* PIZZA HUT: ½ pepperoni (430) or beef (490) pizza.

* WENDY's: chili (250); one burger (440).

* TACO BELL: regular tostada (206); Bell-burger (243); Pinto's, no cheese (231).

HEART HEALTH

MAIN DISHES

MINIATURE MEATBALLS

These flavorful meatballs taste even better when made a day ahead and reheated before serving.

2 Tbsp. soy sauce　　　　　　**½ tsp. ginger**
¼ c. water　　　　　　　　　　**1 lb. lean ground beef**
½ clove garlic, minced

In a large bowl, combine soy sauce, water, minced garlic, and ginger. Add ground beef and mix lightly, but thoroughly. Form into balls about 1 inch in diameter.

Arrange on a lightly oiled baking dish. Bake in a 450°F. oven, uncovered, for 15 minutes. Spear with toothpicks and serve from a hot chafing dish. Yield: About 32 meatballs. Approximate calories per serving: 1 meatball equals 30.

LEMON PEPPER MUSHROOMS

8 large mushrooms　　　　　　**1 Tbsp. mayonnaise**
1 Tbsp. chopped chives　　　　**1 Tbsp. oil**
2 Tbsp. lemon juice　　　　　　**1½ tsp. lemon pepper**

Select large firm mushrooms and wipe with a damp cloth. Remove stems; discard lower half and chop upper half of the stems very fine. In a bowl, combine with the remaining ingredients.

Stuff mushrooms with the mixture. Bake in a shallow pan for 8 to 10 minutes at 450°F. Serve immediately. Yield: 8 servings. Approximate calories per serving: 35.

WONDERFUL MUSHROOMS

1 lb. mushrooms　　　　　　　**¼ c. water or white wine**
1 clove garlic, sliced thin　　　**Freshly ground black pepper**

Wipe mushrooms clean; leave whole but remove stems (which you can use for soup). Lightly oil the bottom of a pan or skillet. Put garlic in bottom of pan. Add mushrooms, water, and pepper. Cover pan. Stir frequently, cooking about 5 minutes. Yield: 4 servings. Approximate calories per serving: 30.

This may be served as a vegetable or used as a sauce on meat, poultry, fish, or baked potatoes. To further enhance the flavor, add about 1 teaspoon of Parmesan cheese to your potato before you spoon on the mushrooms.

WILD RICE WITH MUSHROOMS

1 c. wild rice or long grained rice
   and wild rice combined
⅓ c. green onions or shallots
1 c. fresh mushrooms

Freshly ground black pepper
2 Tbsp. oil
1 Tbsp. margarine

Steam the rice or cook according to directions on the package. Saute fresh mushrooms and green onions in the oil. Stir in margarine and freshly ground pepper. Serve hot. Yield: 6 servings. Approximate calories per serving: 190.

PIZZA SANDWICHES

Sauce:

2 Tbsp. oil
½ c. chopped onion
2½ Tbsp. chopped celery
2½ Tbsp. chopped green
   pepper
1 c. canned tomatoes

6 Tbsp. tomato paste
1 tsp. oregano
⅛ tsp. sweet basil
Freshly ground black pepper
¼ tsp. rosemary (optional)

Saute onion, celery, and pepper in vegetable oil until tender and translucent. Add tomatoes, tomato paste, and seasonings. Cook over low heat on stove top for approximately 30 minutes, stirring occasionally. Yield: Approximately 1½ cups sauce.

BARBECUE ON A BUN

1 lb. ground turkey
1 onion, chopped
1 Tbsp. prepared mustard
½ c. catsup
1 c. tomato sauce (8 oz.)

¼ tsp. ground cloves
1 Tbsp. vinegar
1 tsp. sugar
2 to 3 drops Tabasco sauce
Hamburger buns

Brown meat and onion; drain off fat. Add seasonings and simmer at least 15 minutes. Serve on hamburger buns.

Joanne Gulla, Virginia, MN

HOMEMADE SAUSAGE

1 lb. very lean ground beef
1 tsp. ground sage
½ tsp. dried thyme
½ tsp. garlic powder

1 tsp. black pepper
1 tsp. liquid smoke
½ tsp. crushed red pepper

1. Mix all ingredients together thoroughly; shape into patties.
2. Broil or pan-fry. If pan-frying, pour off fat as it collects.
3. Drain patties on paper towels. Yields 6 servings.

PIZZA

Dough:

1 pkg. active dry yeast
1⅔ c. lukewarm water (95°F. to
 105°F.)

3 Tbsp. oil
4 c. flour

Tomato Sauce:

1 c. finely chopped onion
3 Tbsp. oil
2 cloves garlic, minced
2 (16 oz.) cans low-sodium
 tomatoes (undrained),
 chopped

1 (6 oz.) can low-sodium tomato
 paste
4 tsp. dried oregano
2 tsp. dried sweet basil
2 bay leaves

Sauce (prepare while dough is rising).

1. Saute onion in oil until soft and tender. Add garlic and cook for 2 minutes more. Add remaining ingredients and simmer, uncovered, for 60 minutes, stirring occasionally.

2. Remove bay leaf. If a smoother sauce is desired, puree or put mixture through a sieve.

Topping:

8 oz. low-sodium lowfat cheese
½ c. chopped green onion
¼ lb. fresh mushrooms,
 chopped
1 c. chopped green pepper

1 lb. very lean ground beef or
 low-sodium Homemade
 Sausage (see recipe in
 book), browned and drained

1. Discard yeast in lukewarm water in a bowl. Add oil and stir in flour. Turn onto lightly floured board and knead until smooth. Place dough in an oiled bowl, turning once to coat the surface.

2. Let rise until double in bulk, about 90 minutes. At this point, dough can be punched down, refrigerated for a day or 2, or frozen for future use.

3. Punch down and knead again for a few minutes.

4. Divide dough in half and pat into 2 oiled round 14 inch pizza pans.

5. Add Tomato Sauce and topping ingredients.

6. Bake in a preheated 400°F. oven for 20 to 25 minutes. Yield: 2 pizzas (8 servings each).

RICOTTA LASAGNA SWIRLS

Filling:

1 pkg. fresh spinach	¼ tsp. nutmeg
2 Tbsp. Parmesan cheese	Freshly ground black pepper
1 c. Ricotta cheese (made from partially skimmed milk)	

Cook 8 lasagna noodles. Wash spinach thoroughly; chop finely and put in a pan with a tight fitting lid. Cook over low heat for 7 minutes. Drain and squeeze out excess juice. Mix spinach with cheeses, nutmeg, and pepper.

Spread mixture evenly along entire length of each noodle; roll each one and place on its side, not touching, in an oiled 8x8 inch shallow baking dish.

Sauce:

2 c. tomato sauce	1 Tbsp. oil
2 cloves garlic, minced	½ tsp. basil
½ c. onions, chopped	Freshly ground black pepper

To make sauce, saute garlic and onions in oil. Add tomato sauce, basil, and seasonings; simmer for 15 to 20 minutes. Cover lasagna swirls with the sauce. Bake in oven at 350°F. for 20 minutes.

MOCK SAUSAGE PATTIES

A good idea for those who like a meaty breakfast.

1 lb. lean beef, ground twice	¼ tsp. sage
1 Tbsp. lemon juice	¼ tsp. ginger
Rind of medium lemon, grated	½ c. beef broth
¼ c. fine dry bread crumbs	

Mix together beef, lemon juice and rind, bread crumbs, sage, ginger, and broth; let stand for 15 minutes. Form into 8 patties about ¾ inch thick. Brush a heavy skillet with oil and set over heat for 1 or 2 minutes. Put in the sausage patties and cook for 7 or 8 minutes on each side. Serve hot.

SOUTHERN MEAT LOAF

1½ lb. lean ground beef
1 medium onion, diced
5 slices bread
1 tsp. basil
1 Tbsp. parsley
2 Tbsp. grated Parmesan
　　cheese

½ tsp. garlic powder
Freshly ground black pepper
2 egg whites, slightly beaten
1 (1 lb.) can tomato sauce
1 Tbsp. prepared mustard

Combine the first 9 ingredients and ¼ cup of the tomato sauce; gently mold into a loaf. Pour the tomato sauce into a bowl and, using the can as a measure, add the same amount of water. Mix in the prepared mustard. Pour sauce over loaf and bake at 350°F. for 1 hour. Yield: 6 servings. Approximate calories per serving: 350.

BURGUNDY BEEF

1 lb. lean round steak, well
　　trimmed and sliced into ¼
　　inch strips
½ tsp. garlic powder
½ tsp. pepper
½ tsp. paprika

2 Tbsp. oil
2 Tbsp. flour
¼ c. finely chopped onion
¾ c. water
¾ c. burgundy wine
½ c. sliced fresh mushrooms

1. Season steak strips with garlic powder, pepper, and paprika and brown in oil. Stir in flour.

2. Add remaining ingredients and cover; simmer until meat is tender, about 45 minutes. Yield: 4 servings.

STUFFED BEEF ROLL-UPS

¼ c. margarine
1 c. red wine
2 c. packaged herb stuffing mix
¼ c. minced onion
2 lb. lean round steak, cut ¼
　　inch thick

Freshly ground black pepper
2 Tbsp. flour
2 Tbsp. margarine or oil
1 (10½ oz.) can onion soup
　　(undiluted)

Melt the ¼ cup of margarine. Add wine. Mix lightly with the stuffing mix and onion. Cut the steak into 8 portions; season with pepper. Place a spoonful of stuffing on each steak piece; roll and secure with a string or a toothpick.

Coat each roll in flour and brown in the remaining margarine in a heavy skillet. Pour the soup over all; cover and simmer about 1½ hours or until tender. Yield: 8 servings. Approximate calories per serving: 430.

BRAISED SIRLOIN TIPS

2 lb. beef sirloin tip, cut into 1
   inch cubes
1 (10½ oz.) can beef consomme
⅓ c. red burgundy or cranberry
   cocktail
2 Tbsp. soy sauce

1 clove garlic, minced
¼ tsp. onion powder
2 Tbsp. cornstarch
¼ c. water
4 c. hot cooked rice

Brown meat on all sides in a large heavy skillet. Add consomme, wine (or cranberry cocktail), soy sauce, garlic, and onion powder; heat to boiling. Reduce heat, cover, and simmer for 1 hour or until meat is tender.

Blend cornstarch and water and stir gradually into the stew. Cook, stirring constantly, until gravy thickens and boils. Cook for 1 minute more. Serve over rice. Yield: 8 servings. Approximate calories per serving: 390.

BEEF BOURGUIGNON

5 medium onions, sliced
4 Tbsp. oil
2 lb. lean beef, cut into 1 inch
   cubes
1½ Tbsp. flour
¼ tsp. marjoram

¼ tsp. thyme
Freshly ground black pepper
½ c. beef broth
1 c. dry red wine
½ lb. fresh mushrooms, sliced

In a heavy skillet, cook the onions in oil until tender; remove them to another dish. In the same pan, saute the beef cubes until browned. Sprinkle with flour and seasonings. Add broth and wine. Stir well and simmer slowly for 1½ to 2 hours. Add more broth and wine (1 part stock to 2 parts wine) as necessary to keep beef barely covered.

Return onions to the stew. Add the mushrooms and cook, stirring, 30 minutes longer, adding more broth and wine if necessary. Sauce should be thick and dark brown. Yield: 8 servings. Approximate calories per serving: 375.

MODIFIED BEEF STROGANOFF

1 lb. lean beef
2 Tbsp. margarine
¾ Tbsp. finely chopped onion
1 lb. sliced mushrooms
Salt and pepper

Nutmeg
½ tsp. basil
¼ c. white wine
1 c. plain lowfat yogurt

Pound beef first with mallet until thin. Cut into 1 inch wide strips and then cut beef into ½ inch slices. Melt 1 tablespoon margarine in a nonstick skillet. Saute onion for 2 minutes. Add beef and saute for additional 5 minutes. Turn to brown evenly. Remove from pan and keep hot.

Add remaining margarine to pan; melt and then saute mushrooms. Add beef and onion to pan with seasonings. Add wine and yogurt; gently stir in. Heat, but do not boil. Serve with noodles. Yield: Serves 4. Nutrients per serving: Calories: 263. Protein: 30 grams. Total fat: 12 grams. Total CHO: 8 grams. Alcohol: 0 grams. Cholesterol: 76 milligrams.

Note: If thickening is desired, use 2 teaspoons cornstarch. Calories are the same as flour, but it has double thickening power.

Mary Jane Schmitz, Wadena, MN

MARINATED STEAK

1 thick flank steak or London
    broil (about 1½ lb.)
⅔ c. dry red wine
1 Tbsp. soy sauce

⅛ tsp. oregano, crumbled
⅛ tsp. marjoram, crumbled
Freshly ground black pepper

Mix together the wine, soy sauce, and seasonings. Place the steak in a long glass baking dish and pour the marinade over the meat. Cover and chill at least 12 to 18 hours, turning meat once or twice.

Preheat the broiler. Remove the steak from the marinade. Pat dry and broil 4 inches from the heat for about 5 minutes on each side. To serve, cut thin slices diagonally across the grain. Serve with rice. Yield: 6 servings. Approximate calories per serving: 270.

BEEF KABOBS

1 c. red wine
½ c. soy sauce
1 c. pineapple juice
1 tsp. thyme
1 tsp. rosemary
¼ c. Worcestershire sauce
1 onion, finely chopped
½ tsp. pepper
1½ lb. sirloin, cut into cubes
3 tomatoes, cut into eighths if
    large, or use whole cherry
    tomatoes

3 onions, cut in 1 inch wedges,
    or small whole boiling
    onions
12 whole mushrooms
1 small eggplant, peeled and
    chopped in 1 inch pieces
1 green pepper, cut in large
    cubes
12 small whole potatoes,
    cooked fresh or canned

Make a marinade by mixing the first 8 ingredients together. Pour over the meat. Let stand for 2 hours at room temperature or overnight in the refrigerator.

Alternate the beef on skewers with the vegetables. Broil 3 inches from the heat for about 15 minutes or grill over charcoal, turning frequently and basting with the marinade. Yield: 8 servings. Approximate calories per serving: 320.

MACARONI-BEEF SKILLET SUPPER

1 c. elbow macaroni
1 lb. lean ground beef
1 c. diced onions
1 clove garlic, mashed
2 Tbsp. oil
1 (8 oz.) can tomato sauce

Freshly ground black pepper
1 c. catsup
1 (8 oz.) can mushroom stems
   and pieces, drained
2 Tbsp. Worcestershire sauce
½ tsp. Italian seasoning

Cook the macaroni in boiling water according to package directions; drain and set aside. Saute the meat, onion, and garlic in oil until the meat loses its pink color and onions are tender. Add pepper, tomato sauce, catsup, mushrooms, Worcestershire sauce, and Italian seasoning.

Bring mixture to a boil, then simmer gently for about 5 minutes. Mix in the cooked macaroni and simmer for 5 more minutes. Yield: 8 servings. Approximate calories per serving: 270.

HUNGARIAN GOULASH

2 medium onions
2 cloves garlic, minced
2 Tbsp. oil
1½ lb. lean beef, well trimmed
   and cut into 1 inch cubes
⅓ c. chopped green pepper

1 potato, peeled and grated
¼ tsp. caraway seed
¼ tsp. crushed red pepper
⅛ tsp. pepper
1 low-sodium beef bouillon cube
¾ c. water

1. Saute onions and garlic in oil.
2. Add remaining ingredients and cover.
3. Simmer for 3 hours or until meat is tender. Add more water if needed. Yield: 6 servings.

ZUCCHINI CHEESE CASSEROLE

3 medium zucchini squash
½ c. chopped onion
2 fresh tomatoes, sliced
2 Tbsp. oil

1 lb. lowfat cottage cheese
1 tsp. basil
½ tsp. oregano
⅓ c. Parmesan cheese

Saute zucchini and chopped onion in oil. Whip cottage cheese with basil and oregano in blender. Place alternating layers of zucchini, cottage cheese, and tomato in a 1½ quart casserole dish. Top with Parmesan cheese. Bake at 350°F., uncovered, for 25 to 30 minutes. Yield: 6 servings. Approximate calories per serving: 130.

LAZY BEEF CASSEROLE

A delicious gravy forms during the cooking of this very easy and tender beef dish.

1 lb. lean beef chuck, cut into 1½ inch cubes	¼ tsp. rosemary
½ c. red wine	Freshly ground black pepper
1 (10½ oz.) can consomme (undiluted)	1 medium onion, chopped
	¼ c. fine dry bread crumbs
	¼ c. all-purpose flour

Put meat in a casserole with the wine, consomme, pepper, rosemary, and onion. Mix flour and bread crumbs and stir into the liquid. Cover and bake at 300°F. for about 3 hours. (A lower temperature and longer cooking time may be used if it is more convenient.) Serve with rice or noodles. Yield: 4 servings. Approximate calories per serving: 350 (or 450 with ½ cup rice or pasta).

SUKIYAKI

2 lb. tenderloin or sirloin steak	4 c. fresh spinach leaves, washed and well drained, or shredded Chinese cabbage
3 Tbsp. oil	
½ c. soy sauce	
½ c. beef stock or canned beef broth	1 (5 oz.) can water chestnuts, drained and thinly sliced
1 Tbsp. honey	1 (5 oz.) can bamboo shoots, drained and slivered
1 c. green onion, cut diagonally into ½ inch lengths	1 (16 oz.) can bean sprouts, drained and rinsed in cold water, or 1 lb. fresh bean sprouts
1 c. celery, cut diagonally into 1 inch lengths	
1 c. thinly sliced mushrooms	

For best results, partially freeze the steak before slicing. Remove excess fat. Lay the steak on a board. Using a sharp knife, thinly slice the meat across the grain, diagonally from top to bottom.

Just before cooking, arrange the sliced steak and vegetables neatly on a large platter or tray for easy handling. Heat a large (12 inch) electric fry pan to 400°F. Heat the oil in the pan and quickly saute steak strips, a few at a time, until browned on both sides (about 2 minutes).

Combine the beef stock, soy sauce, and honey; pour over the cooked steak strips. Push the meat to one side of the pan; allow the sauce to begin bubbling and, keeping each vegetable group separate, add the onion, celery, and mushrooms. Cook, tossing over high heat, about 2 minutes. Push each aside as it is cooked.

Again keeping in separate groups, add the spinach or Chinese cabbage, separately, then the sliced water chestnuts, bamboo shoots, and drained bean sprouts, keeping each group apart from the others. Cook and toss, stirring each food until just heated through. Season with pepper.

Serve immediately with rice, accompanied by soy sauce. If more gravy is desired, add an additional ½ cup of broth to the pan before serving. Yield: 10 servings. Approximate calories per serving: 280 (or 380 with ½ cup rice).

CHINESE FLANK STEAK

1 lb. lean flank steak
¼ c. soy sauce
¼ c. cooking sherry
3 slices fresh ginger (the size of
   a nickel)
1 Tbsp. cornstarch
¼ c. oil
1 (6 oz.) pkg. frozen pea pods, or
   10 oz. pkg. frozen Italian

green beans or broccoli
   spears, thawed and drained
¼ to ½ lb. fresh mushrooms,
   sliced
¼ c. chopped green onions
8 water chestnuts, thinly sliced

Slice flank steak across the grain into thin strips, 2 to 3 inches long, ½ to 1 inch wide, and ½ to 1 inch thick. Mix soy sauce, sherry, ginger, and cornstarch; add meat and marinate the mixture for at least 30 minutes at room temperature or 2 hours in the refrigerator. Remove ginger.

When ready to cook, heat skillet with about 1½ tablespoons oil until very hot. Add pea pods or green beans or broccoli and stir rapidly until lightly browned and crisp tender; remove from skillet. Add another tablespoon oil and brown mushrooms (more oil may be needed). Remove from skillet.

Add remaining 1½ tablespoons oil; heat and add green onions, meat, and all of the marinade. Stir rapidly until all of the meat is browned on all sides. Add all other ingredients, including water chestnuts, and stir until heated through. Yield: 4 servings. Approximate calories per serving: 365.

CHINESE BEEF SKILLET

1 (7 oz.) pkg. frozen Chinese pea pods
3 Tbsp. oil
1 lb. flank steak or lean chuck, sliced paper thin across the grain
¼ c. chopped onion
1 small clove garlic, minced
4 c. thinly sliced raw cauliflower flowerets (1 medium head)
1 c. beef broth
2 Tbsp. cornstarch
¼ c. soy sauce
½ c. cold water

Pour boiling water over frozen pea pods and carefully separate them with a fork; drain immediately. Heat electric skillet to about 400°F. Heat 2 tablespoons of the oil; add ½ the beef. Cook briskly, turning meat constantly, for 1 or 2 minutes or until just browned. Remove meat at once.

Let skillet heat about 1 minute and repeat with remaining beef; remove beef. Cook onion and garlic a few seconds in remaining oil. Add cauliflower and broth. Cook, stirring gently, for about 3 minutes until cauliflower is tender crisp.

Mix cornstarch, soy sauce, and water; stir into the broth in the skillet. Add beef and pea pods. Cook, stirring constantly, until the sauce thickens. Serve with rice. Yield: 6 servings, about 1½ quarts. Approximate calories per serving: 285.

CHICKEN TERIYAKI WITH VEGETABLES

2 medium zucchini, sliced
16 cherry tomatoes
16 fresh mushrooms
1 onion, sliced
1½ lb. chicken breasts, boned, split, skinned, and sliced lengthwise
16 wooden or metal skewers

Marinade:

½ c. soy sauce
5 Tbsp. brown sugar, packed
1¼ Tbsp. corn oil
½ tsp. dry ginger
2 Tbsp. sherry

Marinate vegetables and sliced chicken in the refrigerator for 1 hour in a covered container, turning occasionally. Skewer chicken and vegetables on a separate skewer. Broil for 3 minutes on each side. Yield: 8 servings. Approximate calories per serving: 200.

CHINESE CHICKEN WITH PEPPERS AND ONIONS

3 chicken breasts, split and
   skinned
3 medium green or red sweet
   peppers
2 medium onions
5 to 6 Tbsp. soy sauce

6 Tbsp. corn oil
3 pieces fresh ginger (the size of
   a nickel)
3 small hot red peppers or ⅛
   tsp. cayenne
1 tsp. sesame oil

Cut chicken breasts into ½ inch squares. Clean peppers, cut into 1 inch chunks. Slice the onions into quarters and slice those very thinly.

In a wok or a large frying pan, heat 3 tablespoons of corn oil until it begins to smoke. Add the ginger, hot peppers, and chicken to smoking oil. Stir until chicken is thoroughly cooked, about 3 minutes. Remove to a serving dish.

Add 3 more tablespoons of corn oil; heat. Add the onions and peppers; stir-fry till onions become slightly transparent. Return chicken; add soy sauce. Stir for 1 minute. Sprinkle with sesame oil. Serve with rice. Yield: 6 servings. Approximate calories per serving: 200 (or 300 with ½ cup rice).

TURKEY CHOP SUEY

½ c. sliced onions
2 Tbsp. margarine
2 c. diced cooked turkey
1½ c. sliced celery
1 (5 oz.) can water chestnuts,
   drained and sliced
½ c. chicken broth

1 can bean sprouts (don't drain)
2 Tbsp. cornstarch
¼ tsp. salt
¼ c. chicken broth
2 Tbsp. soy sauce
1 small can mushrooms, drained
4 c. cooked rice

Cook onions and celery in margarine over low heat until tender. Add turkey, water chestnuts, broth, and liquid from bean sprouts. Bring to boil. Combine cornstarch, broth, soy sauce, and salt. Add to mixture to cook until thickened, *stirring constantly.* Simmer a few minutes. Add bean sprouts and mushrooms; heat a few more minutes. Serve over hot rice.

Clayone Carlson, Fargo, ND

CRISPY BAKED CHICKEN

1 chicken, cut up
1 c. skim milk
1 c. corn flake crumbs

1 tsp. rosemary
Pepper

Remove all skin and dry pieces. Dip in milk; mix rest of ingredients together and roll in crumbs. Let stand briefly so coating will adhere. Place chicken in foil lined baking dish. Bake at 400° for 45 minutes or more.

Carol Gilbertson, Hawley, MN

CHICKEN MANDARIN

1 (2½ to 3 lb.) frying chicken, cut into serving pieces	½ c. orange juice
¼ c. flour	2 Tbsp. honey
2 Tbsp. margarine	½ Tbsp. soy sauce
2 Tbsp. oil	½ tsp. powdered ginger
4 Tbsp. lemon juice	1 (11 oz.) can mandarin oranges with juice

Wash and dry chicken pieces. Shake in a paper bag with flour to coat. In a skillet, heat oil and margarine. Add chicken and brown each piece. Drain mandarin oranges and set aside. Mix juice from the can with lemon juice, orange juice, honey, soy sauce, and ginger. Pour sauce over the chicken in skillet. Cover and simmer for 30 minutes or until tender. Add mandarin orange sections 5 or 10 minutes before chicken is done. Serve with rice. Yield: 4 servings. Approximate calories per serving: 360 (460 with ½ cup rice).

CHICKEN GUMBO

2 c. chopped cooked chicken	1 fresh jalapeno pepper, seeded
2 Tbsp. oil	½ c. chopped fresh parsley
1 (16 oz.) can low-sodium tomatoes (undrained)	½ tsp. pepper
1 (10 oz.) pkg. frozen okra	1 bay leaf
½ c. low-sodium chicken bouillon	2 cloves garlic, minced
1 c. sliced onion	¼ tsp. dried thyme
	1 c. water
	½ c. rice (uncooked)

1. Brown chicken in oil in large saucepan.
2. Add all ingredients, except rice.
3. Cover and simmer for 10 minutes.
4. Add rice and cook for 25 minutes more until rice is tender, stirring occasionally. Yield: 6 servings.

CHICKEN BREAST CASSEROLE
(Serves 6 to 8)

8 chicken breasts (skin removed)	1 can cream of chicken soup
1 pkg. dry Lipton onion soup mix	1 c. white wine
	½ c. milk

Lay chicken breasts in a Pyrex cake pan and pour dry Lipton onion soup mix over it. Mix cream of chicken soup, white wine, and milk. Pour over chicken and soup; cover and bake at 350° for 1½ to 2 hours. Serve over rice or potatoes.

Joyce McCann, St. Cloud, MN

CHICKEN JAMBALAYA

3 chicken breasts, split and
  skinned
½ c. chopped onion
¼ c. chopped green pepper
1 c. chicken broth
1 c. white wine
¼ c. chopped parsley

½ tsp. basil
1 small bay leaf
½ tsp. thyme
1 c. raw rice
½ c. lean ham, cubed
1 c. canned tomatoes, drained

In a saucepan, bring to a boil the broth, wine, herbs, onion, and green pepper. Place rice, ham, tomatoes, and chicken in a large casserole; pour herb sauce over all. Cover tightly and bake at 350°F. for 25 or 30 minutes. Add seasoning. Turn heat off; allow casserole to remain in the oven for 10 to 15 minutes. Yield: 6 servings. Approximate calories per serving: 350.

CHICKEN AND BROCCOLI WITH MUSHROOM SAUCE

1 (10 oz.) pkg. frozen broccoli
3 Tbsp. margarine
3 Tbsp. flour
1 c. chicken broth
1 (4 oz.) can mushroom slices
  with liquid

1 lb. cooked chicken, sliced (or 2
  c. cooked chicken or turkey)
2 Tbsp. chopped parsley
2 Tbsp. bread crumbs

Cook broccoli according to package directions. Mix margarine and flour together in saucepan. Cook briefly over medium heat. Blend in chicken broth, stirring constantly, until thickened and smooth. Stir in mushrooms and their liquid. Season to taste.

Place broccoli pieces in a shallow baking pan. Cover with sliced chicken and pour mushroom sauce over all. Top with parsley and bread crumbs. Bake at 375°F., uncovered, for 15 to 25 minutes or until bubbly and brown on top. Yield: 4 servings. Approximate calories per serving: 330.

CHICKEN WITH APRICOT GLAZE

1 (2½ to 3 lb.) frying chicken,
  cut into serving pieces
¼ c. flour
2 Tbsp. margarine
2 Tbsp. oil
½ c. apricot jam
1 tsp. marjoram

1 tsp. grated lemon rind
1 Tbsp. soy sauce
1 (16 oz.) can whole peeled
  apricots with juice (there
  should be about 1½ c. juice)
1 large green pepper, cut into ½
  inch sq.

Wash and dry chicken; coat with flour. In a large skillet, brown each piece in heated margarine and oil. After browning, coat chicken pieces with apricot jam. Combine marjoram, lemon rind, soy sauce, and apricot juice; pour over chicken.

Cover pan and simmer until tender, about 40 minutes, basting occasionally. Add green pepper and cook for 5 minutes more. Meanwhile, pit the apricots. Add them to pan just before serving and heat through. Serve with rice. Yield: 4 servings. Approximate calories per serving: 445 (or 545 with ½ cup rice).

CHICKEN FRIED STEAK

1 lb. lean round steak, well
   trimmed
¼ tsp. pepper
¼ tsp. garlic powder
2 egg whites

1 Tbsp. skim milk
1 c. fine low-sodium cracker
   crumbs
3 Tbsp. oil

1. Pound steak to tenderize. Season with pepper and garlic. Cut into serving size pieces.
2. Combine egg whites and skim milk. Dip meat in egg mixture and then into cracker crumbs.
3. Brown coated steak on both sides in oil.
4. Cover and cook over low heat until tender, about 45 minutes. Yield: 4 servings.

CHICKEN DINNER IN THE POT

A very good one-pot dinner. Children like it, too.

2 chicken breasts, split and
   skinned
4 medium size potatoes
2 large carrots
½ lb. fresh green beans (or 1 (10
   oz.) pkg. frozen)

1 large onion
1 Tbsp. dried parsley flakes
Freshly ground black pepper
½ c. dry sherry

Place chicken breasts in a large heavy ovenware pot. (An enamel-coated cast iron pot is best.) Peel potatoes; slice ½ inch thick and place on top of chicken.

Peel and quarter the onion. Peel carrots; quarter lengthwise and cut into 2 inch lengths. Cut ends off the green beans, or separate frozen beans, and place in the pot with onion and carrots. Sprinkle contents of pot with parsley flakes. Season lightly with pepper. Pour sherry over all and cover tightly. Bake at 300°F. for 2 hours or until vegetables are tender. Yield: 4 servings. Approximate calories per serving: 310.

CHICKEN A LA KING

3 Tbsp. oil
4 Tbsp. flour
Freshly ground black pepper
3 c. chicken stock
⅓ c. nonfat dry milk
½ lb. sliced mushrooms

¼ c. diced green pepper
¼ c. chopped pimiento
2 c. cooked chicken
4 Tbsp. sherry
1 Tbsp. chopped parsley

Heat oil in a saucepan. Add flour and cook briefly, stirring. Pour in chicken stock, stirring constantly, until thick and smooth. Season and stir in nonfat dry milk. Cook for 1 minute.

Saute sliced mushrooms and add to sauce, along with chicken, green pepper, and pimiento. Heat through, then add sherry. Adjust seasoning and garnish with parsley. Serve with rice.

SHREDDED CHICKEN WITH GREEN PEPPER AND CARROTS

Color and texture make this a beautiful dish. Quick to cook and delicious.

3 chicken breasts, boned, split,
 and skinned
4 tsp. cornstarch
4 tsp. soy sauce
1 Tbsp. dry sherry
1 egg white, slightly beaten
5 Tbsp. oil

1 whole carrot, thinly shredded
1 green pepper, thinly sliced
1 tsp. fresh ginger, thinly
 shredded or 1 stalk scallion,
 sliced into ½ inch lengths
1 tsp. sugar
2 Tbsp. cold water

Use a very sharp knife to slice chicken breasts horizontally, paper thin. This is easier if breasts are slightly frozen. Cut the slices into strips about ⅛ inch wide and 1½ to 2 inches long. Place in bowl.

Combine ½ of the cornstarch and ½ of the soy sauce with the sherry and egg white. Pour over chicken slivers and let stand for 30 minutes. Heat 1 tablespoon oil in a skillet. Saute carrot slivers for 1 minute.

IN A HURRY - CHICKEN CURRY

Leftover roast or boiled chicken can come to no better end than in this zesty dish of Eastern origin.

2 c. cooked diced chicken or
   turkey
½ lb. thinly sliced fresh
   mushrooms
1 Tbsp. oil or margarine
⅓ c. chopped onion
3 Tbsp. flour

1 c. chicken broth
1½ tsp. curry powder
1 c. finely chopped apple
¼ c. chopped parsley
¾ c. skim milk
1 c. water

In a large skillet, saute chicken, mushrooms, and onion in oil until chicken is lightly browned on all sides. Stir in flour, broth, and curry powder. Add apple and parsley, then pour in milk and water. Simmer, stirring constantly, for 3 minutes or until apple pieces are tender crisp. Serve over rice.

BAKED CHICKEN

1 chicken, cut up into serving
   pieces
¼ tsp. garlic powder
¼ tsp. paprika
⅛ tsp. thyme
¼ c. Parmesan cheese

1 Tbsp. minced parsley
⅓ c. fine bread crumbs
⅓ c. water
1 Tbsp. oil
⅓ c. white wine (optional)
¼ c. margarine, melted

In paper bag, place seasoning, cheese, parsley, and crumbs; coat chicken by shaking a few pieces at a time in the bag. Oil a shallow roasting pan; pour in the water and arrange chicken pieces. Sprinkle chicken with oil and melted margarine. Bake at 350° (uncovered) for 30 minutes. Pour wine over chicken. Lower heat to 325° (cover pan with foil) and bake for 15 minutes longer. Remove foil; raise temperature to 350°. Bake for 10 minutes longer.

Joanne Gulla, Virginia, MN

CHICKEN DIVAN

2 Tbsp. low-sodium corn oil
   margarine
2 Tbsp. flour
1½ c. low-sodium chicken
   bouillon
⅓ c. sliced fresh mushrooms
2 Tbsp. white wine
¼ tsp. pepper

1 (10 oz.) pkg. frozen asparagus
   spears, thawed
4 chicken breast halves (skin
   and fat removed) cooked
   and boned
1 Tbsp. chopped fresh parsley
2 Tbsp. fine dry low-sodium
   bread crumbs

1. Preheat oven to 375°F.
2. Melt the margarine in a small saucepan. Stir in flour and cook for 1 minute.

3. Add chicken bouillon and cook until thickened.

4. Add mushrooms, wine, and pepper.

5. Place asparagus spears in shallow baking dish or 4 individual casseroles. Add chicken and top with sauce. Sprinkle with parsley and bread crumbs.

6. Bake for 20 minutes. Yield: 4 servings.

CHICKEN POT PIE

The vegetables in this pot pie may be any you happen to have on hand. The dish may also be made with other meats, such as beef or pork.

2 c. cooked chicken
1½ c. water
½ c. nonfat dry milk
3 Tbsp. flour
¼ tsp. tarragon
¼ tsp. parsley
Freshly ground black pepper
¾ c. small white onions, cooked

Cooked carrot slices, lima beans, and green peas to total 1½ c. (a pkg. mixed frozen vegetables may be used)
1 recipe pastry crust or Mashed Potato Topping

Beat nonfat dry milk and flour with water until smooth. Add tarragon, parsley, and pepper. Cook over medium heat, stirring constantly, until mixture thickens.

Mix in chicken and vegetables. Pour into 1½ quart casserole. Cover with pastry crust or Mashed Potato Topping. Bake at 400°F. for 20 minutes or until lightly browned. Yield: 4 servings. Approximate calories per serving: 225 (or 340 with topping).

Pastry crust:

½ c. flour   **2 Tbsp. oil**
⅛ tsp. salt

Stir salt and oil into flour. Form into a ball; flatten slightly and place on a sheet of wax paper. Place another sheet on top of dough and roll out quickly. Peel paper off top later; invert dough over filling and seal pie by pressing dough firmly to edge of casserole. Cut steam holes and bake pie at 400°F. for about 20 minutes. Yield: 4 servings. Approximate calories per serving: 110.

Mashed Potato Topping:

2 c. mashed potatoes
½ c. hot skim milk
¼ tsp. pepper
2 Tbsp. margarine, melted

⅛ tsp. rosemary
⅛ tsp. nutmeg
Paprika

Beat together mashed potatoes, margarine, milk, rosemary, pepper, and nutmeg until light and fluffy. Spread over top of chicken mixture and sprinkle lightly with paprika. Bake at 400°F. for about 20 minutes. Yield: 4 servings. Approximate calories per serving: 110.

CHICKEN SALAD CASSEROLE

A hot dish with the character of a salad, this is a good luncheon offering, summer or winter.

2 c. cubed cooked chicken
1 small green pepper, sliced
1 (4 oz.) can mushrooms,
   drained
½ c. slivered water chestnuts

¼ c. mayonnaise
¼ c. skim milk
1 (2 oz.) jar sliced pimiento,
   drained

Simmer green pepper slices in water until nearly tender; drain. Combine milk with mayonnaise. Add pimiento, green pepper, mushrooms, water chestnuts, and chicken. Place in a 1 quart casserole. Cover and bake at 350°F. for 20 minutes. Yield: 4 servings (about 3 cups). Approximate calories per serving: 260.

HAM ROLL-UP

8 thin slices baked ham
8 slices lowfat cheese
   (Mozzarella or lowfat
   Cheddar)

16 asparagus spears (canned or
   frozen, if frozen, thaw first)

Roll each slice of ham around 2 asparagus spears and pin with toothpicks. Place 1 slice of cheese on top of each roll and run under the broiler until the cheese melts. Serve immediately. Yield: 8 servings. Approximate calories per serving: 1 roll equals 200.

HAWAIIAN HAM

Perk up leftover ham in this sweet-and-sour dish.

3 c. lean cooked ham, diced
1 medium onion, sliced
1 small green pepper, sliced in
   rings
1 c. canned pineapple cubes
   with juice
½ c. seedless raisins

2 tsp. dry mustard
¼ c. brown sugar
1 Tbsp. cornstarch
⅓ c. vinegar
1 tsp. Worcestershire sauce
1 Tbsp. soy sauce (optional)

Put the cubed ham in a 2½ quart casserole. Arrange the onion and green pepper rings on top. Drain the pineapple cubes. Reserve the juice and add water to make 1 cup. Place the fruit over the vegetables. Sprinkle with the raisins. Blend mustard, sugar, and cornstarch in a small saucepan. Stir in pineapple juice and vinegar and cook, while stirring, until the mixture boils and is clear. Blend in the Worcestershire and soy sauces. Pour over the ham and vegetables in casserole. Bake, uncovered, at 350°F. for 45 to 60 minutes. Serve over boiled rice. Yield: 8 servings, about 1½ quarts. Approximate calories per serving: 270 (or 370 with ½ cup rice).

BARBECUED PORK CHOPS

1 lb. lean pork chops, well trimmed
3 slices lemon or 3 Tbsp. lemon juice
1 Tbsp. brown sugar, firmly packed
⅓ c. low-sodium catsup
¼ c. water

1. Brown chops in skillet without added fat; drain off fat.
2. Combine remaining ingredients and pour over meat.
3. Cover and simmer for 20 minutes. Remove cover and simmer for 10 minutes more. Add more water if needed. Yield: 4 servings.

BREADED PORK CHOPS
(Lowfat)

Pork chops, fat trimmed
1 egg, beaten (dilute by ½ with water)
Flour
Italian bread crumbs
Salt and pepper to taste

Dip chops in flour, then egg, then crumbs. Brown in Crisco in heavy skillet (about 3 minutes each side). Place in single layer in ungreased roasting pan; cover and bake at 350° until tender (30 to 40 minutes).

Millie Monte, Chisholm, MN

SWEET-AND-SOUR PORK

1½ lb. lean pork loin
2 Tbsp. oil
1 (20 oz.) can pineapple chunks with juice
½ c. water
⅓ c. vinegar
¼ c. brown sugar
2 Tbsp. cornstarch
1 Tbsp. soy sauce
¾ c. thinly sliced green pepper
½ c. thinly sliced onion

Trim all visible fat from the pork loin and cut meat into thin strips. Heat the oil in a skillet and brown the meat strips. Remove the meat and set aside. Drain the pineapple and combine pineapple juice with water, vinegar, brown sugar, cornstarch, and soy sauce. Shake in a glass jar until well mixed.

Cook sweet-and-sour sauce in the skillet until clear and slightly thickened. Add the meat and cook over low heat for about 1 hour. About 5 minutes before serving, add the green pepper and onion slices and the pineapple chunks. Serve over steamed rice. Yield: 6 servings. Approximate calories per serving: 395 (or 495 with ½ cup rice).

LOUISIANA CREOLE ROAST

3 lb. lean roast, well trimmed
2 Tbsp. oil
½ tsp. pepper
1 onion, cut into rings

½ c. chopped celery
½ green pepper, cut into rings
2 (16 oz.) cans low-sodium
　　tomatoes (undrained)

1. Brown meat in oil in large pan or Dutch oven.
2. Season with pepper. Add onion rings, celery, and green pepper, stirring until tender.
3. Add tomatoes and cover; simmer for 1½ to 2 hours until tender, or bake in a 325°F. oven.
4. Remove fat from drippings and thicken for gravy if desired. Yield: 8 servings.

CURRIED TURKEY WITH WATER CHESTNUTS

After the holidays, use leftover turkey in this deliciously different mild curry. Grand for entertaining.

¼ c. oil
1 bunch green onions
1 small stalk celery
1 green pepper, sliced
2 Tbsp. slivered almonds
2 c. water chestnuts, thinly
　　sliced
2 c. diced cooked turkey or
　　chicken

3 Tbsp. flour
1 tsp. curry powder
1 tsp. paprika
½ tsp. sweet basil
1½ c. chicken broth
¼ c. chopped pimiento
1 c. drained pineapple tidbits

Slice green onions and celery diagonally, about ½ inch thick. Heat oil in skillet and saute onions, celery, and pepper until slightly browned. Add almonds, water chestnuts, and cooked turkey. Mix well with flour, paprika, curry powder, and basil. Saute lightly, stirring constantly, until well blended.

Mix in broth, pimiento, and pineapple. Cover and let steam briefly. Season with pepper. Serve on rice. Makes 6 servings. Approximate calories per serving: 280 (or 380 with ½ cup rice).

TURKEY MOUSSE

2 c. diced turkey, cooked
1 env. gelatin
¼ c. cold water
½ c. chicken broth
½ c. mayonnaise
1 Tbsp. lemon juice
1 tsp. grated onion

½ tsp. Tabasco sauce
¼ tsp. paprika
1½ c. lowfat cottage cheese
¼ c. chopped green pepper
¼ c. diced celery
¼ c. chopped pimiento

Soften gelatin in cold water. Add chicken broth to softened gelatin, stirring until dissolved; cool. Add mayonnaise, lemon juice, onion, Tabasco, and paprika.

Whip the cottage cheese in blender until smooth and creamy; add to gelatin mixture, then fold in turkey, green pepper, celery, and pimiento. Pour into a 1 ½ quart mold. Chill until firm. Yield: 10 servings. Approximate calories per serving: 160.

VEAL COLUMBO

⅓ c. wheat germ
1 tsp. crushed oregano
¼ tsp. garlic powder
¼ tsp. onion powder
Freshly ground black pepper
1½ lb. veal cutlet, cut into
　　serving pieces

½ c. skim milk
3 Tbsp. margarine
½ lb. fresh mushrooms, sliced
3 Tbsp. tomato paste
¼ c. Marsala or sherry
2 Tbsp. chopped parsley

Mix wheat germ, oregano, garlic powder, onion powder, and black pepper. Dip veal into milk, then into wheat germ mixture, coating cutlets well. In a skillet, melt margarine, then saute veal in it until golden on both sides.

Combine mushrooms, tomato paste, and wine; pour over veal cutlets and simmer for 10 minutes. Serve garnished with parsley. Yield: 8 servings. Approximate calories per serving: 210.

VEAL PAPRIKA

3 Tbsp. corn oil
1½ lb. cubed veal
1½ onions, chopped
2 Tbsp. paprika (spicy variety, or
　　add ⅛ tsp. cayenne pepper)

1½ c. chicken broth
1 Tbsp. vinegar

Heat oil in heavy pan; brown veal cubes. Remove veal and add onions and paprika; saute for 2 minutes. Return veal to the pot; coat it with paprika mixture using a wooden spoon. Add the chicken broth; bring stew to a boil. Simmer gently for 1½ hours or until veal is tender. Add vinegar before serving. Yield: 6 servings. Approximate calories per serving: 290.

VEAL WITH ARTICHOKES

2 cloves garlic
2 Tbsp. oil
2 lb. veal round, cut into
    bite-size pieces (have
    butcher flatten pieces to ¼
    inch thickness)

1 (1 lb.) can solid pack tomatoes
½ c. sherry or sauterne
¼ tsp. oregano
2 (10 oz.) pkg. frozen artichoke
    hearts

In a heavy skillet, saute the garlic in oil. Remove garlic. Season the veal with pepper; brown in oil. Add the tomatoes, wine, and oregano, mixing well, and the artichoke hearts. Cover and simmer for 45 to 60 minutes or until the meat is tender. Yield: 8 servings. Approximate calories per serving: 310.

PAUPIETTES DE VEAU

2 lb. veal round, sliced ¼ inch
    thick and cut into six 3x4
    inch rectangles
1 (6 oz.) can mushrooms
1 Tbsp. chopped onion
¼ c. plus 2 Tbsp. oil

3 slices bread, broken into small
    pieces
½ tsp. dried parsley
¼ tsp. thyme
Freshly ground black pepper

Brown the mushrooms and onion in 2 tablespoons of oil. Combine the bread, parsley, thyme, and pepper in a bowl. Mix in browned mushrooms and onion. Divide this mixture into 6 portions and place each portion on a piece of meat. Wrap the meat around filling to form a cylinder. Overlap the ends and secure with a toothpick. Brown the paupiettes on all sides in ¼ cup of oil. While meat is browning, make the sauce.

Sauce:

2 Tbsp. flour
Freshly ground black pepper
1 Tbsp. oil

½ c. broth
½ c. dry white wine

Place the browned paupiettes in a casserole dish and pour the sauce over all. Cover and bake at 350°F. for 1½ hours. About 15 minutes before end of baking time, remove cover, spoon some of the sauce over the paupiettes, and continue cooking, uncovered, to glaze the meat. Yield: 8 servings. Approximate calories per serving: 390.

VEAL STEW WITH FENNEL

1½ lb. lean veal stew meat, cut
   in 1 inch cubes
3 Tbsp. oil
Freshly ground black pepper
1 large onion, chopped

¼ c. water
1 tsp. crushed fennel seed
3 small green onions, chopped
2 (10 oz.) pkg. frozen spinach
   leaves

Brown the meat in the oil in a Dutch oven or heavy kettle. Season meat with pepper; stir in the onion and saute until limp, but not brown. Add water, onion, and fennel seed to the pot; cover and simmer the stew over low heat for about 1 hour or until the meat is tender. Add more water, if necessary, during cooking.

Cook spinach separately for about 5 minutes; season to taste. Arrange the meat on a heated serving platter; surround with a border of spinach and garnish with lemon wedges. Yield: 6 servings. Approximate calories per serving: 320.

VEAL SCALLOPINI

4 veal cutlets
1 small clove garlic, quartered
2 Tbsp. oil
1 Tbsp. flour
Freshly ground black pepper
¼ tsp. nutmeg
1 small onion, thinly sliced

½ c. Marsala wine
1 (4 oz.) can sliced mushrooms,
   drained, or ½ lb. fresh
   mushrooms
½ tsp. paprika
2 Tbsp. coarsely chopped
   parsley

Saute garlic in oil over low flame for 5 minutes. Discard garlic. Brown cutlets in the oil. Mix flour, pepper, and nutmeg; sprinkle over browned meat. Add onion and wine. Cover skillet and simmer for about 20 minutes, turning the meat several times. Add more liquid (wine or tomato juice) if necessary.

Add mushrooms; cover and cook for 8 to 10 minutes longer. Serve on a warm platter with the sauce, garnished with paprika and parsley. Yield: 4 servings. Approximate calories per serving: 360.

LAMB-STUFFED CABBAGE

½ lb. cooked lamb, ground
1 c. cooked rice (white or brown)
1 egg (2 egg whites or egg
   substitute equivalent to 1
   egg)
1 small clove garlic, crushed
⅛ tsp. thyme, crumbled
⅛ tsp. rosemary, crumbled

Freshly ground black pepper
1 (15 oz.) can tomato sauce
1 head cabbage (about 2 lb.)
2 Tbsp. margarine
1 c. chopped onion
2 Tbsp. sugar
½ c. water

390

Combine the first 7 ingredients in a large bowl. Add ⅓ of the tomato sauce and mix well with a fork. Trim the outside leaves from cabbage. Cut a small slice, about 3 inches in diameter, from the top end; set aside. Hollow out the cabbage, leaving a shell about ½ inch thick. Make sure the core end is even so the cabbage will set level.

Spoon lamb mixture into the cabbage shell, pressing it down firmly. Fit top back into place; tie with a string. Saute onion in margarine until soft. Add remaining tomato sauce, sugar, and water. Bring to a boil, stirring constantly; remove from heat.

Place cabbage, core end down, in a deep casserole or Dutch oven. Pour sauce over cabbage. Cover and bake in a 350°F. oven for 1½ hours, basting with the sauce 2 or 3 times. Place the cabbage on a heated serving platter; remove string and spoon the sauce over. Cut into wedges to serve. Yield: 4 servings. Approximate calories per serving: 325.

LAMB CHOPS ORIENTAL

4 lean lamb shoulder chops (1 inch thick)
1 (13 oz.) can pineapple chunks, drained (reserve juice)
¼ c. soy sauce
¼ c. vinegar
½ tsp. dry mustard
1 Tbsp. oil
¼ c. brown sugar
1 tsp. cornstarch

Place the chops in a shallow glass dish. Drain pineapple and combine syrup with soy sauce, vinegar, and mustard. Pour over the chops. Cover and refrigerate at least 4 hours, turning the chops occasionally.

Drain the chops, reserving marinade. Heat the oil in a large skillet and brown chops over medium heat. Add ¼ cup of the reserved marinade to the chops in skillet. Cover lightly and cook over low heat for 30 to 45 minutes or until tender.

Mix sugar and cornstarch in a small saucepan; stir in remaining marinade. Heat to boiling, stirring constantly. Reduce heat; simmer for 5 minutes. Add pineapple chunks and heat through. Serve the sauce over chops. Yield: 4 servings. Approximate calories per serving: 335.

CURRIED LAMB

1 lb. lean lamb, well trimmed and cut into 1 inch cubes
1 Tbsp. oil
½ c. finely chopped onion
2 tsp. curry powder
¼ tsp. pepper
1 tsp. ground allspice
1 bay leaf
2 tsp. ground cinnamon
1½ c. water
½ c. raisins

1. Brown meat on all sides in oil.

2. Add remaining ingredients and cook over medium heat for 60 minutes or until meat is tender, stirring occasionally.

ALICE'S BAKED SCALLOPS

1 Tbsp. margarine	½ tsp. thyme
¼ c. dry white wine	1 lb. scallops (bay scallops if in
Juice of 1 lemon	season)

Heat margarine, wine, lemon, and thyme; pour over rinsed scallops. Marinate for 15 to 20 minutes at room temperature. Bake in a 450°F. oven for 5 to 6 minutes. Do not overcook. Yield: 4 servings. Approximate calories per serving: 165.

FLOUNDER FILLETS IN FOIL

4 flounder fillets	½ lb. chopped mushrooms
Margarine or oil	3 Tbsp. dry white wine
Freshly ground black pepper	1 Tbsp. lemon juice
1 Tbsp. shallots or green onions	1 Tbsp. chopped parsley

Saute shallots or green onions in margarine till soft. Add mushrooms and cook for 5 minutes. Stir in wine, lemon juice, and parsley; cook until most of the liquid evaporates.

Lightly grease 4 pieces of heavy-duty foil with margarine or oil. Place a fillet on each piece; season with pepper. Spoon some mushroom sauce over each fillet. Draw edges of foil together and seal. Bake at 400°F. for 20 minutes or until fish flakes. Serve in the foil. Yield: 4 servings. Approximate calories per serving: 225.

STUFFED FISH BEACHCOMBER

1 whole fish (about 2½ to 3 lb.)	½ c. skim milk
2 Tbsp. margarine	1 egg white, slightly beaten
6 Tbsp. diced onions	Freshly ground black pepper
¾ c. sliced mushrooms	½ tsp. curry powder
3 Tbsp. vinegar	2 Tbsp. chopped pickles or
1½ c. day old bread crumbs	relish

Saute onions and mushrooms in margarine for 10 minutes. Add vinegar and simmer for 10 minutes; remove from heat and cool 10 minutes. Soak bread crumbs in skim milk, then squeeze out excess milk and add crumbs to onion mixture. Add beaten egg white, pepper, and pickles or relish mixed with curry powder.

Sprinkle fish on all sides with pepper. Stuff with bread mixture; close opening with skewers or picks. Grease a baking dish or line it with unglazed parchment paper; place fish in it. Brush with oil and bake at 375°F. for 45 minutes or until fish flakes easily when tested with a fork. Yield: 6 servings. Approximate calories per serving: 320.

BRAISED FISH

A beautiful dish with its own delectable sauce. Pour the sauce over rice or soak it up with crusty French bread.

¼ c. oil
1½ lb. pan-dressed fish, or 1 lb.
    firm textured fish fillets
    (such as haddock)
2 Tbsp. flour
½ tsp. sugar
½ tsp. ginger
¼ tsp. garlic powder or 1 clove
    garlic, minced

1 Tbsp. soy sauce
1 Tbsp. sherry
Water
Freshly ground black pepper
Chives or green ends of spring
    onions
2 medium size ripe tomatoes,
    chopped
1 Tbsp. chopped parsley

Dust fillets lightly with flour. In a heavy skillet, heat oil and brown fish on both sides. Combine sugar, ginger, and garlic with soy sauce, sherry, and enough water to make 1 cup; pour over fish. Cover and braise for 10 minutes. Uncover; add black pepper, chives, parsley, and chopped tomatoes. Cook, uncovered, another 5 minutes. Yield: 4 servings. Approximate calories per serving: 335.

OVEN-FRIED FILLETS

1 lb. fish fillets
½ tsp. pepper
½ c. fine dry low-sodium bread
    crumbs

3 Tbsp. low-sodium corn oil
    margarine

1. Preheat oven to 500°F.
2. Lightly season fillets with pepper. Roll in bread crumbs. Place in lightly oiled baking dish and dot with margarine.
3. Bake for 10 minutes or until the fish flakes easily with a fork. Yield: 4 servings.

SO-GOOD POACHED FILLETS

¾ c. water
1 Tbsp. lemon juice
½ onion, sliced

1 Tbsp. vinegar
4 peppercorns
1 lb. fish fillets or fish steaks

1. Place all ingredients, except fish, in saucepan and heat for 5 minutes.
2. Cut fish in serving size pieces and add to liquid.
3. Simmer for 5 to 10 minutes until fish flakes easily with a fork. Yield: 4 servings.

BROILED FISH ROLL-UPS

2 Tbsp. chopped onion
½ c. chopped celery
3 Tbsp. water
2 c. coarse bread crumbs
Freshly ground black pepper
¼ c. cooked chopped spinach

½ tsp. thyme
1½ lb. fish fillets
1 egg white, slightly beaten
¼ c. skim milk
2 Tbsp. flour
½ c. fine cracker crumbs

Preheat broiler for 5 minutes. Combine onion, celery, and water in a saucepan. Bring to a boil; cover and simmer until vegetables are tender. Add bread crumbs, pepper, spinach, and thyme; mix well, adding liquid to moisten if necessary. Place some of the mixture on each fillet. Roll up and fasten with toothpicks. Roll the stuffed fillets in a mixture of egg white and skim milk, then in a mixture of flour and cracker crumbs.

Place fish rolls on a lightly oiled broiler rack and place in the broiler. When almost done on one side, turn carefully and cook until tender (about 10 minutes). Remove toothpicks; garnish with parsley and serve immediately. Yield: 6 servings. Approximate calories per serving: 350.

HALIBUT RAGOUT

A quick and nutritious stew. Serve with your favorite bread.

2 lb. halibut (fresh or frozen)
2 Tbsp. oil
½ c. chopped onion
1 clove garlic, minced
¼ c. chopped green pepper
3 stalks celery, sliced diagonally
3 carrots, cut julienne

1 (28 oz.) can tomatoes
1 c. dry white wine
Freshly ground black pepper
¼ tsp. thyme
¼ tsp. basil
3 Tbsp. minced parsley

Thaw the halibut if it is frozen; cut into 1 inch pieces. Saute onion, garlic, green pepper, celery, and carrots in oil. Add tomatoes, wine, and all seasonings, except 2 tablespoons parsley. Cover and simmer for 20 minutes. Add the halibut; cover and simmer for 5 to 10 minutes more or until done. Sprinkle with the remaining parsley.

MUSHROOM BAKED SOLE

1 medium onion, finely chopped
1/4 c. chopped parsley
1 c. sliced mushrooms
1/4 c. margarine
1 1/2 lb. sole fillets
Freshly ground black pepper
1/4 c. dry white wine
1/2 c. skim milk
1 Tbsp. flour
Paprika

Saute onion, parsley, and mushrooms in 3 tablespoons of the margarine, stirring constantly, until onion is soft. Place 1/2 the fillets in a greased baking dish. Sprinkle lightly with pepper and spread sauteed mixture evenly over fish. Top with remaining fillets; season with pepper. Pour wine over all and dot with remaining margarine. Bake at 350°F., uncovered, for 15 minutes. Remove from oven and drain, reserving the pan liquid.

In a small saucepan, combine flour and milk. Add the reserved pan liquid and cook, stirring constantly, until thickened. Pour over the fish and bake for 5 minutes longer. Sprinkle with paprika and parsley. Yield: 6 servings. Approximate calories per serving: 265.

BEAN SPROUT TUNA CHOW MEIN

1 c. chicken broth
1 Tbsp. soy sauce
Freshly ground black pepper
2 Tbsp. cornstarch
6 stalks celery, cut diagonally
2 medium onions, slivered
1 (6 oz.) can bamboo shoots, drained
1 (4 oz.) can mushrooms, drained, or 4 oz. sliced fresh mushrooms
2 c. freshly grown bean sprouts or 1 can bean sprouts, drained
2 Tbsp. oil
1 (7 oz.) can water packed tuna, drained

Mix chicken broth, soy sauce, and pepper. Stir in cornstarch until dissolved. Slice celery diagonally, 1/8 inch thick. Slice onions in very thin slices or slivers. Cut mushrooms in slices.

Heat oil in frying pan or wok over highest heat. When hot, toss in celery and onions; stir-fry for 1 minute. Add bamboo shoots, mushrooms, and bean sprouts. Stir broth mixture and add to vegetables. Stir and cook just until sauce is thickened. Add tuna and stir until hot and sauce is clear. Serve immediately over fluffy rice. Yield: 4 servings. Approximate calories per serving: 220.

SALMON-BROCCOLI CASSEROLE

2 Tbsp. low-sodium corn oil
   margarine
1 Tbsp. flour
¼ tsp. pepper
¼ tsp. garlic powder
1 c. skim milk
3 fresh tomatoes, chopped

1 tsp. lemon juice
1 (10 oz.) pkg. frozen broccoli,
   thawed
1 (6½ oz.) can low-sodium
   salmon, drained
2 Tbsp. fine dry low-sodium
   bread crumbs

1. Preheat oven to 375°F.
2. Melt 1 tablespoon margarine in saucepan. Blend in flour, pepper, and garlic powder. Add milk and bring to a simmer, stirring constantly.
3. Add tomatoes and lemon juice and cook over low heat for 5 minutes.
4. Arrange broccoli on bottom of casserole. Cover with salmon and top with sauce. Sprinkle with bread crumbs and dot with 1 tablespoon margarine. Bake for 30 minutes. Yield: 4 servings.

TUNA MACARONI CASSEROLE

2 Tbsp. chopped celery
¼ c. chopped onion
2 Tbsp. chopped green pepper
1 Tbsp. oil
1 Tbsp. flour
¼ tsp. pepper
1 c. skim milk
½ c. cubed low-sodium lowfat
   cheese

1 c. unsalted cooked elbow
   macaroni
2 fresh tomatoes, chopped
1 (6½ oz.) can low-sodium water
   packed tuna, drained
2 Tbsp. chopped fresh parsley
1 Tbsp. lemon juice
Paprika

1. Preheat oven to 375°F.
2. Saute celery, onion, and green pepper in oil until tender. Stir in flour and pepper until smooth.
3. Gradually stir in milk and cook, stirring constantly, until thickened. Add cheese and stir until melted.
4. Add macaroni, tomatoes, tuna, parsley, and lemon juice and pour into casserole. Sprinkle with paprika and bake for 30 to 35 minutes. Yield: 4 servings.

TUNA RING

2 (7 oz.) cans tuna, drained
1 c. water
¾ c. dry bread crumbs
½ c. cooked green peas
⅓ c. nonfat dry milk
¼ c. slivered almonds
1 egg (2 egg whites or egg
    substitute equivalent to 1
    egg)

2 Tbsp. finely chopped onion
2 Tbsp. finely chopped green
    pepper
2 Tbsp. finely chopped pimiento
2 tsp. Worcestershire sauce
Freshly ground black pepper

Combine tuna with all other ingredients; spoon into a well oiled 8 inch ring mold. Bake at 350°F. for 45 minutes. Unmold at once. Serve garnished with more pimiento and fresh parsley. Yield: 6 servings. Approximate calories per serving: 300.

MARINADE FOR VENISON, ELK, OR ANTELOPE

1 c. beef broth
1 Tbsp. pickling spice
½ tsp. celery seeds
½ tsp. basil
½ tsp. marjoram
½ tsp. thyme

½ tsp. sage
1 bay leaf
3 peppercorns, crushed
3 whole allspice, crushed
2 Tbsp. lemon juice
¼ c. vinegar

Combine all of the ingredients. Cover venison, elk, or antelope with the marinade. Marinate in the refrigerator for 10 to 12 hours. Remove the meat from marinade and drain well. Cook as desired. Yield: 1¼ cups. Approximate calories per serving: 1¼ cups equals 25.

ENCHILADA BAKE

½ c. dry beans, cooked (or 2 c.
    canned)
1 onion, chopped
1 clove garlic, minced
5 or 6 mushrooms, sliced
1 green pepper, chopped
1½ c. stewed tomatoes
1 Tbsp. chili powder
1 tsp. cumin seed, ground

½ c. dry red wine
8 tortillas
¼ c. grated Mozzarella cheese
    (made from partially
    skimmed milk)
½ c. Ricotta cheese (made from
    partially skimmed milk)
¼ c. lowfat yogurt
6 black olives, sliced

Saute onion, garlic, mushrooms, and pepper. Add the beans, tomatoes, spices, and wine; simmer gently for about 30 minutes. Mix Ricotta cheese and yogurt.

In an oiled 1½ quart casserole, put a layer of tortillas, a layer of sauce, 1½ tablespoons of grated cheese, and 4 tablespoons of cheese-yogurt mixture. Repeat until all ingredients are used, ending with a layer of sauce. Top with cheese-yogurt mixture and black olives. Bake at 350°F. for 15 to 20 minutes. Yield: 6 servings. Approximate calories per serving: 195.

EASY LASAGNA
(Low-sodium, low cholesterol)

About 10 lasagna noodles
(uncooked)
1 lb. ground turkey, cooked and
drained (I use frozen pkg.
Louis Rich turkey)
1 large onion
2 Tbsp. parsley
1 tsp. basil
2 c. water
1 Tbsp. sugar (optional)

12 oz. can tomato paste
(unsalted)
1 qt. tomatoes (canned,
unsalted)
2⅔ c. 2% lowfat cottage cheese
4 oz. Parmesan cheese
1 Tbsp. parsley
1 tsp. oregano
8 oz. Mozzarella (or more)

Mix onion, 2 tablespoons parsley, basil, water, sugar, tomato paste, and tomatoes; add to meat. Mix together cottage cheese, Parmesan cheese, 1 tablespoon parsley, and oregano.

Spray 9x13 inch pan with Pam or grease. Layer ½ sauce, 1 row of uncooked lasagna noodles (I use 5), ½ cheese mixture, then other ½ of sauce, another 5 lasagna noodles, other ½ of cheese, and Mozzarella on top. Bake at 350° for 1 hour, covered, and 15 minutes, uncovered. Makes about 12 servings.

Mary Voss, Owatonna, MN

SALADS AND DRESSINGS

GRAPEFRUIT AND ORANGE SALAD

1 head chicory
1 grapefruit
1 orange

1 small green onion, thinly
   sliced

Wash the chicory; drain well and pat dry. Break or cut up into serving pieces. Peel the grapefruit and orange, taking care to remove all the white membrane. Separate each fruit into sections.

Combine the chicory with the grapefruit and orange sections and green onion. Toss well with oil and vinegar dressing just before serving. Yield: 4 servings. Approximate calories per serving: 50 (or 125 with 1 tablespoon dressing).

ANNA'S BEAN SPROUT SALAD

4 c. fresh bean sprouts
4 c. boiling water
2 Tbsp. soy sauce

1 tsp. sesame oil
2 Tbsp. scallions, chopped

Immerse bean sprouts in boiling water for 1 minute; drain and rinse immediately in cold water. Combine bean sprouts, soy sauce, and sesame oil; toss. Sprinkle scallions on top. Yield: 6 servings. Approximate calories per serving: 35.

SAUERKRAUT SALAD

1 (28 oz.) can sauerkraut
½ c. sugar
1 c. diced celery
1 c. diced green pepper
¼ c. diced onion

Freshly ground black pepper
1 tsp. celery seed
3 Tbsp. diced pimiento
3 Tbsp. vinegar

Drain the sauerkraut for 15 minutes in a colander. Cut with scissors into 1 inch pieces. Mix all ingredients together in a large bowl; cover and store in the refrigerator for 24 hours. (This salad will store indefinitely.) Yield: 10 servings. Approximate calories per serving: 60.

MARINATED OKRA SALAD

1 (10 oz.) pkg. frozen whole okra
¼ c. chopped celery leaves
1 onion, sliced into thin rings
1 bay leaf
½ tsp. celery seed

½ tsp. Italian seasoning
½ c. cider vinegar
2 Tbsp. low calorie Italian
   dressing

1. Cook okra and celery leaves according to package directions on okra. Drain and cool.
2. Combine onion, spices, vinegar, and Italian dressing.
3. Add okra and celery leaves.
4. Cover and chill overnight. Yield: 4 servings.

PICKLED MUSHROOM SALAD

1 (8 oz.) can whole mushrooms (undrained)
¼ c. chopped celery leaves
1 onion, sliced into thin rings
⅓ c. cider vinegar

1 bay leaf
½ tsp. salt
¼ tsp. celery seed
1 tsp. low calorie Italian dressing

1. Combine all ingredients.
2. Cover and chill in refrigerator overnight.
3. Serve on a lettuce leaf if desired. Yield: 4 servings.

COOL CUKE SALAD

1 large cucumber, cut in diagonal slices
2 green onions, chopped
1 c. buttermilk

1 Tbsp. tarragon vinegar
⅛ tsp. paprika
½ tsp. salt
¼ tsp. pepper

1. Combine all ingredients.
2. Chill well. Yield: 4 servings.

BEAN SPROUT SALAD

2 c. fresh or canned bean sprouts
2 c. canned sliced green beans

1 c. chopped parsley
½ tsp. dill seed

Drain bean sprouts and green beans thoroughly. Toss together all 3 items; sprinkle with dill seed and serve with lemon wedges.

Dressing:

1 Tbsp. oil
2 Tbsp. lowfat yogurt

1 Tbsp. catsup
½ tsp. Worcestershire sauce

Mix all dressing ingredients together. Serve with Bean Sprout Salad. Yield: 6 servings. Approximate calories per serving: 50.

CHINESE CHICKEN SALAD

Arrange 4 cups cooked chicken, cut in bite-size pieces, on a platter of Boston or Bibb lettuce.

Sauce A:

4 Tbsp. soy sauce
2 Tbsp. honey

1 clove garlic, crushed

Combine all ingredients for Sauce A and set aside for 5 minutes.

Sauce B:

3 Tbsp. oil
2 scallions, chopped
4 slices peeled fresh ginger
root*
Freshly ground black pepper or
Szechwan pepper

(obtainable at Chinese food
stores)
¼ Tbsp. crushed red pepper

Combine all ingredients for Sauce B in a saucepan and heat for 3 minutes. Mix Sauce B into Sauce A. Pour over the chicken. Yield: 10 servings. Approximate calories per serving: 155.

* Ginger root should be peeled, covered with sherry, and refrigerated before use.

CHICKEN AND RICE SALAD

2 c. cooked unsalted rice,
cooled
2 c. chopped cooked chicken
1 (16 oz.) can low-sodium peas,
drained
1 c. chopped celery

1 c. chopped green pepper
2 Tbsp. finely chopped onion
¾ c. low-sodium mayonnaise
½ tsp. pepper
2 Tbsp. lemon juice
2 Tbsp. chopped fresh parsley

1. Combine rice, chicken, peas, celery, green pepper, and onion.
2. Combine remaining ingredients and toss with chicken mixture.
3. Chill well before serving. Yield: 8 servings.

TURKEY MACARONI SALAD

2 c. chopped cooked turkey
2 c. cooked elbow macaroni,
   cooled
2 stalks celery, chopped
½ onion, chopped

½ c. mayonnaise
1 tsp. prepared mustard
1 tsp. lemon juice
¼ tsp. salt
⅛ tsp. pepper

1. Mix all ingredients together and chill.
2. Serve on lettuce leaf if desired. Yield: 6 servings.

LUNCHEON TUNA SALAD

1 (6½ oz.) can water packed
   tuna, drained
1 (8 oz.) can peas, drained
½ c. finely chopped celery

2 Tbsp. pickle relish
1 Tbsp. lemon juice
¼ c. mayonnaise

1. Toss all ingredients together and chill.
2. Serve on lettuce leaf if desired. Yield: 4 servings.

COUNTRY MACARONI SALAD

1 (7 oz.) pkg. Creamettes elbow
   macaroni (2 c. uncooked)
¾ c. Miracle Whip light (reduced
   calorie salad dressing)
½ tsp. dill weed

1½ c. chopped cooked chicken
1 c. carrot slices
1 c. cherry tomato halves
Lettuce (P.S. Can go light on the
   salt)

Prepare macaroni according to package directions; drain. Add to combined salad dressing and dill weed; mix lightly. Add chicken, carrots, and tomatoes; mix lightly. Chill for several hours. Serve on lettuce covered plates. Garnish with fresh dill weed if desired. Makes 6 servings, 307 calories per 1 cup serving.

Evelyn Fechner, Anoka, MN

DILLED SHRIMP SALAD

3 lb. cleaned and deveined
   shrimp
1 Tbsp. shrimp spice
½ onion, peeled and sliced
1 (5 oz.) can water chestnuts,
   sliced
4 Tbsp. Italian salad dressing

2 Tbsp. chopped fresh dill or 1
   tsp. powdered dill
3 ripe tomatoes
6 fresh mushrooms, sliced
Parsley
1 small head romaine

Cook shrimp in water with the shrimp spice; drain and chill. Toss with the onion, water chestnuts, and dressing. Sprinkle with dill. Serve on romaine lettuce and surround with sliced tomatoes and mushrooms. Yield: 16 servings. Approximate calories per serving: 110.

CHICKEN-VEGETABLE SALAD

2 c. chunked white meat of
    chicken or turkey
½ cucumber, peeled and diced
½ c. diced celery
½ c. water chestnuts, drained
    and sliced
¼ c. diced green pepper

¼ c. chopped pimiento
¼ c. sliced scallions
¼ c. mayonnaise
Salad greens
2 Tbsp. capers
Paprika

Toss the first 7 ingredients with mayonnaise. Serve on crisp salad greens, garnished with capers and paprika. Yield: 6 servings. Approximate calories per serving: 170.

MOM'S FROZEN FRUIT SALAD

2 tsp. unflavored gelatin
6 Tbsp. cold water
2 tsp. confectioners sugar
4 Tbsp. lemon juice
2 Tbsp. maraschino cherry juice
1 c. canned evaporated skim
    milk, chilled (undiluted)

⅔ c. mayonnaise
1 banana, cubed
1½ c. crushed pineapple packed
    in own juice, drained
1 c. sliced maraschino cherries

1. Sprinkle gelatin over cold water in small saucepan. Stir over low heat until gelatin dissolves.
2. Add sugar, lemon juice, and maraschino cherry juice.
3. Whip chilled evaporated milk until soft peaks form.
4. Fold mayonnaise into whipped milk. Do this step immediately or whipped milk will get runny.
5. Fold in gelatin mixture. Fold in fruits.
6. Turn into refrigerator trays, loaf pan, or large mold; freeze.
7. Stir once before mixture is firm.
8. Freeze for 4 to 5 hours or overnight.
9. Slice and serve on salad greens if desired. Yield: 8 servings.

GARDEN RICE SALAD

2 cloves garlic, minced
1 onion, chopped
2 carrots, chopped
1 stalk celery, chopped
⅔ c. fresh parsley, chopped
2 tsp. dried sweet basil
1 tsp. dried oregano

2 tomatoes, chopped
1 (16 oz.) can vegetarian baked
 beans
5 c. cooked rice
1 c. vinegar
2 tsp. salt
¾ tsp. pepper

1. Saute garlic, onion, carrots, celery, parsley, basil, and oregano in a small amount of water until vegetables are tender. Add tomatoes, beans, and rice.

2. Combine vinegar, salt, and pepper and toss with vegetables.

3. Chill overnight before serving. Yield: 12 servings.

FRESH GREEN BEAN SALAD

4 or 4½ c. green beans
½ c. oil
1½ tsp. prepared mustard
1 small clove garlic
¼ tsp. pepper

⅓ c. vinegar
⅓ c. sugar
1 Tbsp. water
Pinch of salt
Parmesan cheese

Cover green beans with 1 inch water; cook for 3 minutes and drain. Put in 12 or 18 inch dish and mix together oil, prepared mustard, garlic, pepper, vinegar, sugar, and water. Add pinch of salt; pour over beans and cover with Parmesan cheese. Can go light on the salt with this recipe or use not salt.

Evelyn Fechner, Anoka, MN

MACARONI SALAD RICOTTA

¼ lb. whole wheat macaroni,
 cooked until tender,
 drained, and chilled
1 c. Ricotta cheese (made from
 partially skimmed milk)
2 tsp. mustard
1 Tbsp. or more lowfat yogurt
¼ c. sliced or chopped ripe
 olives

1 green pepper, chopped
 coarsely
2 scallions with tops, chopped
1 Tbsp. chopped parsley
Red pimiento to taste
½ tsp. dill
½ tsp. basil
Freshly ground black pepper

Make a dressing with the consistency of mayonnaise by thinning the mustard with a tablespoon or more of yogurt and mixing with the Ricotta. Stir in all other ingredients. Serve on a bed of salad greens. Yield: 4 servings. Approximate calories per serving: 170.

FRESH VEGETABLE SALAD BOWL

1 head romaine lettuce
½ lb. fresh button mushrooms
1 lb. cherry tomatoes

1 small head cauliflower
1 lb. very young raw asparagus
spears

Remove outer leaves of romaine, separate stems from mushrooms, and snap off stem ends of tomatoes. Break cauliflower into flowerets and trim stalk end from asparagus. Wash all vegetables, except mushrooms; drain well. Wipe mushrooms with a paper towel.

Place inner leaves of romaine upright around the sides of a deep round salad bowl. Arrange remaining ingredients neatly in the center. Chill until serving time. Serve with your favorite dressing. Yield: 8 servings. Approximate calories per serving: 50.

GUACAMOLE

2 avocados, peeled and mashed
½ tomato, finely chopped
   (discard juice and seeds)
¼ onion, finely chopped
1½ tsp. lemon juice

½ tsp. garlic salt
½ tsp. mayonnaise
5 to 6 drops red pepper sauce
½ c. finely shredded lettuce

1. Combine all ingredients, except lettuce.
2. Store in covered container with avocado seed in center.
3. Remove seed and serve on shredded lettuce. Yield: 4 servings.

SUGARLESS THREE BEAN SALAD

1 (16 oz.) can green beans,
   drained
1 (16 oz.) can wax beans,
   drained
1 (16 oz.) can kidney beans,
   drained
1 (16 oz.) can Italian beans,
   drained (optional)
½ green pepper, chopped
¾ c. chopped onion

¾ c. chopped celery
¼ c. chopped pimento
½ c. vinegar
⅓ c. oil
¾ tsp. pepper
¾ tsp. salt
¾ tsp. Worcestershire sauce
¾ tsp. celery seed
¼ tsp. garlic salt

1. Combine the beans, green pepper, onion, celery, and pimento.
2. Combine remaining ingredients.
3. Pour dressing over bean mixture and mix.
4. Refrigerate in covered container for 12 hours before serving, stirring

occasionally.

5. This salad will keep for several days in the refrigerator. Yield: 16 servings.

BEET SALAD WITH RED ONIONS

2 c. sliced beets, drained
1/4 large red onion, sliced
2 Tbsp. wine vinegar

3 Tbsp. corn oil
Freshly ground black pepper

Place beets in salad bowl. Slice the onion lengthwise into very thin strips. Place in a bowl. Add vinegar, oil, and black pepper. Toss the salad. Marinate for at least 1/2 hour. Yield: 4 servings. Approximate calories per serving: 105.

COOKED SALAD DRESSING

2 Tbsp. cornstarch
2 Tbsp. sugar
1 tsp. dry mustard
1/8 tsp. paprika

1/2 c. water
1 Tbsp. vinegar
1/4 c. margarine
2/3 c. skim milk or buttermilk

Mix together cornstarch, sugar, mustard, and paprika. Add water and cook over low heat, stirring until thickened. Stir in vinegar. Blend in margarine and gradually add milk. Stir until creamy. Store and use as needed. Vary the flavor by adding poppy or caraway seeds or honey. Yield: 1 1/2 cups. Approximate calories per serving: 1 tablespoon equals 25.

ZERO CALORIE DRESSING
(Low-sodium, low-cholesterol)

1/2 c. unsalted tomato juice
1/2 c. unsalted catsup
1/4 tsp. vinegar
Dash of dry mustard

Dash of pepper
Dash of oregano
1/8 tsp. celery seed

Combine all the ingredients in tightly covered jar. Shake well until mustard and oregano have dissolved. Refrigerate at least 4 hours before serving. Yields 1 cup.

Mary Voss, Owatonna, MN

SKINNY DIP
(Low-sodium, low-cholesterol)

¼ tsp. dry mustard
¾ tsp. dry minced onion
½ tsp. water
1 (8 oz.) ctn. lowfat plain yogurt

½ tsp. paprika
½ tsp. dill weed
Crisp vegetables

In a small bowl, combine dry mustard, minced onion, and water; set aside for a few minutes to develop flavor and rehydrate the mustard and onion. Meanwhile, mix together the rest of the ingredients. Stir in onion and mustard mixtures. Chill until ready to serve. Serve with vegetable relishes and/or crackers. Yields 1 cup.

Mary Voss, Owatonna, MN

HERBED SEASONING

2 Tbsp. dried dill weed or basil
  leaves, crumbled
2 Tbsp. onion powder
1 tsp. dried oregano leaves,
  crumbled

1 tsp. celery seed
¼ tsp. grated dried lemon peel
Pinch of freshly ground pepper

Combine all ingredients in small bowl and blend well. Spoon into a shaker that has large holes. Store in a cool dark place. Makes approximately ⅓ cup (about 65 milligram sodium per teaspoon).

Mary Voss, Owatonna, MN

SPECIAL GREEN GODDESS DRESSING

1 egg (or 2 egg whites or egg
  substitute equivalent to 1
  egg)
1 Tbsp. chopped parsley
3 canned anchovy fillets,
  drained

4 green onions with tops
2 Tbsp. tarragon vinegar
¼ c. oil

Place all ingredients, except oil, in a blender. Whip to a liquid consistency. Gradually add the oil, increasing the flow as the mixture thickens. Continue to blend for a few seconds after all the oil has been added. Store in a closed container in the refrigerator until needed. Yield: ¾ to 1 cup. Approximate calories per serving: 1 tablespoon equals 45.

TOMATO DRESSING

1 c. tomato juice
¼ c. lemon juice or vinegar
2 Tbsp. onion, finely chopped

Freshly ground black pepper
1 tsp. chopped parsley
  (optional)

Combine all ingredients in a blender and mix thoroughly, or shake vigorously in a tightly covered jar. Store in the refrigerator. Yield: 1¼ cups. Approximate calories per serving: 1 tablespoon equals 5.

BLENDER MAYONNAISE
(Makes 1½ cups)

⅓ c. Egg Beaters
½ tsp. dry mustard
½ tsp. sugar

¼ tsp. paprika
2 Tbsp. white vinegar
1 c. corn oil

Combine Egg Beaters, mustard, sugar, paprika, vinegar, and ½ cup oil in blender container. Blend on medium high speed just until mixed. Without turning off blender, pour in remaining oil in a slow steady stream. If necessary, use rubber spatula to keep mixture flowing to blades. Continue blending until oil is completely incorporated and mixture is smooth and thick.

Mary Voss, Owatonna, MN

SOUR CREAM

2 Tbsp. skim milk
1 Tbsp. lemon juice

1 c. lowfat cottage cheese

Place all in blender and mix on medium high speed until smooth and creamy. Makes 1¼ cups.

Carol Gilbertson, Hawley, MN

LOW-SODIUM, LOW-CHOLESTEROL MUSTARD DRESSING

¼ c. Egg Beaters*
½ c. sugar
1½ Tbsp. flour
½ c. vinegar

1 tsp. dry mustard
½ c. hot water
1 Tbsp. unsalted margarine

Mix Egg Beaters, sugar, mustard, and flour. Add water and vinegar; cook in double boiler until smooth and thick. Add butter; cool. Store in a covered jar in the refrigerator. Yields 1 pint.

* If eggs are allowed, substitute 3 egg yolks for ¼ cup Egg Beaters.
Mary Voss, Owatonna, MN

LOWFAT, LOW-SODIUM CASSEROLE SAUCE MIX

2 c. nonfat dry milk powder
¾ c. cornstarch
¼ c. unsalted instant chicken
    bouillon
2 Tbsp. dried onion flakes *or* 1
    tsp. onion powder

1 tsp. dried basil
1 tsp. dried thyme
½ tsp. pepper

Blend all ingredients. When ready to use, combine ⅓ cup casserole mix with 1 ¼ cups water to equal 1 can soup.

Mary Voss, Owatonna, MN

HONEY-POPPY SEED SALAD DRESSING

1 c. honey
1 tsp. dry mustard
1 tsp. paprika
2 tsp. poppy seeds

5 tsp. vinegar
1 tsp. lemon juice
1 tsp. grated onion (if desired)
1 c. oil

In a blender or with an electric mixer, blend together all ingredients, except the oil. Gradually add the oil, beating constantly, until mixture thickens. Store in a covered jar in the refrigerator. Yield: 2 cups. Approximate calories per serving: 1 tablespoon equals 95.

LOW-SODIUM, LOW-CHOLESTEROL SALAD DRESSING

½ c. oil
2 Tbsp. lemon juice or vinegar
¼ tsp. paprika

⅛ tsp. dry mustard
1 tsp. sugar

Combine all ingredients and beat; refrigerate in covered jar. Shake well before use. May add dill, onion, garlic, or marjoram. Yields ¾ cup.

Mary Voss, Owatonna, MN

HOMEMADE EGG SUBSTITUTE

6 egg whites
¼ c. nonfat powdered milk
1 Tbsp. vegetable oil

6 drops yellow food coloring
    (optional)

Combine all ingredients in a mixing bowl and blend until smooth. Store in jar in refrigerator up to 1 week. Also freezes well. One fourth cup equals 1 whole egg. Can be used in baking, or fry slowly in a nonstick pan for scrambled eggs.

Marlys Swehla, Albert Lea, MN

SALT SUBSTITUTE

Use equal amounts of ginger, paprika, and grated lemon peel. After 2 weeks, add ½ teaspoon salt. Mixture is ready to use.

Bernice T. Eugenis, Saginaw, MN

FRESH STRAWBERRY SPREAD

2 pt. fresh strawberries or 1 (10 oz.) pkg. frozen strawberries (no sugar added)*
2 Tbsp. cold water

1½ Tbsp. lemon juice
2 tsp. granulated gelatin
¼ c. cold water
Artificial sweetener to substitute for 6 tsp. sugar (I use Equal)

Wash and clean berries; discard hulls. Measure 3 cups. Cut berries in small bite-size pieces and place in a heavy pan with 2 tablespoons cold water and lemon juice. Partially crush berries. Bring to a boil. Stir and cook rapidly for about 5 minutes until berries are just cooked.

Meanwhile, soak gelatin in ¼ cup cold water. Remove berries from heat. Add gelatin; stir to dissolve and blend. When mixture has completely cooled, add the Equal. Turn mixture into small jars; cover tightly and store in refrigerator. Use as a spread on bread toast, muffins, rolls, etc.

* If using frozen strawberries, do not add the 2 tablespoons of cold water.

Mary Voss, Owatonna, MN

EGG SALAD
(Makes 1½ cups)

1 c. Egg Beaters
2 Tbsp. finely chopped celery
2 Tbsp. finely chopped green pepper

½ c. Blender Mayonnaise
Generous dash of ground black pepper
½ tsp. prepared mustard

Pour Egg Beaters into a heavy 8 inch skillet. Cover tightly. Cook over *very low* heat for 10 minutes; remove from heat. Allow to stand, covered, for 10 minutes. Cut into small cubes.

Combine egg cubes, celery, and green pepper. Add Blender Mayonnaise, pepper, and mustard. Toss mixture lightly. Chill before serving. Use as a sandwich filling, or if desired, as a salad on crisp lettuce leaves. (Enough for 4 sandwiches or 3 salads.)

Mary Voss, Owatonna, MN

CUCUMBERS IN MOCK SOUR CREAM

3 medium cucumbers, peeled
   and sliced
1 small onion, chopped fine
1 tsp. sugar

1 c. mock sour cream
2 Tbsp. chopped parsley
Freshly ground black pepper

    Sprinkle cucumbers and onion with sugar; mix well. Chill in the refrigerator for several hours. Drain off water that accumulates. Mix in mock sour cream, parsley, and black pepper. Correct seasonings if necessary. Chill until serving time. Yield: 6 servings. Approximate calories per serving: 50.

HERBED BAKED TOMATOES

4 medium tomatoes
½ tsp. sugar
¼ tsp. onion powder
⅛ tsp. basil
⅛ tsp. oregano

Freshly ground black pepper
½ c. cracker crumbs
1 Tbsp. margarine
Chopped parsley

    Cut top off the tomato and scoop out a small portion of the pulp. Mix together with sugar, onion powder, basil, oregano, and pepper. Stuff tomatoes with this mixture. Top with cracker crumbs; dot with margarine and sprinkle with chopped parsley. Bake at 350°F. for 20 or 30 minutes until the tomatoes are tender. Yield: 4 servings. Approximate calories per serving: 115.

CUCUMBER AND YOGURT DIP

1 cucumber
1 (8 oz.) container plain lowfat
   yogurt

Garlic powder to taste
Dash of Worcestershire sauce

    Scrub cucumber to remove wax. Grate the unpeeled cucumber and drain *very well* until almost dry. Combine with other ingredients. Serve with crackers. Yield: 1¾ cups. Approximate calories per serving: ½ cup equals 45, 1 tablespoon equals 5.

SPICED CHEESE

1 c. lowfat cottage cheese
3 Tbsp. yogurt
1 Tbsp. chopped scallions or
   chives

1 Tbsp. parsley
¼ tsp. dry thyme
Freshly ground black pepper

Place all ingredients in a blender or food processor. Blend thoroughly. Serve on crackers or use as a dip for fresh vegetables, or thin with yogurt to make a salad dressing. Yield: About 1¼ cups. Approximate calories per serving: 1 tablespoon equals 10.

VEGETABLES

CURRIED CELERY

2 c. sliced celery
Boiling water
1 tart apple, pared, cored, and
    chopped
½ c. chopped onion

1 tsp. margarine
1 tsp. cornstarch
1 rounded tsp. curry powder
Freshly ground black pepper

Put celery in a saucepan over heat and pour in boiling water to ½ inch depth; cover. Boil for 5 minutes; the celery should still be crisp. Drain, reserving the cooking water and set celery aside.

Using the same pan, saute the chopped apple and onion in margarine over moderate heat, stirring frequently, until the onion is transparent. Blend in cornstarch and curry powder. Cook for 2 minutes. Add ½ cup of the reserved cooking water and cook for 5 more minutes over low heat. Add the celery and pepper. Yield: 4 servings. Approximate calories per serving: 45.

AVERY ISLAND CELERY

¼ c. margarine
1 medium onion, chopped
1 (16 oz.) can tomatoes
½ tsp. hot pepper sauce

¼ tsp. thyme
4 c. diagonally cut celery
1 (10 oz.) pkg. frozen peas,
    thawed

Melt margarine in a large skillet and cook the onion until just tender but not brown. Drain the tomatoes, reserving liquid. Combine liquid in a skillet with the hot pepper sauce and thyme. Bring to a boil and stir in the celery and peas. Cover and cook for 10 minutes or until barely tender. Add the tomatoes; heat through and place in a serving dish. Yield: 10 servings. Approximate calories per serving: 85.

SAVORY SPINACH

1 (10 oz.) pkg. frozen leaf
    spinach, thawed
2 Tbsp. horseradish

2 Tbsp. chopped Canadian
    bacon, cooked

Cook the spinach in ¼ cup of water until tender, about 4 or 5 minutes. Drain and mix in the horseradish and bacon. Yield: 4 servings. Approximate calories per serving: 50.

STIR-FRY SPINACH

1 lb. loose fresh spinach or   1 Tbsp. oil
     other leafy green vegetable

Wash spinach thoroughly and drain well. Heat oil in skillet or wok over medium high heat and add spinach, turning leaves over several times until they are well coated. Cover and cook for 1 minute. Uncover, stirring for another 30 seconds until spinach is wilted. Do not overcook. Serve at once. Yield: 4 servings. Approximate calories per serving: 60.

DEVILED BEETS

1 Tbsp. margarine
1/4 tsp. dry mustard
1/4 tsp. ground cloves
2 Tbsp. vinegar
1 Tbsp. brown sugar

1/2 tsp. paprika
1 tsp. Worcestershire sauce
3 c. diced cooked beets,
     drained, or small whole
     beets, drained

In a saucepan, melt margarine and mix well with all ingredients, except beets. Toss beets lightly in mixture to coat evenly. Cover and warm over low heat. Yield: 6 servings. Approximate calories per serving: 50.

PANNED BROCCOLI

1 lb. fresh broccoli
2 Tbsp. oil
1 Tbsp. minced onion

1 clove garlic, minced
Freshly ground black pepper
1 Tbsp. lemon juice

Wash broccoli and trim. Peel stems and cut into 2 inch lengths. Separate flowerets by cutting into halves or quarters so they are of uniform size. Blanch (parboil about 10 minutes for stems, less for flowerets). Plunge into cold water for about 3 minutes to set the color and texture. Saute onion and garlic in oil. Add drained broccoli and cook gently until it is tender crisp. This will take only a few minutes. Season with pepper and lemon juice. Serve at once. Yield: 4 servings. Approximate calories per serving: 95.

Variation: Omit lemon juice. Increase the oil. Add 2 or 3 anchovies to sauteed onion and garlic. When broccoli is done, pour entire mixture, including oil, over cooked pasta. Serve sprinkled with Parmesan cheese. Approximate calories per serving: 1/2 cup equals 220.

DILLED GREEN BEANS

Very simple, very quick, and very good!

1 c. beef broth
2 Tbsp. chopped onion
¼ c. chopped green pepper

½ tsp. dill seed
2 (9 oz.) pkg. frozen cut green
  beans

Add onion, pepper, and dill seed to broth and cook for several minutes. Add beans; cook, covered, for 5 to 8 minutes or until beans are just tender. Yield: 6 servings. Approximate calories per serving: 25.

GREEN BEANS OREGANO

1 (9 oz.) pkg. frozen Italian green
  beans
1 c. diced tomato (about 1
  medium tomato)
½ c. diced celery

¼ c. diced green pepper
2 Tbsp. chopped onion
¼ tsp. dried oregano leaves
⅓ c. water
4 lemon wedges

Combine all ingredients in a saucepan and bring to a boil. Separate beans with a fork. Reduce heat; cover and simmer for 6 to 8 minutes or until beans are tender crisp. Serve with lemon wedge. Yield: 4 servings. Approximate calories per serving: 30.

LAYERED VEGETABLES VINAIGRETTE

Dressing:

½ c. vinegar
½ c. oil

½ c. Dijon mustard
Freshly ground black pepper

Mix dressing in a jar; shake well.

Salad:

4 medium carrots
1 lb. green beans
2 tomatoes

2 cucumbers
¼ lb. mushrooms

Scrub or peel carrots and slice into rounds. Steam green beans for 5 minutes; drain. Slice tomatoes, cucumbers, and mushrooms into thin slices. Layer vegetables in a serving dish and top with dressing; refrigerate for 1 hour or more before serving. Yield: 8 servings. Approximate calories per serving: 170.

BEAN SPROUTS PIQUANT

1 Tbsp. margarine
½ lb. fresh mushrooms or use
    canned drained mushrooms
1 (20 oz.) can bean sprouts

¼ tsp. marjoram
¼ tsp. basil
1 tsp. lemon juice

Melt margarine in a large saucepan and cook mushrooms until golden. Stir in drained bean sprouts, herbs, and lemon juice. Cover and let steam for 1 minute. Yield: 6 servings. Approximate calories per serving: 40.

MELENZANA ALLA GRIGLIA - BROILED EGGPLANT

1 large eggplant
½ c. Italian salad dressing
1 tsp. rosemary
¼ tsp. oregano

1 c. tomato sauce
Freshly ground black pepper
2 oz. grated Parmesan cheese

Peel eggplant and cut crosswise in ¾ inch slices. Place in a bowl with salad dressing, rosemary, and oregano, being certain dressing and herbs are spread over each eggplant slice. Let stand for 1 hour; drain.

Arrange eggplant slices on a baking sheet. Broil 3 inches from a medium low flame for about 5 minutes on each side until the slices are tender and lightly browned. Arrange the eggplant and tomato sauce in alternate layers in an 8 inch square baking dish, seasoning each layer lightly with pepper. Top with grated cheese.

Place under broiler again for about 2 minutes or until cheese is brown. Serve immediately. Yield: 6 servings. Approximate calories per serving: 135.

Growing your own sprouts can be an adventure. You can grow sprouts from a wide variety of seeds and grains.

EGGPLANT SPAGHETTI SAUCE

1 eggplant, cut into cubes (you
    don't have to peel it)
3 Tbsp. oil
1 onion, sliced
1 garlic clove, minced

1 green pepper, sliced
1 c. plum tomatoes
1 c. tomato juice
1 tsp. oregano
2 tsp. basil

Saute eggplant in oil about 7 minutes. Add onion, garlic, and pepper; saute for 3 additional minutes or until tender. Combine tomatoes, tomato juice, and herbs. Add to the eggplant mixture. Cover and simmer for ½ hour. Serve over spaghetti. Yield: 6 servings. Approximate calories per serving: 100.

DESSERTS, CAKES, COOKIES, PIES

CHOCOLATE FONDUE

2 c. sugar
¾ c. cocoa powder
2 Tbsp. cornstarch
½ tsp. salt

4 c. cold skim milk
3 Tbsp. tub margarine
1½ tsp. vanilla extract
¼ tsp. butter flavoring

1. Mix sugar, cocoa, cornstarch, and salt together in saucepan.
2. Add skim milk, stirring well.
3. Cook over medium heat to a boil.
4. Lower heat and simmer for 20 minutes. (This can be done in a fondue pot.)
5. Add margarine, vanilla, and flavoring.
6. Dip angel food cake squares, marshmallows, fresh strawberries, banana slices, pineapple cubes, and other fruits. Yield: 5 cups.

LEMON SAUCE

1 c. sugar
2 Tbsp. cornstarch
2 c. water

2 Tbsp. tub margarine
2 Tbsp. lemon juice
2 Tbsp. grated lemon peel

1. Mix sugar and cornstarch in saucepan. Stir in water.
2. Bring to a boil and boil for 1 minute, stirring constantly. Remove from heat.
3. Stir in margarine and flavoring.
4. Serve over pound cake or other dessert. Yield: About 2 cups.

PEACHY DESSERT SAUCE

2 c. sliced fresh or frozen
   peaches

1 Tbsp. lemon juice
Sugar to taste

1. Combine all ingredients in blender until smooth.
2. Serve over cake or sherbet. Yield: 2 cups.

LOW-SODIUM, LOW-CHOLESTEROL ORANGE SAUCE

6 Tbsp. pure currant jelly
3 Tbsp. sugar
Grated rind of 2 oranges

2 Tbsp. orange juice
2 Tbsp. lemon juice
Dash of cayenne

417

Combine jelly, sugar, and grated oranges. Beat about 5 minutes until ingredients are thoroughly blended. Add remaining ingredients and blend well. Chill. Yields 4 servings.

Mary Voss, Owatonna, MN

LOW-SODIUM, LOW-CHOLESTEROL CHOCOLATE SAUCE

¼ c. cocoa	1 Tbsp. flour, sifted
1 c. skim milk	½ tsp. vanilla
¼ c. sugar	

Scald milk in double boiler; remove from heat. Mix dry ingredients. Stir dry ingredients into scalding milk and return to double boiler. Stir until thick. Cook for 10 minutes longer. Add vanilla. Serve hot or cold, 1 to 2 tablespoons per serving. Yields approximately 1 cup.

Mary Voss, Owatonna, MN

CHOCOLATE PUDDING

⅔ c. sugar	2 c. skim milk
2 Tbsp. cornstarch	1 tsp. vanilla extract
½ tsp. salt	2 tsp. tub margarine
2 Tbsp. cocoa powder	

1. Combine sugar, cornstarch, salt, and cocoa in saucepan.
2. Gradually add milk, stirring until smooth.
3. Heat to a boil, stirring constantly. Boil for 2 minutes. Remove from heat.
4. Stir in vanilla and margarine.

LAYERED FRUIT YOGURT PUDDING

Bottom layer:

1½ Tbsp. unflavored gelatin	1½ c. sliced bananas
6 Tbsp. cold water	1 (16 oz.) can pineapple chunks, drained
2 c. cranberry juice	
¾ c. orange juice	½ c. chopped walnuts

1. Soften gelatin in cold water.
2. Heat cranberry juice to simmering and add softened gelatin. Stir over low heat until dissolved and add orange juice.
3. Spread fruit and nuts in bottom of 8x8 inch baking pan.
4. Pour juice mixture over top and chill until set.

Top layer:

1½ tsp. unflavored gelatin	2 Tbsp. sugar
2 Tbsp. cranberry juice	1 c. plain skim milk yogurt

1. Soften gelatin in cranberry juice in small saucepan. Add sugar and stir over low heat until gelatin and sugar are dissolved. Remove from heat and blend in yogurt.

2. Cool to room temperature and pour over bottom layer. Chill several hours.

PINEAPPLE DEEP-DISH DESSERT

5 apples, peeled, cored, and
    sliced
1 (8 oz.) can crushed pineapple
    packed in own juice
    (undrained)

¾ c. brown sugar, firmly packed
3 Tbsp. cornstarch
¼ tsp. ground cinnamon
1 Tbsp. low-sodium corn oil
    margarine

1. Preheat oven to 350°F.

2. Place layers of sliced apples and pineapple in baking dish greased with margarine.

3. Combine sugar, cornstarch, and cinnamon and sprinkle over apples.

4. Dot with margarine.

5. Bake for 35 to 40 minutes. Yield: 6 servings.

STRAWBERRY FROZEN DESSERT

1 (10 oz.) pkg. frozen
    strawberries
3 Tbsp. frozen lemonade
    concentrate
6 Tbsp. sugar

1½ c. evaporated skim milk
1 egg white
1 (9 inch) meringue shell
    (optional)

Combine the strawberries with the lemonade concentrate. Pour the evaporated skim milk into a freezing tray and freeze until mushy around the edges. Put into a chilled bowl and beat to the consistency of whipped cream.

Beat 1 egg white until frothy. Add the sugar slowly, beating well after each addition. Fold in the whipped milk and strawberry mixture. Pour into 3 freezing trays and freeze partially. Place in a chilled bowl and beat again. Return to the freezer for 8 hours or overnight.

Beat again until the dessert is the consistency of ice cream. Freeze until set. Serve plain or in a meringue shell. Yield: 9 servings. Approximate calories per serving: 110 (or 170 with meringue).

RHUBARB CRISP

2 c. cut fresh or frozen
   unsweetened rhubarb
½ c. sugar
2 Tbsp. flour
⅓ c. brown sugar, firmly packed

3 Tbsp. dry oatmeal
¼ c. flour
¼ c. low-sodium corn oil
   margarine, melted

   1. Preheat oven to 325°F.
   2. Put rhubarb in baking dish greased with margarine.
   3. Mix sugar with 2 tablespoons flour and sprinkle on rhubarb.
   4. Combine brown sugar, oatmeal, ¼ cup flour, and melted margarine and sprinkle over top.
   5. Bake for 40 minutes. Yield: 6 servings.

YOGURT SPICE CAKE

½ c. tub margarine
1 c. brown sugar, firmly packed
Egg substitute equivalent to 1
   egg
1⅔ c. enriched all-purpose flour
3 Tbsp. cocoa powder
½ tsp. salt

1 tsp. baking soda
1 tsp. ground cinnamon
½ tsp. ground nutmeg
¼ tsp. ground cloves
¾ c. chopped walnuts
1 c. raisins
¾ c. plain skim milk yogurt

   1. Preheat oven to 350°F.
   2. Cream margarine and brown sugar together.
   3. Add egg substitute and beat for 3 to 5 minutes.
   4. Combine flour, cocoa, salt, soda, spices, walnuts, and raisins.
   5. Add dry ingredients alternately with yogurt to creamed mixture, stirring by hand just to blend ingredients.
   6. Pour into an oiled and floured 8x8 inch baking pan.
   7. Bake for 35 to 40 minutes. Yield: 16 servings.

LOW-SODIUM, LOW-CHOLESTEROL BAKED APPLE DESSERT

½ c. SF margarine
2 c. sugar
1½ c. flour

2 qt. apples, peeled and sliced
½ c. water
2 tsp. cinnamon

   Cream SF margarine. Add sugar gradually. Work in flour and cinnamon; mix well. Remove ¼ of flour mixture (enough for topping). Add water and apples to remaining flour mixture; mix. Pour into ungreased pan (9 inch square). Sprinkle rest of topping over apple mixture. Bake about 1 hour at 350°. Yields 12 servings.

Mary Voss, Owatonna, MN

LOW-SODIUM, LOW-CHOLESTEROL APPLE CRUNCH

1½ qt. apples, sliced
1 c. sugar

¼ c. flour
½ tsp. cinnamon

Mix all ingredients; place in pan. Dot with salt-free margarine.

Salt-Free Crunch Topping:

½ c. oatmeal
⅓ c. brown sugar

½ c. flour
¼ c. SF margarine

Mix dry ingredients. Add SF margarine. Mix until crumbly. Place mixture on fruit and pat firmly (9x9 inch square pan). Bake in 350° oven for 40 minutes or until crust is browned and fruit is tender. Yields 12 servings.

Mary Voss, Owatonna, MN

LOW-SODIUM, LOW-CHOLESTEROL RHUBARB CRUNCH

1 qt. rhubarb, cut fine
1⅓ to 1⅔ c. sugar

⅓ c. flour

Mix all ingredients. Pour mixture into pan. Top with Salt-Free Crunch Topping. Bake at 350° for 40 to 45 minutes. Yields 8 servings.

Mary Voss, Owatonna, MN

LOW-SODIUM, LOW-CHOLESTEROL PEACH CRUNCH

4 c. canned sliced peaches
¼ c. white sugar
¼ c. brown sugar
½ tsp. cinnamon

¼ c. cornstarch
1 tsp. lemon juice
1 Tbsp. SF margarine

Mix sugars, cinnamon, and cornstarch. Add to peaches; heat. Add SF margarine. Heat just until thickened. Add lemon juice. Place in 9x9 inch square baking pan. Cover with Salt-Free Cholesterol Crunch Topping. Bake at 350° for 45 minutes. Yields 12 servings.

Mary Voss, Owatonna, MN

DENVER CHOCOLATE PUDDING CAKE

1 c. all-purpose flour
¾ c. sugar
2 tsp. low-sodium baking
    powder*
3 Tbsp. unsalted margarine,
    melted*
3 Tbsp. cocoa

½ c. skim milk
½ tsp. vanilla
⅓ c. packed brown sugar
⅓ c. sugar
3 Tbsp. cocoa
1 c. cold water or coffee

Sift flour, ¾ cup sugar, and baking powder together in a bowl. Combine margarine and 3 tablespoons cocoa and add to dry ingredients. Beat in milk and vanilla. Pour into lightly oiled 9 inch square baking pan. Sprinkle remaining dry ingredients over top of batter, 1 at a time, but do not mix. Pour water or coffee over top. Bake at 350°F. for 30 to 40 minutes. To serve, invert each piece. Makes 9 servings.

Nutrition information: Three inch square contains 225 calories, 3 grams protein, 5 grams fat, 44 grams carbohydrate, 11 milligrams (½ mEq) sodium, and 0 milligrams cholesterol. Food exchanges per serving: 2 starch, 1 unsweetened fruit, 1 fat.

* If using regular baking powder and margarine equals 145 milligrams sodium per serving (6mEq).

Mary Voss, Owatonna, MN

WILLIAMSBURG ORANGE-WINE CAKE

The wine is in the frosting. A delicious tasting cake.

½ c. margarine
1 c. sugar
4 egg whites (unbeaten)
2 tsp. grated orange rind
1 tsp. vanilla extract

1 c. seedless golden raisins
½ c. chopped walnuts
2 c. sifted cake flour
1 tsp. baking soda
1 c. buttermilk

Cream the margarine and sugar until fluffy. Thoroughly blend in the unbeaten egg whites, orange rind, vanilla, raisins, and walnuts. Sift the flour with baking soda and add to the batter alternately with buttermilk, beginning and ending with the flour mixture.

Pour into a 9x9 inch oiled and floured square cake pan. Bake at 350°F. for 30 to 40 minutes. Yield: 12 servings. Approximate calories per serving: 275 (or 425 with frosting).

Frosting:

½ c. soft margarine
2 c. confectioners sugar

2 Tbsp. sherry

Cream together margarine, confectioners sugar, and sherry until fluffy. Use to frost cooled cake.

WHOLE WHEAT APPLESAUCE CAKE OR CUPCAKES

½ c. oil
¾ c. granulated brown sugar
1 c. applesauce
1½ c. unsifted whole wheat
    flour

1 tsp. baking soda
1 tsp. cinnamon

Oil and flour an 8 inch round or square baking pan or muffin tins. Cream the oil and sugar together and mix in applesauce and baking soda. Add flour and cinnamon, blending thoroughly.

Pour the batter into pan, or make individual cakes in muffin tins. Bake at 375°F. for 30 minutes for an 8 inch cake, about 20 minutes for cupcakes. Yield: 12 cupcakes or one 8 inch pan (9 servings). Approximate calories per serving: 1 cupcake equals 200, 1 square equals 265.

EASY APPLE CAKE

It is very good just as it is, when served soon after baking. Any leftover cake would be delicious served with a lemon sauce.

2 c. diced apples
1 c. sugar
⅓ c. oil
½ tsp. vanilla extract
1 egg, beaten (or 2 egg whites or
    egg substitute equivalent to
    1 egg)

1½ c. unsifted flour
1 tsp. baking powder
1 tsp. baking soda
1 tsp. cinnamon
½ c. raisins

Combine apples and sugar in a mixing bowl and let stand for 10 minutes. Blend oil, vanilla, and egg with the apples, then combine the dry ingredients and mix in well. Stir in raisins. Pour into greased 8 inch square cake pan. Bake at 350°F. for 35 to 40 minutes. Yield: 9 servings. Approximate calories per serving: 290.

LOW-SODIUM, LOW-CHOLESTEROL APPLESAUCE CUPCAKES

1 c. flour
1½ tsp. SF baking powder
1½ tsp. cinnamon
¼ tsp. nutmeg
¼ tsp. ginger
¼ tsp. cloves
⅛ tsp. allspice

½ c. raisins
½ c. applesauce
¼ c. SF margarine
¼ c. Egg Beaters
1 tsp. vanilla
4 Tbsp. sugar

Sift dry ingredients together. Blend Egg Beaters, vanilla, sugar, margarine, and applesauce together. Mix raisins in; gradually stir in the dry ingredients until moistened. Pour into 6 muffin cups. Bake at 350° for 20 to 25 minutes. Yields 6 cupcakes.

Mary Voss, Owatonna, MN

LOW-SODIUM, LOW-CHOLESTEROL BANANA CUPCAKES

½ c. SF margarine
1½ c. brown sugar, packed
1 tsp. vanilla
⅓ c. Egg Beaters
2¼ c. flour

1 Tbsp. SF baking powder
1¼ c. ripe bananas, mashed
1 c. skim milk
1 c. walnuts, chopped

Cream SF margarine, sugar, and vanilla until light and fluffy. Add Egg Beaters to creamed mixture; beat. Mix flour and SF baking powder. Mix bananas with milk. Alternately add dry ingredients and banana mixture to creamed ingredients, starting and ending with dry ingredients. Stir in walnuts. Dish batter into lined cupcake pans, filling ⅔ full. Bake at 350° for 15 to 20 minutes. Yields 28 servings.

Mary Voss, Owatonna, MN

LOW-SODIUM, LOW-CHOLESTEROL LEMON CUPCAKES

¾ c. sugar
¼ c. unsalted margarine
2 egg whites
1 c. flour, sifted
2 tsp. low-sodium baking
    powder

½ c. skim milk
1 tsp. vanilla
2 tsp. lemon extract
2 Tbsp. lemon rind

Cream sugar and margarine; add egg and mix well. Combine dry ingredients and blend into creamed mixture alternately with milk. Add vanilla, lemon extract, and rind and stir into mixture. Fill papered cupcake tins ½ to ⅔ full. Bake at 350° for 20 minutes. Sprinkle with powdered sugar after cooled. Yields 12 cupcakes.

Mary Voss, Owatonna, MN

QUICK ORANGE STREUSEL CAKE

2 c. sifted flour
½ c. sugar
2 tsp. baking powder
1 Tbsp. grated orange rind

1 egg, slightly beaten
½ c. skim milk
½ c. orange juice
⅓ c. oil

Sift together the flour, sugar, and baking powder. Add orange rind. Make a well in the dry ingredients and add beaten egg, milk, orange juice, and oil. Stir until the mixture is dampened but still somewhat lumpy. Turn into an oiled 10 inch pie pan or 8x8x2 inch cake pan.

Topping:

¼ c. flour
½ c. sugar

2 Tbsp. margarine

Mix the flour and sugar together, then cut in the margarine to the consistency of corn meal. Sprinkle over cake batter and bake at 375° F. for 35 minutes or until browned. Yield: 9 servings. Approximate calories per serving: 305.

CINNAMON COFFEE CAKE

1½ c. sifted flour	1 egg white
2½ tsp. baking powder	¼ c. oil
½ c. sugar	¾ c. skim milk

Sift together flour, baking powder, and sugar. Blend in egg white, oil, and milk; stir until flour is moistened.

Topping:

½ c. brown sugar	2 Tbsp. oil
½ c. chopped pecans	2 tsp. cinnamon
2 Tbsp. flour	

Make the topping by mixing together brown sugar, pecans, flour, oil, and cinnamon. Spread ½ of the batter in an oiled 8 inch square pan. Sprinkle with ½ of the topping. Add the remaining batter and sprinkle with the rest of the topping. Bake at 375°F. for 30 minutes or until done. Yield: 9 servings. Approximate calories per serving: 295.

DOUGHNUT PUFFS

2 c. flour	¾ c. skim milk
¼ c. sugar	2 egg whites
1½ Tbsp. low-sodium baking powder	Oil
1 tsp. ground nutmeg	½ c. sugar
¼ c. oil	1 tsp. ground cinnamon

1. Mix flour, sugar, baking powder, and nutmeg.
2. Add oil, milk, and egg whites, mixing well with a fork.
3. Drop from a teaspoon into hot oil and fry for about 3 minutes or until browned.
4. Drain on paper towels.
5. Mix sugar and cinnamon together and roll warm puffs in sugar mixture. Yield: 24 puffs.

MASTER MIX QUICK PEACH COBBLER

2 (29 oz.) cans peach slices (undrained)	3 Tbsp. low-sodium corn oil margarine, melted
½ tsp. almond extract	½ c. skim milk
2⅓ c. low-sodium Master Mix	2 Tbsp. sugar
3 Tbsp. sugar	

1. Preheat oven to 400°F.
2. Heat peaches and almond extract in 9x13 inch baking pan in oven for 15 minutes.

3. Combine Master Mix, 3 tablespoons sugar, margarine, and milk with a fork until a soft dough is formed.

4. Drop dough from a tablespoon onto hot peaches.

5. Sprinkle with 2 tablespoons sugar.

6. Bake, uncovered, for 15 to 20 minutes or until browned. Yield: 8 servings.

RHUBARB BARS

1 c. candy orange slices
1½ c. sugar
3 c. diced rhubarb

3 Tbsp. corn starch
¼ c. cold water
1 tsp. vanilla (reserve)

Dissolve corn starch in cold water. Over low heat, cook all together until thick; cool. Add vanilla.

Crust:

1 c. quick oatmeal
2 c. flour

1 c. brown sugar
1 c. margarine

Combine and mix as for pie crust. Put ¾ in an 11x13 inch pan. Spread cooled filling over all. Sprinkle the rest of crumbs on top. Bake in 350° oven for 30 minutes. Cut in bars.

Viola Antoine, Oakes, ND

GINGER OAT COOKIES

A sweet midday or evening snack needn't be high in fat and calories. This crispy treat contains no egg yolks and absolutely no cholesterol.

½ c. Promise (at room
    temperature, use unsalted)
¾ c. light brown sugar, firmly
    packed
2 large egg whites

2 tsp. vanilla extract
1 c. all-purpose flour
2 tsp. baking powder
¾ tsp. ground ginger
½ c. quick cooking oats

In a large mixer bowl, beat Promise and sugar till light and fluffy. Beat in egg whites and vanilla until smooth. Stir together flour, baking powder, and ginger. Stir in oats. Add dry ingredients to creamed mixture, beating at low speed. Drop by level tablespoonfuls, 1 inch apart, onto greased baking sheet. Bake in a preheated 350°F. oven for 10 minutes or till light brown around edges. Remove cookies from baking sheet. Cool on wire rack.

Yield: Two dozen 2½ inch cookies. Approximately 84 calories, 3 grams fat, 79 milligrams sodium (less if unsalted margarine), and 0 milligrams cholesterol.

Mary Voss, Owatonna, MN

LOW-SODIUM, LOW-CHOLESTEROL SUGAR COOKIES

½ c. unsalted margarine
1 c. sugar
¼ c. Egg Beaters*
1½ c. flour, sifted

1 tsp. low-sodium baking
    powder
1 tsp. vanilla
1 tsp. nutmeg

Combine vanilla, nutmeg, and margarine; mix. Add sugar gradually. Beat egg or Egg Beaters into mixture. Sift flour and baking powder; stir into mixture. Chill for 2 hours or longer. Take ¼ of the dough and roll very thin on floured board. Sprinkle dough with sugar before cutting out cookies. Decorate with nuts, raisins, or spices if desired. Bake on greased cookie sheet for 10 minutes at 400°. Yields 60 cookies (2 inches in diameter).

* If eggs are allowed, substitute 1 egg for ¼ cup Egg Beaters.

Mary Voss, Owatonna, MN

LOW-SODIUM, LOW-CHOLESTEROL OATMEAL RAISIN COOKIES

¾ c. SF corn oil margarine,
    softened
1 c. brown sugar, packed
½ c. sugar
¼ c. Egg Beaters
1 tsp. vanilla
1¼ c. flour

1 tsp. cinnamon
½ tsp. baking soda
¼ c. water
½ tsp. cloves
1 c. raisins
3 c. oatmeal

Cream margarine, sugar, Egg Beaters, water, and vanilla. Stir in remaining ingredients. Drop by rounded teaspoons on cookie sheet. Flatten slightly. Bake for 12 to 15 minutes at 350°. Yields 44 cookies.

Mary Voss, Owatonna, MN

LOW-SODIUM, LOW-CHOLESTEROL BUTTERSCOTCH BROWNIES

1 c. brown sugar
¼ c. vegetable oil
1 egg white
⅓ c. + 2 Tbsp. chopped walnuts

1 tsp. vanilla
1 c. cake flour, sifted
1 tsp. low-sodium baking
    powder

Combine sugar and oil into mixing bowl. Add egg white and beat well. Stir in nuts and vanilla. Fold sifted dry ingredients into mixture. Bake in greased 8x8 inch pan until golden brown or 25 to 30 minutes at 300°. Yields 8 servings.

Mary Voss, Owatonna, MN

LOW-CHOLESTEROL COOKIES

1 c. Promise margarine
1 c. sugar
1 c. sunflower oil
1 egg
1 tsp. cream of tartar
1 tsp. salt

1 tsp. vanilla
3½ c. flour
1 c. oatmeal
1 c. coconut
1 c. Rice Krispies

Mary Hocking, Fargo, ND

LOW-SODIUM, LOW-CHOLESTEROL PEANUT BUTTER COOKIES

1 c. SF peanut butter
½ c. (1 stick) SF margarine
½ c. granulated sugar
½ c. brown sugar, packed

½ tsp. vanilla
¼ c. Egg Beaters
1⅓ c. all-purpose flour
2 tsp. SF baking powder

Cream peanut butter and margarine. Slowly add white and brown sugars, beating until light and fluffy. Add vanilla and Egg Beaters. Beat well. Sift together flour and baking powder. Blend into peanut butter mixture. Drop on cookie sheet. Flatten with fork in crisscross pattern. Bake for about 10 minutes at 350°. Let cool slightly on cookie sheet, then remove and let cool completely. Yields 52 cookies.

Mary Voss, Owatonna, MN

RAISIN OATMEAL COOKIES

1 c. flour
½ tsp. baking soda
1½ c. quick cooking oatmeal
2 egg whites, slightly beaten
¼ tsp. cinnamon

1 c. brown sugar
⅓ c. oil
½ c. skim milk
1 tsp. vanilla
1 c. raisins

Mix flour, soda, and cinnamon. Stir in oats. Combine egg whites, brown sugar, oil, milk, vanilla, and raisins and add to flour; mix. Oil cookie sheets. Bake at 375° for 12 to 15 minutes.

Carol Gilbertson, Hawley, MN

AUNT EMMA'S SHOO-FLY PIE

A Pennsylvania Dutch delight!

Pie pastry for a 9 inch 1 crust pie
1½ c. flour
½ c. firmly packed light brown
   sugar
¼ c. margarine
1 tsp. baking soda

¾ c. boiling water
¾ c. dark corn syrup
¼ tsp. nutmeg
¼ tsp. cinnamon
¼ tsp. cloves

Line a 9 inch pie pan with pie pastry. Combine flour with brown sugar. Cut in the margarine until the mixture resembles corn meal. Pour ⅓ of the crumbs in the pie shell.

Add baking soda to the hot water. Stir in the dark corn syrup and spices and pour ⅓ of the mixture over the crumbs in the pie shell. Continue alternating layers, ending with crumbs on top and bake at 375°F. for 35 minutes. Serve warm or cold. Yield: 8 servings. Approximate calories per serving: 395 (or 315 in 10 servings).

CHOCOLATE INDULGENCE

**4 Tbsp. Promise, melted and
   divided (use unsalted
   margarine)
¾ c. Zwieback crumbs
¼ tsp. cinnamon
¾ c. sugar, divided**

**⅔ c. unsweetened cocoa
2 env. unflavored gelatin
1 c. water
2 c. part skim Ricotta cheese
3 egg whites (at room
   temperature)**

In small bowl, combine 2 tablespoons melted Promise, crumbs, and cinnamon. Press onto bottom of 9 inch springform pan. Bake in a preheated 350°F. oven for 8 minutes. Cool. In medium saucepan, combine ½ cup sugar, cocoa, and gelatin; mix well. Stir in water. Stir over medium heat until sugar and gelatin are dissolved, about 4 minutes. Remove from heat. Stir in remaining 2 tablespoons Promise; cool.

Meanwhile, in large bowl or food processor, beat or process Ricotta until fluffy. Blend in cooled chocolate mixture. In medium bowl, beat egg whites until foamy; gradually beat in remaining ¼ cup sugar until stiff peaks form. Fold egg whites into chocolate mixture. Pour into prepared crust. Chill for 4 hours or until firm. To serve, remove sides of pan. Cut into wedges.

Yield: 10 servings, approximately 207 calories, 9 grams fat, 124 milligrams sodium (less if unsalted margarine), and 15 milligrams cholesterol per serving.

NUTTY CRANBERRY PIE

**Pastry for 1 (9 inch) 2 crust pie
   (unbaked)
1 c. sugar
1½ Tbsp. cornstarch
⅓ c. light corn syrup
¾ c. water**

**1 tsp. grated orange or lemon
   rind
3 c. fresh cranberries
½ c. seedless raisins
¾ c. walnuts, finely chopped
2 Tbsp. oil**

Combine the sugar and cornstarch. Mix the corn syrup and lemon peel with the water and add to the sugar and cornstarch. Bring to a boil, then stir in cranberries and raisins. Boil until the cranberries pop, then remove from heat and add the nuts and oil. Cool until mixture is lukewarm.

Pour cranberry mixture into an unbaked 9 inch pie shell. Top with lattice or regular crust. Bake at 425°F. for 20 minutes, then reduce the heat to 375°F. and bake for 20 minutes. This pie may be served either hot or cold. Yield: 8 servings. Approximate calories per serving: 480 (or 380 in 10 servings).

RASPBERRY CHIFFON PIE

1 (9 inch) pie shell, baked
1¼ c. (10 oz. pkg.) frozen
    raspberries (sweetened)
1 Tbsp. unflavored gelatin
½ c. water (at room
    temperature)
¼ c. plus 2 Tbsp. sugar

1 Tbsp. all-purpose flour
2 Tbsp. lemon juice
⅓ c. ice water
⅓ c. nonfat dry milk
1 Tbsp. lemon juice
2 Tbsp. granulated sugar

Thaw the raspberries and drain, reserving the juice and saving 6 firm berries for garnish. Soften the gelatin powder in water. Combine ¼ cup of sugar with flour in a saucepan. Add the raspberry juice and softened gelatin. Stir and heat slowly until sugar is dissolved. Remove from heat and add 2 tablespoons of the lemon juice and berries. Cool until thick and syrupy, but not set.

Chill the beaters of the electric mixer. In a chilled bowl, combine ice water and nonfat dry milk. Beat until soft peaks are formed (about 3 or 4 minutes). Add the remaining tablespoon of lemon juice and beat another 3 or 4 minutes until stiff. Fold in the 2 tablespoons of sugar, blending well on low speed. Whip this into the raspberry-gelatin mixture. Pour into baked pastry shell and chill until firm. Yield: 8 servings. Approximate calories per serving: 180 (or 145 in 10 servings).

LOW-SODIUM, LOW-CHOLESTEROL PUMPKIN CUSTARD

¼ c. flour
¼ c. sugar
½ c. brown sugar, packed
1 tsp. cinnamon
½ tsp. ginger

2 c. SF cooked squash
2 oz. Egg Beaters
1½ c. liquid reconstituted
    nonfat dry milk (follow
    directions on box)

Mix flour, sugar, and spices. Add to squash and mix. Beat Egg Beaters slightly and add to squash mixture. Add milk gradually. Pour into custard cups. Bake in water bath in 325° oven for 40 to 60 minutes or until knife comes out clean. Yields 1 quart (eight ½ cup servings).

Mary Voss, Owatonna, MN

SF LOW-CHOLESTEROL TWO-CRUST PIE CRUST

2 c. flour   **2 to 3 Tbsp. cold water**
¾ c. SF margarine

Cut margarine into flour until finely blended; chill. Add water and mix until desired consistency is obtained. Form into a flattened rounded edge shape. Roll to desired size. Yields crust for 1 pie. One serving equals 1½ starch and 3 fat exchanges (⅛ pie).

Mary Voss, Owatonna, MN

SOUPS

LENTIL SOUP

1 Tbsp. margarine
1 onion, chopped
2 garlic cloves, finely chopped
1 c. lentils
7 c. water
⅛ tsp. cinnamon

¼ tsp. ginger
¼ tsp. cloves
⅛ tsp. cayenne
1½ tsp. cumin
Freshly ground black pepper

Melt margarine in pan; saute onion and garlic. Add remaining ingredients. Bring to boil; reduce heat and simmer for 1½ hours. Place mixture in blender or food processor and blend. Serve immediately. Yield: Approximately 2 quarts. Approximate calories per serving: 100.

SALAD BOWL SOUP

1 (18 oz.) can spicy tomato
    cocktail juice
1 c. garbanzo beans, drained
¾ c. cubed cooked chicken or
    turkey

1 peeled and mashed avocado
¼ avocado, sliced in 4 pieces
    (for garnish, optional)

Heat the tomato cocktail juice with garbanzos and chicken or turkey meat; simmer for about 5 minutes. Stir in the mashed avocado. Serve immediately garnished with extra avocado slices if desired. Yield: About 1 quart. Approximate calories per serving: 1 cup equals 290.

CREAMY ASPARAGUS SOUP

1 (16 oz.) can cut asparagus with
    liquid
1 c. cooked rice
¼ c. chopped onion

¼ c. chopped celery
1½ c. skim milk
Freshly ground black pepper
Dash of nutmeg

Place canned asparagus and liquid in a blender with onion, celery, and cooked rice. Blend on low speed until pureed. Pour into a saucepan. Stir in milk. Season and heat to boiling point. Serve immediately. Yield: About 1¼ quarts. Approximate calories per serving: 1 cup equals 95.

Variation - Asparagus Watercress Soup: Add ½ cup of chopped watercress to the blender with other ingredients. Blend until pureed and proceed as directed.

432

COLD AVOCADO SOUP

2 (10½ oz.) cans chicken broth,
   chilled
2 ripe avocados, chilled

Dash of lemon juice
1 oz. sherry (or to taste)
Dill weed

Put chilled broth in blender. Dice avocados and add to broth with lemon juice and sherry; blend well. Pour into cups and sprinkle with dill weed. Serve cold. Yield: 3 cups. Approximate calories per serving: 1 cup equals 150.

GREEN SPLIT PEA SOUP

1 c. green split peas
1 Tbsp. margarine
¼ c. chopped onion
4 c. cold water
Freshly ground black pepper

½ tsp. ground marjoram
¼ tsp. thyme
2 Tbsp. parsley
1 diced carrot

Melt margarine in a large saucepan and cook onion until lightly browned. Add water, peas, carrot, and seasoning; cover and simmer for 1 hour or until peas are tender, stirring occasionally. Press soup through a sieve or puree in a blender. Serve immediately. Yield: About 1 quart. Approximate calories per serving: 1 cup equals 85.

YELLOW SQUASH SOUP

2 medium yellow summer
   squash, sliced
2 medium onions, sliced

2 cans chicken broth
Freshly ground black pepper
¼ c. yogurt

Cook squash and onions in chicken broth for 15 minutes or till vegetables are soft. Add pepper and yogurt. Puree soup in blender; serve. Can be served hot or cold. Additional yogurt and pepper may be added to taste. Yield: About 1½ quarts. Approximate calories per serving: 1 cup equals 30.

FRUIT SOUP

1 c. dried prunes
1 c. small dried apricot halves
2 qt. water
1 c. seedless white or dark
   raisins

1 stick cinnamon
2 Tbsp. cornstarch
¼ c. cold water

Soak prunes and apricots in water for 4 hours (or follow package instructions, which may not include soaking). Add raisins and cinnamon stick and bring to a boil; simmer gently, covered, until fruits are tender but still whole. Remove cinnamon stick.

Dissolve cornstarch in cold water. Add to fruit and cook until thickened, stirring constantly. Serve hot or chilled. Yield: About 2 quarts. Approximate calories per serving: 1 cup equals 150.

VEGETABLE BISQUE

¼ c. Promise (use unsalted)
2 medium potatoes, pared and
   diced (about 2 c.)
1 medium size red bell pepper,
   seeded, coarsely chopped,
   and divided
½ c. chopped celery
2 Tbsp. finely chopped onion

½ tsp. ground thyme
¼ tsp. hot pepper sauce
4 c. (16 oz. bag) frozen whole
   kernel corn
1¾ c. (13¾ oz. can) low-sodium
   chicken broth
1 c. water
1¾ c. skim milk

In a large saucepan, melt Promise. Stir in potatoes. Add red pepper, reserving 3 tablespoons for garnish. Stir in celery, onion, thyme, and hot pepper sauce. Stir over medium heat for 5 minutes or until vegetables are tender. Add corn, broth, and water; bring to a boil. Reduce heat; simmer for 20 minutes.

Turn mixture into a food processor or container of electric blender, filling container only halfway. Cover; process until smooth. Repeat with remaining mixture. Return to saucepan; add milk. Heat through. Serve hot, garnished with reserved red pepper. Yield: 8 servings. Approximately 175 calories, 6 grams fat, 108 milligrams sodium (less if unsalted margarine), and 1 milligram cholesterol per serving.

Mary Voss, Owatonna, MN

BEEF-BARLEY VEGETABLE SOUP
(A meal in itself)

3 lb. meaty shin bone (lean), well
   trimmed
1½ qt. cold water
Freshly ground black pepper

3 Tbsp. barley
Vegetables (as for vegetable
   soup)

Place meat in kettle; cover with cold water. Add seasoning. Heat slowly to boiling point; cover and let simmer for 2½ to 3 hours or until meat is tender. Skim off fat. Remove meat and bone. Add barley and vegetables and continue cooking for 45 minutes. Yield: About 2 quarts. Approximate calories per serving: 1 cup equals 185.

TOMATO CORN SOUP

2 Tbsp. oil
¼ c. chopped onion
2 Tbsp. flour
2 c. tomato juice
1 (16 oz.) can (2 c.) cream style
   corn

2 c. skim milk
Freshly ground black pepper
Parsley (for garnish)

In a 2 quart saucepan, heat oil over moderately low heat and cook chopped onion until transparent. Stir in flour and cook, stirring, until slightly thickened. Pour mixture into a blender with tomato juice and corn; blend until smooth.

Pour into a 2 quart saucepan with milk. Place over moderately low heat and cook, stirring constantly. Do not allow to boil. Add pepper to taste. Serve hot garnished with parsley. Yield: About 1½ quarts. Approximate calories per serving: 1 cup equals 155.

TOMATO BOUILLON

A smooth broth whose flavor develops ahead of the cooking. An excellent first course.

4 c. tomato juice
½ bay leaf
2 whole cloves
¼ tsp. dill seed
¼ tsp. basil
¼ tsp. marjoram

¼ tsp. oregano
½ tsp. sugar
Freshly ground black pepper
Chopped parsley
Curry powder (optional)

Place all herbs, except parsley, in the tomato juice and let stand for 1 hour to allow flavors to blend. Heat tomato-herb bouillon to boiling point. Remove from heat and strain. Pour into serving bowls. Garnish with parsley and a dash of curry powder if desired. Yield: 1 quart. Approximate calories per serving: 1 cup equals 50.

VEGETABLE SOUP

3 carrots, finely chopped
1 head cabbage, shredded
2 ribs celery, finely chopped
1 onion, chopped

1 (28 oz.) can tomatoes
6 c. beef broth
Freshly ground black pepper

Place vegetables in a large pot with tomatoes and broth. Bring to boil and simmer, covered, until thick, about 45 minutes. Season to taste with pepper. Yield: 2 quarts. Approximate calories per serving: 1 cup equals 45.

FIVE-MINUTE SOUP

A quick cooking soup, this is best served immediately while the vegetables are fresh and colorful.

4 c. chicken broth
½ raw cucumber, scrubbed,
    unpeeled, and sliced very
    thin
4 raw mushrooms, sliced
2 c. shredded raw green leaf
    vegetable (spinach, lettuce,
    or cabbage)

1 tomato, cubed
½ c. leftover lean meat,
    shredded

Heat the broth. Add the vegetables and meat. Bring to a boil and simmer for 5 minutes. Serve immediately. Yield: About 1½ quarts. Approximate calories per serving: 1 cup equals 45.

MINESTRONE SOUP

3 Tbsp. oil
1 onion, chopped
3 garlic cloves, chopped
2 carrots, chopped
2 stalks celery, chopped
2 potatoes, cubed
4 tomatoes, cubed
1 small zucchini

½ lb. green beans
Black pepper
8 c. water
1 c. white navy beans
½ c. Weight Watchers pasta,
    cooked
1 Tbsp. basil

Heat oil in large pan. Add onion, carrots, garlic, and celery. Saute until the onion is transparent. Add potatoes, tomatoes, zucchini, green beans, black pepper, and water; simmer for 30 minutes. Add white beans and pasta. Add more water if soup is too thick.

In blender, blend basil, 1 clove of garlic, and 1 cup of soup. Return this mixture to soup; mix and serve.

Joanne Gulla, Virginia, MN

PANCAKES, WAFFLES, MUFFINS, BREADS

WHOLE WHEAT AND SOY WAFFLES

1 c. whole wheat flour
¼ c. soy flour
2 tsp. baking powder
2 eggs, separated

1½ c. skim milk
3 Tbsp. oil
2 Tbsp. honey

Preheat waffle iron. Stir together the 2 kinds of flour and baking powder. Beat egg yolks until they are light yellow. Add milk, oil, and honey. Blend well and stir into the dry ingredients. Beat egg whites until stiff and fold into batter. Pour batter onto the hot waffle iron. Yield: About 10 waffles. Approximate calories per serving: 130.

WHEAT GERM PANCAKES

1 c. white flour
2½ tsp. baking powder
1 Tbsp. sugar
½ c. wheat germ

1¼ c. skim milk
2 Tbsp. oil
½ c. lowfat cottage cheese

Stir flour, baking powder, and sugar together. Add wheat germ. Combine milk and oil; stir into dry ingredients until moistened. Stir in cottage cheese only until mixture is slightly lumpy. Drop batter by spoonfuls onto a greased pan. Cook until bubbles appear on upper surface, then turn only once.

Joanne Gulla, Virginia, MN

OATMEAL-BUTTERMILK PANCAKES

1 c. quick oatmeal
1½ c. buttermilk
2 eggs
⅓ c. flour

1 tsp. soda
1 tsp. sugar
½ tsp. salt

Mix all ingredients together. Bake on hot griddle. Makes about 12 cakes.

Optional: Add ½ to 1 teaspoon cinnamon if desired. Oatmeal is good to lower blood cholesterol.

Eloise Hoff, Preston, MN

FRENCH TOAST
(Serves 4)

1 c. Egg Beaters
⅓ c. skim milk
½ tsp. cinnamon

8 slices white bread (day old)
2 to 3 Tbsp. Fleischmann's
   margarine

Combine Egg Beaters, skim milk, and cinnamon in shallow dish and use to coat bread on both sides. Fry in Fleischmann's margarine over medium low heat until golden brown on both sides. Serve hot with syrup.

Mary Voss, Owatonna, MN

FLUFFY COTTAGE CHEESE BLINTZES

1 egg yolk
½ c. lowfat cottage cheese
⅓ c. skim milk

¼ c. flour
3 egg whites

In a mixing bowl, beat egg yolk until thick and lemon colored. Add cottage cheese; beat until almost smooth. Blend in skim milk and flour. Beat egg whites until peaks fold over. Fold into batter. Let batter stand for 5 minutes.

Pour ¼ cup of batter onto a preheated griddle which has been brushed lightly with oil. Bake until the top is bubbly and edges are baked. Turn and bake the other side. Serve at once with mock sour cream or fruit. Yield: 6 small blintzes. Approximate calories per serving: 55.

CHICKEN CREPES

½ c. chopped onion
16 fresh mushrooms, sliced
2 Tbsp. oil
6 Tbsp. flour
1 low-sodium chicken bouillon
    cube

¼ tsp. pepper
¼ c. chopped fresh parsley
3 c. skim milk
⅓ c. white wine
3½ c. chopped cooked chicken
9 Basic Crepes

1. Preheat oven to 350°F.
2. Saute onion and mushrooms in oil.
3. Stir in flour. Add bouillon cube, pepper, and parsley.
4. Gradually stir in milk and cook, stirring constantly, until mixture thickens.
5. Stir in wine and cook for 5 minutes longer.
6. Add ½ of sauce mixture to chicken.
7. Place ¼ cup of the chicken mixture on each crepe. Roll crepes and place, seam side down, in a 9x13 inch baking dish. Top with remaining sauce.
8. Cover and bake for 20 to 30 minutes. Yield: 9 crepes.

438

APPLE-BRAN BREAKFAST MUFFINS

High in fiber and low in fat, these wholesome muffins taste even better spread with Promise.

1½ c. shreds of wheat bran
   cereal
1 c. skim milk
¼ c. Promise, melted (unsalted)
2 Tbsp. molasses
1 large cooking apple, pared,
   cored, and coarsely grated
   (about 1½ c.)

½ c. whole wheat flour
½ c. all-purpose flour
2 Tbsp. toasted wheat germ
2 tsp. baking powder
½ tsp. baking soda
2 large egg whites, stiffly beaten

Lightly grease 12 (3 x 1¼ inch) muffin cups. In a medium bowl, combine bran and milk; let stand for 3 minutes. Stir in Promise, molasses, and apple. Combine flours, wheat germ, baking powder, and baking soda; stir into bran mixture. Fold in egg whites; turn into prepared muffin cups. Bake in a preheated 350°F. oven for 20 to 25 minutes or until done.

Yield: 12 muffins. Approximately 123 calories, 4 grams fat, 282 (less) milligrams sodium, and 3 milligrams cholesterol per muffin.

Mary Voss, Owatonna, MN

ORANGE BRAN MUFFINS

2½ c. flour
1 tsp. salt (optional)
1 Tbsp. soda
3 c. bran cereal
¾ c. sugar

1 tsp. cinnamon
1½ Tbsp. grated orange rind
2 c. plain yogurt
2 eggs or 4 egg whites
½ c. oil

Preheat oven to 375°. In large bowl, combine flour, salt, and soda. Add cereal, cinnamon, and orange rind, mixing well. Briefly, but thoroughly, mix in the yogurt, beaten eggs, and oil. (Do not stir again even while filling pans.) Fill greased muffin cups about ¾ full. Bake for 20 minutes. (You can sprinkle sugar on top of muffins before baking.)

Joanne Gulla, Virginia, MN

OAT BRAN MUFFINS
(No cholesterol)

2¼ c. oat bran
1 c. raisins or currants
1 Tbsp. baking powder
1 tsp. orange rind

⅓ c. sugar
½ c. orange juice
¼ c. oil
White of 3 large eggs

Oven: 375°. Grease muffin tins or use baking cups. Mix oat bran, raisins, baking powder, orange peel, and ¼ cup sugar in large bowl. Add juice and oil. Stir till blended. In small bowl, beat egg whites till soft peaks form. Add remaining sugar; beat till thick and glossy. Stir about ¼ egg whites into mixture to lighten. Fold in remainder. Bake for 20 minutes. Cool.

Joanne Gulla, Virginia, MN

SF LOW-CHOLESTEROL BAKING POWDER BISCUITS

2 c. flour
2 Tbsp. Low Na baking powder
¼ c. nonfat dry milk powder*

2 tsp. sugar
3 Tbsp. SF margarine
½ c. + 2 Tbsp. water*

Blend flour, baking powder, milk powder, and sugar in mixing bowl. Cut in margarine until fat is size of small pea. Add liquid all at once and mix only until all flour is dampened. Knead gently on lightly floured surface. Roll to about 1 inch thickness. Cut into round shapes with pastry cutter and place on ungreased baking sheet. Bake at 450° for 12 to 15 minutes. Yields: 10 servings. One serving (1 biscuit) equals 1 starch and 1 fat exchange.

* Could use skim milk in place of powdered milk and water to equal ½ to ¾ cup.

Mary Voss, Owatonna, MN

APPLESAUCE BREAD

1 c. applesauce
½ c. oil
½ c. sugar
1¾ c. flour
1 tsp. baking soda
½ tsp. salt (optional)

1 tsp. cinnamon
½ tsp. cloves
½ tsp. nutmeg
1 egg or 2 egg whites
1 c. raisins

Mix applesauce, oil, and sugar. Sift in the flour, baking soda, salt, and spices. Add egg (beaten) and raisins. Pour into loaf pan. Bake at 325° for 1 hour and 20 minutes. Baking time may vary.

Joanne Gulla, Virginia, MN

HEALTH BREAD

1 c. quick oats
1 c. whole wheat flour
1 c. Bran Buds
1 c. raisins
1 c. water

1 tsp. salt (optional)
¾ c. sugar (or less)
1 tsp. soda
1 c. sour milk or buttermilk

Preheat oven to 350°. Stir everything together at once. Turn into greased loaf pan. Bake for 50 to 60 minutes.

Joanne Gulla, Virginia, MN

BASIC BREAD

1 cake yeast or 2 env. dry yeast	1 tsp. salt
¼ c. lukewarm water	6 c. sifted flour
1¾ c. skim milk	2 Tbsp. oil
2½ Tbsp. sugar	

Dissolve the yeast in the lukewarm water. Mix sugar and milk together and stir into the dissolved yeast. To this mixture, add salt and 3 cups of flour; beat until smooth. Add the oil.

Gradually mix in the remaining flour until dough is stiff enough to handle. Knead it until it is smooth and elastic. Place dough in a greased bowl, turning to coat all sides with oil. Cover with a clean cloth and let rise in a warm place (about 85°F.) until double in bulk.

Divide into 2 equal parts. Shape into loaves and place into two 10x5 inch loaf pans. Cover and let rise again until doubled in bulk. Bake at 425°F. for 15 minutes. Reduce heat to 375°F. and continue baking for 30 minutes longer. Remove bread from pans and place on wire racks to cool. Yield: Two 1 pound loaves (16 slices each). Approximate calories per serving: 1 slice equals 95.

Variation - Herb Bread: Mix the following herbs into the dough just before kneading: ½ teaspoon of nutmeg, ¼ teaspoon each of thyme, and rosemary, and 2 teaspoons of caraway seed.

DILLY BREAD

1 pkg. dry yeast	1 tsp. salt
¼ c. warm water	1 Tbsp. minced onion
1 c. lowfat cottage cheese,	2 tsp. dill seed
heated to lukewarm	¼ tsp. baking soda
1 Tbsp. margarine	2½ c. all-purpose flour
2 Tbsp. sugar	

Soften the yeast in warm water and combine with cottage cheese. Add sugar and all other ingredients, except the flour. Gradually mix in flour to form a stiff dough and beat well. Let rise in a warm place about 60 minutes or until doubled in bulk.

Punch the dough down and put in well oiled 2 quart round casserole dish or a 9x5 inch loaf pan. Cover and let rise for about 40 minutes. Bake at 350°F. for 40 to 50 minutes. Brush with melted margarine while still hot. Cool for 5 minutes before removing from pan. Yield: One 9x5 inch loaf (16 slices). Approximate calories per serving: 1 slice equals 90.

CINNAMON BREAD

1 recipe for Basic Bread
2 Tbsp. margarine, melted

½ c. sugar
1 Tbsp. cinnamon

Make dough for Basic Bread and let rise the first time. Roll out dough and spread with ½ of the margarine. Mix the sugar and cinnamon together and sprinkle over dough, reserving 1 tablespoon for topping. Roll dough lengthwise like a jelly roll. Shape into a loaf and cut in 2 parts.

Pinch the ends together and tuck under. Place into 2 oiled 10x5 inch loaf pans and spread a little margarine over the top. Let rise until doubled in bulk. Sprinkle each loaf with the remaining ½ tablespoon of cinnamon and sugar mixture. Bake at 375°F. for 50 minutes. Remove loaves from pans and cool on a wire rack. Yield: Two 1 pound loaves (16 slices each). Approximate calories per serving: 1 slice equals 115.

BANANA BREAD

1½ c. all-purpose flour
½ c. sugar
2 tsp. baking powder
1 tsp. baking soda
½ tsp. salt
½ c. wheat germ

3 medium very ripe bananas,
    mashed (about 1 c.)
¼ c. buttermilk
¼ c. oil
4 egg whites

Sift together the flour, sugar, baking powder, baking soda, and salt. Mix in wheat germ. Add all remaining ingredients and beat until well blended. Place in an oiled 8x4 inch loaf pan. Bake at 350°F. for about 1 hour or until done. Yield: 1 loaf (16 slices). Approximate calories per serving: 1 slice equals 130.

OATMEAL BREAD

1½ c. boiling water
1 c. rolled oats
1 tsp. salt
⅓ c. light molasses
1½ Tbsp. oil

1 pkg. dry yeast
¼ c. warm water
4 to 4½ c. all-purpose flour,
    sifted

Pour the boiling water over the oatmeal. Add the salt; stir and cool to lukewarm. Dissolve the yeast in warm water, then add molasses, oil, and dissolved yeast to the oatmeal mixture. Gradually add the sifted flour until dough is stiff enough to handle. Knead the dough on a lightly floured board for about 5 minutes or until dough is smooth and elastic.

Place dough in a lightly oiled bowl, turning to coat all sides of the dough with oil. Cover with a clean cloth and let rise in a warm place (about 85°F.) until double in bulk. Punch down the dough and knead again for a few minutes.

Shape into a loaf and put it in a well oiled 9x5 inch loaf pan. Cover and let rise again (about 1 hour) until doubled in bulk. Bake at 375°F. for 50 minutes. Remove bread from pan and place on a wire rack to cool. Yield: 1 loaf (16 slices). Approximate calories per serving: 1 slice equals 150.

Variation: One quarter cup of wheat germ and/or ½ cup of seedless raisins may be added. Approximate calories per serving: 1 slice equals 170.

CURRANT BREAD

2½ c. all-purpose flour, sifted
⅛ tsp. salt
6 Tbsp. margarine
½ tsp. baking powder
½ c. currants

2 eggs, well beaten (or 4 egg whites or egg substitute equivalent to 2 eggs)
¼ c. skim milk

Cream together flour, salt, and margarine. Stir in the baking powder and currants. Add eggs and milk. Turn into an oiled 8x4 inch pan and bake at 350°F. for 45 to 60 minutes. Yield: 1 loaf (16 slices). Approximate calories per serving: 130.

PUMPKIN-PECAN BREAD

This moist, flavorful bread is a winner any time of the day. It makes an especially good snack.

3½ c. flour
2 tsp. baking soda
1½ tsp. salt
1½ tsp. cinnamon
1 tsp. nutmeg
1 c. sugar
1 c. oil

4 eggs (or 8 egg whites or egg substitute equivalent to 4 eggs)
⅔ c. water
2 c. canned pumpkin
1 c. chopped pecans

Sift together the flour, soda, salt, cinnamon, and nutmeg. Add sugar and stir to mix thoroughly. Make a well in the center of the dry ingredients and add all at once the oil, eggs, water, and pumpkin. Mix well and add the nuts.

Pour batter into four 8x4 inch loaf pans, filling each ½ full. Bake at 350°F. for 1 hour or until a wooden toothpick inserted in the center of the loaf comes out clean. Yield: 4 loaves (16 slices each). Approximate calories per serving: 1 slice equals 85.

FRUIT LOAF

1 recipe Basic Bread
½ c. seedless raisins
½ c. chopped walnuts
¼ c. candied orange peel
¼ c. chopped candied cherries

¼ c. confectioners sugar
1 Tbsp. warm water
1 to 2 drops almond or vanilla
   extract

Make dough for Basic Bread. Mix together the raisins, walnuts, and candied fruit; knead the mixture into the Basic Bread dough. Shape into two 9 inch greased round pans or ring molds. Cover and let rise in a warm place until doubled in bulk. Bake at 350°F. for 1¼ hours.

To make the frosting, mix together the confectioners sugar, warm water, and extract. Use to frost the bread while loaves are still warm. Yield: Two 1 pound loaves (16 slices each). Approximate calories per serving: 1 slice equals 130.

PECAN LOAF
(Makes 1 loaf - 20 slices)

3 c. all-purpose flour
1¼ c. sugar
5 tsp. low-sodium baking
   powder
1½ c. skim milk
¾ c. Egg Beaters
   (cholesterol-free 99% real
   egg product)

⅓ c. Fleischmann's sweet
   unsalted margarine, melted
½ c. pecan halves, coarsely
   chopped

In large bowl, stir together flour, sugar, baking powder, skim milk, Egg Beaters, and margarine just until blended. Stir in pecans. Pour batter into greased 9x5x3 inch loaf pan. Bake at 350°F. for 55 to 60 minutes or until done. Cool in pan for 10 minutes. Remove from pan; cool on wire rack.

Nutrition information: Per serving (1 slice) equals 78 calories, 31 milligrams sodium, 0 milligrams cholesterol, 5 milligrams fat. Exchanges per servings: 2 grains - 1 and 1 fat - 1.

Helen H. Clark, Grand Forks, ND

MISCELLANEOUS HINTS AND DIET SUGGESTIONS

TIPS FOR ADAPTING RECIPES FOR HEART HEALTH
(Low salt, low cholesterol diets)

Use low-sodium baking powder. Substitute 1 teaspoon of baking soda for 4 teaspoons baking powder.

Use low salt peanut butter. (Keep in refrigerator.)

Chocolate should be avoided, but you can use cocoa.

Two egg whites equals 1 egg. (Don't use yolks.) One fourth cup Egg Beaters equals 1 whole egg.

You can use ground turkey in place of ground beef (in most recipes).

You can use "Pam" or similar sprays for greasing pans.

Use unsalted margarine that is low in cholesterol (like Fleischmann's, HyVee, Promise, etc.).

You may use corn oil, safflower, sunflower, and soy bean oils because they contain polyunsaturated fats, which can help reduce cholesterol.

Use Mozzarella cheese or those made from skim milk.

Avoid Coffee-Rich, butter, chocolate, coconut, and palm or coconut oil because they contain saturated fats.

Also avoid *solid* shortenings if possible.

Angel food cake can be substituted for yellow cake.

Mrs. Dash or similar seasoning can be used in place of salt.

Use ice milk instead of ice cream.

Avoid hard cheeses made with whole milk.

Use more chicken (remove skin) and fish than red meat.

Use salt-free bread.

The more *processed* the item is, the more sodium it contains (such as mixes). Try to make from scratch so you know what goes into it.

Use frozen vegetables if fresh vegetables are not available. If using canned vegetables, use the "no salt added" if available.

Do not add salt to food at the table.

Use only ½ to ¾ teaspoon of salt in food preparation per day.

Avoid the following:

Seasoning salts and mixes; garlic salt; onion salt; celery salt; meat tenderizers; monosodium glutamate; soy sauce; ketchup; prepared mustard; prepared horseradish; bottled meat sauce and barbecue sauce; olives; pickles; commercially prepared salted French, Italian, or creamy style salad dressings and commercial gravy or gravy mixes.

Salt-cured meats; meats, fish or fowl that are canned with added salt or smoked; bacon; ham; sausages; salt pork; corned beef; dried beef; processed cold cuts; frankfurters; sardines; process or highly salted cheese and cheese foods; commercial casserole mixes; frozen dinners.

Salted snack foods; salted crackers; salted popcorn; pretzels; potato chips; corn chips; salted nuts (cashew or pistachio included).

Canned soups; dried soup mixes; commercial broth or bouillon.

Sauerkraut; pickled vegetables; pickles; commercially frozen vegetable mixes with sauces; salted canned tomato sauce and paste.

Cultured buttermilk; instant beverage mixes; cocoa mixes; cocktail beverage mixes; club soda; commercial activity drinks, including Gatorade.

Limit the following:

Peanut butter to 2 servings per week. Additional servings of salt-free peanut butter may be used.

Mild-aged cheese, cottage cheese, and Parmesan cheese to 2 servings per week. Additional servings of salt-free cheese may be used.

Antacids, alkalizers, laxatives, and cough medicines may contain significant amounts of sodium. Check the label or contact a pharmacist or your physician for the sodium content.

Chemically softened water contains added sodium and should not be used for cooking or drinking.

Mary Voss, Owatonna, MN

LOWFAT - LOW-CHOLESTEROL - LOW CALORIE FOOD
(Selection and preparation hints)

1. Remove fat from meats before preparing them.

2. Select low fat cuts of meat (tenderize by pounding or marinating).

3. Broil, roast, or bake on a rack to allow fat to drip into a pan.

4. Avoid gravies. Use tomato juice rather than sauce. Cook until thickened.

5. Skim fat off the top of stews and soups (refrigerate and let fat congeal on the top or place in freezer for 20 minutes).

6. Season with herbs and spices rather than fats.

7. Use cornstarch or arrowroot thickened sauces in casseroles rather than condensed soups.*

8. Select water pack canned fish or rinse off the oil.

9. Eat "bulky" foods (raw vegetables and fruits) instead of concentrated calories (fats, sweets, alcohol).*

10. Use plenty of vegetables, cooked quickly in as little water as possible.*

11. Eat fresh rather than canned fruits or select water pack. Drain off the syrup of the light syrup pack varieties.*

12. Select frozen fruits that do not contain sugar. Make jam and jelly using pectin and artificial sweeteners.*

13. Drink coffee or tea without cream or sugar.*

14. Cut the sugar in recipes in half; substitute artificial sweetener for the other half.*

15. Substitute ¼ cup egg substitute for 1 egg in a recipe. Whip egg whites stiff and fold them in just before baking.

16. Use whipped egg whites only in waffles or pancakes.

17. Use whipped toppings with a skim milk base (add to puddings for French creme or to gelatin for Bavarian).

18. Use flavored extracts (chocolate extract for chocolate milk).

446

19. Whip margarine. (One half cup margarine with 2 to 4 tablespoons skim milk; beat in mixer.)*

20. Make gelatin desserts using fruit juice and unflavored gelatin.*

21. Instead of alcoholic beverages, use tonic water or club soda to perk up fruit juice.*

* These suggestions will decrease calories as well as fat and cholesterol.

Mary Jane Schmitz, Wadena, MN

RESTRICTING SALT IN YOUR DIET

Many of your favorite recipes can still be used if you leave out some ingredients and make a few substitutions. Food without salt does taste different than food with salt, but it helps to remember that salt is not the only seasoning. Experiment with spices and herbs, and try cooking with vegetables that add flavor to other foods - onions, green pepper, garlic, tomato, and parsley.

Try the following seasonings on your vegetables and meats:

Carrots - brown sugar, lemon juice, cinnamon, bay leaf, basil, dill, ginger, thyme, cloves.

Asparagus - lemon juice, caraway, unsalted chopped nuts.

Green beans - dill, lemon, marjoram, nutmeg, onion, rosemary, slivered almonds.

Broccoli - lemon juice, oregano, tarragon, basil, dry mustard.

Corn - chives, parsley, green pepper, pimento, tomato.

Peas - mint, mushrooms, onion, parsley, green pepper.

Potato - chives, mace, onion, green pepper, parsley.

Squash - basil, ginger, mace, onion, oregano.

Sweet potato - cinnamon, nutmeg, brown sugar.

Tomatoes - basil, marjoram, oregano, parsley, sage.

Zucchini - lemon juice, garlic, chives, onion powder, bay leaf, basil, dill, oregano. (Add a touch of sugar while cooking vegetables to bring out the flavor.)

Beef - bay leaf, tomato, marjoram, dry mustard, mushrooms, nutmeg, onion, green pepper.

Chicken/turkey - basil, bay leaf, lemon juice, marjoram, onion, pepper, rosemary, sage, sesame seeds, thyme, paprika, cranberry sauce, mushrooms, parsley.

Lamb - curry, garlic, mint, onion, oregano, parsley, rosemary, thyme, broiled pineapple.

Pork - garlic, lemon juice, marjoram, sage, applesauce, cranberries, onion.

Veal - bay leaf, curry, dill seed, ginger, marjoram, oregano, broiled peaches, paprika, apricots, currant jelly, garlic, mushrooms.

Fish/shellfish - bay leaf, curry, dill, garlic, lemon juice, mushrooms, dry mustard, onion, paprika, pepper, green pepper, marjoram, tomato.

Eggs - basil, chives, curry, dry mustard, parsley, green pepper, rosemary, tomato, mushrooms, onion, paprika.

Soups - Cook with fresh vegetables and meaty bones; season with bay leaf, cloves, pepper, and dill.

Spice Blends: These spice blends can be used in cooking as well as at the table in place of salt.

No. 1:

1 Tbsp. mustard (dry)
1 tsp. garlic powder
1½ tsp. pepper
1 Tbsp. onion powder

1 tsp. thyme (optional)
¼ tsp. basil
1 Tbsp. paprika

No. 2:

4 Tbsp. onion powder
2 Tbsp. garlic powder
1 Tbsp. basil

4 Tbsp. paprika
4 Tbsp. parsley flakes

Note: Do not use celery salt, garlic salt, onion salt, flavored or seasoned salts, monosodium glutamate (Accent), poultry seasonings, or commercial spice blends containing sodium.

Mary Jane Schmitz, Wadena, MN

SUGGESTED SUBSTITUTES
(For food high in cholesterol)

1 egg = 1 tablespoon flour for thickening
1 egg = 1 egg white or ¼ cup egg substitute
Butter = equal amount of unsalted margarine
1 tablespoon butter = ¾ tablespoon unsaturated oil
1 cup whole milk = 1 cup skim milk + 2 teaspoons unsalted margarine
1 cup sour cream = 1 cup plain lowfat yogurt
1 ounce chocolate = 3 tablespoons cocoa + 1 tablespoon unsalted margarine

Salt-Free Herb Shake On:

2 Tbsp. ground thyme
2 Tbsp. ground marjoram
1 Tbsp. paprika
2 tsp. dry mustard

½ tsp. garlic powder
½ tsp. onion powder
½ tsp. pepper

Mix well and place in a shaker.

Martha Ayotte, Bemidji, MN

SALT SUBSTITUTE

1 Tbsp. ground herb shaker
1 tsp. ground basil
1 tsp. marjoram
1 tsp. thyme
1 tsp. parsley
1 tsp. savory

1 tsp. mace
1 tsp. onion powder
1 tsp. black pepper
1 tsp. sage
½ tsp. cayenne pepper

Combine all ingredients. Use in place of salt.

Edie Raatz

LOW FAT - LOW CHOLESTEROL
RECIPE MODIFICATIONS

Ingredients	Possible Substitutes
1 whole egg	¼ cup egg substitute 1 egg white and 2 teaspoons oil 2 egg whites
1 cup butter	1 cup preferred margarine ⅞ cup preferred oil
1 cup hydrogenated shortening (or lard)	1 cup preferred oil 1 cup + 3 Tbsp. preferred margarine
1 cup whole milk	1 cup skim milk
1 cup light cream (20%)	3 Tbsp. oil and skim milk to equal 1 cup 1 cup Polyrich 1 cup evaporated skim milk
1 cup heavy cream (35%)	⅔ cup skim milk and ⅓ cup oil 1 cup Polyrich
1 cup sour cream (20%)	¾ cup buttermilk and ¼ cup oil* 1 cup plain, low-fat yogurt 1 cup blenderized low-fat cottage cheese
1 oz. hardened cheeses	1 oz. Mozzarella cheese 1 oz. Ricotta cheese 1 oz. Parmesan cheese 1 oz. (2 Tbsp.) Cottage cheese
1 oz. (1 square) baking chocolate	3 Tbsp. powdered cocoa + 1 Tbsp. oil
1 cup ice cream	1 cup sherbet (made without cream or whole milk) Low-fat, frozen yogurt, frozen tofu desserts Fruit Sorbets
1 oz. bacon (2 slices)	1 oz. lean Canadian bacon* 1 oz. lean ham* 2 Tbsp. Bacon Bits* 2 Tbsp. Bac-Os*
1 Tbsp. bacon fat	1 Tbsp. oil + crushed Bacon Bits (flavor)*
1 can condensed soups: cream of celery cream of chicken cream of mushroom	Homemade allowed white sauce + flavoring 1 cup sauce + ¼ cup chopped celery 1¼ cup sauce + chicken bouillon powder or cube* 1 cup sauce + 1 can drained mushrooms

* Avoid these foods if on salt restriction.

Mary Jane Schmitz
Wadena, MN

450

HOW TO DECREASE YOUR CHOLESTEROL AND FAT INTAKE

	Decrease Use	Go Easy On	Use
Milk Group	Whole milk — regular, evaporated, condensed Hard cheeses Whole-milk cottage cheese, (14% + fat) Ice cream Whole-milk yogurt Imitation milk products — most nondairy creamers, whipped toppings (note type of fat)	2% fat milk, Part-skim mozzarella or ricotta cheese	Skim or 1% fat milk — liquid, powdered evaporated Low-fat yogurt Low-fat American-type cheeses Low-fat cottage cheese (1-2%) Farmer or pot cheese Ice milk
Meat Group	Egg yolks — no more than 3 or 4 a week Organ meats Fatty red meats — beef, lamb, pork Cold cuts Sausage, hot dogs, bacon Spare ribs Canned meats or meat mixtures Duck	Nuts Shellfish Fish canned in oil Peanut butter	Poultry without skin Tuna, water packed Egg whites (2 whites = 1 whole egg in recipes) Dried beans Lean cuts of beef, pork, veal Cholesterol-free egg substitutes
Fruit & Vegetable Group	Added butter, margarine, creams, and sauces Coconut	Avocados Olives	More fresh, frozen, canned, dried fruits and vegetables (avoid heavy syrup calories)
Grain Group	Baked goods — pies, cakes, cookies, doughnuts Deep fried rolls and muffins Egg noodles and breads	Muffins and breads (made with polyunsaturated fats) Angel food cake	Whole-grain breads and cereals (oatmeal, whole wheat, rye, bran) Rice, pasta, noodles (no added fat)
Other Group — Fats (Try to decrease total amount)	Butter Hydrogenated fats Shortening Chocolate Coconut oil Palm oil Lard, bacon fat Sour cream, cream cheese Cream - half & half Most nondairy creamers	Peanut oil Olive oil Mayonnaise Reduced-fat sour cream or cream cheese	Polyunsaturated oils - corn, safflower, soybean, sunflower Margarine with one of the polyunsaturated oils listed first in liquid form Diet margarine Imitation mayonnaise Salad dressing made with polyunsaturated oils listed above or diet dressings.

Mary Voss; Owatonna, MN

MENU COMPARISON

Simple Changes to Cut Calories, Saturated Fat and Cholesterol

OLD	IMPROVED
Breakfast:	**Breakfast:**
Grapefruit half with sugar	Grapefruit half
Fried egg	Cereal with skim milk
Crisp bacon	Canadian bacon
Toast and butter	Toast and soft margarine
Coffee with cream and sugar	Coffee with skim milk (or black)
Break:	**Break:**
Coffee with cream and sugar	Coffee with skim milk (or black)
Sweet roll	Graham cracker
Lunch:	**Lunch:**
Hamburger on bun	Chicken bouillon
French fries with ketchup	Tuna salad sandwich on whole wheat
Coca-Cola	bread with lettuce and tomato
	Skim milk
Dinner:	**Dinner:**
Home fried chicken, cream gravy	Broiled chicken
Glazed carrots	Carrots julienne
Baked potato with sour cream	Baked potato with soft margarine
Tossed salad with 1000 island	Tossed salad with oil and vinegar
dressing	dressing
Roll and butter	Roll and soft margarine
Apple pie	Fresh fruit cup
Coffee with cream and sugar	Coffee with skim milk (or black)
Snack:	**Snack:**
Chocolate sundae	Fresh fruit (as apple)
CALORIES: 3400-3500	CALORIES: 1700-1800
CHOLESTEROL: 700-800 mg.	CHOLESTEROL: 125-200 mg.
SATURATED FAT: 70-75 gm.	SATURATED FAT: 10-15 gm.

Note that in the improved menu, daily intake of calories is halved, cholesterol and saturated fat are reduced even more.

Mary Jane Schmitz
Wadena, MN

MIAMI HEART INSTITUTE DIET
4701 Haridian Avenue
Miami Beach, Florida

Follow this diet exactly and lose 10 pounds in 3 days.

FIRST DAY: Breakfast: ½ grapefruit, 1 slice toast, 2 Tbsp. peanut butter, black coffee or tea

Dinner: ½ cup tuna, 1 slice toast, black coffee or tea

Supper: 2 slices any type meat (3 oz.)
1 cup string beans, 1 cup beets, 1 small apple, 1 cup vanilla ice cream

SECOND DAY: Breakfast: 1 egg, ½ banana, 1 slice toast, black coffee or tea

Dinner: 1 cup cottage cheese, 5 saltine crackers, coffee or tea

Supper: 2 hot dogs, 1 cup broccoli, ½ cup carrots, ½ banana, ½ cup vanilla ice cream, coffee or tea

THIRD DAY: Breakfast: 5 saltine crackers, 1 slice Cheddar cheese, 1 small apple, coffee or tea

Dinner: 1 hard boiled egg, 1 slice toast, coffee or tea

Supper: 1 cup tuna, 1 cup beets, 1 cup cauliflower, ½ cup cantaloupe, ½ cup vanilla ice cream, coffee or tea

This diet works on chemical breakdown and is proven. * Do not vary or substitute any of the above listed foods. Salt and pepper may be used, no other seasoning. Where no quantity is given there are no restrictions.

This diet is to be used 3 days at a time. In 3 days you will lose 10 pounds if the diet is followed exactly.

After 3 days you may resume eating normal food. However, don't overdo it. After 4 days of normal eating, start back on your 3 day diet. You can lose up to 40 pounds in one month if you stick to it.

Do not snack between meals.

Marlys Wendorf
Central Council
St. Cloud, MN

Notes

Diabetic Delights

INFORMATION ON APPLES

VARIETY	CHARACTERISTICS	WHEN AVAILABLE	CHARACTERISTICS OF USE
Yellow Transparent or Lodi	Greenish white to greenish yellow; medium size; tart flavor.	July & Aug.	Excellent for sauce; good for pies. Tanginess makes it preferred as early apple.
Wealthy	Bright red when fully colored; marked with red splashes over greenish skin; medium size.	Late Aug. through Sept.	Good for pies, sauce and eating fresh.
McIntosh	Deep red sometimes striped with green background; white flesh; juicy; medium to large size.	Late Sept. through June	Excellent for eating fresh and sauce; good for baking, pies and in salads.
Jonathan	Solid deep red; small to medium size; firm flesh; sweet-tart flavor.	Late Sept. through June	Excellent for eating fresh, baking and pies; good for sauce. Most versatile of all Michigan apples.
Red Delicious	Yellow colored skin washed with dark red to solid dark red; conical shape with 5 points on bottom; medium to large size; mild sweet flavor.	Oct. through June	Excellent for eating fresh and salad; good for sauce. One of the best for eating fresh.

DIABETIC DELIGHTS

APPETIZERS AND BEVERAGES

CRUNCHY CEREAL SNACK MIX
(Makes 7 cups)

2 c. Corn Chex
2 c. Rice Chex
2 c. Wheat Chex
1 c. salted peanuts

3 Tbsp. margarine, melted
¼ tsp. onion powder
Dash of garlic powder
2 tsp. Worcestershire sauce

1. Combine cereals and peanuts on cookie sheet. Drizzle margarine on top. Sprinkle on onion powder and garlic.
2. Put in preheated 250°F. oven for 15 minutes (if electric skillet is used, preheat skillet to 250°F. and heat, covered, for 15 minutes). Stir mixture several times.
3. Cool by stirring and store in airtight container.

One serving (½ cup) equals 1 bread exchange, 1 fat exchange, 100 calories, 15 grams carbohydrate, 2 grams protein, 4 grams fat.

Angeline Keller, Grand Forks, ND

FROZEN BANANA ROCKETS
(Makes 1 rocket)

½ banana
1 Tbsp. peanut butter

Dry cereal crumbs

Spread banana with peanut butter. Dip into dry cereal. Insert popsicle stick in end of banana and freeze. One Rocket equals 1 fruit, ½ meat, and ½ fat exchange.

Angeline Keller, Grand Forks, ND

SPICY VEGETABLE DIP
(Yield: 1⅓ cups or 12 servings)

1 (8 oz.) ctn. plain lowfat yogurt
¼ c. chili sauce
1 Tbsp. prepared horseradish
1 tsp. grated lemon rind

1 tsp. salt
2 Tbsp. minced celery
1 Tbsp. minced green pepper
1 Tbsp. minced green onion

Combine all ingredients; mix well. Chill thoroughly. Serve as a dip for crisp raw vegetables. Exchange: 2 tablespoons - free.

Angeline Keller, Grand Forks, ND

ORANGE JULI
(Makes about 1 quart)

6 oz. frozen orange concentrate
Sugar substitute equal to 2
   Tbsp. sugar
1 c. skim milk

1 c. water
1 tsp. vanilla
10 to 12 ice cubes

Blend in blender until ice cubes are crushed. Make shortly before serving or mix before using again. One cup equals 1 bread exchange.

Angeline Keller, Grand Forks, ND

HOT COCOA MIX

2 c. nonfat dry milk
5 Tbsp. powdered unsweetened
   cocoa

4 tsp. granulated artificial
   sweetener

Mix dry milk, unsweetened cocoa, and artificial sweetener thoroughly. For a single serving, mix ⅓ cup mixture with ¾ to 1 cup hot water for 1 skim milk exchange. To use entire recipe, add 5 to 6 cups of hot water to mix. One cup equals 1 skim milk exchange.

This Hot Cocoa Mix also mixes well with cold water for a cold chocolate drink.

Angeline Keller, Grand Forks, ND

EGGNOG FOR DIABETICS

1 egg
Few grains of salt
Liquid sugar substitute to taste
1 c. skim milk

¼ tsp. vanilla
Dash of nutmeg
Rum extract to flavor

Beat egg until thick and lemon colored. Add milk, salt, vanilla, and liquid sweetener while still beating. Add rum extract to flavor. Pour into a large glass. Sprinkle with nutmeg. Makes 1 serving. One serving equals 1 skim milk and 1 meat exchange.

From American Diabetes Association, North Dakota Affiliate, Newsletter.

Angeline Keller, Grand Forks, ND

SOUPS

MY FAVORITE VEGETABLE BEEF SOUP

5 oz. uncooked beef (hamburger
 or beef tips)
6 to 8 c. water
14½ oz. can stewed or chopped
 tomatoes
½ head shredded cabbage
4 carrots, diced
2 stalks celery, diced
½ green pepper, chopped

1 c. French style green beans
1 c. sliced mushrooms
1 minced garlic clove or ½ tsp.
 garlic powder
4 beef bouillon cubes or 4 tsp.
 granules
2 packets Equal sweetener
Salt and pepper (if desired)

Brown beef. Add remaining ingredients; simmer as long as you want. Add more water if needed. Entire recipe counts as: 4 protein, 40 optional calories, 18 vegetable.

Mary Voss, Owatonna, MN

GOLDEN VEGETABLE SOUP

1 c. water
½ c. diced celery
½ c. diced carrots
½ c. chopped broccoli or
 cauliflower
1 Tbsp. flour

2 oz. cubed Velveeta cheese
1 oz. diced onion
¼ tsp. salt and pepper
3 oz. raw diced potato
1 c. skim milk

In a 2 quart saucepan, combine water, onion, celery, carrots, potato, and broccoli or cauliflower. Simmer for 15 minutes or until vegetables are tender. Shake together flour and milk; add mixture to undrained vegetables. Add salt and pepper; simmer until thickened. Add cheese; stir until blended. Makes 3 cups. One serving equals 3 vegetable, 2 protein, 1 bread, 1 milk, 30 optional calories.

Note: You can leave out the potato and use both broccoli and cauliflower (omit bread exchange).

Mary Voss, Owatonna, MN

GOLDEN CREAM SOUP

4 (3 oz.) potatoes, peeled and
 chopped
1 c. water
½ c. celery, chopped
½ c. carrots, chopped
½ tsp. salt
Dash of pepper

1 chicken bouillon cube
½ c. onion, chopped
½ tsp. parsley flakes
2 c. skim milk
2 tsp. flour
8 oz. Velveeta cheese, cubed

Combine vegetables, bouillon, spices, and water; boil, covered, until vegetables are soft. Mash with potato masher. Combine milk and flour; mix until smooth. Add vegetable mixture and stir. Add cheese cubes and simmer until cheese is melted. Makes 4 servings: Each equals: Bread exchange, ¾ vegetable exchange, ½ milk exchange, 2 protein exchange (hard cheese), 8 optional calorie exchange.

Jenny Kissel, Bismarck, ND

WEIGHT WATCHER SOUP

1½ c. stewed tomatoes
2 c. water
3 c. shredded cabbage
¼ c. onion
¼ c. celery
1 tsp. parsley flakes
1 tsp. green pepper

2 beef bouillon cubes
1 packet artificial sweetener
16 oz. French style green beans
4 oz. mushrooms
Salt and pepper to taste
Garlic to taste

In large kettle, cook all ingredients, except mushrooms and green beans; add them the last 15 minutes. Unlimited serving size. Total recipe equals 10 vegetable exchange and 20 optional calories (bouillon).

Mary Voss, Owatonna, MN

CLAM CHOWDER

1 c. skim milk
4 oz. minced clams
3 oz. diced potato
¼ c. diced onions
½ c. sliced carrots
½ c. diced celery

½ c. frozen green beans,
 thawed
2 tsp. reduced calorie margarine
1 bay leaf
Dash of Worcestershire sauce
Salt and pepper to taste

Combine all ingredients and cook slowly until all the vegetables are tender. Remove bay leaf. Makes 1 serving. One serving equals 1 milk, 1 bread, 4 protein, 1 fat, 3½ vegetable.

Mary Voss, Owatonna, MN

LO-CAL VEGETABLE SOUP

1 large can tomato juice
1 large can water
6 carrots, sliced or diced in large
 pieces
½ large cabbage

½ large stalk celery
4 beef bouillon cubes
Salt to taste
Tabasco sauce to taste

Cook together; slowly simmer for 1 hour. A favorite noon lunch. Huge bowl can be eaten for less than 100 calories.

Betty Ratzlaff, Fargo, ND

SALADS

DIABETIC SALAD DRESSING

½ c. tomato juice
2 Tbsp. lemon juice or vinegar
1 Tbsp. onion, chopped
Salt and pepper to taste

Chopped parsley (if desired)
Green pepper (if desired)
Horseradish (if desired)
Mustard (if desired)

Combine ingredients in a jar with a tightly fitted top. Shake well before serving.

Betty Ratzlaff, Fargo, ND

EASY LOW CALORIE MAYONNAISE
(16 calories per tablespoon)

1 c. part skim Ricotta cheese
Juice of 1 lemon
1 tsp. salt
½ tsp. dry mustard

1 tsp. celery salt
1 hard cooked egg
Few drops of sweetener
   (optional)

Peel the egg and put in blender along with all the rest of ingredients. Mix about 2 minutes or until egg is thoroughly dissolved and it is creamy smooth; refrigerate to thicken.

Can be used with onion soup for a California dip. Add 1 tablespoon chopped pickles or drained pickle relish to ½ cup mayonnaise for low-cal tartar sauce. Can also be frozen. Stir to restore smooth texture after defrosting.

Marie Capen, Duluth, MN

SUNSHINE GELATIN

1 env. unflavored gelatin
¾ c. orange juice
1 c. grated carrot

1 (8¾ oz.) can crushed
   pineapple packed in
   unsweetened juice

Soften gelatin in ¼ cup orange juice. Bring remaining orange juice to a boil. Mix in juice-gelatin mixture and stir until dissolved. Add grated carrot and pineapple in its juice. Stir well. Pour into mold and refrigerate until firm. Yield: 6 servings. Exchanges: 1 serving equals 1 fruit, ⅓ vegetable. Calories: 49 per serving. C = 12, P = .5, F = 0.

Angeline Keller, Grand Forks, ND

SEVEN LAYER SALAD
(Diabetic)

½ head lettuce (about 3 c.)
½ c. chopped celery
¼ c. chopped green onion
¼ c. chopped green pepper
1 c. frozen green peas, thawed
½ c. Weight Watchers Reduced
   Calorie Mayonnaise

1 tsp. Hidden Valley Ranch
   dressing mix (dry)
2 packets Equal
4 oz. grated Parmesan cheese

Clean, drain, and chill lettuce; tear into bite-size pieces. In a sealed bowl, layer lettuce, celery, onion, green pepper, and peas. Sprinkle with Equal. Mix dry dressing mix with mayonnaise; spread over top of vegetables. Sprinkle evenly with cheese. Cover and refrigerate for several hours or overnight. Makes 4 servings. Each serving equals 2 vegetable, 3 fat, ½ bread, 1 protein.

Mary Voss, Owatonna, MN

SAUERKRAUT SALAD

1 large can sauerkraut and juice
1 can shredded green beans
   (using ¼ c. juice)
1 small jar sliced mushrooms,
   drained
1 small jar pimentos, drained
1 medium green pepper,
   chopped

1 c. celery, cut up
1 carrot, shredded
1 tsp. onion flakes
Little black pepper
About 7 to 9 tsp. sweetener

Mix and will keep in refrigerator for a long time.

Jenny Kissel, Bismarck, ND

TUNA SALAD

2 oz. tuna
1 oz. cubed cheese
½ c. cooked macaroni
2 Tbsp. chopped onion

2 Tbsp. diced celery
4 tsp. reduced calorie
   mayonnaise
1 Tbsp. chopped pimento

Mix all ingredients together; chill. Makes 1 serving. Exchange: 1 bread, 3 protein, 2 fat, 1 vegetable.

Mary Voss, Owatonna, MN

CHICKEN SALAD

½ c. cooked macaroni
4 oz. cooked cubed chicken
½ c. diced celery
½ c. pineapple tidbits

1 Tbsp. reduced calorie
  mayonnaise
1 packet sweetener

Mix together all of the ingredients; chill. Serve on lettuce leaf. Makes 1 serving. Exchange: 1 bread, 4 protein, 1 fruit, 1 vegetable, 1½ fat.

Mary Voss, Owatonna, MN

POTATO SALAD

4 hard-boiled eggs
12 oz. cooked potatoes
½ c. chopped celery
¼ c. chopped green onion
⅛ c. sliced radishes
⅛ c. chopped pimento
8 diced pimento olives
½ c. Weight Watchers
  mayonnaise

½ c. Weight Watchers plain
  yogurt
1 env. Hidden Valley Original
  Ranch dressing mix
1 Tbsp. ketchup
1 Tbsp. mustard
1 tsp. vinegar
2 packets Equal sweetener

Combine eggs, potatoes, celery, onion, radishes, pimento, and olives. Make dressing from remaining ingredients; mix together. Chill. Makes 4 servings. Each serving equals 1 protein, 1 bread, ½ vegetable, 3 fat, 20 optional calories.

Mary Voss, Owatonna, MN

BEV'S SUPER SUMMER SALAD

1 pt. blueberries
1 pt. strawberries
1 c. green grapes and/or red
  seedless grapes
2 peaches, diced with peel on
1 c. cherries, pitted and halved
  or 2 bananas, thick sliced

1 (11 oz.) can mandarin oranges,
  drained
1 (20 oz.) can chunk pineapple in
  own unsweetened juice,
  drained (save juice for
  sauce)

Sauce:

1 c. reserved pineapple juice
  (add water to make 1 c.)
¼ c. lemon juice
2 Tbsp. and 2 tsp. cornstarch
Sweetener to equal ¾ c. sugar (I
  use ¾ Sprinkle Sweet *or* 18

pkg. Equal *or* half and half -
if Equal, add *after* partly
cooled)

Mix cornstarch and sugar substitute (not Equal). Add liquids; bring to boil and boil for 1 minute using either microwave or stove top, stirring as needed. Chill and serve over fresh fruits. This makes a large salad of about 20 servings. The sauce is very thick and must be stirred vigorously before adding to fruits, then gently folded in.

Sauce equals: 18 calories per tablespoon or 6 calories per teaspoon. Makes about 20 tablespoons so each serving of salad is about 1 fruit exchange plus 18 calories. (You could just use any fruits you like - count the portions and add the sauce by the teaspoon or tablespoon and count the calories in them.)

Jenny Kissel, Bismarck, ND

SUMMERTIME SALAD

1 c. crushed drained pineapple
   (canned in its own juice)
1 small pkg. sugar-free pistachio
   pudding mix

1 c. lowfat yogurt (plain)
2⅔ c. lowfat cottage cheese
½ c. Cool Whip

Combine pineapple, dry pudding mix, yogurt, cottage cheese, and Cool Whip; mix well. Makes 8 servings of ½ cup each. Each serving equals: ¼ fruit, ¼ milk, 1 protein, 17 optional calories.

Jenny Kissel, Bismarck, ND

CHEESE PINEAPPLE SALAD

1 pkg. lemon or lime
   (NutraSweet) jello
1 c. boiling water
1 (No. 2) can crushed pineapple

1 c. small curd cottage cheese
½ c. celery, sliced
½ c. walnuts

Dissolve gelatin in boiling water and cool until syrupy. Stir in remaining ingredients. Put in jello mold and chill.

Frosting:

1 (3 oz.) pkg. cream cheese
1 Tbsp. mayonnaise

1 tsp. lemon juice

Blend and beat till smooth.

Or:

½ c. plain or lemon yogurt
1 Tbsp. mayonnaise

1 tsp. lemon juice

Blend and beat till smooth.

Carol Reynolds, Hibbing, MN

MACARONI SALAD SUPREME

Mix together:

4 c. cooked ring macaroni	1 c. chopped celery
8 oz. cooked chicken, diced	½ c. chopped green pepper
4 oz. hard cheese, cubed	½ c. chopped radishes
4 hard-boiled eggs, chopped	1 bunch green onions, chopped

Dressing:

½ c. Weight Watchers blue label salad dressing	2 tsp. chicken bouillon granules
½ c. plain yogurt	¼ tsp. pepper
1 Tbsp. vinegar	1 tsp. dry mustard
1 packet Equal sweetener	1 tsp. Mrs. Dash or other seasoning

Make dressing. Toss with other ingredients; chill. Makes 8 servings. One serving equals 1 bread, 2 protein, ½ vegetable, 1 fat, 14 calories.

Mary Voss, Owatonna, MN

MAIN DISHES

CASEROLE SAUCE MIX

2 c. nonfat dry milk (crystals
   suggested)
¾ c. cornstarch
¼ c. instant chicken bouillon
2 Tbsp. dried onion (flakes or
   chopped)

1 tsp. dried basil, crushed
   (optional)
1 tsp. dried thyme, crushed
   (optional)
½ tsp. pepper

Combine all ingredients; mix well. Store in a glass jar or other airtight container. Makes 3 cups, equal to 9 cans condensed soup. To use, combine ⅓ cup mix with 1 cup water. Cook and stir till thickened. If you like, add mushrooms, celery, or bits of chicken to resemble the soup you usually use. (Note: Powdered milk has been used and works fine.)

For easy fixings, microwave in glass casserole for 2 to 3 minutes, stirring twice. Add other ingredients, such as cooked vegetables, meats, and noodles and heat for a delicious low calorie, lowfat main dish.

The neat thing is this mix tastes good and the statistics are good news. One recipe, serving 4 or more people, adds only the following amounts of fats, calories, and sodium: Fat (grams): Casserole Mix .2, canned mushroom soup 23.8. Calories: Casserole Mix 95, canned mushroom soup 330. Sodium (milligrams): Casserole Mix 710, canned mushroom soup 2,370.

Your new version of mushroom soup will cut calories and sodium by more than ⅔ and fat a 100 times. Most of us need to cut down on all three.

Mary Hocking, Fargo, ND

TURKEY POT PIE
(Makes 4 servings)

2 c. diced cooked turkey
1½ c. water
½ c. nonfat dry milk
¼ c. flour
1 tsp. salt (optional)
¼ tsp. tarragon

¼ tsp. parsley
⅛ tsp. pepper
¾ c. small white onions, cooked
1 (10 oz.) pkg. frozen peas and
   carrots
Pastry crust

1. Preheat oven to 400°F.
2. Mix nonfat dry milk and flour with water until smooth. Add salt (if used), tarragon, parsley, and pepper. Cook over medium heat, stirring until mixture thickens.
3. Mix in chicken and vegetables. Pour into 1½ quart casserole.
4. Cover with pastry crust. Seal pie by pressing dough over casserole.
5. Cut steam holes in dough. Bake for 20 minutes or until lightly browned.

One serving, including crust (¼ recipe) equals 1 bread exchange, 3½ lowfat meat exchanges, 1 vegetable exchange, ½ fat exchange, 311 calories, 20 grams carbohydrate, 29 grams protein, 14 grams fat.

Pastry Crust (makes 4 servings):

½ c. flour	2 Tbsp. oil
⅛ tsp. salt	

1. Stir salt and oil into flour. Form into a ball; flatten slightly and place on a sheet of wax paper. Place another wax paper sheet on top of dough and roll out quickly.

2. Peel off top layer of paper; invert dough over filling and strip off second layer of paper. Totally cover top of filling with dough.

One serving (¼ recipe) equals 1 bread exchange, ½ fat exchange, 100 calories, 15 grams carbohydrate, 2 grams protein, 3 grams fat.

Angeline Keller, Grand Forks, ND

CHEESE STUFFED SHELLS
(Diabetic)

16 jumbo pasta shells (3 oz.)	1 Tbsp. dried parsley
1⅔ c. cottage cheese	¼ tsp. dried oregano
1 c. shredded Mozzarella	¼ tsp. pepper
½ c. grated Parmesan cheese	1 tsp. seasoned salt
1 egg, beaten	¼ tsp. garlic powder

Cook shells according to package directions. While shells are cooking, make sauce.

Sauce:

½ c. chopped onion	½ tsp. salt
½ garlic clove, minced	⅛ tsp. pepper
2 c. tomato juice	3 packets Equal sweetener
½ c. tomato paste	2 tsp. cornstarch

Simmer sauce, covered, for 10 minutes.

To make filling, stir together cheeses, egg, and seasonings. Divide filling; fill each shell. Place in baking dish. Pour sauce over and around filled shells. Bake, covered, at 350° for 30 minutes. Makes 4 servings. One serving equals 1 bread, 3 protein, ¾ vegetable, ½ fruit, 5 optional calories.

Mary Voss, Owatonna, MN

CHEESEBURGER PIE

1 c. tomato paste
4 oz. onion, chopped
1 beef bouillon cube
1 tsp. sweetener
½ tsp. chile powder

8 oz. cooked (boiled) ground
beef or veal
4 oz. grated hard cheese
2 c. cooked rice

Combine first 5 ingredients; simmer with meat for 8 to 10 minutes. Add 3 ounces cheese and rice; stir until cheese is melted. Pour in a 9 inch pie tin. Sprinkle with other 1 ounce of cheese. Bake for 30 minutes at 375°. Divide into 4 servings. Each serving equals 2 ounces meat, 1 choice (rice), 1 ounce cheese, 1 something extra.

Jenny Kissel, Bismarck, ND

CRAB FETTUCINE
(Diabetic)

12 oz. can evaporated skim milk
1 Tbsp. margarine
1 Tbsp. cornstarch
11 oz. shredded crab or baby
shrimp

1½ tsp. Seafood Cajun Magic
4 oz. can sliced mushrooms
1 oz. Parmesan cheese
3 c. cooked fettucine

In large pan, combine milk, margarine, and cornstarch; heat until smooth and slightly thickened. Add seasoning and mushrooms. Stir in seafood and cook until heated through. Add cheese and toss with hot fettucine. Serve immediately. Makes 6 servings. One serving equals ½ milk, ½ fat, 2 protein, 1 bread, 1 vegetable, 5 optional calories.

Mary Voss, Owatonna, MN

TURKEY GOULASH
(Serves 4)

1 lb. ground turkey
2 diced onions

½ c. chopped green pepper

Brown ground turkey with onions and green pepper.

Add:

Salt and pepper to taste
Onion powder to taste
Garlic powder to taste
1½ tsp. chili powder
2 (28 oz.) cans tomatoes, finely
chopped

1 large can mushroom pieces
with liquid
2 packets beef bouillon
3 oz. uncooked elbow macaroni

Bring to a boil all ingredients, except macaroni. Add macaroni, but do not stir in. Continue to boil, uncovered, till macaroni absorbs all of the liquid and is tender, about 20 minutes. Divide evenly. Each serving equals: 3 protein, 1 bread, and 5 calories. (Freezes well!)

Jenny Kissel, Bismarck, ND

QUICK VEGETARIAN CHILI
(Serves 8)

15½ oz. can Great Northern
   beans, drained
15½ oz. can kidney beans,
   drained
15½ oz. can garbanzo beans,
   drained
16 oz. can whole tomatoes

16 oz. can stewed tomatoes
   (optional)
1 (6 oz.) can tomato paste
½ c. chopped onion
1 garlic clove
1 tsp. chili powder

Combine all ingredients and simmer for 15 minutes. Each serving equals: 3 protein, ¼ cup tomato paste, vegetables.

Jenny Kissel, Bismarck, ND

BEST LASAGNA IN THE WORLD!

1 lb. lean ground beef
1 c. chopped onion
2 tsp. seasoned salt
1 to 2 tsp. chili powder
1 tsp. garlic powder
3 packets Equal sweetener
29 oz. can tomato sauce
6 oz. can tomato paste

8 oz. can mushrooms, drained
3½ c. water
12 oz. shredded Mozzarella
   cheese (3 c.)
1 c. cottage cheese
¾ c. Ricotta cheese
½ c. Parmesan cheese
9 oz. *uncooked* lasagna noodles

In a large pan, brown beef with onion and seasonings. Stir in tomato sauce, paste, mushrooms, and water; simmer for 10 to 15 minutes. The mixture should be thin. Mix together cottage, Ricotta, and Parmesan cheeses.

Spray 9x13 inch pan with Pam. Layer ⅓ of uncooked noodles, ⅓ of cheese mixture, ⅓ of the sauce, and ⅓ of the shredded Mozzarella. Continue with 2 more layers of each until pan is filled. Bake at 350° for 1 to 1½ hours. Cut into 8 equal pieces. Freeze if desired. Makes 8 servings. One serving equals 4 protein, 1½ bread, 1½ vegetable, 30 optional calories.

Mary Voss, Owatonna, MN

DESSERTS, COOKIES, CAKES

STRAWBERRY COTTAGE CHEESECAKE

¾ c. graham cracker crumbs (6
    sq. 2½ inches)
2 Tbsp. reduced calorie
    margarine, melted
3 packets Equal sweetener
1 (3 oz.) pkg. strawberry
    "sugar-free" jello

3 c. lowfat cottage cheese
1 (10 oz.) pkg. frozen
    strawberries (1½ c.)
6 packets Equal sweetener
1 Tbsp. cornstarch
Red food coloring (if desired)

Combine cracker crumbs, margarine, and 3 Equal. Press into 8 inch pie pan. Bake at 375° for 10 minutes; cool. Combine jello in 1 cup boiling water; cool. Combine cottage cheese and cooled jello in blender. Process until smooth. Pour into cooled crust.

In a small saucepan, cook strawberries, cornstarch, and Equal for 1 minute. Pour glaze over cheesecake; chill. Makes 6 servings. Each serving equals ½ bread, 1½ protein, ½ fat, ¼ fruit, 10 optional calories.

Mary Voss, Owatonna, MN

CHOCOLATE MOUSSE

1 pkg. chocolate ALBA Fit 'n
    Frosty
1 env. Knox unflavored gelatine

½ c. "very" hot water
2 packets Equal sweetener
3 or more ice cubes

Put very hot water in blender; sprinkle with Knox gelatine. Let stand to soften; process until blended. Add ALBA and sweetener; process again until blended. Add ice cubes; process on high. If mousse is too thick, add a small amount of water. If it is too thin, refrigerate until set. Makes 1 serving. Exchange: 1 milk.

Mary Voss, Owatonna, MN

CREAMY GELATIN DESSERT

1 env. dietetic lemon or lime
    gelatin
1 c. cottage cheese
Artificial sweetener equal to ¼
    c. sugar

1 (15 or 16 oz.) can unsweetened
    crushed pineapple

Drain pineapple and save the juice. Dissolve gelatin in 1 cup hot water as directed on package. In blender, combine cottage cheese, artificial sweetener, and pineapple juice (to which water is added to equal 1 cup). Blend to milkshake consistency. Add mixture to gelatin with crushed pineapple. Place in 4 covered containers (margarine containers are a perfect size) and chill until set. *Very good!* Yield: 4 large servings.

Substitution: One serving without nuts equals 1 fruit substitute and 1 meat substitute; with nuts, 1 fruit, 1 meat, 1 fat. *Very good!*

Angeline Keller, Grand Forks, ND

PINEAPPLE CHEESECAKE

20 oz. can crushed pineapple packed in its own juice
2 packets unflavored gelatin
½ c. hot water
1⅓ c. skim milk powder (no water added)

1½ packets sugar substitute (equal to 3 tsp. sugar)
2 tsp. vanilla
½ tsp. lemon juice
½ tsp. butter flavoring

Place drained pineapple in blender with ½ of its juice. Add gelatin and hot water; blend for 2 minutes. Add dry milk and remainder of juice, sugar substitute, vanilla, butter flavoring, and lemon juice. Blend for 3 minutes. Pour into 10 inch pan; sprinkle lightly with cinnamon and allow to set for 1 hour. Yield: 8 servings. Exchanges: 1 serving equals ½ fruit exchange, ½ milk exchange.

Angeline Keller, Grand Forks, ND

HAWAIIAN DELIGHT CHEESECAKE

¼ c. graham cracker crumbs
2 Tbsp. (2 env.) unflavored gelatin
½ c. water
1 (8¼ oz.) can water pack pineapple tidbits
1 (12 oz.) ctn. creamed cottage cheese

3 eggs, separated
1 Tbsp. unsweetened lemon juice
¼ c. skim milk
2 tsp. Pillsbury's liquid sweetener
1 tsp. vanilla
⅛ tsp. salt

Sprinkle 3 tablespoons graham cracker crumbs on bottom of 9 inch square pan. Soften gelatin in water. Drain pineapple tidbits, reserving juice. Bring reserved juice, adding water, if necessary, to make ¾ cup, to a boil and dissolve softened gelatin.

In small mixer bowl, beat cottage cheese at high speed until smooth, about 3 minutes. Add egg yolks, milk, lemon juice, sweetener, vanilla, and salt; beat well. Blend in dissolved gelatin. Chill until mixture is thick but not set.

Beat egg whites until soft peaks form; gently fold into gelatin mixture. Spoon over crumbs in pan. Sprinkle remaining crumbs over filling. Top with pineapple tidbits and chill until firm, at least 4 hours. Makes 9 servings. *Very good!*

One serving equals 96 calories per serving. Exchanges: 1 meat exchange and 1B vegetable exchange.

Angeline Keller, Grand Forks, ND

RAISIN RICE PUDDING

2 c. water
½ tsp. salt
½ c. white rice (uncooked)
¼ c. raisins
2 Tbsp. cornstarch

1⅓ c. skim milk
1½ tsp. vanilla
6 packets artificial sweetener
1 tsp. cinnamon (if desired)

Bring water and salt to a boil in medium size saucepan. Stir in rice and raisins. Return to a boil, then reduce heat to low; cover and simmer for 30 minutes. Mix cornstarch and milk; add to rice and stir until mixture thickens. Remove from heat. Stir in vanilla, sweetener, and cinnamon. Garnish with nutmeg just like grandma did! Makes 4 servings. Each serving equals ½ bread, ½ fruit, ⅓ milk, 15 optional calories.

Mary Voss, Owatonna, MN

RICE PUDDING

2 eggs, slightly beaten
2 c. skim milk
1 c. cooked rice
¼ c. raisins

½ tsp. vanilla extract
½ lemon
Dash of nutmeg
Artificial sweetener to taste

Divide rice and raisins into 4 custard cups. Mix remaining ingredients, except nutmeg, and pour into cups. Sprinkle nutmeg over each cup and bake in 350° oven for 45 minutes. Yield: 4 servings. Exchanges: 1 serving equals 1 bread, ½ milk.

Angeline Keller, Grand Forks, ND

GLORIFIED RICE
(Serves 6)

Mix together:

1 (6 serving size) pkg. Jell-O
    Sugar-Free instant vanilla
    pudding mix, prepared
    according to pkg. directions
3 c. cooked and cooled rice
1 (20 oz.) can crushed pineapple
    canned in its own juice,
    drained

1 sliced banana
2 c. cottage cheese
8 packets Equal

Divide evenly into 6 servings. Each serving equals: 1 protein, 1 fruit, 1 milk, and 1 bread.

Jenny Kissel, Bismarck, ND

DIABETIC RICE PUDDING

2 c. cooked rice
2 c. milk
¼ c. Brown Sugar Twin
2 eggs

1 tsp. vanilla
¼ tsp. salt
½ c. seedless raisins
Cinnamon or nutmeg

Preheat oven to 350°. Scald milk. Beat brown sugar substitute, egg, vanilla, and salt to blend. Slowly add and stir milk into egg mixture. Blend in cooked rice and raisins. Pour into 1½ quart casserole. Set in pan containing 1 inch hot water.

Bake for 55 minutes or until knife inserted in middle comes out clean. Remove from oven and sprinkle with cinnamon or nutmeg before serving.

Marie Capen, Duluth, MN

EGG CUSTARD

2 eggs, slightly beaten
2 c. milk
1 Tbsp. liquid artificial
    sweetener (or to taste)

½ tsp. vanilla
Pinch of salt

Beat ingredients together and pour in 4 dessert size Pyrex baking dishes. Place dishes in a pan of hot water and bake at 300° for 50 to 60 minutes until set; chill. Yield: 4 servings. Exchanges: ½ milk, ½ meat, 1 fat.

Note: One teaspoon brandy flavoring, 1 tablespoon grated orange rind, or 1 teaspoon almond flavoring may be added instead of the vanilla to vary the flavor.

Angeline Keller, Grand Forks, ND

PUMPKIN CUSTARD

1 env. unflavored gelatin
¼ c. cold water
3 egg yolks
1¼ c. canned pumpkin
½ c. skim milk
1 Tbsp. sugar substitute
    solution

½ tsp. salt
½ tsp. cinnamon
½ tsp. nutmeg
½ tsp. ginger
3 egg whites, beaten stiff

Sprinkle gelatin on cold water and let stand for 5 minutes. Put egg yolks into top of double boiler and beat slightly. Add pumpkin, milk, sugar substitute solution, salt, and spices; cook until thick. Add soaked gelatin and cool.

Fold in stiffly beaten egg whites. Pour into molds and cool in refrigerator. Makes 6 servings. (For diabetics, 1 serving is ½ a milk exchange.)

Angeline Keller, Grand Forks, ND

HOLIDAY TAPIOCA PUDDING
(Makes 2 cups)

2 Tbsp. instant tapioca
2 c. skim milk
¼ c. low-cholesterol egg
    substitute

2 egg whites
¾ tsp. vanilla
Granulated sugar substitute to
    taste

1. Cook tapioca and skim milk in the top of a double boiler until tapioca becomes transparent.
2. Slowly add hot tapioca and milk mixture to egg substitute; return to double boiler.
3. Cook until mixture thickens; stir constantly.
4. Cool and add vanilla.
5. Beat egg whites until very stiff; fold into mixture.
6. Add granulated sugar substitute to taste by lightly sprinkling over the top of mixture; fold in.
7. Cool. Serve in parfait glasses.

One serving (½ cup) equals 1 nonfat milk exchange, 80 calories, 12 grams carbohydrate, 8 grams protein.

Angeline Keller, Grand Forks, ND

OLD-FASHIONED BREAD PUDDING
(Serves 6)

12 slices bread (40 calories per
    slice), cubed
¾ c. raisins
2 c. skim milk

3 eggs
5 scoops Weight Watchers
    sweetener
1 tsp. cinnamon

Cube bread. Add raisins. Spray a 9 inch square pan. Place raisin-bread mixture in pan. Beat together skim milk, eggs, sweetener, and cinnamon; pour over bread mixture. Bake at 350° for 40 to 45 minutes. Each serving equals 1 bread, 1 fruit, ½ protein (egg), and ⅓ milk.

Jenny Kissel, Bismarck, ND

BANANA PUDDING

16 sq. graham crackers
1 pkg. vanilla sugar-free
    pudding mix (Virginia uses
    D-Zerta brand)

2 c. skim milk
4 small bananas
2 egg whites
½ tsp. vanilla

Prepare pudding mix according to directions using the 2 cups skim milk. Line the bottom and sides of a 6½ x 9 x 2 inch baking dish with graham crackers. Add 2 sliced bananas and ½ of the pudding. Cover with another layer of graham crackers and the remaining 2 sliced bananas. Cover with the remaining pudding. Beat the egg whites until they form peaks. Add vanilla and spread over top of pudding. Brown in 375° oven. Yield: 8 servings. Exchanges: 1 serving equals 2 bread, 1 fruit, and ½ nonfat milk. Calories: 1 serving equals 220.

Angeline Keller, Grand Forks, ND

PINEAPPLE SNOW
(Makes 8 servings)

1 env. unflavored gelatin	1½ c. unsweetened pineapple
2 Tbsp. sugar	juice
⅛ tsp. salt	2 egg whites
½ c. water	

1. Combine gelatin, sugar, and salt in saucepan. Add water. Place over low heat, stirring constantly, until gelatin is dissolved. Remove from heat.
2. Stir in pineapple juice.
3. Chill until the mixture begins to thicken.
4. Add egg whites and beat with electric beater until mixture begins to hold its shape.
5. Spoon into dessert dishes; chill until firm.

One serving (¾ cup) equals 1 fruit exchange, 44 calories, 9 grams carbohydrate, 2 grams protein, 0 grams fat.

Angeline Keller, Grand Forks, ND

DIABETIC ANGEL FOOD-FRUIT DESSERT

1. Bake 1 angel food cake.
2. Tear up cake in small pieces and put in two 9x13 inch cake pans.
3. Make 2 sugar-free (small packages) vanilla Jell-O pudding per instructions on Jell-O package.
4. Add 12 ounces of sour cream.
5. Spread 3 and 4 over angel food cakes.
6. Slice strawberries or peaches, or whole blueberries and cover pudding-cream mixture.
7. Top with Cool Whip (large tub).
8. Decorate with leftover fruit.
9. Keep refrigerated.

Bobbie Gludtmendro, Fargo, ND

PISTACHIO BLUEBERRY DESSERT

1 (small) pkg. sugar-free	1 ctn. Weight Watchers plain
pistachio instant pudding	yogurt
2 c. skim milk	1 c. blueberries

Mix together pudding and milk. Stir in yogurt; fold in blueberries. Chill. Makes 4 servings. Each serving equals 1¼ milk, ½ fruit.

Mary Voss, Owatonna, MN

RAISIN NUT BALLS

1/4 c. chopped raisins
3 Tbsp. chunky peanut butter
2 tsp. honey
2 tsp. shredded coconut
1 tsp. lemon juice
1/4 tsp. cinnamon

1/3 c. nonfat dry milk powder
1 pkg. chocolate flavored low
    calorie drink mix (ALBA)
1/4 c. water
2 to 2 1/2 inch graham cracker
    sq., crushed

Combine raisins, peanut butter, honey, coconut, lemon juice, and cinnamon. Add dry milk and ALBA; mix with spoon, then using your fingers, knead until blended. Add water and mix well. Cover and refrigerate for 45 minutes. Make into 18 balls and roll in graham cracker crumbs. Chill for 1 hour. Makes 2 servings. One fruit exchange, 1 milk, 1/2 bread, 1 1/2 fat, 1 1/2 protein, 30 optional calories.

Jenny Kissel, Bismarck, ND

GUMDROP CHEWS

1 can fruit flavored diet soda
1/2 c. lemon juice
1/2 tsp. vanilla
3 to 4 drops desired food
    coloring

Artificial sweetener to equal 1 c.
    sugar
5 env. unflavored gelatin

Mix 1/2 can soda and all other ingredients in small mixing bowl. Boil remaining soda and add to mixture, stirring until gelatin is dissolved. Pour into 9x13 inch baking dish and refrigerate until firm. Cut into squares or cut out with cookie cutters. Exchange: Free food.

Angeline Keller, Grand Forks, ND

DIABETIC COOKIES

1 1/4 c. water
2 c. raisins or 1 c. each of raisins
    and dates, cut up

1/3 c. shortening
1/4 tsp. nutmeg
1 tsp. cinnamon

Boil this together for 5 minutes. Cool to warm.

2 eggs
1/2 tsp. salt
1 tsp. soda
1 Tbsp. hot water
2 Tbsp. Sucaryl or liquid
    sweetener

2 c. flour
1 tsp. baking powder
1/2 to 1 c. walnuts

Add 2 eggs. Beat in 1 egg at a time. Add salt. Dissolve soda in hot water; add. Add Sucaryl or liquid sweetener, flour, baking powder, and walnuts. Drop from spoon on a greased cookie sheet. Bake in 350° oven.

Elizabeth Klug, Dickinson, ND

PEANUT BUTTER COOKIES WITH NO SUGAR
(Diabetic recipe)

1½ c. sifted flour
1½ tsp. baking powder
½ tsp. salt
¼ c. margarine
½ c. peanut butter

1½ tsp. vanilla
1 egg, well beaten
⅓ c. orange juice
Artificial sweetener to substitute
  for 24 tsp. sugar

Preheat oven to 400°. Sift together flour, baking powder, and salt. Cream together margarine, peanut butter, and vanilla. Add egg, orange juice, and sweetener; blend well. Add dry ingredients gradually; mix well after each addition.

Measure 1 level tablespoon dough for each cookie. Roll between hands to form ball. Place 2 inches apart on an ungreased cookie sheet; flatten with fork. Bake for about 15 minutes. Yield: 24 cookies. Food exchanges per serving: 2 cookies equals 1½ bread exchange and 2 fat exchange.

Joanne Eklund

PEANUT BUTTER COOKIES

2 eggs
1¼ c. graham cracker crumbs
  (about eighteen 2 inch
  crackers)
¼ c. chunky peanut butter

Nonnutritive sweetener
  equivalent to ½ c. sugar
2 Tbsp. milk
2 tsp. double acting baking
  powder

About 30 minutes before serving: Preheat oven to 350°F. In medium bowl with mixer at high speed, beat eggs until thick and lemon colored. With wooden spoon, gradually beat in remaining ingredients until smooth. With hands, roll rounded measuring teaspoonfuls dough into balls. Place 2 inches apart on cookie sheets. With tines of fork, press cookie down in crisscross fashion. Bake for 10 minutes. *Good.* Makes 2 dozen cookies. Exchanges for 3 cookies: 1 bread and 1 fat.

Dough too soft to roll. *Drop* from spoon. Did not press with fork. Got *36* (1½ inch) cookies.

Angeline Keller, Grand Forks, ND

CHOCOLATE SMUNCHIES

1 (4 serving) pkg. sugar-free
  chocolate pudding
2 c. skim milk

2 c. peanut butter
64 graham cracker sq.
2 c. Cool Whip

Mix pudding with skim milk according to package directions. Mix peanut butter with pudding. Divide equally on 32 graham cracker squares. Top each with 1 tablespoon of Cool Whip and top with second graham cracker square. Freeze until ready to use. Makes 32 smunchies. Each 1 equals: 1 bread, 1 protein, 1 fat, 25 optional calories.

Mary Voss, Owatonna, MN

GINGERBREAD COOKIES

1 c. diet margarine	3 c. all-purpose flour
⅓ c. granulated sugar	1 c. whole wheat flour
⅓ c. molasses	2 tsp. ginger
1 egg	1 tsp. baking soda
2 Tbsp. vinegar	½ tsp. salt

1. Cream margarine with sugar.
2. Stir in molasses, egg, and vinegar.
3. Stir flours together with ginger, baking soda, and salt.
4. Blend flours slowly into margarine.
5. Chill for 3 hours or overnight.
6. On lightly floured surface, roll until ⅛ inch thick.
7. Cut into shapes. Use cookie cutter or top of juice glass.
8. Place on tin foil lined cookie sheet.
9. Bake at 375° for 10 to 12 minutes. Makes 60 cookies.

One serving (1 cookie) equals ½ starch/bread exchange and ½ fat exchange.

Wally Littlefield, Fargo, ND

PINEAPPLE BARS

1 c. crushed pineapple with juice	2 Tbsp. diet margarine
2 tsp. cornstarch	1 Tbsp. brown sugar replacement
¼ tsp. lemon juice	1 tsp. cinnamon
1 tsp. vanilla extract	¼ tsp. baking soda
1½ oz. oatmeal	

Combine 4 ingredients and heat until thickened; cool slightly. Mix remaining ingredients until crumbly. Pat ¾ mixture in pan. Add pineapple mixture. Sprinkle remaining crumb mixture on top. Bake at 350° for 25 to 30 minutes. Two servings: 1 fruit, 1½ fat, 1 bread optional.

Jenny Kissel, Bismarck, ND

MUNCHIES

½ c. seedless raisins
16 graham crackers (2 x 2½ inch sq.)
½ c. nonfat dry milk
1 tsp. vanilla
½ c. walnuts
½ c. water
½ c. peanut butter
1 tsp. cinnamon

Simmer raisins and water over low heat. Remove and cool. In 6 x 9 inch cake pan, place 8 graham crackers, side by side, to cover bottom. Mix the nonfat dry milk, peanut butter, vanilla, cinnamon, walnuts, and raisin-water mixture until well blended. Pour over the graham crackers in pan and place 8 more crackers on top. Cover with plastic wrap and refrigerate. Cut into 16 bars. Yield: 16 servings. Exchanges: 1 serving equals ½ milk, 1 fat, and ½ fruit exchange. Calories: 105.

Angeline Keller, Grand Forks, ND

BABY RUTH BAR

1 pkg. chocolate ALBA
¾ oz. Grape-Nuts
1 Tbsp. peanut butter
1 Tbsp. water

Mix ALBA and Grape-Nuts in a small bowl. Add peanut butter and blend together with a fork. Add water and mix. Shape into a roll; wrap in Saran Wrap and freeze. Makes 1 serving. Exchanges equal 1 milk, 1 bread, 1 protein, 1 fat.

Mary Voss, Owatonna, MN

BROWNIES: A BAKER'S TWO DOZEN

1 sq. unsweetened chocolate (or 1 oz. no-melt type)
½ c. shortening
2 Tbsp. liquid sweetener
2 eggs, beaten
1 c. sifted cake flour (or 1 c. regular minus 2 Tbsp.)
2 tsp. vanilla
½ tsp. salt
½ tsp. baking soda
¼ c. chopped nuts

Melt chocolate and shortening in saucepan over low heat. Remove from heat. Add sweetener, vanilla, and eggs; stir until well blended. Add dry ingredients; mix until blended. Stir in nuts. Pour into greased 8 inch square pan. Level batter. Bake in 325° oven for 20 minutes. Cool; cut into 26 squares. Exchange: 2 brownies equal ½ bread, 1½ fat, 96 calories.

Angeline Keller, Grand Forks, ND

HOLIDAY FRUITCAKE
(Makes 12 servings)

½ c. raisins or currants
5 dates or prunes, finely snipped
5 figs, finely snipped
16 dried apricot halves, finely
   snipped
1 orange rind, grated
½ c. margarine
1 egg

1 tsp. vanilla
1¼ c. all-purpose flour
½ tsp. baking soda
1 tsp. baking powder
¼ tsp. cinnamon
¼ tsp. nutmeg
⅛ tsp. cloves

1. Combine raisins, dates or prunes, figs, apricots, and orange rind in a small bowl and set aside.

2. Cream margarine until light and fluffy.

3. Add egg and vanilla.

4. Stir in flour, soda, baking powder, and spices.

5. Pour in fruit mixture and beat until blended.

6. Bake in 325° oven for 45 to 55 minutes; cool. Store in an airtight container for at least 3 days for better slicing. Be sure to make the cake 3 to 4 days before serving; the longer it sets the better it tastes. If cake is to be stored longer than a week, wrap it in foil and refrigerate until used.

Note: To add that traditional rum or brandy flavor to the cake, heat 2 tablespoons rum or brandy in a small saucepan just until boiling. After the alcohol has boiled, cool it and pour it gently over the cake. Wrap cake in foil and refrigerate until needed.

Heating the rum or brandy drives off the alcohol, leaving only the carbohydrates and flavor. No food exchange value adjustment needs to be made when such a small amount is used. One serving (1/12 recipe) equals 1 bread exchange, 1 fat exchange, 1 fruit exchange, 155 calories, 25 grams carbohydrate, 2 grams protein, 7 grams fat.

Angeline Keller, Grand Forks, ND

RHUBARB CAKE

2½ c. rhubarb, cut finely
¾ c. sugar
⅓ c. vegetable oil
1 egg
1 c. sour milk, buttermilk, or
   plain yogurt
2 c. flour (whole wheat pastry
   flour makes a more
   nutritious cake)

1 tsp. baking soda
1 tsp. cinnamon
¼ tsp. allspice
¼ tsp. cloves
¼ tsp. nutmeg

Cream sugar, oil, egg, and milk together. Add dry ingredients; mix well. Stir in rhubarb. Spread batter in a 9x13 inch cake pan. Bake at 350° for 35 to 40 minutes. Makes 15 servings. One serving equals 1 bread, 1 fruit, and 1 fat exchange.

Angeline Keller, Grand Forks, ND

LOW CALORIE SPONGE CAKE

½ c. nonfat dry milk	3 eggs
1 c. sifted flour	¾ c. sugar
1½ tsp. baking powder	2 tsp. grated lemon peel
Dash of salt	

In small saucepan, heat milk until bubbles form around edge of pan; remove from heat and set aside. Preheat oven to 350°F. Sift flour, baking powder, and salt; set aside. In small bowl of electric mixer at high speed, beat eggs until thick and lemon colored. Gradually add sugar, beating until mixture is smooth and well blended, about 5 minutes.

At low speed, blend in flour mixture just until smooth. Add warm milk and peel, beating just until combined. Immediately pour batter into ungreased 9 inch angel food pan. Bake for 30 minutes or until cake tester inserted in center comes out clean. Invert pan over neck of bottle; let cool completely. Serve plain. Serves 10 (90 calories each).

Jenny Kissel, Bismarck, ND

SPICE CUPCAKES

1 c. sifted flour	1 egg
2 tsp. baking powder	½ c. water
¼ tsp. salt	1 Tbsp. shortening
½ tsp. cinnamon	1 Tbsp. salad oil
¼ tsp. nutmeg	½ tsp. vanilla
⅛ tsp. ginger	

Sift dry ingredients together. Beat egg and add water, salt, oil, and vanilla. Divide batter equally among 8 cupcakes. Set muffin pan in shallow pan of water and invert oblong cake pan over the muffin pan. Bake at 350° for 20 minutes. Remove cover for 5 minutes.

Frosting:

½ c. cottage cheese, sieved	½ tsp. salt
1 tsp. shortening	1 Tbsp. melted butter

Combine ingredients, beating until smooth. Flavor as desired and spread.

Jenny Kissel, Bismarck, ND

DIETETIC SPONGE CAKE
(Good)

6 eggs, separated
½ tsp. cream of tartar
½ c. cold water
2 Tbsp. lemon juice
2 Tbsp. liquid sweetener (equals
   1 c. sugar)

1 Tbsp. vanilla
1⅓ c. flour
1 tsp. baking powder
½ tsp. salt

In large mixing bowl, beat egg whites until foamy. Add cream of tartar and continue beating until stiff, but not dry. In small bowl, beat egg yolks until thick and lemon colored (about 5 minutes).

Combine water, lemon juice, sweetener, and vanilla. Combine flour, baking powder, and salt. Add alternately with liquid to yolks. Beat at medium speed for 2 minutes. Thoroughly fold yolk mixture into beaten whites. Bake in ungreased 9 or 10 inch tube pan at 325° for 55 to 60 minutes. Invert until completely cooled. Makes 12 servings.

Note: 1 serving equals 1 fruit exchange and 1 meat exchange.

Angeline Keller, Grand Forks, ND

BREADS, PASTRIES, PIES

BANANA NUT BREAD

1 lb. (3 or 4) ripe bananas,
   mashed
1½ Tbsp. liquid sugar substitute
2 eggs, well beaten

1¾ c. cake flour
3 tsp. baking powder
¼ tsp. salt
¼ c. chopped walnuts

Sprinkle sugar substitute over bananas and stir. Blend in eggs. Sift together flour, baking powder, and salt. Add walnuts. Blend thoroughly into banana mixture. Pour batter into greased loaf pan (approximately 4x7 inches). Bake at 350° for 25 minutes, then reduce heat to 300° and continue baking an additional 35 to 40 minutes until done and golden brown on top. Yield: 20 servings. Old exchanges: ½ bread exchange, ½ fruit exchange, ⅓ fat exchange. Revised exchanges: Same.

Angeline Keller, Grand Forks, ND

BRAN MUFFINS

⅓ c. whole wheat flour
½ tsp. baking soda
¾ c. All-Bran cereal
¼ c. raisins
½ tsp. baking powder
1 egg

¼ c. apple juice concentrate
¼ c. skim milk
2 tsp. sugar substitute
¼ tsp. cinnamon
¼ tsp. nutmeg
¼ c. pecans, chopped

Mix all dry ingredients. Add combined liquids and stir until moistened. Do not overstir. Pour batter into well greased muffin pans. Bake at 350° for 15 to 20 minutes or until golden brown. Yield: 6 muffins. One serving equals 1 muffin. Exchanges: 1 serving equals 1 bread and ½ fruit exchange. Sodium: 1 serving equals 92 milligrams. Calories: 1 serving equals 100.

Angeline Keller, Grand Forks, ND

POTATO LEFSE
(Recipe from Mildred Larson)

4 c. boiled and riced potatoes,
   packed
⅓ c. shortening
1 Tbsp. sugar

1¼ tsp. salt
¼ c. milk
1½ c. flour

Mix together potato, shortening, sugar, salt, and milk when potatoes are warm. Cool the mixture. Add flour. Make 32 balls. Roll thin on floured board. Bake on ungreased griddle at 400°. When top bubbles, turn. Bake until light brown. Storage after cooking: Layer patties on a towel. After cooling, wrap in Glad Wrap. Freeze. Yield: 32 patties. To serve: Add margarine and dietetic jelly. Roll and eat.

Angeline Keller, Grand Forks, ND

PASTRY FOR ONE-CRUST PIE

1 c. sifted flour
½ tsp. salt
¼ c. sunflower, safflower, or
    corn oil

2 Tbsp. cold milk

Mix sifted flour and salt. Measure into measuring cup the oil and cold milk. Pour oil and milk into flour mixture. Stir with fork; press into a ball. Roll between two (12 inch square) sheets of waxed paper. Remove top sheet of paper, then lift pastry and lower sheet of paper. Place pastry in pie pan with paper side up. Remove paper and fit pastry into pan. Form a fluted edge on pastry. Do *not* prick pastry. Pour filling into pastry lined pan and bake as directed. Each serving (including pastry) equals: 1 bread exchange + 1½ fat exchanges + ½ milk exchange.

Angeline Keller, Grand Forks, ND

PUMPKIN PIE

Mix:

2 eggs, slightly beaten
1 (16 oz.) can solid pack
    pumpkin
2½ Tbsp. Sugar Twin brown
    sugar replacement
½ tsp. salt

1 tsp. cinnamon
½ tsp. ginger
¼ tsp. cloves
1 large (13 fl. oz.) can
    evaporated skim milk

Pour into a 9 inch pie shell. Bake in 425°F. oven for 10 minutes. Reduce temperature to 350°F. and bake for 30 minutes or until a knife inserted into center of pie filling comes out clean.

Angeline Keller, Grand Forks, ND

NO SUGAR APPLE PIE

Apples
Cinnamon
Dash of salt

6 oz. apple concentrate
2 Tbsp. flour

Make favorite 2 crust pastry. Slice apples in bottom of crust. Sprinkle with cinnamon and dash of salt. Boil apple concentrate and flour till thick. Pour sauce over apples. Put crust on top and bake till done.

Carol Reynolds, Hibbing, MN

LOW-CAL APPLE PIE

½ c. uncooked rolled oats
6 c. thin sliced apples
⅔ c. pineapple juice

2 Tbsp. raisins
½ tsp. cinnamon
Grape-Nuts (to sprinkle on top)

Layer oats in bottom of 8x8 inch pan. Add apples; pour juice over and sprinkle with raisins and cinnamon. Cover with foil and bake for 1 hour at 350°. Remove foil; cover with Grape-Nuts and bake for 15 minutes more. Serve with Cool Whip.

Bernice T. Eugenis, Saginaw, MN

SUGAR-LESS APPLE PIE
(Diabetic)

2 crust pie shell
Apples, sliced
1 (6 oz.) can apple juice
    concentrate

3 Tbsp. Minute tapioca
Cinnamon
Butter

Make 2 crust pie shell. Fill with apples (sliced). Add apple juice concentrate, Minute tapioca, and cinnamon. Dot with butter. Put top crust on and back in *conventional* oven. Do *not* microwave.

Ollie Kearney, Owatonna, MN

NEW ENGLAND APPLE PIE
(Sugar-free)

Pastry:

2 c. flour
⅔ c. butter or oleo

6 or 7 Tbsp. water

Makes top and bottom crust.

Filling:

¾ c. raisins
¾ c. water
6 c. peeled sliced apples
1 Tbsp. lemon juice

1 tsp. cinnamon
½ tsp. nutmeg
Dash of ginger
Dash of cloves

Boil raisins and water. Remove from heat and cover for 10 minutes. Add apples, lemon juice, cinnamon, nutmeg, ginger, and cloves. Put in crust and cover with crust. Bake at 350° for 40 minutes.

May add a little Sugar Twin.

Sandy Luce

SUGAR-LESS PEACH PIE
(Diabetic)

Pie shell
½ c. orange juice concentrate
½ c. water

2 Tbsp. corn starch
3 Tbsp. peach or orange jello
Peaches

Boil up orange juice concentrate, water, and corn starch. Add peach or orange jello. Add peaches and put in baked pie shell.

Ollie Kearney, Owatonna, MN

RAISIN PIE
(Sugar-Free)

1⅓ c. raisins
2 c. water
3 egg yolks
½ Sugar Twin
1 Tbsp. vinegar

1 Tbsp. butter
2 Tbsp. flour
½ tsp. vanilla
⅓ c. heavy cream

Simmer raisins and water for 5 minutes. Add remaining ingredients, except butter and vanilla, to raisin mixture. Cook until thick. Add butter and vanilla last. Pour into baked pastry crust. Top with meringue.

If using sour cream, don't use vinegar.

Sandy Luce

STRAWBERRY YOGURT PIE

Crust:

8 graham crackers (2½ inch sq.), made into crumbs

8 tsp. reduced calorie margarine, melted

Mix together and press into 9 inch pie pan. Bake for 5 to 10 minutes at 350°; cool.

Filling:

3 (8 oz.) ctn. Weight Watchers strawberry yogurt

2 c. Cool Whip
1 c. fresh sliced strawberries

Stir together yogurt and Cool Whip with wire whisk. Fold in strawberries. Pour into cooled crust; refrigerate for 3 hours. Cut into 8 equal pieces. Each serving equals ½ bread, ½ fat, ⅜ milk, ½ fruit, 50 optional calories.

Mary Voss, Owatonna, MN

CHOCOLATE PEANUT BUTTER PIE

1 c. graham crackers, crushed

4 Tbsp. crunch peanut butter

Mix ingredients together and line an 8 or 9 inch pie pan. Bake at 350° for 5 minutes.

Filling:

**1 pkg. chocolate sugar-free
   pudding (follow directions
   on box)**

1 c. Cool Whip

Add Cool Whip to chocolate pudding. Pour onto crust and chill. Cut into 4 servings. One serving equals 1 bread, 1 protein, 1 fat, 1 milk.

Wally Littlefield, Fargo, ND

REESE'S PEANUT BUTTER PIE

**8 graham cracker sq.
2 Tbsp. diet margarine, melted
1 (4 serving) pkg. low calorie
   chocolate "cooked"
   pudding**

**2 c. skim milk
6 Tbsp. peanut butter**

Mix graham cracker crumbs and melted margarine. Press into 8 inch pan. Bake at 350° for 8 minutes, then cool. Prepare pudding according to package directions. Mix in peanut butter while pudding is still warm. Pour into baked crust; chill for 3 hours. Makes 4 servings. Each serving equals 1 bread, 2¼ fat, 1 milk, 1½ protein.

Mary Voss, Owatonna, MN

Notes

Gluten Free

A HANDY SPICE AND HERB GUIDE

ALLSPICE—a pea-sized fruit that grows in Mexico, Jamaica, Central and South America. Its delicate flavor resembles a blend of cloves, cinnamon and nutmeg. USES: (Whole) Pickles, meats, boiled fish, gravies. (Ground) Puddings, relishes, fruit preserves, baking.

BASIL—the dried leaves and stems of an herb grown in the United States and North Mediterranean area. Has an aromatic, leafy flavor. USES: For flavoring tomato dishes and tomato paste, turtle soup; also use in cooked peas, squash, snap beans; sprinkle chopped over lamb chops and poultry.

BAY LEAVES—the dried leaves of an evergreen grown in the eastern Mediterranean countries. Has a sweet, herbaceous floral spice note. USES: For pickling, stews, for spicing sauces and soup. Also use with a variety of meats and fish.

CARAWAY—the seed of a plant grown in the Netherlands. Flavor that combines the tastes of Anise and Dill. USES: For the cordial Kummel, baking breads; often added to sauerkraut, noodles, cheese spreads. Also adds zest to French fried potatoes, liver, canned asparagus.

CURRY POWDER—a ground blend of ginger, turmeric, fenugreek seed, as many as 16 to 20 spices. USES: For all Indian curry recipes such as lamb, chicken, and rice, eggs, vegetables, and curry puffs.

DILL—the small, dark seed of the dill plant grown in India, having a clean, aromatic taste. USES: Dill is a predominant seasoning in pickling recipes; also adds pleasing flavor to sauerkraut, potato salad, cooked macaroni, and green apple pie.

MACE—the dried covering around the nutmeg seed. Its flavor is similar to nutmeg, but with a fragrant, delicate difference. USES: (Whole) For pickling, fish, fish sauce, stewed fruit. (Ground) Delicious in baked goods, pastries and doughnuts, adds unusual flavor to chocolate desserts.

MARJORAM—an herb of the mint family, grown in France and Chile. Has a minty-sweet flavor. USES: In beverages, jellies and to flavor soups, stews, fish, sauces. Also excellent to sprinkle on lamb while roasting.

MSG (MONOSODIUM GLUTAMATE)—is a vegetable protein derivative for raising the effectiveness of natural food flavors. USES: Small amounts, adjusted to individual taste, can be added to steaks, roasts, chops, seafoods, stews, soups, chowder, chop suey and cooked vegetables.

OREGANO—a plant of the mint family and a species of marjoram of which the dried leaves are used to make an herb seasoning. USES: An excellent flavoring for any tomato dish, especially pizza, chili con carne, and Italian specialties.

PAPRIKA—a mild, sweet red pepper growing in Spain, Central Europe and the United States. Slightly aromatic and prized for brilliant red color. USES: A colorful garnish for pale foods, and for seasoning Chicken Paprika, Hungarian Goulash, salad dressings.

POPPY—the seed of a flower grown in Holland. Has a rich fragrance and crunchy, nut-like flavor. USES: Excellent as a topping for breads, rolls and cookies. Also delicious in buttered noodles.

ROSEMARY—an herb (like a curved pine needle) grown in France, Spain, and Portugal, and having a sweet, fresh taste. USES: In lamb dishes, in soups, stews and to sprinkle on beef before roasting.

SAGE—the leaf of a shrub grown in Greece, Yugoslavia and Albania. Flavor is camphoraceous and minty. USES: For meat and poultry stuffing, sausages, meat loaf, hamburgers, stews and salads.

THYME—the leaves and stems of a shrub grown in France and Spain. Has a strong, distinctive flavor. USES: For poultry seasoning, in croquettes, fricassees and fish dishes. Also tasty on fresh sliced tomatoes.

TURMERIC—a root of the ginger family, grown in India, Haiti, Jamaica and Peru, having a mild, ginger-pepper flavor. USES: As a flavoring and coloring in prepared mustard and in combination with mustard as a flavoring for meats, dressings, salads.

GLUTEN FREE

In preparing this section, I have found through a friend and volunteering at a health food store, that a lot of people have an intolerance to flour and its related products. The information I have gathered is from many different sources and hope it will give some variety and new ideas for affected people and new information to those not knowledgeable about "GF" (Gluten Free) diets and foods.

Anyone wanting more information can contact the following organizations for recipes, questions, or food facts.

They are:

Celiac Sprue Association
United States of America, Inc.
2313 Rocklyn Drive, Suite 1
Des Moines, IA 50322

Midwest Gluten Intolerance Group
5660 Rebecca Lane
Minnetonka, MN 55345

I would like to thank the preceding organizations for the information provided for this book.

Barb Fivecoate

GLUTEN FREE PRODUCT TIPS

Airline Meats: Fifteen major airlines were recently surveyed and it was found that virtually all offer lacto-ovo vegetarian, strict vegetarian, fruit platter, seafood, lowfat cholesterol, low- or no-salt, and kosher meals. Some also serve Hindu, Moslem, Oriental, bland, and low-fiber meals. Most airlines ask for a 24 hour advance notice, but they can sometimes accomodate passengers with only an hour or two notice.

Short flights usually offer only little snacks - and no choice - while coast-to-coast flights usually offer a choice of meat, chicken, or fish. Several airlines are able to offer a GF diet, but can do best with their strictly vegetarian or fruit offerings for celiac patients. Special meals cost no more, so if you want to avoid the airlines version of Russian roulette, remember to ask for a special meal when you make your reservation and double-check it when you hand over your money.

In four recent flights, I made use of vegetarian offerings. They were well done, nicely served, often included rice, and didn't cause a hitch in my diet. The next time you fly, learn what the food choices will be at the same time you plan your routing. I think you'll be pleased with the results.

United Airlines has started offering GF meals, according to Douglas Gorab, Manager Food and Beverages. The starch offering - plain rice cakes. Gorab asks that those who try the meals write him about their experience (P.O. Box 66100, Chicago, Illinois 60666).

Heinz Instant Baby Foods (dehydrated) include these GF items: Apples, bananas, peaches, carrots, squash, sweet potatoes, creamed peas, creamed corn, mixed vegetables, rice cereal with bananas and apple juice, rice cereal with pears and apple juice, mixed fruit, apples and bananas, apples and apricots, apples and peaches, and apples and pears. None of the dinners are GF. The products contain no added sugar, salt, modified starch or tapioca, preservatives, artificial colors or flavors, or MSG. The calorie value per canister ranges from 40 to 80 calories. For more information, the toll free phone number is 800-872-2229. (From Eva W. Sherman, Consumer Representative.)

Lipton Onion Soup Mix contains wheat flour in the hydrolyzed vegetable protein so it is *not* GF (Gluten Free).

3-Musketeers Candy Bar now contains barley so it is *no longer* GF.

Chiclets and Peppermint Chiclets are gluten free. (Letter from Mary Richardson, Director Consumer Affairs, Warner Lambert Co.)

These Campbell's soups are gluten-free: Old-Fashioned Vegetable Beef, Split Pea with Ham, Country Vegetable.

Beatrice Foods responded with the following gluten-free list:

Tomato Products: Hunt's ketchup, tomato sauces and pastes, meatloaf fixin's tomato sauce, all natural barbecue sauce.

Bean Products: Hunt's Big John's Beans 'n Fixin's, chili beans, pork and beans, red kidney beans, small red beans.

Pudding Products: All snack packs.

Popcorn Products: Orville Redenbacher's Gourmet popping corn, microwave popping corn, caramel crunch popcorn, sesame crunch popcorn snack, gourmet granola crunch popcorn snack is *not* GF.

Oriental Products: La Choy fancy mixed Chinese vegetables, chop suey vegetables, bamboo shoots, water chestnuts, fried rice, bean sprouts, pork chow mein, beef chow mein, chicken chow mein (and dinner), shrimp chow mein (and dinner), meatless chow mein, vegetable chow mein, beef pepper oriental (and dinner), sukiyaki, sweet and sour oriental with pork, sweet and sour oriental with chicken, sweet and sour pork, fried rice with meat, and Chinese pea pods.

Sloppy Joe Products: Hunt's original Manwich and Mexican Manwich.

Soup Products: Soup Starter homemade soup mix and chicken vegetable flavor.

Dry Beverage Products: Swiss Miss cocoa products.

Peanut Butter Products: Peter Pan crunchy-creamy peanut butters (also salt free and sodium free).

Nut Products: Fisher almonds, cashews, fancy mixed nuts, cashews/almonds, honey roasted, peanuts, sunflowers, black walnuts, and English walnuts.

The following products are also gluten-free:

Ortega Products: Ortega taco shells, tostada shells, taco sauce (mild and hot), chile products (includes salsa and tomatoes and chiles products), hot pepper products, and pimentos.

Lawry's original spaghetti sauce seasoning blend with imported mushrooms and extra rich and thick spaghetti sauce seasoning blend.

Spin Blend salad dressing.

Estee cream of mushroom soup.

Sunkist Fun Fruits.

Campbell's pork and beans.

B&M barbecue beans.

Old El Paso taco dinner.

Campbell's chunky chili beef soup.

Pepperidge Farm soups.

Heinz vegetarian beans.

Oregon cherry fruit filling.

Royal instant pudding.

Hormel's Dinty Moore beef stew, Dinty Moore chicken stew, Dinty Moore burger chuck stew, Dinty Moore 7 vegetables in beef gravy, and Hormel chili.

Swiss Miss puddings.

Heinz distilled white vinegar.

Kraft Light 'N Lively yogurt.

Quaker's Van Camp's New Orleans style red kidney beans.

Keebler's Zesty Cheddar Cheeblers.

Chun King chow mein vegetables, bean sprouts, water chestnuts, bamboo shoots, and soy sauce.

Hawaiian Punch (all forms).

Patio: 6 count cheese enchiladas, cheese enchilada dinner, and tortillas.

Del Monte: All canned fruits, vegetables, fruit juices, fruit drinks, all dried fruit products, and canned puddings.

My-T-Fine: All flavors packaged pudding and pie filling mixes.

Heublein Food Products: A.1. Steak Sauce, Escoffier Sauce Diable, Escoffier Sauce Robert, Grey Poupon Dijon mustard, Steak Supreme Steak Sauce.

Tomato Cocktail: Snap-E-Tom.

Cooking wines and wine vinegars: Regina cooking burgundy, Regina cooking sauterne, Regina cooking sherry, Regina champagne vinegar, Regina red wine vinegar, Regina red wine vinegar with garlic.

Byerly's at St. Louis Park (aisle 4) now carry:

Wel-Plan: Pasta in macaroni, short cut spaghetti, spaghetti rings, custard cream cookies, sweet cookies - lemon flavored, low protein corn and tapioca starch crackers.

Dietary Specialties: Chocolate cake mix, brownie mix, blueberry muffin mix, white bread mix (hurrah!).

In addition, they now again carry: Aproten-low protein rusks, DP low protein bread in cans.

Star Kist and Chicken of the Sea tuna report that their tuna is GF.

Jell-O Pudding Pops are gluten-free.

Thank You smooth 'n creamy pudding (now carried at Byerly's) are gluten-free. The flavors are: Rice, tapioca, chocolate, and vanilla.

New products since the Byerly's list was printed include Pacific Products Quick 'n Creamy Brown Rice Hot Cereal; Health Valley Cheddar Lites; Weight Watchers Crispbread and Harvest House; Kellogg's Fruit Marshmallow Krispies (contain *malt* flavoring); Liberty Orchards Aplets, Cotlets, Grapelets, Fruit Festives (dried fruit).

Some gluten-free products that you may want to be aware of: Barbara's Corn Flakes (9 ounce); Barbara's Brown Rice Crisps (11 ounce). Both products are sweetened with fruit juices.

Product News: All of *Wrigley's chewing gums* are GF, including Spearmint, Doublemint, Juicy Fruit, Big Red, Freedent, Hubba Bubba, and Orbit sugar free gum. Write to *Campbell's Soup Co.*, Camden, New Jersey 08101 for a list of GF soups and other products.

Ragu Foods, Inc., Rochester, New York, has 2 GF spaghetti sauces: Homestyle flavored with meat (no sugar added recipe) and Chunky Garden-style. Both are described as "100% Natural Ingredients, No preservatives, and No Additives." There is a toll free telephone number for consumers: 1-800-243-5804 (in CT, call 1-800-852-8558).

Eskimo Pie Products are GF except for the Bavarian Ice Cream Roll and Eskimo Pie Crispy. (Tina B. Seay, Consumer Affairs Dept., Eskimo Pie Corp.)

Ralston Purina's Sunflakes Cereal has corn and rice as its base so it is GF. *When cooking with corn meal,* you can avoid graininess in breads, etc. by following this method. Add the liquids in the recipe to the meal; boil the mixture a few minutes, then let it set for awhile to break down the meal.

Hershey's GF Products (besides those in the *GF Commercial Product Brochure* now include: Golden almond chocolate bar, Rolo caramels in milk chocolate, Skor toffee bar, and chocolate milk (2% lowfat). (List from Hershey's Foods Corp.)

Spice Islands Beau Monde Seasoning is GF. The ingredients are salt, dextrose, onion, celery seeds, and tricalcium phosphate. (Mary Cantini, Consumer Services, Specialty Brands Inc.)

Farmer Brothers Coffee, a brand used in some restaurants, does not contain gluten or any additives or diluents. (Han Y. Rhyu, Technical Director, Farmer Brothers Co.)

R.C. Bigelow Teas which are GF include: Constant Comment, Earl Grey, Orange Pekoe, Irish Breakfast, Peppermint Stick, English Teatime, Cinnamon Stick, Plantation Mint, Lemon Life, Chinese Fortune, Looking Good, Orange and Spice, I Love Lemon, Feeling Free, Fruit and Almond, Mint Medley, Sweet

Dreams, Early Riser, Nice over Ice, Apple Orchard, Chamomile Mint, Orange and C, Lemon and C, Almond Orange, Mint Blend, Hibiscus and Rose Hips, Peppermint, Chamomile, and Spearmint. (Naomi Dull, Consumer Relations, R.C. Bigelow Inc.)

Schweppes Beverages which are GF include: Ginger ale, Tonic, Bitter Lemon, Club Soda, Seltzer Water, and Collins Mixer. (Letter from R.J. Larwood, Dominion Beverage Co.)

Chewing Gums: Beech Nut (Cinnamon, Fancy Fruit, Peppermint, and Spearmint); Beechies Candy Coated (Fruit, Peppermint, Pepsin, and Spearmint); Bubble Yum Bubble Gum - and Sugarless (all flavors); Fruit Stripe Gum - and Bubble Gum (all flavors); Replay Gum (all flavors); Carefree Sugarless and Bubble Gum (all flavors).

Planters Bars: Peanut/Raisin, Walnut/Apple, Almond/Apricot, and Almond/Pineapple; Jumbo Block, and Peanut Candy.

Cough Drops: Beech Nut and Pine Bros. (Assorted Honey and Wild Cherry).

Planters Nuts: Most are GF *except* Sesame Nut Mix.

For thickening sauces, gravies, cream pies, etc., substitute equal amounts of rice flour for wheat flour. Cream of Rice (dry) or crushed dry GF rice cereal makes an excellent breading for chicken, fish, cutlets, and croquettes, according to the Council.

Chico-San Crispy Rice Cakes (100% all natural whole grain brown rice) featured these snack ideas in a recent ad - for toppings, try: Melted cheese and jalapeno peppers, peanut butter and jelly, cottage cheese and tomato, cream cheese and olives, carrot-raisin salad, scrambled egg and bacon bits, taco sauce and Cheddar cheese, chicken salad, egg salad, tuna and melted cheese.

For a free Chico-San Crispy Rice Cakes recipe book, write to: P.O. Box 1055, Boston, MA 02277-1055. Be sure to include your name and address.

Plantain Flour (made from a fruit similar to bananas) is recommended for baking - combined with rice flour - by a Pennsylvania member. He substitutes it for ¼ to ⅓ of the rice flour in a GF recipe. This has a beneficial effect on the texture of pancakes, cakes, and bread. "There are times when one does not even notice the difference from wheat flour texture. It does not have any strong flavor of its own, but has a brownish color, and gives a little of the effect of buckwheat in pancakes," he says. For pancakes, he uses a combination of baking powder, baking soda, buttermilk, and beaten egg whites for leavening. "Unfortunately," he adds, "plantain flour does not stick things together. For that we use tapioca starch which helps give a springy and spongy texture." He buys the flour from Baldinger's Foods of All Nations, Zelienople, PA 16063. (The flour is a product of Columbia and is distributed by Goya House in the USA.)

Nabisco Brands, Inc. has published a brochure of *Allergen-Free* Products. If you want the 34-page brochure, write to: Consumer Information Center, Nabisco Brands, Inc., East Hanover, NJ 07936. Listed here are GF items (do not contain wheat, barley, oats, or rye): Coconut Macaroon Soft Cakes; Cheese 'n Crunch Cheese Flavored Snack; Planters Tortilla Chips-Traditional; Cheese Curls, Cheez Balls, and Corn Chips. *Puddings:* Royal Sugar Free Instant Pudding (banana cream, butterscotch, chocolate, chocolate chocolate chip, chocolate mint, dark 'n sweet, lemon, pistachio nut, toasted butter almond, toasted coconut, and vanilla); Royal Cooked Puddings (banana cream, butterscotch, chocolate custard, dark 'n sweet, flan with caramel sauce, key lime and lemon pie fillings, vanilla, and vanilla tapioca).

Candies: Pearson's and Curtiss Candies - Mint Parfait, Peanut Butter Parfait, Baby Ruth and Butterfinger candy bars; Charleston Chew Candy (chocolate, strawberry, and vanilla); Bridge Mix; Coconut Squares, Welch's Cortina Chocolate and Dark Chocolate Covered Cherries; Cortina Thin Mints; Chocolate Covered Peanuts and Raisins; Fudge Bar; Nut Fudge Squares; Pom Poms Caramels, Sugar Babies Caramels, Sugar Mama and Daddy Caramels.

Uncle Ben's Converted Rice and Select Brown Rice are GF. However, Uncle Ben's Wild Rice, Rice Florentine, and Flavored Rice are *not* GF (contain hydrolized vegetable protein).

Rice Council of America recommends these substitutes for 1 cup of wheat flour:

¾ c. rice flour	1 scant c. corn meal (fine)
1 c. corn flour	⅝ c. potato starch flour (10
¾ c. corn meal (coarse)	Tbsp.)

The Rice Council also recommends that you use this method to have a smoother texture when baking with rice flour: Mix the rice flour with the liquid called for in a recipe. Bring to a boil, then cool before adding other ingredients.

Coarse flours need not be sifted before measuring, according to the Council. However, coarse meals and flours require more leavening than wheat flour - use 2½ teaspoons of baking powder for each cup of coarse flour.

Homemade Vegetable Soup, beef stew, lasagna, chili, and spaghetti sauce all freeze well. Make them in large quantities and freeze them in meal size portions for later use. Tomato juice can be added in small amounts to the chili and spaghetti sauce to freshen up the taste when heating after thawing. An extra dash of seasoning at warm-up time also adds a new flavor to these "plan-overs."

Need a new idea for your brown-bag lunch? Try these: Ham, cheese, and mustard rolled in a soft tortilla (corn). Brown rice or a pasta salad. Turkey strips with your favorite dressing as a dip. A cored apple, cut in half - with peanut butter or cheese spread in the center. (Courtesy of Dow Consumer Products Dept.)

Cotton seed flour may be a future food choice for celiacs. This high protein flour (up to 64% protein in weight, compared to 12 to 15 % for wheat flour) does not contain gluten, according to *Changing Times* (page 10, June, 1985). Ways to use it in baking are being tested at Texas Women's University. The flour isn't on the market yet, but cottonseed kernels (called Cot-n-nuts) are in some stores. They have more protein and less fat than peanuts.

Gluten-Free Products are available from:

Red Mill Farms - New products include Dutch Chocolate Cake, Banana Nut Cake, and Coconut Macaroons. Write to Red Mill Farms, 290 South 5th Street, Brooklyn, NY 11211, or phone (212) 384-2150 for information about ingredients and prices.

Dietary Specialties - formerly Henkel Corporation, has GF pasta, cookies, bread, baking mix, and wheat starch. Writh to Dietary Specialties, P.O. Box 227, Rochester, NY 14601 for prices, or call (716) 263-2787.

Vita-Wheat, Inc. - has GF bread, cookies, and fruit cake available. Rice bread is available in two varieties, one with eggs and milk and one without. All other GF products are made without egg or milk. Write to Vita-Wheat, Inc., 1839 Hilton Road, Ferndale, MI 48220 or call (313) 543-0888.

Ener-G Foods, Inc. - carries 31 baked GF products and 20 mixes, starches, flours, and other products for the GF diet. Send a business size self-addressed, stamped envelope to Ener-G Foods, Inc., P.O. Box 24723, Seattle, WA 98124, (206) 767-6660. New products include Italian croutons and rice bread made without yeast, sugar, eggs, or milk.

MAIN DISHES

CHICKEN-RICE DISH

1 (6 oz.) box Uncle Ben's long grain and wild rice
2½ oz. sliced mushrooms

Favorite chicken pieces, cut into individual servings
Fleischmann's oleo

1. Pour rice into baking pan.
2. Add 2⅔ cups water.
3. Add 1 tablespoon Fleischmann's oleo.
4. Place chicken pieces (skin side up) on top of rice.
5. Pour melted Fleischmann's oleo on top of chicken pieces.

Bake for 1½ hours at 375° or 400° in preheated oven. (Adjust oven temperature for browning.)

When the gluten-free mushroom soup is available, substitute for oleo and pour over chicken pieces.

LASAGNA

1 (8 oz.) pkg. Aproten macaroni
1 lb. ground beef
1 (15 oz.) can tomato sauce
1 (6 oz.) can tomato paste
½ tsp. salt

1 tsp. Italian seasoning
1 lb. dry cottage cheese
2 c. Mozzarella cheese, grated
½ c. Parmesan cheese

Brown ground beef; drain. Add tomato sauce, tomato paste, and seasonings; simmer slowly for 20 minutes. Prepare macaroni product according to package; drain. Arrange ⅓ of the macaroni in bottom of greased baking dish. Top with ⅓ of the meat sauce, ⅓ of the Mozzarella, and ⅓ of the cottage cheese. Repeat layers twice, ending with cottage cheese. Top with Parmesan cheese. Bake in 350° oven for 30 minutes. Let stand for 10 minutes.

RICE SOUFFLE

2 c. cooked rice
1 medium onion, chopped
¾ tsp. garlic salt
Dash of sweet basil
Dash of Beau Monde
3 eggs, beaten

¼ c. oil
1 c. cheese, grated
1 c. milk (½ evaporated, ½ regular milk)
¼ c. dried parsley
1 tsp. salt

Mix ingredients. Bake in greased dish at 350° for 45 minutes.

TACO-HAMBURGER CASSEROLE

2 lb. ground beef
2 Tbsp. margarine
½ c. chopped onions
½ c. chopped celery
½ c. chopped green pepper
1 tsp. garlic powder

2 Tbsp. taco seasoning
Salt and pepper to taste
10 oz. frozen mixed vegies
1 c. sour cream
1 c. shredded Mozzarella cheese

Brown beef, onions, celery, and green pepper in margarine. Add seasonings, mixed vegies (which have been thawed), and sour cream; simmer for 10 minutes, but do not boil. Put in 9x13 inch pan and put the Mozzarella cheese on top (I used 2 cups on the top).

Topping:

2 eggs, beaten
1 c. milk
1 Tbsp. oil
½ c. potato flour
½ c. rice flour

1 tsp. xanthan gum
¼ tsp. garlic powder
1 Tbsp. dry parsley (optional)
⅓ c. Parmesan cheese

Beat eggs and add milk and oil. Mix the flours, xanthan gum, garlic, parsley, and cheese; add to the egg mixture. Pour on top of casserole and bake at 400° for 30 minutes.

MINA DE ESPINACA Y TOMAT

1 medium onion, chopped
1 garlic clove
2 Tbsp. butter or margarine
16 oz. chopped tomatoes,
    including most juice
10 oz. frozen spinach, thawed
    and well drained

Season to taste (Italian herb mix
    is very good)
2 large eggs
Crispy cakes (plain or Italian
    seasoning)
4 to 6 oz. cheese (Swiss,
    Mozzarella, etc.)

Saute in a large skillet the onion, garlic, and margarine. Add to the onion mixture the tomatoes, spinach, and seasoning. Use enough crispy cakes to make 3 layers in small (8x8 inch) pan (mine is 7x10 inches and take 5 per layer). Beat eggs. Coat pan with oil. Dip crackers in egg for 1 layer and cover bottom of pan. Add ⅓ of vegetable mixture. Sprinkle with 1 to 2 ounces cheese. Repeat with crackers, vegetable layer, and cheese. Top with last layer of crackers and sprinkle with cheese. Bake for 20 to 25 minutes at 375° until cheese is melted and casserole is bubbly.

Variation: 6½ ounces of drained and flaked tuna may be added to tomato mixture when it is almost finished simmering.

MIXED VEGETABLE CASSEROLE

1 (8 oz.) pkg. frozen French style
    green beans
1 (8 oz.) pkg. frozen baby lima
    beans
1 (8 oz.) pkg. frozen peas
3 green peppers, cut into strips

1½ c. heavy cream
1½ c. GF mayonnaise
Salt and pepper to taste
¾ c. grated Parmesan or
    Cheddar cheese

Put vegetables and peppers into a pan with just enough boiling water to keep from burning; cook only until thawed. Drain and cool. Whip cream until stiff; mix with mayonnaise and remaining ingredients. Put vegetables into a 3 quart casserole; cover with sauce. (Casserole can be refrigerated at this point to be baked later in the day.)

Bake, uncovered, at 325°F. for 50 minutes or until puffy and lightly browned. Makes 8 servings.

TUNA RICE PATTIES

2 c. cooked rice
2 eggs, beaten
1 (6 to 7 oz.) can tuna

1 Tbsp. chopped onion
Salt and pepper as desired

Flake tuna; mix all ingredients lightly and shape into patties. Fry in a small amount of corn oil in skillet until brown. Makes 4 to 6 patties.

CHOCOLATE CRUMB CRUST

4 c. Cocoa Puff cereal

½ c. melted margarine

Crush Cocoa Puff cereal to make 1½ cups crumbs. Mix in melted margarine. Press into two 8 inch pie pans or one larger pie pan. Bake at 400°F. for 8 minutes. Use with a favorite pie filling.

Nancy Linnemann

SAUCE MIX (DRY) FOR CASSEROLE

2 c. instant dry milk
¾ c. cornstarch
¼ c. instant GF chicken bouillon
2 Tbsp. dried onion flakes
    (optional)

½ tsp. pepper
1 tsp. basil, crushed (optional)
1 tsp. thyme (optional)

In a bowl combine the dry milk, cornstarch, bouillon, onion flakes, and seasonings. Mix well. Store in airtight container. Makes 3 cups of mix, equal to 9 cans (10½ ounce size) condensed cream soup.

To make sauce equivalent to 1 can of soup, combine ⅓ cup of the mix with 1 ¼ cups water in a saucepan. Cook and stir over low heat until thick. If desired, add 1 tablespoon of butter and some chopped cooked celery or sliced mushrooms.

Note: A similar recipe from Jeannette Kralemann gave these directions for microwave cooking of sauce. Put ⅓ cup of mix and 1¼ cups water in a microwave cooking dish; stir well. Cook and stir every minute until thickened.

CONFETTI RICE AND CHEESE

2 c. cooked rice	1 egg
½ c. chopped fresh parsley	1 c. milk

Beat egg. Stir in milk. Mix everything together. Place in oiled casserole. Bake at 350° until set, about 45 minutes.

ITALIAN BROCCOLI AND MACARONI

1 stick margarine	Salt to taste
1 medium onion, diced	½ lb. Mozzarella cheese, diced
2 (10 oz.) pkg. frozen broccoli	6 to 8 Tbsp. Parmesan cheese
1 lb. Aproten macaroni (4 c. dry), cooked and drained	4 eggs, beaten plus enough milk to equal 2 c. liquid
1 lb. Ricotta cheese	

Melt margarine in skillet. Add frozen broccoli and onion. Cook until broccoli is done. Mix Ricotta cheese into broccoli mixture. Add 1 pound cooked macaroni; salt to taste. Put ½ mixture in Pam-sprayed 15x11 inch pan. Sprinkle Parmesan and ½ of Mozzarella cheese on top; repeat. Pour egg-milk mixture slowly over top. Bake in 350° oven for 30 minutes. Put foil over top while baking if cheese gets too brown.

POTATOES - GRATIN DAUPHINOIS
(Scalloped potatoes)

2 lb. potatoes, sliced	Salt and pepper
1 c. milk or half & half	Nutmeg
¼ lb. margarine (or butter)	

Spread the potatoes in a greased baking dish; season. Spread small pieces of margarine over the surface. Pour on milk. Bake in moderate oven approximately 1 hour. (Cover the dish until the last 15 minutes.)

CORN MEAL CREPES

2 eggs
½ tsp. salt
⅓ c. corn meal

2 Tbsp. oil
½ c. cornstarch
½ c. milk

Beat eggs slightly. Add salt, corn meal, oil, cornstarch, and milk. Mix well. Keep mixing the batter, the corn meal settles.

I tried these with the automatic crepe maker, but the batter wouldn't stick to the cooking surface. So a crepe pan would work better.

BAKED FISH-VEGETABLE DINNER

3 large potatoes, peeled and
    sliced thin
Salt substitute
½ lb. fresh mushrooms, sliced
1 lb. zucchini, cut into ⅛ inch
    slices
4 large tomatoes, peeled,
    seeded, and sliced

2 green onions, sliced thin
1½ lb. fish fillets (haddock,
    perch, flounder, or sole)
2 Tbsp. corn oil margarine
1 tsp. fresh thyme, chopped, or
    ½ tsp. dried thyme
Pepper, freshly ground
Lemon slices

Preheat the oven to 350°F. Generously coat a 2 quart baking dish with margarine. Arrange the potatoes in the dish; sprinkle lightly with salt substitute. Cover with foil; bake for 15 minutes. Uncover and place the sliced mushrooms, zucchini, tomatoes, and green onions over the partially cooked potatoes.

Place the fish fillets over the vegetables; cut a few diagonal slashes in the fish. Dribble melted margarine over fish; sprinkle with the herbs and pepper. Bake, uncovered, until the fish is slightly browned and flakes easily. This may take 10 to 20 minutes, depending on the thickness of the fillets. Do not overcook. Garnish with lemon slices. Makes 4 to 6 servings.

PARTY STUFFED TOMATOES

4 large ripe tomatoes
½ c. uncooked long grain rice

Lettuce cups
Filling of choice (follows)

Tomato Cups: Cut away top of each tomato and cut out wedges around the sides to form a zigzag edge. With a spoon, scoop out the seeds and pulp. Carefully turn the tomatoes upside-down on paper towels to drain while preparing one of the fillings. Cook the rice by label directions; cool. Mix rice with the other filling ingredients. Gently stuff the Tomato Cups. Cover loosely with plastic wrap and refrigerate until serving time.

Ham-Rice Filling:

Cooked rice
1 c. diced cooked ham
1 small chopped carrot
¼ c. cooked peas
1 Tbsp. finely chopped parsley

⅓ c. GF vinegar
⅔ c. salad oil
¼ tsp. salt
⅛ tsp. pepper

In a bowl, combine the cooked rice with cooked ham, carrot, peas, and parsley. Mix vinegar, salad oil, salt, and pepper in a screw-top jar; shake well. Pour ⅔ cup of this dressing over the rice mixture; toss until ingredients are coated. Spoon into Tomato Cups and chill. Serve on lettuce. Pass remaining dressing to spoon over.

Shrimp-Rice Filling:

1 Tbsp. butter
1 tsp. curry powder
2 Tbsp. chopped green onion
Cooked rice
1 (4½ oz.) can drained shrimp
2 more Tbsp. chopped green
    onion

Little chopped dill
⅓ c. GF vinegar
⅔ c. oil
¼ tsp. salt
⅛ tsp. pepper

Heat butter in a small skillet. Add curry powder; cook for 1 minute over low heat. Add 2 tablespoons chopped green onion; saute until tender, about 2 minutes. Cool. In a bowl, combine the cooked rice with drained shrimp, 2 more tablespoons chopped green onion, the cooked onion, and curry. If desired, add a little chopped dill.

Mix GF vinegar, oil, salt, and pepper in a screw-top jar; shake well. Pour ⅔ cup of the dressing over the mixture; toss until ingredients are coated. Spoon into Tomato Cups and chill. Serve on lettuce. Pass remaining dressing to spoon over.

SWEET POTATOES IN ORANGE CUPS

6 medium (8 oz.) oranges,
    halved
2 (18 oz.) cans sweet potatoes
¼ c. butter or margarine
½ c. brown sugar
½ tsp. cinnamon

¼ tsp. nutmeg
½ tsp. salt
⅛ tsp. pepper
Chopped nuts, mini
    marshmallows, or crushed
    drained pineapple

Squeeze juice from orange halves, reserving ½ cup juice. Scrap out inside of oranges, removing as much of white membrane as possible. Thoroughly mash potatoes and add butter, brown sugar, reserved orange juice, and spices until smooth. Fill 12 orange cups with potato mixture. Arrange in 9x13 inch baking dish.

Bake, covered with foil, in a 350° oven for 20 minutes. Garnish tops; bake, uncovered, until heated through and garnish is lightly browned, 20 to 25 minutes.

For microwave, bake on HIGH, uncovered, for 5 minutes. Add garnish topping and microwave an additional 7 to 10 minutes.

Variations: Spoon mixture into buttered 2 quart casserole and bake as previously directed.

SPECIAL AU GRATIN POTATOES

12 potatoes
½ lb. Cheddar or sharp
   American cheese, diced
1 diced green pepper
1 small jar pimento

Salt and pepper to taste
½ c. butter, melted
½ c. milk
1 medium onion, chopped
   (optional)

Boil potatoes in their jackets. Peel, dice, and put them in a long cake pan or large casserole. Add rest of ingredients and bake for 1 hour at 350°; stir occasionally.

CHICKEN WITH VEGETABLES

2 whole chicken breasts (about
   2 lb.)
1 egg white
1 tsp. cornstarch
1 tsp. salt
1 tsp. light soy sauce
Dash of white pepper
8 oz. bok choy (about 4 large
   stalks)
8 oz. pea pods
¼ c. cold water
2 Tbsp. cornstarch
2 Tbsp. oyster sauce

½ tsp. sugar
3 Tbsp. vegetable oil
3 Tbsp. vegetable oil
1 tsp. finely chopped ginger root
2 cloves garlic, finely chopped
1 tsp. salt
1 c. sliced mushrooms
½ c. sliced canned bamboo
   shoots
½ c. sliced canned water
   chestnuts
¾ c. chicken broth
2 tsp. dry white wine

Remove bones and skin from chicken; cut chicken into ½ inch slices. Mix egg white, 1 teaspoon cornstarch, 1 teaspoon salt, the soy sauce, and white pepper in glass or plastic bowl; stir in chicken. Cover and refrigerate for 30 minutes.

Separate bok choy leaves from stems. Cut leaves into 2 inch pieces; cut stems into ¼ inch slices (do not combine leaves and stems). Remove strings from pea pods. Place pea pods in boiling water; cover and cook for 1 minute. Drain. Rinse under running cold water; drain. Mix water, 2 tablespoons cornstarch, the oyster sauce, and sugar.

Heat wok until 1 or 2 drops of water bubble and skitter. Add 3 tablespoons vegetable oil; rotate wok to coat side. Add chicken; stir-fry until chicken turns white. Remove chicken from wok.

Add 3 tablespoons vegetable oil; rotate to coat side. Add ginger root and garlic; stir-fry until garlic is light brown. Add bok choy stems and 1 teaspoon salt; stir-fry for 30 seconds. Add mushrooms, bamboo shoots, and water chestnuts; stir-fry for 1 minute.

Stir in chicken, bok choy leaves, chicken broth, and wine. Cover and cook for 2 minutes. Stir in cornstarch mixture; cook and stir until thickened. Add pea pods; cook and stir for 30 seconds. Makes 6 servings.

MICROWAVE MEATLOAF

1 lb. ground beef	¼ c. crushed GF corn chips
1 egg	1 onion, chopped
1 c. crushed canned tomatoes	½ tsp. garlic powder
(or GF tomato puree)	1 tsp. GF soy sauce

Mix all ingredients. Put into a prepared microwave baking pan. Cook on HIGH for 5 minutes. Cook on MEDIUM for 17 minutes.

CHICKEN WITH FUN SEE

6 medium dried black mushrooms	1 Tbsp. cornstarch
2 whole chicken breasts (about 2 lb.)	1 Tbsp. cold water
	1 Tbsp. dark soy sauce
1 egg white	1 tsp. sugar
1 tsp. cornstarch	⅓ c. vegetable oil
1 tsp. salt	1 clove garlic, finely chopped
1 tsp. light soy sauce	1 tsp. finely chopped ginger root
Dash of white pepper	2 Tbsp. vegetable oil
4 oz. cellophane noodles (bean thread)	1½ c. thinly sliced celery cabbage
4 oz. pea pods	½ c. shredded canned bamboo shoots
2 green onions	1½ c. chicken broth

Soak mushrooms in warm water until soft, about 30 minutes; drain. Rinse in warm water; drain. Remove and discard stems; shred caps. Remove bones and skin from chicken; shred chicken. Mix egg white, 1 teaspoon cornstarch, 1 teaspoon salt, 1 teaspoon soy sauce, and the white pepper in glass or plastic bowl; stir in chicken. Cover and refrigerate for 20 minutes.

Soak noodles in cold water for 20 minutes; drain. Cut noodles into 3 to 4 inch pieces. Remove strings from pea pods. Place pea pods in boiling water. Cover and cook for 1 minute; drain. Immediately rinse under running cold water; drain. Cut green onions into 2 inch pieces. Mix 1 tablespoon cornstarch, the water, 1 tablespoon soy sauce, and sugar.

Heat wok until 1 or 2 drops of water bubble and skitter. Add ⅓ cup vegetable oil; rotate wok to coat. Add chicken, garlic, and ginger root; stir-fry until chicken turns white. Remove chicken from wok.

Add 2 tablespoons vegetable oil; rotate to coat side. Add mushrooms, celery, cabbage, and bamboo shoots; stir-fry for 1 minute. Stir in chicken and chicken broth; heat to boiling. Add noodles; heat to boiling. Stir in cornstarch mixture; cook and stir until thickened. Add pea pods; cook and stir for 30 seconds. Garnish with green onions. Makes 6 servings.

GOLDEN OVEN-FRIED CHICKEN

½ c. margarine
1 clove garlic, minced
1 c. GF corn flake crumbs
¼ c. grated Parmesan cheese
¼ c. finely chopped almonds
   (optional)

2 Tbsp. minced parsley
1 tsp. salt
¼ tsp. ground thyme
⅛ tsp. pepper
2½ to 3 lb. chicken, cut up or
   quartered

Preheat oven to 400°F. In a 13x9 inch pan, melt margarine with garlic. In a bowl or shallow pan, combine remaining ingredients, except chicken; mix well. Dip chicken pieces in garlic butter, then in the crumb mixture. Place, skin side up, in the garlic butter in pan. Bake, uncovered, for about 1 hour or until tender; baste occasionally with pan drippings. Makes 4 servings.

CORN CHOWDER

1 (16 oz.) can whole kernel corn
¼ c. chopped onion
2 Tbsp. margarine or bacon
   drippings
1 c. corn liquid (add water to
   make amount needed)

1 c. diced raw potato
½ tsp. salt
¼ tsp. pepper
2 Tbsp. GF flour
2 c. milk

Drain corn; save liquid. In a 1½ quart saucepan, cook the chopped onion in fat until tender. Add corn liquid (and enough water to make 1 cup), the peeled diced potato, salt, and pepper. Cook until potato is tender. Add corn.

Put the GF flour and milk into a shaker or screw-top jar; shake to blend. Add to the corn mixture. Cook, stirring constantly, for about 5 minutes or until slightly thickened. Makes 4½ cups of chowder.

SHRIMP MOLD

1 (8 oz.) pkg. cream cheese	1¼ c. GF tomato sauce
1 c. GF mayonnaise	1 c. chopped celery
1 env. unflavored gelatin	⅓ c. chopped green onion
¼ c. cold water	12 oz. halved precooked shrimp

Soften cream cheese; mix with mayonnaise. Soften gelatin in ¼ cup cold water. Heat tomato sauce to boiling. Mix gelatin into sauce until dissolved; slowly pour into cream cheese mixture. Mix with beater or wire whip. Stir in celery, onion, and shrimp. Pour into gelatin mold. Chill for several hours or overnight until firm. Unmold. Serve with rice crackers or celery sticks.

TURKEY RICE SALAD

Use this when there's leftover turkey.

1 c. cubed cooked turkey	Favorite fruits
3 c. chilled cooked rice	

Combine cubed cooked turkey with chilled cooked rice. Add favorite fruits, such as cubes of red skinned apple and wedges of fresh orange - or halves of green grapes.

Dressing - Mix:

½ c. plain yogurt	2 tsp. lemon juice
2 Tbsp. orange juice	Dash of cinnamon
2 tsp. honey	

Top with toasted slivered almonds at serving time.

FRUITED PORK CHOPS

6 pork chops (1½ lb.)	⅛ tsp. ground nutmeg
1 c. apple juice	Dash of pepper
1 (8 oz.) pkg. mixed dried fruit	1 Tbsp. GF flour or cornstarch
½ tsp. salt (optional)	¼ c. water
⅛ tsp. ground allspice	

Trim outside fat from chops; rub fat over bottom of 12 inch skillet (with ovenproof handle). Heat till fat is lightly browned; discard fat. Brown chops lightly on both sides. Add apple juice, dried fruit, salt, spices, and pepper; cover. Bake at 350°F. for 1 hour or until fork tender.

Remove chops to a warm platter; spoon fruit over top. Skim and remove fat from pan liquid. Blend flour and water till smooth; stir into pan liquid. Cook and stir over medium heat until thickened. Serve with meat and fruit. Makes 6 servings, 280 calories each.

SALMON-RICE PIE

1 c. water
1/3 c. rice
1/8 tsp. salt
1 tsp. margarine
2 eggs
1 (6½ oz.) can water packed
salmon or tuna, drained

3/4 c. skim milk
2 c. fresh or frozen peas
1/2 tsp. parsley flakes
1/4 tsp. pepper
1/8 tsp. nutmeg
4 slices lowfat Swiss cheese

Spray inside of a 9 inch pie pan with vegetable pan spray. In saucepan, heat water, rice, and salt to boiling. Reduce heat; cover and simmer for 14 minutes. Stir in margarine and 1 of the eggs; press rice mixture into pan to make crust.

Spread salmon (with bones) or tuna over rice. Heat milk and peas to simmer. Add parsley, pepper, and nutmeg. Beat remaining egg; gradually stir in milk mixture. Pour over salmon. Layer cheese slices over top. Bake at 350°F. for 25 minutes. Makes 6 servings, each providing 247 calories, 20 grams protein, 8 grams fat, and 239 milligrams calcium.

STIR-FRY

4 boneless chicken breasts, cut
into 1 inch pieces
2 Tbsp. soy sauce (GF)
2 Tbsp. cooking sherry

1/2 tsp. ginger
1 tsp. garlic salt
2 Tbsp. cornstarch

Marinate chicken in preceding mixture for 30 minutes.

1 bunch onions
3 stalks celery
1 c. broccoli flowerets

1 (No. 20) can sliced water
chestnuts, drained

Chop diagonally the onions and celery. Add about 1 cup broccoli flowerets and sliced water chestnuts. Stir-fry vegetables for 2 to 4 minutes in 1/4 cup oil and remove. Stir-fry chicken in 1/4 cup oil until done. Return vegetables to pan to heat through. Serve over rice.

CHOW MEIN CASSEROLE

1 lb. lean ground beef
3/4 c. chopped celery
3/4 c. chopped onion
1/2 c. uncooked rice
1/2 tsp. salt
1 1/4 c. boiling water
1 (3 oz.) can mushroom stems
and pieces

1 (6½ oz.) can sliced water
chestnuts
1 Tbsp. brown sugar, packed
2 Tbsp. GF soy sauce
1 1/4 c. GF chicken broth
1 tsp. margarine or butter

Cook beef in large skillet. Add celery and onion; continue cooking till tender. Put rice and salt in greased 2 quart casserole; pour in boiling water. Add all the other ingredients; cover. Bake at 350°F. for 30 minutes. Stir. Bake, uncovered, for 30 minutes more or until rice is tender. Makes 4 servings.

OVEN OMELET

6 slices cheese
6 to 12 slices bacon, fried and
   crumbled

8 eggs
1 c. milk
½ c. shredded Swiss cheese

Place cheese slices in bottom of buttered 9 or 10 inch pie pan. Beat eggs and milk. Add bacon and Swiss cheese. Pour over cheese slices. Bake at 350° for 30 minutes.

ZUCCHINI PIZZA CRUST

3 c. grated zucchini
3 eggs, lightly beaten
⅓ c. rice flour or corn meal

¼ tsp. salt
½ tsp. nutmeg
Toppings (as desired)

Grate zucchini (about 3 large zucchini) using a medium grater or the food processor. Press liquid from zucchini. Combine the beaten eggs with rice flour or corn meal, salt, and nutmeg. Mix with the zucchini. Spread evenly over a 9x12 inch baking sheet (with sides) or a 12 inch pizza pan.

Bake at 450°F. for about 12 minutes or till firm. Remove from oven and top as desired with GF tomato sauce, chopped onion, bacon pieces, mushrooms, cheese, and other toppers. Return to a 350°F. oven and heat until sauce is bubbly and cheese is melted (12 to 15 minutes). Makes 4 servings.

SLOW-COOKED GLAZED CARROTS

1½ c. orange juice
½ c. light brown sugar
½ tsp. salt
⅛ tsp. ginger

2 Tbsp. quick cooking tapioca
1 Tbsp. butter or margarine
8 to 10 fresh carrots, peeled and
   thinly sliced

Combine orange juice, sugar, salt, ginger, butter, and tapioca in a small bowl. Place carrots in an electric slow cooker. Add orange juice mixture and stir well. Cover and cook at LOW for 8 to 10 hours or at HIGH for 6 to 8 hours. Stir well before serving. Makes 6 to 8 servings.

RICE ALA DONNA
(Lasagne)

2 c. cooked rice
½ lb. Mozzarella cheese, cubed
½ lb. Parmesan cheese

1 qt. spaghetti sauce
1 lb. sweet Italian sausage

Steam sausage and then saute until golden. Cool and slice into ¼ inch slices. Butter large Pyrex dish and put in one layer of rice. Sprinkle with cubed Mozzarella, Parmesan, sausage slices, and several spoonfuls of spaghetti sauce. Repeat layers until all ingredients are used. Bake at 350° for about 20 minutes or until heated through.

CORN OYSTERS

3 c. sweet corn, cut and scraped
   from the cob
1 egg

½ tsp. salt
½ c. rice flour
1 tsp. baking powder

Add egg; beat in by hand. Add other ingredients and mix well. If mixture is too thick, add a bit of water or milk. Drop by spoonfuls on a hot greased griddle so they are the size of fried oysters. Brown on both sides and serve warm or with cocktail or tartar sauce. If you have a sweet tooth, eat them with butter and syrup.

SALADS

PEAS PIZZICATO

2 pkg. (10 oz.) frozen baby peas,
    thawed
1 c. sour cream
½ tsp. salt

1 green onion, chopped
6 bacon slices, cooked and
    crumbled
Freshly ground pepper

Thaw peas and drain (do not cook); toss with remaining ingredients. Makes 8 servings, about 135 calories per serving.

For fewer calories, you might substitute plain yogurt for sour cream.

HIGH RISE SALAD

1 small head lettuce, shredded
2 to 3 large carrots, grated
4 ribs celery, sliced

1 (10 oz.) pkg. frozen peas,
    cooked and drained
4 green onions, sliced

Dressing:

1 c. sour cream
1 c. Kraft mayonnaise

1 tsp. lemon juice

Layer ½ of each of the following in order: Lettuce, carrots, celery, peas, onions; repeat layers. Mix together dressing ingredients and frost top of salad. Garnish with bacon pieces from 4 slices bacon or Sizzlean, cooked crisp and crumbled.

PIZZA SALAD

½ lb. bulk sausage (GF)
1 head lettuce
1½ c. ripe pitted olives
1 c. Jack cheese strips
1 c. cherry tomatoes (halves)

1½ c. garlic flavored GF
    croutons
Oregano Dressing (recipe
    follows)

Crumble bulk sausage and saute in skillet until browned; drain off fat. Break lettuce into pieces in a salad bowl. Top with sausage, olives, cheese, tomatoes, and croutons. Drizzle with dressing; toss. Makes 4 servings.

Oregano Dressing - Mix together:

½ c. salad oil
6 Tbsp. GF vinegar

2 tsp. crushed oregano
½ tsp. garlic salt

Chill well.

FRISCO CHICKEN SALAD

2 c. cooked brown rice
2 c. chopped cooked chicken
½ c. raisins (optional)
2 Tbsp. green onion slices

2 Tbsp. sunflower seeds
GF creamy salad dressing
1 (11 oz.) can mandarin orange
   segments, drained

Combine rice, chicken, raisins, green onion, sunflower seeds, and about ⅔ cup of creamy pour-on dressing (your choice). Mix lightly. Add orange segments; gently mix. Chill. Serve on lettuce. Makes 4 servings.

RIGATINI SALAD

1 box Rigatini (Aproten)
1⅓ c. Hellmann's mayonnaise
2 Tbsp. finely chopped onion
2 c. finely chopped celery

1 medium green pepper,
   chopped
1 medium red apple, chopped

Cook Rigatini as directed. Combine all ingredients, except Rigatini. Add Rigatini and toss. Cover; chill at least 1 hour to blend flavors.

TACO SALAD

⅔ c. chopped onion
1 clove garlic, minced
2 Tbsp. salad oil
1 lb. ground beef
1 (8 oz.) can GF tomato sauce
2 Tbsp. water
1 tsp. chili powder
1 tsp. salt
1 head lettuce

½ c. GF French dressing
4 c. GF corn chips
3 tomatoes, cut in thin wedges
½ c. sliced green onion
Ripe olives
½ c. sour cream or shredded
   cheese
Bottled GF taco sauce

Cook onion and garlic in oil until tender crisp. Add beef; brown and drain off fat. Add tomato sauce, water, chili powder, and salt; cook, covered, over low heat for 10 minutes. Finely shred lettuce to measure 6 cups; toss with dressing.

On each plate, spread some corn chips; top with some of the meat mixture, lettuce, tomato, onion, olives, and sour cream. Pass the taco sauce. Makes 6 servings.

SALAD MANDARIN

1 medium head Bibb or Boston
   lettuce, torn
11 oz. mandarin oranges, chilled
   and drained
½ medium avocado, peeled and
   thinly sliced

½ c. coarsely chopped pecans,
   toasted
2 green onions, thinly sliced
⅓ c. commercial Italian dressing

Combine first 6 ingredients in a medium bowl. Add Italian dressing, tossing gently. Serves 6.

WALDORF SALAD

2 c. diced apple
1 c. julienne celery sticks
½ c. broken walnuts
¼ c. mayonnaise
1 Tbsp. sugar

½ tsp. lemon juice
Dash of salt
½ c. whipped cream
½ c. raisins (optional)

Combine celery, nuts, apple, and raisins. Mix mayonnaise, lemon, sugar, and salt and add to whipped cream. Fold into apple mixture.

IN-THE-PINK SALAD

20 oz. crushed pineapple
1 c. water
6 oz. strawberry jello
16 oz. whole cranberry sauce

3 Tbsp. lemon juice
¼ tsp. ground nutmeg
2 c. sour cream
½ c. chopped pecans (optional)

Heat pineapple juice and water to boiling; remove from heat and stir in jello until dissolved. Blend in rest of ingredients and pour into 2 quart mold. Chill until firm. Yield: 8 to 10 servings.

CRANBERRY MOLDED SALAD

1 env. plain gelatin
6 oz. cream cheese, softened
2 Tbsp. mayonnaise or salad
   dressing
2 Tbsp. sugar

16 oz. whole cranberry sauce
8 oz. crushed pineapple, drained
½ c. chopped pecans
1 c. heavy cream

Sprinkle gelatin over ¼ cup cold water in small bowl and let stand for 5 minutes to soften. Add ¼ cup boiling water; stir to dissolve. Set aside to cool.

Combine cream cheese, mayonnaise, and sugar in large bowl and beat until smooth. Beat in gelatin mixture. Stir in cranberry sauce, pineapple, and pecans. In second bowl using clean beaters, beat cream until stiff and fold into cranberry mixture. Pour into 2 quart mold or 6 to 8 individual molds. Chill in refrigerator for 6 to 8 hours or overnight. Makes 8 servings.

EMERALD ISLE MOLD

1 (3 oz.) pkg. lime jello
1 c. boiling water

¾ c. grapefruit juice
1 (8 oz.) pkg. cream cheese

Dissolve jello in boiling water; add grapefruit juice. Gradually add to softened cream cheese; mix until well blended. Pour into 1½ quart mold. Chill until firm.

1 (3 oz.) pkg. lime jello
1 c. boiling water
1 c. ginger ale

1 c. grapefruit sections
1 c. diced apples
¼ c. chopped nuts

Dissolve lime jello in boiling water. Add ginger ale. Chill until slightly thickened. Fold in fruit and nuts. Pour over molded gelatin layer. Chill until firm.

MINTED FRUIT SALAD

1 c. GF salad dressing or
 reduced calorie dressing
1 c. chopped red apple
1 c. chopped green apple
2 c. canteloupe chunks

1 c. celery slices
1 c. walnut halves
½ tsp. ground ginger
2 Tbsp. finely chopped fresh
 mint

Gently mix all ingredients; chill well. Makes 6 to 8 servings.

CHRISTMAS FRUIT SALAD

1 c. pineapple chunks
1 c. sugar
1½ Tbsp. cornstarch
2 eggs
¼ tsp. salt
1½ c. milk
Juice of 1 lemon or 2 Tbsp.
 ReaLemon

3 bananas, diced
3 apples, peeled and diced
1 c. chopped pecans
8 oz. miniature marshmallows
¼ c. red and/or green
 maraschino cherries

Drain pineapple; reserve ½ cup juice. Combine sugar, cornstarch, eggs, salt, milk, and pineapple juice. Cook in top of double boiler until thick. Stir in lemon juice. Cool. Add fruits and nuts. Serve with whipped cream.

BLUEBERRY SALAD

1 (3 oz.) pkg. grape jello
1 c. boiling water
1 (16 oz.) can crushed pineapple

1 can blueberry pie mix
1 c. whipped cream
Chopped nuts

Dissolve grape jello in boiling water. Add crushed pineapple. Add blueberry pie mix. Let set a couple of hours. Top with whipped cream. Sprinkle with chopped nuts.

CRANBERRY SALAD

1 lb. fresh cranberries, washed
    and ground fine
1 c. sugar

1 pt. whipping cream
1 c. miniature marshmallows
2 c. crushed pineapple, drained

Add sugar to cranberries and let stand in refrigerator for 2 hours. Whip cream and fold in the marshmallows. Add drained pineapple to cream and set in refrigerator for 2 hours. Combine the cream mixture with cranberry mixture and refrigerate until serving time.

BROCCOLI SALAD

1 (16 oz.) pkg. frozen broccoli
    (bite-size)
1½ c. chopped celery
¼ c. chopped onion
3 hard cooked eggs, sliced
1 tsp. dill weed

1 tsp. sugar
1 tsp. lemon or lime juice
1 c. GF mayonnaise
½ tsp. salt
3 oz. pimento stuffed olives,
    sliced

Break apart the frozen broccoli. Mix all ingredients; chill overnight. (You may prefer to precook the broccoli a short time and cool it before adding it to the salad.)

CALIENTE SALAD

15½ oz. can kidney beans,
    drained
1 diced cucumber
1 small onion, diced
1 green pepper, diced
3 large tomatoes, diced
4 slices bacon, crisply fried and
    crumbled

½ c. mayonnaise
1 tsp. chili powder
Dash of cayenne powder
Salt and pepper to taste
2 c. lettuce, torn

Combine all ingredients, except bacon and lettuce; refrigerate. Add bacon and lettuce just before serving.

PINK CHAMPAGNE SALAD

1 (8 oz.) pkg. cream cheese
¾ c. sugar
1 (15¼ oz.) can crushed
    pineapple, drained

10 oz. frozen strawberries
2 sliced bananas
1 (9 oz.) pkg. Cool Whip

Mix together softened cream cheese and sugar. Add fruit and Cool Whip. Place in 9x13 inch salad pan; refrigerate.

BREADS, MUFFINS

Tip: Muffins and biscuits made of flours other than wheat often have a better texture when made in small sizes.

RICE BRAN MUFFINS

1 c. Jolly Joan Rice Bran
½ c. brown sugar, packed
2 eggs or Jolly Joan Egg
    Replacer
1 tsp. soda

2 c. Jolly Joan Rice Mix
¼ c. margarine
¼ c. molasses
1 c. buttermilk, milk, or soy milk

1. Stir soda into molasses until foamy and light in color; set aside.
2. Cream brown sugar and margarine.
3. Beat in eggs, then rice bran.
4. Beat in the buttermilk, molasses, and soda.
5. Beat in the rice mix.
6. Spoon into greased muffin pans ½ to ¾ full. Bake at 375° for 30 minutes. Makes 18 muffins.

APPLE-CINNAMON MUFFINS

Mix together:

1 egg
2 Tbsp. oil

¾ c. milk
½ grated apple without skin

Mix together:

1 c. Soyo/Fearn Rice Baking Mix   ¼ to ½ tsp. cinnamon

Add egg mixture to dry ingredients and mix until smooth, but still somewhat lumpy. Fill greased muffin tins ⅔ full. Bake at 400° for 20 minutes.

PUMPKIN BREAD

2 eggs
1 c. sugar
¾ c. vegetable oil
⅓ c. sifted rice flour
⅓ c. sifted soy flour
⅓ c. sifted potato starch flour

½ tsp. salt
1 tsp. baking powder
1 tsp. baking soda
1 tsp. cinnamon
½ c. chopped nuts
1 c. canned pumpkin

Beat eggs until light and fluffy; gradually add sugar and beat well. Add oil and mix. Sift dry ingredients together and add alternately with pumpkin. Stir in nuts. Pour into lightly greased pan. Bake at 350° for 45 minutes or until done, or put in larger pan for bars.

DATE-NUT BREAD

1 c. dates, cut up
1 c. boiling water
1 tsp. soda
2 Tbsp. shortening
1 c. sugar
1 egg

½ tsp. salt
1 tsp. vanilla
1½ c. rice flour
½ c. potato starch flour
½ c. nuts
¾ tsp. xanthan gum

Pour boiling water over dates and soda; let cool. Cream shortening and sugar, then add egg, vanilla, and date mixture. Add the dry ingredients and nuts. Pour into 2 small loaf pans and bake at 350° for 40 minutes or until tested done.

BANANA BREAD

⅓ c. Crisco
⅔ c. sugar
2 eggs
1½ c. rice flour
¼ c. potato starch

¾ tsp. xanthan gum
2 tsp. baking powder
¼ tsp. soda
½ tsp. salt
2 c. mashed bananas

Mix in order given. Pour into 2 small loaf pans and bake at 350° for about 50 minutes or until tested done.

PUMPKIN BREAD

1⅔ c. Jolly Joan Corn Mix (or
    similar product)
1½ c. sugar
1 tsp. soda
½ tsp. cinnamon
⅓ c. butter or margarine

2 eggs
⅓ c. water
1 c. pumpkin
¾ c. raisins (optional)
½ c. nuts (optional)

Pour into 1 large loaf pan or 2 small pans. Bake at 350° for 1 to 1¼ hours.

ROLLS

¾ c. rice flour
¼ c. soy flour
¼ tsp. baking soda
2 tsp. baking powder
⅛ tsp. salt (optional)

1 Tbsp. sugar
1 egg
¼ c. cottage cheese
½ c. buttermilk or sour milk
2 Tbsp. melted butter

Combine first 6 ingredients. In mixer bowl or blender, place egg, cottage cheese, milk, and melted butter. Mix or blend well. Add this to dry ingredients and mix well. Divide into rings or custard cups that are greased well. Rings must be placed on a greased cookie sheet. Bake at 350° for 30 minutes.

CORN-CHEESE BREAD

1 c. cream style corn
1 c. yellow corn meal
3 eggs
Salt (optional)
½ tsp. soda
¾ c. buttermilk

⅓ c. melted white shortening or
   oil
¾ c. grated sharp Cheddar
   cheese
2 Tbsp. butter

Preheat oven to 400°F. In a mixing bowl, combine the corn, corn meal, eggs, soda, and buttermilk; season with salt as desired. Mix well. Add the shortening and ½ cup of cheese. Stir to blend.

Meanwhile, put the butter in an oven-safe 9 inch skillet (should have high sides), preferably of black iron. Place in the oven to heat until butter melts without browning. Pour the batter into the skillet. Sprinkle with the remaining cheese and bake for 30 minutes or until the bread is firm and golden brown on top. Yield: 8 servings.

RICE BRAN MUFFINS

⅓ c. rice bran
½ c. brown sugar
2 eggs or egg replacer
1 tsp. soda

1⅓ c. Jolly Joan rice mix
¼ c. margarine or butter
¼ c. molasses
1 c. buttermilk or Soyquick*

Stir soda into molasses until foamy and light in color; set aside. Cream brown sugar and margarine; beat in eggs and then rice bran. Pour in buttermilk, molasses, and soda. Beat in rice mix. Spoon into greased muffin pans, filled ½ to ¾ full. Bake at 375° for 30 minutes. Makes 12 large muffins.

* Milk substitute available from Ener-G Foods, Inc.

QUICK-RAISED RICE BREAD

2 eggs
1 c. plain yogurt
2 Tbsp. oil
½ tsp. baking powder

1½ tsp. baking soda
2 Tbsp. sugar or honey
2 c. GF Rice Baking Mix

Put all ingredients in a bowl and mix well together. Pour into a greased and dusted (with GF flour) loaf pan (9x5x3 inches). Bake at 375°F. for about 35 to 45 minutes or until it tests done.

BREAKFAST MUFFINS

2 eggs
½ c. oil
½ tsp. vanilla
1 c. rice flour
½ c. soy flour
2 Tbsp. potato starch flour or
    potato flakes

¾ c. sugar
1 tsp. cinnamon
2 tsp. baking powder
½ tsp. soda

Beat together the eggs, oil, and vanilla. Sift together the flours, sugar, cinnamon, baking powder, and soda. Mix the dry ingredients with oil-egg mixture. Spoon batter into greased muffin cups (or use paper liners) so each is ½ full. Bake at 350°F. for 15 to 18 minutes until browned. Makes 16 to 20 muffins, depending on size of cups. This also can be baked in a greased loaf pan at 325°F. for 1 hour.

Muffin variations: Add any of the following combinations to the egg-oil mixture:

1 c. mashed banana (reduce
    sugar to ½ c. and omit
    cinnamon if desired)
1 c. applesauce (reduce sugar to
    ½ c.)
1 c. shredded apple (may be
    necessary to add a small

amount of water or milk if
    apple is dry)
1 c. shredded zucchini and ¼ c.
    chopped nuts

TAMALE SPOONBREAD

1 (1 lb.) can tomatoes
    (undrained)
1 (3½ to 4 oz.) can chopped
    green chilies (undrained)
2 Tbsp. butter
½ tsp. salt
½ tsp. crushed oregano

¼ tsp. ground cumin (optional)
¾ c. corn meal
1 tsp. baking powder
6 eggs, separated
½ tsp. cream of tartar
¼ c. (1 oz.) shredded Cheddar
    cheese

Butter bottom and sides of a 2 quart casserole; dust with corn meal. In large saucepan, combine tomatoes (chopped), chilies, butter, salt, and the herbs. Cook and stir over medium heat until butter melts. Stir in corn meal and baking powder. Cook, stirring constantly, until mixture thickens, 3 to 4 minutes. Remove from heat.

In a large bowl, beat egg whites and cream of tartar until stiff but not dry. Separately, beat yolks slightly. Blend a little of corn meal mixture into yolks; mix with all of corn meal mixture. Fold mixture into whites. Pour into dish. Sprinkle with cheese. Bake at 375°F. for 40 minutes or until an inserted knife comes out clean. Serve at once. Makes 4 servings.

BARS, COOKIES, DESSERTS

MAGIC COOKIE BARS

½ c. butter or margarine
1½ c. GF corn flake crumbs
1 (14 oz.) can sweetened
    condensed milk

1 (6 oz.) pkg. chocolate chips
1 (3½ oz.) can flaked coconut
1 c. chopped nuts

Preheat oven to 350°F. (325°F. for glass baking dish). In a 13x9 inch baking pan, melt butter; evenly sprinkle crumbs over it. Evenly pour sweetened condensed milk (not evaporated milk) over it. Top with remaining ingredients, spreading evenly over mixture. Press down gently. Bake for 25 to 30 minutes or until lightly browned. Cool well before cutting. Makes 24 bars. Store, loosely covered, at room temperature.

PEANUT-BUTTER CAKE

2 eggs, separated
½ c. smooth peanut butter
⅓ c. butter or margarine,
    softened
¾ c. honey
1 tsp. vanilla
1 c. milk

1½ c. rice flour
2 Tbsp. potato flour
3 Tbsp. corn starch
3 tsp. baking powder
½ tsp. salt
½ tsp. cinnamon

Separate eggs; beat egg whites till stiff and set aside. In a large bowl using electric mixer, cream peanut butter and butter together. Add warm honey and egg yolks; beat until mixture is light and fluffy. Stir in vanilla.

Meanwhile, carefully heat the milk to just below simmering. Add rice flour while stirring briskly. To the peanut butter mixture, add potato flour, corn starch, baking powder, salt, and cinnamon. Gradually add the milk mixture. Gently fold in beaten egg whites. Gently spread batter in 2 greased and rice floured 9 inch cake pans.

Bake at 325°F. for about 30 minutes or until cake tests done. Batter also may be used for cupcakes. Bake about 25 minutes. Cool on wire racks. Remove from pans and frost with Cocoa-Peanut Butter Frosting.

Cocoa-Peanut Butter Frosting:

1 (6 oz.) pkg. semi-sweet
    chocolate bits
½ c. smooth peanut butter
2 Tbsp. butter or margarine

1 tsp. vanilla
2½ c. sifted confectioners sugar
⅓ to ½ c. light cream

Melt chocolate chips over hot water. In medium size mixing bowl, using electric mixer at low speed, blend together peanut butter, melted chocolate, butter, and vanilla. Add powdered sugar alternating with cream (or evaporated milk) until spreading consistency. Makes about 1¾ cups of frosting.

MACAROON KISSES

2 egg whites
1 c. sugar
½ tsp. vanilla

¾ c. flaked coconut
2 c. rice cereal (optional)

Beat egg whites until stiff. Continue beating while gradually adding sugar. Blend in vanilla, coconut, and cereal. Drop by teaspoon on greased cookie sheet. Bake at 375° until lightly browned, 8 to 10 minutes. Let cool on sheet before removing. Makes about 30.

MELTING MOMENT COOKIES

½ c. cornstarch
½ c. powdered sugar
1 c. white rice flour

¾ c. butter
½ tsp. almond extract

Sift together cornstarch, powdered sugar, and flour. Mix butter and extract into first mixture until dough turns soft; chill 1 hour. Form into ¾ to 1 inch size balls. Put on ungreased cookie sheet and bake at 350° for 10 minutes or until edges are light brown. *Cool* before removing from cookie sheet.

Frosting:

¼ c. oleo or butter
2 c. powdered sugar, sifted

⅛ tsp. almond extract

Melt oleo or butter. Add powdered sugar and almond extract. Add enough milk to make spreading consistency. Frost and garnish with sugar decorations.

ALMOND BARK BARS

1 lb. almond bark
1 c. chunky peanut butter
4 to 5 c. Rice Krispies

1 c. peanuts
1 tsp. almond flavoring

Melt the almond bark. Blend in rest of ingredients and spread in buttered 9x13 inch pan. Chill in refrigerator or let stand overnight.

You can use chocolate or butterscotch bark as well.

TOFFEE BARS

Apple-Cinnamon Crispy Cakes
1 c. brown sugar
1 c. butter or margarine

Chopped nuts (optional)
Chocolate bits (optional)

Line cookie sheet with foil (for ½ batch an 8x8 or 7x10 inch pan works fine). Cover pan with Crispy Cakes (for 7x10 inch pan it takes 5). Boil the sugar and margarine together for 3 minutes; pour over crackers, making sure all are covered. Bake for 5 minutes or until the crackers float.

Sprinkle with chopped nuts and/or chocolate bits if desired. (Nuts should be put on *before* baking so they stick to the cakes.) Cut or pull apart before they are completely set. Freezes well.

BUCKEYE BALLS

1½ c. peanut butter
½ c. margarine or butter (room
    temperature)
1 tsp. vanilla

1 (16 oz.) pkg. confectioners
    sugar
1 (6 oz.) pkg. chocolate pieces
2 Tbsp. vegetable shortening

Line a baking sheet with wax paper. In medium size bowl, mix peanut butter, butter, vanilla, and sugar with hands to form a smooth dough. Mixture will be very stiff. Shape dough into balls. Place on wax paper and put in refrigerator.

In the top of double boiler over simmering, not boiling, water, melt chocolate and shortening together. When smooth, pour into a small bowl or measuring cup. Remove peanut butter balls from refrigerator. Insert a wooden pick into a ball and dip into melted chocolate so that ¾ of ball is coated. Return to wax paper, chocolate side down, and remove pick. Repeat with all balls. Refrigerate on wax paper 30 minutes or longer until chocolate is firm, not sticky.

To store, remove balls from wax paper and place in plastic containers with wax paper between layers to keep separate.

JELLO COOKIES

4 small pkg. jello (or 2 large
    pkg.)

3 env. Knox unflavored gelatine
4 c. boiling water

Stir together flavored and unflavored gelatin in bowl. Pour boiling water into gelatins and stir until dissolved. Pour onto low flat pan. *Chill.* When ready to serve, cut in shapes or use cookie cutter.

COCONUT DROPS

1 egg white, well beaten
½ c. sugar

1¾ c. coconut

Beat sugar into egg white. Stir in coconut. Drop by small spoonfuls on oiled pan. Bake at 425° for about 7 minutes or until lightly browned. Makes 2 dozen.

FLOURLESS PEANUT BUTTER COOKIES

1 c. chunky peanut butter
1 c. sugar

1 egg, slightly beaten
½ tsp. vanilla

Mix peanut butter and sugar. Add egg and vanilla. Shape into 1 inch balls on ungreased cookie sheet. Press with fork to flatten. Bake at 350° for 12 to 15 minutes. Makes 3 dozen.

RAISIN CLUSTERS

½ c. butter or margarine
¾ c. sugar
1 c. chopped raisins
1 beaten egg
1 Tbsp. milk (or Isomil)

1 tsp. vanilla
¼ tsp. salt
½ c. chopped nuts
3 c. puffed rice cereal
Coconut

Melt margarine. Add sugar, raisins, egg, milk, vanilla, and salt; bring to boil. Boil for 2 minutes. Add cereal and nuts; mix thoroughly. Cool slightly. Roll into balls with buttered fingers and coat with coconut. *Cool* before serving.

OVERNIGHT MERINGUES

2 egg whites
⅛ tsp. salt
⅛ tsp. cream of tartar
8 Tbsp. sugar

¼ c. finely chopped nuts
1 sq. chocolate
1 tsp. vanilla

Beat egg whites until stiff. Add salt and cream of tartar; beat. Beat in 6 tablespoons sugar, 1 tablespoon at a time. Beat until stiff, glossy, and smooth. Fold in last 2 tablespoons sugar, nuts, chocolate, and vanilla. Heat oven to 350°. Drop by rounded spoonfuls on baking sheet. Place on center rack. Turn oven off; leave in overnight. Store in airtight container.

APPLE CRISP

5 c. peeled apple slices
1 Tbsp. lemon juice
2 c. Rice Krispies
⅓ c. brown sugar

⅓ c. potato starch flour
¼ c. margarine
¾ tsp. cinnamon

Place apple slices in 8 inch square baking dish; sprinkle with lemon juice. Coarsely crush cereal. Combine cereal with remaining ingredients. Mix until crumbly; sprinkle over apples. Bake at 375° for 30 to 40 minutes or until apples are tender and topping is golden brown.

Can use a gluten-free cereal flake in place of the Rice Krispies.

HONEY COOKIES

½ c. butter or margarine
½ c. raw honey
1 c. brown rice flour
½ c. potato starch
⅓ c. raw sunflower seeds
⅓ c. chopped nuts

1 tsp. soda
1½ tsp. baking powder
½ tsp. cinnamon
¼ tsp. cloves
¼ tsp. allspice

Cream butter and honey. Mix all dry ingredients and then combine with creamed mixture. Drop by teaspoon and bake at 350° for 8 to 10 minutes.

COCOA MINI MERINGUES

3 egg whites
¼ tsp. cream of tartar
¾ c. sugar
2 Tbsp. cocoa

Whipped topping
Mini chocolate chips
Fruit (optional)

Beat egg whites and cream of tartar in small bowl until foamy. Beat in sugar, 1 tablespoon at a time, and beat until stiff and glossy. Don't underbeat. Sprinkle sifted cocoa in meringue and gently fold in. Cover 2 baking sheets with aluminum foil. Drop meringue by level measuring tablespoons about 1½ inches apart on aluminum foil. Make small indentation in center of each with tip of spoon.

Bake for 10 minutes in 275° oven. Turn off oven, leaving cookies in oven with door closed for 1 hour. Remove from oven and cool away from draft. Top each with 1 teaspoon whipped topping and garnish with fruit or mini chocolate chips. They can be wrapped in aluminum foil and frozen for 2 weeks.

Variations:

2 tsp. cocoa	4 drops food coloring
½ tsp. grated orange peel	½ tsp. almond or peppermint
½ tsp. grated lemon peel	extract

Also, divide meringue mixture into 3 parts and fold into each part *one* of the variation ingredients as shown.

SCOTCH CRISPIES

1 (12 oz.) pkg. butterscotch
   morsels
1 c. peanut butter

6 c. oven-toasted rice cereal (I
   use puffed rice)

1. Melt butterscotch morsels and peanut butter over hot water (not boiling). Stir until smooth.
2. Toast puffed rice in oven until golden brown.
3. In large bowl, mix butterscotch mixture and rice cereal; mix well.
4. Press mixture into foil lined 13x9x2 inch pan.
5. Chill for an hour or so before cutting into squares. Makes 48 (1½ inch) squares.

SCOTCHEROOS

Combine:

1 c. sugar   1 c. light corn syrup

Cook in 3 quart saucepan over moderate heat, stirring frequently, until mixture begins to bubble. Remove from heat.

Stir in:

1 c. chunky peanut butter   6 c. Rice Krispies

Press into buttered 9x13 inch pan.

Melt in double boiler over hot water (or microwave for 3 minutes):

1 c. real chocolate chips   1 c. butterscotch chips

Stir until blended; remove from heat. Spread evenly over bars. Cool until firm. Cut and serve.

REESE-TYPE CUPS

1 qt. peanut butter (Skippy)   2 lb. powdered sugar
1 lb. margarine, softened

Mix well; roll into balls. Dip into 18 ounces Nestle's chocolate chips and ⅜ pound paraffin wax, melted in *double boiler.* Makes about 200 to 300 pieces, depending on size.

MAGIC COOKIE BARS

½ c. margarine or butter
1½ c. low protein gluten-free
cinnamon crackers from
Ener-G-Foods
1 (14 oz.) can Eagle Brand
sweetened condensed milk
(not evaporated)

1 (6 oz.) pkg. semi-sweet
chocolate morsels
1 (3½ oz.) can flaked coconut
(1⅓ c.)
1 c. chopped pecans

Preheat oven to 350° (325° for glass dish). In 13x9 inch baking pan, melt margarine in oven. Sprinkle crumbs over margarine; mix together and press into pan. Pour sweetened condensed milk evenly over crumbs. Top evenly with remaining ingredients; press down firmly. Bake for 25 to 30 minutes or until lightly browned. Cool thoroughly before cutting. Store, loosely covered, at room temperature.

FUDGE BROWNIES

2 sq. unsweetened chocolate
⅓ c. corn oil
1 c. sugar
2 eggs
½ c. nuts (optional)
½ c. less 1 Tbsp. rice flour

2 Tbsp. plus 1 tsp. potato starch
flour
½ tsp. baking powder
½ tsp. salt
1 tsp. vanilla

Melt chocolate with oil over hot water. Beat in sugar and eggs. Stir in sifted dry ingredients. Pour into well greased 8 inch square pan. Bake at 350° for 30 to 35 minutes. When slightly cool, cut into squares.

SWEET SURPRISE COOKIES

7 oz. jar marshmallow creme
1 c. peanut butter (chunky)

1½ c. Rice Krispies

Mix all and roll into balls. Dip in almond bark of your choice. Makes about 40.

NUT GOODY BARS

6 oz. chocolate chips
6 oz. butterscotch chips
1 c. creamy peanut butter
1 c. salted peanuts
½ c. margarine

¼ c. milk
2 Tbsp. vanilla pudding mix (not instant)
3 c. powdered sugar
1 tsp. maple flavoring

Melt chips and peanut butter over low heat. Spread ½ of mixture in a wax paper lined 9x13 inch pan; refrigerate until cool. Add peanuts to remaining mixture; set aside.

In pan, melt margarine. Stir in milk and vanilla pudding mix. Bring to a boil and remove from heat. Add powdered sugar and maple flavoring. Beat till smooth and spread on refrigerated mixture. Spread peanut mixture on top and refrigerate to set. Cut bars.

CHOCOROONS

2 sq. unsweetened chocolate
2 Tbsp. margarine
⅔ c. sugar
2 eggs

¼ tsp. salt
1 tsp. vanilla
2⅔ c. coconut

Melt chocolate with margarine over low heat or over hot water. Mix all ingredients, except coconut; beat well. Stir in coconut. If desired, add ¼ cup chopped nuts. Drop from a teaspoon onto a greased cookie sheet. Bake for 15 minutes at 325°F. Ingredients may be doubled or tripled to make more cookies.

APPLE PUDDING CAKE

½ c. shortening
1 c. sugar
1 egg
2 Tbsp. milk
1 c. rice flour

½ tsp. salt
½ tsp. cinnamon
1 tsp. soda
½ tsp. baking powder
2 c. chopped apple

Cream shortening and sugar. Beat in egg; add milk. Sift dry ingredients together; add them to the creamed mixture. Beat well. Stir in the chopped apple. Add ½ cup of chopped nuts or raisins if desired. Bake in a greased 9x13 inch pan at 350°F. about 40 minutes (325°F. in a glass pan). Cool. Cut into bars. This makes 32 or more bars, depending on how you cut them.

CHOCOLATE BUTTERSCOTCH SCOTCHEROOS

1 c. sugar
1 c. light corn syrup
1 c. peanut butter
6 c. crisp GF rice cereal

1 (6 oz.) bag semi-sweet
 chocolate bits
1 (6 oz.) bag butterscotch bits

In a large saucepan, combine the sugar and corn syrup. Bring just to a boil; remove from heat and stir in peanut butter. Mix in rice cereal. Press into a buttered 9x13 inch pan. Melt chocolate and butterscotch morsels in a double boiler over hot water; spread over cereal mixture. Chill. Cut into squares. Makes 48 bars (1x2 inches).

CHOCOLATE CHIP BARS
(Recipe courtesy of Byerly's)

½ c. sugar
⅓ c. brown sugar
½ c. margarine
1 egg
½ tsp. vanilla
½ tsp. salt

1 tsp. potato flour
½ tsp. soda
5 Tbsp. cornstarch
⅔ c. rice flour
6 oz. mini chocolate chips

Cream sugar and margarine. Beat in egg, vanilla, salt, and potato flour. Add cornstarch and rice flour; mix well. Stir in chocolate chips. Spread in greased 8x8 inch pan; refrigerate for 20 minutes. Bake at 375° until golden brown (about 25 to 30 minutes). Makes 16.

NO BAKE CORN FLAKE-BAKER'S BARS

1 c. Karo light syrup
1 c. sugar
12 oz. crunchy peanut butter
5 c. corn flakes
12 oz. Baker's sweet chocolate
    flavored chips

1 tsp. vanilla
1 tsp. Fleischmann's oleo
6 oz. butterscotch chips

A. *Lightly* boil syrup and sugar.
B. Add peanut butter prior to removing from flame.
C. Add corn flakes.

Meanwhile:

A. Melt chocolate chips and butterscotch chips in double boiler.
B. Add butter and vanilla to chips. Put bars on greased cookie sheet by patting with greased hands. Spread last mixture on top of bars. (Add a few drops of hot water to ease spreading.) Let stand for 30 minutes and cut into bars. Refrigerate in closed container.

FORGOTTEN COOKIES

2 egg whites
¾ c. granulated sugar
1 (6 oz.) pkg. semi-sweet
　chocolate pieces or 1 c.
　raisins or chopped nuts

Beat egg whites in a deep medium size bowl with mixer at high speed until soft peaks form. Continue to beat while slowly adding sugar; beat until a stiff meringue forms. Fold in chocolate pieces or raisins or chopped nuts.

Drop by heaping teaspoonfuls onto greased cookie sheets. Place in a 375°F. oven and turn off heat; leave in oven until it cools to room temperature, or overnight. Remove from cookie sheets and store in airtight containers. Makes 2 ½ dozen.

MARSHMALLOW BARS

1 (12 oz.) bag semi-sweet
　chocolate chips
1 (12 oz.) bag butterscotch chips
1 c. peanut butter

1 (10 oz.) bag colored miniature
　marshmallows
1 (1 lb.) bag Spanish peanuts

In double boiler or over low heat, stir chocolate chips, butterscotch chips, and peanut butter together until melted or well blended. Remove from heat and stir in marshmallows and peanuts. Spread immediately in greased 9x13 inch pan. Chill until set before cutting into bars. Keep the bar size small - these are sweet! Makes about 4 dozen bars.

PEANUT BUTTER BARS

1 c. sugar
1 c. Karo syrup (light)

2 c. peanut butter (18 oz.)
2 c. crushed corn flakes*

Cook sugar and Karo syrup until clear or dissolved. Stir in peanut butter and corn flakes. Spread in buttered 9x13 inch pan. Cut into squares immediately. (These freeze well.)

* Six and one half cups corn flakes equals 2 cups, crushed.

TROPICAL FRUIT-NUT BARS

1 (20 oz.) can crushed pineapple
3 env. (1 oz.) unflavored gelatin
¼ c. honey

1½ c. chopped walnuts
1 c. raisins
¼ c. flaked coconut

Drain pineapple well (save juice), pressing out juice with back of spoon. In saucepan, sprinkle gelatin over reserved juice; let stand for 1 minute. Stir over low heat until gelatin is dissolved. Stir in pineapple, honey, walnuts, raisins, and coconut. Turn into an 8 or 9 inch square pan. Chill. Cut into bars.

LEMON NUT BALLS

¾ c. powdered milk
2 c. sifted powdered sugar
¼ stick margarine, melted

4 Tbsp. lemon juice
Chopped nuts

Mix together the dry milk, sugar, margarine, and lemon juice. Form into small balls. (You may need to add more powdered sugar for the right consistency to handle.) Roll in chopped nuts; refrigerate to "set." Makes about 1½ dozen cookies.

INCREDIBLE PEANUT BUTTER COOKIES

1 c. peanut butter
1 c. sugar

1 large egg
1 tsp. vanilla

In an electric mixer bowl, combine all ingredients and beat until well mixed. Roll dough into balls the size of a small walnut. Place balls 2 inches apart on a lightly greased cookie sheet. Flatten balls with the tines of a fork. Bake at 325°F. for about 13 minutes. Place on a wire rack to cool. Makes about 2½ dozen cookies.

Note: These also can be mixed by hand.

NO CRUST PUMPKIN PIE

Corn flake crumbs for crust
½ c. light brown sugar
½ c. Jolly Joan rice mix
1 can evaporated milk
2 eggs

1 (16 oz.) can pumpkin
1 tsp. vanilla
1 tsp. cinnamon
½ tsp. ginger
¼ tsp. cloves

Preheat oven to 350°. Butter a 9 or 10 inch pie plate and dust with very fine corn flake crumbs; set aside. Beat remaining ingredients until smooth and pour into pie plate. Bake for 50 to 55 minutes. (May be served with whipped cream or nondairy topping if desired.)

CRANBERRY NUT PIE

1¼ c. cranberries
¼ c. brown sugar
¼ c. chopped walnuts
1 egg

½ c. sugar
¼ c. cornstarch
⅓ c. melted margarine

Preheat oven to 325°. Butter a 9 inch pie plate and layer fresh or frozen cranberries on bottom. Sprinkle with brown sugar and nuts. In a bowl, beat egg until thick; gradually add sugar, beating well. Stir in cornstarch and melted margarine; blend well. Pour mixture over cranberries and bake about 45 minutes. May be served with ice cream or Cool Whip.

PUMPKIN PIE

Crust:

1 c. rice flour
½ tsp. salt
1 tsp. sugar

1½ Tbsp. milk
⅓ c. oil

Mix in pie pan and pat into shape.

Filling: See recipe on Libby's pumpkin pie can. Follow directions on can and bake as directed.

SPONGE CAKE

9 eggs
1¾ c. sugar
½ c. lemon juice and ground up
    rind

1 scant c. potato starch
2 tsp. baking powder
Pinch of salt

Separate 7 of the eggs and beat until dry. In another bowl, beat the 7 yolks plus 2 whole eggs. Add sugar, lemon juice and rind, and beat thoroughly. Sift the dry ingredients and add to egg yolk mixture. Fold all this into the dry beaten whites. Put into *an ungreased* angel food pan. Bake at 350° for 40 to 50 minutes, then cool upside-down.

YUMMY YELLOW CAKE

1 c. rice flour
⅓ c. cornstarch
½ tsp. salt
1 c. sugar
½ c. shortening
3 tsp. baking powder

4 eggs, separated
¾ c. buttermilk
1 tsp. almond extract
1 tsp. vanilla
¼ tsp. xanthan gum

Sift dry ingredients into a bowl. Add shortening, egg yolks, and ½ cup of the buttermilk. Beat for 3 minutes at medium speed of the mixer. Add remaining buttermilk, flavorings, and xanthan gum; beat for 2 minutes.

Beat egg whites till stiff peaks form; fold batter into whites. Pour into a greased 13x9 inch pan or 2 layer cake pans (8 inches). Bake at 350° for 25 to 30 minutes or until cake tests done. Frost as desired or use as the base for strawberry shortcake.

TEXAS APPLE STREUSEL

4 large apples, pared and sliced
2 Tbsp. lemon juice
¼ c. corn flour (or rice or potato flour)
½ tsp. cinnamon

½ c. brown sugar, firmly packed
2 Tbsp. melted margarine
½ c. chopped pecans and/or shredded coconut
¼ tsp. nutmeg

Toss apple slices with lemon juice; place in a slightly greased 9 inch baking pan. With a fork, blend flour, spices, sugar, and margarine. Add pecans and/or coconut; mix well. Sprinkle evenly over apples. *Conventional oven:* Bake at 350° for about 35 minutes. *Microwave:* Cook on HIGH for 12 to 14 minutes. Rotate dish every 5 minutes. Let stand for 5 minutes. Serve with half & half or GF ice cream. Makes 4 servings.

SOUR CREAM COFFEE CAKE

1 c. butter or magarine
1½ c. sugar
3 eggs
1 tsp. vanilla
1 tsp. lemon juice
1 c. mashed potatoes
2 c. white rice flour, sifted

2 tsp. baking soda
3 tsp. baking powder
Pinch of salt
1 c. dairy sour cream
½ c. sugar
2 tsp. cinnamon

Cream butter with the 1½ cups sugar. Stir in eggs, vanilla, and lemon juice. Add mashed potatoes. Sift together flour, soda, baking powder, and salt. Add dry ingredients alternately with sour cream to egg mixture. Pour ½ of batter into a greased 10x13 inch pan or 2 square pans (8 inches).

Mix the ½ cup sugar and cinnamon. Sprinkle ½ of this on top of batter. Pour in remaining batter; sprinkle with rest of the mixture. Bake at 350° F. for 35 minutes or until done.

PEANUT BUTTER BALLS

½ c. peanut butter
2 Tbsp. honey
½ c. peanuts, coarsely chopped

¼ c. dry skim milk
½ to 1 c. coarse GF cereal
    crumbs

Mix the peanut butter and honey. Stir in nuts and dry milk to make a stiff dough (add more dry milk if necessary). Roll into 1 inch balls. Roll in cereal crumbs and store, covered, in refrigerator. Makes 18 to 20 balls.

APPLE CAKE

½ c. shortening
1¼ c. white sugar
1 c. brown sugar
2 eggs
2 c. diced apples
1 tsp. salt
1 tsp. cinnamon

1 tsp. baking powder
1 tsp. soda
2¼ c. rice flour
1 c. buttermilk
½ tsp. xanthan gum
¼ tsp. cloves (optional)

Cream shortening and sugar. Add eggs, beating well. Add diced apples. Sift dry ingredients and add alternately with buttermilk. Pour into greased and floured 9x13 inch pan.

Sprinkle with topping made of:

¼ c. sugar
1 tsp. cinnamon

½ c. nuts (if desired)

Bake at 350° for 40 to 45 minutes.

Honey may be substituted for *some* of the sugar.

RICE PUDDING WITH MERINGUE

½ c. long grain rice
1 qt. milk
2 egg yolks
¼ tsp. vanilla

¼ c. sugar
¼ tsp. salt
2 egg whites

Cook rice, milk, and salt in double boiler for about 2 hours, stirring occasionally. Add egg yolks, sugar, and vanilla, which have been mixed together. Put in casserole. Beat egg whites, adding gradually 4 tablespoons sugar. Brown in 350° oven.

CRANBERRY PUDDING

1 c. raw cranberries
¼ c. sugar
¼ c. nuts
1 egg
½ c. sugar

½ tsp. baking powder
¼ c. potato flour
¼ c. white rice flour *or* ¼ c. garbanzo flour*
6 Tbsp. melted butter

Generously grease 8 or 9 inch pie plate. Spread cranberries over bottom of plate. Sprinkle with ¼ cup sugar and nuts. Beat egg, ½ cup sugar, flour, baking powder, and melted butter until thoroughly combined. Pour batter over cranberries. Bake in 325° oven until crust is golden brown (35 to 45 minutes). Serve warm or cold with Butter Sauce. Serves 6.

Butter Sauce:

1 c. sugar
½ c. butter

½ c. cream

Combine all ingredients in heavy saucepan. Bring to boil, stirring constantly. Boil for 1 minute. Serve warm.

* Garbanzo flour available from Valley Co-op in Burnsville. It is a very fine and light flour.

SUN FLAKE CRISPIES

1 c. sugar   1 c. white Karo syrup

Bring sugar and syrup to boil; take off the stove.

Add the following:

1 c. peanut butter
1 tsp. vanilla
½ c. peanuts

4 c. Sun Flakes
½ c. coconut

Put on cookie sheet. Cool and cut.

CHOCOLATE BARS

Crust - Combine as for pie crust:

½ c. soy flour
½ c. potato starch flour

3 tsp. sugar
½ c. chopped nuts

Spread in 9x13 inch pan; press down. Bake for 10 minutes in 375° oven; cool.

First layer:

8 oz. pkg. cream cheese (at room temperature)

1 c. powdered sugar
1 c. Cool Whip

Soften cream cheese at room temperature. Combine with powdered sugar; beat until creamy. Fold in Cool Whip. Spread mixture over cooled crust.

Second layer:

2 (small) pkg. pudding   **Cool Whip**
2 c. milk

Combine pudding with milk and cook over stove until thickened, stirring frequently (or in microwave). Chill. After pudding has chilled, stir pudding and spread on top of first layer. Top with remainder of Cool Whip (use 8 to 9 ounce Cool Whip). Refrigerate until ready to serve.

Very good with lemon pudding also.

MISCELLANEOUS TREATS AND SNACKS

LEMON FRUIT SAUCE

Mix:

½ c. GF salad dressing   ½ tsp. ground ginger
½ c. lemon flavored yogurt

Serve over a mixture of fresh fruit. Makes 1 cup sauce.

ORANGE SMOOTHIE

In blender container, put:

⅓ c. orange juice   ½ c. vanilla flavored yogurt

Cover and blend. Makes 1 cup.

ELEPHANT MILK

In blender container, put:

¾ c. milk   1 Tbsp. honey
2 Tbsp. creamy peanut butter

Cover and blend. Makes 1 cup.

POPCORN CRUNCH

1 roaster (1 qt.) popped popcorn   1 c. margarine
  (1 c. unpopped)   ½ c. white Karo syrup
1⅓ c. sugar   1 tsp. GF vanilla (imitation)

Combine sugar, margarine, and Karo in heavy pan over medium heat. Heat to just barely softball stage. Add the vanilla and mix. Pour over popcorn; coat well. Store in airtight container.

GLUTEN-FREE/LACTOSE-FREE ICE CREAM

¾ c. sugar   1 egg
1 env. unflavored gelatin   2 tsp. GF vanilla (imitation)
Dash of salt
4 c. Coffee Rich nondairy
  creamer

Combine sugar, gelatin, salt, and 2 cups Coffee Rich in saucepan. Bring to a boil. Beat egg in a bowl. Very slowly add 1 cup of hot mixture to the egg. Return egg mixture to saucepan and cook for 2 minutes. Let cool. Add 2 cups Coffee Rich and vanilla. Freeze overnight.

Next morning, beat ice cream with electric rotary beater and pour into 1½ quart container. Ready to eat in a few hours.

MICROWAVE PEANUT BRITTLE

1 c. raw Spanish peanuts
1 c. white sugar

½ c. white Karo syrup
⅛ tsp. salt

Stir together in 1½ quart casserole; microwave on HIGH for 7 to 8 minutes, stirring well after 4 minutes.

Add:

1 tsp. butter or margarine

1 tsp. vanilla

Stir well and microwave on HIGH another 1 to 2 minutes. Add 1 teaspoon baking soda. Stir well until fluffy. Pour out on greased cookie sheet. Cool for 1 hour. Break into pieces.

PEANUT BUTTER CHEWS

1 c. peanut butter
1 c. sugar
½ c. Carnation evaporated milk

4 tsp. cornstarch
½ c. chocolate chips (optional)

Bake at 350° for 10 to 12 minutes.

FAST CHOCOLATE PECAN FUDGE

½ c. butter or margarine
¼ c. cocoa
4 c. powdered sugar

1 tsp. vanilla
⅔ c. evaporated milk
1 c. chopped pecans

Melt butter in saucepan; remove from heat. Stir in cocoa, then powdered sugar and vanilla. Add evaporated milk. Stir constantly over low heat until warm and smooth. Extra beating may be needed to make smooth. Add nuts. Pour into 8x8 inch pan; chill. Cut into squares.

SALT-FREE BEEF JERKY

2 lb. lean boneless meat, cut
    into strips
1 Tbsp. pepper

1 c. water
3 cloves garlic, crushed
1 Tbsp. GF vinegar

Combine all ingredients. Stir occasionally to insure all strips; marinate evenly for 10 to 12 hours in the refrigerator. Place a wire rack over baking sheet and arrange single layers of beef strips so that they don't overlap. Bake in very slow oven (150° to 175°) for 10 to 12 hours. Store in airtight container at room temperature.

POPCORN CAKE

4 qt. popped popcorn	¼ c. oil
1 (11 oz.) pkg. M&M's candies	½ c. margarine
½ to ¾ c. peanuts	1 (10 oz.) pkg. marshmallows

Mix the popcorn, candies, and peanuts. Melt together the oil, margarine, and marshmallows. Pour over popcorn mixture and mix all well. Put into a greased Bundt pan; pack in well, then turn out.

HOT BROWN RICE-FRUIT CEREAL
(Makes 1 serving)

½ c. cooked brown rice	1 tsp. honey
¼ to ⅓ c. cooking apple, chopped	⅓ to ½ c. sesame milk (recipe follows)
1 Tbsp. raisins	

Cook the rice with a dash of cinnamon and nutmeg to taste. Mix it with the other ingredients (if apple is not tart, add ¼ teaspoon lemon juice). Bake, covered, in a toaster oven at 350°F. for 20 minutes or in microwave oven (with cover askew - or slit plastic film) on MEDIUM HIGH for 4½ minutes. Serve as is or with plain yogurt.

You may cook enough rice for several days at one time. Mix each portion in an ovenproof cereal bowl and refrigerate. This makes a hot breakfast which is quick to fix each morning. Other dry fruits may be used.

Sesame "Milk":

1 Tbsp. toasted sesame seeds	¼ c. water

In blender, blend toasted sesame seeds with water until seeds are thoroughly ground. This may be made in larger quantities and stored in the refrigerator. These proportions can be used to make "milk" from any nuts or seeds.

BLINTZ PANCAKES

4 beaten eggs	1 Tbsp. sugar
1 c. plain yogurt	2 Tbsp. potato starch
1 c. cottage cheese	¼ c. rice bran
½ tsp. salt	⅔ c. brown rice flour

Beat eggs in bowl. Add other ingredients and mix well. Bake on greased griddle. These are good plain or with butter. They may also be served with sugar or fruit sauces.

ONION RINGS/HUSH PUPPIES

2 eggs
½ tsp. salt
1 tsp. lemon juice
1½ c. brown rice flour
2 Tbsp. potato flour

3 Tbsp. corn starch
1½ tsp. baking powder
¾ to 1 c. milk
Onions
Oil (for frying)

Beat eggs. Add salt and lemon juice. Add dry ingredients, unsifted. Add ¾ cup milk. If too thick, add more. Mix well and coat onion rings. Deep-fry until golden.

This batter may also be used to coat fish pieces for deep-frying. This batter makes a lot of onion rings, so if you run out of them and have leftover batter, you may make hush puppies by adding corn meal to thicken, garlic salt, and minced onion. Drop by spoonfuls into deep fryer.

TUNA TREATS

1 (7½ oz.) can tuna, packed in
    water, with liquid
1 egg

⅓ c. rice flour
1 Tbsp. chopped onion
½ tsp. baking powder

Flake tuna in liquid with a fork. Add all other ingredients and mix well. Mixture should be thick enough so you have to push it off a teaspoon with another spoon into hot fat. Add more flour if necessary. Turn once to brown on all sides; drain and serve hot.

COCKTAIL SAUCE

Mix together:

½ c. catsup
1 tsp. horseradish

Dash of Worcestershire sauce
Dash of lemon juice

TARTAR SAUCE

Mix together:

½ c. mayonnaise
1 Tbsp. finely minced onion
1 Tbsp. finely minced green
    pepper

1 tsp. parsley
1 tsp. sweet pickle relish
Dash of lemon juice (if desired)

MOCK HOLLANDAISE SAUCE

¼ c. dairy sour cream
¼ c. mayonnaise or salad
    dressing

1 tsp. lemon juice
½ tsp. prepared mustard

Combine ingredients in a small saucepan. Cook and stir over low heat until heated through; do not boil. Serve on asparagus, etc.

POTATO PIZZA

1½ c. GF thin white sauce
½ c. shredded process Cheddar
    cheese
4 c. thinly sliced potatoes
1 lb. ground beef
1 (15 oz.) can GF tomato or pizza
    sauce

½ c. chopped onion
½ Tbsp. sugar (optional)
Dash of salt
Dash of oregano
8 slices Mozzarella cheese
½ c. grated Parmesan cheese

Mix white sauce with shredded cheese; pour into the bottom of a greased 9x13 inch pan. Layer potatoes over the sauce. Brown the ground beef in a skillet; pour off grease. Spread beef over potatoes. Mix the tomato sauce with onion, sugar, salt, and oregano; pour over the meat and potatoes. Cover with foil and bake at 375°F. for 1 hour or until potatoes are done. Remove foil.

Top the casserole with Mozzarella cheese; sprinkle the Parmesan cheese over top. Return to oven until the cheese melts, about 15 minutes.

SNACK AND SANDWICH HINTS

Make favorite sandwiches, using GF bread. Wrap moist fillings separately. One or 2 chicken drumsticks make hearty eating (cook several at a time and keep them in the freezer). For nibbling, cut cheese into slices or wedges; wrap in plastic wrap.

Other ideas:

Rice crackers or cakes
Raw vegetables
Dried fruit
Fresh fruit

Peanut butter
GF nuts
Popcorn
GF chips

Soft corn tortillas (Azteca, Zapata, and Mosquitos brands) are GF and good to use several ways. Try them as noodles for soup; cut into strips, fry in a little oil or heat in microwave, and add to soup, or, crisp them in oven and make crumbs to coat fish or chicken, or, use as crumbs in meatloaf mixture.

MEATBALLS FOR SOUPS

In a large bowl, combine:

1 lb. ground beef
¼ c. uncooked regular rice
2 tsp. chili powder (if desired) or
   season with just a bit of

oregano, thyme, or garlic
   powder and pepper
1 tsp. salt
1 egg

Mix; shape into 1 inch meatballs. Brown in a large skillet. Drain on paper towels and add to the soup pot.

VEGETABLE DIP

⅔ c. mayonnaise (do not use
   Miracle Whip)
⅔ c. sour cream
2 tsp. dill weed

2 tsp. seasoning salt
2 tsp. parsley flakes
2 tsp. onion flakes

Mix; let stand overnight to blend flavors. Serve with raw vegetables.

CURRY DILL DIP

1 c. mayonnaise
1 c. sour cream
1 Tbsp. dried parsley
1 tsp. dried onion flakes or 2
   Tbsp. finely chopped green
   onion

1 tsp. dill weed
1 to 2 tsp. curry powder
1 tsp. seasoned salt

Combine all ingredients; refrigerate at least 1 hour. Serve as dip for raw vegetables, chips, and crackers. Can also be used as topping for hot vegetables.

SHRIMP DIP

1 (8 oz.) pkg. cream cheese
1 can shrimp, chopped
1 c. ripe olives, chopped
1 tsp. lemon juice

1 Tbsp. mayonnaise
1 tsp. Beau Monde seasoning
1 Tbsp. chili powder

AVOCADO SCOOP

Spread 1 container frozen avocado dip (Calavo brand) on plate and layer on top:

Chopped lettuce
Chopped tomatoes

Chopped green onion
Grated Cheddar cheese

Serve with tortilla chips to use as a scoop.

INDEX OF RECIPES

BARBECUE

BAR-B-Q'S 5
BARBECUE CHICKEN 4
BARBECUE SAUCE 3
BARBECUE SAUCE 4
BARBECUE SAUCE 3
BARBECUED CORNED BEEF 2
BARBECUED RIBS 6
BARBEQUE RIBS 5
BARBEQUED BEANS 1
BASTING SAUCE FOR GRILLED
    CHICKEN 4
BEST-EVER BQ SAUCE FOR
    TURKEY INJECTION 4
CHINESE BARBEQUED PORK 5
EASY BARBECUE SAUCE 3
FRESH BARBECUED SALMON 1
INDIA JELLIED SNAKE 1
KABOB (MARINADE) SAUCE 2
MARINADE SAUCE 2
WORLD'S BEST STEAK BASTE 3

CROCK POT COOKING

BAKED APPLE 7
BEEF STEW 9
BEEF-AND-KIDNEY STEW 11
BRAISED OXTAILS, SPANISH
    STYLE 12
BREAD PUDDING 7
CHEESE AND POTATO
    CASSEROLE 16
CHILE CON CARNE 14
CORNED BEEF AND CABBAGE 16
CORNED BEEF AND CABBAGE 17
CROCK POT BAR-B-Q RIBS 9
CROCK POT BEANS 15
CROCK POT DRESSING 7
CROCK POT RIBS AND SAUCE
    MIX 14
EASY CHILI 15
FORGOTTEN STEW 10
GREEN BEAN CASSEROLE 15
HEARTY BEEF STEW 10
HEARTY POTATO-SAUERKRAUT
    SOUP 8
HOT VEGETABLES DISH 16
IRISH LAMB STEW 11
KATY'S HOMEMADE POTATO
    SOUP 8
MEAT LOAF WITH TOMATO
    SAUCE 12
MEATBALLS WITH RICE 13
NO PEEK STEW 10
PARTY MEATBALLS 7
PAT'S STEW 11
SPLIT PEA SOUP 9
STEAMED FRANKS 13
STUFFED CABBAGE ROLLS 17

STUFFED GREEN PEPPERS WITH
    TOMATO SAUCE 17
SWISS STEAK 13
VEGETABLE BEEF SOUP 8

COOKING FOR A CROWD

BARBECUED HAMBURGERS 28
BARBECUED HAMBURGERS 28
BARBEQUED HAMBURGER 28
BASIC WHITE SAUCE 21
BBQ MEAT BALLS 27
BIG A'S MEAT LOAF 26
CABBAGE WALDORF SALAD 24
CAULIFLOWER AND BROCCOLI
    SALAD 23
CHICKEN HOT DISH 30
CHICKEN HUNTINGTON 30
CHILI CON CARNE 33
CHOW MEIN 29
COCOA OR HOT CHOCOLATE 20
COFFEE 20
COFFEE 20
COLE SLAW 25
CREAMED CHICKEN WITH
    PIMENTO ON RICE 30
EIGHT REUBEN SANDWICHES 26
FESTIVE DAIRY PUNCH 20
FRENCH DRESSING 22
FRENCH DRESSING 22
FRUIT JELLO 23
HAM LOAF 27
HAMBURGER AND CROUTON
    HOT DISH 31
HAMBURGERS 26
HARDY CHILI FOR HARDY
    APPETITES 32
LETTUCE AND ORANGE SALAD 24
MASTER MIX FOR BISCUITS,
    MUFFINS, AND CORN BREAD 21
MAYONNAISE 22
MEAT BALLS 27
NOODLE PIZZA 31
POTATO SALAD 25
POTATO SALAD TO SERVE 100 24
QUANTITIES TO SERVE 100 19
QUANTITIES TO SERVE 50 19
RANCH BEANS 29
SCALLOPED CHICKEN WITH RICE 29
SCALLOPED POTATOES 31
TACOS 32
THOUSAND ISLAND DRESSING 22
TUNA, EGG, AND MACARONI
    SALAD 23

ETHNIC FOODS

BREADS
APPLE KUCHEN...................35
BIG BREAD ROUNDS.............35
BLUEBERRY PIEROGI -
   DUMPLINGS.................47
BOHEMIAN RAISIN BISCUIT
   KOLACHY...................46
FLAT BREAD....................37
FLAT BREAD - NORWEGIAN........37
FRENCH BREAD.................37
FRENCH SOURDOUGH BREAD.......37
GERMAN APPLE STRUDEL.........43
GERMAN CHICKEN AND
   DUMPLINGS.................47
GERMAN KUCHEN DOUGH AND
   FILLING....................38
HONEY DATE-WALNUT BREAD.......35
HONEY LEKUCHEN...............39
IRISH SODA BREAD.............46
ITALIAN CHEESE TWISTS.........39
JAN'S PIZZA BUNS.............40
JULEKAKE.....................40
KRINGLA - NORWAY.............40
MANNA BREAD.................36
MOM'S KUCHEN................36
NORWEGIAN COFFEE BREAD.......41
NORWEGIAN COFFEECAKE.........41
NORWEGIAN STYLE FOODS -
   GRANDMA'S KUMLA...........35
OSLO KRINGLE - NORWEGIAN
   PASTRY....................42
PIEROGI......................48
POTICA.......................42
PULL-APART GARLIC BREAD.......42
RUSSIAN ZUCCHINI BREAD.......43
SPAETZLE - DUMPLINGS..........47
STROMBOLI....................43
SUGAR KRINGLES...............40
SWEDISH BROWN BREAD..........44
SWEDISH COOKY RINGS -
   KRINGLOR..................45
SWEDISH POTATO PANCAKES -
   RARIVNA POTATISPLATTAR......45
SWEDISH TOAST...............45

CASSEROLES
A FRENCH DINNER FOR 4.........49
AS A SALAD OR BUFFET DISH......62
BULGOGI - KOREAN BBQ BEEF......65
CABBAGE HOT DISH.............52
CABBAGE ROLLS...............51
CABBAGE ROLLS...............51
CHICKEN ADOBO - PHILLIPPINE
   ISLANDS...................58
CHICKEN STIR-FRY WITH
   VEGETABLES................59
CHICKEN TETRAZZINI...........54
CHILI RELLENOS...............69
CHOP SUEY...................53
CHOW MEIN...................64
CRISPY OVEN-FRIED MEXICAN
   CHICKEN...................60

DENMARK FRIKADELLER
   MEATBALLS.................67
EASY PORK AND VEGETABLE
   WOK.......................64
EGG FOO YONG................74
EGG ROLLS...................65
ENCHILADAS..................59
ENGLISH SAUSAGE ROLLS........55
FETTUCCINE ALFREDO - ITALIAN....67
FLEISCH KEICKLIN.............61
FRIED RICE - CHINESE.........67
FRIED RICE ORIENTAL..........57
GERMAN STUFFED PORK CHOPS....62
GERMAN-STYLE BRATWURST
   AND SAUERKRAUT............55
GREEK MOUSSAKA - LAMB AND
   BEEF DISH.................68
GRILLED CHICKEN TACOS........60
HUNGARIAN CABBAGE BAKE.......52
INDONESIAN-STYLE BEEF AND
   BANANAS...................69
IRISH BOILED CORNED BEEF
   DINNER....................50
IRISH CORNED BEEF CURED IN
   A PLASTIC BAG..............50
IRISH CORNED BEEF CURED IN
   THE REFRIGERATOR...........49
IRISH LAMB OR MUTTON STEW.....71
IRISH LAMB STEW.............73
ISABELLE'S OLLIE BOLLEN........57
ITALIAN CHICKEN PARMESAN......58
KLUSKAS - POLISH RAW POTATO
   DUMPLINGS.................66
KNISHES.....................66
LA TOURTIERE - FRENCH MEAT
   PIE.......................53
MAHNDU - KOREAN EGG ROLL.....65
McGREW KRAUTBURGERS.........68
OLD-FASHIONED IRISH STEW......70
ORIENTAL EGG FOO YONG........71
ORIENTAL PORK FRIED RICE......71
ORIENTAL STEW...............72
PAUL'S SWEET AND SOUR
   CHICKEN WINGS.............58
PENNSYLVANIA DUTCH SWEET
   AND SOUR TURKEY...........60
POLISH GOEMPKI - PIGS IN
   BLANKETS..................57
POLYNESIAN CHICKEN...........57
QUESADILLAS WITH PICADILLO
   FILLING....................63
ROUMANIAN NOODLE
   CHARLOTTE.................75
SAUERBRATEN................63
SCRAMBLED EGGS WITH
   TOMATOES..................66
SOUFFLE DEMOULE,
   MOUSSELINE................76
SOUR CREAM ENCHILADAS........74
SPAETZLE....................73
SPANISH RICE................73
STIR-FRY BEEF AND
   VEGETABLES - CHINESE.......52
STIR-FRY CHICKEN LIVERS.......53

STIR-FRY WITH BEAN SPROUTS 54
STUFFED CABBAGE ROLLS - A
   LA ITALIANO 51
STUFFED TOFU 61
SWEET-SOUR RED CABBAGE 75
TOAD-IN-THE-HOLE - ENGLISH 70
TOMASO SELLENTINO LA SAGNA 56
WILD RICE/WHITE RICE GROUND
   BEEF CASSEROLE. 75
WON TONS - CHINESE. 56

COOKIES, BARS, CAKES
ABERGAVENNY NUTS - ENGLISH 80
ANISE DROPS - GERMAN 78
ANISE DROPS - GERMANY 78
BOUREKAKIA - GREEK WALNUT
   ROLL 81
CANADIAN BARS. 85
CARDAMOM COOKIES - SWEDISH. . . . 83
CHINESE COOKIES 84
COCONUT BALLS -
   SWITZERLAND 79
COFFEE KISSES - FRENCH. 81
CREAMY PUFF KISSES -
   HUNGARY 80
CZECHOSLOVAKIAN COOKIES   . . . 84
DANISH APPLE CAKE. 90
FATTIGMAND. 88
GERMAN COOKIES 82
GORO - NORWAY. 88
IRISH DROP COOKIES 84
ISRAEL 79
ITALIAN COFFEE CAKE. 90
JABLKA NA SZARLOTKE - APPLE
   CAKE FILLING. 90
KRUM BAKE 86
KRUM BAKE - NORWEGIAN 86
KRUM BAKER. 86
KRUMBAKA. 85
KRUMBAKE. 89
LARGE RAISIN BUTTERMILK
   SCONES - ENGLISH 87
LES MADELEINES 78
MEXICO WEDDING CAKES 78
NEW YEAR CAKES (GALETTES) -
   BELGIUM 80
ORIENTAL RICE KRISPY BARS. 85
POLISH WAFERS - POLAND 82
RAISIN SCONES - ENGLISH 87
ROSETTES - NORWAY 88
ROSQUITAS PARA TE - LITTLE
   WREATHS FOR TEA 81
SANDBAKKELS. 89
SANDBAKKELSE 83
SANDBAKKELSE 84
SHORTBREAD - DENMARK 80
SPRITZ. 83
SWEDISH HEIRLOOM COOKIES 84
SZARLOTKA - APPLE CAKE. 89
TEA COOKIES - RUSSIA. 82
WAR CAKE 89

CREPES AND PANCAKES
CREPES. 92
PAUUUKAKKO 94
POTATO PANCAKES. 93
POTATO PANCAKES - PLACKI
   KARTOFLANE 92
SMOREN - PANCAKE CRUMBLES 92
SWEDISH PANCAKES 93
SWEDISH PANCAKES - PLATTER 94
WELSH PARSLEY PANCAKES -
   CREMPOG LAS. 93

DESSERTS
APPLE CAKE WITH VANILLA
   SAUCE - SWEDISH 95
BEIGNET AUX POMMES. 96
BREAD AND BUTTER PUDDING -
   ENGLISH 97
CARAMEL PECAN PUMPKIN PIE -
   IRISH 100
KULTA - VELLIS 96
MOUSSE AU CHOCOLAT 97
NANA'S HOLIDAY RAISIN
   PUDDING. 99
RASPBERRY SYLLABUB -
   ENGLISH 99
RICE CUSTARD PUDDING -
   RISGRYNSKAKA 95
ROMMEGRAT 97
ROMMEGROT - NORWEGIAN
   CREAM MUSH 97
SERNIK - CHEESECAKE. 100
SWEDISH RICE PUDDING 99
SWEDISH RICE PUDDING 98
TOSCAS - SWEDISH TARTS. 95
TRIFLE - ENGLISH. 98

FISH
BAKED LUTEFISH 102
LAKSLOOTA - FINNISH 102
PICKLED FISH - GERMAN 102
TUNA ZUCCHINI SUISSE -
   FRENCH. 102

LASAGNA AND PIZZA
BEEFY MEXICAN LASAGNA. 104
ESKIMO PIZZAS. 104
FEISTA LASAGNA. 104
MARIE'S EASY LASAGNA. 106
MEXICAN PIZZAS. 105
SPAGHETTI PIE 105

LEFSE
LEFSE 108
LEFSE 108
LEFSE - SCANDINAVIAN. 107
POTATO LEFSE. 107
TINA'S FAVORITE LEFSE 107

MEATS
CHORIZO. 114
DANISH MEAT BALLS 110
HUNGARIAN VENISON ROAST 112

NORWEGIAN MEAT BALLS - KJOD
KAGER.........................111
NORWEGIAN SYLTA.................114
PIGS FEET SULTANA...............110
POLISH EASTER BROTH.............112
POLYNESIAN MEAT BALLS..........111
PORK CHOPS - HUNGARIAN
STYLE 110
PORK CHOW MEIN.................113
POTAGE A LA RUSSE..............109
SUNDAY BEEF ROAST -
SONDAGSSTEK 109
VIENNESE HAMBURGER 112

PASTA
AFRO-ITALIAN-AMERICAN
SPAGHETTI SAUCE 115
GNOCCHI - ITALIAN DUMPLINGS 115
ITALIAN SAUCE WITH MEATBALLS...115
ITALIAN SPAGHETTI SAUCE 116
PASTA VAZZOO 116
SPAGHETTI SAUCE...............116

SALADS
GERMAN POTATO SALAD..........118
HOT GERMAN POTATO SALAD 118
SIENISALAATLE - FINNISH FRESH
MUSHROOM SALAD 119
SLOVENIAN POTATO SALAD 118

SAUCES
QUICK PLUM SAUCE - CHINESE 120
SWEET AND SOUR SAUCE -
CHINESE STYLE.................120

SOUPS
CABBAGE-KRAUT STUFFING FOR
PIEROGI......................122
CHEESE SOUP - GERMAN DISH 121
CLEAR BEET SOUP - CZYSTY
BARSZCZ CZERWONY 122
SAUERKRAUT SOUP -
KAPUSNIAK...................122
TOFU SOUP 121
WILD RICE SOUP 121

VEGETABLES
CABBAGE MARINARA - GERMAN....123
CANTONESE VEGETABLES 124
COLCANNON - IRISH 124
PIECZARKI MARYNOWANE -
PICKLED MUSHROOMS 125
PIECZARKI NADZIEWANE -
BAKED STUFFED MUSHROOMS...125
RED CABBAGE....................123
STIR-FRIED MIXED VEGETABLES ...125
STUFFED VEGETABLES - GREEK
STYLE 123
TERIYAKI-SAUCED VEGETABLES -
ORIENTAL 124

DRESSINGS AND SALADS

APRICOT SALAD 128
BEEF-POTATO SALAD 128
BONNIE'S FRENCH DRESSING......127
BUTTERMILK COOKIE SALAD......129
CABBAGE-FRUIT SALAD..........129
CHERRY JELLO SALAD 129
CHICKEN AND CELERY SALAD 130
CHICKEN SALAD 129
CHICKEN SALAD 130
CHICKEN SALAD 130
CHICKEN SALAD SUPREME 131
CHICKEN-ORANGE SALAD.........131
CHOCOLATE PUDDING SALAD 131
COLESLAW DRESSING............127
CORNED BEEF SALAD............132
DEE'S THOUSAND ISLAND
DRESSING.....................127
EASY SALAD 132
FLORENTINE SALAD.............132
FRENCH DRESSING 127
FRENCH DRESSING 128
FRUIT SALAD...................133
FRUIT SALAD...................133
FRUIT SALAD...................133
HOLIDAY SALAD 134
JELLO-APPLESAUCE SALAD 134
MEDITERRANEAN RICE SALAD 134
MID-EAST SALAD................134
PASTA SALAD..................135
PASTA VEGETABLE SALAD 135
POTATO SALAD 135
QUICK MIX SALAD 135
SALAD 132
SAUERKRAUT SALAD 136
SESAME SOY DRESSING.........128
SEVEN-UP SALAD 136
SHRIMP MACARONI SALAD........136
SUMMER SALAD 137
TUNA LUNCHEON SALAD 137
WILTED LETTUCE SALAD.........137

MICROWAVE

HOW TO GET THE BEST FROM
YOUR MICROWAVE 139
MICROWAVE HINTS...............142

**APPETIZERS, SNACKS, AND
CANDIES**
BACON WANDS 149
CARAMEL CORN 143
CARAMEL NUT ROLLS...........150
CHEESE AND ZUCCHINI SNACKS ...146
CREAM CHEESE MINTS..........154
CREATE-A-HOT-DIP.............147
CRUNCHY TOFFEE IN THE
MICROWAVE 154
ELAINE'S MICROWAVE CARAMEL
CORN.........................143
GARLIC WALNUT NIBBLERS 146
GRANOLA 143

MICROWAVE CARAMEL CORN 144
MICROWAVE CHEX PARTY MIX. 145
MICROWAVE DIVINITY. 150
MICROWAVE PEANUT BRITTLE. 151
MICROWAVE PEANUT BRITTLE. 151
MINI PIZZAS 149
MUSHROOM-CHEESE CANAPES. 149
NO FAIL FUDGE. 153
NO-FAIL FUDGE. 152
NO-FUSS CARAMEL CORN 145
ORIENTAL MEATBALLS 148
PEANUT BRITTLE 151
POTATO STICKS. 144
SPECIAL FUDGE SAUCE 152
SPICY FRANKS 146
SUGARED SPICED NUTS. 147
TASTES LIKE MORE PRETZELS 144
TOFFEE PIECES. 153
TWO-LAYER FUDGE IN THE
    MICROWAVE 153
VELVEETA FUDGE 152

SOUPS, SALADS,
    SANDWICHES,
    MISCELLANEOUS
BROCCOLI AND HAM SOUP 155
BROCCOLI SALAD. 156
CLAM CHOWDER. 155
DELUXE SCRAMBLED EGGS. 157
EASY REUBEN SANDWICHES. 157
MICROWAVE TOMATO SOUP 156
OATMEAL. 157
TACO SALAD 156

FISH, POULTRY, MEATS
BAKED CHICKEN A LA KING. 160
BAKED FISH 159
CREAM SAUCE 158
EASY BEEF STEW. 168
EASY CHICKEN RICE 161
FISH AND SEAFOOD. 158
FIVE MINUTE PORK CHOP 163
FOUR BEAN HOTDISH 167
GLAZED CHRISTMAS HAM 163
GOLD NUGGET BEEF LOAF 167
LASAGNA 168
MICROWAVE COOKING. 170
MICROWAVE MEAT BALL STEW 168
MOCK CHOW MEIN. 166
MUSHROOM BEEF RICE 169
PORK BARBEQUE SEASONING 164
PORK CHOPS WITH STUFFING 163
QUICK CHICKEN DINNER 160
ROAST TURKEY. 162
SAUSAGE-BREAD STUFFING. 162
STIR-FRY TOMATO BEEF 169
STUFFED GREEN PEPPERS 166
STUFFED PEPPER POT 166
SUMMER LASAGNA 159
SWEET AND SOUR MEATBALLS. 165
SWEET AND SOUR PORK. 164
SWEET AND SOUR TURKEY. 161
SWEET-SOUR MEAT BALLS 164
TUNA CASHEW CASSEROLE 159

TURKEY NOODLE BAKE 161

VEGETABLES
AU GRATIN POTATOES 173
BAKED POTATOES 173
CARROT CASSEROLE 172
CHEESY BROCCOLI CASSEROLE . . . 171
CHEESY BROCCOLI ONION
    CASSEROLE 171
CHILI POTATOES 174
CREAMY CABBAGE. 172
DELUXE POTATOES 174
DILLED ZUCCHINI 177
FANTASTIC POTATO SALAD 175
FROSTED CAULIFLOWER 172
GARDEN VEGETABLE
    CASSEROLE 178
HARVARD BEETS. 171
HOT GERMAN POTATO SALAD 176
HOT GERMAN POTATO SALAD 176
MICROWAVE SCALLOPED
    POTATOES 175
PARMESAN POTATOES 175
POTATO LASAGNA. 174
POTATOES-PARMESAN CHEESE 174
SUMMER GARDEN TREAT 177
VEGETARIANS DINNER. 177

DESSERTS
APPLE DESSERT 179
BAKED APPLES 179
BAKED APPLES 179
BRAN BARS 183
CHEESECAKE FONDUE 184
DELUXE RICE CEREAL BARS. 183
EASY RHUBARB CRISP 181
EASY RICE PUDDING 180
EASY RICE PUDDING. 181
FIVE MINUTE CHEESE CAKE 184
FROSTING. 183
FUDGE BROWNIE PIE 186
HOW TO MICROWAVE PUMPKIN. 182
IMPOSSIBLE FRENCH APPLE PIE . . . 186
LEMON MERINGUE PIE 187
MICROWAVE LEMON BARS 183
MICROWAVE PIE CRUST 186
MICROWAVE PUMPKIN 182
ORANGE ZUCCHINI CAKE. 185
PEACH CRISP 180
PEACHY BUTTER BRICKLE CAKE . . . 184
PINEAPPLE DOWNSIDE-UP CAKE . . . 185
PUMPKIN PIE. 188
RHUBARB CRISP. 182
SPICED PEACHES. 180
SWIRLED AMARETTO
    CHEESECAKE. 181

POTPOURRI

DIPS AND HORS D'OEUVRES
CHEESE BALL 192
CHICKEN CANAPES 190
CHICKEN NIBLETS 190

CRAB PUFFS 192
DIP 189
GALA SOUR CREAM DIP 189
GARLIC MUSHROOMS 192
HOT CRAB SPREAD 191
JALAPENO CHIP DIP 191
MEXICAN DIP 190
SHRIMP AND CRAB DIP 189
SUPER SEAFOOD SPREAD 191
TERESA'S CORNED BEEF
   CHEESE BALL 191
TERIYAKI BEEF STRIPS
   APPETIZER 192
VEGETABLE DIP 189

SOUPS
CORN AND CHEESE SOUP 195
E-Z CHEESE BROCCOLI SOUP 195
GOLDEN CREAM SOUP 195
HURRY-HEARTY SOUPS 194
POTATO SOUP 194
SOUP COMBINATIONS 194
SOUP TRICKS 194

VEGETABLES
BBQ POTATOES 201
BEETS IN ORANGE SAUCE 197
BROCCOLI BAKE 200
BROCCOLI SOUFFLE 200
CALIFORNIA POTATOES 197
CARROT PENNIES 197
CREOLE CORN 198
GREEN ONION PIE 200
HEALTH DRESSING 197
PAM'S YUMMY CORN 198
POTATO ONION BAKE 200
SPINACH CHEESE BAKE 199
SWEET POTATO PIE 198
SWISS VEGETABLE 199
TWICE-BAKED YAMS 198

CASSEROLES
BAKED BEANS 202
BEEF BURGER SUPPER 210
BEEF TOMATO RICE STEW 207
BEEFY BUMWICHES 211
BROCCOLI AND HAM QUICHE 212
CELERY HOT DISH 202
CHICKEN CHOW MEIN 205
CHICKEN-WILD RICE CASSEROLE . . . 203
CHOW MEIN HOT DISH 205
COUNTRY GARDEN DINNER 207
EGG HOTDISH 212
FLUFFY WILD RICE 202
HAMBURGER HASH BROWN HOT
   DISH 208
HEARTY BEEF 'N POTATO
   CASSEROLE 209
HURRY-UP BAKED BEANS 202
IMPOSSIBLE TURKEY PIE 206
OVEN OMELET 212
PIZZA CASSEROLE 209
POTATO HOTDISH 208
SANDY'S LAZY DAY LASAGNE 209

SAUSAGE FILLED CREPES 211
SIX SOUP HOT DISH 207
SOUPER STROGANOFF 210
SPAGHETTI PIZZA 210
SPECIAL IDEAS 202
SURPRISE HOT DISH 208
TEN MINUTE DINNER 207
TURKEY LOAF 206
TURKEY STRATA 206
TURKEY WILD RICE CASSEROLE . . . 204
WILD RICE CASSEROLE 205
WILD RICE CASSEROLE 203
WILD RICE CASSEROLE 203
WILD RICE FISH CASSEROLE 204
WILD RICE PATTIES 204

MEATS
BAKED HAM-POTATO CASSEROLE . . . 219
BARB E. QUE PORK CHOPS 221
BEEF POT ROAST 213
BREAKFAST SAUSAGE 219
BROILED HAMBURGER 215
CALIFORNIA ROAST 213
COUNTRY HAM WITH RED EYE
   GRAVY 219
CUBED STEAK HAYSTACKS 214
DOWN SOUTH BARBEQUE 220
GIBLET GRAVY 216
GOURMET PORK CHOPS 221
HOMEMADE SHAKE AND BAKE
   FOR CHICKEN 217
HOMEMADE TACO SEASONING
   MIX 217
LAZY DAY STROGANOFF 215
LEMON-MARINATED CHUCK
   ROAST 213
LIVER STEAK 214
MEAT BALLS 214
ORANGE GLAZED SPARERIBS 220
PORCUPINES 214
PORK CHOPS AND POTATOES 220
PORK CHOPS WITH CHICKEN
   RICE SOUP 221
RYP'S MOCK-FILLET MIGNON 215
SAUCE FOR CHICKEN OR PORK
   CHOPS 216
SKILLET-GLAZED HAM FOR TWO 218
SLOPPY RIBS 220
SPAGHETTI SAUCE 217
SPAGHETTI SAUCE . . . . , . 218
SPAGHETTI SAUCE 218
SUPER BOWL SUNDAY
   SANDWICHES 215
TERIYAKI MARINADE FOR BEEF,
   CHICKEN, OR PORK 216
TWICE-COOKED NOODLES WITH
   PORK 222

POULTRY
BAKED CHICKEN BREAST 223
BAKED CHICKEN DRUMMIES 225
BAKED CHICKEN WITH SAUCE 224
BARBEQUE CHICKEN 224
BROILED CHICKEN BREASTS 223

CHICKEN HOT DISH 224
CHICKEN LASAGNA MADE WITH
  UNCOOKED NOODLES 226
DUCK. 225
GRILLED CHICKEN TACOS 226
MRS. HOVIS' FRIED CHICKEN 223
TOMATO SAUCE AND CHICKEN -
  ITALIAN. 225
UNFORGETTABLE CHICKEN
  WINGS 224

FISH
CRAB LASAGNA. 229
ESCALLOPED SALMON OR
  SALMON LOAF 228
FISH MARINADE 229
GARY'S SALMON FILLETS. 227
LOBSTER TAILS ON THE GRILL. . . . 227
RICE AND SALMON BALLS 227
SALMON CUSTARD CASSEROLE 227
SALMON LOAF. 228
SALMON LOAF. 228
SALMON STEAKS 227

BREADS
BAKED FRENCH TOAST. 230
BATTER RHUBARB BREAD 237
BRAN MUFFINS APLENTY. 232
BUTTERED BREAD CRUMBS 230
BUTTERHORNS 233
CHEESE BUBBLE BREAD 235
CINNAMON ROLLS 233
COWBOY BREAD 236
CRANBERRY NUT BREAD 236
DATE LOAF 237
FLAT BREAD. 232
GARLIC CROUTONS 230
GOLDEN CROWN ROLLS. 234
HOMEMADE CROUTONS 230
HONEY WHOLE WHEAT BREAD 238
JAM AND CHEESE LOAF
  MORNING BREAD 235
KANIP - STRIPS OF DUMPLINGS 231
MANDARIN ORANGE BREAD. 236
MUFFINS. 232
PERFECT PASTA 231
POPOVERS THAT POP 231
POTATO PANCAKES. 230
RHUBARB ROLLS 234
SOUR CREAM COFFEE CAKE. 234
SOUTHERN GAL BISCUITS 233
STRAWBERRY BREAD 237

BARS
APPLE OATMEAL BARS 241
APPLE ROLY POLY 242
APPLESAUCE BARS 241
BROWN SUGAR CHEWS 247
BROWNIES 244
BUTTERSCOTCH BARS 244
CHOCO-WALNUT BARS 243
CHOCOLATE CHIP SPICE BARS. 247
COCA-COLA BARS. 239
CREAM CHEESE BARS 244

CRISPY DATE BARS 243
GOOEY CLUSTERS BARS 247
HELPFUL HINT. 239
NO BAKE GRAHAM CRACKER
  BARS 240
ORANGE-FROSTED
  WALNUT-SPICE BARS 245
PEANUT BUTTER BARS. 246
PEANUT BUTTER-CHOCOLATE
  BARS 246
PECAN PIE BARS 240
PRIZE BUTTER BARS. 246
RICE KRISPIES CARAMEL BARS 239
RUM RAISIN CUSTARD BARS 245
RYAN'S FAVORITE CHOCOLATE
  MINT BROWNIES 242
SUPER GOOD APPLE BARS 240

FROSTINGS AND CAKES
BANANA NUT CAKE 252
BEST RUM CAKE EVER. 249
BLACKBERRY CAKE 252
CHOCOLATE CHIP FROSTING. 249
CHOCOLATE ZUCCHINI CAKE. 250
FROSTED CHIFFON CAKE. 253
GINGERBREAD WITH
  CHOCOLATE CHIPS. 253
LAZY DAISY CAKE 250
MILLIER NO-BAKE FRUIT CAKE 252
NUTRITIOUS DATE CAKE. 250
OLD COUNTRY BUFFETS HOT
  FUDGE PUDDING CAKE 251
QUICK CHOCOLATE FROSTING 249
SUPER GERMAN CHOCOLATE
  AND COCONUT CAKE. 251

COOKIES
AUNT ROSE'S GINGER COOKIES . . . 261
AUNT SARAH'S GINGER BALLS. 261
BITS 'O BRICKLE COOKIES. 256
CHOCOLATE ROCKIES 259
COCONUT AND DATE COOKIES. 257
CREAM WAFERS 254
CRISPY SUGAR COOKIES 260
DATE DROP COOKIES 258
DATE NUT BALLS 256
DEVILS FOOD DROP COOKIES 257
GINGER COOKIES. 261
GUMDROP OATMEAL COOKIES 255
MOLASSES COOKIES 262
MY MOST FAVORITE COOKIE 260
NO ROLL SUGAR COOKIES 258
OATMEAL SNACKS 260
100 GOOD COOKIES. 254
ORANGE CHEESE CHOCOLATE
  CHIP COOKIES. 259
PINEAPPLE-COCONUT DROPS 256
POWDERED SUGAR SPRITZ. 255
PUMPKIN COOKIES. 259
PUMPKIN COOKIES. 259
SALTED PEANUT CRISPS. 254
SOFT PUMPKIN COOKIES 255
SWIRLED LEMON COOKIES 258

XMAS COOKIES 257

PIES
COTTAGE CHEESE TARTS 263
CREAM CHEESE PIE CRUST 263
CRUSTLESS CUSTARD PIE 263
MOM'S SOUR CREAM APPLE PIE . . . 264
PIE CRUST 263
RASPBERRY, GOOSEBERRY,
  BLACKBERRY, OR CURRANT
  PIE 264
RHUBARB PIE 264
SOUR CREAM PIE 265

DESSERTS
AMAZING RHUBARB COBBLER 268
APPLE COBBLER 267
APPLE CRISP 266
APPLE FLAKE CRUNCH 267
BUTTERFINGER DESSERT 269
CHERRY CHEESECAKE 272
CHERRY DELIGHT 271
CHOCOLATE DE CREME
  DESSERT 270
CHRISTMAS APPLE SLICES 266
COUNTRY APPLE DESSERT 267
CUPCAKE CUSTARD 269
FROZEN PUMPKIN DESSERT 270
FRUIT DELIGHT 271
KIWI DELIGHT 270
LEMON DESSERT 271
LEMON FRUIT FREEZE 271
ORANGE FLUFF 270
ORANGE SAUCE - DESSERT 272
PEANUT BUTTER PARFAIT
  DESSERT 272
PINEAPPLE MACADAMIA CHEESE
  PIE 273
RHUBARB COBBLER 268
RHUBARB STRAWBERRY
  CRUNCH 268
RHUBARB TORTE 269
SPEEDY APPLESAUCE DESSERT . . . 266

JAMS AND JELLIES
BAKED CRANBERRIES 275
CHOKECHERRY SYRUP 274
CRANBERRY BUTTER 275
PEACH CONSERVE 274
RHUBARB JAM 275
RHUBARB JELLY 274
ZUCCHINI ORANGE JAM 274

PICKLES
MARINATED CUCUMBERS 276
OVERNIGHT PICKLES 277
PICKLED EGGS 276
REFRIGERATED PICKLES 276

DRINKS
A HEALTH DRINK 278
APPLE JUICE 278
FLAVORED MILK DRINKS 279
HOT APPLE CIDER 278

HOT MULLED CIDER 278
MELON COOLER 280
MEXICAN HOT CHOCOLATE 280
RHUBARB SLUSH 279
SUNSHINE WEDDING PUNCH 279
TOMATO JUICE 279

CANDY
BUTTER CRUNCH CANDY 283
CARAMELS 282
CARAMELS 282
CHOCOLATE MINTS 284
CLUB SODA CRACKER'S CANDY 281
DIVINITY 284
ENGLISH BUTTER TOFFEE 282
ENGLISH CHRISTMAS LOAF
  CANDY 286
ENGLISH TOFFEE 283
HOT FUDGE SAUCE 283
HUNGARY MAPLE CANDIED
  WALNUTS 285
PEANUT BUTTER FUDGE 285
PECAN FUDGE 283
PENUCHE CANDY 285
POPCORN BALLS 286
QUICK AND MILD CHOCOLATE
  CANDY 285
SOUR CREAM CANDY 284
SPICED PEANUTS SNACK 281
SUGAR AND SPICE PECANS 286
TRIPLE TREATS CANDY 281

HELPFUL HINTS

A BISCUIT TIP 291
AMAZING ANIMAL HINTS 341
BASIC SEASONINGS 291
BURNT AND SCORCHED PANS 290
CARPET CARE HINTS 337
CHEESE GUIDE 356
CLEANING HINTS 313
CLEVER CLOTHING HINTS 319
COFFEE FILTERS 292
COOK WITH HONEY 292
COOKING SUGGESTIONS 289
COOKING TIPS 288
COOKING TIPS SUBSTITUTES 288
CROWD PLEASERS 348
DAILY CALORIE NEEDS FOR
  WOMEN AND MEN 361
DEFINITELY DESSERT 296
EVERYBODY'S FAVORITES 299
FANTASTIC FURNITURE HINTS 330
FOOD FRESHNESS 309
FOR THE BIRDS 342
FREEZING HERBS 292
FRESH FROM THE OVEN 295
GARDENING - GREEN THUMB
  HINTS 344
GENERAL CLEANING TIPS 339
HELPFUL HINTS 323
HELPFUL HINTS 328
HELPFUL HINTS 321

HELPFUL HINTS 292
HELPFUL HINTS 290
HINTS 288
HINTS - FOR THE BIRDS. 343
HOUSEHOLD HINTS 287
HOW TO CORRECT MISTAKES IN
    COOKING. 300
HOW TO USE CLEANING FLUID. 322
KITCHEN CLEAN-ER-UPERS 306
MEASURE OF FOOD PER
    PURCHASING UNIT 358
MEDICINAL 294
NAVY BEANS FOR SOUP. 291
NEW DESIRABLE WEIGHTS. 360
NUTRITION TIP 292
PERFECT PARTY PLEASERS. 297
PLANNING FOR A CROWD 349
POTPOURRI 298
PREPARING BEANS TO COOK
    FOR A RECIPE. 291
REMOVE STAIN FROM HANDS 291
SEASONING GUIDE. 351
SHORTCUTS IN THE KITCHEN 302
SKIN AND BODY CARE HINTS 333
STAIN REMOVAL HINTS 317
SUBSTITUTIONS FOR COOKING 288
SUPER SOUPS AND
    SCRUMPTIOUS SALADS. 299
TABASCO. 288
TEMPTING MAIN DISH IDEAS. 294
TERMS USED IN RECIPES 293
TERRIFIC CAR HINTS. 336
THE CODED LOAD 287
THE STEPS. 323
THREE SOLUTIONS TO REMOVE
    WHITE WATER RINGS AND
    SPOTS 323
TIMETABLE FOR ROASTING
    TURKEYS. 350
TO AVOID SCRAPING CARROTS. 291
WEIGHTS AND MEASURES. 346
WEIGHTS AND MEASURES IN
    THE METRIC SYSTEM. 346
WHAT CAUSES RINGS 322
YIELDS, EQUIVALENTS &
    SUBSTITUTIONS. 352

HEART HEALTH

MAIN DISHES

ALICE'S BAKED SCALLOPS. 392
BAKED CHICKEN. 383
BARBECUE ON A BUN. 368
BARBECUED PORK CHOPS. 386
BEAN SPROUT TUNA CHOW
    MEIN. 395
BEEF BOURGUIGNON 372
BEEF KABOBS 373
BRAISED FISH 393
BRAISED SIRLOIN TIPS 372
BREADED PORK CHOPS 386
BROILED FISH ROLL-UPS 394
BURGUNDY BEEF 371

CHICKEN A LA KING. 382
CHICKEN AND BROCCOLI WITH
    MUSHROOM SAUCE 380
CHICKEN BREAST CASSEROLE. 379
CHICKEN DINNER IN THE POT 381
CHICKEN DIVAN. 383
CHICKEN FRIED STEAK. 381
CHICKEN GUMBO 379
CHICKEN JAMBALAYA. 380
CHICKEN MANDARIN 379
CHICKEN POT PIE. 384
CHICKEN SALAD CASSEROLE 385
CHICKEN TERIYAKI WITH
    VEGETABLES 377
CHICKEN WITH APRICOT GLAZE. . . . 380
CHINESE BEEF SKILLET 377
CHINESE CHICKEN WITH
    PEPPERS AND ONIONS 378
CHINESE FLANK STEAK. 376
CRISPY BAKED CHICKEN 378
CURRIED LAMB 391
CURRIED TURKEY WITH WATER
    CHESTNUTS 387
EASY LASAGNA 398
ENCHILADA BAKE 397
FLOUNDER FILLETS IN FOIL. 392
HALIBUT RAGOUT. 394
HAM ROLL-UP 385
HAWAIIAN HAM 385
HOMEMADE SAUSAGE. 369
HUNGARIAN GOULASH 374
IN A HURRY - CHICKEN CURRY 383
LAMB CHOPS ORIENTAL 391
LAMB-STUFFED CABBAGE. 390
LAZY BEEF CASSEROLE 375
LEMON PEPPER MUSHROOMS 367
LOUISIANA CREOLE ROAST 387
MACARONI-BEEF SKILLET
    SUPPER. 374
MARINADE FOR VENISON, ELK,
    OR ANTELOPE 397
MARINATED STEAK. 373
MINIATURE MEATBALLS 367
MOCK SAUSAGE PATTIES 370
MODIFIED BEEF STROGANOFF 372
MUSHROOM BAKED SOLE 395
OVEN-FRIED FILLETS 393
PAUPIETTES DE VEAU. 389
PIZZA. 369
PIZZA SANDWICHES. 368
RICOTTA LASAGNA SWIRLS 370
SALMON-BROCCOLI CASSEROLE . . . 396
SHREDDED CHICKEN WITH
    GREEN PEPPER AND
    CARROTS 382
SO-GOOD POACHED FILLETS. 393
SOUTHERN MEAT LOAF. 371
STUFFED BEEF ROLL-UPS 371
STUFFED FISH BEACHCOMBER. 392
SUKIYAKI. 375
SWEET-AND-SOUR PORK. 386
TUNA MACARONI CASSEROLE. 396
TUNA RING. 397
TURKEY CHOP SUEY. 378

TURKEY MOUSSE 388
VEAL COLUMBO 388
VEAL PAPRIKA 388
VEAL SCALLOPINI 390
VEAL STEW WITH FENNEL 390
VEAL WITH ARTICHOKES 389
WILD RICE WITH MUSHROOMS 368
WONDERFUL MUSHROOMS 367
ZUCCHINI CHEESE CASSEROLE 374

SALADS AND DRESSINGS
ANNA'S BEAN SPROUT SALAD 399
BEAN SPROUT SALAD 400
BEET SALAD WITH RED ONIONS . . . 406
BLENDER MAYONNAISE 408
CHICKEN AND RICE SALAD 401
CHICKEN-VEGETABLE SALAD 403
CHINESE CHICKEN SALAD 401
COOKED SALAD DRESSING 406
COOL CUKE SALAD 400
COUNTRY MACARONI SALAD 402
CUCUMBER AND YOGURT DIP 411
CUCUMBERS IN MOCK SOUR
   CREAM 411
DILLED SHRIMP SALAD 402
EGG SALAD 410
FRESH GREEN BEAN SALAD 404
FRESH STRAWBERRY SPREAD 410
FRESH VEGETABLE SALAD BOWL . . . 405
GARDEN RICE SALAD 404
GRAPEFRUIT AND ORANGE
   SALAD 399
GUACAMOLE 405
HERBED BAKED TOMATOES 411
HERBED SEASONING 407
HOMEMADE EGG SUBSTITUTE 409
HONEY-POPPY SEED SALAD
   DRESSING 409
LOW-SODIUM,
   LOW-CHOLESTEROL MUSTARD
   DRESSING 408
LOW-SODIUM,
   LOW-CHOLESTEROL SALAD
   DRESSING 409
LOWFAT, LOW-SODIUM
   CASSEROLE SAUCE MIX 409
LUNCHEON TUNA SALAD 402
MACARONI SALAD RICOTTA 404
MARINATED OKRA SALAD 399
MOM'S FROZEN FRUIT SALAD 403
PICKLED MUSHROOM SALAD 400
SALT SUBSTITUTE 410
SAUERKRAUT SALAD 399
SKINNY DIP 407
SOUR CREAM 408
SPECIAL GREEN GODDESS
   DRESSING 407
SPICED CHEESE 411
SUGARLESS THREE BEAN
   SALAD 405
TOMATO DRESSING 407
TURKEY MACARONI SALAD 402
ZERO CALORIE DRESSING 406

VEGETABLES
AVERY ISLAND CELERY 413
BEAN SPROUTS PIQUANT 416
CURRIED CELERY 413
DEVILED BEETS 414
DILLED GREEN BEANS 415
EGGPLANT SPAGHETTI SAUCE 416
GREEN BEANS OREGANO 415
LAYERED VEGETABLES
   VINAIGRETTE 415
MELENZANA ALLA GRIGLIA -
   BROILED EGGPLANT 416
PANNED BROCCOLI 414
SAVORY SPINACH 413
STIR-FRY SPINACH 414

DESSERTS, CAKES, COOKIES, PIES
AUNT EMMA'S SHOO-FLY PIE 428
CHOCOLATE FONDUE 417
CHOCOLATE INDULGENCE 429
CHOCOLATE PUDDING 418
CINNAMON COFFEE CAKE 425
DENVER CHOCOLATE PUDDING
   CAKE 421
DOUGHNUT PUFFS 425
EASY APPLE CAKE 423
GINGER OAT COOKIES 426
LAYERED FRUIT YOGURT
   PUDDING 418
LEMON SAUCE 417
LOW-CHOLESTEROL COOKIES 428
LOW-SODIUM,
   LOW-CHOLESTEROL APPLE
   CRUNCH 421
LOW-SODIUM,
   LOW-CHOLESTEROL
   APPLESAUCE CUPCAKES 423
LOW-SODIUM,
   LOW-CHOLESTEROL BAKED
   APPLE DESSERT 420
LOW-SODIUM,
   LOW-CHOLESTEROL BANANA
   CUPCAKES 423
LOW-SODIUM,
   LOW-CHOLESTEROL
   BUTTERSCOTCH BROWNIES 427
LOW-SODIUM,
   LOW-CHOLESTEROL
   CHOCOLATE SAUCE 418
LOW-SODIUM,
   LOW-CHOLESTEROL LEMON
   CUPCAKES 424
LOW-SODIUM,
   LOW-CHOLESTEROL OATMEAL
   RAISIN COOKIES 427
LOW-SODIUM,
   LOW-CHOLESTEROL ORANGE
   SAUCE 417
LOW-SODIUM,
   LOW-CHOLESTEROL PEACH
   CRUNCH 421

LOW-SODIUM, LOW-CHOLESTEROL PEANUT BUTTER COOKIES.............. 428
LOW-SODIUM, LOW-CHOLESTEROL PUMPKIN CUSTARD...................... 430
LOW-SODIUM, LOW-CHOLESTEROL RHUBARB CRUNCH 421
LOW-SODIUM, LOW-CHOLESTEROL SUGAR COOKIES........................ 427
MASTER MIX QUICK PEACH COBBLER 425
NUTTY CRANBERRY PIE........... 429
PEACHY DESSERT SAUCE 417
PINEAPPLE DEEP-DISH DESSERT ... 419
QUICK ORANGE STREUSEL CAKE 424
RAISIN OATMEAL COOKIES........ 428
RASPBERRY CHIFFON PIE 430
RHUBARB BARS 426
RHUBARB CRISP.................. 420
SF LOW-CHOLESTEROL TWO-CRUST PIE CRUST 431
STRAWBERRY FROZEN DESSERT... 419
WHOLE WHEAT APPLESAUCE CAKE OR CUPCAKES............. 422
WILLIAMSBURG ORANGE-WINE CAKE 422
YOGURT SPICE CAKE 420

SOUPS
BEEF-BARLEY VEGETABLE SOUP ... 434
COLD AVOCADO SOUP 433
CREAMY ASPARAGUS SOUP 432
FIVE-MINUTE SOUP 436
FRUIT SOUP..................... 433
GREEN SPLIT PEA SOUP 433
LENTIL SOUP.................... 432
MINESTRONE SOUP.............. 436
SALAD BOWL SOUP.............. 432
TOMATO BOUILLON................ 435
TOMATO CORN SOUP............. 435
VEGETABLE BISQUE.............. 434
VEGETABLE SOUP 435
YELLOW SQUASH SOUP 433

PANCAKES, WAFFLES, MUFFINS, BREADS
APPLE-BRAN BREAKFAST MUFFINS 439
APPLESAUCE BREAD.............. 440
BANANA BREAD 442
BASIC BREAD 441
CHICKEN CREPES................. 438
CINNAMON BREAD 442
CURRANT BREAD 443
DILLY BREAD 441
FLUFFY COTTAGE CHEESE BLINTZES 438
FRENCH TOAST.................. 437
FRUIT LOAF 444
HEALTH BREAD 440

OAT BRAN MUFFINS.............. 439
OATMEAL BREAD................. 442
OATMEAL-BUTTERMILK PANCAKES 437
ORANGE BRAN MUFFINS 439
PECAN LOAF 444
PUMPKIN-PECAN BREAD.......... 443
SF LOW-CHOLESTEROL BAKING POWDER BISCUITS.............. 440
WHEAT GERM PANCAKES 437
WHOLE WHEAT AND SOY WAFFLES..................... 437

MISCELLANEOUS HINTS AND DIET SUGGESTIONS
HOW TO DECREASE YOUR CHOLESTEROL AND FAT INTAKE........................ 451
LOW FAT - LOW CHOLESTEROL RECIPE MODIFICATIONS.......... 450
LOWFAT - LOW-CHOLESTEROL - LOW CALORIE FOOD 446
MENU COMPARISON.............. 452
MIAMI HEART INSTITUTE DIET...... 453
RESTRICTING SALT IN YOUR DIET 447
SALT SUBSTITUTE............... 449
SUGGESTED SUBSTITUTES 448
TIPS FOR ADAPTING RECIPES FOR HEART HEALTH............ 445

DIABETIC DELIGHTS

APPETIZERS AND BEVERAGES
CRUNCHY CEREAL SNACK MIX..... 455
EGGNOG FOR DIABETICS.......... 456
FROZEN BANANA ROCKETS........ 455
HOT COCOA MIX................. 456
ORANGE JULI................... 456
SPICY VEGETABLE DIP 455

SOUPS
CLAM CHOWDER................. 458
GOLDEN CREAM SOUP........... 457
GOLDEN VEGETABLE SOUP........ 457
LO-CAL VEGETABLE SOUP 458
MY FAVORITE VEGETABLE BEEF SOUP 457
WEIGHT WATCHER SOUP 458

SALADS
BEV'S SUPER SUMMER SALAD 461
CHEESE PINEAPPLE SALAD........ 462
CHICKEN SALAD 461
DIABETIC SALAD DRESSING....... 459
EASY LOW CALORIE MAYONNAISE 459
MACARONI SALAD SUPREME....... 463
POTATO SALAD 461
SAUERKRAUT SALAD.............. 460
SEVEN LAYER SALAD............. 460
SUMMERTIME SALAD.............. 462
SUNSHINE GELATIN 459

TUNA SALAD 460

MAIN DISHES
BEST LASAGNA IN THE WORLD! 467
CASSEROLE SAUCE MIX 464
CHEESE STUFFED SHELLS 465
CHEESEBURGER PIE 466
CRAB FETTUCINE 466
QUICK VEGETARIAN CHILI 467
TURKEY GOULASH 466
TURKEY POT PIE 464

DESSERTS, COOKIES, CAKES
BABY RUTH BAR 477
BANANA PUDDING 472
BROWNIES: A BAKER'S TWO
    DOZEN 477
CHOCOLATE MOUSSE 468
CHOCOLATE SMUNCHIES 475
CREAMY GELATIN DESSERT 468
DIABETIC ANGEL FOOD-FRUIT
    DESSERT 473
DIABETIC COOKIES 474
DIABETIC RICE PUDDING 471
DIETETIC SPONGE CAKE 480
EGG CUSTARD 471
GINGERBREAD COOKIES 476
GLORIFIED RICE 470
GUMDROP CHEWS 474
HAWAIIAN DELIGHT
    CHEESECAKE 469
HOLIDAY FRUITCAKE 478
HOLIDAY TAPIOCA PUDDING 472
LOW CALORIE SPONGE CAKE 479
MUNCHIES 477
OLD-FASHIONED BREAD
    PUDDING 472
PEANUT BUTTER COOKIES 475
PEANUT BUTTER COOKIES WITH
    NO SUGAR 475
PINEAPPLE BARS 476
PINEAPPLE CHEESECAKE 469
PINEAPPLE SNOW 473
PISTACHIO BLUEBERRY
    DESSERT 473
PUMPKIN CUSTARD 471
RAISIN NUT BALLS 474
RAISIN RICE PUDDING 470
RHUBARB CAKE 478
RICE PUDDING 470
SPICE CUPCAKES 479
STRAWBERRY COTTAGE
    CHEESECAKE 468

BREADS, PASTRIES, PIES
BANANA NUT BREAD 481
BRAN MUFFINS 481
CHOCOLATE PEANUT BUTTER
    PIE 484
LOW-CAL APPLE PIE 482
NEW ENGLAND APPLE PIE 483
NO SUGAR APPLE PIE 482
PASTRY FOR ONE-CRUST PIE 482
POTATO LEFSE 481

PUMPKIN PIE 482
RAISIN PIE 484
REESE'S PEANUT BUTTER PIE 485
STRAWBERRY YOGURT PIE 484
SUGAR-LESS APPLE PIE 483
SUGAR-LESS PEACH PIE 484

GLUTEN FREE

GLUTEN FREE PRODUCT TIPS

MAIN DISHES
BAKED FISH-VEGETABLE DINNER . . . 498
CHICKEN WITH FUN SEE 501
CHICKEN WITH VEGETABLES 500
CHICKEN-RICE DISH 494
CHOCOLATE CRUMB CRUST 496
CHOW MEIN CASSEROLE 504
CONFETTI RICE AND CHEESE 497
CORN CHOWDER 502
CORN MEAL CREPES 498
CORN OYSTERS 506
FRUITED PORK CHOPS 503
GOLDEN OVEN-FRIED CHICKEN 502
ITALIAN BROCCOLI AND
    MACARONI 497
LASAGNA 494
MICROWAVE MEATLOAF 501
MINA DE ESPINACA Y TOMAT 495
MIXED VEGETABLE CASSEROLE 496
OVEN OMELET 505
PARTY STUFFED TOMATOES 498
POTATOES - GRATIN DAUPHINOIS . . . 497
RICE ALA DONNA 506
RICE SOUFFLE 494
SALMON-RICE PIE 504
SAUCE MIX (DRY) FOR
    CASSEROLE 496
SHRIMP MOLD 503
SLOW-COOKED GLAZED
    CARROTS 505
SPECIAL AU GRATIN POTATOES 500
STIR-FRY 504
SWEET POTATOES IN ORANGE
    CUPS 499
TACO-HAMBURGER CASSEROLE 495
TUNA RICE PATTIES 496
TURKEY RICE SALAD 503
ZUCCHINI PIZZA CRUST 505

SALADS
BLUEBERRY SALAD 511
BROCCOLI SALAD 511
CALIENTE SALAD 512
CHRISTMAS FRUIT SALAD 510
CRANBERRY MOLDED SALAD 509
CRANBERRY SALAD 511
EMERALD ISLE MOLD 510
FRISCO CHICKEN SALAD 508
HIGH RISE SALAD 507
IN-THE-PINK SALAD 509
MINTED FRUIT SALAD 510
PEAS PIZZICATO 507

PINK CHAMPAGNE SALAD.........512
PIZZA SALAD 507
RIGATINI SALAD..................508
SALAD MANDARIN................509
TACO SALAD 508
WALDORF SALAD 509

BREADS, MUFFINS
APPLE-CINNAMON MUFFINS.......513
BANANA BREAD 514
BREAKFAST MUFFINS 516
CORN-CHEESE BREAD............515
DATE-NUT BREAD 514
PUMPKIN BREAD.................514
PUMPKIN BREAD.................513
QUICK-RAISED RICE BREAD.......515
RICE BRAN MUFFINS 515
RICE BRAN MUFFINS 513
ROLLS 514
TAMALE SPOONBREAD 516

BARS, COOKIES, DESSERTS
ALMOND BARK BARS.............519
APPLE CAKE 531
APPLE CRISP....................522
APPLE PUDDING CAKE 525
BUCKEYE BALLS.................520
CHOCOLATE BARS 532
CHOCOLATE BUTTERSCOTCH
    SCOTCHEROOS 526
CHOCOLATE CHIP BARS 526
CHOCOROONS....................525
COCOA MINI MERINGUES 522
COCONUT DROPS................521
CRANBERRY NUT PIE 529
CRANBERRY PUDDING 532
FLOURLESS PEANUT BUTTER
    COOKIES 521
FORGOTTEN COOKIES.............527
FUDGE BROWNIES 524
HONEY COOKIES 522
INCREDIBLE PEANUT BUTTER
    COOKIES 528
JELLO COOKIES 520
LEMON NUT BALLS 528
MACAROON KISSES 519
MAGIC COOKIE BARS 524
MAGIC COOKIE BARS 518
MARSHMALLOW BARS.............527
MELTING MOMENT COOKIES 519
NO BAKE CORN FLAKE-BAKER'S
    BARS 526
NO CRUST PUMPKIN PIE 528
NUT GOODY BARS................525
OVERNIGHT MERINGUES 521
PEANUT BUTTER BALLS...........531
PEANUT BUTTER BARS 527
PEANUT-BUTTER CAKE 518
PUMPKIN PIE....................529
RAISIN CLUSTERS 521
REESE-TYPE CUPS...............523
RICE PUDDING WITH MERINGUE ...531
SCOTCH CRISPIES 523
SCOTCHEROOS...................523

SOUR CREAM COFFEE CAKE.......530
SPONGE CAKE 529
SUN FLAKE CRISPIES 532
SWEET SURPRISE COOKIES 524
TEXAS APPLE STREUSEL..........530
TOFFEE BARS 520
TROPICAL FRUIT-NUT BARS 527
YUMMY YELLOW CAKE 529

**MISCELLANEOUS TREATS AND
    SNACKS**
AVOCADO SCOOP.................540
BLINTZ PANCAKES 536
COCKTAIL SAUCE 537
CURRY DILL DIP 539
ELEPHANT MILK 534
FAST CHOCOLATE PECAN FUDGE...535
GLUTEN-FREE/LACTOSE-FREE
    ICE CREAM....................534
HOT BROWN RICE-FRUIT
    CEREAL......................536
LEMON FRUIT SAUCE 534
MEATBALLS FOR SOUPS..........539
MICROWAVE PEANUT BRITTLE......535
MOCK HOLLANDAISE SAUCE 538
ONION RINGS/HUSH PUPPIES 537
ORANGE SMOOTHIE...............534
PEANUT BUTTER CHEWS 535
POPCORN CAKE 536
POPCORN CRUNCH 534
POTATO PIZZA 538
SALT-FREE BEEF JERKY 535
SHRIMP DIP 540
SNACK AND SANDWICH HINTS 538
TARTAR SAUCE 538
TUNA TREATS 537
VEGETABLE DIP..................539

Notes

Notes

Notes

This Cookbook is a perfect gift for Holidays, Weddings, Anniversaries and Birthdays.

★ ★ ★ ★ ★ ★

Cookbook Publishers, Inc. is pleased to have the privilege of publishing this fine cookbook.

Would you like a personalized cookbook for your own favorite organization? For complete information write to:

COOKBOOK PUBLISHERS, INC.
2101 Kansas City Road
P.O. Box 1260
Olathe, Kansas 66061-1260

Pine to Prairie Cookbooks

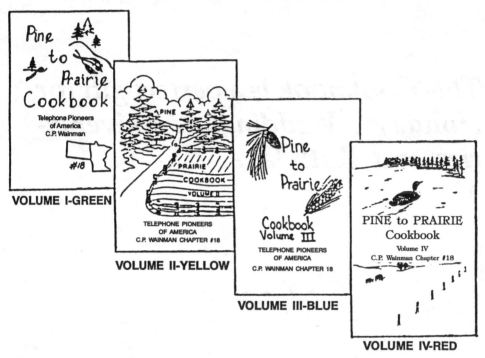

VOLUME I-GREEN

VOLUME II-YELLOW

VOLUME III-BLUE

VOLUME IV-RED

Please allow 4 to 6 weeks for delivery

Wainman Cookbook Coupon

Please Send me the following cookbooks:

☐ VOLUME I ☐ VOLUME II ☐ VOLUME III ☐ VOLUME IV

Please enclose $6.00 per book plus $2.50 per book postage and handling.

Name _____

Address _____

City, State, Zip _____

Mail to: Cookbook
Telephone Pioneers of America
Northwestern Bell
200 South 5th St., Room 1300
Minneapolis, MN 55402